JESUS SYMBOL OF GOD

JESUS

SYMBOL OF GOD

Roger Haight, S.J.

ORBIS BOOKS

Maryknoll, New York 10545

The Catholic Foreign Mission Society of America (Maryknoll) recruits and trains people for overseas missionary service. Through Orbis Books, Maryknoll aims to foster the international dialogue that is essential to mission. The books published, however, reflect the opinions of their authors and are not meant to represent the official position of the society. To obtain more information about Maryknoll and Orbis Books, please visit our website at www.maryknoll.org.

Library of Congress Cataloging-in-Publication Data

Haight, Roger.
    Jesus, symbol of God / Roger Haight.
       p. cm.
    Includes bibliographical references and index.
    ISBN 1-57075-247-8 (cloth)
    1. Jesus Christ—Person and offices. 1. Title.
BT202.H24   1999
232—dc21   98-49921
                                                          CIP

To My Colleagues at
Weston Jesuit School of Theology,
Faculty, Staff, and Students

Contents

Preface

In the middle of the last decade of the twentieth century, the Jesuits held a General Congregation in which elected delegates from around the world gathered in Rome. During its three months of deliberations the congregation developed position documents on fundamental issues of ministry in the church. One of these documents was on inculturation, a theme that had been under intense discussion in the churches of Asia, Africa, and Latin America since Vatican II.

Inculturation is treated as the incarnation of Christian faith and life within the diversity of human experiences that are codified in the languages, ideas, values, and behavior patterns that make up a culture or subculture. A metaphor for an inculturating evangelization is planting a seed, so that the plant "draws its nourishment from the earth around it and grows to maturity."[1] Inculturation does not mean that the gospel message is accommodated to human culture, but rather that the substance of the gospel is allowed to take on the form of a local culture. "Inculturating the Gospel means allowing the Word of God to exercise a power within the lives of the people, without at the same time imposing alien cultural factors which would make it difficult for them truly to receive that Word."[2]

The great paradigm for inculturation occurred when the church proclaimed its faith to Hellenistic culture in terms that it could understand and was in turn shaped by this culture. This process is just beginning in a self-conscious way in many parts of the world today. Asian and African Jesuits expressed their experiences of alienation because of the split between their own cultural experience and the still-western character of the church. Also, without using the word "postmodernity," the document spoke of the current intellectual milieu of western industrial societies as a culture and of the task of inculturation relative to it. "We cannot speak to others if the religious language we use is completely

---

1. "Our Mission and Culture," *Documents of the Thirty-Fourth General Congregation of the Society of Jesus*, John L. McCarthy, ed. (St. Louis: The Institute of Jesuit Sources, 1995), #3, p. 50.
2. "Our Mission and Culture," #3, p. 50.

foreign to them: the theology we use in our ministry cannot ignore the vista of modern critical questions within which we too live."[3] As in the process of Hellenization, the effort at addressing contemporary intellectual culture will also affect the language by which we understand our own faith. "In a predominantly secular context, our faith and our understanding of faith are often freed from contingent cultural complications and, as a result, purified and deepened."[4]

This book is written in the spirit of this dialogue with postmodern culture. It follows the imperative of Vatican II's *Gaudium et Spes* to address the contemporary world, to make faith intelligible in terms that it can understand. It is not written as part of a debate inside the Roman Catholic Church, but rather seeks to join with Christian theologians of all denominations in representing Christian faith in a way that is intelligible to educated people at the beginning of the third millennium, those both inside and outside the church who transcend national boundaries and share a set of values and ideas that constitute a subculture.

The intentionality and implied audience of the work have influenced its method and many of its features. I shall explain that method at length in the opening chapters. But a simple listing of some characteristics of the work may provide useful guidelines for reading it.

I undertook this christology convinced that Christianity in the twenty-first century must confront new problems and issues that will generate genuinely new understandings and behavior patterns in and by the churches. The generalized symbol for the cultural factors mediating these changes is "postmodernity." But at the same time Christianity, in this case in its theology and christology, must remain faithful to its originating revelation and consistent tradition. For this reason a good part of this work is dedicated to representing and analyzing the tradition.

In the course of this work, both in terms of method and content, I shall explain why the basis of christology is soteriology, why every Christian understanding of Jesus Christ has its source in the experience of salvation. This elementary structure of the priority of soteriology to christology, not agreed upon by all theologians, finds expression in extensive historical and constructive reflection on the meaning of salvation.

The apologetic intention of this christology leads to a method that is frequently characterized as "from below." This designates a methodical point of departure, not the end point, which is a "high" christology. But this methodological procedure also inculcates a structure or framework of thought in which the historical figure, Jesus of Nazareth, is always in play as the source and ultimate referent in affirmations about Jesus Christ. This framework is reflected in frequent appeals to the imagination as integral to the process of knowing, for imagination is the bridge between concrete

---

3. "Our Mission and Culture," #20, p. 59.
4. "Our Mission and Culture," #22, p. 60.

reality and our understanding of it.[5] The framework accounts for the interest in the historical Jesus. If God has taken flesh in Jesus, however this is explained, it would be strange if Christians were not curious to know all they could about the historical person, Jesus. The framework explains why, although this is a christology, it is entitled "Jesus." If this were a christology from above, it would be entitled "Christ, the Sacrament of God," where sacrament is explicitly a symbol of human encounter with God.[6] Because this is a christology from below, Jesus is called "Symbol of God," for although this symbol is a sacrament and never "merely" a symbol, "symbol" is the broader and more recognized interdisciplinary category. In the christology of this book, the symbol mediates in both directions: it draws human consciousness toward God, and it mediates God's presence to the human spirit.

This is an essay in systematic theology and christology. As a work of systematic theology, however, it does not intend to contain the subject matter in a totalizing manner and does not result in "a system." Generally speaking, postmodernity's historical and pluralistic consciousness have taken the teeth out of the totalizing pretentions of systems of thought. Rather, the systematic character of this work is defined, first, by a consistent perspective and method. I attempt to present a continuous argument from the first to the last chapter, so that positions reflected in the constructive portion will not be adequately understood apart from the early chapters that lead there. Second, the work is systematic also because it deals with a certain range of topics that are deemed relatively adequate to constitute a broad treatment of the subject matter.

But these same two indicators underline the severe limitations of this and any other systematic work. There are other legitimate perspectives and methods in Christian theology and christology that will yield other genuine insights. And this christology does not treat all the sources for christology or all the problem areas in the discipline. It is a broad but in no way comprehensive work in the light of today's knowledge and christological scholarship. Moreover, I can hardly be satisfied that the many subdisciplines and subtopics that actually feed into this christology have been adequately examined. The Lucan scholar will lament: "What has he done to my Luke?" And the Augustinian will pale at the rapid representation of Augustine's world. But these are the inevitable limitations of a synthetic work. In considering the historical tradition I have tried to stay close to texts, use a variety of commentators in reading them, and seek non-polemical, generally accepted historical interpretations, but always

---

5. Gerald J. Bednar, *Faith as Imagination: The Contribution of William F. Lynch, S.J.* (Kansas City: Sheed & Ward, 1996), 58.

6. As in Edward Schillebeeckx's neo-Thomist classic, *Christ the Sacrament of the Encounter with God* (New York: Sheed & Ward, 1963). The title, *Jesus Symbol of God*, is a translation of the title of Schillebeeckx's work in a new framework, "from below."

with the intent of the systematic theologian hermeneutically to draw the historical meaning forward into present-day relevance. This book is not intended as an introductory text, and I have not generally defined common theological terms with those who will meet them for the first time in view, but rather only occasionally to indicate how I am using a particular term.

I have been greatly helped along the way with this work in christology, and I am deeply grateful to many. William Dych, S.J., Otto Hentz, S.J., Paul Knitter, William Reiser, S.J., and Robert Schreiter, C.PP.S., all read the first draft of this book and suggested extremely valuable revisions. Daniel Harrington, S.J., and Robert Daly, S.J., read substantial sections of the manuscript and also offered expert corrections. Cheryl Waschenko also read the first draft and helped me clarify many points in the argument. Brian Doyle assisted me in setting up the work bibliographically. I am indebted as well to the Jesuit Community at Centre Sèvres in Paris for welcoming me warmly into their midst for five months as I began this project, and to the Jesuit Community at the Ateneo de Manila University who welcomed me back for four months as I finished a first draft, both during the course of a sabbatical year in 1996.

PART I

QUESTIONS OF METHOD

CHAPTER 1

Theology and Christology

The period of the end of the twentieth and the beginning of the twenty-first century is increasingly being called postmodern. More will be said about postmodernity later on, but one of its characteristics is a consciousness of pluralism at every level of thinking about humanity: its nature, its history, its purpose, its God. Because the church's theology reflects the world in which it exists, this pluralism characterizes the church at large. Christian theology is a pluralistic discipline, and this pluralism reaches into each denominational church. The few premises that are shared by all Christian theologians are often not enough to ensure mutual understanding, and far from enabling agreement.

As a consequence, it becomes imperative that a constructive theological statement begin with a sketch of its fundamental presuppositions and premises. In this chapter, therefore, I will outline some of the principles and conceptions that help to define the theological matrix of this christology. More particularly the chapter will first lay out some distinctions concerning theology itself, of which christology is a subdiscipline. This initial discussion of theology will include principles to which I will constantly appeal in the course of the argument. In a second part, this chapter will define the place of Jesus Christ in the world of Christian faith and its theology. It will be important to have a clear conception of the place of Jesus of Nazareth within Christian faith in order to understand what is going on in the discipline of christology and how it relates to Christian theology more generally. Then, in a third section, I will briefly discuss the discipline of christology itself. In the light of the previous discussion I hope to be able to clarify the central place of christology within Christian theology. I will conclude this initial chapter with a consideration of the situation of christology and how it dictates the questions that will shape this christology.

CHRISTIAN THEOLOGY

The standard definition of theology as "discussion of God" conceals large differences of conception and practice. It thus becomes necessary to say something of the sources of theology and to make the distinctions that will help situate this essay in the world of theological discourse. Three loci fundamental to theology are faith, revelation, and scripture. I add to these a fourth concerning the symbolic character of theological language. Discussion of these will provide an initial indication of the premises of this work.[1]

Faith is a universal form of human experience. Religious faith involves a religious experience that entails an awareness of and loyalty to an ultimate or transcendent reality. Unfortunately the term "experience" itself has become problematic in its generality and vagueness. But it is not necessary to develop a theory of religious experience in order to explain the meaning and significance of the category of experience relative to faith. Faith in its primary sense is an intentional human response, reaction, act, or pervasive and operative attitude. What is preserved in the insistence that faith is experiential may be seen in three familiar distinctions: first, following Newman, faith is primarily a real, concrete, and particular apprehension and assent as opposed to a merely notional one.[2] Second, faith is primarily and more properly "direct" faith, the object of which is engaged by the person of faith, as distinct from indirect faith, which believes something to be the case on the word of another. With indirect faith the object remains notional. Third, as distinct from theoretical knowledge, Maurice Blondel proposed a "possessive knowledge" which he related to the Johannine idea of "doing the truth." Possessive knowledge is the result of engagement with the object of faith through one's action. The object of faith becomes so internalized that it possesses and is possessed by the knower. The object of one's real faith is the principle of one's action.[3] Once again, faith has an experiential dimension. The other side of each of these distinctions is not irrelevant or unimportant. But one should recognize that faith is primarily an elemental, existential human response, so that when it is said that theology rests on faith, one is always finally led back to some existential human experience at its source.

Faith is not knowledge; but faith is cognitive. In this paradoxical tension the term "knowledge," properly speaking, is taken to refer to the domain of knowledge of things of this world. Despite the wide variety of finite things to be known and ways of knowing them, and even though faith is more analogous to certain specific forms of knowing than to others, still the object of religious faith is precisely that which transcends the finite

---

1. This initial section recapitulates material that is developed at greater length in Roger Haight, *Dynamics of Theology* (New York: Paulist Press, 1990).

2. In real assent the mind "is directed towards things, represented by the impressions which they have left on the imagination." John Henry Newman, *An Essay in Aid of a Grammar of Assent* (New York: Longmans, Green, & Co., 1898), 75.

3. Maurice Blondel, *Action (1893): Essay on a Critique of Life and a Science of Practice*, trans. by Oliva Blanchette (Notre Dame, Ind.: University of Notre Dame Press, 1984), 419, 441.

world we know. This transcendence of its object accounts for one aspect of a specifically religious faith. But religious engagement with a transcendent unknown can still be cognitive. This conviction cannot be demonstrated, since to do so would imply objectively knowing the object of faith. Those who possess religious faith consider it self-authenticating. But the longevity and vitality of many different religious traditions suggests a real contact with reality.[4] The significance of this thesis for theology can be seen negatively in both terms of the tension. If faith were an objective knowledge circumscribed by our world, the object of faith would cease to be transcendent; and if faith were not cognitive, its real object would be either humanity itself or some other finite object and hence intentionally illusory. Both of these charges are sometimes made against theology: the first, of idolatry, from inside the discipline; the second, of projection, from outside. They seem equally destructive of what theology intends.

Beliefs are expressions of faith and as such are distinct from faith. This distinction, which is typical of modern theology's turn to the subject, has come under attack for being too individualistic in its conception of the foundations of religion and theology, and not conscious enough of the historical differentiations of faith itself. These criticisms merit consideration and must be addressed, but in the end they are not mortal. Faith usually involves the corporate faith of a community. Although faith correlates with a deep dimension of human awareness and commitment, it is distinguishable but never separable from the beliefs which express the object of faith in propositional form. It is not that faith is untouched by beliefs, for faith and belief dialectically determine each other; but faith can retain a measure of autonomous identity within different expressions of belief. One can be related to God as creator whether or not Genesis is an historical account of creation. Thus the distinction still serves to make its point: it allows for development and change in a religious tradition, while at the same time preserving a core identity and sameness. Beliefs may change while faith at its deepest level remains constant, even as it is modified. Without some such distinction, theology that is both faithful to a historical norm and free to become inculturated in a variety of historical forms would be impossible.

Some convictions concerning the nature of Christian revelation derive from christology. Yet revelation itself has been subjected to extensive reflection, and one can make some general statements about revelation that function as premises to christology.

Although formally distinct, authentic religious faith and revelation are two aspects of the complex phenomenon of religious experience. Revelation is faith being met by, or even stimulated and initiated by, the ultimate. Revelation is the encounter in faith with the transcendent. In

---

4. See Peter Byrne, *Prolegomena to Religious Pluralism: Reference and Realism in Religion* (New York: St. Martin's Press, 1995) for an extended discussion of the realism of religious faith, especially 167–90.

Christian terms, revelation is the presence of God encountered in faith, always in such a way that God takes the initiative in freedom: revelation is God's self-presence, self-communication, and self-gift. Since revelation is a correlative of faith, it shares a parallel structure. That is, in speaking about revelation one must make distinctions that are analogous to those in the language of faith. For example, one can differentiate dimensions of revelation analogous to faith and belief. The core revelational experience, its center of gravity, is best conceived in Christian terms in the language of personal encounter with God.[5] The thematizations of such an experience in concept, language, or active response represent a distinct dimension of the revelatory experience. Moreover, one must reckon on various levels of these thematizations as reflection becomes more abstract and distant from revelational experience. For example, one can distinguish a) spontaneous expression within the experience of original revelation itself, b) the more routinized yet still primary religious language of a community, c) its still more abstract doctrinal forms which are the result of dialectic and debate and form the landmarks of a tradition, and d) the ongoing theological interpretations of these revealed beliefs.[6]

The significance of an experiential conception of revelation for theology can be summed up most pointedly in a negative and a positive inference. Negatively, the final criterion for Christian theological interpretation cannot lie in another theological interpretation. The "orthodoxy" of a particular theological position cannot be another theology, because all such interpretations are human projects, historically conditioned, and in themselves relative to the encounter with God's presence that they express and mediate. Positively, however, the measure of orthodoxy must be said to lie in the faith of the community. It should be clear that the content of this revelatory encounter is unknowable apart from the community's religious language. But when it comes to measuring whether a new interpretation of the meaning of this language is authentic or not, one cannot rest content with comparing words and concepts; one must look toward the community's experience of God's presence and ask whether or not a theology preserves and elicits that existential experience. Without distinctions within the structure of revelation analogous to these, theology could not move forward, but would be condemned to repeating the words of the past. These principles will be recalled in the course of this work for they bear directly upon issues in christology.

Scripture represents the major universally recognized source for Christian theology. But historical consciousness has undermined the mere

---

5. Edward Schillebeeckx, *Revelation and Theology*, 2 (New York: Sheed & Ward, 1967), 89. These themes are expanded in Haight, *Dynamics of Theology*, 51–86.

6. Michael L. Cook differentiates symbols, metaphors, and stories within the structure of revelation. These provide a basis for conceptual theological analysis, doctrinal statements, and creedal symbols. See "Revelation as Metaphorical Process," *Theological Studies*, 47 (1987), 390–95.

citation of a scriptural text as warrant and proof for theological positions. Respect for the sometimes sharp differences between a biblical perspective on reality and our own has rendered the use of scripture in theology a more complicated affair. In the modern period both liberal and evangelical theologians have recognized that one cannot simply identify revelation with the texts of scripture. One needs a theory of the nature of scripture, revelation, theology, and how they interrelate.

The view of scripture and its use in theology that is operative in this christology binds together several elements. First is a view, derived from the Christian tradition, of the universal and potentially revelatory presence of God to humanity. The problem of revelation is not its scarcity, but the plurality of its manifestations. Second, whenever revelation occurs it is always mediated; that is, it makes an historical appearance and becomes manifest through historical events, things, places, persons. In the language of Karl Rahner, transcendental revelation is never given as such; it only appears in categorical manifestations.[7] Third, for Christianity, Jesus is the central mediation of God in history. The whole of Christianity revolves around Jesus of Nazareth as the constitutive mediation of God's revelation for Christian faith. Fourth, the whole of scripture, but especially the gospels, in the absence of Jesus of Nazareth, constitutes the ever-present second-order mediation of God's revelation whose original source was Jesus. In other words, as the classic original witness to Jesus and God revealed through Jesus, the scriptures continue to make present in an overt but secondary way to the community the original mediation of the revelation that occurred in Jesus.[8] All of these elements will be considered again in greater detail in the context of specific applications.

On the basis of the theory that is scarcely developed in these propositions, one can conceive of how scripture can be authoritative for the church and operate as a source for theology. One may assume the negative stipulation that scripture cannot be used in such a way that the mere citation of a passage is enough to establish a theological position. Even if one can show that inspiration and inerrancy still bear some meaning in today's world, the quotation of a scriptural text cannot by itself establish any theological position for belief. Use of scriptural texts must take into account the differences that obtain between an original meaning of a passage and its meaning in a present situation. Citation of scripture text, therefore, must employ some hermeneutical method that gives an account of interpretation.

Positively, scripture, as the ever-present second-order mediation of what occurred in the event of Jesus of Nazareth, continually influences

---

7. Karl Rahner, *Foundations of Christian Faith: An Introduction to the Idea of Christianity* (New York: Seabury Press, 1978), 51–53.

8. The church too performs this function in conjunction with scripture; there is no antithesis here, for the two institutions imply each other. The church wrote or established the scriptures; the scriptures serve as the church's constitution; the church interprets the scriptures which norm the church.

theology by shaping the consciousness of the community and the theologian in it. The specifically Christian scriptures, written within the Christian communities under the influence of the Jewish scriptures, were gradually recognized as the classical witness to the faith of the new religion. In this way they began to act as the constitution of the community in a very fundamental sense. The scriptures became the basis of the church's teaching, the authority upon which it reflected to solve new problems, the inspiration of faith, the source of the language of prayer and worship. The scriptures continue to shape the consciousness of the Christian church. They provide a common language for self-understanding, a reference point for interpreting Christian beliefs, and inspiration for moral choices. As the source for interpretation, the scriptures work their way into the interpretations themselves.[9]

More particularly, however, in relation to specific theological problems or positions, scripture displays its authority by disclosure and elaboration. A given text of scripture involves both meaning and reference to a world outside the text.[10] In a religious text, this reference is to an existential or experiential mode of being in the world that involves encounter with transcendence. The text of scripture finds its authority precisely within the encounter with transcendence that it mediates, and not merely as an objectively constituted meaning. The authority of a scriptural text cannot be isolated from the experiential faith and revelatory encounter that bestow that authority in the first place. But this disclosure is still not enough for the public discipline of theology: it must be elaborated by thematic reasoning and argument. To establish a position theologically, the theologian must enter into a process of dialectical reasoning and discussion of alternative positions. Without argument theology becomes a function of blind traditionalism or current feeling.

The terms "symbol" and "symbolic" are used frequently in this essay. They serve as a reminder of the kind of human awareness that lies at the foundation of theology and of the status of its language. Symbolic knowledge and language correspond to the tensive character of the relation between faith and beliefs, revelatory encounter and its discursive expression. The ontology of symbol and how it functions specifically in christology will be taken up again below; it will also be the subject of Chapter 7. In what follows I want simply to underline some rudimentary notions about symbol in order to lay out further some of the premises of this work.

A symbol is that through which something other than itself is known. A symbol mediates awareness of something else. Sometimes the only way this "other" can be known is through some symbolic mediation. For exam-

---

9. The work of David Kelsey, *The Uses of Scripture in Recent Theology* (Philadelphia: Fortress Press, 1975) is useful in sorting out the elements involved in this issue.

10. Paul Ricoeur, "The Hermeneutical Function of Distanciation," *Hermeneutics and the Human Sciences: Essays on Language, Action and Interpretation*, ed. by John B. Thompson (Cambridge: Cambridge University Press, 1981), 140–42.

ple, there are layers of the self that do not lie on the surface, open to our own immediate self-awareness, but must be revealed through other forms of activity such as dreaming or writing or painting or behaving. Image, text, picture, and story can function as symbols and mediate knowledge of something other than their overt design, namely, a state of consciousness hidden from immediate self-awareness. Psychology and art are completely at home with symbolic forms of knowing. Religious symbols are analogous, and they point to and mediate transcendent realities in response to religious questioning.

The knowledge that is engendered through symbol is not an attenuated form of cognition, but an extension of the range of human awareness. The kind of knowledge mediated by symbols may be called engaged participatory knowledge.[11] This means that it is the product of becoming conscious existentially and experientially of that which is mediated by the symbol. It will be shown later that the symbol has a tensive and dynamic structure that stimulates the mind to activity. It provokes it to reach for the further meaning that lies within the symbol itself. Only by an actively engaged participation can the human mind reach a meaning deeper than the empirical or higher than the terrestrial. Because theology deals with transcendent reality, and the data of faith is received through revelation, theology is a symbolic discipline.

Two axioms flow from the symbolic character of theology, and they interact dialectically. The first may be expressed negatively: because theology is symbolic, its assertions are not direct statements of information about God. Information here connotes a kind of objectified datum that is asserted about God the way information about other things of this world are known. While the observation seems obvious enough, still, theologians are sometimes so drawn into the linguistic, textual, and cultural world of a tradition that meaning becomes taken for granted and begins to function like ordinary non-symbolic language. One loses the agnosticism that Thomas Aquinas proposed was an element of all theological assertion, and begins to think that religious language mediates comprehension and control over the subject matter. Respecting the transcendent character of faith and revelation, theology communicates no immediate information about God. This negative axiom invites a critical attentiveness to theological prose: how is the author dealing with transcendent subject matter?

The second axiom may be expressed positively: the symbolic assertions of theology communicate through the engaged participatory experience which they invite and actively engender. The symbolic assertions of theology draw one into the mystery of the transcendent. The fact that they are not informative of facts does not lessen their epistemological value; symbolic religious assertions uncover and mediate to consciousness areas that would otherwise remain closed. But cognitive awareness has to find

---

11. Avery Dulles, "The Symbolic Structure of Revelation," *Theological Studies*, 41 (1980), 60–61.

its basis in some form of engaged participatory encounter with its object. In the final analysis, the meaning and truth of the symbols of tradition have to be found in the present-day experience of the community.

These two principles, when they are taken together, point to theology as a discipline that is always in motion through history. Theology is no hard physical science; it does not advance by the accumulation of facts. Rather theology is a constant entertainment of perennial questions, whose answers are not there waiting to be discovered. Nor is there any religious authority which possesses all the answers or any comprehensively complete answer. Theology must be an ongoing discussion open to all parties who bring symbolic answers to the most basic of human questions.

On the basis of these brief considerations of the foundations of theology, I propose a brief characterization of the discipline and a summary of some of its axioms. The question of how these premises are incorporated into the method of this work in christology will be taken up in Chapter 2.

Theology is reflection on the nature of reality from the perspective of the symbols of the Christian faith. This conception is similar to that of Thomas Aquinas's notion of sacred doctrine, which included considerations on all things in heaven and on earth in the light of the principles of revelation.[12] This expansive notion of theology is inclusive: it includes explicit reflection on God and on the world. It also includes turning back in a critical examination of the symbols of faith themselves, as in the case of christology.

Perhaps the most important aspect of this discipline flows from its foundation in faith and revelation. The epistemology of faith and revelation ultimately determines one's conception and practice of theology. As theology is conceived here, elementary tensions are at work at every moment in the process of theological interpretation and affirmation. On the one hand, faith and revelation are not knowledge in the sense of any form of knowledge that we have of this world, because their object is essentially transcendent. It is always a mistake in categories to confuse a theological assertion with a datum of knowledge or a piece of information. And yet, on the other hand, faith and revelation are in their own generic way cognitive: by an existential faith and an engaged participation one encounters transcendent reality as given, as present. This experiential dimension of faith and revelation, however, exists nowhere without a reflective and interpretive human response. These interpretations unfold at various degrees of distance from the core of revelatory experience: spontaneous religious action or expression in primary religious language, written religious language such as that found in scripture, abstract and normative language found in creeds, elaborations of discrete beliefs in doctrines, reflection on these beliefs in theology, principles of action flowing from beliefs formulated in moral, practical, and spiritual theology.

---

12. Thomas Aquinas, *Summa Theologica: Complete English Edition in Five Volumes* (Westminster, Md.: Christian Classics, 1961), I, q. 1.

The engaged participatory awareness of faith is not individualistic; the real presence of transcendence to it is experienced by a community along the route of its tradition. There is no way to isolate an individual apart from his or her social, historical, and cultural situation. Tradition in its most fundamental sense consists in the historical reality of the lived faith of the whole community. The distinction between belief and faith preserves this tension and allows for a dynamic, dialectical interaction between them. From different perspectives faith both changes and remains constant in history, across time and cultures; beliefs, too, may change and still consistently reflect a perduring faith. Existential faith gives beliefs their realism; changing beliefs give faith a flexibility to engage new cultures.

The idea of a symbol is essentially tensive, dynamic, and dialectical; a symbol mediates something other than itself by drawing or leading beyond itself to a deeper or higher truth. By conceiving theology as a symbolic discipline and by consistently using the language of symbol, one is able to ensure respect for its elementary character. Symbols do not provide objective information about God; but symbols draw human consciousness and life into a deeper world of encounter with transcendent reality. This represents epistemologically a symbolic realism.

Symbols and symbolic knowledge can be defined and distinguished from metaphor, literal speech, analogy, myth, parable, and so on in a variety of ways.[13] There is no standard usage. In this essay, the symbolic draws its logic less from a conceptual analysis of predication and more from a phenomenological analysis of the dynamics of religious experience. Symbolic predication preserves the realism of the analogy of being, but does so on the basis of an engaged, participatory encounter with transcendence. To say that religious language is symbolic and metaphorical, therefore, does not impugn realism in predication but provides an alternative analysis of the logic of predication. Also, insofar as analogical predication includes the classical three-fold structure of affirmation, negation, and reaffirmation in a higher mode, one finds another commonality with the symbolic.[14] However, in the epistemology of religious symbols this *triplex via* is strictly dialectical: for example, God "is" personal, and God "is not" personal as humans know personal. This means that predications about God should not be considered literal, because this always risks a non-dialectical reduction of the infinite to the limitations of the finite medium.[15] But symbolic language, even though not literal, is still revela-

---

13. See the discussion of symbol, metaphor, literal speech, and analogy by Michael L. Cook, *Christology as Narrative Quest* (Collegeville, Minn.: Liturgical Press, 1997), 32–39.

14. Aquinas, ST, I, q. 13, a. 2.

15. The very notion of literal language about God is actually quite complex, and I have generally tried not to use the term because of the variety of meanings "literal" can have and the ways such literal speech can be explained. See Cook, *Christology as Narrative Quest*, 36–38. Sometimes the term "literal" is used simply to indicate that something "is *really* so."

tory and cognitive. As such it both is and is not "objective" knowledge. It can be called objective because of the realism of symbols; they mediate a real and revelatory awareness of their transcendent "object" as opposed to subjectivist projection. But infinite, transcendent, incomprehensible reality is not "an object" and cannot be contained or measured by the limits of the concepts drawn from this world. The very experience of transcendence exceeds the conceptualized or objectified or linguistic representation of it. Therefore one cannot reduce either transcendent reality or cognitive participatory knowledge of it to "objectified" thematic knowledge. The reader will be able to discern the sometimes positive and sometimes negative meaning of the term "objective" from the context.

From a doctrinal perspective, scripture is essentially a book of religious symbols. The multiplicity and complexity of these symbols can hardly be exaggerated, nor can the different ways in which scripture is brought to bear on theological proposals. More will be said on this question relative to christology in the chapters which follow. But at least the symbolic usage of scripture should be clear at this point. Mere citation of scripture, as testimony to a past belief, by itself bears little weight for belief today; the dynamic process by which scriptural testimony can win authority is one of disclosure and elaboration, that is, symbolic mediation and argument.

This preliminary sketch of how theology is conceived in this work will gain more substance in the course of the development, especially when we take up the question of method in christology. But the next task is to locate the place of Jesus Christ in the tradition and world of Christian faith.

JESUS CHRIST AS SYMBOL OF GOD

The relation between Christian theology broadly conceived and christology reflects the place in Christianity of Jesus Christ himself. It is probably the case that no reflective Christian is unaware that Jesus Christ stands at the center of Christian faith, and this indeed is what will be defended here. But it will not be unproductive to explain the implications of the obvious in technical terms.

We begin with the principle that all revelation is historically mediated. In the language of Karl Rahner, transcendental revelation, which is the universally present and thematically unconscious awareness of God's grace or personal self-communication, never exists as such, but always and only in the form of categorical, this-worldly, historical experience. Rahner's reflections at this point are epistemological. Beyond that, on the basis of Christian doctrine, Rahner argues for the universal presence and personal self-communication of God to all human beings. But this universal presence can only enter explicitly, reflectively, and thematically as an object into human consciousness by virtue of an historical mediation. One needs the symbolic mediation of an external event or an objective and specifying medium to give an otherwise vague awareness a particular name.[16]

Rahner's insight can be transposed analogously into a historical and social context of the history of religious groups. John Hick makes such a move by reinterpreting the epistemological principle of Thomas Aquinas that whatever is known or received by a knower is known according to the "form" or mode or condition of the knower.[17] Hick uses this as part of his explanation of the pluralism of religions. He postulates a certain presence, impact, or pressure of ultimate reality on all peoples. But the recognition of the Real, that is, ultimate transcendent reality, will always take on the form and character dictated by the situation and circumstances of the culture of the people involved.[18] Reverting to the theological framework of Rahner, one can understand his distinction between the transcendental and categorical aspects of religion in epistemological terms that include a social and historical perspective. With this distinction one can construe the history of religions theologically in a dramatic, historical, and narrative way. Wherever God's transcendent presence is experienced by a group, the awareness and conceptualization of this divine reality will take on a form and character that is marked by the specific situation, language, culture, and symbols that mediate it to consciousness. The symbols of a specific culture provide the form of a particular religious consciousness. "Religion is the substance of culture; culture is the form of religion."[19]

At this point it will be helpful to distinguish two kinds of symbols: conceptual or conscious symbols and concrete symbols. Conscious symbols are the words, notions, concepts, ideas, sayings, or texts that mediate a deeper consciousness of a level of reality that goes beyond their overt meaning. The metaphor is a good example of a conscious symbol; descriptions of how the metaphor functions resemble the dynamics of symbols. A concrete symbol, by contrast, is an object. The term refers to things, places, events, or persons which mediate a presence and consciousness of another reality. For example, the human body mediates a presence of the human spirit on several levels: to others by gesture and speech; to conscious self-awareness by reflection on one's action; ontologically, in different ways as construed in different metaphysical systems.

---

16. Rahner, *Foundations*, 51–55.

17. John Hick, *An Interpretation of Religion: Human Responses to the Transcendent* (New Haven: Yale University Press, 1989), 153; also *God Has Many Names* (Philadelphia: Westminster Press, 1980), 48–49, with reference to Aquinas, *Summa Theologica*, II–II, q. 1, a. 2.

18. Rahner and Hick agree in principle that God is mediated to a people through the actual religious forms that are in place in a culture. See Karl Rahner, "History of the World and Salvation History," *Theological Investigations*, 5 (Baltimore: Helicon Press, 1966), 97–100, and "Christianity and the Non-Christian Religions," ibid., 121–31; and Hick, *An Interpretation of Religion*, 162–65, 233–51.

19. Paul Tillich, *Theology of Culture* (New York: Oxford University Press, 1964), 42.

In the light of these two premises, that all faith and revelation are historically mediated, and that symbols can be divided into conscious and concrete symbols, we can state in a straightforward way the place of Jesus Christ in the Christian religion: for Christians, Jesus is the concrete symbol of God.

Jesus was a concrete figure in human history. The term "Jesus" is first of all a proper name and in this work it always refers to Jesus of Nazareth. As a proper name it prescinds from the epistemological or historical questions of how and how much we can know of Jesus. It is used with the same simple directness that one intends in using a name to refer to a friend, such as Jane. One does not self-consciously refer to "the historical Jane." This directness is possible on the basis of the virtually universal agreement that Jesus of Nazareth existed. Jesus was an early first-century Jew who later came to be recognized by some, or many, depending on the perspective, as the Messiah, anointed one, or Christ. The title "Christ" quickly developed into a second proper name, so that he became known as Jesus Christ most probably after his death. The name Jesus of Nazareth, then, is the best direct designator of Jesus during the course of his earthly life.

People encountered God in Jesus, and they still do. This seemingly innocent proposition contains a tough knot of conflicting interpretations: what does "to encounter God in Jesus" mean? The double assertion, that people encountered God in Jesus in the past and in the present, is also problematic. Is the medium of this encounter really Jesus or the memory of Jesus? But we do not have to solve these problems now in order to accept the generalized formula that, both during his life time and after his death, a good number of Jews were so moved religiously by Jesus that in a large variety of ways they experienced God and God's saving presence mediated by him. The entire New Testament, along with some extra-biblical literature, together confirm the first-century Jesus movement which can be shown to extend back into Jesus' lifetime. Therefore, in a precise sense that is yet to be determined, Jesus is the mediation of God's presence to Christianity. This is the first and most basic meaning or logic underlying whatever literary meaning is found in the predication that Jesus is the Christ.

One can say that the idea that Jesus is symbol of God means in a direct and as yet unsophisticated way that Jesus is a mediation of the experience of God in history. One has a rudimentary christology in this statement, but one too undifferentiated to serve for very much. Yet even at this level of vagueness it accomplishes what is intended here, namely, to define in a first, historical, and genetic way the place of Jesus Christ in Christian faith which has the ultimate, transcendent reality of God as its object. Jesus Christ is the mediator of specifically Christian faith. This statement will require a great deal more reflection and nuance, because the state of the question today offers conflicting interpretations of this very formula. Yet despite the work that still needs to be done, the formula establishes Jesus Christ at the center of Christian faith and revelation with the literalness that the metaphor of a circle conveys: there can only be one center of a circle. Jesus who is called Christ is the single central, but not exclusive, determinant of the character of Christian faith. This principle can take on important critical significance, for example, in contrast to the position St. Paul has sometimes assumed in interpretations of Christian faith.

CHRISTOLOGY AND THEOLOGY

Christology is a subdiscipline of theology; it is the study and discussion of Jesus Christ, or of Jesus as the Christ. As such it has become itself a vast discipline under the umbrella of which one finds other subdisciplines to which theologians dedicate careers: New Testament christology, the history of christology, patristic christology, contemporary christology. A large corpus of literature surrounds the discussion of Jesus Christ in relation to liberation, ecology, other religions. Regarding christology as an integral discipline, it is good to distinguish between the christological problem narrowly conceived and a broader sense of christology.

CHRISTOLOGY NARROWLY CONCEIVED

Christianity has its foundation in the encounter of God in and through Jesus. The focus of the Christian imagination on Jesus as a medium of God raised, and still raises, the question of how God was present to or in Jesus. And how in his turn was Jesus related to God? This is the christological question in its purest and most narrowly defined form. It was said earlier that theology as a reflection on all of reality in the light of Christian symbols does not preclude theological reflection on its own symbols. Such is the case here. In the narrow christological question, the focus falls on Jesus himself and his status in relation to God and other human beings as the Christ.

The history of the christological question is as old as christology itself: just who is Jesus of Nazareth? How are we to situate or categorize him relative to God and to other human beings? New Testament christologies respond to these questions in a variety of ways. And a good part of patristic theology of the early centuries was given over to speculative attempts at understanding the relationship between Jesus Christ and God, culminating in the definition of the divinity of the Son, or Logos, at Nicaea in the fourth century and the classical christological formula of Chalcedon in the fifth century.

The narrow christological question cannot be neglected; nor can christology bypass the classical responses to this question that were fashioned in the patristic period.[20] These councils govern the language and under-

---

20. Taking classical soteriology and christology seriously in many respects goes against the trend of current christology. Some believe that the criticisms of classical

standing of the mainline churches. It is clear that the christological question has become a new question that is not answered by the old formulas; we need new language. But we must take up these classic formulas in any adequate christology for, however problematically, they continue to shape christological consciousness after 1500 years. There are only three options possible relative to these classical formulations: to avoid them, to repeat them, or to interpret them. One cannot avoid them because the question of just who Jesus was in ontological terms always remains; it will not go away and is not unimportant. One cannot just repeat the classical formulas, because they do not have the same meaning in our culture as they did when they were formulated. To repeat them, therefore, is to interpret them in a sense that was not intended by them. Therefore, one has no choice but to engage the classical councils and to explicitly interpret them for our own period. Christologies that try to leap over the classical doctrines fail in comprehensiveness.

CHRISTOLOGY BROADLY CONCEIVED

Encountering God in and through Jesus was the origin of Christianity and is its constant ground. Both in its historical becoming and its genetic structure Jesus functions as the medium of the Christian encounter with God. This focal point of Christian faith, however, is expansive: it grows and flowers forth in the broad vision of Christian faith. Christology, then, is more fully conceived as the study of the generating source of Christian faith. It remains the central piece in the Christian vision; its reach extends to the whole drama of salvation as this is conceived in Christian symbols. Although christology in some respects is reflection turned in on its own central symbol, it should also be understood in the more expansive way as reflection on the center and basis of the Christian symbol system itself. Hans Küng, for example, was correct in centering his broad interpretation of Christian existence in Jesus Christ.[21] Christology provides the basis for the enlarged Christian vision which encompasses all reality.

Christology, therefore, possesses an intrinsic dynamism that is oriented outside itself. It is part of a Christian theology that has as its scope an understanding of all things, of reality itself, in the light, reductively, of an encounter with God as mediated by Jesus. This book intends such an expansive christology. Despite its title, which seems to favor a preoccupation with the narrow christological problem, and despite the many problems concerning the internal meaning of the Christian symbols that

---

christological language show that it positively distorts the person and role of Jesus Christ as he is presented in the New Testament witness. Others want to bypass classical christology by an exclusive appeal to evangelical language or by representing christology in an existential or narrative form.

21. Hans Küng, *On Being a Christian* (New York: Doubleday, 1976).

make up an integral christology, the orientation of this essay is toward developing an understanding of Jesus Christ that will illumine our world and life in it.

THE SITUATION OF CHRISTOLOGY

What is the situation of christology at this time? Few areas in theology have been as volatile over the past two decades as christology. Many of the leading theologians of our time have proposed their christologies; a plethora of christologies respond to particular issues; the discipline itself is divided into a number of subdisciplines that require specific expertise and have generated their own bodies of literature. More and more, what is subsumed within the area of christology appears to be a confusing mass of accumulating data. In what follows I will begin to bring some order into this sprawling discipline by first enumerating some of the major movements within it. This will demonstrate the pluralism that now reigns within christology. I shall then suggest that the consciousness implied in these many different trends in christology may be called postmodern. And, finally, I will pinpoint a set of questions that are implied in these christological movements, questions which will enter into the logic of this present work.

CHRISTOLOGY TODAY

No one should doubt the pluralistic character of christology today, even within a single church. What follows is a straightforward description of currents within christology. It will be useful simply to place before the intellectual imagination a cross section of what this pluralism entails. Instructive in this overview are the distinctively different approaches to christology, the problems to which they respond, and the way in which they correlate with distinctive elements of our historical situation.

Transcendental Christology

Transcendental christology is a response to extrinsicism in Christian thought, the idea that God's address to human existence in Jesus Christ comes entirely from the "outside" and runs counter to human interests and the inner exigencies of human freedom. To show that Jesus Christ is precisely the fulfillment of the human, this christology begins with transcendental phenomenology of human existence and finds a universal inner dynamism that reaches out for absolute truth, goodness, freedom, and being. In Jesus the divine has condescended to meet this need. Therefore, God in Jesus as the Christ does not represent a heteronomous suppression of the human, but its integral and ideal realization: incarnation does not stand over against the human, but completes and fulfills it absolutely. Hypostatic union, describing the union of the Eternal Word and the human in Jesus, is really the ideal case of what happens or can happen in all human beings who accept God's presence in grace.[22]

Jesus Research

Jesus research is back in earnest. Because it is a subdiscipline of the study of the New Testament, to participate requires the skills of the historian and the biblical scholar. But even the non-specialist will notice that, despite the attempt to objectify the quest by establishing norms and criteria, a great deal of divergence about some quite fundamental matters concerning Jesus still reigns. The diversity within the Judaism of his time allows for remarkably different interpretive categories.[23] There may be consensus on certain data about Jesus that are considered in some measure historically authentic. But one finds no consensus about how this data may be construed in a holistic way.[24] A number of things can be said about Jesus of an historical nature. But it must also be admitted that what we do not know far outweighs what we do, and that questioning on any given point quickly leads to the answer "We do not know." Yet this historical research is having an impact on christology. We are challenged to determine how this historical investigation influences christology in principle, and what its particular contribution might be.

Narrative Christology

A focus on the historical Jesus lends itself to a narrative christology which exploits what we can know about Jesus. It probes his commitment to the reign of God and examines his faith insofar as such is discernable in his actions. The way Jesus lived and acted assumes great importance in a narrative christology. Although it is impossible to write a biography or "Life" of Jesus, one can construe the general pattern of his public ministry. Narrative christologies take different forms which serve different intents. Some narrative christologies have achieved brilliant success in telling the story of Jesus in a way that is both technically exact and utterly engaging for Christian life.[25] Political and liberation theologians plead for a narrative christology that is simultaneously a practical theology. The salvation Jesus

---

22. Karl Rahner's christology is an example of transcendental christology, and this brief characterization has Rahner in mind. Rahner's christology will be more fully, but still schematically, represented in Chapter 15.

23. Daniel J. Harrington, "The Jewishness of Jesus: Facing Some Problems," *Catholic Biblical Quarterly*, 49 (1987), 1–13.

24. Helpful descriptions of some of the main trends in Jesus interpretation are found in Marcus Borg, *Jesus—A New Vision* (New York: HarperCollins, 1987) and *Meeting Jesus Again for the First Time* (New York: HarperCollins, 1994).

25. The christology of Hans Küng, *On Being a Christian*, and the work of Edward Schillebeeckx, *Jesus: An Experiment in Christology* (New York: Seabury Press, 1979), are good examples of narrative christologies.

Christ mediates to the world must never be understood apart from its historical unfolding in concrete instances. Faith is the praxis of hope, and theology's role is to keep alive the narrative of salvation. Only a narrative account can appeal to praxis in response to historical suffering.[26] For still others, narrative simply represents on epistemological grounds the most primitive and basic structure of human experiencing and knowing. Primary contact with reality arises within the matrix of duration; memory of the past, attention to the present, and anticipation of the future together form the framework of experiencing. Narrative thus represents most closely the imaginative encounter of humans with the concrete and temporally unfolding world prior to conceptual and analytical construal. The various stories of Jesus, therefore, really provide the apperceptive foundations of christology.[27]

Existential Christology

If narrative christology depends on what we can know of Jesus, little though it be, existential christology is conscious of what we do not and cannot know because of the historical sources and what, for theological reasons, should not engage us. Epistemologically, no historical data or anything that Jesus did can establish faith; God did not act through Jesus in historically empirical ways. God acts through Jesus as through a medium, so that the salvific event occurs in the drama of revelation and faith in each believer and in the community as a whole. Several quite different forms of christology today share at least a distrust of the turn to Jesus. Existential christology sees the point of all christology as the encounter with God through faith that constitutes salvation. This may be expressed as a kerygmatic or Word-event christology: Jesus is God's Word or the medium of God's self-revelation and self-communication. The logic of Christianity itself is carried in the preached word, the message of God's being Emmanuel and a present, authenticating, and empowering force for living. In terms of method, this christology may be content to leave the historical Jesus in the shadows behind the New Testament as document; it will exploit the text, the genres, the stories as stories, the parables, and the sayings with literary or rhetorical criticism, in order once more to let the kerygma of Jesus mediate its power in Christian life. It is not Jesus precisely as an historical figure that is important, although Jesus as a person is presupposed. The significance of Jesus lies in how he impacts people, and thus how he is interpreted.[28]

---

26. Johann Baptist Metz, *Faith in History and Society: Toward a Practical Fundamental Theology* (New York: Seabury Press, 1980), 163–66. See James Matthew Ashley, *Interruptions: Mysticism, Politics, and Theology in the Work of Johann Baptist Metz* (Notre Dame, Ind.: University of Notre Dame Press, 1998), 129–34.

27. Cook, *Christology as Narrative Quest*, 39–49.

28. Rudolf Bultmann, *Jesus Christ and Mythology* (New York: Charles Scribner's Sons, 1958). The work of Schubert M. Ogden provides a more recent example of existential christology, although it is not exhaustively described as such. See his *Christ without*

Liberation Christology

The underlying structure of liberation christology incorporates many of the features enumerated thus far. It differs from existential christology in focusing on Jesus and assumes a narrative style in presenting him. But it is analogous to existential christology in its concern for salvation and its use of hermeneutics in approaching Jesus. What makes liberation christology distinctive, then, is its hermeneutical principle or key which in some respects has become symbolized in the phrase "option for the poor." Jesus is interpreted from the point of view of the social and cultural situation of destitution that allows people barely to survive in subhuman conditions.[29]

Existential and liberation christologies are not necessarily as antithetical as they are often depicted: the one privatized, the other socially conscious; the one denying the relevance of the historical reality of Jesus, the other in danger of using the discipline of history uncritically. In fact, existential Word christology can be liberationist, and the term "existential" need not be reduced to "individualistic."[30] Liberation christology is explicitly hermeneutical and concerned with salvation; it never seeks the "historical facts" of Jesus' life for their own sake.

Feminist Christology

Like liberation theology generally, feminist theology is differentiated and complex. Many regard it as closely allied with liberation christology, insofar as they share a common dialectical framework, the formal structure of oppression and liberation. There are material bonds as well: most of the world's poor are women. As far as the hermeneutical logic of theology is concerned, therefore, feminist theologians may refer to themselves as liberation theologians.[31] But at the same time the distinctive problematic of patriarchal structures, particularly as they have shaped the Christian tradition itself, provide this theology with a particular focus with universal import. In the measure that androcentrism has controlled the meaning of Jesus

---

Myth (New York: Harper & Row, 1961) and *The Point of Christology* (New York: Harper & Row, 1982).

29. The best example of Latin American liberation christology is Jon Sobrino, *Jesus the Liberator* (Maryknoll, N.Y.: Orbis Books, 1993; a second volume is forthcoming). The shift from an existential to a social hermeneutical perspective is clearly sketched by Dorothee Soelle, *Political Theology* (Philadelphia: Fortress Press, 1974).

30. For example, Schubert M. Ogden proposes his existential christology as essentially liberationist. See his essays, "The Concept of a Theology of Liberation: Must Christian Theology Today Be So Conceived," *On Theology* (San Francisco: Harper & Row, 1986), 134–50, and *Faith and Freedom: Toward a Theology of Liberation* (Nashville: Abingdon Press, 1979).

31. For example, Rosemary Radford Ruether, *Sexism and God-Talk: Toward a Feminist Theology* (Boston: Beacon Press, 1983), and Elisabeth Schüssler Fiorenza, *In Memory of Her: A Feminist Theological Reconstruction of Christian Origins* (New York: Crossroad, 1983), both consider themselves liberation theologians.

Christ, feminist christology has been forced to question how a male savior figure can offer salvation for women. In broader terms, however, feminist christology deals with every form of oppression and their interconnections. The God mediated by Jesus Christ calls into question all dominating power.[32]

Inculturated Christology

Liberation christology is inculturated; it responds to the concrete negativities of an historical context, and thus it takes on the character of the culture to which it responds. But the problematic of inculturation is more general than that of liberation, and it can become more radical. For inculturation makes the issues that are involved in interpretation explicit, and it underscores the necessity of change and difference in understanding. Christianity today is for the first time in its history self-consciously becoming a world religion; change, development, and inculturation are not just happening, but happening with planned intent. Jesus Christ must become African, Indian, Sri Lankan, Filipino, and Bolivian, in the same measure in which he became Greek and Latin, and profoundly reinterpreted by successive waves of western culture. Pluralism, sameness within differences, the possibility of mutual recognition within cross-cultural communication, Christian identity focused on and through Jesus amid different understandings of salvation, these are the themes which have risen to the surface and will assume great importance in the years to come.[33]

Jesus Christ and Other Religions

Another area in the study of Jesus Christ concerns his relation to other religions. For christology in those areas which are dominated by the other religions of the world this issue is central to the project of inculturation, to Christian identity, and thus to christology. It is not a corollary to ecclesiology, missiology, or christology; it defines the point of departure.

At the turn of the twentieth century Ernst Troeltsch raised the question of the absoluteness of Christianity, which reductively becomes a christological question, as a touchstone for emergent historical consciousness. But, for Karl Barth, Troeltsch symbolized all that was wrong with liberal theology, and the reaction against the constructive program of Troeltsch and others was complete. But this response merely suppressed the issue, and now it is back. The measure in which this issue is recognized today, not only by theologians but also by educated Christians generally, and the amount of discussion it is receiving in courses of theology and comparative religion, indicate the degree in which general consciousness has

---

32. Elisabeth Schüssler Fiorenza, *Jesus: Miriam's Child, Sophia's Prophet: Critical Issues in Feminist Christology* (New York: Continuum, 1994), 3–31.

33. For example, Robert Schreiter, ed., *Faces of Jesus in Africa* (Maryknoll, N.Y.: Orbis Books, 1991) and R. S. Sugirtharajah, ed., *Asian Faces of Jesus* (Maryknoll, N.Y.: Orbis Books, 1993).

become historically conscious. And the fact that one finds little, if any, consensus on the status of Jesus relative to other mediations of God in history shows that this is a genuinely open question, one which defines an attitudinal matrix that is prior to other christological issues.[34]

Other Religious Interpretations of Jesus

The confluence of Jesus research, comparative religious studies, and interreligious dialogue is producing more explicit interpretations and representations of Jesus from the perspective of other religions.[35] Such studies objectify and reflect back to Christians, often by contrast, their own understanding of Jesus in a starkly clear way. They provide a mirror by which Christians may judge the degree of their success in portraying Jesus to the world. And they display the possibilities of different and new interpretations.

Process Christology

Process thought is an attempt to accommodate the experience of historicity and change that has called the paradigm of classical consciousness into question. With a coherent philosophical base, and in terms more dynamic than those of substance philosophy, it reformulates issues that demand categories of fluidity and action. For example, the incarnation is understood dynamically within a framework of God's ongoing communicating presence to the world. The duality of the humanity and divinity within the unity of Jesus finds a distinctive constructive interpretation in which God's self-presence and human freedom reciprocally interact. Fundamentally, the standard christological issues are reinterpreted by the categories of process.[36]

Specific Christological Issues

Some of the fundamental questions that must be discussed within the discipline of christology are also undergoing a review. What has been outlined up to this point concerns the way the discipline of christology itself is approached, its structure and method. But there are also debates concerning some of the elementary topics that perennially have defined its

---

34. More than any other in the United States, Paul Knitter has kept this question before the minds of theologians. His latest works are *One Earth Many Religions: Multifaith Dialogue & Global Responsibility* (Maryknoll, N.Y.: Orbis Books, 1995), *Jesus and the Other Names: Christian Mission and Global Responsibility* (Maryknoll, N.Y.: Orbis Books, 1996), and Leonard Swidler and Paul Mojzes, eds., *The Uniqueness of Jesus: A Dialogue with Paul F. Knitter* (Maryknoll, N.Y.: Orbis Books, 1997). Each of the first two of these volumes contains an extensive bibliography on this issue.

35. See Paul J. Griffiths, *Christianity through Non-Christian Eyes* (Maryknoll, N.Y.: Orbis Books, 1990).

36. Norman Pittenger, *Catholic Faith in a Process Perspective* (Maryknoll, N.Y.: Orbis Books, 1981), esp. 73–101 and *The Word Incarnate* (New York: Harper & Row, 1959). Also John Cobb, *Christ in a Pluralistic Age* (Philadelphia: Westminster Press, 1975).

content. The following four crucial topics yield wide-ranging and different interpretations.

First, what is the meaning of incarnation? It has become apparent that demythologization is not a response to something negative, that a mythic understanding of reality is common and even demanded by some aspects of life. But can we not achieve a more open and critical understanding of Jesus' origin with God than what is naively suggested by the myth when it is taken not as myth but as literal? Are there any analogues or symbolic references that may guide our understanding at this point? Demythologization is a valid process, but it demands new categories for remythologizing how God was at work in Jesus. And primary religious language must be reappropriated on the theological level with critical conceptualizations.[37]

Second, many christologies today interpret the councils of Nicaea and Chalcedon in an effort to make them intelligible. But this concern is not universal. Some christologies interpret these doctrines historically, as functions of the past and without further comment, and thus also with little intelligibility in our situation. Sometimes these doctrines are bracketed in favor of evangelical language. More commonly, when these doctrines are acknowledged, they are subjected to historical criticism. But the question raised by these various strategies is the same: what can these doctrines mean positively in our various social and cultural situations today? There is more consensus in the critique of these doctrines than in a constructive response to this question.

Third, Logos christology itself, which has been the paradigm for all christology from the beginning of the patristic period, is now being called into question. Are there not other New Testament christologies that can be appropriated by various cultures in the way Logos language was adopted by Greek culture? Does not Spirit christology possess stronger warrant in the New Testament, more intelligibility for an historicist imagination, and greater emotive power for the Christian life than Logos christology?[38] Are there still other New Testament christologies that might form a basis for an integral christology?

Fourth, historical consciousness is affecting the trinitarian foundation for christology.[39] As long as one's consciousness is shaped dogmatically by the systematic coherence of the doctrines of Christ and the immanent

---

37. Karl-Josef Kuschel, *Born Before All Time? The Dispute over Christ's Origin* (New York: Crossroad, 1992), represents a dialogue between exegetes and theologians on this issue.

38. So argues Paul W. Newman, *A Spirit Christology: Rediscovering the Biblical Paradigm of Christian Faith* (Lanham, Md.: University Press of America, 1987).

39. Catherine Mowry LaCugna, in *God for Us: The Trinity and Christian Life* (San Francisco: HarperCollins, 1991), traces the historical development of the doctrine of the trinity and reinterprets it in a way that restores primacy to the trinitarian economy that lies at the center of Christian faith and life.

trinity, the latter doctrine acts as a support for one's understanding of Jesus Christ. But for an historically differentiated manner of thinking, the doctrine of the immanent trinity depends on christology, so that it must be rethought in terms of all the problems that have been set forth here. The doctrine of God's trinitarian economy of salvation is the centerpiece of Christianity itself, but it is becoming difficult to propose the doctrine of the immanent trinity as the premise or starting point for a critical and apologetic christology.

In sum, the discipline of christology today can be characterized as pluralistic. There are many different methodological approaches to Jesus Christ and different positions on the topics that are normally treated within it. This first characterization of the situation of christology, then, defines it with reference to the actual movements and developments that are occurring in the discipline. This situation may also be understood in the more general terms of the consciousness that accompanies these developments.

POSTMODERN CONSCIOUSNESS

The meaning and valuation assigned to the term "postmodernity" are certainly not uniform today. In Chapter 11, in the course of developing further the situation of christology today, I shall outline the sense of postmodernity that is at work in this book. But even at this initial stage I want briefly to indicate that the movements and problems that are driving christology reflect a cultural thematic. Whether the elements of this current situation clearly transcend modernity may be debated. But reflective appraisal of contemporary modes and qualities of thought are of critical importance.

Some of the elements of current consciousness are widespread in the educated world and might be considered as part of a general awareness. The limits of our general picture of reality, of the cosmos, the planet, and human existence, are being expanded exponentially by science. The still vague new picture of reality that is coming into focus is being mediated on many fronts, through physics, astronomy, paleontology, biology, genetics, and so on. The historical consciousness of modernity is gradually becoming radicalized, spawning movements such as deconstructionism and a trenchant relativism. Pluralism too has become more radical; it threatens and it attracts; but there seems to be no important question that yields a consensus. A social understanding of human existence has become dominant for many; individualism does not correspond to the social construction of the human. But this promising new way of thinking also threatens to undermine the value of the individual subject. And thus, in full reaction, much of western culture clings to individualism with an almost religious tenacity. A consciousness of massive social evil is also part of late twentieth-century awareness. Because of the increase in the world's population and the mounting failure to distribute equitably the goods of the earth, the statistics of human suffering increasingly attack any optimistic sense of history. How are human beings to regard the future? Surely the vision of evolutionary progress is gone, and the grounds of hope are obscure.

The actual movements in christology today reflect and in some cases explicitly address issues that arise out of this new cultural milieu. Thus one can formulate in broad terms the questions that are latent in our situation.

QUESTIONS FOR CHRISTOLOGY TODAY

I conclude this chapter with an attempt to formulate more carefully the questions that are raised by these movements in christology and the cultural consciousness they reflect. Many questions must be addressed by any systematic christology simply to be adequate to the task. But some questions are particularly vital and critical at this juncture of history, and they help determine the distinctive character that a christology must assume today. The joining together of these particular problematic issues will help to account for the character of this work.

The first question concerns Jesus of Nazareth. A Christian cannot really respond to others about the nature of Christianity without some idea of who Jesus was. Historical consciousness forces this upon us. How is Jesus to be understood in his public appearance and ministry? The vigor with which Jesus research is going forward lends a certain immediacy to this question. But, on a deeper level, one will have to reflect on how this research enters into and affects the more formal discipline of christology. This issue is most important for understanding the structure of christology itself, and the question has to be addressed both theoretically and practically in terms of content.

The second question to which this christology addresses itself is the resurrection of Jesus. This is a standard topic in any christology because it is such a central consideration. Because of the many different approaches to the structure and meaning of Jesus' resurrection, every christology should present a coherent interpretation of what many Christians take to be the very core of Christian faith.

Third, christology must address the humanly caused and systemically ingrained human suffering that so characterizes our world situation today. Although human suffering cannot be reduced to social suffering, liberation christologies, including feminist, black, and womanist christologies, have brought to the fore at its most telling point the problem of evil and suffering for christology. The negativity of human existence reaches its most mysterious, widespread, and scandalous form in social suffering and oppression imposed by human beings on other innocent human beings. It is true that the larger and even more difficult problems of ecology and the management of nature have to form the context for dealing with sheer poverty and human degradation. Also, the larger questions of the culture and identity of those who are marginalized by society cannot be neglected in addressing the social injustice they endure. But needless human suffering has to form a focusing question for christology, not because christology will bear a messianic solution to these problems, but because Jesus cannot be the Christ and salvation cannot be real without having some bearing on this situation.

The fourth and perhaps most catalytic of the christological questions being asked today concerns the relation of Jesus Christ to other religions and mediations of ultimate reality. The consciousness that gives rise to this question is new; educated people take historical limitations, distinctiveness, and pluralism for granted. But what is most important here is the recognition that this question itself is an open one because it rests on new cultural suppositions, and that, as a real question, it must induce new christological thinking. One cannot develop a christology independently of this question and attach the solution as a kind of appendix. The historical situation of christology today, one which enters intrinsically into one's way of thinking about Jesus Christ, is already defined by an attitude that is accepting of other religions in principle and an appreciation of interreligious dialogue, and this must find expression in christology.

The fifth question concerns the meaning of salvation. This term is one of the most frequently used in the Christian vocabulary. But like other symbols which point to realities that are deeply existential and transcendent in their source, the term "salvation" can become vague and superficial. Moreover, the ancient mythological stories of how Jesus saved have lost their power; instead of functioning as life-giving symbols, they have become objective, literal, incredible, and even embarrassing. One needs a new language of salvation, one that addresses the historical suffering experienced in our world, and the present-day consciousness that is scandalized by it, and at the same time is faithful to the scriptural and classical witness about Jesus saving.

And, finally, the sixth major question that must be addressed by any christology, but which is particularly pressing today, concerns Jesus' divinity. Along with this there must also be some reflection on the dependent doctrine of the trinity, since these two doctrines developed in such close association with each other. This investigation will unfold in several layers, then, for it entails a historical interpretation and retrieval of the classical doctrines, a constructive proposal that will be faithful to scripture and the doctrinal tradition, and at the same time try to meet the exigencies of current consciousness.

Such is the situation of christology, in its relationship to Christian theology generally, and particularly in terms of the consciousness it must address and the questions to which it must respond. The chapter which follows will take up the question of method in such a way that these questions will be integrated into the construction of a christology that addresses our situation.

CHAPTER 2

The Method of Christology

The review of the developments in christology in the last chapter shows the vitality of the discipline. It is evolving on many simultaneous and in some degree independent fronts. When one brings all of these areas together and takes the measure of the many fundamental questions that are being asked, one must also ask whether christological beliefs are on the verge of passing into a new configuration. If such were the case, it would not necessarily mean that the core of Christian faith would also change, for faith is distinct from belief, and its fundamental commitment has continually undergone changing beliefs through the centuries. But at the same time, the adjustment of beliefs that often accompanies a genuinely new understanding can constitute a new vision of things.

How are we to cope with these many diverse conversations that make up the situation of christology today? How can so many fundamental questions be handled at one time on a level that transcends superficiality? Is there a way to establish a measure of control, or at least some integration, relative to these many developments? The response to these questions lies in the area of method. In what follows, I will characterize a fundamental approach to these issues, a strategy for understanding that will encompass the various christological questions that are being debated. Added to this will be the definition of a method or way of proceeding that corresponds to this heuristic strategy. The only way to integrate these areas of development into some unity is to establish a consistent framework and method that prove themselves by generating a coherent understanding that is relatively adequate to the questions and the data.

This chapter, then, will unfold in three sections. The first will consider the heuristic framework that will govern this christology. The second will describe its method as a hermeneutical method of critical correlation. The third section will outline the criteria of theology as applied to christology.

A GENETIC STRUCTURE OF UNDERSTANDING

A genetic structure of understanding is one whose form or logic corresponds to the genesis of christology. In other words, one's understanding of what is going on in christology is learned from the historical process of how christology first evolved. The burden of this section is to explain this heuristic framework for christology. But this also involves responding to some other questions along the way. A number of standard issues pertain to the topic of method in christology, and one must touch upon them, sometimes for no other reason than to locate oneself in a tradition.

BEGINNING WITH JESUS

A standard issue relative to Christian theology generally is whether it should have an apologetic character, and what this would mean. This has direct bearing on the starting point of christology. One could define the alternatives by measuring the distance between the approaches of Friedrich Schleiermacher and Karl Barth. If one regarded Schleiermacher's *Discourses on Religion* as integral to his later systematic work in christology, despite the differences, one has a classic example of an apologetic theology.[1] Religion and Christianity make sense because they fulfill the very aspirations of human existence as understood by the cultured people of his time. By contrast, Barth sees no reason whatsoever for revelation or theology to be beholden to the philosophy or science or culture of the day.[2] His christology is one of firm, declarative assertion, paragraph after paragraph. Schleiermacher and Barth have been raised to the level of symbols, and all are familiar with the extremes of the positions and their dangers. The question is whether there might be a more broadly acceptable meaning of apology.

Apology means, first of all, taking one's audience seriously. If one wants to be understood, one must take into account the audience or the variety of audiences to which one seeks to communicate. Early in its existence the church adopted a missionary posture as it spread beyond the eastern Mediterranean and addressed the Greco-Roman world. This mission church, bent on evangelizing Greek and Roman culture, was forced to enter into the culture with which it sought to communicate. Christology like any other theological subdiscipline must be apologetic in this first sense of entering into the culture with which it is intended to communicate.

Christology is apologetic in a second sense: it makes an effort to explain christological faith and belief. The equation of apology and explanation

---

1. Friedrich Schleiermacher, *On Religion: Speeches to Its Cultured Despisers* (New York: Harper & Row, 1958), 1–25.
2. Karl Barth, *Church Dogmatics*, I, 1, *The Doctrine of the Word of God* (Edinburgh: T. & T. Clark, 1975), 3–44.

does not entail a reduction of faith, which is the basis and source of christology, to explanatory reason. Faith can never be subject to adequate explanation and will never be explained away. Christology begins and ends in faith; it communicates from and appeals to faith. But christology must transcend fideism, that is, pure assertion of this faith, without any account of its inner logic or its coherence with what is known to be true from other sources. Critical reason, therefore, has a role in the development of christology from within faith itself.

Christology is apologetic in a third sense: it appeals to something that Christians and all others alike share in common, namely, a public figure, Jesus of Nazareth. One of the ways in which apology makes contact with its audience is by establishing the common ground between the speaker and those who are addressed. Some believe that, if one accepts any given cultural norm or anthropology as a standard, or as a basis for building a christology and communicating Christ, Jesus Christ will inevitably be compromised in the end. But this overstates the case and misses the point of beginning with Jesus. The first disciples "began" with Jesus. And all human beings thereafter potentially can share a common knowledge of Jesus of Nazareth, a human being and a public figure who in some measure has been preserved in the gospel portraits. In this respect it does not matter that Jesus is construed differently from different points of view; he is a common subject matter for conversation.

The primary reason for beginning christology with Jesus of Nazareth, then, is the apologetic character of Christian faith itself. The impulse to communicate and explain is entailed in the missionary dimension of faith; it flows from the conviction of faith's universal relevance. The public appearance of Jesus, in turn, is the historical datum that allows for the possibility that christological faith be shared by all human beings.

Karl Rahner helped to clarify the language of the discipline when he distinguished two different approaches in christology in terms of a point of departure: christology from above and christology from below.[3] Since the patristic period christology unfolded from above, that is, it began on the basis of authority, with an understanding of an exalted Christ as presented in the Johannine tradition, or, later, a construal of God as differentiated into a trinity. In the course of its development such a christology also accounted for the true humanity of Jesus, his consubstantiality with human beings. With these shared convictions as a starting point this christology as it were "descends," following the pattern of the incarnation itself. By contrast, Rahner noted the modern trend in christology which unfolded from below. It began on the basis of a consideration of Jesus of Nazareth, and continued with an interpretation of his resurrection. After an examination of New Testament christologies and, perhaps, patristic christologies as well, this approach led to a consideration of the divinity of Jesus the Christ. With its

---

3. Karl Rahner, "The Two Basic Types of Christology," *Theological Investigations*, 13 (New York: Seabury Press, 1975), 213–23.

starting point consisting in Jesus of Nazareth, this christology "ascends," following the pattern of resurrection and exaltation.[4] For his part Rahner considered the two methods equally valid.

If the term "valid" were used in a more practical sense to connote apologetically sensitive, communicative, engaging, credible, and successful, it might well be argued that christology from above is precisely not valid today. Of course, there may be sectors within the church where one only need appeal to the authority of Christian sources to justify language about Jesus Christ. One cannot dismiss completely the theoretical possibility of a convincing christology from above. But if one reflects on the measure to which the intellectual culture of those outside the church is also within the church, as is witnessed by the developments in christology, one may find it difficult to ignore that questions are being asked within the church itself that require an approach from below that is apologetic in intent. The whole Christian community is in search of a viable christology for today, and it is not possessed by anyone in such a manner that it can be proclaimed on the sole basis of authority.

Christology, then, begins with Jesus; christology from below is one that begins with Jesus of Nazareth. On the one hand, the logic for this is utterly simple: Jesus is the subject matter, or the object, of christology. Christology is reaction to and interpretation of Jesus. Christology came into existence for the first time as a response to Jesus; it developed out of an encounter with God in and through Jesus during and after his lifetime. Since christology is about Jesus, there is nothing more simple than to realize that he remains its point of departure even today. On the other hand, however, nothing is ever as simple as it seems. In using the proper noun "Jesus" to designate Jesus of Nazareth, we have up to this point prescinded from the question of whether, how, and in what measure one can know something about Jesus. These issues are hotly debated today within the discipline of New Testament studies and christology, and the work being done to address them has a significant bearing on christology.

JESUS RESEARCH AND ITS IMPACT ON CHRISTOLOGY

I shall not review the history of the quest for the historical Jesus, beginning with questions posed by eighteenth-century rationalism, the flowering of the quest in the nineteenth century, the questioning of its premises and rejection of its relevance for christology by German evangelical theology in the early twentieth century, and its gradual return to prominence on new premises beginning in the middle of this century. Research on Jesus is a vital area of scholarship at the turn of the twenty-first century.

---

4. It is important not to confuse this language with the terms that characterize as "low" or "high" those christologies that emphasize, often to the neglect of the other, either the humanity or the divinity of Jesus Christ. Christology from below may generate a high christology.

In what follows I will analyze various aspects of this research from the narrow perspective of its bearing on christology. Broadly speaking, one can discern two distinct concerns and hence approaches to Jesus in the literature. One is intent on presenting an accurate historical representation of Jesus in his own context. Another is concerned with understanding Jesus as a figure who is relevant to today's world. After schematizing the logic of both, I will describe the impact of this material on christology generally and on this essay in particular.

Jesus research is historical investigation of Jesus of Nazareth. One of the first concerns of this study is purely historical: it seeks to present an accurate historical portrait of Jesus within the context of first-century Palestine. Historical research is concerned with the epistemological and historical questions of whether, how, and with what measure of success one can reconstruct the person of Jesus. Given the fact that the direct sources available for this project are for the most part the synoptic gospels, and that these are documents written out of a tradition of a faith commitment that already sees in Jesus one who was sent by God, and that expresses this faith in the stories about him, how can one get back to the way Jesus actually appeared? Relative to this issue, the phrase, the "historical Jesus," is an epistemologically technical term that refers to Jesus insofar as he has been reconstructed by the historian.

This material is relevant to christology insofar as it responds to questions such as the following that may be asked about Jesus. Has religious interpretation of Jesus, such as that found in the gospels, created someone other than Jesus as he actually was during his lifetime? Can the historical interpretations of Jesus, the various portraits of the historical Jesus, yield a consensus on the person Jesus of Nazareth? Will such an historical portrait of Jesus provide a "basis" for all future interpretations thereby ensuring a norm for christological interpretation?[5]

Regarding the first two questions concerning the historical project itself, those engaged in it believe that one can get behind the faith-filled evangelical accounts of Jesus and make some judgments about Jesus, his public life, and his teaching. These are never very detailed pictures, and when one reflects for a moment on what one does not and cannot know about Jesus, they seem a pale shadow of the actual person, especially the person entertained by faith. John Meier explains the project of the historian in terms of an application of certain agreed upon criteria of historicity.[6] The

---

5. The term "basis" is particularly ambiguous in the setting of this discussion. It takes on a spectrum of meanings between a hard sense of "warrant" or "proof," and a soft sense of being "the object of reference." It is important to attend to the particular usage and not take its meaning for granted.

6. John P. Meier, *A Marginal Jew: Rethinking the Historical Jesus*, 1, *The Roots of the Problem and the Person* (New York: Doubleday, 1991), 21–40, 167–95. But these criteria are not universally agreed upon. For example, another considerably different set of criteria are offered by John Dominic Crossan, *The Historical Jesus: The Life of a Mediterranean Jewish Peasant* (San Francisco: HarperCollins, 1991), xi–xxxiv.

historian is very careful in isolating what may be considered the more or less authentic historical sources for making any judgments. On a more theoretical level of literary hermeneutics, Eric Hirsch argues historically and philosophically that authorial intent is the basis of all interpretation of past texts. His position on hermeneutics supplies reasons for wanting objective criteria to tie down meaning that stands at the source of a tradition to the particular historical moment of its appearance. The reception of past historical meaning into new situations he calls "significance" in order to distinguish it from the original historical meaning.[7] By analogy, the quest for the historical Jesus seeks a reconstruction of Jesus in terms of how he was understood during his lifetime, as distinct from later interpretations of him.

A major ambiguity characterizes the quest for the historical Jesus that, as far as I can see, cannot finally be adjudicated. This concerns an a priori imaginative assessment of the degree to which the portraits of Jesus in the synoptic gospels correspond to Jesus of Nazareth. Each author who takes up the question has some judgment on this, even though it may remain implicit, and collectively they vary considerably. Some authors work with a deep suspicion that the portrait found in the synoptics is distant from the "real" Jesus;[8] others work on an assumption of a basic continuity between the two.[9] This is one of the a priori subjective factors that will always preclude a consensus on Jesus.

Within this first concern for reconstructing the historical Jesus one finds two different trends among the researchers which can be seen to complement each other. The first belongs to those authors who work on what may be called "the genre of Jesus." They are interested in a broad characterization of the kind of person he was, the role he assumed, the public image he projected or with which he was labeled. Jesus was a Jew, but what type of Jewish figure was he? On the assumption that a decision

7. Eric D. Hirsch, *Validity in Interpretation* (New Haven: Yale University Press, 1967), 1–23, 245–64. See also E. D. Hirsch, *The Aims of Interpretation* (Chicago: University of Chicago Press, 1976), passim. Although I do not subscribe to the hermeneutical theory of Hirsch, it may be conceded that he has a nuanced appreciation of how the intent of an author may be approached, and that this helps in establishing the historicity or historical individuality of a past text. In contrast to Hirsch, however, it must be insisted that in the same measure that meaning is reduced to the intent of the particular author, it is also distanced from future situations, so that its "significance" is attenuated. A more adequate theory of meaning, therefore, locates it in the encounter of the interpreter with the reality to which the text is a witness.

8. Rudolf Bultmann would be typical of such a position. Although he recognized the historical figure of Jesus in his work *Jesus and the Word* (New York: Charles Scribner's Sons, 1934), still, his extended use and perfecting of form critical analysis allowed him to see the measure in which the synoptic stories reflected the life situation of the early Christian communities.

9. Edward Schillebeeckx, in his work *Jesus: An Experiment in Christology* (New York: Seabury Press, 1979), exemplifies a critical stance that joins historical conservatism with a conviction about a certain continuity between the synoptic material and Jesus.

about genre is a first broad hermeneutical decision about how the details of witness about Jesus are to be understood,[10] this analysis is important. It unfolds on a broader and more abstract plane that transcends and subsumes decisions about the historicity of this or that pericope or saying. But it provides a gestalt that directs interpretation. For example, Geza Vermes tries to establish that Jesus was a wonder-worker, a holy man who performed exorcisms and was able to cure at a distance. This accounts for his being noticed by the crowds.[11] Edward Sanders interprets Jesus as a charismatic prophet dramatically announcing the restoration of Israel.[12] Prophetically symbolic actions directed toward the temple in Jerusalem especially account for the events that led to his public execution. Burton Mack presents Jesus as an itinerant and iconoclastic teacher of wisdom with a band of followers in the style of a Cynic philosopher.[13]

The discipline of christology can learn from all of these portraits of Jesus. They are not equally credible, and criticism by the exegetes and historians themselves will measure those which are more and less adequate to the data. But christology does not have to unfold on the basis of a choice between these hypothetical constructions. One can learn from all of these large schematic outlines of the person of Jesus without having to make decisive judgments.

The second style of search for the historical Jesus proceeds in a more piecemeal fashion. It is slower to project or hypothesize the genre of Jesus and stays with the details. It analyzes the sayings of Jesus, the parables of Jesus, his prophetic actions, certain themes such as the kingdom of God, his exorcisms, the events that have been called his miracles. Pericope by pericope, each story is analyzed in its parallels and development; source criticism, form criticism, and redaction criticism are all marshaled to help in a judgment about this or that aspect of Jesus' historical appearance. This is the method of Meier as he patiently sifts the literature and applies the criteria of authenticity. His results are modest but solid. For example, Meier shows that it is historically certain that Jesus performed wonderful actions of healing and exorcism that attracted attention, without, however, being able to give a description of exactly how these events transpired.[14] Gerd Theissen could perhaps be characterized as an author who combines both an approach through particulars

---

10. See Hirsch, *Validity in Interpretation*, 222, with reference to the analogous problem of determining the meaning of a text.

11. Geza Vermes, *Jesus the Jew: A Historian's Reading of the Gospels* (Philadelphia: Fortress Press, 1973).

12. E. P. Sanders, *Jesus and Judaism* (Philadelphia: Fortress Press, 1985).

13. Burton L. Mack, *The Lost Gospel: The Book of Q and Christian Origins* (San Francisco: Harper, 1993).

14. See John Meier, *A Marginal Jew*, 2, *Mentor, Message, and Miracles* (New York: Doubleday, 1994), 967–70, where he summarizes an exhaustive survey and analysis.

and the broader generalizations.[15] One senses in his work a non-skeptical attitude toward the broad correspondence between the synoptics and Jesus. Theissen represents Jesus in general Hellenistic categories of the first century as a philosopher and poet, but also in more strictly Jewish terms as an eschatological prophet and possible messiah.

A significantly different kind of Jesus research is conducted by those who are concerned about understanding Jesus in such a way that he is relevant to today's world. These authors move a step closer to the discipline of christology, and, in fact, some of them may be considered as working within the field of christology. Their intentionality may be called historical, but it is not purely historical in the sense of interpreting the past in its own past context or recreating a portrait of the past. Rather the concern here is to overcome a historicism which would hold that all data from the past is individual, particular, and so historically circumscribed that it cannot be normative for another different situation. The more the understanding and meaning of a past event, person, or text is tied to the past, the less is it relevant for our self-understanding in the present. The christological concern is evident: unless the meaning of Jesus can be released from the past and shown to be relevant beyond its limited horizon, christology becomes impossible.

It is important to appreciate the theory that underlies this concern for Jesus, lest it be judged as unhistorical simply because it is not the same historical concern as re-presenting the ostensible past. Inspired by Martin Heidegger, theologians such as Rudolf Bultmann and Schubert Ogden release the saving content of Jesus from the empirical-historical detail of his life and find it in the existential reality of the encounter with God that is mediated in the New Testament message or the Jesus kerygma. Ogden is a good example because he has been writing for some time and has exerted a strong influence in christology. Ogden distinguishes between the empirical-historical Jesus and the existential-historical Jesus.[16] Both of these terms refer to Jesus, but they differ epistemologically in the manner in which Jesus is perceived or appreciated. The distinction does not concern Jesus, therefore, but ourselves, the knowers, with respect to the different ways of knowing and appreciating Jesus. Because the gospels are existentially engaged and faith-filled appreciations of Jesus, they cannot be the basis for reconstructing an empirical-historical Jesus, nor would such a step be christologically significant, since faith, which is directed toward a transcendent God, cannot find a "basis" in any empirical-historical

---

15. See, for example, the combination of certain details about Jesus and his teaching and the broad generalizations that Gerd Theissen offers in his narrative portrayal of Jesus in *The Shadow of the Galilean: The Quest of the Historical Jesus in Narrative Form* (London: SCM, 1987).

16. Schubert M. Ogden, *The Point of Christology* (San Francisco: Harper & Row, 1982), 41–63, 113–26.

data.[17] What is generated by Jesus research in the end is not an empirical-historical Jesus but an existential-historical Jesus, that is, the portrait of Jesus as contained in the Jesus kerygma, which is the earliest witness of faith to Jesus. In this way, Ogden both saves the quest for the now existential-historical Jesus or Jesus kerygma, and finds a way of seeing the relevance of this Jesus to present-day faith.

Generally, the intentionality of the hermeneutical theories of Hans-Georg Gadamer and Paul Ricoeur can be seen as relevant to this wing of those who are interested in the historical Jesus. Also inspired by Heidegger, Gadamer shows how foreknowledge and questioning on the one hand, and fusion of horizons and application on the other, enter into the structure of all knowing: knowing is interpreting, out of a tradition and into a present-day situation.[18] For Ricoeur, the intrinsic meaning of a past text transcends its original limitations by a distanciation from its author, situation, and audience. And by an indigenous surplus of meaning, a text acquires new meanings in new situations, meanings which are also intrinsic to the original. Appropriation in any given situation involves being altered and changed by a new, real, and referential existential possibility that is really contained in the past document but not explicitly or consciously intended in its future form.[19]

The logic governing this hermeneutical theory intends that interpretation be faithful to the intrinsic meaning of the past, in its particularity and circumscribed by its situation. At the same time interpretation breaks open that particularity and grasps its universal relevance in an expanded meaning that has a bearing on life today and is accompanied by a claim to truth. This is a different project than the purely historical one of recreating the past because, while it respects appreciation of the past as past, it also utterly transforms that understanding by placing it in an explicit relationship with the questioner in the present. Many of those who do christology today, and who look back to the "historical Jesus," should be understood as working within this paradigm: feminist theologians, liberation theologians, political theologians, theologians dedicated to inculturation. They are intent on presenting portraits of Jesus which correspond to the historical Jesus, but which are also intended to be relevant to spe-

---

17. The same valid point is frequently made by saying that one cannot pass from empirical history to christological assertion except by a leap of faith. Note, however, that one could also say, from another perspective and making a different point, that one could not have any idea of God with specific content without some "basis" in history.

18. Hans-Georg Gadamer, *Truth and Method* (New York: Seabury Press, 1975), 235–40, 245–78, 289–94, 325–41.

19. Paul Ricoeur, *Hermeneutics and the Human Sciences* (Cambridge: Cambridge University Press, 1981), 131–44, 182–93. Also Paul Ricoeur, *Interpretation Theory: Discourse and the Surplus of Meaning* (Fort Worth: Texas Christian University, 1976), 25–44.

cific aspects of life in our current world. For example, Elisabeth Schüssler Fiorenza represents Jesus as the source and foundation of a movement of a discipleship of equals; without using the obviously anachronistic term, Jesus is implicitly understood as embodying feminist values.[20] Jürgen Moltmann's Jesus, whom he refers to mainly as Christ, is responsive to many of the human and political dilemmas we experience today.[21] In Edward Schillebeeckx's work *Jesus*, Jesus is the bearer of God's salvation in response to all forms of human suffering in a portrayal that clearly has our present world in view. Jon Sobrino's liberationist interpretation of Jesus responds to the massive human suffering caused by social injustice in Latin America and beyond.[22] Asians and Africans interpret Jesus in categories that are indigenous to their various cultures and respond to religious sensibilities of the place.

Most of the theologians listed here would agree with Ogden that they are working with an existential-historical Jesus in two respects: with respect to the sources and with respect to the existential concern they bring to the project. Very few theologians claim to "base" their christology on a recreation of an empirical-historical Jesus. Faith cannot be mediated "on the basis of," in the sense of being caused by, historical evidence. But this does not mean that the quest for the historical Jesus, even in its more strictly historical version, has no relevance at all for christology.

Regarding the bearing of Jesus research on christology, this line of investigation is one of the factors that is transforming the discipline. Of course, there are different ways of addressing this question, and from certain points of view Jesus research does not affect christological understanding at all. Some doctrines about Jesus do not stand or fall on the basis of a more detailed knowledge of Jesus. But from another perspective one can see how the ongoing results of this investigation are having their effect. Three things stand out here.

First, Jesus research reinforces the conviction that Jesus is the "basis" of christology in the sense that Jesus is the object or subject matter of christology. A Christian cannot escape interest in Jesus of Nazareth; popular interest in the results of Jesus research shows that this theoretical consideration corresponds to a spontaneous desire to know. People have a practical curiosity about the way Jesus actually appeared. This

---

20. See Elisabeth Schüssler Fiorenza, *In Memory of Her: A Feminist Theological Reconstruction of Christian Origins* (New York: Crossroad, 1983), 26–36, 39–40, where she explains her hermeneutical historical method.

21. Jürgen Moltmann, *The Way of Jesus Christ: Christology in Messianic Dimensions* (Minneapolis: Fortress Press, 1993).

22. Jon Sobrino's first extended essay in christology, *Christology at the Crossroads* (Maryknoll, N.Y.: Orbis Books, 1978), illustrates well this hermeneutical intent. He gives a detailed analytical account of his hermeneutical method in *Jesus the Liberator: A Historical-Theological Reading of Jesus of Nazareth* (Maryknoll, N.Y.: Orbis Books, 1993), 11–63.

curiosity can never be fully satisfied. But at the same time what we can and do know about Jesus is both sufficient and necessary for christology.[23] That this knowledge is based on the Jesus kerygma and is mediated from and to an existential-historical concern in no way precludes a priori that it refers and corresponds to Jesus of Nazareth in a way that is historically true.

This insistence on Jesus being the subject matter of christology has some consequences. It entails the thesis that statements about Jesus Christ always have to have some connection with Jesus of Nazareth. If Jesus is the subject matter of christology, the interpretations of Jesus as the Christ must remain interpretations of Jesus. What is being called for here is a joining together of a historical and a theological imagination. When, later on, I consider Jesus as a mediator of God's salvation, and the Christian doctrine that Jesus is divine, these theological assertions will have to be kept in tension with a historical imagination that keeps the human being Jesus, in however a general way, in view.

A second consideration shows further the way in which Jesus research is affecting christology. It has to do with the imagination. Historical investigation and interpretation of Jesus affects christology through the imagination. This can be briefly shown on the basis of the role of imagination in human knowing.

Imagination, or the imagination, is something with which everyone is familiar, but, as a part of the complex functioning of the human mind, it is exceedingly difficult to define. Using Aristotelian and Thomistic categories, the imagination is one of four inner senses that always accompanies human knowing, because all knowledge is drawn out of the data of the external senses and mediated to understanding through, among other things, concrete images that are in turn stored in the memory. The imagination also contains a creative power to construct new forms and meanings. For example, from the image of "gold" and of "a mountain" the imagination can construct a "golden mountain."[24] This creative power is most important for creative intelligence and for construing human possibilities into the future. It will become an important factor in resurrection faith. But for the moment I dwell on how theoretical knowledge is always tied to concrete images. In the case of Jesus, where possible, these images should be supplied by history.

The mechanics of faculty psychology should not distract from what is relevant here, namely, that as embodied knowing all human knowledge bears an element of the concrete that imaginatively accompanies it. Even the more abstract of our conceptions always bear with them an

---

23. I shall comment on the warrants of this sufficiency and necessity further on.

24. See Thomas Aquinas, *Summa Theologica: Complete English Edition in Five Volumes* (Westminster, Md.: Christian Classics, 1961), I, qq. 77–79, on the various powers of the human soul and their functions in intellectual knowing.

imaginative residue that is the trace of our physical being in the world. This function of the imagination means that all understandings of Jesus Christ are accompanied by some imaginative portrayal, however implicit this may remain. For example, the liturgical, catechetical, and generally devotional mediations of Jesus Christ, by which the life of faith of most Christians is cultivated, will always be accompanied implicitly by an imaginative construal of Jesus that corresponds with the devotional, liturgical, hymnic, and doctrinal language. What is said here of ordinary Christians applies as well to theologians insofar as they too presumably take part in the Christian community.

At this point one can see how Jesus research comes to bear on the understanding of Jesus Christ. It impacts the imagination and re-schools it by supplying more directly historical images that more closely correspond to the historical person Jesus. This influence is both negative and positive. Negatively, historical Jesus research calls into question unhistorical or "purely dogmatic" conceptions of Jesus, that is, those conceptions of Jesus Christ that have been severed from a concrete or historically realistic imagination, and operate in a quasi-docetist fashion. Positively, historical research enriches the imagination and proposes a historically concrete construal of the Christian mediation of God who is Jesus of Nazareth. What is described here in neutral, technical terms, however, can represent a dramatic transition in the life of an individual Christian or, over a longer period of time, a community. This is going on at present.

A third way of formulating how Jesus research is affecting christology, one that is closely related to the first two, concerns the relation between what christology affirms of Jesus in understanding him to be the Christ and Jesus' historical self, including his self-consciousness or his self-understanding. It is often presumed that what is affirmed by christology about Jesus does in fact correspond to his own consciousness about himself or his understanding of himself and his historical role. More than just a popular belief, some christologies unfold on the basis of this principle as a tacit premise. This is the reason, for example, why many christologies are interested in establishing some form of "implicit christology" in Jesus' own lifetime. The problem of the historical Jesus becomes particularly acute for an historicist imagination that defines or limits the intrinsic meaning of a past event by the actual consciousness that defined it in the past.[25] The actual meaning and function of Jesus are limited by his historical self-conscious intentions.

---

25. I am using "historicist" here in the sense seen in Hirsch earlier, where the strict meaning of a text, or by extension an event, is limited to its authorial intent. If one worked in such a system of understanding, for the intrinsic meaning of Jesus of Nazareth, as distinct from his later significance, to be the bearer of God's salvation in messianic terms, not to mention being the Logos of God, he would have had to possess such an awareness and intentionality.

But it is becoming increasingly clear through Jesus research that some later New Testament interpretations and, a fortiori, dogmatic interpretations were not part of Jesus' self-understanding. The majority of the portraits of the historical Jesus in fact presuppose and are constructed on the basis of naturalist assumptions and the principle of analogy, that is, that one cannot expect to find in the life of Jesus something that is utterly unknown anywhere else. Surely Jesus did not display any consciousness that he had two natures and was hypostatically united to the divine Word. Various other examples will be brought forward in the course of this work, but what is important here is the point. History appears to undercut the imaginative portrait of Jesus that has accompanied certain dogmatic conceptions of him. Historical reconstruction also heightens the tension involved in the distinction between Jesus' intrinsic historical meaning and his later significance for us. What Christians affirm about Jesus must be intended to apply to him in his earthly career.

As a response to this problem, historical research into Jesus seems to impel the following thesis: later interpretations of Jesus may capture his intrinsic meaning and reality even though they may not have been part of Jesus' self-consciousness or self-understanding. In other words, one can affirm something to be the case about Jesus, especially in his relation to God or in his relation to ourselves, that was not necessarily part of Jesus' consciousness. This principle will have a major role to play in the theology of salvation. There will undoubtedly be debate over the extent to which this principle may be applied. Not everyone will be content to see it applied at every juncture. But Karl Rahner prepared the ground for such a thesis by distinguishing levels of consciousness in Jesus so that, theoretically speaking, Jesus did not have to be explicitly conscious of the depth of his relation to God.[26] But whatever its range of application, this principle can play a major role in christology. Negatively, the thesis proposed here relieves the necessity that later New Testament claims about Jesus or present-day construals of him correspond exactly to Jesus' consciousness or self-understanding. Positively, it frees christology to find categories for expressing the intrinsic meanings of Jesus that truly refer to the Jesus of history, are analogous with those of the tradition, but in their difference are also more directly relevant to our present situation.

In sum, the effect of Jesus research on christology can be understood in a dialectical way through the mediation of the concrete, historical imagination and the role of the imagination in all knowing. On the one hand, historical research encourages christology to keep close to the most primitive kerygma or witness to Jesus. This closeness will function as a kind of negative norm that will chasten predications about Jesus that are not realistic or credible. But on the other hand, and dialectically related to the first

---

26. Karl Rahner, "Dogmatic Reflections on the Knowledge and Self-Consciousness of Christ," *Theological Investigations*, 5 (Baltimore: Helicon Press, 1966), 193–215.

principle, christological affirmation is not positively limited to the primitive witness to Jesus of Nazareth. Reconstructions of the historical Jesus do not in any sense have the last word in christology.

A GENETIC STRUCTURE OF UNDERSTANDING

The phrase, "a genetic structure of understanding," is designed to provide in broad terms a first characterization of the method of this work. This method has been described as having an apologetic dimension, being initiated from below and ascending, beginning with Jesus, and recognizing the impact of the new wave of Jesus research on the imagination of all Christians, theologians included. A genetic structure of understanding draws these elements together in the insight that one can grasp the logic of christology by tracing the history of the original development of christology. The structure of christology is represented in the New Testament as the implicit story of the genesis of the first christologies. The elements for the development are found in the pages of the New Testament: Jesus, his impact on disciples, the disciples encountering God in Jesus in one way or another, the experience of God's salvation in Jesus, interpretations of who Jesus was, interpretation of God's relation to Jesus and of Jesus' relation to God, and in the light of this, interpretations of God, of human existence, of the dynamic relation between God and human beings. A *genetic* structure, then, is first of all a history, a story, a drama in which the unfolding of events have a beginning and, in some respects, an end with the proclamation of Jesus as the Christ and a more developed understanding of what this might mean.

This genesis, however, has a *structure*, and it will be analyzed in more detail in Chapter 7. This structure revolves around Jesus and his being the historical mediation of God to human existence. This is the structure of Christian faith, of the faith of each individual Christian and of the community as it moves through history. It is thus a dynamic structure in the sense that it describes an event that keeps recurring. Jesus continues to mediate the presence and consciousness of God to the Christian community for its salvation. Thus one can see repeated in the life of the community, and in its understanding of who Jesus Christ is, this formal genetic structure of Jesus being the historical mediation of God to human existence. Let this serve as a first formal characterization of the christological approach of this book.

A HERMENEUTICAL METHOD OF CRITICAL CORRELATION

Given today's pluralism in theology, a systematic account of any topic requires an explanation of the method that is being employed. The description of a method should be clear enough to provide a schematic map of what will unfold in the pages of a work. I will try to present a straightforward description of the dynamics of understanding, or the pattern of interpretation that is operative here. I propose in two interactive moments a hermeneutical method that involves a critical correlation of tradition and present-day experience.

A HERMENEUTICAL METHOD

The tradition of hermeneutical thought that began with Schleiermacher has gained a new importance for theology through the interpretations of Heidegger, Bultmann, Gadamer, Ricoeur, Tracy, Jeanrond, Schneiders, and others.[27] Generally these authors are concerned with the interpretations of texts. But what they describe is more than a method of understanding texts. To understand anything is to interpret it, and a thoroughgoing hermeneutical theory transcends epistemology to become an anthropology. To be human is to interpret. Thus we will have to ask what it means to interpret a person, to apply hermeneutical theory to Jesus of Nazareth, as well as past texts.

Many things recommend hermeneutical theory as an area of thought from which to draw fundamental ideas relating to theological method. Hermeneutical theory is historically conscious and appreciates the deep threat of a relativistic pluralism that historicity seems to mediate. But even in its historical consciousness this hermeneutical theory seeks to overcome a radical historicism and to reflect in its theory of knowing the deep continuity in human existence that is continually mediated by history.[28] Hermeneutical theory is a congenial resource for disciplines like ethics, law, and theology which make appeal to a normative tradition.

---

27. Among the works to which I am indebted in these reflections are the following: Rudolf Bultmann, "The Problem of Hermeneutics," *New Testament and Mythology and Other Basic Writings*, ed. Schubert M. Ogden (Philadelphia: Fortress Press, 1984); Gadamer, *Truth and Method*; Werner G. Jeanrond, *Text and Interpretation as Categories of Theological Thinking* (New York: Crossroad, 1988) and *Theological Hermeneutics: Development and Significance* (New York: Crossroad, 1991); Paul Ricoeur, *Conflict of Interpretations*, ed. Don Ihde (Evanston: Northwestern University Press, 1974), *Interpretation Theory*, and *Hermeneutics and the Human Sciences*; Edward Schillebeeckx, *The Understanding of Faith: Interpretation and Criticism* (New York: Seabury Press, 1974); Sandra M. Schneiders, *The Revelatory Text: Interpreting the New Testament as Sacred Scripture* (San Francisco: HarperCollins, 1991); David Tracy, *The Analogical Imagination: Christian Theology and the Culture of Pluralism* (New York: Crossroad, 1981) and "Part Two," in Robert M. Grant, *A Short History of the Interpretation of the Bible*, 2nd ed. (Philadelphia: Fortress Press, 1984), 151–87.

28. I understand the "anthropological constants" proposed by Edward Schillebeeckx to be both historically conscious and "classical" insofar as they reflect the unity of the human species and universally relevant categories that can serve as bases for communication. See Schillebeeckx, *Christ: The Experience of Jesus as Lord* (New York: Seabury Press, 1980), 731–43.

The Logic of Hermeneutics

The logic of hermeneutical theory can be appreciated in two fundamental movements. The first is a certain release of meaning from its particularity in the past; the second is a retrieving of this meaning in a new particular situation.

First, the condition for appreciating the claim that meaning of the past has on the present is precisely the release of past meaning from its individual instanciation in the past. When meaning is construed as bound by or tied to the concrete and specific situation of the past, in the same measure it cannot be relevant to other different situations. This tether to the past is cut at different levels.[29] At the level of understanding, the formulation of meaning into a public language, involving what Thomas Aquinas called abstraction, effects a certain idealization of meaning that makes it public and available to others. Thus a personal experience does not remain locked in the private realm of one's individual experience but is rendered communicable through language and speech. Then, beyond this, through the technology of writing, meaning is dramatically abstracted and rendered universally communicable. Ricoeur calls this distanciation: writing creates a distance between the written meaning and its original author, situation, and audience. In a straightforward historical sense, meaning has been freed from, that is to say, allowed to transcend, its particular historical conditions and made more broadly available. For example, the ten commandments, which began as the social rules of a tribe of people in the Middle East, became in their written form a universal ethical norm. A negative example, that is, a failure to release meaning from the past, would be to claim Jesus' relevance for a present time and place because it is similar to that of Palestine in the first century. This failure in finding the ideal meaning of the past undermines Jesus' universal relevance by implying that Jesus is less relevant to a dramatically different situation. As we will see, there must be an analogy between the past and the present, but at the same time the similarity must transcend the particularity of the past. The relevance of Jesus must be attached to his being consubstantial with human beings in every situation.

The second condition for appreciating the meaning of a past text, and especially for the affirmation of its truth, is the retrieval of that meaning within the context of a new particular situation. An idea's ideal meaning, or a text's abstract and universal meaning, cannot remain disconnected from the present world of the human beings who would affirm its truth. It must have a bearing upon and correspond to reality as it is known and lived in a concrete situation. This process of retrieving is given a variety of names by different authors. It is called a fusion of horizons by Gadamer, and also applicability. It is called appropriation by Ricoeur. In each case

---

29. The issue here is whether meaning and especially truth is completely circumscribed by the past, or whether, while always retaining some relation to the past, it also transcends the past, to become applicable as truth in other circumstances.

an idea or meaning can only be affirmed as true by being drawn into the world of meaning of the one who makes the affirmation. The New Testament, for example, relates how Jesus walked on the Sea of Gennesaret. This can be a literal story, or it can be a symbolic story. On the one hand, in our world, people do not walk on water, and one must surmise that they did not do so in Jesus' time either. On the other hand, the point of the story is not to relate a mere fact, but to communicate the identity of Jesus that is only grasped by faith. Therefore, this story has to be received as symbolic, if one is to grasp its true and intended meaning.

This double movement of entering into the past in order to draw it forward in a meaningful claim of truth for life in our world is both spontaneous and filled with tensions. An integral entry into the past involves an historical method that appreciates the past as past, in its particularity and strangeness relative to the present. Universally relevant meaning never exists ideally, as it were, merely clothed in the externals of concreteness. All human understanding is historically and imaginatively conditioned. But the true referent of a past text that bears universal relevance will correspond to a form of human existence that precisely transcends its particular past incidence.[30] One can thus recognize in the past text, for example, a human engagement in the world that is precisely a possibility for existence today. One recognizes an existential human response to reality that is universally relevant, authentic, and true, so that it makes a claim on one's own response to the world of today. Surely the theory of communication, interpretation, and understanding that is outlined here presupposes a common anthropology that serves as the bond that links human beings and texts across time and cultures. This belief in a common humanity of a single species contests a radical pluralism, sometimes reflected in the empirical studies of cultural anthropology, that would undermine the unity of the race. The presupposition in this hermeneutical theory is that human beings can communicate with each other meaningfully across cultural barriers, even though it may be exceedingly difficult at times.

Hermeneutics of a Person

The hermeneutical tradition of Heidegger that includes Gadamer, Ricoeur, and others contains an existential ontology or anthropology. It describes human existence as interpreter; to be human is to act self-consciously and freely, to know, to understand, to interpret. Thus hermeneutical theory may be applied to an understanding of any classical text, work

---

30. Because of the break with their concrete past situations, one cannot restrict the reference and truth of texts to the ostensive world in which they were written. Paul Ricoeur thus describes a second order, existential reference to a potential world that is held out as a real possibility for all who would grasp it intentionally and in action. For example, a work of fiction may have a forceful existential reference, a truth pertaining to the real existential order, that is truer than a literal, descriptive text. Ricoeur, *Hermeneutics and the Human Sciences*, 140–42.

of art, religious object or symbol, event, or person. What is analytically clear in the understanding of texts also applies to knowledge of all reality; to know is to interpret. When we meet other human beings, we interpret them. We do not perceive their inner selves; we interpret them through their public selves, that is, their words and their gestures. So too with Jesus. We will never be able to get into Jesus' mind or psyche. But we can interpret his public person in his actions, his words, and the orientation of his life; one can interpret the internal meaning of Jesus from the external witness of his life.

One must answer today the long debated question of whether we can know enough about Jesus in order to make him the focus of christology in an explicit, methodological way. In this christology the response is that we can and we do, so that this knowledge that we have of Jesus is both necessary and sufficient for christology. The evidence for this view will be laid out in Chapter 3. But from the outset, one must understand the claim with considerable nuance. One can recover the main outlines of the worldview of Jesus, and one can arrive at a generalized portrait of him that is "substantially" accurate. By substantially I mean "pertaining to the substance of the person," not in any historical detail, but still corresponding to his historical actuality. It is not the case that we know nothing about Jesus. The suppositions or bases for this knowledge is the conviction that the gospels were written or constructed according to the fundamental structure of Christian faith. That is, although, as form criticism has shown, they are statements of faith about Jesus now perceived as risen, and already viewed as Messiah, they were also written about Jesus and his mediation of God. They were written within the context of an imaginative memory of Jesus, so that they enjoy a historical substratum. There is no reason to dichotomize subject and object, subjective faith and the memory of its object, Jesus. The distinctions between the historical (*historisch*) and historic (*geschichtlich*) Jesus,[31] the Jesus of external and internal history,[32] the empirical-historical and the existential-historical Jesus,[33] are valid and useful distinctions. They define exactly the character of the sources for a reconstruction of a historical Jesus and the way Jesus is received in faith. But these distinctions of the way Jesus is approached and perceived are not exclusive of each other, and the poles of each distinction can critically interact and complement the other. The interaction of these two approaches to Jesus, the one historical and the other theological, lies at the basis of the consideration of Jesus in this book. Although the development here is dependent on the work of exegetes, the tension between theology and history remains a critical con-

---

31. Meier, in *A Marginal Jew*, 1, 26–31, gives a brief history of this distinction.

32. H. Richard Niebuhr, *The Meaning of Revelation* (New York: Macmillan, 1960), 59–73.

33. As employed by Schubert M. Ogden in *The Point of Christology*, 41–63 and passim.

cern. Christology must remain conscious of the question of the historicity of what is asserted about Jesus.

Can Jesus be the object and norm of interpretations? The answer to this question can be a firm yes. But this too must be nuanced. Since we do not know much about Jesus, historical knowledge of him can provide a direct answer to relatively few of the most fundamental religious questions. One does not turn to Jesus for information. The final relevance of Jesus does not merely lie in the fact that he is an object or subject matter of the New Testament texts, so that he can be the subject matter of our interpretation. Much more pointedly, Jesus is the medium of God and the revealer of human existence in an encounter with God. As a text is a witness to reality, so too, analogously, Jesus is a witness to reality. The subject matter of christology transcends Jesus without leaving him behind. The concrete Jesus of history is concomitantly transparent; he is the revealer of God, who is the subject matter of Christian faith and who claims authority over human existence. To the question of how Jesus functions as a norm, the response must be equally nuanced. I will develop below how Jesus, as he is critically retrieved by historical research, can function as a negative norm for christology but not as a positive norm.

CRITICAL CORRELATION

A method of correlation entails bringing together the present and the past, bringing into conjunction our present situation and the tradition about Jesus from a past that extends right up to the present. I understand tradition in a broad sense that includes the witness of scripture. Interpretation occurs in the meeting, sometimes the confrontation, between the tradition and our present situation. The engine of interpretation always consists in the question that one addresses to the subject matter that is being interpreted. One always brings an interest, a pre-understanding, and a certain preoccupation or attention to the project of understanding. In the course of the development of this christology we will have to put a finer point on the questions raised by our situation that were outlined in Chapter 1. But some questions may not be appropriate to a particular object of interpretation, and thus the tradition can call the present situation into question. The critical character of this method arises from the dialectical or interactive relationship between the past, the present, and the future, and between different cultural interpretations of Jesus, and these will be reflected in the norms for christology that will be outlined further on.

Correlation as it is understood here represents a transposition of basic insights from hermeneutical theory into a method for theology.[34] Correlation

---

34. David Tracy succinctly represents how the hermeneutical theories of Gadamer and Ricoeur can be reformulated into a theological method in his chapters entitled "Part Two" in Grant, *A Short History of the Interpretation of the Bible*, 151–87. Edward Schillebeeckx's work from the 1970s onward consistently employs this method broadly

involves among other mechanisms a fusion of horizons and appropria-tion.[35] Horizon is the background and field of vision in which all the par-ticular things we understand are arranged. We judge things by their relationships within a horizon: their nearness and distance, what they are, their size, their importance, their relationship to other things. The metaphor designates culture, society, and situation which indeed provide the horizon of intelligibility and understanding. Everything that is and everyone who would understand anything always exist in a particular sit-uational, socially constructed, cultural horizon. Understanding something from the past or from another culture occurs in a fusion of horizons: what is to be understood and its horizon are drawn into the horizon of the pre-sent in which those who would understand are located. To a certain extent, on the level of understanding, we can transcend our present situation and horizon. We can, for example, know that life in first-century Palestine was different than it is today in Palestine, and different again from life every-where else in the world. To appreciate that difference is the self-transcen-dence which characterizes the freedom of the human spirit. But we cannot escape our present horizon in the judgment of truth. The affirmation of truth can only occur as an act of responsibility in the present moment. For exam-ple, to say no more than that John the Evangelist affirms that Jesus was divine, apart from being historically unnuanced, can be an evasion of this responsibility. The speaker today must not only try to estimate what such a view meant in the Johannine community; one who makes such an affirma-tion must also know what he or she means by such a statement and explain it. The tradition must be critically received into the present situation.

Ricoeur, however, with his analysis of appropriation stresses how our present horizon can be expanded by the past, and, I would add, the future. A responsible present is not cut off from its past. When the past is appro-priated, our present horizon is expanded and our world is changed by being impacted from a wider world and the questions that it addresses to us. Therefore, the judgment of truth is not a narrow or isolated tyranny of the present.[36] To exist as a human being is to exist in solidarity with other human beings, across time and into the future. To reject in principle an openness and active listening to the witness of other voices from the past and across contemporary cultures is equally irresponsible. The tradition, therefore, must be allowed to criticize the present situation.

It remains to underline the open character of the discipline of christol-ogy. This can be seen from two points of view. The first corresponds to Jesus being the subject matter of christology. Insofar as christology is reflection on Jesus Christ, Christian tradition provides the sources for an

---

conceived. See Mary Catherine Hilkert, "Hermeneutics of History: The Theological Method of Edward Schillebeeckx," *The Thomist*, 51 (1987), 97–145.

35. On the fusion of horizons, see Gadamer, *Truth and Method*, 268–74; on appropri-ation, see Ricoeur, *Hermeneutics and the Human Sciences*, 182–93.

36. Ricoeur, *Hermeneutics and the Human Sciences*, 142–44, 190–93.

ongoing history of interpretation; wherever new questions are posed to the tradition, in some measure new answers will be forthcoming. But, secondly, the subject matter of theology generally, and hence christology, also transcends Jesus Christ; it includes interpretation of all reality. In the fashioning of the Christian vision of all things, Jesus provides the central source and witness to their ultimate transcendent ground. But the very scope of the theological enterprise requires that other witnesses and other traditions enter into this critical conversation and correlation. In other words, the Christian tradition itself can be called into question in the broadest theological conversation of interreligious dialogue that now characterizes our situation. Christology has thus entered into a new phase in the history of Christianity, as it transpires within the context of global questions of mutual understanding among the religions and the demand to establish common ethical norms. This new context renders the project of christology not only open-ended but also more nuanced and complex. More than ever, the Christian community experiences the need for some clear norms in this work.

THE CRITERIA FOR CHRISTOLOGY

The criteria for theology and for christology in particular do not provide a measure for authenticity and truth with the clarity of physical science. There is no template against which one can measure the adequacy of a christological proposal, with the exception, perhaps, of some clear cases of extreme positions. The changing situation of the Christian community, the pluralism of approaches, and the multiple interrelated questions that make the need for criteria so pressing at the same time render them less clear-cut and decisive. One can state the criteria or norms for christology in a way that makes them appear as clear standards, but, in fact, they function more like questions or areas of consideration that need to be adequately addressed and explained. And they do not overcome pluralism, but admit a variety of positions. Three criteriological points drawn from theology in general find an application in christology as well. These are faithfulness to the tradition, intelligibility in today's world, and empowerment of the Christian life.[37]

In the first criterion of faithfulness to the Christian tradition the term "tradition" includes scripture, which is the classic statement of the earliest

---

37. These three criteria may be subdivided and expanded. Reducing the number to three is a way of underlining the fundamental structure of Christian faith and the place of Jesus Christ in it: Jesus is rendered intelligible as the religious and moral power of Christian faith. See the discussion of five criteriological considerations by Robert J. Schreiter, *Constructing Local Theologies* (Maryknoll, N.Y.: Orbis Books, 1985), 117–21, and his *The New Catholicity: Theology between the Global and the Local* (Maryknoll, N.Y.: Orbis Books, 1997), 81–83.

tradition. Tradition refers directly to the historical life of the community, which is available existentially as the corporate mode of existence that Christians share and objectively through the historical witnesses from the past.[38] Christology is a discipline that represents the faith of a religious community which exists in historical continuity and solidarity with its past. That past is the source of the identity and the formal self-understanding of the community in the present. Often a community's self-identity depends on its being in continuity with its past, especially its genesis and foundation. This historical dynamic takes on more dramatic dimensions in the light of the revelation that was mediated to what became the Christian community in the event of Jesus Christ. The history of Christian doctrine represents a corporate commitment to protect the revelation mediated by Jesus Christ from the corrosive influences of history. The point of criteria in christology is precisely to keep the community faithful to its original faith in Jesus Christ, while at the same time interpreting that faith in a manner that is comprehensible in new situations. Appropriate Christian language about Jesus Christ, therefore, must be faithful to the tradition.[39] A considerable amount of attention in this book will be given to the scriptural data for christology and the early theological tradition where christological language was solidified into doctrines.

The tradition in this respect must be understood as differentiated, and it helps to understand some of its different aspects and their relative importance. Christology must be faithful, first of all, to Jesus of Nazareth who is both the subject matter and the source of christology. Interpretation must be faithful to the object of interpretation. That object is found first of all in the Jesus kerygma, the earliest existential witness of faith in Jesus of Nazareth. But this Jesus kerygma itself can be critically appropriated through historical Jesus research. Some of the results of this inquiry, that is, some aspects of the constructed historical Jesus, can thus provide norms and criteria for christological understanding. This is the case most clearly with negative judgments: reconstruction of the historical Jesus can operate as a negative norm in christology. This means that christology cannot affirm of Jesus of Nazareth what is positively contradicted by a consensus of scholarship. One cannot, for example, interpret Jesus in such a way that the reign of God occupied no place in his message. One cannot on the basis of Jesus affirm that ultimate reality is in the end impersonal. Positively, historical portraits of Jesus open up the creative imagination and function as a guide to understanding Jesus Christ in the present, but

---

38. The meaning of tradition here is drawn from Maurice Blondel, *The Letter on Apologetics and History and Dogma* (New York: Holt, Rinehart and Winston, 1964), 264–87.

39. This theological perspective stands in contrast to that of Wilfred Cantwell Smith who considers Christianity to be what it is historically at any given time; it has no norms from the past. See his *Towards a World Theology: Faith and the Comparative History of Religion* (Philadelphia: Westminster Press, 1981), 21–44, 154–61.

they do not function as a positive norm for christology. Christology can, must, and does transcend what history has to say about Jesus. This christology will attend to the data about Jesus proposed by Jesus research.

Christology must also attend and be faithful to New Testament christologies as the first and more formally normative statements of the faith of the community in Jesus as the Christ. Such is the logic of the formation of the canon; New Testament christologies that were gathered became the classical expressions and witnesses to the faith of the Christian community.

Finally, christology requires fidelity to the history of soteriology and christology across the history of the church. Obviously those events in which critical decisions were made, as in the Councils of Nicaea and Chalcedon, have a preeminent authority in the history of the church and its christology. Special attention will have to be given to these landmarks in the history of the church's christology. All of this data from tradition constitute sources for christological reflection and function as norms or criteria. They are the data to be interpreted in constructing a christology for today. There must, therefore, be a certain equilibrium of historical norms.[40] They cannot all be applied in some literal fashion that would in effect cancel their collective force. Rather, all of these normative data have to be interpreted, balanced, and measured in conjunction with still other norms. This christology will attend to significant moments in the history of the church and try to interpret faithfully what is found in this data.

A second criterion for christology is intelligibility in today's world, including internal coherence. Negatively, although this is a common phenomenon, one cannot logically affirm a belief that stands in contradiction with what one knows to be true in a wider context. In other words, the principle of non-contradiction rules out a compartmentalization of christological beliefs held in a private sphere that do not correlate with what we positively know to be the case from other spheres of life. More positively, one's christological faith should find expression in belief structures or ways of understanding that fit or correspond with the way reality is understood generally in a given culture. This does not imply that christological beliefs will be reduced to what can be explained by reason. It is one thing to say that something is intelligible; it is quite another to reduce its truth to what can be demonstrated by reason. The whole of christology transpires within the context of a commitment of faith. But if christological belief is to criticize and challenge certain ideas and values in a culture, it must be comprehensible. In brief, christology must be intelligible or credible; it must make sense. Coherence adds to intelligibility a demand that christology itself add up to a unified whole, that there be no contradictions within itself, that its elements fit into a unity of intelligibility, or an integral vision of life.

---

40. Francis Schüssler Fiorenza, "The Jesus of Piety and the Historical Jesus," *Proceedings of the Catholic Theological Society of America*, 49 (1994), 90–99, shows that ordinary Christian piety forms part of the criteriological balance.

Here too the formal criterion of intelligibility of itself often will not be able to resolve specific problematic issues. What is self-evidently intelligible in one culture may not be so in another; what one person in a given culture takes for granted, another may never have imagined and thus reject out of hand. The criterion of intelligibility, therefore, proposes a formal area for discussion; it prescribes reasoned discourse. It contains the ideal and the imperative that Christian faith not fall back into either fideism or fundamentalism, that it be open to the new experiences that history and the world continually open up to new generations. Intelligibility represents a quest for new and deeper understanding of how Jesus Christ fits as part of the intelligible world of God's creation.

There are several areas in which the intelligibility of the christology formulated in the patristic period labors under stress. One area in particular concerns the unique and exalted character of Jesus Christ in face of the existence and vitality of other world religions, together with the generally positive evaluation of these religions in principle. The norms of intelligibility and coherence demand that one reconcile the universal relevance of Jesus Christ with the conviction that other religions have a role in world history under God's providence. Another closely related element concerns the mode of understanding the traditional doctrine of Jesus' divinity. These questions are not isolated points that can be attended to in passing. They touch the center of christological belief and understanding, and they are felt by most educated Christians. The demand for intelligibility on these points generates some of the main themes of this christology.

A third criterion for theology and hence for christology is empowerment of the Christian life. A christology that fulfills the first two norms but does not touch Christian life in a way that opens up possibilities for Christian existence is inadequate. This is so because the point of all understanding is to direct human action in a way that corresponds more deeply with reality.

This criterion of empowerment should be understood as touching various levels of the Christian life. The following are three such levels: first, christology has to have some resonance with actual existential Christian life. This does not mean that the discipline of christology must appeal directly to the existential experience of all Christians. Rather, the language and logic of christology must take into account and correlate with the fact of Christian faith and life. One of the sources of christology is the actual faith life of the Christian community which may unfold without any intellectual sophistication. The fact as well as the content of this level of naive faith and belief of an experiential kind must be accounted for in christology.

A second level is that of ethical coherence and integrity. Christology should correspond to and engender a Christian way of life that responds to the ethical challenges of our time.[41] Neither the Christian community

---

41. For example, Schubert Ogden, in *The Point of Christology*, 148–68, explains his liberationist interpretation of Jesus Christ on the basis of the criterion of moral or ethical credibility in our situation.

nor Jesus Christ can be understood apart from life in the world. Jesus has to be considered within the context of an understanding of and attitudes toward the larger portion of human beings who share other religious traditions. Jesus must be appreciated in connection with the moral responsibility that is engaged by the inordinate amount of social injustice and suffering that currently afflict humanity. A demand for ethical coherence and credibility means that Jesus must be understood in such a way that he provides an impulse to Christian faith and life that responds to the social ethical crises that face humanity.

A third level of empowerment concerns the symbol of salvation. Christology must describe salvation today in such a way that it corresponds intelligibly to what people actually experience. This view of salvation must represent something that can be experienced in this world, so that christology reflects a living spirituality of the community and leads to or opens up a way of life that makes sense. A concern for the criterion of empowerment, that a christology stimulate a Christian life of discipleship, will play a major role in this christology.

These first two chapters provide an initial orientation to the premises, the method, and the direction which this christology will take. Many of these purely formal considerations will be found to conform to certain well-known patterns of theology today; others will take on more clarity in the actual development of christological material. We begin by taking up the various levels of data and witness in the scriptural sources.

PART II

BIBLICAL SOURCES

CHAPTER 3

Appropriating Jesus in Christology

A consideration of the biblical sources for christology in four short chapters requires hard decisions about what is most important for the interpretation of Jesus Christ. I have also had to impose a specific focus on each of these topics. The limitations of this part of the work will be evident to anyone familiar with the data available for analysis. My hope is that these four investigations at least will provide a biblical framework for the constructive effort in Part Four. Each of the four topics seems to be essential to the logic of christology: the person Jesus, his historical mediation of God, the historical experience of his disciples that he was raised by God, and a survey of some of the first christological and soteriological interpretations of him. Together these chapters set forth the narrative structure, if not the actual story, of the genesis of christology.

Christology began with Jesus of Nazareth, and it must begin with Jesus today. This point of departure finds an echo in the curiosity about Jesus that Jesus research feeds. It would be hard to imagine anyone who is interested in human existence from a religious perspective not being drawn to know more about Jesus. We have already described the diverse ways historical research on Jesus is being pursued and the reasons for its impact on christology. In this chapter and the next I will review some of the results of this investigation, first in terms of the characterizations of the kind of persona or role Jesus displayed, and then in terms of his representation of God.

The present chapter contains four different holistic interpretations of Jesus and, within the context that they provide, a summary sketch of his public career. But I shall begin with a reflection on the approach and method that is assumed in this investigation.

A HISTORICAL-HERMENEUTICAL APPROACH

Gerd Theissen, in his narrative interpretation of Jesus of Nazareth, constructs a story in which the protagonist is commissioned by Roman authorities to find out who this Jesus of Nazareth is and to deliver a report.

He is always one step behind Jesus as he pursues his inquiry through Galilee; he never meets him or hears him preach, but must rest content with the reports of people representing various constituencies: peasants, Zealots, people in the towns, Romans, religious leaders, and so on. The story, which is constructed with finesse and supplemented with technical commentary, functions as an allegory. The contemporary of Jesus represents all who inquire after Jesus and must be satisfied with testimony about him. But it is the character of the testimony that becomes paradigmatic. Each witness reflects a perception of Jesus from the perspective of his or her group. As the story unfolds, new perceptions of Jesus are added to the whole picture, which is thus constantly being altered as the focus is readjusted. Jesus continually takes on new meaning. Narrative interpretation is thus open-ended. "This open-endedness matches the actual process of scholarly research."[1]

The allegory implies that the meaning of Jesus is itself not static, but "overflows," and keeps on overflowing as Jesus is brought into relationship with ever new situations and problems and peoples. The meaning of Jesus cannot be contained; it is not, as it were, a given, a substance that takes on new accidental connotations in new relationships. Rather, the new relationships themselves constitute new meanings and relevancies *of Jesus*. Moreover, this does not end in his lifetime. Just as the real historical meaning of Jesus can be seen continually to expand in relation to the situations and groups he encountered during his lifetime, so too it continues to expand through time. Jesus is also related to our time today, and to the multiple situations, peoples, and groups that make up our world. And this ever new meaning is always potentially the meaning of Jesus, that is, Jesus of Nazareth back then.

Needless to say, many different interpretations of Jesus mark the landscape of Christian consciousness today. In this chapter and the next I do not consciously intend to propose another independent portrait of Jesus. I take Jesus research to be a technical study of the exegete and historian. Were the theologian to quit for a time the discipline of theology in order to enter the world of scripture scholarship and learn from the inside the criteria of evidence and judgment, he or she would at the same time become another partisan voice within what is essentially a pluralistic discipline. Thus the interpretations of Jesus which follow will be proffered from within the context of systematic theology and remain dependent upon the historical work of others. But at the same time, these interpretations rely on a theological method that has been shaped by hermeneutical theory, and hermeneutics may provide a bridge between the disciplines of scripture and systematic theology, in this case, christology. A further development of this proposition will serve as an explanation of the method of this chapter.

---

1. Gerd Theissen, *The Shadow of the Galilean: The Quest of the Historical Jesus in Narrative Form* (Philadelphia: Fortress Press, 1987), 55.

The overarching framework of thought was noted in Chapter 1. People encountered God in Jesus, so that Jesus became the historical event in history that provided the focal point for the Christian experience of God. A genetic understanding of christology goes back to Jesus as that to which all Christian interpretations of him and God refer. From the point of view of hermeneutical theory, Jesus is a classic symbol. David Tracy defines the classic from a hermeneutical perspective in this way: "classics are those texts [or persons] that bear an excess and permanence of meaning, yet always resist definitive interpretation. . . . Though highly particular in origin and expression, classics have the possibility of being universal in their effect."[2] Classics are universally relevant and bear a certain timeless quality. But this is so not by ceasing to be individual, particular, and historically conditioned. A classic is not abstract and deliberately vague and general, nor is its universality theoretical. Its timelessness is a "mode of historical being"; it overcomes the distances of time and culture "in its own constant communication"; it is timeless by being contemporaneous with other ages.[3] It keeps on mediating meaning in different situations. As a concrete universal, a classic must possess a certain polyvalence. This consists in a fundamental and intrinsic character that opens it up to many different perceptions, construals, and relevancies in new situations.[4] This openness to many meanings, despite its being one thing, reveals its universality as a kind of dynamism toward communicating with all, and uniting people in its message and indirectly in itself.

One can understand the discipline of christology and the relationship between theologians and historians within this framework of interpreting Jesus as a classic person. Some knowledge of Jesus is necessary for christology for several reasons. Jesus is the subject matter of christology; on one level, christology is about Jesus. Without knowledge of Jesus, the discipline would have no real content, and the idea of the risen Christ who relates to us today would be empty. The risen Christ is Jesus, and we know nothing concrete about the risen Christ apart from Jesus, because all such knowledge is drawn from some historically mediated experience. The

---

2. David Tracy, *Pluralism and Ambiguity: Hermeneutics, Religion, Hope* (San Francisco: Harper & Row, 1987), 12. A classic is "always retrievable, always in need of appreciative appropriation and critical evaluation, always disclosive and transformative with its truth of importance, always open to new application and thereby new interpretation." David Tracy, *The Analogical Imagination: Christian Theology and the Culture of Pluralism* (New York: Crossroad, 1981), 115.

3. Hans-Georg Gadamer, *Truth and Method* (New York: Seabury Press, 1975), 256–57.

4. Classics share this polyvalence with symbols that reflect universal dimensions of human experience. Such symbols have a pre-linguistic depth that defies their being adequately transcribed into logical or conceptual references. Paul Ricoeur shows how this has been demonstrated by studies of psychoanalytic, poetic, and religious symbols. This depth dimension is a primary factor in their opening up multiple meanings, interpretations, and references. See Paul Ricoeur, *Interpretation Theory: Discourse and the Surplus of Meaning* (Fort Worth: Texas Christian University, 1976), 45–69.

interpretations of Jesus that make up the New Testament lead back to him, because they derive from him. Although these confessional documents are virtually our only window on Jesus, they are not the source of Jesus, but Jesus is the ultimate source of them. An understanding of Christianity in its historical origins, then, demands some knowledge of Jesus. A sense of historicity is leading theologians and Christians generally to put more stock in the saving power of Jesus' public career and ministry, in contrast to the almost exclusively dogmatic Pauline concentration of the dynamics and power of salvation in Jesus' death. The revelation of God that is mediated by the human career of Jesus is taking on much more significance today in Christian spirituality.

Having made the case for the necessity of a consideration of Jesus in christology, it is equally important to distinguish quite sharply the properly theological goal in the study of Jesus from that of the historian and exegete as such. This differentiation will also serve to clarify the relationship between theology and history. A first distinction can be formulated in terms of the pre-understanding brought to the study and the way Jesus is known and encountered. The object of the historian's inquiry is an empirical-historical knowledge of Jesus, that is, a knowledge of Jesus as he appeared in history. On this basis, the search unfolds on naturalist premises of the historian, according to the canons of evidence agreed upon within the discipline. By contrast, the theologian brings to the quest of the historical Jesus a religious question and an existential-historical concern. At the origin of Christianity, it was said, was the fact that people encountered God in or through Jesus, and it is that phenomenon that lies at the base of the theological interest in Jesus.

A second distinction lies in a difference of horizon of interpretation. The historian seeks to interpret Jesus within the context of the relationships that constituted the world of Jesus during his lifetime. History is an exercise of self-transcendence of the human spirit, its ability to understand the other as other. The historian seeks to transcend his or her present context in order to grasp Jesus precisely as having existed in another context. In this sense, the interpretation, which is still an interpretation, seeks objectivity. Even though such objectivity remains an ideal that can never be perfectly realized, some interpretations still appear better than others, because they account more adequately for the data. The theologian, by contrast, seeks to draw Jesus forward and understand him within the context of the present situation. It is still Jesus, the figure from the past, who is thus interpreted, but he is interpreted within the framework of the new and wider horizon of the present situation. The present-day situation is what the historian must try to transcend in order not anachronistically to read into the data present concerns; the present-day situation is the key to the theologian's understanding of how the Jesus of the past can be relevant today.

The distinction between an empirical-historical and an existential-historical concern helps to show why empirical history alone can never generate faith, because the encounter with God in Jesus qualitatively surpasses empirical data and knowledge. But existential and participatory engagement with a medium of faith does not rule out, but positively includes, interest in an empirical-historical knowledge of the medium. It should not be imagined that the move toward an examination of the historical Jesus as fundamental for christology is opposed to a christology that works from the faith testimony of New Testament texts. The theologian engages history, not as a chronological prior step, but as a logically prior moment of theological interpretation before drawing it forward into the present. A theologian's concern for the historical Jesus represents a critical dimension of theological interpretation, one which helps to prevent fideistic projection of unwarranted meaning on the originating historical medium of Christian faith.

In the course of this chapter I shall examine four broad portraits of the historical Jesus, that is, critical historical reconstructions of the kind of person that he was. These portraits attempt to identify the public appearance of Jesus during his ministry. These personae or public roles can be compared to genres in literature. Genre, as I am using the term, refers to the structure and form of a work, that which makes it to be the kind of work that it is. A genre in literature is thus made up of a set of conventions that define a particular form and thus a kind of literature. As knowledge of genre opens up a certain interpretation of a text, so too, analogously, knowledge of Jesus' public status opens up a line of interpretation of his message and its meaning.

The functions of genre are multiple. But two aspects of genre are instructive: how it functions relative to the production of texts, and to the reception and interpretation of texts. First, relative to the production of texts: "The primary purpose of such norms and conventions is to facilitate communication."[5] If one has something to say, one should put it in the form that will make its content as clear as possible. A business letter is not written in rhyming couplets; a religious dogma in a conciliar decree is different than a recipe in a cookbook. If one chooses the wrong genre, one may compromise the communication. Genre, then, is a set of conventions determining the form of communication and is meant to enhance it.

Second, relative to reception and interpretation of texts, grasping a genre is a first act of interpretation. Generally speaking, interpretation should correspond to the objective meaning of the text. The first clue of what that meaning might be is provided by genre. "The genre provides a sense of the whole, a notion of typical meaning components."[6] On the one hand, genre

---

5. Werner G. Jeanrond, *Theological Hermeneutics: Development and Significance* (New York: Crossroad, 1991), 87. "When we wish to express ourselves in speech or writing we choose the genre of our expression very carefully because much of the initial reception of our text which normally structures the process of reading will depend on our choice of genre." Ibid., 86.

6. Eric D. Hirsch, *Validity in Interpretation* (New Haven and London: Yale University Press, 1967), 222.

is chosen to direct reception or interpretation; and, on the other hand, the interpretation of the reader should correspond to the genre. The whole is a key to the meaning of the parts; by a hermeneutical circle, the elements of a text take on a meaning consonant with the kind of text one is reading. Thus establishing the genre is the first, broad act in interpretation.

In the sections which follow I shall sketch four "genres" of Jesus. These are general assessments of the type of religious figure he was. The assumption in trying to determine the "genre" of Jesus is that his genre is consonant with his message. This interpretation of the kind of person he was, then, becomes as well the first act of interpreting his message.[7]

JESUS AS PROPHET

The identification of Jesus as eschatological prophet has a distinct recent history beginning with the publication by Johannes Weiss of *Jesus' Proclamation of the Kingdom of God* in 1892.[8] Weiss' goal was to counter the modern conceptions of the kingdom in liberal theology which were alien to Jesus' own self-understanding. "The kingdom of God as Jesus thought of it is never something subjective, inward, or spiritual, but is always the objective messianic kingdom, which usually is pictured as a territory into which one enters, or as a land in which one has a share, or as a treasure which comes down from heaven."[9] This inbreaking of God's thoroughly supernatural power was clearly future, as the Lord's prayer indicates, but it was so near that one could use language of its being felt as beginning and present. The rule of God stood opposed to Satan's kingdom, and Jesus understood his own ministry to be defeating Satan's rule on earth through the power of God as Spirit.[10] As Jesus conceived it, "the kingdom of God is a radically superworldly entity that stands in diametric opposition to this world. This is to say that there *can* be no talk of an *innerworldly* development of the kingdom of God in the mind of Jesus."[11] Thus Weiss presented Jesus as the prophet of the end-time who lived within a religious worldview significantly alien to a modern horizon. "It is extremely difficult for us to think our way into this self-consciousness," according to Weiss, because, as he saw it, Jesus' "soul in some way lived in God in a fashion analogous to nothing we can imagine."[12]

---

7. Two works surveying various broad interpretations of Jesus are Marcus J. Borg, *Jesus: A New Vision: Spirit, Culture, and the Life of Discipleship* (San Francisco: Harper & Row, 1989) and Ben Witherington, III, *The Jesus Quest: The Third Search for the Jew of Nazareth* (Downers Grove, Ill.: InterVarsity Press, 1995).

8. Johannes Weiss, *Jesus' Proclamation of the Kingdom of God*, ed. by Richard H. Hiers and D. Larrimore Holland (Philadelphia: Fortress Press, 1971).

9. Weiss, *Proclamation*, 133.

10. Weiss, *Proclamation*, 74–79.

11. Weiss, *Proclamation*, 114.

12. Weiss, *Proclamation*, 128.

This view of Jesus as eschatological prophet continued to find expression in the works of Albert Schweitzer,[13] Rudolf Bultmann,[14] and Günther Bornkamm. In Bornkamm's conception, which is more attentive to the parables than that of Weiss, Jesus' being a prophet is not so radically defined by an apocalyptic worldview. As in Bultmann, Jesus is depicted as a prophet and a rabbi who teaches with an inner, autonomous authority. But at the same time, Jesus appears within a tradition of religious expectation of the reign of God to come.[15] Reginald Fuller is explicit about Jesus' self-understanding in terms of eschatological prophecy; he was confident in this role and of being vindicated in the end. "Take the implied self-understanding of his role in terms of the eschatological prophet away, and the whole ministry falls into a series of unrelated, if not meaningless fragments."[16] Like his proclamation, Jesus' deeds actualize the kingdom of God; God is working eschatologically within Jesus' ministry of healing and exorcism. "His ministry was eschatological-prophetic in the sense that he was not merely proclaiming a future salvation, but was actually inaugurating it."[17] Ben Meyer's view of Jesus is similar: Jesus understood his public career as a divine mission to Israel; he was to bring the work of Moses and the prophets to a definitive completion. He did this by proclaiming and by acting out in public symbolic actions the advent of the kingdom of God.[18] "In sum, once the theme of national restoration in its full eschatological sweep is grasped as the concrete meaning of the reign of God, Jesus' career begins to become intelligible as a unity."[19]

Edward Schillebeeckx, after surveying various basic types of christology of the early church, finds that the idea of eschatological prophet is behind them all. As a common root understanding, it most probably extended back into Jesus' own lifetime and probably characterized his self-understanding.[20] For Theissen, the role of prophet approaches Jesus' center of gravity. As a prophet, Jesus is a religious figure who mediates God, God's word, and God's will. Jesus preached the kingdom of God, and in the name of God Jesus confronted ideas and practices that were in place, preached reversals of commonly accepted ways of doing things,

---

13. Albert Schweitzer, *The Quest of the Historical Jesus* (New York: Charles Scribner's Sons, 1951), passim.

14. Rudolf Bultmann, *Jesus and the Word* (New York: Charles Scribner's Sons, 1934), 120–27. Bultmann also conceives Jesus as a rabbi, who taught, disputed, interpreted the law, told parables, and so on.

15. Günther Bornkamm, *Jesus of Nazareth* (New York: Harper & Brothers, 1960), 56–67.

16. Reginald H. Fuller, *The Foundations of New Testament Christology* (London: Lutterworth Press, 1965), 130.

17. Fuller, *Foundations*, 129.

18. Ben F. Meyer, *The Aims of Jesus* (London: SCM Press, 1979), 169.

19. Meyer, *Aims*, 221.

20. Edward Schillebeeckx, *Jesus: An Experiment in Christology* (New York: Seabury Press, 1979), 401–38.

criticized religious institutions, confronted people with a message from God.[21]

An extensive case for understanding Jesus as a prophet is made by E. P. Sanders.[22] In Sanders's view, Jesus was a prophet of Jewish restoration. The center of his preaching was the kingdom of God, and this was understood by Jesus to involve a new Israel, a restoration of the social, political order, such that God's will would prevail, making it God's kingdom on earth. Sanders constructs this view of Jesus on the basis of a careful analysis of a number of pieces of historical evidence. It synthesizes and explains basic points about Jesus which seem to be the most historically certain.[23] First, Jesus was a disciple of or associated with John the Baptist. While there are differences between the messages of the two, in several respects Jesus continues the prophetic teaching of John that Israel repent in preparation for a coming judgment.[24] Second, Sanders holds that the appointment of the twelve by Jesus is probably authentic, and that it represents a symbolic act pointing to the restoration of the twelve tribes. Third, the early church clearly had an eschatological consciousness, and it is most reasonable to assume that this consciousness came from Jesus. Fourth, Jesus expected the destruction of the temple and its restoration, a belief about Jewish restoration that was known at the time. And, fifth, Jesus' dramatic acting out of his convictions in Jerusalem, that is, predicting the destruction of the temple, was enough to explain his death. Jesus' public execution is a datum that demands a coherent explanation beyond teachings about God's forgiveness and love.[25]

What was the nature of the kingdom or reign or rule of God that Jesus saw being ushered in? According to Sanders, this is not a reign of God outside of history and in another world; it is God establishing a rearrangement of this world according to God's will for the order of things. It will occur not by human but by God's intervening power. God's time has arrived; God is about to intervene in history and reestablish the nation Israel according to God's rule. Sanders integrates this sharp prophetic image of Jesus with his teaching through parables and his healing. He sees Jesus' ministry coming to a climax in Jerusalem prior to his death. There, in dramatic symbolic actions, Jesus depicted the destruction and restoration of the temple in the new Israel.[26]

---

21. Theissen, *The Shadow of the Galilean*, 129–53.

22. E. P. Sanders, *Jesus and Judaism* (Philadelphia: Fortress Press, 1985) and *The Historical Figure of Jesus* (London: Penguin Books, 1993).

23. These are summarized in Sanders, *Jesus and Judaism*, 222; see also *Historical Figure*, 10–14.

24. John P. Meier provides an extensive historical analysis of the relationship of Jesus and John in *A Marginal Jew*, 2, *Mentor, Message, and Miracles* (New York: Doubleday, 1994), 17–233.

25. Sanders, *Jesus and Judaism*, 232.

26. Sanders, *Jesus and Judaism*, 61–76. Jesus did not expect the end of the world in

Like Weiss, Sanders has preserved the other-worldly source and the supernatural, interventionist character of the kingdom of God that unified Jesus' teaching and actions. How is this aspect of Jesus' message, which is so intimately connected with his prophetic identity, to be appropriated? The category of symbol provides a way to understand this language of the imminent coming of the kingdom of God. A symbol, it was said, is something that communicates by pointing to something else. In a religious symbol, like the kingdom of God, that "something else" is transcendent or other-worldly, is not known directly or objectively, but only by faith and hope, and always through some historical symbol. The symbol mediates the object of faith. The kingdom of God as used by Jesus was such a symbol, and one should understand Jesus' language here as religious and symbolic language.[27] Jesus, then, did not have an objective knowledge of a concrete arrangement called the kingdom of God, or a direct knowledge of a particular design of society and history, or a knowledge that this kingdom would arrive at a certain time and in a specific way. Such an understanding of symbol is precisely a misunderstanding. This is religious language about transcendent reality, expressing a faith conviction that God will act. It shares an urgency and prophetic clarity, but this should not be construed as representing a non-symbolic and direct objective knowledge of how God will act in history.[28]

The contention here is not simply that the kingdom of God is to be interpreted as a symbol today, but also that it was used symbolically by Jesus himself. Jesus undoubtedly did not have a theory of religious symbol. But since all religious language is always symbolic, whether he was explicitly conscious of it or not, Jesus was using this religious language

---

the sense of destruction of the cosmos. He looked for a divine, transforming "miracle," God intervening as God had in Israel's past history. So too, now, God would create an ideal society, a restored Israel. *Historical Figure*, 183–84.

27. Norman Perrin writes that "in the proclamation of Jesus 'Kingdom of God' was used as a tensive symbol, and that it was used to evoke the myth of God acting as king. The challenge of the message of Jesus was to recognize the reality of the activity of God in the historicity of the hearer's existence in the world, and especially in the experience of a clash of worlds as the hearer came to grips with the reality of everyday human existence." Norman Perrin, *Jesus and the Language of the Kingdom: Symbol and Metaphor in New Testament Interpretation* (Philadelphia: Fortress Press, 1976), 197. See Chapter II, "The Interpretation of Kingdom of God in the Message of Jesus," 15–88, passim. Sanders agrees that one should not attribute to Jesus literal views of a gross nature: people in Jesus' time also used metaphorical language. "When dealing with this sort of material, we can never be sure how literally to take it. . . . When it comes to analyzing what ancient Jews thought, we must remain uncertain about this point." *Historical Figure*, 186.

28. See A. E. Harvey, *Jesus and the Constraints of History* (Philadelphia: Westminster Press, 1982), 94–97, for a brief analysis of the logic of prophetic and apocalyptic discourse. It is an appeal to a common perception of a future that is needed and desired, over against the current negative state of affairs. It does not live on direct knowledge of the future, but on a hope and expectation of a future that is strong and near enough to be experienced as at work, influencing the present.

symbolically and metaphorically. Jesus is not therefore to be understood as predicting an event of which he had direct knowledge, and which would happen at a certain time or in a certain way. Rather, he is expressing the conviction that God will act for human salvation and that God's action is even now ready to occur, however it will happen concretely.[29] This does not eliminate great differences in the religious imagination of then and now. But one can appreciate the religious character of Jesus' language back then, even as one appreciates similar language of prayer and expectation today. This kind of language is used all the time in religious preaching. It is the symbolic language of faith and hope.

N. T. Wright follows Sanders in construing Jesus as a prophet. In the words Luke attributes to Cleopas on the way to Emmaus, Jesus was "a prophet mighty in deed and word" (Luke 24:19). When one surveys the historical elements of the story of Jesus on which there is a general consensus, and views them as a whole, there emerges a portrait of Jesus as a prophet of the kingdom of God in the apocalyptic tradition. This picture neatly fits with the situation of Palestine and Galilee of the first century, with the popular movements of that period, and with what we know of Jesus' predecessor, John the Baptist.[30]

The texts referring to Jesus as a prophet create an unmistakable impression. Jesus was a "leadership" and an oracular prophet. He gathered disciples and explained the goals of his movement: the renewal and restoration of Israel. An itinerant, he taught the people in the towns and villages. He actively symbolized his message in dramatic actions, as in the temple precincts in Jerusalem. He also imitated some of the classical prophets in his actions. "Jesus believed himself called to work as a prophet, announcing the word of Israel's God to his wayward people, and grouping around himself a company who . . . would be regarded as the true people of YHWH."[31]

As a prophet mighty in word, Jesus spoke the oracles of judgment and promise. Like John, Jesus too spoke of imminent catastrophe: the kingdom of God was about to begin and it would involve radical change. On the one hand, the current generation is judged harshly; Israel was on the road to ruin. On the horizon lay "a judgment consisting of a great national,

---

29. I do not make this claim on the basis of historical research or of any knowledge of what Jesus was thinking. It is rather an a priori claim based anthropologically on an understanding of human existence and a theory of religious knowledge. There is a certain tendency, without real warrant, to project on people of the past a naive understanding of religious language.

30. N. T. Wright, *Christian Origins and the Question of God*, 2, *Jesus and the Victory of God* (London: SPCK, 1996), 147–62. According to Wright, "the best initial model for understanding [Jesus'] praxis is that of a prophet; more specifically, that of a prophet bearing an urgent eschatological, and indeed apocalyptic, message for Israel." Ibid., 150. Wright summarizes his portrait of Jesus in "How Jesus Saw Himself," *Bible Review* (June, 1996), 22–29.

31. Wright, *Jesus*, 196.

social and cultural disaster, ultimately comprehensible only in theological terms."[32] On the other hand, for those who repented and accepted the message, the kingdom of God proffered welcome and peace. But Jesus also depicted the kingdom of God in parable. Practically all of the parables of Jesus can be understood, according to Wright, as representations of the history of Israel; it is heading toward the climax of its history in which its present reality will be undone and replaced with God's rule. Viewing Jesus as a prophet and Israel as the subject matter opens up the historical meaning of the parables. These are not timeless truths, but pointed indictments which are cryptically spoken because of their explosive, prophetic content.[33]

The gospels are filled with the mighty deeds of the prophet Jesus. These unexpected, marvelous acts fit the person and his message: they overcame the negativity of Satan, they promised the rule of God. In Wright's account, the miracles of Jesus did not really "stick out" as they do for a rationalistic spirit; they were an integral part of his being the prophet of the kingdom. They were works of power, and thus signs of God acting. Socially, they drew those who were marginated from the community by sickness back into Israel. They were also subversive, because they went around the religious authority in place, and were thus branded by association with the power of Satan.[34] In sum, Jesus believed that the judgment and vindication of Israel was being ushered in through his prophetic activity.

A distinct variation of the interpretation of Jesus as an eschatological prophet envisages the coming kingdom of God in the concrete terms of social transformation within the towns and villages of Palestine. Such is the view of Richard Horsley. Jesus had an apocalyptic orientation and framework of thinking; it was commonly expected that God would act finally in the history of Israel for its restoration. God in fact was already effecting this revolution, and Jesus consciously participated in the movement. But it was not to be a revolution through armed rebellion, or a top-down reformation. Rather, the rule of God would transform society from below. God was bringing the old order to an end and effecting a renewal of individual and social life in the towns and villages. The rule of God and the restoration of Israel were to be accomplished as a social reconstruction of personal and social life.[35]

Given this imaginative framework, the sense and direction of the ministry of Jesus falls into place. The kingdom of God is God's initiative; and Jesus participated in ushering it in. But this kingdom of God is in the midst of people; it means wholeness of life under God's rule. Concretely, entering or being in the kingdom of God meant being in a society and community that embodied God's will and values. The kingdom of God

---

32. Wright, *Jesus*, 185.

33. Wright, *Jesus*, 174–82.

34. Wright, *Jesus*, 186–96.

35. Richard A. Horsley, *Jesus and the Spiral of Violence: Popular Jewish Resistance in Roman Palestine* (Minneapolis: Fortress Press, 1993), 190–93, 321–24.

involved "renewal of the fundamental social-political form of traditional peasant life, the village."[36] For example, Jesus' teaching attacked the oppressive character of patriarchy and proposed more egalitarian familial relations. His teaching on love of enemies called for a new spirit of cooperation and mutual assistance in village life. But also, on a broader level, as a Jewish prophet, Jesus "pronounced oracles and parables of judgment against the ruling institutions of Jewish Palestine, the Temple and the high priesthood."[37]

In this view, therefore, one should not think of the kingdom of God as an other-worldly place, nor as involving God intervening in the world, for the world is generally under God's rule, and God is always present to historical life. Rather, one must interpret Jesus' works and actions concretely as having a bearing on the villages, which were the principle arena of his activity. "Jesus was apparently a revolutionary, but not a violent political revolutionary. Convinced that God would put an end to the spiral of violence, however violently, Jesus preached and catalyzed a social revolution."[38]

In sum, the centering characteristic of Jesus as a religious figure in first-century Palestine was his prophetic preaching of the kingdom of God for the restoration of Israel. This provides the framework for interpreting him; other aspects of his story would be integrated into this one.

JESUS AS TEACHER

A very large percentage of the gospel material represents Jesus teaching or as a teacher, so that it is common enough to designate him as such. But there were different kinds of teachers in Jesus' time. In what follows I will briefly represent two forms of this distinctive genre of Jesus, the one a recent development growing out of North American Jesus research, the other an effort to locate Jesus in the Jewish sapiential tradition. In the first case, as it is presented by John Dominic Crossan and Burton Mack, Jesus appears as a Jewish teacher who resembled a popular Cynic philosopher; in the second, represented by Ben Witherington, III, Jesus was a sage within the tradition of Ben Sira and the Wisdom of Solomon.

Crossan's view of Jesus is contained in *The Historical Jesus: The Life of a Mediterranean Jewish Peasant.*[39] This essay embodies a number of noteworthy methodological moves. Crossan generally leans toward caution against accepting the historical authenticity of the synoptic narratives as they stand. All the evidence he considers must pass through the criterion of multiple attestation. He also shifts the horizon or backdrop against

---

36. Horsley, *Spiral of Violence*, 324.

37. Horsley, *Spiral of Violence*, 285.

38. Horsley, *Spiral of Violence*, 326.

39. John Dominic Crossan, *The Historical Jesus: The Life of a Mediterranean Jewish Peasant* (San Francisco: Harper, 1991).

which Jesus is portrayed: instead of reading Jesus within the framework of his tradition as represented in the Hebrew scriptures, Crossan uses cultural anthropology and historical and social recreations of his contemporary Galilee to locate Jesus. Instead of situating him as continuous with his past religious history as reflected in the scriptures, Crossan defines Jesus within a "secular," social, and cultural matrix characterized by class, other social distinctions, and the political dynamics of colonization and occupation.[40]

Crossan depicts Jesus as a peasant, originating from the lower classes of society and, as an artisan, actually ranked below a peasant. At the same time, however, Jesus was influenced by the cultural and social Hellenization that affected the Galilee of his time. In his public ministry, therefore, Jesus took on a role that resembled that of a popular Cynic philosopher. A Cynic is a wisdom figure, a popular philosopher and itinerant sage. Cynicism was also a lifestyle, and the Cynic acted out his message. In it freedom was cherished and poverty embraced as a condition for inner liberty. Cynicism could also reflect social reaction against oppression. Crossan correlates data concerning this type of figure gathered from Greco-Roman sources with the instructions of Jesus regarding the mission of his disciples. Their prescribed actions and dress are very similar to that of the Cynic: cloak, knapsack, and staff. They were poor, itinerant preachers.[41]

It is in the content of his message and the meaning of the kingdom of God that one sees the distinctiveness of this portrayal of Jesus, especially in contrast to the line of interpretation begun by Weiss. According to Crossan, Jesus began as a disciple of John the Baptist who preached repentance in the light of an imminent coming of God, but who later broke with the Baptist, probably because he no longer accepted the apocalyptic message. The kingdom of God that Jesus preached, then, consisted in the internalization of God's rule, a rule that transcends and judges all human rule.[42]

> The sapiential Kingdom looks to the present rather than the future and imagines how one could live here and now within an already or always available divine dominion. One enters that Kingdom by wisdom or goodness, by virtue, justice, or freedom. It is a style of life for now rather than a hope of life for the future. This is therefore an ethical Kingdom, but it must be absolutely insisted that it could be just as eschatological as was the apocalyptic Kingdom. Its ethics could, for instance, challenge contemporary morality to its depths.[43]

How did Jesus' preaching unfold in practice? Those who made up the kingdom of God included the destitute, degraded, unclean, and expendable

---

40. Crossan, *The Historical Jesus*, xxviii–xxxiv.
41. Crossan, *The Historical Jesus*, 72–88, 340–41.
42. Crossan, *The Historical Jesus*, 259, 266.
43. Crossan, *The Historical Jesus*, 292.

classes of society. It was radically egalitarian. Crossan consistently depicts
Jesus as one standing in opposition to official or institutionalized structures of religious authority. Thus Jesus' power as a healer is an implied
criticism of religious institutions.[44] "Open commensality profoundly
negates distinctions and hierarchies between female and male, poor and
rich, Gentile and Jew. It does so, indeed, at a level that would offend the
ritual laws of *any* civilized society. That was precisely its challenge."[45] As
Crossan sees it, Jesus' implicitly prophetic activity of healing and fellowship at meals became an egalitarian movement through the mission of the
disciples. In this way Crossan is able to integrate various aspects of the
Jesus tradition into this large definition of Jesus' genre. It is not an exclusive category: Jesus' healing, exorcizing, mixing with sinners, and
prophetic critique become integrated into it. He accepts, for example, the
possibility of a dramatic gesture against the temple in Jerusalem that led
to Jesus' execution.[46]

But in the end, it was Jesus himself, in his charismatic authority as an
itinerant teacher, who threatened the temple. Crossan thus summarizes
his position: "My proposal is that when we cross apocalyptic and sapiential with scribes and peasants, it becomes necessary to locate Jesus in the
quadrant formed by sapiential and peasant. What was described by his
parables and aphorisms as a here and now kingdom of nobodies and the
destitute, of mustard, darnel, and leaven, is precisely a kingdom performed rather than just proclaimed."[47]

Burton Mack is another author who finds in the comparison between
Jesus and the life and motives of the Cynic philosopher reason to liken
Jesus to this type of figure. But Mack too has a distinctive approach to the
Jesus material which should be noted at the outset. In his search for historical authenticity, Mack focuses on Q, behind which he sees a community. Through a close analysis of the texts he isolates "the remains of the
earliest collections of sayings in the Q tradition, the layer of Q material
called Q prime."[48] This material, which is dated around 45–55 CE, is the
oldest witness to Jesus, and it forms the primary source for Mack's reconstruction. These texts put us in contact with the earliest stage of the Jesus
movement. They are made up mostly of sayings in which life in general
is considered and standard norms and values are criticized. "When

44. Crossan, *The Historical Jesus*, 138, 157–58, 266–73, 298–300, 324–25.

45. Crossan, *The Historical Jesus*, 263.

46. Crossan, *The Historical Jesus*, 355–60.

47. Crossan, *The Historical Jesus*, 292.

48. Burton L. Mack, *The Lost Gospel: The Book of Q and Christian Origins* (San
Francisco: Harper, 1993), 107. Two other interpretations of Jesus as a teacher influenced
by currents of Hellenism not considered here are V. K. Robbins, *Jesus the Teacher: A
Socio-Rhetorical Interpretation of Mark* (Philadelphia: Fortress Press, 1984) and F. G.
Downing, *Christ and the Cynics: Jesus and Other Radicals in First Century Traditions*
(Sheffield: JSOT Press, 1988).

viewed together, moreover, these sayings make a comprehensive set of sage observations and unorthodox instructions. They delight in critical comment upon the everyday world and they recommend unconventional behavior."[49] The sayings take the perspective of the underdog and criticize various forms of social custom. They do not suggest a program of systemic or social change, even when society might encourage discriminatory values. But there is always a suggestion of a better way to live. Sympathy clearly lies with the poor and the humble. The sayings recommend simplicity, an unencumbered life, a freedom from anxiety, and a closeness to nature.[50]

At this point Mack expands on the parallels between Jesus' teaching and the practical popular philosophers called Cynics. The similarity appears surprising because people are accustomed to hearing the words of Jesus against the background of the prophetic language of the Hebrew scriptures. In fact the Cynic might be understood as the Greek analogue to the Hebrew prophet. "The crisp sayings of Jesus in Q prime show that his followers thought of him as a Cynic-like sage."[51] As Mack portrays them, Cynics were public figures, social critics who embraced a public life of renunciation, debaters who called into question the status quo of accepted cultural or social patterns of behavior. "Thus the marketplace was the Cynic's platform, the place to display a living example of freedom from social and cultural constraints, and a place from which to address townspeople about the current state of affairs."[52] Like satirists, political cartoonists, and stand-up comedians, they set forth an alternative set of values and lifestyle. The Cynic could also be compared to a physician who offers a diagnosis of society and a cure. The Cynic is not necessarily erudite. "Their task was not to pose as teachers of truths people did not know, but to challenge people to live in accordance with what they did know."[53] Rather than seek the reform of social systems, they appealed to individuals to become self-reliant and live according to the wisdom of nature. The Jesus movement began as a local Jewish variety of Cynicism in the rough and ready circumstances of Galilee before the war. The movement was much more concerned with morals and action than with beliefs. Although it did not aim at social reform, it was concerned with roles in society and had an egalitarian bent.[54]

What shape did the kingdom of God assume in Jesus' Cynic-like preaching? There are a few sayings in Q prime that refer to the kingdom of God. None are apocalyptic, and none assume this view as its frame of

---

49. Mack, *The Lost Gospel*, 110.
50. Mack, *The Lost Gospel*, 111–12.
51. Mack, *The Lost Gospel*, 115.
52. Mack, *The Lost Gospel*, 116.
53. Mack, *The Lost Gospel*, 119.
54. Mack, *The Lost Gospel*, 114–21.

reference. But a strong link binds the rule of God and the pattern of counter-cultural practices that Q recommends.[55] In the general contrast between law and nature as the basis for social thought and a philosophy of life, the kingdom of God language of Q prime leans on the side of nature. The idea of kingship refers to the sovereignty of the individual's power to resist the prevailing social order or custom. One is king by being responsible and counter-cultural, by following an alternative lifestyle and vision. "That is why the language of the rule of God in Q refers not only to the challenge of risky living without expectation that the social world will change, but also to the exemplification of a way of life that like-minded persons might want to share."[56] In short, the kingdom of God is not apocalyptic and social, but a challenge to individuals to lead a responsible, simple, radical life. The interpretations of Crossan and Mack thus agree at several basic points.

Ben Witherington also calls Jesus a sage. But his interpretation of Jesus shares little more than that with Crossan and Mack. His construction of the meaning of this genre is considerably different than that of a Hellenized Jew. He is critical of the comparison of Jesus with a popular Cynic philosopher on several accounts, most forcefully insisting that parallels are not proof. More constructively he suggests that the Cynic influence, which had gained a foothold in Palestine in the first century, may have influenced not Jesus but the development of the Jesus tradition.[57]

Witherington's own thesis is that one finds in the Jesus tradition a further development of the Wisdom tradition, especially as found in Ben Sira, the Wisdom of Solomon, and Qoheleth. "In the Gospels one hears a sage who expressed himself primarily in Wisdom forms of utterance or in sapiential *adaptation* of eschatological and legal forms of utterance, or finally in the prophetic adaptations of the Wisdom form *mashal* [parable]."[58] Witherington is convinced "that the vast majority of the Gospel sayings tradition can be explained on the hypothesis that Jesus presented himself as a Jewish prophetic sage, one who drew on all the riches of earlier Jewish sacred traditions, especially the prophetic, apocalyptic, and sapiential material, though occasionally even the legal traditions."[59] The term "sage," then, is the most appropriate and comprehensive category for categorizing Jesus. Even though he used other traditions, prophetic, eschatological, and so on, Jesus cast the material in sapiential forms. For this reason "sage" is heuristically the most all-encompassing and satisfying genre of Jesus.[60]

---

55. Mack, *The Lost Gospel*, 124.

56. Mack, *The Lost Gospel*, 127.

57. Ben Witherington, III, *Jesus the Sage: The Pilgrimage of Wisdom* (Minneapolis: Fortress Press, 1994), 117–45.

58. Witherington, *Jesus the Sage*, 117.

59. Witherington, *Jesus the Sage*, 158.

60. Witherington, *Jesus the Sage*, 201.

Witherington offers some concrete reflections on Jesus' teaching activity. Jesus not only had disciples but probably understood them as such. This means that they learned from the teacher. Jesus taught with the authority of a teacher of the wisdom of God. One thus has an explanation for how the Jesus tradition began.[61] Witherington is less expansive, however, on the theme of the kingdom of God. In his view it seems to be less an independent center of Jesus' teaching and more a theme that gets filtered through a sapiential lens, especially that of the parable. Prophetic themes are, as it were, taken up into the sapiential horizon. Justice is transformed within the framework of God's transcendent wisdom that is disclosed in parable: the kingdom of God relativizes justice; the kingdom of God turns the orderly structure of society on its head. "The dominion of God has its own economy."[62]

Witherington's most far-reaching hypothesis is that Jesus referred to himself as the embodiment of Wisdom.[63] He thinks that Jesus, reflecting on the tradition, was encouraged by precedents to see himself in such a way that he took "the considerable step from presenting himself as a sage to presenting himself as the embodiment of Wisdom in the flesh."[64] This is not an improbable progression, because earlier texts show persons presenting themselves as a "living symbol" or "figure of God's message." "Jesus did not merely announce the inbreaking of God's dominion on earth, he believed that he brought it, and thus in some sense even embodied it."[65]

The genre of teacher is thus differentiated. We will not consider other interpretations of Jesus as teacher, such as Rabbi or Pharisee, but move to Jesus as healer. It should be noted, however, that the appreciation of Jesus as teacher is gaining ground today.

JESUS THE HEALER

By the criteria of historicity, especially of multiple attestation, there is overwhelming evidence that Jesus performed exorcisms, healings, and

---

61. Witherington, *Jesus the Sage*, 179.

62. Witherington, *Jesus the Sage*, 200.

63. Witherington, *Jesus the Sage*, 201–8. He proposes this thesis on the basis of some of the Matthean wisdom christology texts. Especially relevant are Matt 11:25–27; 11:28–30; 12:42; 8:20. I shall consider the wisdom christology of Matthew in Chapter 6.

64. Witherington, *Jesus the Sage*, 203.

65. Witherington, *Jesus the Sage*, 204. "What is especially daring about the idea of Jesus taking the personification of Wisdom and suggesting that he was the living embodiment of it, is that while a prophet might be seen as a *mashal* or prophetic sign, no one, so far as one can tell, up to that point in early Judaism had dared to suggest that he was a human embodiment of an attribute of God—God's Wisdom. . . . Some explanation for this remarkable and anomalous development must be given, and the best, though by no means the only, explanation of this fact is that Jesus presented himself as both sage and the message of the sage—God's Wisdom." Ibid.

"mighty deeds" that transcended normal explanation. Geza Vermes has developed these and other data into a coherent, encompassing portrait of Jesus.[66]

Regarding method, Vermes is interested in a historian's and not a theologian's quest for the historical Jesus: his aim is to fill out the earliest kerygma about Jesus contained in the gospels. But in contrast to a skepticism about the historical authenticity of the gospels, he professes a "guarded optimism concerning a possible recovery of the genuine features of Jesus. . . ."[67] But his most important move lies in the use of sources outside the gospels to recreate the situation of Jesus, especially the religious situation. Jesus was an Aramaic-speaking Galilean Jew, according to Vermes; therefore he examines the Galilee of Jesus. Jesus was a charismatic figure; therefore he analyzes analogous figures of the period and of whom there are reports in Jewish literature. The gospels only provide a skeletal outline of Jesus. Vermes proceeds by analogy to put more flesh and substance on the bare bones of the gospel portraits of Jesus. He builds on the fit or analogy between a particular situation, or standard role, or custom, or typical practice and that of Jesus. Jesus did what charismatic figures did; therefore Jesus was a charismatic; and what we know of charismatics helps fill out the portrait of Jesus. In this way what the evangelists say about Jesus becomes historical and real by the way it corresponds or is true to the historical situation.[68]

In Geza Vermes's reconstruction, Jesus was an itinerant "holy man" or *hasid* who engaged in exorcism, healing, and teaching. He thus gained a certain notoriety and following, and he enjoyed a certain authority. In the final analysis he was executed mainly for political reasons by the religious and civil leaders because, with his following, he posed a real or imagined threat to the social-political status quo. Let me briefly expand on some of the elements of this picture.

First of all, Vermes says much about Jesus simply by virtue of his being a Galilean. It was a backwater region relative to Judea and Jerusalem. Galileans had a reputation of being less strict in following the details of religious practice; Galilee itself harbored Zealots and rebels. Simply to be from Galilee would make one an object of distrust in the eyes of religious authority in Jerusalem and the secular Roman authorities. Although Jesus was not a Zealot, he seems to have been executed as one.[69] The reason was most probably preemptive caution, the attempt to head off potential problems before they actually arose.

---

66. Geza Vermes, *Jesus the Jew: A Historian's Reading of the Gospels* (Philadelphia: Fortress Press, 1981). Vermes has revised but not substantially changed his position, originally published in 1973, over the years. See his "Jesus the Jew," in the anthology *Jesus' Jewishness: Exploring the Place of Jesus within Early Judaism*, ed. by James H. Charlesworth (New York: Crossroad, 1991), 108–22.

67. Vermes, *Jesus the Jew*, 235, n. 1.

68. Vermes, *Jesus the Jew*, 42.

69. Vermes, *Jesus the Jew*, 43–44, 49–50.

Second, the primary category that Vermes uses to capture Jesus is that of holy man. A holy man is a charismatic figure who is defined by Vermes by what he does. He has the ability to heal, but without being a professional physician. His healing power is connected with being able to mediate God's authority and power over sickness. He is an exorcist, able to drive out spirits, and this is very closely connected with healing. Such a religious figure can also forgive sins. Vermes is clear on the fact that this power to forgive sins was not extraordinary for this kind of figure. Jesus' roles "as healer of the physically ill, exorciser of the possessed, and dispenser of forgiveness to sinners, must be seen in the context to which they belong, namely charismatic Judaism."[70]

Third, Jesus was also a teacher; this was not alien to being a charismatic figure. He taught in parables, which was typical. He addressed crowds of people, not just a small band of initiates, and seemed to prefer "the uneducated, the poor, the sinners and the social outcasts."[71] But at the same time he attracted followers, disciples, and a core of twelve.

Fourth, Jesus accumulated authority. In Vermes's view this authority did not come from study, but from charismatic power. It had its center in the conjunction of Jesus' teaching with his ability to heal and drive out spirits. Jesus, then, could also be characterized as a prophet who performed great deeds. Vermes minimizes the novelty of the content of Jesus' teaching and tends to link Jesus' authority and appeal mainly to his charismatic power. More generally, in all of these roles, Jesus was not, as it were, exceptional or unique. Vermes finds in Jewish literature other analogous figures who did much the same thing as Jesus around the same time. In the end "the person of Jesus is to be seen as part of first-century charismatic Judaism and as the paramount example of the early Hasidim or Devout."[72]

In some degree and according to different aspects, the genre of Jesus outlined by Vermes is supported by other scholars. For example, Edward Schillebeeckx sees the miracle tradition as part of the substance of Jesus' public career. Behind many of the miracle stories there is some kind of authentic historical tradition: Jesus was a healer and exorcist. He displayed such a power that people had to judge whether it was from God or from the devil. The gospel message is that Jesus worked by the power of God, always for human good. He thereby revealed a God completely on the side of human existence, and he himself mediated this saving power of God in act in history. In his miracles Jesus proffers divine help and fellowship with this God.[73] This is confirmed by Meier's extensive analysis

---

70. Vermes, *Jesus the Jew*, 58.

71. Vermes, *Jesus the Jew*, 26–27.

72. Vermes, *Jesus the Jew*, 79. "Once the Gospel report concerning his person and work is analyzed, the secondary traits removed, and the essential features inserted into the context of contemporary political and religious history, Jesus of Nazareth takes on the eminently credible personality of a Galilean Hasid." Ibid., 83.

73. Schillebeeckx, *Jesus*, 179–200.

of the miracle tradition mentioned earlier. He examines the miracles globally, by type of miracle, and in each individual report. Although the sources do not yield any detailed historical knowledge about specific incidents, that Jesus performed a variety of "wonderful" works is certain.[74]

Like the other genres of Jesus, this one too should be understood in an inclusive way that encompasses other aspects of Jesus. It does not exclude Jesus' teaching or the prophetic dimension of his ministry. For example, Sean Freyne sees in the miracle tradition a threat to the temple and religious authorities, and thus a deeper reason for Jesus' execution. Freyne accepts Vermes's view of Jesus as a *hasid*, healer, exorcist. A telling historical index is the Beelzebub controversy since it displays even Jesus' enemies recognizing his doing powerful deeds; he acts with divine power and authority. "Should the crowds who were impressed by Jesus' mighty deeds be equally enthusiastic about his teachings and link the two together, then the temple system itself and the centrality of Jerusalem, as the seat of divine power and presence, was in danger of collapsing."[75] The peasantry, which was his audience, would have been impressed by his mighty deeds. But it was in Jerusalem that the threat was felt, not in Galilee. There Jesus' wonderful deeds give at least symbolic meaning to the claim of destroying the temple; the threat is implicit in Jesus' actions and becomes real insofar as Jesus attracts crowds.[76] According to Freyne, then, one can explain the conflict generated by Jesus' ministry without postulating revolutionary conditions in Galilee; the conflict is generated by the holy man's activity itself.[77]

JESUS AS SAVIOR OR LIBERATOR

I indicated at the head of this chapter that Jesus research unfolds on different levels, and hermeneutical theory helps to sort them out. Besides various attempts to understand Jesus within the situation of his lifetime in first-century Galilee and Jerusalem, one finds interpretations of Jesus that are more explicitly hermeneutical. By that I mean that, in more or less explicit terms, their goal is to understand Jesus more universally and in a context that includes today's world. It is still Jesus who is intended—the

---

74. Meier, *Mentor, Message, and Miracles,* 507–1038.

75. Sean Freyne, *Galilee, Jesus and the Gospels: Literary Approaches and Historical Investigations* (Philadelphia: Fortress Press, 1988), 236.

76. Freyne, *Galilee,* 232–39.

77. These "genres" of Jesus are flexible, and may be contracted or expanded. For example, Marcus Borg describes Jesus the healer within a wider genre of a Spirit-filled, ecstatic, charismatic figure. I will treat this aspect of Jesus in Chapter 6 under the title of Spirit christology. Borg actually uses four or five different "types" to describe different characteristics that all coalesce in the one person, Jesus. Besides *Jesus: A New Vision,* see his popular *Meeting Jesus Again for the First Time: The Historical Jesus and the Heart of Contemporary Faith* (San Francisco: HarperCollins, 1994).

Jesus of the past. But what is known of Jesus historically is, as it were, drawn forward and interpreted within a present-day horizon. To say that this occurs "more or less" explicitly refers to the fact that some authors aver to what they are doing, while others do not, so that in some cases one wonders whether a given author knows what is going on.

The category of "appropriation," a crucial one in interpretation theory, can be used to represent what is happening here. As indicated earlier, appropriation means making a message from another or past situation one's own in one's own situation; it entails social-existential interpretation of something; it includes affirmation of its truth and commitment to what is affirmed. It is not, insists Ricoeur, subjectively reducing the message to one's own experience.[78] But at the same time, appropriation in the present also entails new meaning for the text or symbol from the past. Not only does the text mediate a new appreciation of reality for the interpreter, but also, in so mediating this meaning to a new situation, the text itself takes on new meaning. It is important that one recognize that this meaning is intrinsic to the text or its subject matter of the past, even though this particular meaning could not have been recognized in the past.

The genre of Jesus as savior or liberator is proposed here as one that has been continually applied to Jesus after his death and, in the light of an Easter experience, right up to the present. The term "liberator" is used as a rough equivalent of savior. In both cases, the terms refer to Jesus. In its reflective form this reference to Jesus would be based on the critical research and reflection of the historian. It would also include an existential, participatory engagement with Jesus that appreciated him as savior or liberator. It will be shown in later discussions that a foundational experience of Jesus such as this underlies all New Testament christology, the very notion of Christian salvation, and ultimately christology itself. As it is used here, this genre is a heuristic category. It contains the primal religious question that is addressed to Jesus: what is the religious appeal of Jesus? What does he hold out for human existence and the world in terms of ultimate reality? This genre of Jesus, therefore, formally shifts the perspective on Jesus in two ways: Jesus is being drawn forward and being presented in the light of faith's perception of him; and this is occurring in an ever-present time. This category for understanding, appreciating, and appropriating Jesus today is found in a large number of studies of Jesus, particularly those done with theological intentions. In current theological interpretations of Jesus the genre of savior or liberator is most pronounced among various forms of liberation theology.

In the analysis of Juan Luis Segundo, Jesus was a prophet who combined religious and political concerns.[79] The center of Jesus' preaching was

---

78. Paul Ricoeur, *Hermeneutics and the Human Sciences* (Cambridge: Cambridge University Press, 1981), 182–93, esp. 190–93.

79. Juan Luis Segundo, *The Historical Jesus of the Synoptics* (Maryknoll, N.Y.: Orbis Books/ Dove / Sheed & Ward, 1985).

the kingdom of God, and this referred to the historical, social, and political sphere, or an arrangement of life in history that was also religious. The kingdom of God had its grounding in the will of God; it would be established by God; but it would exist in this world, consist in social-political arrangements among human beings, and not be established apart from human agents. This kingdom of God that Jesus preached was thus a movement in history. Jesus inaugurates a movement that works for this kingdom of God by recruiting disciples who were to continue his work. The kingdom of God, for Jesus, was not to be merely a kingdom of religious virtues. On the contrary, although grounded in God's will and empowerment, it consists in a social-political situation in which humanity, whose essence is freedom or liberty, flourishes.

Jon Sobrino entitles his interpretation of Jesus *Jesus the Liberator*.[80] In his view the reign of God assumed the place of ultimate reality in Jesus' life: it was that for which Jesus lived and died. The kingdom is a hoped-for utopia in the midst of the sufferings of history. It is a historical reality that is sought, a transformed social condition that stands opposed to the anti-kingdom of injustice. Although as an eschatological reality it is open to all, it is addressed directly to the poor in this world, to those who are at the bottom of society. The kingdom of God represents the most basic and elemental will of God; it represents God's desire for life over death. It also represents God's plan for human existence; God is for the life and the integrity of creation. All humanity can be divided into those whose life is fundamentally secure and those for whom it is not, those who merely survive in a condition precariously near to death. God's kingdom supports their life, survival, integral existence, and well being. Jesus is understood at bottom as the agent of the kingdom of God. His ministry consisted in realizing the kingdom of God, that is, making it a historical reality by his actions: his healing by God's power, his exorcisms, his welcoming of sinners, his preaching which challenged people to become his followers. The central message, however, embraces everything: "the Kingdom of God is coming for the poor and outcast; it is partial, and therefore causes scandal."[81]

According to black liberation theologian James Cone, simply by attending to the Jesus of history and the meaning of the term "black," one must insist that Jesus was and is black. On the one hand, Jesus was the Oppressed One, and failure to see his complete identification with the poor and oppressed is to distort the historical person. The stories of his birth, his identification with sinners at his baptism, his ministry of concern for the poor, his referral of the kingdom to the poor because they were

---

80. Jon Sobrino, *Jesus the Liberator: A Historical-Theological View* (Maryknoll, N.Y.: Orbis Books, 1993). This work refines his earlier *Christology at the Crossroads: A Latin American Approach* (Maryknoll, N.Y.: Orbis Books, 1978). See also two works of Leonardo Boff, *Jesus Christ Liberator: A Critical Christology for Our Time* (Maryknoll, N.Y.: Orbis Books, 1978) and *Passion of Christ, Passion of the World: The Facts, Their Interpretation, and Their Meaning Yesterday and Today* (Maryknoll, N.Y.: Orbis Books, 1987).

81. Sobrino, *Jesus the Liberator*, 100.

poor, and the cycle of his death and resurrection, all identify Jesus' person and ministry with the poor and the oppressed. But today blackness most accurately interprets the reality of what Jesus was. Given the data about Jesus, blackness alone can define his past and present significance: "what else, except blackness, could adequately tell us the meaning of his presence today?"[82] Thus Jesus is able to empower liberation precisely because Jesus *is* "black."[83]

Elisabeth Schüssler Fiorenza locates the center of Jesus' vision and action in the *basileia* of God and finds four characteristics that defined his movement.[84] First, in contrast to John the Baptist, Jesus mediated a notion of God's reign that is already in our midst and already experientially available. It is arriving and experienced in the healing and curing ministry of Jesus himself. Second, the *basileia* stands for God recreating human wholeness. The salvation of the kingdom is human integrity and fulfillment; it is humanization. Third, the *basileia* is inclusive of all; it excludes no one; it is especially addressed to those who need it most, the poor and the marginated. God's reign is "inclusive of every person in Israel and . . . engenders the wholeness of every human being."[85] Fourth, the *basileia* of God involves reversals of our ordinary appreciations of things.

As for the *praxis* of the *basileia*, Schüssler Fiorenza sees it addressed to three constituencies in particular: the poor, the sick and crippled who were the object of Jesus' ministry of healing, and the group summed up with the phrase tax collectors, sinners, and prostitutes. In general, the kingdom was addressed centrally to those excluded and marginated from society, and these constituted the majority of Jesus' followers. The movement that was thus constituted during his lifetime consisted of a discipleship of equals within the sphere of this inbreaking *basileia*, and in it key roles were played by women. The egalitarian movement begun by Jesus thus reclaims the status of women and all who are marginalized.[86]

In Edward Schillebeeckx's treatment of Jesus the implicit questions found in the authors just surveyed are, as it were, recapitulated in the concentrated reality of human suffering, especially the massive social suffering that human beings inflict on each other.[87] What is the meaning of the human existence that, on the one hand, sees an excess of meaning-destroying corporate suffering and, on the other, dreams of a better, more humane

82. James H. Cone, *A Black Theology of Liberation: Twentieth Anniversary Edition* (Maryknoll, N.Y.: Orbis Books, 1990), 120.

83. Cone, *A Black Theology of Liberation*, 123, 110–28.

84. Elisabeth Schüssler Fiorenza, *In Memory of Her: A Feminist Theological Reconstruction of Christian Origins* (New York: Crossroad, 1983).

85. Schüssler Fiorenza, *In Memory of Her*, 120.

86. Schüssler Fiorenza, *In Memory of Her*, 99–157. Schüssler Fiorenza refines the earlier discussion in *Jesus: Miriam's Child, Sophia's Prophet: Critical Issues in Feminist Christology* (New York: Continuum, 1994).

87. Schillebeeckx, *Jesus*, and *Interim Report on the Books Jesus and Christ* (New York: Crossroad, 1981).

future? An appropriation of Jesus today has to be positioned within this fundamental secular and religious question of salvation. With this question as his guide, Schillebeeckx reads Jesus as a prophet, a prophet who was also an exorcist, a healer, and a teacher. The center of Jesus' public ministry was the kingdom of God, so that a consideration of the person of Jesus has to be entered through this symbol. The kingdom of God is the efficacious will, values, and actual reigning of God in history; it is grace and salvation. For the God of Jesus, whom he called Father, is a God of life. God is completely for the human, a God of human well-being: God's cause is humanization.

Schillebeeckx reads the whole of Jesus' teaching and ministry as a kind of transparency of this humane God. Taking this kingdom of God as a center, he sees the parables disclosing a dissident God. In the reversals of the parables, God's values appear as transcendent and other than human ways, disruptive of the present order of things, and always in the interests of human welfare. The same is true of Jesus' praxis. Schillebeeckx finds a fundamental ethics in the kingdom of God, reflected in the Sermons on the Mount and on the Plain. Jesus' own praxis of the kingdom confronted law, authority, and custom. He mixed with the poor, sinners, prostitutes, and tax collectors. Jesus' God was a subversive God.

In sum, the appropriation of Jesus as savior or liberator is open to a variety of nuances. On the one hand, Jesus' public career possessed a variety of facets; on the other hand, Jesus always communicates meaning to human existence by responding to the implied questions of those searching for a salvation or liberation.

THE JESUS TO BE APPROPRIATED

Who and what was Jesus? Was he a Jewish *hasid* or holy man who went around healing and also teaching? Was he a Jewish peasant who adopted the ways of a Cynic sage and whose teaching about the kingdom should be understood by each one individually? Was he a wisdom teacher in the tradition of Ben Sira? Or was Jesus a prophet single-mindedly committed to announcing and mediating a dramatic restoration of Israel through God's power? Was Jesus really a kind of pharisaic teacher in the school of Hillel debating the fundamental meaning of the law?[88] It is difficult to answer the initial question definitively. Yet all of these genres help to illumine the distinctiveness of Jesus. I do not mean to recommend harmonization. One cannot build an historically sound composite picture of Jesus by simply adding together these many historical reconstructions, because of the diversity of the suppositions, evidence, and perspectives

---

88. Harvey Falk, *Jesus the Pharisee: A New Look at the Jewishness of Jesus* (New York: Paulist Press, 1985).

that are brought to bear. But we do learn more about Jesus from these many essays than we would without them. And there is much data that they share in common.

In concluding this chapter on Jesus I shall not attempt to recreate him in his time or in a narrative form.[89] Such an essay is roughly possible, and more than a few are available. I presuppose the historical narrative accounts of Jesus already considered. What follows, by contrast, is a more modest attempt at a summary of data that begins to bring Jesus into slightly sharper focus. Instead of making first-century Palestine the horizon of interpretation, this presentation is influenced by today's situation and the question of salvation and human liberation as it is experienced today. But at the same time it deals with Jesus. On the basis of the reconstructions of exegetes and historians, I move to the level of conceptual analysis and propose this summary in propositional form. I look for aspects of Jesus and his ministry that are less controversial, more or less agreed upon by many of the questers, and hence representative of a consensus in abstract terms. I intend neither a narrative account of a historical Jesus, nor a homiletic recreation of the person, but simply a particular appropriation of some of the results of Jesus research. Jesus is presented in language that opens up or generalizes from the concrete particularities of his situation.

The Reign of God

Jesus preached the reign of God. Most exegetes conclude that this was the very center of Jesus' message to first-century Palestine. On one level it is probably impossible to pin down exactly all that Jesus meant by the phrase, the rule of God. But on another level it is straightforward and can be understood by all: "we know perfectly well what he meant in general terms: the ruling power of God."[90] Christians regularly pray in the prayer taught by Jesus that God's "will be done, on earth as it is in heaven" (Matt 6:10). This is the reign of God.

The phrase, the reign of God, is a religious symbol pointing to a transcendent sphere.[91] Insofar as it refers to *God's* reign, it is reality effected by

---

89. Michael L. Cook, in *Christology as Narrative Quest* (Collegeville, Minn.: Liturgical Press, 1997), provides a foundational rationale for christology as narrative. In his critique of the historical reconstruction of Jesus, Luke Timothy Johnson insists that "the *meaning* of Jesus is given, not by any of the single pieces, or their historical probability, or the qualitative balance among them, but by the structuring of the narrative as such. The meaning is given by the story." *The Real Jesus: The Misguided Quest for the Historical Jesus and the Truth of the Traditional Gospels* (San Francisco: Harper, 1996), 154. I accept this role of a narrative portrayal of Jesus. But it should not be held in opposition to historical research into the data behind the story or conceptual analysis of the content of the story.

90. Sanders, *Jesus and Judaism*, 127.

91. Perrin, *Jesus and the Language of the Kingdom*, 196–98.

transcendent power that cannot be circumscribed by human imagination, and cannot be defined in precise conceptual or factual terms. The kingdom of God is eschatological; it ultimately encompasses the future, the end-time, the completion and fulfillment of history. Such a kingdom is utopic, and to think of its arriving at a certain time and place is to misconceive the symbol. Jesus, as far as we know, never defined exactly how the kingdom of God would appear; he did not say how it would be ushered in. But the kingdom of God makes sense against the background of the profound negativities of human life; it appeals to human desire and hope for what should be and could be by God's power in the face of human impotence.[92] Because of its ultimate transcendence, it will be conceived in many different ways.

But in Jesus this kingdom of God is not far off or unrelated to this world. In his teaching it is imminent, about to come upon the world; Jesus is its herald; in some respects he is its agent,[93] and the reign of God comes to light in his teaching and action. Several dimensions of the rule of God may be experienced as concentrated together in Jesus: the reign of God of the future is linked up with his person and action; Jesus' praxis makes God's rule present; and this is held out as a cause and a mission that attracts disciples.[94]

In making the reign of God the center of his preaching, Jesus was theocentric. Jesus did not preach himself; his person and work do not appear as the focus of his own teaching. He spoke rather of God, whom he called Father. God, God's will, God's values, God's priorities dominated all that was remembered about what Jesus said and did. When the New Testament speaks of Jesus as obedient, or as having a mission from the Father, it reflects the centrality of the kingdom of God in Jesus' life as a cause. The consistent picture of Jesus is of one who is completely committed and faithful to making concrete and actual God's will and values in history. The fact that the reign of God was so central to Jesus' life and teaching makes it normative for the Christian theologian: christologies that neglect it are inadequate, and, positively, Christians must find some meaning for the reign of God in their theological understanding of the world.

Parables and Sayings of Jesus

The transcendent and symbolic character of the reign of God is reflected in the fact that much of Jesus' teaching about it is in the form of parable. A parable is figurative language, an extended simile or metaphor, not necessarily exclusive of allegory, which communicates in narrative form

---

92. The dynamics of a negative experience of contrast, as described by Edward Schillebeeckx, open up the meaningfulness of such religious symbols as the kingdom of God. See, for example, his *God the Future of Man* (New York: Sheed & Ward, 1968), 153–55, and *Church: The Human Story of God* (New York: Crossroad, 1990), 5–6.

93. Sanders, *Jesus and Judaism*, 153.

94. Schillebeeckx, *Jesus*, 150–54.

something disclosive of God, the world, or human life. Research on the parables has distinguished various redactional levels in the gospel versions, so that parables have become a privileged source for hearing the authentic voice of Jesus.[95] They show Jesus using the stories and references of everyday life in Galilee to open up dimensions of reality from the point of view of God's reign. "The kingdom of God is like" thus refers to the ordinary world as it would be under the efficacious rule of God. The parables, which construe everyday life as symbolic of God's meaning and presence, are Jesus' way of communicating an appreciation of God's rule.

What do the parables open up to the imagination? They portray God, and I shall consider them at greater length in the next chapter. The one Jesus called Father is personal and loving. The story of the Prodigal Son depicts God as compassionate, welcoming, forgiving, accepting, completely bent on the wholeness, integrity, completion, and fulfillment of human beings, who are God's children. The parables also portray human existence, individual life and the corporate life of Israel. They represent aspects of a way of life consonant with the kingdom of God. The story of the Good Samaritan in characterizing the meaning of the neighbor by depicting a kind of universal love, mutual care, and concern that extends even to the enemy is simply shocking. This is human life guided by the values of God.

Analyses of the parables show that they consistently contain a kind of reversal of common patterns of thinking, a puzzling ending that overturns what is expected. God's will, in relation to common human ways of thinking and behaving, is a surprise. This same kind of reversal is also found in a number of Jesus' sayings, such as the beatitudes and woes (Luke 6:20-26), the command to love and care for those who hate us (Luke 6:27-28), and so on. The poor, those who suffer, and the persecuted are the happy ones; the kingdom belongs to them and not to the rich. With these judgments Jesus is standing in the line of the prophets. The kingdom of God is judgment against situations of human suffering and oppression; the reign of God will reverse these dehumanizing conditions. Preaching often depicts Jesus as a prophet. History functions positively in bringing forward the authentic voice and actions of Jesus that give the title its content.[96]

The New Testament says that Jesus spoke with authority. One could infer this from the emergence of the Jesus movement. Jesus made an impact on people; he was remembered as one who had authority.[97] But authority in religious matters is ultimately mediational; it is the ability to disclose and mediate the authority of God or ultimate reality in one way

---

95. John R. Donahue, *The Gospel in Parable: Metaphor, Narrative, and Theology in the Synoptic Gospels* (Philadelphia: Fortress Press, 1988), brings together the wealth of current interpretation of the parables. Perrin provides a history of parable interpretation up to the mid-1970s in *Jesus and the Language of the Kingdom*.

96. Bornkamm, *Jesus of Nazareth*, 190.

97. Bornkamm, *Jesus of Nazareth*, 170, 179.

or another. Some of Jesus' authority is revealed in the parables. While some of these stories remain obscure today, or subject to multiple interpretations, many are utterly simple, clear, and radical. They often surprise the imagination with a God who offends by being so compassionate. This God is so loving and accepting of all human beings that they seem judged, or at least exposed, in the light of this goodness. In a world of sin God's love is counter-cultural; it confronts people prophetically. But to the victims of this sin, the poor, the marginated, the dehumanized, this transcendent love offers hope and an encouragement to struggle against their situation.

Jesus' Wondrous Acts

Exegetes are more or less convinced that Jesus was a healer of some kind, an exorcist, one who attended to the negativities of life. He also offered forgiveness of sin. It is most difficult to determine what exactly the events behind any given miracle story were. They are undoubtedly embellished, and in some cases created later to make a point about how Jesus was perceived by faith. The particular historicity of the events behind the miracle stories is simply not known. But this is not really important. In principle, miracle stories of themselves can tell us nothing of the divine origin of Jesus. Moreover, in some instances a literal imagination can obscure and conceal Jesus' mediation of the divine. Especially in secular cultures today, the more Jesus is depicted as a supernatural miracle worker, the less is he a credible mediator of God's transcendent and sovereign power. Although it is historically certain that Jesus cared for the sick and those who suffered, exactly how this was manifested is secondary. Divine power in Jesus' life is mysterious. We cannot know its mechanism or how it operated.

But at the same time it seems historically accurate to say that people in Jesus' time, and probably Jesus himself, understood God to be at work in his ministry. God as Spirit, that is, symbolically, the presence and power of God, in some way was working in and through Jesus as he attended to those who suffered.[98] Jesus' care for human suffering dramatizes how the cause of God is the cause of humanity. The God of Jesus is a God who is intrinsically concerned about the wholeness of human beings. That God is all-inclusive and egalitarian is manifested in Jesus' reaching out to those on the margins. In the same measure this God is the God of all. The universality implicit in monotheism is a universality of God's being related to and concerned with every single human being. God wills the integral development of the freedom of every human being toward wholeness and completion. Such is the message of Jesus.

---

98. James D. G. Dunn, *Jesus and the Spirit* (London: SCM Press, 1975), 52. See Maurice Wiles, "Religious Authority and Divine Action," *Working Papers in Doctrine* (London: SCM Press, 1976), 132–47, for a reflection on the meaning of God acting in history.

This disclosure spontaneously and necessarily spills over today into the social and political spheres and reaches the structural dimensions of public institutional life. Jesus did not have the sense of history that we possess today, a twenty-first century experience of the social structure of existence and human solidarity. But the disclosure of a God who is compassionate, boundless, and egalitarian love is simple and all-encompassing. This love automatically subsumes within itself, as it apparently did in Jesus' ministry, a radical desire to attend to human suffering, to resist it, to cure it, to overcome it in whatever form it takes and whatever its causes are. A christology that does not include this has left Jesus behind, not drawn him into present-day life.

Jesus' Freedom for Others

The category of freedom is highly interpretative when it is applied to Jesus, because of all that it connotes in a twenty-first century western culture. I use it here to collect a number of actions or patterns of actions that historians attribute to Jesus. In all of them Jesus seems to display a spontaneous self-transcendence. He thus reflects in his own behavior a kind of dedicated action that corresponds with his message of the kingdom.

Multiple sources attest to the fact that Jesus had a reputation for associating with people of ill repute, with publicans and prostitutes, with those who were the outcasts of his society. Jesus also reached out to public sinners; he offended people with his offer of forgiveness of their sin and acceptance of them. Jesus possessed the freedom necessary to interpret the law: he appears to be saying that the kingdom of God cannot be contained in a codified form; it always overflows in favor of God's compassion and our love of neighbor.

These simple points, which are developed much more fully in kerygmatic stories and historical reconstructions, mediate some powerful religious messages. The kingdom of God is not simply the left hand of God's judgment; it is, finally, the right hand of God's loving concern, God's compassionate forgiveness of sinners and acceptance of them as persons. This love is universal and egalitarian; no one falls out of its scope. In all the gospels, the theme of Jesus reaching out to those who are neglected, oppressed, and suffering simply dominates the narratives. It is not surprising that these ideas are translated into action. There is solid backing in Jesus for the premises of feminist, black, liberation, and political theologies, and for human support of all persecuted minorities. Jesus exemplifies the inner freedom of self-transcendence needed to engage the problems of others, and Jesus teaches that such freedom is the birthright of all and should not be shackled by any external bondage.

The Ethics of Jesus

At this point one must speak of the ethics of Jesus. One way of going about this would be to consult the sayings of Jesus, in the Sermon on the Mount or on the Plain, and gather together some of his maxims on righteous or ethical behavior. This could lead to a construction of an ethics of rules. Or basic principles could be discerned underlying Jesus' particular teachings that have universal relevance but historically changing application.[99] But the foundations of Jesus' ethics are more solidly, although less specifically, grounded in the disclosure of God that he mediates by his teaching and through the implicit logic of his activity. The concrete mediation of God's compassionate love for all who suffer announces a call for followers and draws people into discipleship. This is God's cause, God's project in the world, God's plan for history. God's project is such that it demands a fundamental option, a life commitment, an all-encompassing loyalty and fidelity that wraps itself around all particular choices in life. Edward Schillebeeckx draws this out further. There is a linkage in Jesus between the future and the present which stimulates "religious and ethical conduct in accord with the kingdom of God."[100] God's sovereignty over history and human praxis are connected by Jesus. This is reflected in his moving around and doing good, his taking sides with the dispossessed and the outcasts, his parables and sayings, his association with sinners. Thus the kingdom of God and praxis for the wholeness of being, especially of others, are closely associated. Human beings living according to the values of the kingdom of God *is* God's sovereign love manifested in history; service of the neighbor *is* the rule of God registered in human life. Human beings caring for others "is the visible form and aspect in which the coming of God's kingdom is manifested. . . ."[101] This is the form that the kingdom of God takes. On the premise of faith that Jesus is a religious mediation of God, one can read the kingdom of God in the behavior of Jesus. Once again, the basic conception is simple and foundational.[102]

The ethics of Jesus, then, are not formulated in a legal code; as far as particular maxims or teachings are concerned, they are not original. Jesus does not add new content to ethical reasoning, or, if he does at any particular point, this is not what is central. Rather, the ethics reflected in Jesus, whatever the source, become the ethics of the kingdom of God. This means that what is correct and morally virtuous by the dictates of human

---

99. In this way the social gospel movement drew its social ethics from Jesus. See, for example, Shailer Mathews, *The Social Teaching of Jesus: An Essay in Christian Sociology* (New York: Macmillan, 1897); Francis Greenwood Peabody, *Jesus Christ and the Social Question: An Examination of the Teaching of Jesus in Its Relation to Some of the Moral Problems of Modern Social Life* (New York: Macmillan, 1900); Walter Rauschenbusch, *The Social Principles of Jesus* (New York: Association Press, 1916).

100. Schillebeeckx, *Jesus*, 153.

101. Schillebeeckx, *Jesus*, 153.

102. On the premise that Jesus is sacrament of God's self-revelation, Schillebeeckx develops the relationship of Jesus to ethics in *On Christian Faith: The Spiritual, Ethical and Political Dimensions* (New York: Crossroad, 1987), 47–84, and in "Glaube und Moral," *Ethik im Context des Glaubens* (Fribourg: Universitätsverlag, 1978), 17–45. Part of this earlier essay is translated as "Religion and Ethics," *The Schillebeeckx Reader*, ed. by Robert Schreiter (New York: Crossroad, 1984), 260–68.

reasoning may also be construed as having its source and destiny in God. People are responsible before, and to, God. Everyday moral reasoning and prudence are thereby transformed.[103] What Jesus discloses for his followers as an ethical, holy life united to God is one that is completely immersed in history. A life fully engaged in society will reflect the sacrality and absoluteness of God's will when it contributes to the good of the whole community. This represents the sapiential dimension of Jesus' teaching. But in a world of injustice this formal and fundamental ethics will assume a liberationist content. The prophetic dimension of discipleship judges and resists everything that kills, diminishes life, and curtails freedom.

Jesus' Death

From a historical standpoint an appropriation of Jesus' death involves a measure of critical nuance. At the start of the Christian movement the death of Jesus as a religious-political criminal on a cross was inexplicable; it seemed to contradict the possibilities and expectations of Jesus' mission. Gradually, however, the followers of Jesus interpreted his death in the light of the Jewish scriptures in a variety of ways: it was a martyr's death, a prophet's death, a sacrificial death, an atoning death, a redeeming death. As a result, most Christians today know of Jesus' death dogmatically and understand it in abstract symbolic categories. But when this tradition bends back on history and takes on a literal or descriptive reference to the way things happened, the resulting interpretations can be seriously misleading. It begins to seem as though God wanted and even planned that Jesus die the way he did. Here we have a good example of how a critical, historical imagination can cut through distorted perceptions of the meaning of second-order kerygmatic teaching.

Jesus' death was the end of his life on earth, his last action in his life's passion; it was not only done to him, but something he did. It must be construed in its historical dynamics. For there is a deep logic in Jesus' death that all can recognize, prescinding from the question of the responsibility of this or that group, which has no direct theological import.[104] Jesus' death was due to his message, his preaching it, and his actions. His crucifixion was determined by the measure in which he confronted people or challenged their interests. Jesus' death flowed from the radicality and seriousness of his

---

103. H. Richard Niebuhr, *The Meaning of Revelation* (New York: Macmillan, 1960), 175–91.

104. Raymond Brown accepts some historicity of both judgments against Jesus, the one of the Sanhedrin, the other of Pilate, mainly on the basis of multiple attestation and the reasonable expectation that these events would have been remembered. Raymond E. Brown, *The Death of the Messiah: From Gethsemane to the Grave* (New York: Doubleday, 1994), 425, 555–60, 725, 753. But reconstructing in any exact fashion the motives for the decisions that led to Jesus' death is difficult. "It is impossible to conclude from the Gospels what sequence of events brought Jesus to the cross." Gerard S. Sloyan, *The Crucifixion of Jesus: History, Myth, Faith* (Minneapolis: Fortress Press, 1995), 40.

message; from his perspective, it was a function of his fidelity to his mission or cause, the cause of God, a mission of salvation to the people around him. Jesus gave his life for the kingdom of God, and all the evidence points to the fact that he gave it freely.[105]

The troubling aspects of Jesus' death lie in the questions that can be asked about it.[106] Was there an inevitability in Jesus' death? And if there is some human historical necessity, lying in some maxim that says all such prophetic witness will ultimately be destroyed, does this disclose something about the human condition? The answers to these questions may carry with them a terrifying revelation about humanity; they lead to reflections about God and ultimate justice in the universe. At this level Jesus begins to appear as a mediating symbol and a response to fundamental religious questions. But at this level, too, Jesus' death must be connected with the whole of his life; it absolutely cannot be separated and made a datum of reflection in itself. Jesus' death says that Jesus endured in his life to the very end; he summed up his dedication to God's cause against the negativities of human existence in a final act of trusting commitment.

CONCLUSION

The quest for the historical Jesus is not and will never be conclusive. Despite this historical inconclusiveness, the quest is important as a corrective of manifestly false interpretations of Jesus, and as a stimulus of a concrete historical imagination relative to his person. But the theologian must move beyond the quest, because, after the most adequate historical reconstruction has been accomplished, the theologian still must interpret Jesus for our time. And the theologian cannot wait; interpretation must and does go forward, even though the Jesus question is not settled.

The distinctive role of the theologian's interpretation focuses upon appropriation of Jesus into our current horizon and situation. This requires some knowledge of who Jesus was in his own lifetime. Reconstructing the

---

105. The distinction between history and theological interpretation is important in the matter of Jesus' death. Relative to the historical reasons and motives for Jesus' being put to death, there is some agreement that it was caused proximately by Jesus' prophetic activity in the temple area, which was perceived by those in authority within the framework of a knowledge of his ministry in Galilee. On the part of Jewish leaders, particularly the priests, this was seen as a threat to the temple cult and perhaps their authority. On the part of the Romans, one can postulate a fear of general unrest stimulated by a preacher of the kingdom of God with a following. Jesus was executed as "King of the Jews." But to move from historical reconstruction to theological significance is a qualitatively different step, and one should be wary of assigning metaphysical implications to particular events. Of the genres of Jesus presented here, the prophetic interpretation best explains the historical logic of his execution. See, for example, Sanders, *Jesus and Judaism*, 61–76, 294–318, and *Historical Figure*, 249–75.

106. These questions are posed by Hans Küng in *On Being a Christian* (Garden City, N.Y.: Doubleday, 1976), 334–42.

historical Jesus is the work of exegetes and historians; in the end, it is not the task of theologians as such to judge what can or cannot be known by the historian. But for the theologian, the desire to root the interpretation of Jesus in a real historical person and the need for some critical leverage over the multiplicity of interpretations of Jesus imply a necessity of being in dialogue with the historian. At every point history critically appraises widespread kerygmatic images of Jesus that are ambiguous, while the general character of the same historical Jesus opens up possibilities that may empower Christian life.

The interpretation of Jesus for our time will have the same structure as it did when people first encountered Jesus. Jesus was a person in whom people encountered God. The basis for Jesus' central place in Christian faith rests in the fact that he continues to be one in whom people encounter God. In the next chapter the discussion will turn to the theme of how God appears in the ministry of Jesus.

CHAPTER 4

The God of Jesus

This chapter takes up the teachings of Jesus. More specifically, it will examine the image or perception of God conveyed through Jesus. The reason for this focus will become apparent in the chapters dealing with the structure of christology and the notion of salvation, but an indication of the rationale is appropriate at this point. I presuppose the principle that all contact with God is mediated historically, and that for Christian faith Jesus is the event in history where that encounter occurs. The foundation of Christianity and christology lies in the fact that disciples and others encountered God in Jesus, so that Jesus forms the central point of mediation for Christian revelation of and encounter with God. So rudimentary is this principle that, when asked about the nature and reality of God, the Christian can respond that God is like Jesus.[1] This does not mean that the Christian's knowledge and encounter with God comes exclusively through Jesus Christ, but that Jesus supplies the central symbol and norm for understanding God. It becomes imperative, therefore, to inquire about the conception of God that Jesus represented.

This chapter will examine Jesus and his teaching with a kind of double vision. On the one hand, Jesus and his teaching as these are portrayed in the New Testament and critically examined by scriptural exegetes make up the object of investigation. But, on the other hand, Jesus is a witness and mediator of God. Therefore the chapter also looks through Jesus to the object or subject matter of his teaching. Also, beyond the formal teaching, I shall consider the reference to God that is contained in Jesus' actions. Because of his function in the Christian religious imagination, Jesus himself can be considered a parable of God, so that one can discern implicit teaching or a revelatory mediation of God in Jesus' activity.

I begin with a brief statement about the tradition about God that is contained in the Hebrew scriptures. There was a time when the differentiation of Jesus' teaching from that of Jewish tradition was a criterion for its

---

1. Juan Luis Segundo, *Christ in the Spiritual Exercises of St. Ignatius* (Maryknoll, N.Y.: Orbis Books, 1987), 22–26.

authenticity. Scholars gauged most important and significant in Jesus' teaching what could be differentiated from that of the Jewish community. But Jesus was a Jew who was brought up in and shaped by Jewish religious tradition. It would be surprising if the God of Jesus were not substantially the God of his Jewish upbringing. So deep and solid is this continuity that one must expect that, beyond whatever minor differentiations that might be found, Jesus' teaching and mediation of God substantially ratify and confirm this tradition. In a second section, I shall examine some of the distinctive ways in which Jesus mediates the God of Jewish tradition. And the third concluding section will contain a synthetic recapitulation of the characteristics of the God who is encountered in Jesus.

GOD IN JEWISH TRADITION

The point of these initial reflections is to try to encapsulate in some measure the tradition, the heritage, the religious framework in which Jesus was formed. From an objective point of view, it is foolish to think that one could capture the idea of God in the Jewish scriptures in a few pages. But if one situates this sketch in a world where many religions offer their views of ultimate reality, and atheism respectably affirms the universe devoid of an intelligent creator, one can at least hope to describe in large terms some of the characteristics, if not the intricate distinctiveness, of Jewish monotheism. Nothing more is aimed at here than can be done in a brief space, and, given the scope of this work, it must be sufficient. Some consideration of the very source of Jesus' teaching is necessary to situate it and measure the depths of its tradition. The short-hand way I have chosen to describe the religious consciousness of the Jewish scriptures considers the three kinds of writing in turn: historical, prophetic, and didactic. Given these blocks of data I shall characterize a number of elements of the teaching about God according to the genres of literature and some key texts.

God Saves

Claus Westermann has pointed out that in the Jewish imagination God does not possess a nature with many characteristics, but God acts. God is savior only because God saves. Israel meets God in God's act of saving and thus forming Israel.[2] The original and most basic Jewish creed was a narrative of God saving. The story was written down, retold, sung, and remembered (Exod 14:1-15:21). The story was reduced

---

2. Claus Westermann, *What Does the Old Testament Say about God?* (Atlanta: John Knox Press, 1979), 25–29. Cited hereafter as *Old Testament God*. Also David J. A. Clines, "Images of Yahweh: God in the Pentateuch," *Studies in Old Testament Theology*, ed. by Robert L. Hubbard et al. (Dallas: Word Publishing, 1992), 79–98. This volume will be cited hereafter as *Studies*.

to the short form of a creed for purposes of ritual (Deut 26:5–11). The story unfolds in a straightforward narrative structure that contains the event of salvation: our ancestors went down to Egypt; the Egyptians oppressed us; we cried to Yahweh out of our need; Yahweh heard us and saw our affliction; Yahweh saved us by bringing us out of Egypt and to this place; and now I bring this first fruit which the Lord has also given; and I worship and rejoice.[3] This narrative and its pattern preserve a memory of what God had done, and shape a kind of experience of God that occurs over and over again; they define the broad outline of how God is experienced.

It goes without saying that God is personal. It is simply taken for granted that God possesses the range of responses that human beings possess. Yahweh interacts with human beings. God in this account is not far off but very close to and concerned about what goes on in human history. God's dialogue with human beings is one that is always bent on their salvation. This salvation overcomes all kinds of adversity. It may be the social and political salvation of a people that is recounted in Exodus, or it may be a personal salvation that is reflected in some of the psalms. Out of need one prays to God for salvation; God hears; God responds.

God Acts in History

That God acts in history is implied in the story of God saving. But in our age where God seems absent from history, the experience of God being so close as to take part in the events of history needs to be underlined. That God acts in history means that God has a role, takes a part, participates in the unfolding of earthly events.[4] This direct way of stating things need not imply that this faith was entirely naive. Although the Jewish scriptures recount various theophanies, God for the most part remains transcendent, not visible or available to the senses. There were no physical representations of Israel's God; all shrines were imageless (Isa 44:9-11). God was sovereign and free, and could not be summoned or controlled by human beings.[5] But God's presence and power could be pointed to by various symbols such as Word or Breath or Spirit. In the creation narrative, God's Word effects the reality it speaks: "God said, 'Let there be light,' and there was light" (Gen 1:3). Ezekiel's vision of the valley of dry bones that come to life by the power of God depicted as wind, breath, or spirit dramatizes the immanent, creative, life-giving energy of God present and working in the world (Ezek 37:1-14). The figurative speech here

---

3. Westermann, *Old Testament God*, 30.

4. History is the chief medium of the revelation of God; "God who acts" is the more general category, and "God who speaks" the narrower notion. Such is the thesis of G. Ernest Wright. "Biblical theology is first and foremost a theology of recital, in which Biblical man confesses his faith by reciting the formative events of his history as the redemptive handiwork of God." *God Who Acts: Biblical Theology as Recital* (London: SCM Press, 1952), 38.

5. Anthony Phillips, *God B.C.* (Oxford: Oxford University Press, 1977), 4, 90.

reflects the quality of the experience. Wind is unseen but felt, invisible in itself but visible in its effects. Breath too is invisible energy and power; with it there is life, without it death. The transcendent and creative power of God is neither directly experienced nor merely postulated; it is experienced in what occurs; it is read in the text of historical events as the positive ground of what happens.

The God who acts in history is sovereign king. "The Lord will reign for ever and ever" (Exod 15:18). "I am the Lord, your Holy One, the Creator of Israel, your King" (Isa 43:15). On the day of the Lord, "the Lord will become king over all the earth" (Zech 14:9). God rules; God is surrounded by a heavenly court; God engages in battle.[6] This foundational image of God, which emerged during the monarchy, is important for understanding Jesus' image of the kingdom or rule of God.

God also acts in history through agents. The agents may be angels or human beings.[7] God raises up charismatic leaders and prophets and priests to mediate God's will and influence in history. That kingship was a sacred office and that kings were God's agents imply that God also worked through the social and political structures of the nation. God even reaches outside Israel to find an agent of salvation for God's people in the invading Cyrus (Isa 41:24). It takes effort to transcend a present-day western perspective in order to appreciate this experience of God's active presence in the unfolding of life in everyday society and history without caricaturing it as simplistic. On the one hand, kings and prophets behave like everyone else, and every event has its own explanation. On the other hand, God is a deeper energy within things, and Jewish religious experience of these institutions transforms them so that they are understood as the media of how God acts in history.

The law is a good example of God at work within institutions. The commandments and the law of Israel can be explained in social political terms as comparable to those of other similar societies. But the commandments came to be understood as part of a covenant between God and the people of Israel (Exod 24; Deut 5:1-21). This was not merely an agreement of the past, but an ever-binding covenant of God's will and human obedience that defined a pattern of life. Moreover, the law which governed human affairs was shaped to reflect God's saving action. In the laws of Exodus one finds a great deal of law that protects people in society. Individual laws were formulated to reflect compassion for those in need (Exod 22:25-27). "You shall not pervert the justice due to the sojourner or to the fatherless, or take a widow's garment in pledge; but you shall remember that you were a slave in Egypt and the Lord your God redeemed you from there; therefore I command you to do this" (Deut 24:17-22). God present

---

6. John D. W. Watts, "Images of Yahweh: God in the Prophets," *Studies*, 138–42.

7. Moses is such a mediator; kings, priests, and prophets are mediators. See Claus Westermann, *Elements of Old Testament Theology* (Atlanta: John Knox Press, 1982), 73–84. Cited hereafter as *Elements*.

and active in history according to the basic paradigm of compassion and salvation colors everything. "Charity is part of law because it helps to restore that order which God wills and which law maintains."[8] Law, then, reflects God and God's will; and God is love, goodness, and compassion toward the weak.

God Judges Sin and Punishes the Sinner

I move to the basic motifs of the prophetic literature. Simply put, the prophets announce God's judgment on sin. God's election and graceful presence to Israel was conceived in the form of a covenant which was structured by law. According to the ideal, Israel would reflect the character of God. There should be no one in need in the covenanted community of God's chosen people. The community was to mirror God's gracious nature. A lack of peace, harmony, and just relations in the community meant a rupture between the community and God.[9] The underside of the history of Israel up to the Babylonian conquest of Jerusalem in 586 BCE is a history of sin, which in the view of Hebrew scriptures is endemic to human existence, but which nevertheless evoked prophetic threats of disaster for the nation. This sin is against God's compassionate will; it opens up in the community a condition of distance or estrangement from God. "When you spread forth your hands, I will hide my eyes from you; even though you make many prayers, I will not listen; your hands are full of blood" (Isa 1:15). Thus God raised up prophets who complained about Israel's sin, lack of faith, and breaking of the covenant, and threatened the community with the severest punishment, destruction of the community and the covenant itself.

It is important to recognize that this other side of God, God's anger, judgment, and punishment, correlates exactly with God's love and compassion for those who are dependent on others and mistreated. God reacts against the injury of the weak *because* God loves and has compassion. And God's judging is precisely a continuation of God's saving activity: God judges and warns in order to preserve the existence of Israel within the context of the covenant agreement.[10] The covenant texts continually encourage Israel to remember what God has done on its behalf. But people forget, and the prophets are there to remind them. The prophets censure sin and sinners in strong, blunt terms: "you who hate the good and love the evil, who tear the skin from off my people, and their flesh from off their bones" (Mic 3:2). These prophetic denunciations reveal further a God who is more interested in justice, in compassionate behavior obedient to God's loving will, than all the accoutrements of reli-

---

8. Phillips, *God B.C.*, 19. The laws of Deuteronomy "have two main objectives—to ensure that Israel remains loyal to her God and that charity continues to be exercised in favour of dependent members of society." Ibid., 27.

9. Phillips, *God B.C.*, 22–26.

10. Westermann, *Old Testament God*, 56.

gion. Some of the prophetic texts are dramatic: "to the melody of your harps I will not listen. But let justice roll down like waters" (Amos 5:23-24; see Mic 6:6-8).

God Finally Forgives and Accepts

The witness of the prophets after the destruction of Jerusalem and the Babylonian exile adjusts to the new conditions. The message of Jeremiah is gentler: "I will forgive their iniquity, and I will remember their sin no more" (Jer 31:34). It reflects once again the compassion of God for a leveled Israel after its people had suffered their punishment. It speaks of a new unconditional covenant based on pure grace (Isa 55:3), the pure love of God, and less dependent upon an obedience to the law. God will never again be angry or rebuke Israel: "my steadfast love will not depart from you" (Isa 54:9-10). Phillips presents the shift in the notion of God and God's relation to Israel from the pre-exilic to the post-exilic period as a shift toward a more interiorized relationship between God and the people. What was a quasi-contractual arrangement conditioned upon obedience to the covenantal agreement meant that obedience brought prosperity and sin brought prophetic warning, judgment, and final punishment. What emerges in the perception of God thereafter is a recognition of the illogical, gratuitous depth of divine mercy. "The Mosaic covenant was a straight arrangement between Israel and her God, so that no matter what individuals did within the community, the whole community was liable for any breach of law."[11] In the restored covenant, after Babylon, there would be more individual accountability. In the new arrangement "the law is to be a matter of individual obedience—the covenant relationship is to be with those whose hearts are for God, no matter what the rest of the people do."[12]

The compassion of God asserts itself in a classic tensive balance with God's judgment against human sin. The psalms especially bring to expression the experience of God as compassionate, both to Israel and to individuals. God is mercy and forgiveness; God is compassionate like a father. "As a father has compassion for his children, so the Lord has compassion for those who fear him" (Ps 103:13). This testimony to God's compassionate fatherhood is important for understanding Jesus' construal of God.

God Creates, Provides, and Blesses

Distinctive features in the Jewish conception of God are preserved in the creation narratives and wisdom literature. The stories of God creating reality in the primeval beginning contain a clear affirmation of the universal

---

11. Phillips, *God B.C.*, 37.
12. Phillips, *God B.C.*, 38, with reference to Jer 31:27-34. Knowledge of the Lord will no longer have to be taught, but will be interiorly known. "I will put my law within them, and I will write it upon their hearts; and I will be their God, and they shall be my people" (Jer 31:33).

sovereignty and power of God. God's creating is a "creation by word": what God speaks comes into existence. The world, its history, the cosmos itself, all have their source in the one God. This God, then, is not limited by the sphere of the history of Israel; God is not merely Israel's God. There is a clear, intended affirmation in these narratives of the universal sovereignty of God. God is Lord of all history and all reality.[13] This dependence upon God is continual, so that God is not just the past source of a new independent reality. This is seen in the Noah cycle in which the world is destroyed: the story of the flood is correlative to creation. The existence of the whole world and all of history continues to depend on God.

Westermann insists that in the Jewish scriptures God not only saves but also blesses. Often emphasis falls on the distinction of the Jewish God from the gods of other religions: the God of Israel is not a God of nature but of history. God is one who acts in history in a saving way and not an object of a fertility cult. But this distinction should not cancel out God's presence in the natural workings of the world in which God blesses human life. In contrast to the dramatic events of salvation, God's blessing is a quiet, continuously flowing, and often unnoticed presence which can be associated with an idea of providence. "Blessing is realized in a gradual process, as in the process of growing, maturing, and fading."[14] These are the everyday processes in which people are married, have children, work, and prosper. Blessing has to do with the things that surround a full existence, especially in the context of the family and the general social and economic maintenance of society from one generation into the next. In sum, the whole sphere of the working of nature also belongs to God; it is not only ordered by God's wisdom, but it is also a place of God's working power and beneficent influence.

God Is the Indecipherable Source of Wisdom

The priest discerned the law of God, and the prophet God's word, while the wise offered counsel based on a reading of the character of God and human existence in and through the patterns of nature and society (Jer 18:18).[15] Wisdom is reflection that is based on the premise that God the creator is behind the order one witnesses in the world, in physical nature, in human nature, in society. It seeks to understand human existence in terms of the patterns of everyday life, and it tries to understand God as the source and creator of the logic one observes in the world. "Wisdom, then, complemented law, for like law it sought to achieve and maintain that divine order which God had inaugurated at creation but which was ever threatened by man's folly, his predilection for disorderly conduct."[16] Wisdom lit-

---

13. "The concepts of the whole, of the whole of humanity, and of the whole of the world first emerged in this talk about creation." Westermann, *Elements*, 87.

14. Westermann, *Old Testament God*, 44; also *Elements*, 102–14.

15. Phillips, *God B.C.*, 51.

16. Phillips, *God B.C.*, 52.

erature also probes the moral order of the world, the relation between proper behavior and happiness. The assessment of the coherence of history is not uniform. Proverbs is optimistic about a correspondence between human behavior and God's blessing: "No ill befalls the righteous, but the wicked are filled with trouble" (Prov 12:21; see also Prov 12:2 and 3:9-10). Ecclesiastes is pessimistic about finding any moral order or happiness in life: "And I thought the dead who are already dead more fortunate than the living who are still alive; but better than both is he who has not yet been, and has not seen the evil deeds that are done under the sun" (Eccl 4:2-3).[17]

The Book of Job goes to neither of these extremes. Job himself knows that the innocent suffer; it is false that "no ill befalls the righteous." Yet Job clings to God and implicitly to a moral universe. But this represents no calmly conceived middle or moderate position; it is held from within the excruciating pain of a suffering that seemed to contradict the premise of faith, and the overwhelming religious experience of absolute mystery. Somehow, in a way that is utterly beyond human discernment and transcends all understanding, God remains the basis of a coherent universe despite evil and the suffering of the innocent. God's justice is unfathomable.[18]

In sum, then, who is the God whose name was written in the heart of the Jewish tradition in which Jesus was raised? God was personal and responsive: one prayed to God in the praise and laments of the psalms, and God listened and responded. This is at the center; this is where it begins. In prayer one remembered what God had done and did: God saves the community Israel and individuals within it; God blesses everyday life. In prayer one recognized that God's love overflows in righteous anger at sins of injustice, threatens and exacts punishment, but always in the interests of conversion and salvation. God also listens to sorrow and lamentation, shows compassion, and forgives. This God who is so close and available, however, is also larger than the universe. God is the creator king who is universally sovereign and provident; God is the source of whatever intelligibility there is through the gift of law and as the deeper source of the order of things. But God still remains transcendent mystery.

GOD IN JESUS' MINISTRY

Disciples and others encountered God in Jesus. But who is the God who is mediated through Jesus' ministry? Against the background of the Jewish

---

17. The mystery of God reaches a certain intensity in the writings. For example, Qoheleth "simply denies that anyone can make sense of what God is doing." Roland E. Murphy, "Images of Yahweh: God in the Writings," *Studies*, 193. See Eccl 3:11, 8:17, 11:5.

18. John J. Scullion, "God in the Old Testament," *The Anchor Bible Dictionary*, 2, ed. by Noel Freedman (New York: Doubleday, 1992), 1046.

conception of God I take up the way God appears in the historical ministry of Jesus. But let me begin with an explanation of the hermeneutical perspective that governs these reflections and the caution that the words and the analysis can never encompass the encounter itself.

I shall not attempt a critical, historical, developmental account of the origins of Jesus' teachings. This would require a consideration of intertestamental literature that exceeds the present theological intent. Rather, I propose simply to gather together some of the prominent witnesses to the way God appeared in Jesus' words and ministry. The order of the material presented here is hardly systematic; the goal is to recapitulate and comment upon the strands of testimony that preserve Jesus' mediation of God. But the method of presenting this material does involve a systematic option. I am interested in staying as close as possible to texts which offer an historically authentic witness to the voice of Jesus. But I am not exclusively concerned with limiting the interpretation of their witness to the meaning they bore in their particular historical context. Implicitly, I operate out of a present-day horizon that is concerned with how these textual witnesses can be construed today, while at the same time remaining faithful to the historical ministry of Jesus. Interpreting parables illustrates this strategy. In some of Jesus' polemical parables, knowledge of the particular audience he addressed would help to determine their exact historical meaning. But when that particular audience is unknown, and with it the historical intention of Jesus, such a parable may still possess a structured content that renders its meaning quite clear, but in a more general and universal way. As a still more pointed example, Jesus' teaching may or may not have included an ostensive reference to a jubilee year, but whether it did or not, his teaching commanded a concern for the poor. Or, again, whatever Jesus was referring to in a particular saying on the kingdom of God, he always meant something about the will of God. The goal, then, is neither to abandon the historical witness of Jesus, nor to limit interpretation to its original situation, but to underline its more universal meaning and implication.

THE SYMBOL OF THE KINGDOM OF GOD

Mark reports that "after John was arrested, Jesus came into Galilee, preaching the gospel of God, and saying, 'The time is fulfilled, and the kingdom of God is at hand; repent, and believe in the gospel'" (Mark 1:14-15). It is generally agreed among historians that these two verses state with relative accuracy the beginning of Jesus' ministry. Jesus probably spent some time under the influence of John the Baptist.[19] Despite the differ-

---

19. John P. Meier, *A Marginal Jew: Rethinking the Historical Jesus*, 2, *Mentor, Message, and Miracles* (New York: Doubleday, 1994), 116–30. "So strong was the impact of John on Jesus that, for a short period, Jesus stayed with John as his disciple and, when he struck out on his own, he continued the practice of baptizing disciples." Ibid., 129.

ences, there are some basic similarities in the framework and the message of both: the kingdom of God is near, and it calls for conversion. Most exegetes and historians also agree that the notion of the kingdom of God lies at the heart of the message of Jesus. One can take it as a centering point which radiates influence on all of the teaching of Jesus. Nothing that Jesus said or did is completely unrelated to the kingdom of God, because it condenses and expresses the vision, cause, or mission for which he lived. Thus the notion or idea of God that Jesus mediates is not far from, and certainly cannot be divorced from, what he meant by the kingdom of God. The problem, however, lies in the fact that there is no agreement on what exactly the kingdom of God means. As far as we know, Jesus not only did not define the kingdom of God, but described it in so many different ways and in such figurative language that it is constant fertile ground for divergent interpretations. We have seen that a generic interpretation of Jesus as prophet, wisdom figure, healer, or liberating savior will yield different views of the kingdom of God and consequently the God represented by Jesus.

A hermeneutical approach to the kingdom of God can absorb this ambiguity into itself and achieve positive results. The kingdom of God is a religious symbol.[20] It does not represent factual or conceptual knowledge of particular data or a specific state of affairs. The kingdom of God is not a phrase that describes and thus stands for something else in a clear and stable one-to-one relationship. As a religious symbol the kingdom of God points to something else that is experienced religiously and thus specifically as other and transcendent. If the kingdom of God is understood not as a symbol but as a conception, or as an expression of positive knowledge, it is misunderstood, and this results in confusion. Questions are asked that cannot be answered, such as, when is it coming? or what will it look like? This religious symbol does not convey defined knowledge but, appealing to a tradition of religious experience, evokes many different forms of hope for God's kingly activity to become effective in life and history.[21]

Norman Perrin proposes the following archeology of the symbol: it rests foundationally on the analogy or metaphor of God being depicted

---

20. Many systematic theologians hold that religious language is of its own nature intrinsically symbolic. Thus all the language of the scriptures that refers to God or other transcendent realities is symbolic. But Norman Perrin has taken the notion of a religious symbol and expressly applied it to the idea of the kingdom of God in Jesus' preaching. This represents a valuable contribution on the part of an exegete to theological interpretation. Norman Perrin, *Jesus and the Language of the Kingdom: Symbol and Metaphor in New Testament Interpretation* (Philadelphia: Fortress Press, 1976). See the brief commentary on Perrin in Chapter 3, n. 27.

21. Perrin, *Jesus and the Language of the Kingdom,* 33–34. According to Perrin it is wrong to speak of the kingdom of God as a conception as distinct from a symbol, "because it is an imprecise use of language and hides the possibilities for understanding and interpretation that are present when the kingdom is recognized as a symbol." Ibid., 77.

as a king. As such it joins together two stories or modes of kingship, one relating to God's being creator and sustainer of the world, the other relating to God's being active in history in behalf of Israel. These two conceptions of God were merged in Jewish religious experience, and the symbol of the kingdom of God functions by appealing to and evoking this fundamental religious tradition.[22] When Jesus proclaimed the kingdom of God he was using symbolic language, language that evoked the living tradition of an experience of God acting in history as king. This language challenged people to recognize the reality of God present and active in the events of the everyday empirical world on a level that is not identical with but transcends the empirical.[23]

Once one recognizes the symbolic character of the expression, the kingdom of God, and the source of its meaning in a tradition of religious language and experience, one can also assimilate some of the generalizations about the kingdom made by exegetes and theologians. The kingdom of God is the result of *God's* action in history; God freely acts to establish the kingdom. But this does not require a literal application of a fantastic imagination. Israel knew God acting in history through human agents. Jesus himself was construed as one of those agents acting in the power of God as Spirit (Luke 11:20).

The kingdom of God looks to the future; it is an eschatological and final condition; it is, as Sobrino says, a hoped-for utopia in the midst of the suffering of history.[24] But it seems that Jesus experienced the presence of God's influence as close, near, and even beginning in the present time. Jesus may well have said that "the kingdom of God is in the midst of you" (Luke 17:21). The kingdom of God, then, even though it encompasses the end-time, is not something utterly other-worldly, because it points to God acting in history. God's divine power has its effects in history. The kingdom of God, insofar as it points to God's saving power, rights the wrongs and negates the negations of historical reality.

The historical effects of God's reigning constitute a social transformation. In an Israel occupied and ruled by Roman authority, people could not fail to hope for God's restoration of Israel as *God's* people. The kingdom of God also meant God's justice would replace injustice: the poor and the marginalized would be reintegrated into society. But the kingdom of God as God's will being done in history does not exclude the individual and his or her responsibility before the demands of life and the neighbor.

---

22. Perrin, *Jesus and the Language of the Kingdom*, 16–22.

23. See Perrin, *Jesus and the Language of the Kingdom*, 196. The symbolic character of "king" and "kingdom" relative to God does not begin to address the question of whether this is a viable symbol in secular, postmodern, and cybernetic societies and cultures.

24. Jon Sobrino, *Jesus the Liberator: A Historical-Theological View* (Maryknoll, N.Y.: Orbis Books, 1993), 70.

I do not mean to level the various interpretations of Jesus and his understanding of the kingdom, which are clearly different, to a common denominator. The symbol of the kingdom of God that Jesus preached may be construed to reach further than any single interpretation allows. But at the same time, the characterizations of the kingdom offered by Sanders, Wright, and Horsley presented in the last chapter seem to capture best the framework of Jesus' preaching.

In sum, the symbol of the reign of God points to God acting in history for salvation. It appeals to a tradition of religious experience that remembers God's action in the past and, from within a horizon of apocalyptic expectation, expresses in various ways a critical need for God's intervention now. Because of its symbolic character, the content of the kingdom of God is diffuse; it is reflected in Jesus' sayings, parables, blessings, symbolic actions, ethics, prayer, and, generally, the contours of his whole ministry. To complete the circular argument, it may be noted that this proliferation of various aspects, expectations, and interpretations of the reign of God shows its symbolic character.[25] I will look briefly at all of these aspects of Jesus' ministry that are preserved in the gospels in order to fill out the picture of God in Jesus' ministry.

GOD IN SOME OF JESUS' SAYINGS

In an exegetical study examining how Jesus depicted God in his ministry, Jacques Schlosser considers some of the words and sayings attributable to the historical Jesus.[26] Jesus frequently referred to God simply as God, that is, using the generic term *"theos."* Jesus also regularly referred to and addressed God as Father, and I shall comment on this name below.

Some qualities of God that appear in Jesus' sayings include God's transcendent power: God is God. God is represented as knowing all, even the inner workings of a human being; God sees all. God is represented as good, and this goodness is another quality of God's otherness; God alone is good (Mark 10:17-18).[27] God is, of course, personal, and Jesus encourages people to praise God, to glorify the Father, to sanctify God's name, not only with words, but also with their life and behavior. God appears as the Holy One, the one who is glorious. Also, prayer of petition presupposes that God is well disposed toward human beings and desirous of human welfare.

God acts. In continuity with the tradition of the Jewish writings, Jesus the Jew presents God as a person who enters into personal relationships

---

25. Perrin, *Jesus and the Language of the Kingdom*, 43.

26. Jacques Schlosser, *Le Dieu de Jésus: Étude exégétique. Lectio Divina*, 129 (Paris: Éditions du Cerf, 1987), 21–51, for a survey of various words used by Jesus to designate God.

27. Schlosser, *Le Dieu de Jésus*, 54–57.

with human beings. God is most specifically construed as an acting God; God does things which encompass the whole of history. Jesus refers directly to God's action of creating and blessing (Mark 10:6; Luke 12:6-7). Jesus presupposes God's actions in the Jewish tradition of the past and, in keeping with his view of the kingdom of God, looks toward God's action in the present and immediate future. Two aspects of God's action are judgment and salvation. God judges; God can cast people into Gehenna; God settles accounts; God condemns (Luke 6:37); God chastises (Luke 18:14; Matt 23:12). And God also saves, is merciful, justifies, forgives. A variety of texts point to each of these saving actions.[28]

God is a God of the living; God's saving activity reaches to the end of life in resurrection. In a story of Jesus in controversy with the Sadducees over the resurrection of the dead, Jesus argues on the basis of God being the God of the fathers, Abraham, Isaac, and Jacob. Since God is the God of the living and not the dead, there must be resurrection. Revealed in this exchange is a notion of God that combines God's creative power and God's faithfulness in saving love. God does not let go of what God has chosen. God is a God of the living and of life, a saving power against death.[29] It is hard to escape the power in the simplicity: a God of life prevails over death.

Finally, it is fairly certain that Jesus referred to and called God Father. This is not original to Jesus, for there are numerous references and invocations directed to God as Father in Jewish tradition. In Wisdom, for example, the righteous person "boasts that God is his Father," and that he "is God's son," whom God will liberate from his enemies (Wis 2:16, 18). The connotation of the term generally is that God has power and authority, and that God is characterized by love and personal concern. There are many instances in the gospels in which Jesus refers to or invokes God as Father. Luke has Jesus say: "I thank thee, Father, Lord of heaven and earth, that thou hast hidden these things from the wise and understanding and revealed them to babes; yea, Father, for such was thy gracious will" (Luke 10:21). The text combines a direct appeal to God as Father, God's sovereignty, God's concern for salvation, and God's partiality to those who are weak and dependent. The tendency is for God to be understood as the Father of the righteous or of disciples, but I consider the universality of God's love further on.[30]

That Jesus' preferred address to God was "Abba," and that this term was the equivalent of a child's calling God "daddy," thus establishing a unique, familial, and personal relationship between Jesus and God, is a thesis that was widely accepted after being argued by Joachim Jeremias beginning in the 1960s. Recently, however, this thesis has been criticized

---

28. Schlosser, *Le Dieu de Jésus*, 73–76.
29. Schlosser, *Le Dieu de Jésus*, 77–91.
30. See Schlosser, *Le Dieu de Jésus*, 105–77.

so that, on the whole, it is an unlikely proposition in the detail with which Jeremias proposed it.[31] The term "Abba" does not seem to have the meaning popularly ascribed to it, but is adult language. More generally, Jesus' reference to God as Father is also criticized by feminist scholars.[32] The intention of the feminist critique is to break a normative bond between present-day Christian language for God and patriarchal institutions and androcentric thought patterns.

After the historical arguments have been settled, a hermeneutical approach to Jesus' language about God is helpful in distinguishing universally relevant meaning from meaning that is entrenched in historically limited ideological interests. Three things may be said here with certainty. The first is that Jesus undoubtedly referred to God as Father, and the term "Abba" at least reflects that. The second is that one cannot make the case for exclusive use of the term "Father" for God on the basis of Jesus' ministry.[33] The third is that one can make a case on the basis of Jesus' ministry against an ideological, that is, androcentric or patriarchal, use of "Father" for God. Jesus' conception of God as Father was actually a critique of domineering patriarchy: "Far from being a sexist symbol, the 'father' was for Jesus a weapon chosen to combat what we call 'sexism.'"[34]

GOD IN JESUS' PARABLES

Because exegetes can get fairly close to an original structure of many of the parables, and because Jesus characterized the kingdom of God most fully in parables, they may be seen as a privileged *entrée* into Jesus' view of God. The parable has a structure that makes it a symbol especially apt for disclosing what cannot be defined. It is common today to refer to the tensive and paradoxical character of the parables: they often employ reversals, sometimes sharp logical surprises, to make their point. "By

---

31. See, for example, Geza Vermes, *Jesus and the World of Judaism* (Philadelphia: Fortress Press, 1983), 41ff.; James Barr, "'Abba Isn't 'Daddy,'" *Journal of Theological Studies*, NS 39 (1988), 28–47; James Barr, "'Abba, Father' and the Familiarity of Jesus' Speech," *Theology*, 91 (1988), 173–79.

32. See, for example, Mary Rose D'Angelo, "*Abba* and 'Father': Imperial Theology and the Jesus Traditions," *Journal of Biblical Literature*, 111 (1992), 611–30; and her "Theology in Mark and Q: *Abba* and 'Father' in Context," *Harvard Theological Review* 85 (1992), 149–74.

33. "The difficulty with the appeal to Jesus' use of father to restrict other options in naming toward God [is that it] presses speech that was pluriform, subtle, and subversive into an exclusive, literal, and patriarchal mold, and simply does not do justice to the evidence at hand." Elizabeth A. Johnson, *She Who Is: The Mystery of God in Feminist Theological Discourse* (New York: Crossroad, 1992), 82.

34. Robert Hamerton-Kelly, *God the Father: Theology and Patriarchy in the Teaching of Jesus* (Philadelphia: Fortress Press, 1979), 103. According to Hamerton-Kelly, who follows Jeremias on this, Jesus' use of the term "father" in his setting meant something similar to "mother" in developed modern society. Ibid., 81.

their paradoxical qualities the parables become metaphors of the transcendent."[35] A brief hermeneutical appraisal of the structure and dynamics of a parable will help to explain the interpretations which follow.

Among others, two things seem important here. First, because a parable can be considered an extended metaphor, it uses the everyday language of ordinary situations to describe an aspect of a reality that completely transcends these situations. In other words, a parable, like a metaphor, is symbolic; it describes, discloses, or reveals something that is other than itself. And, secondly, because the kingdom of God is transcendent and other, so that the language points to but does not represent it, the mind must actively go to work on the parable in order to discover its meaning. It does not lie unambiguously on the surface. If someone says that Harry Truman was a bull, a knowledge of his biography will not immediately yield the point. Like a metaphor, a parable will only reveal its meaning to active, reflective interpretation. Parables "tease the mind into ever new perceptions of reality; they startle the imagination; they function like symbols in that they 'give rise to thought.'"[36] As a result, scholarship cannot tie down the meaning of parables, and the history of their interpretation is one of pluralism and change.

I cannot do justice to either the tradition of the parables or contemporary parable research in such a brief space. I have chosen five parables, arbitrarily and without any other logic than what they themselves may communicate, to illustrate more of Jesus' teaching on God.

The parable of *The Rich Fool* (Luke 12:16-21) tells of a man whose harvest was so full that he planned to build larger barns to store his ample goods so that he could relax and enjoy himself for years to come. "But God said to him, 'Fool! This night your soul is required of you; and the things you have prepared, whose will they be?'" (Luke 12:20). The contrast is clearly laid out: material security versus the sphere of God; immediacy and self-concern versus loftier values and concern for others. This is not just about the suddenness of death. To gather earthly goods for an early retirement and the easy life in the face of the coming kingdom of God is just plain stupid.[37] To lay up treasure for oneself is not to be rich toward God (Luke 12:21). This parable helps to define the terrain of religious meaning. The reign of God is a sphere of meaning that transcends and overturns the value of hoarding treasure for one's pleasure. The sphere of God is one of ultimate meaning, of life and death, existence and non-existence, completely other and infinitely more important. And if the harvest of God's blessing

---

35. John R. Donahue, *The Gospel in Parable: Metaphor, Narrative, and Theology in the Synoptic Gospels* (Philadelphia: Fortress Press, 1988), 16.

36. Perrin, *Jesus and the Language of the Kingdom*, 106.

37. Joachim Jeremias, *The Parables of Jesus* (London: SCM Press, 1972), 165. The colloquialism is mine, recalling the saying: "The fool says in his heart, 'There is no God'" (Ps 14:1).

is itself the kingdom of God, the parable warns against its private use at the expense of the interests of the whole community.[38]

The parable of *The Seed Growing Secretly* is narrated in Mark 4:26-29. The kingdom of God is like the following scenario: the farmer plants, he does nothing as the earth in some unknown way generates slow growth until the harvest is ready, and he harvests it. This is a parable which would have had a definite meaning in a specific context of its being told. Does it say that the long history of God's dealing with Israel has reached a climax because the kingdom of God is here?[39] Was it originally spoken against the Zealots for trying to bring about the kingdom of God by force: the kingdom of God will only be effected by God independent of human work.[40] In either case, the contrast lies between the secret, independent power of growth and the power of human labor. The parable seems to point to the kingdom of God as including God's providential care, God's power and energy in nature that are the very sources of life. As I noted, the Jewish scriptures called this blessing. God's kingdom includes God's agency in the quiet growth and fulfillment that transpires within the sphere of nature. But the kingdom is also, at the opportune moment, occurring in Jesus' ministry.[41]

The parable of *The Mustard Seed* (Mark 4:30-32), which Mark places right after The Seed Growing Secretly, is short enough to be quoted: the kingdom of God "is like a grain of mustard seed, which, when sown upon the ground, is the smallest of all the seeds on earth; yet when it is sown it grows up and becomes the greatest of all shrubs, and puts forth large branches, so that the birds of the air can make nests in its shade" (Mark 4:31-32). One way of interpreting this parable is to try to recreate the situation of its telling: the kingdom of God is a full-grown shrub, it is here, and people are entering it. Or Jesus is saying that his little band of followers will be transformed by God into a more massive historical movement and become the kingdom of God.[42] Another way of understanding the parable is to recognize the distance of the parable from its original situation and audience, and to attend to the elements of its structure. Once again one sees the clean contrast between beginning and end, the smallest and the largest. The kingdom of God is God's work, and its results will be unexpected and extraordinary. The parable draws the imagination into a sphere that by contrast transcends earthly and human insecurity to offer shelter, protection, and a home. The kingdom of God is the sphere of

---

38. Bernard Brandon Scott, *Hear Then the Parable: A Commentary on the Parables of Jesus* (Minneapolis: Fortress Press, 1989), 138–39; Donahue, *Gospel in Parable*, 178.

39. C. H. Dodd, *The Parables of the Kingdom* (London: Nisbet & Co., 1935), 176–80.

40. Jeremias, *The Parables of Jesus*, 151–52.

41. Pheme Perkins, *Hearing the Parables of Jesus* (New York: Paulist Press, 1981), 83; Donahue, *Gospel in Parable*, 35–36.

42. The first represents the realized eschatology of Dodd, *The Parables of the Kingdom*, 189–91; the second interpretation is that of Jeremias, *The Parables of Jesus*, 149.

shalom, of peace with justice. But there is another contrast at work here, between the mustard bush and the tall cedar, planted on a mountain, to which Ezekiel compared Israel (Ezek 17:22-24). This parable, insisting that small is beautiful, presents a more realistic and unheroic account of how Israel might understand the kingdom of God in its midst.[43]

The Workers in the Field (Matt 20:1-16) compares the kingdom of God to the story in which the owner of a vineyard hired workers early in the morning for a day's wage. He then hired more workers throughout the day even to the last hours. He then ordered that the last hired be paid first, but they all got the same day's wage, those hired early in the morning and those hired late in the day. This is followed by a second part in which those who worked a full day complain of the injustice. To this the land-lord replies that his behavior contains no contractual injustice, only gen-erosity, and they should not begrudge his grace. This straightforward story reveals more as one continues to examine it under the light of reflection. I prescind from its possible historical context as a rebuke to the righteous, who may have complained about Jesus associating with sinners: the king-dom is open to all; all are equal in the kingdom. The point of the parable must lie in the inconsistency, in the question which everyone will ask: is not the landlord really unjust in this scenario, not in terms of a legal agree-ment, but humanly speaking? No parable contradicts more forcefully the basic order of society: equal pay for equal work.[44] The parable seems to suggest that what may appear as injustice is really God's incomparable, overflowing generosity to those who need it. "It is a striking picture of the divine generosity which gives without regard to the measures of strict jus-tice."[45] The parable confronts its audience with the sharpest contrast between God's grace and human justice.[46]

The Prodigal Son (Luke 15:11-32) is probably one of the three or four best known of Jesus' parables. It is a simple story in two acts and three char-acters. But it is hard to decide whose story it is and where the focus lies: the father, the younger son, the older brother? The youngest of two sons claims his inheritance, goes off, fails, and hits bottom. But he comes to his senses, turns toward home with a prepared speech of repentance, and is met by the father who sees him while far off and, moved by compassion, receives him back unconditionally and with a celebration, because he was dead and now he is alive. In the second act, the older brother is filled with resentment and anger at never being so treated, even though he remained faithful. Yet he too is re-accepted by his father. This parable may reflect

---

43. Scott, *Hear Then the Parable*, 386–87; Donahue, *Gospel in Parable*, 37; Perkins, *Hearing the Parables*, 85–88. Also N. T. Wright, *Jesus and the Victory of God* (London: SPCK, 1996), 240–41, on both of these "growing" parables.

44. Donahue, *Gospel in Parable*, 81.

45. Dodd, *The Parables of the Kingdom*, 122. Jeremias believes that this parable reflects Jesus' and God's special compassion for the poor, those hired last who would have had nothing to bring home to their families. Jeremias, *The Parables of Jesus*, 37.

46. Scott, *Hear Then the Parable*, 296–98.

the resentment of those considered righteous at Jesus' proposing an easy access to the kingdom of God for sinners.[47] But the deeper and broader meaning arises out of the contrast which, lest it be missed, is stated twice: between being lost and being found or saved, between being dead and being restored to life. And that which makes the difference between life and death is the simple, directly focused, extravagant, unconditional, overflowing, compassionate, forgiving love of God. In this case the fatherhood of God points toward loving care. As in the last parable, so too here, this love of God can appear to be scandalous when one begins to measure it, as did the brother. The God portrayed here by Jesus is a love that exceeds human logic.[48]

In sum, the parables disclose a God that stands over against common, self-interested human values. In the reversals of the parables, God's values appear as transcendent and other than human ways, disruptive of the present order of things, and always in the interests of human welfare. Since God is a God of infinite love and concern for humanity, the kingdom of God becomes a judgment against anti-human behavior and a promise of salvation in the pure goodness of God. Finally, one should not forget the manner in which the genre of parable itself communicates: by depicting God and God's kingdom in the everyday forms of Galilean life, Jesus reinforces the idea of a God perceived as present to and active within the patterns of human existence. This becomes more explicit in Jesus' symbolic actions.

GOD IN JESUS' SYMBOLIC ACTIONS

People encountered God in Jesus. This proposition cannot be confined to the mediation of Jesus' preaching and his oral message. It must extend generally to his person and specifically to his actions. Ordinarily, when a public figure offers a policy that must be taken on faith, one looks for signs of authenticity and credibility. It was expected that the prophet communicate in symbolic actions; teachers in the Cynic tradition mirrored some of their themes in their behavior and life-style. Demonstration is a less explicit but at times more forceful mode of communicating basic ideas. The gospel records contain a number of different kinds of actions performed by Jesus that are considered more or less historically authentic, and they communicate something about his conception of God.

---

47. Dodd, *The Parables of the Kingdom*, 120–21; Jeremias, *The Parables of Jesus*, 131–32.

48. Perkins, *Hearing the Parables*, 53–62; Donahue, *Gospel in Parable*, 151–58; Scott, *Hear Then the Parable*, 99-125. Wright reads the parable allegorically as telling the story of Israel's turning on God, being carried off into exile, coming to its senses, and returning to God. And now in Jesus' ministry the promise of reconciliation in the kingdom is coming to pass. The older brother is like those who did not go into exile, Samaritans, who resent the return of true Israel. Wright, *Jesus*, 125–31.

Healing

It is practically unanimous that Jesus was an exorcist and a healer. Jesus had some sort of leverage over devils or evil spirits.[49] "If it is by the finger of God that I cast out demons, then the kingdom of God has come upon you" (Luke 11:20). A good deal of material from multiple sources testifies that Jesus also healed, among crowds and on an individual basis. There are indications that he used some rudimentary ritual (Mark 8:22-26).[50] Mark tells the story of Jesus healing the mother of Simon's wife: "He came and took her by the hand and lifted her up, and the fever left her; and she served them. That evening, at sundown, they brought to him all who were sick or possessed with demons. . . . And he healed many who were sick with various diseases, and cast out many demons" (Mark 1:31-32, 34). Since sickness, Satan, and sin were related, exorcism, healing, and even forgiveness of sin could be intertwined. The prophet helped the sick, and the physician implored God for the right diagnosis and attributed the cure to God. Generally, an exorcist "was believed to be acting as God's agent in the work of liberation, healing, and pardon."[51] One can imagine that some of the people who witnessed Jesus were convinced that he was acting through the power of God as Spirit that was active in him.[52]

What is the notion of God that is opened up in this scenario? Of Luke 11:20 just cited, Norman Perrin says: "Jesus is deliberately evoking the myth of the activity of God on behalf of his people, and claiming that the exorcisms are a manifestation of that activity in the experience of his hearers."[53] This conveys a God who is personal, good, and concerned with human well-being. This is a God who stands opposed to and acts against that which diminishes or negates human wholeness: sin, sickness, possession. What this God effects through the mediation of Jesus was called in the Jewish tradition a form of salvation; it could be called liberation. It appeared in Jesus' action as the power of God which cured and restored to human beings their full potential for life in this world.

Associating with Social Outcasts

Luke depicts Jesus responding sharply to those who rejected his ministry: "John the Baptist has come eating no bread and drinking no wine; and you say, 'He has a demon.' The Son of man has come eating and drinking; and you say, 'Behold, a glutton and a drunkard, a friend of tax collectors and sinners!'" (Luke 7:33-34). It seems fairly certain that Jesus

---

49. This is a contextual way of putting it, with devils and spirits being the cause of various symptoms. Today one might simply say that Jesus had the power to heal.

50. Geza Vermes, *Jesus the Jew: A Historian's Reading of the Gospels* (Philadelphia: Fortress Press, 1981), 22–25.

51. Geza Vermes, "Jesus the Jew," *Jesus' Jewishness: Exploring the Place of Jesus within Early Judaism*, ed. by James H. Charlesworth (New York: Crossroad, 1991), 115; see also Vermes, *Jesus the Jew*, 59–69.

52. James D. G. Dunn, *Jesus and the Spirit* (London: SCM, 1975), 41–67.

53. Perrin, *Jesus and the Language of the Kingdom*, 43.

directed his attention to people who stood outside the margins of society, and that this was a disturbing factor in his ministry and message for the religiously upright. Jesus associated with sinners, tax collectors, and prostitutes, a phrase that occurs a number of times in the gospels. Jesus associated with those who were excluded from society. The outcasts of the community made up a good proportion of his followers; these included the uneducated, those whose salvation was denied because of their religious ignorance and moral failure.[54] Historians also make much of the fact that Jesus ate meals with public sinners. Sitting down at table with those normally shunned sends a strong message: it dramatically contradicts the spontaneous and sacral distinctions in society and is thus egalitarian. Crossan states the case sharply: "Jesus' kingdom of nobodies and undesirables in the here and now of this world was surely a radically egalitarian one, and, as such, it rendered sexual and social, political and religious distinctions completely irrelevant and anachronistic."[55] A distinct category of those to whom Jesus reached out are the economically poor. "Blessed are you poor, for yours is the kingdom of God" (Luke 6:20). To no one else is the kingdom of God so expressly appointed in Jesus' teaching. This partiality for the poor is also reflected throughout the gospel stories.[56]

These actions of Jesus communicate forcefully the character of the God whom he served. They say that God has a special concern for all who are weak, deprived of the necessities of life, and oppressed. This God wants human beings to flourish; God thus desires the conditions in which they can be healthy and whole. The God of Jesus, in being for those who are weak and neglected, is likewise against all patterns of behavior or structures of society that diminish or dehumanize people. The behavior of Jesus on behalf of people who were marginalized because of social and religious conventions had to have been strongly resented by those with social authority and power, and was probably one of the reasons for his execution. Jesus' association with sinners and with the poor unfolded within the social framework of a religious imagination and tradition. Jesus made claims about God's will, preferences, and coming kingdom.

Jesus and the Temple

Another major symbolic gesture of Jesus, one which many think probably led directly to his arrest, was his action at the temple in Jerusalem. "He entered the temple and began to drive out those who sold and those who bought in the temple" (Mark 11:15). Some view this as a symbolic

---

54. Elisabeth Schüssler Fiorenza, *In Memory of Her: A Feminist Theological Reconstruction of Origins* (New York: Crossroad, 1983), 126–30, 141–42; Joachim Jeremias, *New Testament Theology: I. The Proclamation of Jesus* (London: SCM Press, 1971), 108–21.

55. John Dominic Crossan, *The Historical Jesus: The Life of a Mediterranean Jewish Peasant* (San Francisco: Harper, 1991), 298; see also 261–64.

56. See Jon Sobrino, *Christology at the Crossroads: A Latin American Approach* (Maryknoll, N.Y.: Orbis Books, 1978), 79–87.

"cleansing" of the temple of irreligious activities. This interpretation presupposes that the temple was or had been profaned; Jesus was reacting against externals in the name of interior or pure spiritual worship. Others believe that this is unlikely, because the principal function of the temple was to be a place of sacrifice, and sacrifice required the availability of animals and hence trade. There could be no sacrifice without exchange of money. To attack trade would implicitly undermine and attack God's provisions. By contrast, Jesus' action would have been perceived by those who saw it as an attack on the temple; the action symbolized the destruction of the temple in view of its restoration. In Sanders's view, this symbolic meaning is testified to by multiple sayings which speak of destroying and restoring the temple (e.g., Mark 14:58). "Jesus either threatened or predicted that *God* would put an end to the present temple: that is, that the end was at hand."[57] In other words, Jesus predicted the imminent coming of judgment and the new age.

These are clearly different interpretations of Jesus' symbolic action, entailing different messages about the reign of God in Jesus' preaching. But neither one changes radically the portrait of God found in Jesus' message. Jesus is clearly denouncing something in the temple precincts, and if it is not the practices of selling, it could be a whole system that needed restoration. In both cases God's prerogatives appear to be compromised by human self-interest: God's transcendence and glory and God's rule are at stake. Either interpretation fits with elements of Jesus' ministry seen thus far. But a symbolic reading of Sanders's view concerning Jesus' imminent expectations should be highlighted lest they appear too literal and fantastic. For example, Sanders tends to view Jesus as a visionary who was mistaken about the coming kingdom of God, which was conceptualized in specific terms.[58] By contrast, I suggest a hypothesis in which a) Jesus did not know specifically how the kingdom of God would be ushered in; b) God's action in establishing it need not be imagined apart from this-worldly and historical agency; and c) as a function of religious hope, Jesus' expectation was too diffuse and open-ended to be considered a "mistake." The kingdom of God was God's presence in power for judgment and blessing.

GOD IN JESUS' ETHICS OF THE KINGDOM

There are elements of Jesus' teaching that bear on ethics which entail his conception of God. Once again, this discussion involves generaliza-

---

57. E. P. Sanders, *Jesus and Judaism* (Philadelphia: Fortress Press, 1985), 73, 61–76; see also his *The Historical Figure of Jesus* (London: Penguin Books, 1993), 249–75.

58. "According to Sanders, the kingdom proclaimed by Jesus was to be otherworldly in origin, one brought about by God and not by military insurrection. Then God would step in and provide a new temple, a restored people of Israel, and a renewed social order in which 'sinners' have a place." Daniel J. Harrington, "Retrieving the Jewishness of Jesus: Recent Developments," *New Theology Review*, 11 (1998), 13.

tions on the basis of elementary aspects of Jesus' teaching. I limit the reflection to two themes, both of which are contained in parables and sayings:
love of neighbor, and wealth and poverty.

Everyone knows the story of *The Good Samaritan*: "A man was going
down from Jerusalem to Jericho. . ." (Luke 10:29-37, prefaced by 25-28).
The parable is so well known that the title has lost its original paradoxical character—a Samaritan cannot be good—and become merely representative of one who helps another. Jesus' hearers identified with the Jews
in the story, not the Samaritan.[59] But here too one must look at the reversals to open up the meaning and the dramatic, one might say explosive,
power of this teaching. The one who showed that he knew what being a
neighbor was and embodied it was a Samaritan, one who was hated by
Jews. The greater the enmity between Jew and Samaritan, the more the
story lacks verisimilitude, the more the impact of this teaching, and the
more its point is driven home. There is a second reversal in the text, not
structural and perhaps not as essential, but still preserved in the parable.
The lawyer asked who his neighbor was, as though trying to define objectively with more precision the limits of his duty. The response of the parable, underlined in Jesus' interpretation, is subjective: "Go and do likewise"
(Luke 10:37). Imitate a Samaritan. There are no limits to concern or love
for others; in fact, one should actively make oneself the neighbor of one's
enemies.[60] The supposition of this parable is that it adds to Jesus' characterization of how things work in the kingdom of God, which in turn
reflects the nature of God. There are no enemies under God's rule. Jesus
teaches a universal love that extends to one's enemies, whether they be
personal enemies in the village or those of a particular group or nation.
Since the enemy is good, the barriers between insiders and outsiders are
broken down. This is another example of Jesus turning the world of his
fellow Jews upside down.[61]

The rationale behind the commandment of universal love which is
implicit in this parable of the kingdom of God becomes explicit in some
of Jesus' sayings. One of the clearest of these is the following: "You have
heard that it was said, 'You shall love your neighbor and hate your
enemy.' But I say to you, Love your enemies and pray for those who per-
secute you, so that you may be sons of your Father who is in heaven; for
he makes his sun rise on the evil and on the good, and sends rain on the
just and on the unjust" (Matt 5:43-45). The point of the saying concerns
the motivation for love of enemies: this is the way God relates to evil people, and we are to be perfect even as God is. To love in return those who

---

59. This parable provides an example of some of the paradox involved in interpretation itself. In order to communicate the point of this parable today, one must change
the protagonist from a virtuous figure, a good Samaritan, to the most despised of all.

60. Jeremias, *The Parables of Jesus*, 204–05.

61. Perkins, *Hearing the Parables*, 117–23; Donahue, *Gospel in Parable*, 129–34; Scott,
Hear Then the Parable, 189–202; Wright, *Jesus*, 304–07.

love you is to operate on the basis of the solidarity of the clan, and to revert back to the level of publicans and pagans. This universalism of God's concern is also found in the Jewish scriptures.[62] But the matter was not settled. This text has the merit of being a clear statement, against alternative views, on a debated issue. There is no reticence here; it is stated cleanly and not softened or rationalized; it reflects God's transcendent justice. "The fact of the unlimited divine goodness is presented with calm assurance, like a primary given, one that cannot be escaped and which imposes itself on the basis of its own evidence."[63]

Another moral issue that reflects a conception of God in Jesus' teaching concerns wealth. In contrast to the blessing of the kingdom of God for the poor, Luke reports Jesus saying: "But woe to you that are rich, for you have received your consolation" (Luke 6:24). This saying is also represented dramatically in the parable *The Rich Man and Lazarus* (Luke 16:19-31). The rich man was clothed elegantly and feasted; Lazarus, outside his gates, was poor and diseased. Lazarus died and was carried by angels to Abraham's bosom; the rich man died and ended up in torment in Hades. The contrast, and then the reversal, could not be stronger or more symmetrical. Blessing and woe, heaven and hell, for the poor and the rich: in the end God's justice prevails, contrasting life situations and moral stances reap their proper rewards, and all things are leveled off. The parable contains no new teaching: the Law and the Prophets instructed on the seduction to idolatry of riches and the obligations of justice. And it forcefully presents a God of righteousness who responds to the question of why the evil flourish.[64] Scott believes the parable represents the kingdom of God as one of solidarity between rich and poor. The point is made through a threat: it must happen now; tomorrow is too late.[65]

The social gospel movement at the turn of the twentieth century and liberation theology both make much of Jesus' teaching on riches. Jon Sobrino, for example, deals with this material with considerable nuance. Riches in Jesus' teaching are not an evil in themselves. This is shown on the basis of the fact that abundance is a blessing of God. Rather, riches become evil because of what they do to the human person or group. First, they become a blockage between those who are wealthy and God, operating as a kind of idol of self-interest that makes absolute claims upon human existence. Second, riches become a barrier between people. The

---

62. Jonah 4:11; Ps 145:9; Sir 18:13.

63. Schlosser, *Le Dieu de Jésus*, 260; see 235–60.

64. Perkins, *Hearing the Parables*, 67–72; Donahue, *Gospel in Parable*, 169–72.

65. "The story is a metaphor for the unnoticed menace that Jesus' announcement of the kingdom of God places on ordinary life." Scott, *Hear Then the Parable*, 159. Wright's interpretation, by contrast, follows his pattern of seeing the story as a story of Israel. Thus, as in the story of the Prodigal Son, the focus falls on Lazarus; he is Israel being reborn and recreated. This is happening in Jesus' ministry as shown by his attention to the poor. Wright, *Jesus*, 255–56.

rich are often described in contrast and opposition to the poor. Wealth is considered evil precisely because it is held at the expense of the poor, and this is why it is condemned. In the end, Sobrino sees Jesus denouncing riches as a moral and not an ontological problem; they are a curse, they dehumanize the rich, they make it difficult for people to open themselves to God and to the neighbor. Behind this stance of Jesus, of course, is God. This is the God whose judgment on the effects of riches is in inverse proportion to God's love, which reaches out especially to those who are mistreated and suffer.[66]

GOD IN JESUS' PRAYER

The gospel accounts of Jesus report that he went off to pray. The gospels characterize Jesus at prayer, recount many of his counsels to pray and his sayings about prayer, and describe how he taught his disciples to pray. A look at Jesus' prayer and the attitudes implied in it will reveal another aspect of Jesus' God to whom the prayer is addressed.

One may take the prayer that Jesus taught his disciples as a model: "Father, hallowed be thy name. Thy kingdom come. Give us each day our daily bread; and forgive us our sins, for we ourselves forgive every one who is indebted to us; and lead us not into temptation" (Luke 11:2-4). The prayer consists in an invocation, two wishes or hopes, and three petitions. All should call God Father as Jesus himself does. May God's name be sanctified and vindicated; may God's rule among human beings be finally achieved or accomplished. The three requests placed before God are for God's continued sustenance and blessing, for God's forgiveness, and for God's protection against final apostasy. Each of these elements of Jesus' prayer have close parallels in Jewish writings making the prayer thoroughly Jewish.[67]

What does this prayer tell of the God to whom it is addressed? We are helped in this by some of the sayings of Jesus on prayer that Luke gathers together in subsequent verses (Luke 11:9-13). God is personal and responsive. God is Father in the loving, compassionate sense of one who forgives. Disciples should pray with humility and yet confident reliance that they will be heard (Luke 11:10). God's goodness and loving blessing will surpass that of earthly parents (Luke 11:11-13). The supposition in this prayer is that God more than desires human welfare and fulfillment. God is, as it were, present, available, and ready to bestow blessing on those who merely turn to God, acknowledge God's holiness, and internalize God's fatherhood by acting like brothers and sisters who forgive each other.

---

66. Jon Sobrino, *Jesus the Liberator*, 170–74.

67. Joseph A. Fitzmyer, *The Gospel According to Luke, The Anchor Bible*, 28 (Garden City, N.Y.: Doubleday, 1985), 899–901.

Jesus as the Symbol or Parable of God

It is often said that Jesus himself is a parable of God. The refrain of this chapter has been that people encounter God in Jesus. This is translated in more technical theological language to read as follows: Jesus is the historical mediation of God for the Christian imagination. Juan Luis Segundo rephrased this insight into an axiom, referred to in the opening paragraph of this chapter, that he used to capture functionally the meaning of Jesus' divinity, namely, that "God is like Jesus." Christians know the nature and character of God by focusing their attention on Jesus. This examination of how Jesus mediated God, even though it has been carried out on a very generalized hermeneutical level, allows us to say a bit more about how Jesus reveals God.

A parable, even when it is formally presented as an extended simile with the phrase "the kingdom of God is like," functions more like a metaphor. I indicated earlier how in a metaphor one thing is identified with something different, as in "My husband is a bear." What immediately strikes the listener or reader is the non-identity between the implicitly compared items. The creative imagination is thus set in motion to formulate the similarity or point of identity: is he a teddy or a grizzly? So too, analogously, to say that Jesus is a parable of God introduces paradox, tension, and ambiguity in Jesus' mediation of God. One must recognize immediately that as a human being Jesus is Jesus, is not God, but points away from himself to God. Only then can the human mind begin to recognize certain contours of God within the reality of Jesus. This reality of Jesus is made up not simply of Jesus' oral teaching, in terms of sayings, announcements, controversy, interpretations of the tradition, and parables. It extends to Jesus' actions, his exorcising, curing, gathering disciples, associating with public sinners, departing from religious custom, and more formal symbolic prophetic actions. Putting these elements together, it becomes clear that what mediated the kingdom of God during Jesus' public ministry was not this teaching, nor that action, nor a specific parable he told. It was the whole person who had an impact on disciples and was remembered after his death. This explains why the ideal presentation of Jesus as the medium of God will assume a narrative form. The detail with which a narrative portrayal of Jesus is possible is problematic, but the principles of historiography allow for some creative reproduction on a generalized level.[68] I cannot discuss here the criteria by which some narrative christologies fail and others succeed. But this can be said: first, the idea that Jesus is the parable of God requires that Jesus be recognized as a concrete human being perceivable in imaginative terms. And, secondly,

---

68. R. G. Collingwood, *The Idea of History* (New York: Oxford University Press, 1956), 241–42; Roger Haight, "The Impact of Jesus Research on Christology," *Louvain Studies*, 21 (1996), 222.

it is the ensemble of the aspects of Jesus, unified in his faith in the kingdom of God and his action, that mediates a conception of God.

Finally, it is true that we know little in any specific detail about this Jesus. And since it is the whole event of Jesus that mediates God to the human imagination, Jesus releases symbolically, like a parable, many different aspects of God. But at the same time, given the tradition in which Jesus stood, we do get a certain idea of what God is like in his ministry. I conclude, then, with a schematic attempt to characterize God as God is encountered in Jesus.

SYNTHETIC REFLECTIONS ON THE GOD OF JESUS

This final section does not attempt what cannot be done, namely, to circumscribe the God of Jesus. It should rather be considered an invitation to put some holistic shape to the view of God who is encountered in Jesus. To a certain extent one is forced to recapitulate the data of the gospels on the God of Jesus in objective terms. The imagination tends to perform this task whether one intends it or not. But the aim here is to represent something more existential and subjective: how do people encounter God in Jesus? A comparison between the first two sections of the chapter would indicate a first answer to this question: Jesus' God is not substantially different than the God of Jewish tradition.[69] Jesus' representation is distinctively his: he told these parables, used those sayings, and so on. But the God of Jesus is in no substantial way other than the God of Israel. One cannot interpret Jesus' being the Christ on the basis of a unique or new message about the character of God.

God Is Personal

In some respects the experience and conviction that God is personal is a presupposition of Jesus from his Jewish heritage. God is not impersonal; the totality of the world and nature and ultimate reality are not finally impersonal. The unimaginably vast canopy of space, an emptiness filled with rocks and fire, is not all there is, but is itself filled with a personal presence, intelligence, and moral goodness. We are not alone in the universe. This language reflects a present-day perspective, but Jesus expressed substantially the same conviction in the language of the providential care of a personal God who attends to everything: the creator of heaven and earth cares for the lilies of the field and the sparrow. Jesus prayed or spoke to God. In the Jewish tradition God is often depicted

---

69. Rudolf Bultmann, *Theology of the New Testament*, 1 (New York: Charles Scribner's Sons, 1951), 23, generally concurs. But at the same time, he points out distinctive dimensions of Jesus' God, and offers a dehistoricized and individualist interpretation of the way God is encountered in Jesus, which is unwarranted. Ibid., 25.

anthropomorphically as reacting with feeling and interacting with human beings. God has chosen a people; God is with them; God is personal. The ultimate reality is neither fate and necessity nor the utter contingency of what is arbitrary, random, and a function of chance. Rather, as in the parable of The Workers in the Field, God deals with each human being individually: God's relations to human beings are not reducible to the objective standards of law or social convention. God is personal.

In Jesus this God is Father. Jesus was not unique in teaching this, but this language was definitely his own. When Jesus prayed he addressed God as Father, and when he taught others to pray, he taught them to do the same. The metaphor of God as a father has rich meaning, and it brings into a concrete image many of the characteristics and operations of God relative to the created world and ourselves. It would be hard to imagine that the experience of God as Father was not very close to defining Jesus' own conception of God. But three things are also clear today: the first is that notion of fatherhood is socially constructed. The term means different things in different cultures. The second is that the fatherhood of God has become in some respects ideological. God's fatherhood has been used to distort reality and unjustly serve the interests of some against the interests of others. Feminist theology has taught us that. The third is that, although God is personal, God is not characterized by gender after the fashion of finite reality. One can give no ontological weight to gender in God. This is proved by the transcendence of God and illustrated by the female images that are used of God in the scriptures. Female language about God opens up aspects of God's personhood that male metaphors cannot.[70] Ironically, fidelity to Jesus' language about God as a personal father includes breaking open that metaphor to other personal images. Jesus cannot be used to justify an ideological use of Jesus' name for God. Indeed, Jesus' conception of the fatherhood of God is critical of human patriarchy.

God Is Transcendent

The transcendence of God was presupposed by Jesus; it was part of his tradition. It was not always so, as the Jewish scriptures testify. But long before Jesus' time the God of Israel was the one God of all, and not one among many. God was transcendent, that is, going beyond and infinitely surpassing all finite reality of which God was creator. God is holy, awesome, completely other; God is omnipotent and sovereign ruler of all that God created. As such, God can inspire holy fear and attentive reverence. These qualities of God were not expressed in a systematic, philosophical way by Jesus and his tradition. They are a function of God's being creator

---

70. Johnson, *She Who Is*, 54. As in all predication about God, calling God personal functions symbolically. God is not a person, because all the limitations of persons as we know them are denied in the recognition of *God's* personhood; but, positively, the symbol encourages the creative imagination to invest God with transcendent *personhood*.

of the world, provident Lord of history, the one who rules and is to come in power and might.[71]

Much could be said about the significance of God's sovereign power that is part of God's transcendence. But one thing is clear from the ministry of Jesus: God's transcendence is subversive. It is customary for sociologists to view religion as a conservative force in society. In its domesticated form it tends to sacralize the status quo and help socialize people into standard patterns of behavior. But religion always has the potential to be the opposite, especially when the patterns of society rest on or embody injustice. When a transcendent God of justice claims one's loyalty, nothing else may stand in its way. God in God's transcendence desacralizes the world, demystifies the present order, relativizes all the "absolutes" that history creates. Jesus was a prophet because his God is transcendent. Jesus communicates in his teaching and in his action that God's ways are other than human ways.

God Is Love

The transcendence of God which elicits a holy fear is not at all the last word of Jesus about God. Far from it. In Jesus' words and ministry God is represented as not unfriendly but friendly and benevolent. God is personally concerned about human existence, and God wills absolutely what is good for it, its ultimate happiness and fulfillment. God is concerned about the whole of God's creation. But relative to personal human existence, God's personal concern is love. God loves human beings. This means that God is not merely transcendent, but immanent and close. This closeness cuts through much of the formalism and ritual of religion: God is always readily at hand. For love is the desire to be united with something else, "the drive towards the unity of the separated."[72] Thus God approaches human beings by the gift of God's own personal self.

There are some characteristics about this loving God revealed by Jesus which appear paradoxical, but are not, because they describe an infinite love. First, God's love is universal; it reaches to all equally. What Jesus pointed to was a God whose love was boundless: without conditions and all inclusive. As Schillebeeckx puts it, although Jesus addressed his ministry to Jews and not to Gentiles, his message was pure openness; he removed all the frontiers from God's love.[73] Jesus does not create barriers between people but tears them down. Such love characterizes God's very nature.

A second characteristic of God's love is that it reaches to individuals, and would not be greater for any individual person were he or she the

---

71. The basic metaphor of the kingdom of God rests on the experience of God as sovereign Lord and ruler. Schillebeeckx notes that "reverence for God's exalted nature is fundamental to Jesus' message and to his ministry." *Jesus* (New York: Seabury Press, 1979), 142.

72. Paul Tillich, *Love, Power, and Justice: Ontological Analyses and Ethical Applications* (New York: Oxford University Press, 1960), 25.

73. Schillebeeckx, *Jesus*, 146.

only human being. This is displayed in many of Jesus' actions of compassion. But the parable of the Prodigal Son is exemplary: here is a God who so loves the delinquent son that, even before he turns to God, God is there accepting him. The love of God is unconditional, love without any prior stipulations. This love is an inclusive category; it includes compassion, mercy, and forgiveness. God is depicted as reacting to, feeling for, and being affected by any pain suffered by the human beings who are God's own offspring.

A third characteristic is that Jesus displays a partiality, or compassionate preference for the poor and others who are weak and marginalized. When Jesus, the parable of God, ate and drank with prostitutes and public sinners, he brought them evidence of God's special love for them.[74] Like the prodigal son, the lost had to be found, the dead brought back to life. This is God's compassion which, like a parent's love, reaches out in solicitude and takes special care of the weak child because he or she needs it to reach full potential. Only in an infinite love can these three characteristics, universality, specific individual concern, and partiality for the wounded, merge without contradiction.[75]

Jesus, it was said, was theocentric. Ironically, what he presents to the world is a God who is anthropocentric. God's cause is the cause of human existence. God is a God who is for humanity, as creator and thus one who is intrinsically interested and concerned about the well being of what God creates.[76]

God Is Savior

Being savior is the effectiveness of God's love; it is the directing of God's love toward those who need it; it is mercy for the sinner, compassion for those who suffer, assistance for those whose freedom is bound in one form of captivity or another. One can summarize Jesus' message about God as a whole in terms of salvation: "Jesus presents God as salvation for human existence."[77] The kingdom of God is another term for this salvation: it is God's saving power for an absolutely meaningful future. God's absolute will is for the salvation of all, according to Jesus. Such is the consequence of the utter gratuity or grace of God's love. It comes prior to and without any conditions. It reaches toward total salvation, the overcoming of suffering, the fullness and completion of the *humanum* in all of its aspects.

---

74. Schillebeeckx, *Jesus*, 145.

75. Jon Sobrino, in *The Principle of Mercy: Taking the Crucified People from the Cross* (Maryknoll, N.Y.: Orbis Books, 1994), explores the dimension of mercy in the love of God that is revealed in Jesus, and proposes it as one of the foundation stones for liberation theology.

76. But God creates all of creation, of which human existence is a part. One cannot understand the anthropocentrism of the God of Jesus as license for humanity to demean itself by destroying the environment that constitutes human existence.

77. Schillebeeckx, *Jesus*, 142.

This teaching is really found in every aspect of Jesus' teaching; the kingdom, which is salvation, is the very framework of that teaching. It is found explicitly in such places as the beatitudes which address those who suffer. Salvation is the implicit content of Jesus' healing ministry, and his reaching out toward those who suffer in any way. Jesus represents God as savior. God's internal and sovereign will is for salvation and, in the end, God alone is the guarantor of the defeat of evil in every form.

God of Justice and Judgment

The God of Jesus is a God of justice and judgment, not despite God's desire for salvation but because of it. This God is interested in human life and the way it is lived in this world. Jesus points to a God who is concerned about morality, about law, about how people conduct themselves, about who is victim and who is the cause of the oppression. This is not a God who is aloof and indifferent to what goes on in human society and in individual behavior.

Most exegetes are agreed that the phrase "the kingdom of God" gets close to the sum and substance of Jesus' message. The kingdom of God is nowhere defined conceptually; it is profusely illustrated by parable; it is a transcendent reality with many meanings and nuances; it has a bearing on life in this world. God's kingdom can be depicted as God's will for the world, the rule of God in the sense of human society unfolding according to God's will. The rule of God is the rule of God's values and ways among human beings. This rule of God is a rule of justice, and God is a God of justice.

The God of Jesus is also a God of judgment against injustice. The kingdom of God is a utopic ideal for society in the sense that it is where oppression and suffering will be overcome. The kingdom of God is the criterion for Jesus' judgment which reflects God's judgment. "God's lordship is also a judgment upon our history."[78] This thematic of judgment is a dominant pattern in Jesus' ministry. One sees it in the constant reversals of common human values in his sayings and in the parables. A trenchant example is contained in the beatitudes which prophetically announce God's No to suffering and poverty. Jesus' preaching of the kingdom of God is itself an implicit judgment on the present situation and a call to conversion. Jesus and Jesus' God are radical, counter-cultural, and subversive.

Is God, the Father of Jesus, on the side of the oppressed and the underdog? Yes, God is the protector of the poor. This becomes immediately apparent negatively in the manifest error of any idea of Jesus being on the side of the wealthy, the powerful, the influential. And, like a parent, God certainly does not stand on the sidelines and watch neutrally as someone stronger brutalizes one of God's children. The God of Jesus is a God of justice and of judgment upon injustice because God is love.[79]

---

78. Schillebeeckx, *Jesus*, 143.
79. How can one explain a love of God which is egalitarian and reaches out to all,

This chapter provides an exceedingly broad sketch of the God mediated through Jesus and his ministry. This notional portrait of God is of course totally transformed in a religious encounter. There the experience of God's presence breaks the boundaries of words. In mediating God, Jesus represents salvation. The data of this chapter, therefore, will take on a systematic importance when it becomes necessary to explain theologically the salvation mediated by Jesus. For the present, however, I turn to the experience of Jesus' being raised and alive with God.

---

and at the same time is biased toward the poor? This point may be illustrated with an analogy or parable, since there is no other way to understand God. Suppose that in a family of several children one child is handicapped. Would not parental love, not to mention the love of sisters and brothers, take on a special creative function that would try to restore and make up what is not given by nature? Such a gift of more or extra love, which is really not quite that, is a natural reaction of the parental relationship, and should also be that of brothers and sisters.

Another side of this excess of love for one's own, and in a special way for those who need one's love because of their deprivation, is protectiveness. This protectiveness can flare into a fierce anger when someone bullies someone who is weak and defenseless. This is exactly the logic of the outrage of the prophets and their language of the anger of God at the way the poor and the weak were treated in Israel. God is depicted as saying: "When you attack the weak ones who are my favored, you attack me." And positively: "Whatever you do for the least of my children you do for me" (Matt 25:40).

CHAPTER 5

Jesus' Resurrection

Western Christianity enjoyed a quiet, confident belief in Jesus' resurrection up to the nineteenth century. But the Enlightenment and nineteenth-century historical criticism raised many questions. Reason doubted the plausibility of a person being raised from the dead and appearing publicly. When critical historiography was applied to biblical texts, the historicity of the resurrection narratives was called into question.[1] As a result, theological reflection on the resurrection of Jesus has taken on an apologetic character. This means that theology includes the task of explaining the resurrection of Jesus within a context of the fundamental problems or questions that arise from the conjunction of history and theology. For example, how are we to balance a critical historian's approach to the New Testament data pertaining to the resurrection and the theologian's reading of the same data as kerygma or the Word of God? How does one move from historical witness to a theological assertion of the resurrection that is intelligible to our world? Although these questions appear technical, an apologetic structure also responds to the exigencies of people within the churches. On the one hand, the gospels present what appear to be straightforward stories of an empty tomb being discovered, Jesus appearing to the disciples, Jesus being alive and interacting with the disciples. On the other hand, to read these texts naively as simple descriptive narratives is to misread them, for at bottom this is not what they are. And to so misread them as to encourage a naive, childlike belief does not help Christians integrate their faith with the rest of their lives. Basic adult catechesis must deal with this issue; the adult faith of the ordinary Christian is being forced to enter a certain postcritical or second naivete. It follows that the apologetic character of current resurrection theology also corresponds to the catechetical task of sorting out and explaining the elements of faith within the churches.

---

1. Joseph Moingt, *L'Homme qui venait de Dieu* (Paris: Éditions du Cerf, 1993), 347; Thorwald Lorenzen, *Resurrection and Discipleship: Interpretive Models, Biblical Reflections, Theological Consequences* (Maryknoll, N.Y.: Orbis Books, 1995), 37–42.

The structure of such a critical and apologetic approach to the resurrection of Jesus cannot avoid a certain tension between history and theology. This involves staying close to the New Testament data on Jesus' resurrection, and considering the testimony of the disciples, the narratives of the appearances and the empty tomb, and the confessions concerning the risen Christ. It also involves submitting these data to critical reflection, interpreting the testimony that is given, and trying to construct an understanding of the resurrection that both makes sense of this data and is intelligible to people living at the beginning of the third millennium. But this task of correlation is complicated by a pluralism of interpretations both on the level of scriptural data and theological reconstruction. There is no firm consensus on the character of the resurrection in the New Testament witnesses, which are multiple, nor on the historicity of the appearance narratives or the empty tomb tradition. And there is a whole spectrum of theological construals of the nature and significance of the resurrection in Christian faith.

This pluralism puts constraints on a chapter that tries to deal with the resurrection of Jesus in a short space. At least one must be clear in one's goals. My aim here is to propose one way of understanding what it means to say that Jesus is risen. The question implies attempting to explain theologically the Christian belief that Jesus is alive because God raised Jesus out of death. What is the structure of this Christian confession? What is the evidence? And what logic provides its intelligibility? But given the complexity and pluralistic character of the discussion, I will begin with a definition of the premises, presuppositions, and methodological options that help constitute the framework of this chapter. Christians generally agree that Jesus is risen. But since no consensus prevails on what this means, or how its meaning is to be interpreted, the least one can do in a single chapter is to be clear about the method governing one's own position.

This chapter, therefore, will unfold in the following way: the first section will define a hermeneutical perspective on the resurrection. The second will survey the kind of testimony to the resurrection presented to us by the New Testament witness. The third section will develop a theoretical reconstruction of the genesis of the Christian belief in Jesus' resurrection. And the fourth and concluding section will comment on the significance of the resurrection and this theological interpretation of it.

A HERMENEUTICAL PERSPECTIVE

I begin this discussion of the resurrection of Jesus with a clarification of the perspective that will guide it, an initial definition of what the term "resurrection" means in this christology, and a statement of principles and presuppositions that will be operative in the argument.

In what sense is the orientation of these reflections called hermeneutical? All understanding is at the same time interpretation. But with the term "hermeneutical" I want to call attention to the deliberate attempt to form a bridge between history and theology, and to do this in a number of different senses. The hermeneutical theories of Gadamer and Ricoeur have as one of their concerns the interpretation of the past as meaningful and true in and for the present situation. A hermeneutical perspective, therefore, explicitly intends to be faithful to the witness of the past, and to interpret it in such a way that it comes to bear on present-day consciousness. Hermeneutical theory thus participates simultaneously in the disciplines of history and constructive theology; it forms a bridge that so connects historical and present-day meanings as to render them interdependent. A hermeneutical perspective also tries to hold together attention to data, in the sense of empirical or imaginable events, and the constructive task of discovering transcendent theological meaning that is mediated by these events. It seeks to balance history, in the sense of what happens in this world, with transcendent reality by using the category of symbol.

THE SYMBOL OF RESURRECTION

In the introduction to this chapter I referred to the pluralism that characterizes the discussion of the resurrection of Jesus on almost every level.[2] This pluralism descends to the very meaning of the symbol "resurrection," which is not a univocal idea even in the New Testament. What is the object of this belief? The meaning of resurrection cannot be decided cleanly by the New Testament witness. And yet the essential meaning of resurrection is a matter of systematic importance, for it will influence the interpretation of all the issues that attend the discussion. For example, if one thinks that resurrection is the resuscitation of a corpse, one will tend to read the story of the empty tomb in literal, historical terms. If one thinks the resurrection means Jesus living on in the faith of the community, one can discount the question of the historicity of the empty tomb stories as irrelevant. The pluralism of the meaning of resurrection in the New Testament, however, does not provide license to decide the meaning of the resurrection on an a priori basis. One should be guided in one's conception by the data of the New Testament. In effect, the pluralism at the level

---

2. Two examples of typologies of understandings of the resurrection are those of David Fergusson, "Interpreting the Resurrection," *Scottish Journal of Theology*, 38 (1985), 287–305, who distinguishes radical, liberal, and traditional types, and Lorenzen, *Resurrection and Discipleship*, 11–111, who describes traditional, liberal, evangelical, and liberationist positions. John Galvin, "The Resurrection of Jesus in Contemporary Catholic Systematics," *Heythrop Journal*, 20 (1979), 123–45, surveys the range of different theories among Catholic theologians of the nature of the resurrection of Jesus, the genesis of faith in the resurrection, and the place of the resurrection in Christian faith. Hans Küng, in *On Being a Christian* (Garden City, N.Y.: Doubleday, 1976), 370–81, provides a handy description of a variety of different theories on how faith in the resurrection came about historically.

of the New Testament witness forces one to define at the outset the meaning of the symbol, at least in a preliminary way. But in so doing, we shall try faithfully to incorporate New Testament data.

Exegetes point to two quite distinct symbolizations of the destiny of Jesus at his death.[3] The first finds a center of gravity around the equivalent of the English word "resurrection" itself. It is reflected in many texts. For example, during the course of his discourse at Pentecost, Peter speaks of Jesus' resurrection in this way: "This Jesus God raised up, and of that we all are witnesses" (Acts 2:32). In another speech, later on in Acts, Peter uses almost the same formula: "They put him to death by hanging him on a tree; but God raised him on the third day and made him manifest; not to all the people but to us, who were chosen by God as witnesses, who ate and drank with him after he rose from the dead" (Acts 10:39-41). "The Lord has risen indeed, and has appeared to Simon" (Luke 24:34). This basic creedal statement exists in various forms: God raised him, or, he was raised, or, he rose. The metaphor lying behind this general conception of the resurrection from death is an awakening from sleep and rising. It is distinctive in that it proposes the resurrection as a discrete event within a series of events in the continuous life of Jesus. Thus, Jesus lived, was executed and died, was buried, and then rose, and appeared to the disciples who ate and drank with him, and, finally, he ascended into glory. But the central burden of this symbol is the restoration of life to Jesus; it communicates that he is alive with new life by God's power. "It means the complete restoration to life of Jesus of Nazareth at every level of his being."[4]

The second conception of what happened to Jesus at his death is quite different from the first. It is contained in such terms as "exaltation" and "glorification." One also finds it in many texts. For example, during the same discourse in the second chapter of Acts, Peter continues as follows: "Being therefore exalted at the right hand of God, and having received from the Father the promise of the Holy Spirit, he has poured out this which you see and hear" (Acts 2:33). Jesus was "taken up in glory" (1 Tim 3:16). This second line of imagery is found especially in some of the christological hymns. In this language of exaltation and glorification, the symbol is developed in contrast with descent, humility, and an earthly condition here below; it describes Jesus' destiny as ascent, glorification, a state of being with God above, exaltation (Phil 2:6-11). "Both ascension and exaltation derive from the symbolism of the lifting of the righteous man up to heaven."[5] Jesus after his death is now in a state of glory; he is

---

3. I am dependent on Xavier Léon-Dufour, *Resurrection and the Message of Easter* (New York: Holt, Rinehart and Winston, 1974), 5–45, for this analysis. This work is cited hereafter as *Resurrection*. Edward Schillebeeckx, *Jesus: An Experiment in Christology* (New York: Seabury Press, 1979), 533–44, deals with the distinction and relation between the notions of resurrection and exaltation.

4. Léon-Dufour, *Resurrection*, 20.

5. Léon-Dufour, *Resurrection*, 35.

Lord. The metaphor is not one of resurrection but of glorification: over against his humility in the flesh and death, Jesus is now revealed to be exalted in another sphere.[6]

Comparing the two symbols, both affirm or express that Jesus did not remain in the power of death but is alive. But they do so with different emphases. Resurrection, to be awakened, emphasizes the continuance of life; exaltation emphasizes being lifted up out of this empirical world. Resurrection tends to locate Jesus restored to life in this world where he appeared. Exaltation carries Jesus out of this world where there are no longer appearances nor a succession of events in time; Jesus' being glorified is a single mystery. These two patterns coexisted, showing that there can be different symbols to express the same experience, that "resurrection" is not the exclusive term for indicating the New Testament message about the destiny of Jesus after his death.[7]

How is this symbol of Jesus being resurrected to be interpreted today, especially in the light of the discussions that surround various aspects of "resurrection"? Although it is difficult, if not impossible, to arrive at a positive concept of Jesus' resurrection, a number of outside limit-statements can be established that help to define the symbol, at least in relation to other interpretations of it. A first fundamental point is that it is certain that the early disciples believed that Jesus himself was alive, had been raised, and was exalted in glory with God. In other words, the New Testament witness is not merely to an existential or communitarian phenomenon, that Jesus lives on in the faith of the community, but is "realist" and "objective," if such terms are appropriate, in affirming that God so acted in Jesus' behalf that he is alive. The existentialist interpretation of Jesus' resurrection includes a valuable perspective and rich insights into the experience and effect of Jesus' resurrection in the community of disciples.[8] We shall borrow from the existentialist position in understanding how faith in Jesus' resurrection came about and the impact this faith had on the community. But it falls short of the position represented here in its agnosticism about the real continuity of Jesus' existence as an individual with God.

Second, Jesus' resurrection was not a return to life in this world, was not a resuscitation of a corpse, was not a resumption of an existence con-

---

6. Léon-Dufour, *Resurrection*, 29.

7. Léon-Dufour, *Resurrection*, 38–45.

8. Rudolf Bultmann, "New Testament and Mythology," *Kerygma and Myth: A Theological Debate* (New York: Harper & Row, 1961), 33–44, and "The Primitive Christian Kerygma and the Historical Jesus," in Carl Braaten and Roy A. Harrisville, eds., *The Historical Jesus and the Kerygmatic Christ: Essays on the New Quest of the Historical Jesus* (Nashville: Abingdon Press, 1964), 15–42; Willi Marxsen, "The Resurrection of Jesus as a Historical and Theological Problem," in C. F. D. Moule, ed., *The Significance of the Message of the Resurrection for Faith in Jesus Christ* (London: SCM, 1968), 15–50, *The Resurrection of Jesus of Nazareth* (Philadelphia: Fortress Press, 1970), and *Jesus and Easter: Did God Raise the Historical Jesus from the Dead?* (Nashville: Abingdon Press, 1990).

tained in or limited by the space-time continuum. Rather, Jesus' resurrection was a passage into "another world," an assumption into the sphere of the ultimate and absolute reality who is God and who, as creator, is other than creation. What occurred in the resurrection of Jesus pertains to another order of reality that transcends this world because it is God's realm. Transcendence does not mean "unrelated to finite reality." God is transcendent, but as creator and savior God is also engaged with finite reality. But God is infinitely and qualitatively other than created reality, and being in "God's sphere" implies transcending this world in a way that human imagination cannot follow. For this reason it is better to say that Jesus' resurrection is not an historical fact, because the idea of an historical fact suggests an empirical event which could have been witnessed and can now be imaginatively construed.

The language used here stands in contrast to those who speak of Jesus' resurrection as an historical fact or datum. For example, Wolfhart Pannenberg, who places the resurrection at the center of his christology, affirms that the resurrection was a public historical event open to the scrutiny of historians. He is motivated by an apologetic concern and understands revelation as being mediated through history. But he does not answer the critical epistemological questions of how the historical event of the resurrection appeared or might be imagined by historians.[9] Nicholas Lash also insists, first, that the resurrection of Jesus is a fact. "If the doctrine of the resurrection is true, it is factually true, and the fact to which it refers is a fact about Jesus."[10] But he goes on to characterize the resurrection as an "historical fact," "at least in the sense that no attempt to estimate the truth of stories about Jesus can ignore the historian's testimony."[11] Lash does not want the resurrection to be divorced from historical reference, to be considered merely or entirely a subjective perception on the part of the disciples, but as related to public testable data. While those reasons are solid in themselves, they do not, I think, justify calling the resurrection a historical fact. To do so tends too strongly to associate the resurrection with the empirical, making it a this-worldly event, and subject to an imaginative construal. Such historicizing undermines the fundamental nature of the resurrection as a transcendent object of faith.

Third, the resurrection was the exaltation and glorification of the whole individual person, Jesus of Nazareth. The one who was resurrected is no one else than Jesus, so that there is continuity and personal identity between Jesus during his lifetime and his being with God. But this resur-

---

9. Wolfhart Pannenberg, *Jesus—God and Man* (Philadelphia: Westminster Press, 1968), 88–106, insists on the public historical character of the resurrection by arguing for the historicity of the appearances referred to by Paul in 1 Cor 15:1-8 (as distinct from the appearances in the gospels) and the empty tomb narratives.

10. Nicholas Lash, "Easter Meaning," *Heythrop Journal*, 25 (1984), 12. In other words, the idea of a fact corresponds to what I have described as the realistic truth of the resurrection concerning Jesus.

11. Lash, "Easter Meaning," 13.

rection need not entail the assumption of his physical corpse. One should conceive the symbolism operating in the other direction: the idea of the disappearance of Jesus' body is a way of signifying that the integral person, Jesus of Nazareth, was resurrected.[12] Jewish anthropology demanded in some way at least an attenuated body for the integrity of the person. The insistence of the texts on the disappearance of Jesus' body is thus an insistence on Jesus' real resurrection. The bodily resurrection of Jesus thus means that Jesus in his whole integral identity has been assumed into God's life. But the resurrection may be conceived as a meta-historical and meta-empirical happening at the moment of death, and does not require the disappearance of Jesus' corpse. Identifying the resurrection with the empirical disappearance of the body of Jesus may be seen as a category mistake that tends to distort the symbol.

Finally, it seems important to insist again on the transcendent character of Jesus' resurrection. What happened to Jesus in and through his death is transcendent; it is an eschatological reality that transpired in a region that is not circumscribed by the physicality of the finite world. Jesus was not, as far as we know, transferred to another space and time. Because being exalted is transcendent, the term "resurrection" is symbolic in pointing attention to another order of reality, that of existing within the creator God's own life, which cannot be grasped directly or immediately. Being resurrected is an object of faith-hope: faith, as an engaged commitment to the reality symbolized in the story of Jesus; hope, as openness to the future, and as involving concern about one's own destiny. At their source in the human spirit as such, at the core of human openness to all reality and to the future, faith and hope are identical. Faith in the message of Jesus and hope for absolute being with God form the ground of the recognition of the resurrection of Jesus. This faith-hope fully engages and is partly driven by the creative side of the imagination. The sheer openness to reality that characterizes the human spirit is channeled through the imagination to envisage possibilities that transcend actuality. Here the imagination "sees" real possibilities on the basis of creative extrapolation from the present. In this dynamic sense, faith-hope in the resurrection gains expression as a function of the creative imagination. This will be developed more fully in the course of this chapter, but at this point it serves to define the region of the meaning of resurrection. The resurrection is not a datum lying on the surface of history, or in the region where dead bodies are buried. As a transcendent reality resurrection can only be appreciated by faith-hope.[13]

---

12. Galvin, "The Resurrection of Jesus," 126, 132–34.

13. Gerald O'Collins makes a distinction between a physical resurrection, suggesting a reanimation of Jesus' corpse, and a bodily resurrection, suggesting the resurrection of Jesus' personal reality or self. This helps to clarify the meaning of "bodily." Gerald O'Collins, *Jesus Risen: An Historical, Fundamental and Systematic Examination of Christ's Resurrection* (New York: Paulist Press, 1987), 122.

Almost all of the theological problems connected with resurrection revolve around a sensible, imaginative construal of it. In earlier chapters I underscored the active role of the imagination that is engaged by Jesus research. When we begin to talk of the resurrection, however, this function of the imagination causes problems. "The reality of the resurrection itself therefore is completely *intangible* and *unimaginable*."[14] Use of the imagination, of course, is encouraged by the New Testament witness which, although it does not describe or portray the resurrection itself, is filled with testimonies to Jesus alive in vivid, imaginative stories about Jesus appearing. The stories propose objective, public, extraordinary events with a divine cause. God is thus shown as intervening in such a way that the immediate effects are visible, and God or God's angelic envoys appear as an immediate presence and cause of historical events. The reader is naturally drawn into these stories, and imagination is schooled in this concreteness. But the sensible imagination is precisely what tends to render the resurrection incredible today. As long as the resurrection itself is tied to the sensible representations, one will operate at a level of understanding that caricatures the symbol and unnecessarily causes problems for faith. It inevitably leads to a set of questions that mislead: "Where was Jesus when his body was being prepared for burial and finally laid in the tomb?" "What happened to Jesus' body?" "What kind of body was Jesus' resurrected spiritual body that passed through walls?" These questions are inappropriate to the reality of resurrection. It will become clear in the course of this chapter that the imaginative accounts of the New Testament are symbolic vehicles for expressing faith in and asserting the reality of Jesus' resurrection.

In sum, what is the nature of the resurrection? It is the assumption of Jesus of Nazareth into the life of God. It is Jesus being exalted and glorified within God's reality. This occurred through and at the moment of Jesus' death, so that there was no time between his death and his resurrection and exaltation. This is a transcendent reality which can only be appreciated by faith-hope. I take this to be a middle and mediating position between an existentialist and an empirical-historicist interpretation of the New Testament witness.

THE OBJECT OF HISTORICAL INQUIRY

Since the resurrection of Jesus is an indescribable and unimaginable transcendent reality, how is it to be studied with an historical and genetic method in christology? This question can be answered unambiguously: through the reactions of the disciples who recognized and were affected

---

14. Küng, *On Being a Christian*, 350. Küng is clear and perceptive in drawing attention to this problem. The imagination tends to bind the transcendent reality of Jesus' being exalted to describable earthly conditions and thereby reduce its transcendent character.

by this transcendent event. In other words, the analysis which follows focuses its attention on the New Testament witness, and pursues an investigation of the resurrection through the reactions and testimony to it of the first witnesses. The resurrection has a bearing on history through those who recognized it in faith and have provided a public witness to their experience. The New Testament is the record of the witness of faith to Jesus resurrected.

It is generally if not universally agreed that with the execution of Jesus the disciples were left confused and discouraged. There is evidence that they left Jerusalem, perhaps fled, in the wake of what was taken to be the disaster of Jesus' crucifixion. But at the other end of the New Testament witness one finds a Jesus movement that evolves into the Christian church and an autonomous faith and religion. The historical question that is posed here is directed toward the disciples: what happened to them to cause this reversal? The witness of the gospels says that they encountered Jesus risen, but what is this Easter experience of the disciples? How are we to understand the dynamics of what occurred in their lives to reverse the trajectory of despair initiated by the sudden and violent death of Jesus? A critical, hermeneutical method in christology approaches the resurrection not only by a theological analysis of the texts of the New Testament, that is, by an internal literary criticism, but also by an inquiry into the experience behind the early testimony to the resurrection as this is recorded in the New Testament. The experience of the resurrection is the bridge, the connection, between Jesus' own public ministry and the christologies that were developed and recorded in the New Testament. It also forms a bond uniting the first disciples with Christians today.

One of the principles that will govern this inquiry into the Easter experience that led to the affirmation that Jesus is risen is the principle of analogy. There are several ways of expressing this principle and its implications.[15] A positive statement of the principle is that one must understand historical events within a unified ontological framework. This means simply that if one is to understand something and affirm that it is true, one has to be able to grasp its intelligibility and its possibility of existence. And this can only be done on the basis of some analogy with what one experiences as being intelligible and true within the sphere of common human experience today. Of course, one must be rather careful not to allow one's own personal experience to short-circuit the broad range of common human experience. A negative statement of the same idea is that one should ordinarily not expect to have happened in the past what is presumed or proven to be impossible today.

The question of the uniqueness of the resurrection of Jesus provides an example of how the principle of analogy is relevant. Jesus' resurrection is often depicted as a completely unique event and totally unexpected. But Paul is explicit in affirming the analogy between Jesus' resurrection and

---

15. See Roger Haight, *Dynamics of Theology* (New York: Paulist Press, 1990), 172–73.

our own in the following terms: "But in fact Christ has been raised from the dead, the first fruits of those who have fallen asleep. For as by a man came death, by a man has come also the resurrection of the dead. For as in Adam all die, so also in Christ shall all be made alive. But each in his own order: Christ the first fruits, then at his coming those who belong to Christ" (1 Cor 15:20-23). The resurrection of Jesus and the resurrection of all human beings are interdependent concepts, that of Jesus being the "first fruits" or prototype of the latter. Paul states that there is a kind of reciprocal condition of possibility that obtains between the two concepts. "For if the dead are not raised, then Christ has not been raised. If Christ has not been raised, your faith is futile and you are still in your sins. Then those also who have fallen asleep in Christ have perished. If for this life only we have hoped in Christ, we are of all men most to be pitied" (1 Cor 15:16-19).

If one can make the distinction within the symbol of resurrection between dimensions corresponding to the ideas of resurrection narrowly conceived and exaltation seen earlier, one might say that what happened to Jesus at his death differs from the destiny of other human beings not insofar as it is resurrection but insofar as it is exaltation or glorification.[16] This would provide a way of distinguishing the unique identity and destiny of Jesus of Nazareth, a concept which is still to be discussed. The analogy and correlation between Jesus' resurrection and the resurrection that Christians hope will be the destiny of all human life lends credibility to the genesis of faith in Jesus' resurrection. The principle of analogy legitimates this continuity while at the same time allowing that Jesus' resurrection remains distinct and different from the object of a common human hope. The principle means that the resurrection of Jesus is in some respects *sui generis*, while in others it should be understood within the realm of the possibilities of human hope.

The principle of analogy generates another application that is clearly enunciated by Edward Schillebeeckx: "There is not such a big difference between the way we are able, after Jesus' death, to come to faith in the crucified-and-risen One and the way in which the disciples of Jesus arrived at the same faith."[17] The "not such a big difference" should be interpreted as meaning that there is an analogy between the two. There are differences stemming from the fact that the disciples had a vivid memory of Jesus during his lifetime, and in many cases a personal contact with him. But one must distinguish between the differences of context and situation on the one side and the sameness that characterizes the structure of the experience and affirmation on the other. The disciples' basic experience is that

---

16. Gerald Bostock, "Do We Need an Empty Tomb?" *The Expository Times*, 105 (1994), 203. The principle will also have a bearing on the consideration of the empty tomb stories. Christians see no contradiction in using the language of resurrection during the very act of burying the dead.

17. Schillebeeckx, *Jesus*, 346.

Jesus lives in God's glory. This essential experience "is accessible to all Christians, who remain dependent on the initial disciples for the knowledge of the historical Jesus which enables them to believe and hope that [the] transcendental desire for resurrection has been fulfilled in him."[18] This principle of the continuity of Christian experience across the differences of circumstance and historical situation allows one to understand more intimately the deep structure of what is going on within, or what is represented by, the gospel narratives. The principle of analogy works in both directions; it gives the inquirer leverage in understanding the past, and it gives the texts of the past a right to be heard in our distinctly different situation today.

To sum up this first stage of our discussion of the resurrection, this symbol is not to be understood in imaginative categories as something that occurs within the concrete environment of our everyday world. The imagination accompanies all understanding, and it inevitably causes difficulties when applied to this transcendent reality. It is not the imagination that ties human conception to sensible data, but the imagination that constructs new possibilities of being that informs the concept of resurrection. Resurrection should be conceived as belonging to the transcendent sphere, an object of faith-hope which is that of God. But at the same time, we can approach the resurrection obliquely on the basis of the New Testament witness to this faith-hope and its object by means of an inquiry into the human experience that generated the initial conviction that Jesus was alive with God.

THE NEW TESTAMENT WITNESS

Earlier I quoted examples of creedal formulas, concise confessional statements of the kerygma. There are no direct or immediate witnesses to the resurrection in the New Testament, and I have indicated why that is the case in principle. I now want briefly to consider the indirect kinds of witness to the resurrection contained in the New Testament, namely, narratives about the discovery of his tomb empty and appearances of Jesus. I begin with the earliest and perhaps single most authoritative witness of all, Paul, who although he is completely silent about an empty tomb, lists a series of occasions in which Jesus appeared to people. And still more astonishingly, Paul's testimony includes what seems to be an eye-witness account of an appearance of Jesus to him. This whole treatment will amount to little more than a taking of a position, since I will deal only schematically with the evidence and only by examples. The two examples

---

18. Galvin, "The Resurrection of Jesus," 128, paraphrasing Karl Rahner, "Hope and Easter," *Christian at the Crossroads* (New York: Seabury Press, 1975), 90–91. "The evidence of the disciples *and* our own inner evidence of the experience of the living power of Jesus . . . together form one testimony: he lives." Rahner, ibid., 90.

of appearances are the one to Paul and to the disciples on their way to Emmaus. The point is to show how the data may be handled hermeneutically, for space does not allow exhaustively building a case.

St. Paul: Kerygma, Appearance, and Calling

The fifteenth chapter of 1 Corinthians is an extensive discussion of the theme of resurrection that begins with Paul's witness to the message that he himself received. It is clear, direct, and forceful:

> (v. 3) For I delivered to you as of first importance what I also received, that Christ died for our sins in accordance with the scriptures, (4) that he was buried, that he was raised on the third day in accordance with the scriptures, (5) and that he appeared to Cephas, then to the twelve. (6) Then he appeared to more than five hundred brethren at one time, most of whom are still alive, though some have fallen asleep. (7) Then he appeared to James, then to all the apostles. (8) Last of all, as to one untimely born, he appeared also to me.

The text is important because of the number of significant features it contains. I begin by commenting on the classic formula of the kerygma about Jesus: "he was raised." Second, among the appearances that Paul lists is the one to himself. Luke's description of that appearance in Acts deserves attention. And, thirdly, I shall briefly note the aspect of calling that is intrinsic to the appearance narratives.

The Kerygmatic Formula

Paul's statement in v. 4 that "he was raised on the third day in accordance with the scriptures" is the oldest statement of the Easter message and its most authoritative form. Since Paul received it himself, presumably on his conversion, it is part of the earliest tradition and can be dated within five years of Jesus' death. The meaning of the formula is "that his whole self in his entire psychosomatic existence was transformed and entered thereby into the eschatological existence."[19] As was noted earlier, this is an eschatological and meta-historical event correlated with a general expectation of a resurrection of the dead (1 Cor 15:16).

The Appearance to Paul

The passage 1 Corinthians 15:1-8 contains a straightforward statement that Jesus appeared to many, in different situations and constellations of circumstances. An apologetic note is struck in v. 6 when Paul says some of the

---

19. Reginald H. Fuller, *The Formation of the Resurrection Narratives* (Philadelphia: Fortress Press, 1980), 18. See also 30–34, 48–49, 169–70. Edward Schillebeeckx analyzes the New Testament data and interprets it in *Jesus*, 320–97, 516–44.

witnesses are still alive, as if to invite verification. More than any other single text, this one lends credibility to the phenomenon of appearances generally. But one does not have to check the other witnesses, because Paul himself is one: Jesus appeared to Paul (v. 8). Paul uses a standard expression for Jesus' appearances in characterizing Jesus' appearance to him. This indicates that in Paul's mind Jesus' appearance to him was equivalent to the earlier appearances.[20] One thus has a personal testimony to an appearance of Jesus.

According to Paul, Christ "was seen" by him, or Christ "appeared to him," or Christ "showed himself" to him. The verb *ophthē* can carry all of these meanings. But in 1 Corinthians 9:1 Paul changes the passive character of his receiving a vision into an active voice: "Am I not an apostle? Have I not seen Jesus our Lord?" The term used in these cases, "to see," "to be seen," or "to show oneself," "to let oneself be seen," is a standard term, used frequently, and thus approaching a technical expression. But should it be understood in a physical sense of seeing, or in a deeper symbolic sense pointing to a religious experience, an encounter, or recognition, or sudden new awareness of Jesus as one who is alive? Or, still more removed from a direct or immediate encounter with Jesus, can the term symbolize an objective conclusion or an inference or more generally mediated conviction *that* Jesus is risen, alive, and exalted with God? A direction for answering these questions has already been set in principle with the characterization of theology as such as a symbolic discipline. All language about transcendent reality is symbolic of experience that is historically mediated. The divergent responses to the question show that one cannot determine the exact nature of this experience by critical-historical means. But one can examine the clues in the New Testament that point toward the symbolic character of the language of the appearances. What are the indications that appearance-language is a way of expressing religious experience?

One way of going about this is to take the case of Paul as paradigmatic. This seems legitimate since his is the only firsthand or personal witness to such an appearance that we possess. Also, he himself ranks his experience of an appearance with those of the other leaders of the community. There are two avenues in which Paul's experience may be examined: first, through his own characterization of it, and second, through Luke's narrative description of it in Acts in the genre of an appearance story (Acts 9:3-19; 21:6-21; 26:12-23).[21] Each of these approaches will contribute to an understanding of the character of the "appearances" of Jesus.

---

20. Léon-Dufour, *Resurrection*, 57. Yet, in referring to himself as "one untimely born," Paul also seems to differentiate himself from the others in a way that is not completely clear.

21. This strategy is used by Fuller, in *Resurrection Narratives*. "What we know of Paul's appearances . . . can be applied . . . to the interpretation of the earlier appearances" (43). Others agree with this principle, for example, Pheme Perkins, *Resurrection: New Testament Witness and Contemporary Reflection* (Garden City, N.Y.: Doubleday, 1984), 200; Kenan B. Osborne, *The Resurrection of Jesus: New Considerations for Its Theological Interpretation* (New York: Paulist Press, 1997), 90–95.

The only New Testament witness who describes the appearances of the risen Jesus does so from a personal, experiential standpoint in terms of religious experience. Paul's own characterization of his own experience is not as a vision. His experiences are not objectified and open for examination. Rather, his language about his experience of the risen Jesus indicates that it is a religious revelation, an internal "seeing" in which God takes the initiative. Referring to his experience on the road to Damascus, he speaks of God who "had called me through his grace," and "was pleased to reveal his Son to me" (Gal 1:15-16). "Paul is a transformed individual, and this transformation is described in a variety of terms: a revelation, being seized by Christ, knowing Christ, seeing Christ, an appearance. In all of this, God is presented as the initiator, and through the event Paul is given a mission."[22] Paul's own characterization of his own experience forms a hermeneutical principle for understanding Luke's narrative account of it as a phenomenal event.

Luke's story of the appearance of the risen Christ to Paul is well known: Paul, on his way to Damascus, at around midday encounters a great light, falls to the ground, hears the voice of the Lord who identifies himself as Jesus, is struck blind, is instructed to go to the city, where he is healed and prepared to be the Lord's instrument in the apostolate or mission to the gentiles. It is commonly judged that the three versions of this story (Acts 9, 22, 26) are not historical narratives in the sense of accurately recounting events as they happened. Rather, they are constructions to make a point, communicate a message, in a narrative form, as was customary at the time. As the speeches in Acts were constructed by Luke, so too were the three narratives of Paul's encounter. Just as Paul's speeches in Acts were not transcriptions, neither are these narratives reportorial. Luke may have had a tradition with which to work. In fact, the accounts have a similar structure to other appearances and commissioning accounts in Jewish scripture. But the bottom line is that Luke creatively put together the story of Paul's conversion through an appearance just as he creatively constructed Paul's and others' speeches.[23] The common theme in the three accounts is light. But exactly what this light was and how it was experienced is not clear, for it was "not an ordinary experience capable of ordinary apprehension or neutral observation, but a revelatory event."[24] Some

---

22. Osborne, *The Resurrection of Jesus*, 95. In the end, whether the revelatory experiences came through the physical eye or the mind's eye is irrelevant; the point is that the appearances are revelations from God. See Fuller, *Resurrection Narratives*, 30–31. Fuller's view of the New Testament language about the resurrection resembles the logic of symbol: "All such language is analogical. Language was made for the description of events in this age; the New Testament has the problem of conveying events which belong to the eschatological age, but which are disclosed through this-worldly, historical events." Ibid., 33.

23. Osborne, *The Resurrection of Jesus*, 101–03.

24. Fuller, *Resurrection Narratives*, 47.

exegetes believe that Paul was referring to this light when he wrote the following with reference to the source of his ministry: "For it is the God who said, 'Let light shine out of darkness,' who has shone in our hearts to give the light of the knowledge of the glory of God in the face of Christ" (2 Cor 4:6). In sum, there was a before and after to Saul, and this is what the story depicts. "Reduced to basics, what happened involved the (by definition incommunicable) personal experience of the risen Lord, and the ritual acceptance into the community. To give narrative life to that bald statement, Luke employs models and symbols available to him in the tradition."[25]

Calling and Mission

The experience that Jesus was alive and with God carried the themes of calling and an impulse to continue Jesus' work. The initiative in these experiences, according to the witnesses, came from God. The missionary dimension of the experience involved spreading the movement that had begun with Jesus. This is the explicit message of Paul, and of Luke's depiction of the content of Paul's experience. In the third account of the appearance, Jesus himself announces Paul's mission. The appearance stories are analogous to accounts of the vocation or calling of the prophets in the Jewish scriptures. Willi Marxsen understands the appearance stories as intimately linked to, if not reduced to, a call to mission; they contain the imperative that Jesus' message and cause must be carried forward.[26]

This theme is formalized in the appearance on the mountain to the eleven that constitutes the conclusion of Matthew's gospel. Of the eleven who gathered at the mountain in Galilee which Jesus had appointed, some worshiped him when he appeared, while others doubted. But Jesus said:

> All authority in heaven and on earth has been given to me. Go therefore and make disciples of all nations, baptizing them in the name of the Father and of the Son and of the Holy Spirit, teaching them to observe all that I have commanded you; and lo, I am with you always, to the close of the age (Matt 28:18-20).

This engagement with the risen Jesus in such a way that one actively joins his cause and movement is implicit in all the appearance stories. And the strongest warrant for the belief that Jesus is risen lies in the effects of the experience that these stories express. This is the other end of the

---

25. Luke Timothy Johnson, *The Acts of the Apostles* (Collegeville, Minn.: Liturgical Press, 1992), 167. What Luke does is to put "in narrative terms what is essentially an internal transformation." Ibid.

26. See Küng, *On Being a Christian*, 376–77; Marxsen, *The Resurrection of Jesus of Nazareth*, 83–86; Léon-Dufour, *Resurrection*, 213–17.

change that came over the disciples and Paul. In fact, the Jesus movement began to spread within the synagogues. The movement begun in Jesus that seemed to end with his death then began to take off and to spread with the enthusiasm and zeal of a divine mission. This surge of human energy was not simply Jesus risen; it was *because* Jesus was raised.

THE EMPTY TOMB

There are several versions of the discovery of the empty tomb. They contain a good number of common elements among them along with differing details. The one in Mark 16:1-8, upon which I focus attention, is the shortest of them. In Mark, three women, Mary Magdalene, Mary the mother of James, and Salome, early in the morning of the first day of the week, went to the tomb of Jesus to anoint the body. Worried about who would roll back the heavy stone in front of the tomb, they found it already rolled away when they arrived, and inside a young man who was really an angel. He delivers the message that Jesus is risen and charges the women: "go, tell his disciples and Peter that he is going before you to Galilee; there you will see him, as he told you" (Mark 16:7). The women left, astonished and afraid, and said nothing.

Once again, we ask the question of the historicity of this story. Does it tell the story of the origin of Christian faith in the risen Jesus in authentically historical terms? And again, apart from the fact that my understanding of the resurrection does not support the necessity of an empty tomb in principle, it must be said that history cannot determine the authenticity of these accounts. But neither can history disprove an empty tomb, and a number of exegetes support its historicity. "The empty tomb story was not the Evangelist's creation, but tradition with a long history behind it. Basic to it . . . was an alleged factual report, the discovery of the empty tomb by the women. This alleged factual report was then used as a vehicle for the proclamation of the resurrection."[27] But what is at stake here is not the fact of an empty tomb, which in itself is quite distinct from resurrection, but whether the resurrection of Jesus requires it. As far as I can see, the strongest argument against such a necessity rests upon an understanding of the nature of resurrection as transcendent and upon the analogy of Jesus' resurrection with that of others, as it is reflected in 1 Corinthians 15. Of course, one can make up scenarios at one's convenience to explain the removal of Jesus' body by someone or other.[28] But this is

---

27. Fuller, *Resurrection Narratives*, 171. Fuller says that one simply cannot decide whether or not there is a historical basis for the story. "It is impossible for us at this distance to check the reliability of the women's report." Ibid. Pheme Perkins agrees that the tradition is old, and that one cannot really controvert it. But she adds: "Finding the tomb empty was not the source of early Christian belief that Jesus had been raised." Perkins, *Resurrection*, 94.

28. See, for example, Bostock, "Do We Need an Empty Tomb?" 201–03, who makes a case for the priests removing Jesus' body.

ultimately a work of fancy. Once the imagination is allowed a place in depicting the resurrection in empirical terms or spatial-temporal categories, one also creates problems that are as impossible to solve as they are irrelevant to the point of the resurrection itself.

But at the same time the story of the empty tomb does tell us something about the community which employed it to communicate its faith. For the creation and the telling of the story itself presupposes the faith in the resurrection that it expresses. Thus a brief analysis of the structure of the story will enable us to say something about the character of the early faith in the resurrection.

The story in its simplest form has three elements: the women who go to the tomb, the stone rolled back and the tomb empty, and the annunciation of the Easter message. Each of the three elements represents a dimension of the Easter faith of the disciples of Jesus. First, insofar as it is a narrative, the women are the point of continuity in the story. From beginning to end it is the story of their learning of the resurrection of Jesus. These women, then, are presented as the first witnesses to the resurrection and thus at the source of the post-Easter Jesus movement. They are proposed by this tradition as the model in coming to faith in the resurrection.[29] Given the low status of women as witnesses in the existing culture, the positioning of these women in this way must bear some significance concerning their historical role.

Second, the tomb is the zone of death. The tomb being opened and the body of Jesus gone means that death has been overcome. Jesus is alive. He is not here in the place of the dead.[30]

Third, the message of Jesus risen is announced by an angel. This means that it is a revelation that comes from God and is not inferred. "The resurrection is announced by a heavenly messenger, and is a revelation made to the community, not the community's view of the events."[31]

In sum, how may the stories of the empty tomb in their various forms be interpreted today? These stories are symbolic: they give expression to the faith of the community that Jesus is risen. Whether and to what degree there is a kernel of historicity behind them cannot be determined historically. But they dramatize the content of faith. Given Jewish anthropology and conceptions of bodilyness, it is hard to conceive of a more explicit vehicle to communicate the faith of the new Jesus movement: Jesus is risen. The content of this faith is not a datum that can be deduced; it is revealed by God. And given the prejudice against the testimony of women in Jewish society, one has to wonder about the prominent position given

---

29. Léon-Dufour, *Resurrection*, 135.

30. Morna D. Hooker, *The Gospel According to St. Mark* (London: A & C Black, 1991), 385. "He is not here" also means not in and of this world, but "the transformation of the body into an eschatological mode of existence and his immediate assumption into heaven." Fuller, *Resurrection Narratives*, 57.

31. Léon-Dufour, *Resurrection*, 112.

them by this story. Women played a prominent role sustaining Jesus' public ministry; it appears that this role is accented in the new post-Easter Jesus movement.

THE APPEARANCE AT EMMAUS

There are many appearance stories in the New Testament, as well as reports of appearances of which we have no account. In John's gospel, Jesus' appearances are compressed into a short temporal framework. In Luke's gospel, Jesus appeared over a period of forty days and then was exalted, although most commentators agree that this framework is literary and not historical. One may entertain the possibility of a shorter or a longer time period in the course of which the disciples experienced Jesus as alive and present, especially longer if the appearance to Paul is counted. One cannot know concretely how the disciples experienced Jesus as risen. "We cannot presume to reach the direct experience of those who became convinced that Jesus had been raised, since our earliest sources are quite reticent in that regard. From Paul we may presume that it is a spiritual experience that carried with it the conviction of a revelatory encounter with God."[32] A case can be made that the time it took the disciples to recognize that Jesus was risen was somewhat protracted. How long? We really do not know. The stories of the apparitions were first told or composed within a context of faith that Jesus had been raised. They are expressions of that faith. They are not reports of events as they happened, not chronicles of unfolding events. They were created afterwards as expressions of faith meant to appeal to or elicit faith in Jesus risen on the part of the hearer.[33] A first premise for interpreting them is to understand their genre; they are examples of kerygmatic preaching.

I have chosen to focus attention on the story of the apparition to the two disciples on their way to Emmaus (Luke 24:13-35). The story is called a "legend," a "tale," or a crafted short story. Luke undoubtedly possessed his own sources or traditions on which he worked. "Consequently, the intention of the story is not to bring historical facts to our knowledge in

---

32. Perkins, *Resurrection*, 94.

33. The position reflected here is that the word "appearances" does not accurately portray the kind of experience the disciples had in coming to an awareness that Jesus was alive and exalted with God. It may be contrasted with the position of those who defend the appearances as the primary way in which the disciples came to know that Jesus had been raised, and that these appearances consisted in "an experience that was unique and not merely interior but involved some external, visual perception." Gerald G. O'Collins, *The Resurrection of Jesus Christ: Some Contemporary Issues* (Milwaukee: Marquette University Press, 1993), 18. O'Collins has written extensively on the resurrection and has consistently defended the historicity of the appearances as sensible experiences of some kind. Besides the works previously cited, see also his *Interpreting the Resurrection: Examining the Major Problems in the Stories of Jesus' Resurrection* (New York: Paulist Press, 1988).

an objective way. Instead it has to do with the *doctrine* which is brought to our attention in the form of a narrative so that we might become receptive to its implied theological content."[34] The genre leads H. D. Betz to conclude that "nothing told in the narrative is incidental; every detail has its significance. It is the intention of this legend to narrate what is essential to the origin and nature of the Christian faith."[35] My interest in this story, however, is not quite the same as Betz's, who draws out its theological and doctrinal content. I am interested more in the way this story illustrates the origin of Christian faith in the sense of its historical genesis. Despite the fact that this story is not to be read as an exact historical account of specific events, the subject matter of this carefully crafted story concerns the emergence of faith in Jesus risen. If the disciples in this story are taken as representatives of the earliest disciples of Jesus generally, the story will be seen to explain in a general but historical way how faith in the resurrection of Jesus was generated.[36]

The story is well known. On the first day of the week, two disciples were on their way to Emmaus from Jerusalem when they were joined by Jesus, whom they were prevented from recognizing. When they expressed their near despair at the execution of Jesus, including the curious reports of the empty tomb, Jesus in his turn interpreted for them at length the events concerning himself in terms of the scriptures. When they came to the village, he stayed to eat with them. "When he was at table with them, he took the bread and blessed, and broke it, and gave it to them. And their eyes were opened and they recognized him; and he vanished out of their sight" (Luke 24:30-31). In their excitement they returned immediately to Jerusalem to report to the eleven.

Exegetes break down this story into its principal elements and arrange them in the form of an outline differently, according to the various interests of the authors and the different kinds of analysis to which the story is subjected.[37] I propose to comment on six elements of the narrative: 1) the situation, 2) the discussion of Jesus, 3) the use of the scriptures, 4) the initiative of God, 5) the recognition of Jesus in the breaking of the bread, 6) the concluding confession of the kerygma.

First, the story reflects fairly accurately, even though broadly, the historical situation of the followers of Jesus after his death. "But we had

---

34. Hans Dieter Betz, "The Origin and Nature of Christian Faith According to the Emmaus Legend," *Interpretation*, 23 (January, 1969), 33.

35. Betz, "Emmaus Legend," 38.

36. John Galvin, who has considered this issue extensively, seems to be moving toward the position that theologians should prescind from the discussion of the historical genesis of faith and deal more extensively with the content of resurrection faith. John Galvin, "The Origin of Faith in the Resurrection of Jesus: Two Recent Perspectives," *Theological Studies*, 49 (1988), 42. There is merit to Galvin's concern, but the apologetic theme in this christology also impels some consideration of this issue.

37. For example, Betz, "Emmaus Legend," 38–45, deals with the story theologically; Fuller, *Resurrection Narratives*, 186, outlines the story kerygmatically.

hoped that he was the one to redeem Israel" (Luke 24:21). Fuller believes that this verse seems "to recapture precisely the actual historical mood of the disciples between Good Friday and the Easter revelations, and therefore to belong to the original pre-Lucan narrative."[38] "Historically there can be no doubt that Jesus' disciples had placed in the prophet from Nazareth their highest and ultimate eschatological hopes for themselves and for their nation. His death on the cross had brought an end to those hopes and expectations."[39]

Second, it would be hard to imagine the followers of Jesus not subjecting his public ministry that culminated in his recent arrest and execution to an intense and protracted discussion. This historical phenomenon is not mentioned in passing but underscored by repetition. The disciples were "talking with each other about all these things that had happened" (Luke 24:14). The subject matter was "Jesus of Nazareth, who was a prophet mighty in deed and word before God and all the people" (Luke 24:19). And, of course, they conversed about "how our chief priests and rulers delivered him up to be condemned to death, and crucified him" (Luke 24:20). A number of things about this are important, but I shall highlight only two. One is that this discussion was an exercise of memory; the disciples remembered Jesus and the events leading up to his death. The other is the narrative form of this memory; Jesus was remembered through what he had said and done, which in turn made him to be the prophet he was.[40]

Third, through the help of Jesus as stranger, the disciples reflected on the life and fate of Jesus in the light of the scriptures. This element of the story too reflects the historical fact that the early Jesus movement and community interpreted Jesus in the light of the scriptures: the New Testament is the product of just such a reflection. This element of the story correlates with the character of the primitive kerygma received by Paul, "in accordance with the scriptures" (1 Cor 15:3, 4). The followers of Jesus found in the Jewish scriptures their principal worldly resource to begin to understand after his death just what happened in the Jesus event.

Fourth, the story reflects the sense that God is operative in the coming to awareness of Jesus being alive and exalted. The disciples are passive to the action of God upon them. It is God who withholds the identity of Jesus as stranger from their recognition, just as God is the agent when "their eyes were opened" (Luke 24:31). Recognition of Jesus risen and alive came as a revelation from God and not merely as an inference or conclusion based on objective data.

Fifth, there is a clear reference to the eucharist in this story. It recalls the Last Supper (Luke 22:19) and contains a classic Lucan way of referring to

---

38. Fuller, *Resurrection Narratives*, 105.
39. Betz, "Emmaus Legend," 38.
40. Betz, "Emmaus Legend," 38–39.

the eucharist. "The lesson in the story is that henceforth the risen Christ will be present to his assembled disciples, not visibly (after the ascension), but in the breaking of the bread. So they will know him and recognize him, because *so* he will be truly present among them."[41] But beyond this message of the story, it may also reflect historically where and how the disciples came to recognize that Jesus was alive. It is possible that this story enshrines a tradition of the way in which a revelatory encounter with Jesus occurred. "There is no apparent reason why the eucharistic meal should not have provided the occasion for some at least of the resurrection appearances, more probably those which occurred to groups rather than those to single individuals."[42] Such a view postulates that the followers of Jesus resumed or continued their gatherings and meals together, and that "they recognized him" (Luke 24:31).

Sixth, the story ends with a statement of the concise formula of the kerygma, "The Lord has risen indeed" (Luke 24:34), as if to say that this is the climax of this narrative. Actually, it is the conclusion of another untold story of Jesus' appearance to Simon. But, more generally, it is the climax of the whole drama of the gradual conversion of the community represented in these two disciples.

In sum, given its narrative structure, this story looks like it could represent, or at least reflect, in a general but ultimately historical way the manner in which the disciples came to faith in the exalted Jesus. Whether or not there were two disciples traveling to Emmaus, distancing the story from such a particular, specific event allows it to represent a community of disciples who are disoriented, but who are still in possession of the vivid memory of Jesus. This community did in fact reflect arduously on the meaning of Jesus in the light of Jewish scriptures, and, as it turned out, did continue the practice of the eucharistic meal, a practice learned in the company of Jesus. It seems quite possible therefore that the story represents broadly the historical route the disciples took to arrive at the affirmation of faith that Jesus is risen. Its historicity, then, applies especially to the structure of the story; the story bears reference to the community. This simultaneously symbolic and historical reference explains why the story would have been an ideal vehicle for kerygmatic preaching. Its structure allows the preacher to develop the logic of faith and the listener to grasp it. This view also fits with the theory that christology developed chiefly within the context of worship and cult.

---

41. Joseph A. Fitzmyer, *The Gospel According to Luke* (Garden City, N.Y.: Doubleday, 1985), 1559. In Betz's view, the story teaches that the resurrected Jesus is present both in the word-event of engaging the scriptures and in the common eucharistic meal. Betz, "Emmaus Legend," 40, 41.

42. Fuller, *Resurrection Narratives*, 109.

THEORETICAL RECONSTRUCTION OF THE
GENESIS OF FAITH IN THE RESURRECTION

The first two parts of this chapter provide an interpretation of the New Testament data concerning the resurrection. I pass now to a general theory of the structure of this faith in Jesus' resurrection. At the start, I should note the theoretical character of this reconstruction. We cannot determine concretely how faith in Jesus' resurrection arose. The New Testament does not provide the kind of information that would yield such an inference with any clarity. The wide variety of conceptions of this process is enough to prove that essays at describing or "explaining" how resurrection faith came about are at best hypothetical. But such theoretical characterizations of the epistemology of the resurrection help to establish its analogy with faith experience today and thus its credibility. I present this reconstruction around four points.

THE ROLE OF FAITH-HOPE

The element of hope is highlighted in Karl Rahner's transcendental theology and christology. One of Rahner's principal concerns in his christology is to show an intrinsic consistency between human existence itself and what Christians believe about Jesus Christ. His is an apologetic christology which, to make Jesus Christ intelligible to human beings today, places christological belief in correlation with anthropology. Rahner thus tries to bring out the internal continuity between Jesus Christ and human beings, between what happened to Jesus and the destiny of all. On the basis of this underlying principle, Rahner highlights the role played by hope in the faith that recognizes, grasps, or appreciates that Jesus is risen. For he is, as Paul said, the first of many.[43]

This hope is understood within the framework of philosophical and theological anthropology. It is not merely a psychological phenomenon. Nor is it simply a craving for individual survival. As I will insist later on, one cannot logically hope for one's own salvation without implicitly including the salvation of all. On the considerably deeper level of the dynamic and teleological character of human existence itself, Rahner understands hope as the fundamental posture of the openness of the human spirit to being itself. At this level, faith and hope are scarcely distinct, for hope in this sense is the ground out of which faith arises. "In the word 'hope' this one unifying 'outwards from the self' attitude into God as the absolutely uncontrollable finds expression. Hope, therefore, represents this unifying medium between faith or vision and love. . . ."[44] This

---

43. Karl Rahner, "Resurrection," *Sacramentum Mundi: An Encyclopedia of Theology*, 5 (New York: Herder and Herder, ND), 323–24, 329–31.

44. Karl Rahner, "On the Theology of Hope," *Theological Investigations*, 10 (New York: Herder and Herder, 1973), 250.

explains the term "faith-hope"; in this discussion I try to keep the fundamental orientation of human existence toward being, this fundamental trust, closely linked with faith. This faith-hope has transcendental roots; its origin is an element of human existence as such; as a fundamental confidence and trust in being itself, it includes a desire for permanence in existence. This transcendental faith-hope "constitutes the anthropological horizon for an understanding of what is meant by resurrection."[45] Jesus' resurrection appears as the confirmation and the fulfillment of this hope.

JESUS OF NAZARETH AS THE EXTERNAL REFERENCE FOR THE "EXPERIENCE" THAT JESUS IS ALIVE

The second element of this theory is the role played by Jesus of Nazareth during his lifetime, that is, in his public ministry. The affirmation that Jesus is risen is an object of faith-hope. It arises out of a participatory or engaged experience of transcendence, and is not a piece of objective information. As such, like all matters of faith, it is revealed; it is given to human awareness through a religious experience taken to be revelatory. But all revelation is mediated to human experience through an external medium or datum which symbolically represents the content of revelation. Revelation is not a purely a-historical inner communication of God to an individual consciousness. One has to ask about the external medium, the external thing, event, or situation which gave rise to an awareness of Jesus' resurrection. In traditional common-sense readings of the New Testament narratives, such a medium is either the appearances of Jesus alive or the experience of an empty tomb or an angelic announcement which mediated belief in the resurrection. Jesus is alive and risen because he was seen; Jesus is alive because the tomb was empty and the angel said he is risen. A critical-historical appreciation of the resurrection narratives, however, requires that a similarly critical and apologetical theology of the resurrection seek a different historical foundation. In the view proposed here, the external event that helped mediate a consciousness of Jesus risen was Jesus himself during his ministry. Or, to be more exact, after his death, the disciples' memory of Jesus filled this role.

Some exegetes and theologians believe that they can find sufficient grounds in the historical Jesus to warrant a belief in his resurrection. Whether or not the disciples actually believed in his resurrection before his death, Jesus provided sufficient indications to warrant this belief.[46] Other theologians explicitly reject the view that Jesus during his lifetime

---

45. Galvin, "The Resurrection of Jesus," 126.

46. See John P. Galvin, "Resurrection as *Theologia crucis Jesu*: The Foundational Christology of Rudolf Pesch," *Theological Studies*, 38 (1977), 513–25, and "The Origin of Faith in the Resurrection of Jesus," 25–44; also "The Resurrection of Jesus," 135–36.

supplied the grounds for belief in his own resurrection. The resurrection amounts to new content about Jesus dead and risen, and thus the kingdom of God, and these are precisely not found in a living Jesus. In this sense, Jesus of Nazareth is not a sufficient basis for faith in the resurrection because it is impossible to conclude to the resurrection of Jesus from the content of Jesus' life.[47] I suggest a position between these two that combines the insights of both. It seems clear that one cannot infer objectively a potential knowledge of Jesus' resurrection from a critical reading of the New Testament record of his teaching during his lifetime. But although the historical Jesus of Nazareth is not the sufficient ground for an affirmation of his resurrection, he is its necessary ground. One cannot affirm a resurrection of Jesus without reference to Jesus of Nazareth. Moreover, one must account in some way for the resurrection of *Jesus*. The one affirmed to be risen was Jesus, and such an affirmation necessarily presupposes a memory of him. Further, there must have been something about Jesus that impelled a hope in *his* resurrection. Jesus is thus the external historical cause that gave rise to the faith-hope in his resurrection, but he is not the sufficient or adequate cause.

What then are the historical "grounds" for belief in Jesus' resurrection? What I am calling "grounds" here are not the only factors leading toward faith in Jesus risen. Nor should "grounds" be construed as something probative or impelling faith with necessity. We are speaking of those factors that focus the attention on Jesus as the object of God's action. On that supposition, these historical grounds are found simultaneously in Jesus' teaching and in his person. First, with regard to his teaching, the disciples had a vivid, experiential recollection of Jesus' teaching. This memory included "their recollection of their relationship with Jesus, and recalling his ministry and his message of the kingdom of God; remembering his warning that they might display a lack of faith; remembering their experience of the God of grace whom they had come to know in the presence of Jesus; and recalling how he helped people in distress, how he ate and drank with sinners and promised salvation to them."[48] The content of Jesus' teaching about God, God's goodness, love, and fidelity, is primary here. And this should be measured against the background of the problem of good, evil, and ultimate justice, which the death of Jesus raised for the disciples.[49] The impulse must be approached in the cosmic framework of the moral coherence of human existence in which the very idea of resurrection first arises

---

47. Galvin, "The Resurrection of Jesus," 130–31, explaining the position of Walter Kasper. See Walter Kasper, *Jesus the Christ* (New York: Paulist Press, 1976), 124–43, for a nuanced discussion of the scriptural data and grounds of faith in the resurrection. Relative to the appearances, Kasper is clear that these are not to be construed as "objectively tangible events." An appearance was "an experience in faith," but not in the sense that the object, Jesus exalted, was the product or projection of faith. Ibid., 139.

48. Lorenzen, *Resurrection and Discipleship*, 75–76, paraphrasing Schillebeeckx.

49. See the analysis of the parable *The Rich Man and Lazarus* in Chapter 4.

through a contrast experience. The truth of Jesus' message of God as final savior, as it came to bear on Jesus' particular situation, is the first factor suggesting the resurrection of Jesus.

The second factor, Jesus' person, is something that ultimately cannot be clearly portrayed, but must be postulated. It stems from the fact that Jesus made an impact on people, that he so stood out above the content of his message, which was not original in its substance, that people encountered God in him. Because it was Jesus whom people experienced as risen, and not someone else, one must assume that Jesus had a forceful religious impact on people. It is this factor that Bornkamm tries to define with his category of "authority." Jesus displayed this authority in his teaching, his healing, and his overall comportment.[50] But in the end, this impact that Jesus had on his disciples during his lifetime cannot be reconstructed. It was an existential reality, only the remnants and traces of which could survive in objectified forms. No amount of imaginative and rhetorical skill can substitute for this authority and its existential influence on those who actually experienced it. This is precisely where the difference between the original disciples and all of those who come after them lies. Those who actually encountered and were influenced by the authority of Jesus, and who were led to faith and the affirmation of his resurrection for the first time, represent something that could happen only once. This is the logic behind apostolicity which Paul seeks to defend for himself with his own experience of the risen Jesus. But at the same time Paul is a witness to the possibility of someone who did not know Jesus in the flesh having an analogous experience.

Another way of putting this is to ask why the individual Jesus was raised from death. The answer must be because of the way he lived his life. It is difficult to think of any other reason than the one given in the hymn cited by Paul in his letter to the Philippians: he was raised because of the way he lived; he was obedient to God's rule and therefore was he exalted (Phil 2:8-9). I take this not merely in the moral sense of reward: he earned it. Rather, primarily, and stressing God's initiative, linking Jesus' resurrection to his life means that God has ratified Jesus' form of existence as revelatory of God's values and rule. Jesus' life, especially in its care for every form of human suffering, represents God's own plan for human existence. Thus the objective datum, the external historical event, that pointed to or mediated the further experience that Jesus was and is alive and risen was the experience of the disciples of Jesus himself during his lifetime and the memory of it. This kind of life, the life of this man, leads to life in God. It was the realization that the fidelity of God, the loving creator, lies within or encompasses the fidelity of this man, and this entails resurrection.

---

50. Günther Bornkamm, *Jesus of Nazareth* (New York: Harper & Brothers, 1960), 60–61.

AN INITIATIVE FROM GOD AS SPIRIT

The third element in the genesis of faith in the resurrection of Jesus is
the initiative of God operative in the human subject who comes to this
awareness. One who so encounters God in Jesus as to affirm that Jesus is
now, after his death, alive in the life of God does so on the basis of the initiative of God as Spirit.

This initiative of God in the faith-hope in Jesus' resurrection is urged
by several reasons. First, religious experience normally bears the theme of
having been initiated by God; it is not accounted for by human potential-
ities alone. All authentic and lasting religious experiences display the character of having been given gratuitously by God.[51] Second, such a divine
initiative is a way of saying that what is experienced here is not mere projection. Christians hold that Jesus really is alive. Affirming that this conviction is due to its being revealed by God is a way of assuring its realism:
how else would one be convinced that this is the case? Third, Christian
theology generally attributes all saving faith to the initiative of God's
grace, here understood as God's Spirit. This intellectual anti-Pelagianism
and anti-rationalism in the end rests on the quality of the experience of
faith itself: it comes from God's initiative. A fourth reason lies in the transcendent character of the resurrection; it is known in a revelatory religious
experience and not in an empirical, historical perception or an objective
inference from such an event. Fifth, the agency of God as Spirit is a theologically reasonable way to account for the change that occurred in the
lives of the disciples. Of all the historical data, this change is the most
remarkable. After the death of Jesus the disciples appear to have been confused, scattered, and disillusioned. Still later they were united, confident,
and preaching Jesus alive. A revelatory faith experience can account for
the shift from the cycle of disaster, discouragement, and despair to the spiral of a vibrant, enthusiastic, and hope-filled community that is seen in the
embryonic church. Sixth, there is an overwhelming witness in the New
Testament to the internal influence of God as Spirit within the Jesus movement from its beginning. I take it that this "pouring out of the Spirit" is a
symbolic phrase that interprets the corporate experience at the beginning
of the Jesus movement. This "enthusiasm" both caused and accompanied
the emergent group's recognition that Jesus was alive. With different
accents, Paul, Luke, and John all have vivid statements about the role of
God as Spirit working within the nascent faith experience of Jesus risen
and exalted.

The function of this doctrinal element in the theory of the origin of faith
in the resurrection should be clear. The language of the agency of God as
Spirit underlines the conviction, internal to faith itself, that faith-hope in

---

51. William James, in *The Variety of Religious Experiences* (New York: Collier Books,
1961), 300–01, 332–36, comments on the manner in which religious consciousness is not
completely within human control, and the manner in which it is self-authenticating.

Jesus' exaltation is itself a gift of divine origin. Thus one cannot objectively establish the truth of this faith by historical or rational argument. But at the same time, God as Spirit operates within a human experience that is historically and rationally constituted. The testimony of the Spirit is not direct illumination, not immediately experienced, not an unmediated Word of God. On the contrary, the experience of God present and immanent is precisely mediated by the memory of Jesus. This element of an initiative from God must be combined with the focus on a memory of Jesus; together they form a mediated experience of God's power of resurrection. A purely fideistic interpretation of the Easter experience must be rejected as strongly as a purely rational explanation.

How should this experience of an initiative from God be named? What kind of experience was it? The answer to this question is still more tenuous and exegetes propose various models of experience by highlighting different strands of evidence. Was it a conversion experience? Or an experience of forgiveness?[52] Whatever the best name for this experience may be according to exegetical data, clearly, as was seen in the case of Paul, it was a call to continue the ministry of Jesus. This seems to be a necessary and integral factor in the whole affair. A participatory encounter with the God who raised Jesus out of death cannot, by definition, leave one indifferent to the cause for which Jesus lived. Indeed, such an encounter presupposes some interest and engagement with this event. Paul is no exception here: in persecuting followers of Jesus he was deeply, although mistakenly, engaged with the cause of God; upon his conversion, he measured the depth of his error by the length of his calling and mission in the name of the risen Christ.

APPEARANCES AND STORIES OF THE EMPTY TOMB AS
EXPRESSIONS OF THIS RESURRECTION FAITH

To round off the elements of this theoretical reconstruction of how faith in the resurrection of Jesus first came about, I simply recall the point already made: the stories of appearances and the empty tomb are ways of expressing and teaching the content of a faith already formed. Most exegetes agree on this. On the one hand, then, most of the theories which strive to maintain that the appearance narratives have empirical, historical referents do so by various forms of deliberate ambiguity in the meaning of historical reference: such phrases as the disciples "somehow encountered," or the narratives describe "some historical event," explain little. On the other hand, those who insist on the naive realism of the appearance stories may be falling into the trap of those who deny Jesus was personally risen. Meaning is not totally determined by immediate reference; it is not the case that the affirmation "Jesus is risen" could only be

---

52. Schillebeeckx, in *Jesus*, 390–92, proposes that the root experience of the first disciples was one of forgiveness that somehow involved Jesus himself forgiving.

true if Jesus were "physically" encountered or the tomb were really empty.[53] The fact that some realities can only be known metaphorically or symbolically need not be a philosophical or theological embarrassment. It is a mark of their transcendence. The appearance stories are very clear and positive statements that Jesus is risen, and there is no reason to believe that their authors intended them to be anything less than such positive symbols. There is a middle ground between fundamentalism and a purely existential interpretation of the resurrection. A critical theology, which subjects these symbols to the reflection to which they give rise, should have no problem with the symbolic character of the New Testament witness to the resurrection.

In sum, these four elements provide a framework within which one can understand the genesis of the belief in the resurrection of Jesus. It arises out of a basic faith in God as mediated by Jesus, and a lingering commitment to the person of Jesus as the one in whom the disciples encountered God. This faith is faith-hope; that is, it rests on the anthropological foundation of a fundamental trust in existence and an openness to the power of being. The character of ultimate being, however, is revealed by Jesus to be personal, good, loving, concerned about human existence, and saving. After Jesus' death, the memory of Jesus did not die before faith in this God blossomed into a belief that Jesus was alive and exalted within God's saving power. This belief, however, which arose along the continuum of a memory and commitment to Jesus and his message about God, was new. To the best of our knowledge, this conviction was lacking immediately after Jesus' death. But there was a change in the disciples, from little faith to a fuller faith that included belief in Jesus' resurrection. This experience is attributed to God as Spirit at work within the disciples in tandem with the memory of Jesus and his message.[54]

---

53. Gerard J. Hughes, "Dead Theories, Live Metaphors and the Resurrection," *Heythrop Journal*, 29 (1988), 325–27. Hughes is here defending a real resurrection of Jesus against Marxsen and G. W. H. Lampe. He sees both as being influenced by overly skeptical forms of philosophy and a biblical criticism that undermines the historicity [read actuality] of the resurrection. Metaphors are used in science and understood realistically, that is, they are considered as successfully referring to their objects, when they explain the data through which the object is manifested, but which is itself beyond direct experience. So too theology is called upon to explain the experiences we have, including their referents, and it is successful and realistically true in the measure in which, with its metaphors or symbols, it accounts for experience. Ibid., 326.

54. This theory is in fundamental agreement with the proposal of Peter Carnley in his magisterial study, *The Structure of Resurrection Belief* (Oxford: Clarendon Press, 1987). The key terms of his theory are "remembering" and "knowing," which correlate respectively with history and experience. Memory of the historical Jesus is an integral and essential element of resurrection faith. Knowing, in the sense of encountering Jesus as risen in an experience of Christ as Spirit, is the other essential element in the structure of Easter faith. Recognition of the role of God as Spirit in the experience of resurrection of Jesus takes pressure off the necessity of having to decide what is going on

THE SIGNIFICANCE OF THE RESURRECTION

The significance of the resurrection lies in the notion of salvation. One cannot adequately convey the place of resurrection in christology outside of the fuller context of meaning which is pointed to by the symbol of salvation and which is fundamental to christology. The meaning of salvation will thus occupy us at length in the consideration of New Testament christology, the history of redemption theories, and a constructive conception of salvation for today. But at the same time it is important to indicate at least briefly the theological significance of the resurrection of Jesus generally and with special attention to the interpretation proposed here.

Let me begin by speaking generally of the place of the resurrection in the economy of salvation that God accomplished and accomplishes in Jesus. The resurrection of Jesus and human reception of the revelation of this resurrection together make up an integral and essential part of God's salvation as understood by Christians. Relative to what God accomplished in Jesus, two things deserve notice: the first is that God, who created Jesus, calls this human being back into God's own life. What God begins in love, because of the complete boundlessness of that love, continues to exist in that love, thus overcoming the power and finality of death. The second is that what God did in Jesus, God always does and has always done. For the salvation accomplished in Jesus Christ consists in revealing the true nature and action of God. Therefore, what God did in Jesus, God has been doing from the beginning, because to save is of the very nature of God. God is one whose concern about the life of what God creates never fails; God's power of life, then, is never finally defeated by death.

This objective salvation, so to speak, is actualized in its Christian form in human existence by means of its being revealed in Jesus. Salvation becomes an experienced reality in the disclosure that God effects through Jesus; salvation is in turn something that is recognized, accepted, internalized, and lived by Christians. A full concept of salvation includes both objective and existential dimensions. This does not mean that God is less a savior relative to people who are ignorant of God, or that people are not saved if they are unaware of the full reality, including the religious sacrality, that makes up human life. It simply means that people participate in life more fully precisely in being more fully aware of their own reality. To be aware of God as savior, and that one is embraced by a divine love that is also a power of resurrection, adds a dimension to self-conscious human

---

historically in the empty tomb and appearance narratives. Carnley also gives prominent consideration to a eucharistic framework for this experience (325). I have added the third anthropological dimension of transcendental hope as also essential to resurrection faith, and rounded out the theory with a clear statement that the historicity of the empty tomb and appearance narratives is not essential to resurrection faith-hope.

existence. This faith-hope transforms a two-dimensional life of finite time and space into a life with eternal depth and breadth and height. In the end it relativizes suffering and death by an infinite cosmic context of love and eternal life. Resurrection transforms human existence in the end and, when grasped in faith, the experience of life in this world.

But something should be said about the significance of the specific interpretation of the resurrection of Jesus that is offered here. Beyond the obvious concern for credibility, at what other points is this view of the resurrection distinctive?

Jesus Is the Focal Point of Initial Christian Faith

One way to appreciate a first aspect or quality of this interpretation of the resurrection is to contrast it with another. Jon Sobrino warns that "the most radical temptation facing Christianity is the temptation to focus one-sidedly on the risen Christ."[55] This results in turning Christianity into "religion" in a pejorative sense of an attachment to an other-worldly transcendent power, rather than a way of life lived in this world within the sphere of God's love and justice. When the resurrection takes on central importance, the events of the life of Jesus that led to his death tend to be left behind. Although they are not forgotten, because the gospels continue to be read, they are at least minimized by their relationship to the resurrection which, after all, is symbolic of final victory and renders Jesus transhistorical and always present. This in turn can have a dramatic effect on one's understanding of the Christian life and the significance of participation in the world of everyday affairs, especially the social issues that concern the life and death of so many. Sobrino strongly accuses the church of having failed in this regard in the course of history.

Accepting the warnings of Sobrino, this interpretation of the resurrection tries to retain Jesus at the center of christology. Jesus of Nazareth remains the concrete focal point of primitive Christian faith in the resurrection itself. In other words, the external, objective, and historical referent for Christian faith in the resurrection of Jesus is the Jesus of history, the person Jesus in his pre-Easter life. Negatively, the objective referent of Christian faith is not Jesus' teaching abstracted from his person. The object of faith is not a kerygma of the church about Jesus, for faith in Jesus is prior to such a kerygma, and the kerygma itself, which is about Jesus, grows out of faith precisely as encounter with Jesus. Nor does the basic content of Christian belief in resurrection or eternal life exist apart from the person of Jesus. Christian faith in the resurrection of human beings generally is an extrapolation of faith that *Jesus* is risen. Christian faith is faith in God mediated by this man Jesus, who, because of the way he lived and by the power of God, is now perceived to be alive with God. This is evident from the gospels themselves: they are about Jesus who lived in history and is now alive and risen.

---

55. Jon Sobrino, *Christianity at the Crossroads* (Maryknoll, N.Y.: Orbis Books, 1978), 278.

Uncentering of the Resurrection in Christian Faith

This phrase, "uncentering the resurrection," develops another aspect of the preceding observation. The focusing of Christian faith on the historical Jesus implies a certain "repositioning" of the resurrection in the structure of Christian faith. This observation should not be construed to imply any minimization of belief in the resurrection of Jesus within Christian faith. What is at stake here is how resurrection fits within the structure of Christian faith. This is to be understood relative to some interpretations of Christian faith as being centered on the resurrection and on Jesus risen. Therefore, again, contrast with other positions may be the best way to present what is aimed at here.

Hans Küng writes that the resurrection is the core of Christian faith, "without which there is no content to Christian preaching or even to faith." The resurrection is taken "not only as the basic unit, but also as the permanent, constitutive core of the Christian creed."[56] Resurrection has assumed center stage; other aspects such as the life and ministry of Jesus, and the symbol of incarnation, have lost a certain relative prominence. Walter Kasper, while at times closely associating the resurrection with Jesus' life and death, at other times speaks of the resurrection as a new, underivable act of God that adds new content to the message of the earthly Jesus.[57] One often finds the reasoning that Jesus' message was falsified by the manner of his death, a statement that seems to presuppose either that there have not been other far more dramatic manifestations of evil in our world, or that one would have expected an intervention of God to save Jesus from his execution. Thus, finally, the resurrection is regularly interpreted as the validation or ratification or legitimation of Jesus' message which, in an implied sense, would not have been able to be perceived as true without a new revelation of Jesus' resurrection and consequent victory.

The problem with this language is not that it is wrong, for it is susceptible to benign interpretation. But it makes it appear as though the person of Jesus, seen in his earthly teaching and actions as a whole, was not and is not in himself a revelation of God, or not a revelation of God sufficient enough not to require another external divine initiative. It gives rise to the following interpretation of Jesus' resurrection which is at best misleading: with the crucifixion Jesus' whole life was voided; it was a catastrophic event because it contradicted his message of God's love. But then there was a further event, recognized as integral in itself, a miracle, a new divine initiative, the resurrection. By this new act of God, then, Jesus' life was validated. Therefore the resurrection, as a distinct and discrete event in response to the cross, is taken as the center of faith, and is that upon which the whole of Christian faith rests. And, given this conviction about the finality of the resurrection, nothing else matters. The focus of faith becomes

---

56. Küng, *On Being a Christian*, 346; also 380–81.
57. Galvin, "The Resurrection of Jesus," 130–31, paraphrasing Walter Kasper.

Jesus now, risen and present to us as a revelation of our future. Given that relationship to Jesus risen, the memory of his life pales into relative insignificance. It is the mere condition for the possibility of resurrection.

No. A genetic christology from below alters such a perspective. Jesus' message is true, and his life a revelation of God, even if, contrary to fact, there had been no explicit experience of resurrection. Jesus' life, what he said and did, is the center of faith. Jesus' ministry and message mediate a revelation of God. Its content is the love and fidelity of God. In remembering Jesus, his message and life, and by the gracious initiative of God as Spirit in their lives, the disciples came to realize that Jesus is an authentic revelation of God. Moreover, they came to recognize that Jesus now lives with God partly through Jesus' own representation of God during his public ministry. Thus one may speak of the resurrection as God's confirming and validating Jesus' life, but not as an event independent of or isolated from Jesus' life. Resurrection is a part of Jesus' life as its transcendent end.

Analogy with Present Christian Faith

According to the witness of Paul seen earlier, there is a fundamental analogy, that is, similarity admitting difference, between the resurrection of Jesus and the resurrection of all human beings. There is also an analogy between faith-hope in the resurrection today and the Easter faith-hope of the first disciples. Resurrection faith today is not belief in an external miracle, an empirical historical event testified to by disciples, which we take as a fact on the basis of their word. Although that may describe in fact the belief of many Christians, it is no ideal. A reflective faith-hope today will affirm Jesus risen on the basis of a conviction that Jesus' message is true; because God is the way Jesus revealed God to be, Jesus is alive. This reflection is not deduction; it is a discursive description of the content of the Christian experience just analyzed. Christians today cannot experience Jesus in exactly the same way as his first disciples. Faith-hope in the resurrection is mediated through a Jesus who is represented in and through the Christian community in a variety of different ways. But, finally, belief in Jesus' resurrection rests on an appreciation of the message and life of this man, and the religious experience that his life is a revelation of the way God is, and of the way human life is led back to God. Faith-hope in the resurrection is based on the existential faith that Jesus revealed God as God truly is: a God of love; a God of fidelity; a God who as the author of life is also the finisher of life; and a God who saves from final death those who respond to this God. In sum, first, the historical basis for faith in Jesus' resurrection is the historical life of Jesus himself, and the power of his ministry to reveal a resurrecting God. Second, the religious basis consists in existential revelation and faith which are the products of the initiative of God's grace. And, third, both of these are enveloped within a fundamental, transcendental hope in the future. With regard to the first element, present-day knowledge of Jesus is analogous to Paul's, who did not know Jesus in the flesh. With regard to the second two factors, a present-day recognition of Jesus as alive is generically the same.

We can now conclude with a summary response to the question this chapter seeks to answer, namely, what does it mean to say that Jesus is risen? What is the logic of this statement? This is an affirmation of faith-hope that expresses a religious commitment and a trust on the part of the self and the community. Whether spoken by the first disciples or disciples today, there is a fundamental continuity in the structure of the conviction. It affirms that Jesus is ontologically alive as an individual within the sphere of God. It is pronounced partly on the historical grounds of Jesus' teaching and life, his message and his person, and at the same time it is based on a religious encounter with God's revelatory Spirit or grace. This resurrection is construed as God's declaration that Jesus' life is a true revelation of God and an authentic human existence. Because recognition of the resurrection involves the self in a performative and engaged way, it is a call to mission, and as such, through hope and commitment, it becomes salvific. More must be said about this salvation in the course of this book. Resurrection for Jesus, as the end and finality of his life, was an intrinsic part of it, not something added on. So too is resurrection for human beings generally. But even here there is a tension. On the one hand, what is revealed in Jesus' resurrection is not that all human life is raised, but that faithful human existence such as his is called back into God's love. On the other hand, what one finds in Jesus' own teaching is a God of unconditional love reaching out pointedly toward sinners. Only on this latter premise can we hope for this salvation.

CHAPTER 6

The Pluralism of New Testament Soteriologies and Christologies

The resurrection of Jesus, or, historically, the Easter experience that Jesus is alive and exalted, marks a transition in the relationship of the disciples to Jesus. On one side of the resurrection there was surely interpretation of Jesus, for to understand is to interpret. But it is not easy to arrive at more than a speculative estimation of how the disciples interpreted Jesus during his lifetime. On the other side interpretation takes a qualitatively new turn. The Easter experience is thus often referred to as the point of departure and cause of formal christology. This indicates that Jesus is now interpreted more explicitly in categories that indicate a distinctive and in some cases unique relationship to God. Many of these interpretations of Jesus are available, for the New Testament consists in the direct literary witness of early, if not the earliest, soteriologies and christologies.

This chapter will review and comment upon some of the soteriologies and christologies that are found in the New Testament. But it is important to be clear about the goal that governs the treatment of such a vast topic in a short space. The aim is not to offer new exegetical analyses. Rather, writing as a systematic theologian, I want, first of all, to document the fact of the pluralism of soteriologies and christologies in the normative New Testament teaching. And, secondly, I want to reflect on the significance of this pluralistic data for systematic christology today. Specifically, I want to address three issues raised by the New Testament interpretations of Jesus. The first regards the relationship between soteriology and christology, or, as it is sometimes put, the relation between a functional approach to Jesus that attends to what he did and a more ontological approach to Jesus that inquires about his identity, or even his being, in relation to God and to other human beings. The second line of questions concerns the fact of the pluralism of New Testament conceptions of Jesus. What are the reasons for this pluralism? What is its relevance for christology today? The third area of reflection concerns the normative role of the New Testament for theology and christology today. How are we to conceive of a pluralistic document being normative? Or, what is normative in the New Testament's christologies? I begin this investigation with some preliminary reflections.

PRELIMINARY REFLECTIONS

A few minutes in the New Testament christology section of a theological library will reveal a formidable body of literature, enough to convince one that some preliminary comments are needed as an orientation to the treatment of this material.

A first reflection concerns the depth and extent of the pluralism of New Testament christology. On one level, this pluralism lies on the surface of the New Testament writings. The different authors and communities are not all saying the same thing about Jesus. One wonders today why the remarkable differences of interpretations were not attended to or highlighted in classical christology, given the fact that they are so obvious today. Historical consciousness has accentuated our attentiveness to differences among the New Testament authors. The same historicity, however, also influences exegetes and interpreters today, and pluralism also marks the exegetical interpretations of any given New Testament christology. For example, is Philippians 2:6-11 a relatively "low" second Adam christology, or is it a relatively "high" wisdom christology?[1] Since there is some agreement that this text reflects an early pre-Pauline hymn, the difference in interpretation could reflect rather different assessments of the manner in which first-century christology developed. The extent of this exegetical pluralism allows me to clarify further the purpose of this chapter. This does not include airing the various sides of the intricate debates over specific New Testament passages, and certainly not adjudicating them or defending a position. One of the goals is simply to represent the broad lines of some of the christologies of the early church that are represented in the New Testament. The point is to show that they are really different, for this is positive data that must be self-consciously engaged in constructive christology.

But this generously broad goal still does not resolve the practical problem of dealing with New Testament christology in an orderly, methodical way, no matter what the length of the chapter. Is there any satisfactory procedure for harnessing the historical diversity of the New Testament books and their different interpretations of Jesus? One method would be to build types that collect into various groupings christologies that have a common

---

1. James D. G. Dunn, *Christology in the Making: A New Testament Inquiry into the Origins of the Doctrine of the Incarnation* (Philadelphia: Westminster Press, 1980), 113–25, defends the first position, while Ben Witherington, III, *Jesus the Sage: The Pilgrimage of Wisdom* (Minneapolis: Fortress Press, 1994), 257–66, defends the second.

structure or share certain chosen characteristics.[2] Another approach would be to develop independently the soteriology[3] and then the christology of each book or author[4] of the New Testament. And still another procedure would be to isolate major thematic concepts in specific New Testament works or across several books and analyze their historical background and intrinsic logic.[5] Any of these ways or a mixture of them can help to gain some control over a historical development that sprawls over the last two-thirds of the first century, in different communities, at different times, exemplifying different levels of development, represented by different authors or groups of authors, expressed in different genres of literature and categories, and responding to different life situations and problems.

In this chapter, however, I will have to be satisfied with a short-hand method of analyzing the christologies of the New Testament, one that is consonant with the point of the chapter. I have chosen five christologies or types of christology which I will illustrate by an analysis of texts which contain or exemplify them. This combines the concreteness of exegetical analysis with hermeneutical generalization. One of the goals here is to show that from a theological standpoint one can move from a pluralism that first appears as a confusing morass of different interpretations to a recognition that the pluralism in New Testament christology is valuable and freeing; it has positive constructive implications.

I have not chosen the one christology which provided a new name for Jesus of Nazareth: Jesus as messiah or christ. After Jesus of Nazareth was recognized by his followers as being the messiah, or Christ, the title Christ began to function as a name, and his followers came to be called Christians. The term "Christ" also has other functions. For example, whereas the name Jesus tends to point to Jesus of Nazareth during his earthly life, there is a certain tendency to allow the name Christ to point to Jesus in his risen and exalted state and sometimes to a pre-existent Christ. This is probably due to the distinction between the Jesus of history and the Christ of faith that arose with critical-historical investigation of Jesus. In any case, because I have used the proper name of Jesus to

---

2. For example, Earl Richard, in *Jesus: One and Many: The Christological Concept of New Testament Authors* (Wilmington: Michael Glazier, 1988), 74–75, distinguishes three types of christology in the New Testament witness: 1) exaltation and enthronement, 2) agency christology, 3) wisdom or pre-existent christology. Edward Schillebeeckx proposes four types of christology in the early church: 1) parousia christology, 2) divine-man christology, 3) wisdom christology, and 4) Easter christologies. All four are rooted in a concept of Jesus as the eschatological prophet which was probably predicated of Jesus, at least in the form of a question, during his lifetime. Edward Schillebeeckx, *Jesus: An Experiment in Christology* (New York: Seabury Press, 1979), 401–38.

3. Edward Schillebeeckx, in *Christ: The Experience of Jesus as Lord* (New York: Seabury Press, 1981), analyzes holistically the conception of salvation in each book of the New Testament, with the exception of the synoptic gospels (112–462), and then synthesizes his findings by enumerating the symbols he finds there (463–514).

4. This is the approach of Richard in *Jesus: One and Many.*

5. Such is the approach of Dunn in *Christology in the Making.*

refer to Jesus of Nazareth, and because I do not want to break the bond between an exalted Christ and Jesus of Nazareth, I will generally refrain from referring to Christ but always to Jesus Christ to indicate the risen and exalted one.

This brief analysis of New Testament christologies is also governed by the principle that there is a close connection between soteriology and christology. A specific view of how Jesus saved implies a christology, and a given christology also implies in a more or less explicit way a soteriology. I will reflect at greater length on the relationship of reciprocity between *agere* and *esse* in Jesus, and the logic of the relationship between soteriology and christology in the structure of Christian faith, in the final section of this chapter. And still later, in Chapter 7, the relationship will be drawn up into a more general theory of religion. The principle is announced here to explain why in the analysis of each of the christological texts I will include a comment on the explicit or implicit experience of salvation that is reflected in it.

Finally, I must repeat that the perspective of this account of New Testament christology remains that of a hermeneutical theologian. This means that a double concern or question guides these reflections. The first relates to the historical meaning of the text as a witness to the experience of the Christian community during the first formative and normative century. The second question relates to the bearing of this christology on the Christian community today. In meeting the first concern I remain more or less dependent upon a variety of exegetes whose task it is to unveil the historical meaning of the text within the context and according to the life situation which generated it. In meeting the second concern I will pose such questions as the following to these christologies: what is the structure or logic of the christology and can it be generalized? What experience of Jesus lies behind this christology? What soteriology accompanies or is implied in this christology? What concrete meaning or existential mode of life is referred to by the christology? And, finally, what kind of experience does it open up as a possibility for life in the world today?[6]

FIVE NEW TESTAMENT CHRISTOLOGIES

Each of the following New Testament christologies will be developed briefly according to a two-part scheme: an exegetical account of the texts, and an interpretative analysis of the structure of the christology, the perception of Jesus implied in it, its implied soteriology, and the kind of possible human experience it can give rise to today.

---

6. These questions are suggested by the analysis of "appropriation" by Paul Ricoeur in "Appropriation," *Hermeneutics and the Human Sciences*, ed. by J. B. Thompson (Cambridge: Cambridge University Press, 1981), 182–93.

JESUS CHRIST AS LAST ADAM

The classic text embodying the interpretation of Jesus Christ as the last Adam is Romans 5:12-21 (also 1 Corinthians 15:21-23, 45-49). Two verses capture the essence of the image:

> (18) Then as one man's trespass led to condemnation for all men, so one man's act of righteousness leads to acquittal and life for all men. (19) For as by one man's disobedience many were made sinners, so by one man's obedience many will be made righteous.

The two verses represent the structure of the parallelism between Adam and Jesus Christ on which the fundamental idea of this christology rests. Jesus Christ is compared and contrasted with Adam. The point of correspondence is that they are both one person in whom the destiny of all has been determined. They are "epochal" figures in the sense that whole blocks of history have been shaped by them: Adam for the present age from the beginning; Jesus Christ for the future beginning now. The contrast consists in the nature of their acts and their corresponding effects. Adam's was an act of disobedience, and it began a history of sin in which all are implicated. Jesus Christ's act was one of obedience, and he is the initiator of a new epoch of righteousness.[7]

Before attending to any of the details of the image one should consider its size, the sheer scope of the vision it contains, the breadth of the context in which Jesus Christ is considered. The obvious reference is to the story of creation, so that even though the reading of Jesus Christ is through Jewish history, the framework for understanding him includes all creation and the whole of human history. All of human history is divided into two parts, the period of sin up to Jesus Christ and the history after it until the future end. The image draws into itself a theological vision of the whole of history.

This christology is a good example of the identity of Jesus Christ being defined by what he did. This is developed by Paul in the comparison and contrast with Adam. Adam was one person whose act influenced the whole of history, for through him sin and thus death spread to all human beings (v. 12). Adam's act was one of disobedience (v. 19). Paul is very clear in depicting the situation of humankind under the control of the powers of sin and death; it is a condition from which no one is exempt; Adam's act led to the condemnation of all human beings (v. 18). The condition of humankind that Paul envisages is one of hopelessness and despair. Sin, which Paul personifies, reigned, and the result was death (v. 21).

In a parallel manner Jesus Christ is one person who determines the whole course of future history. In him, in effect, a new race of human beings has begun. He is the second, but really eschatological or final

---

7. James D. G. Dunn, *Romans 1-8* (Dallas: Word Books, 1988), 296.

Adam. In contrast to Adam, Jesus' act was one of obedience, and by it all human beings are led to acquittal, righteousness, and life (vv. 18–19). Where sin reigned, grace is poured out in the wake of the righteous act of Jesus Christ; where death ruled, life is promised (v. 21). The contrast is a classic description of salvation, a reversal of an evil and desperate situation by the power of God working through the agency of Jesus Christ.

What exactly did Jesus Christ do that initiated or caused the reversal of the effects of Adam's sin? In direct parallel and contrast with Adam's disobedience, the act of Jesus Christ was obedience. As Adam's sin misdirected history, so the righteous act of Jesus Christ reverses the course of destruction within human history. Paul seems to suggest "a recapitulation or rerunning of the divine program for man in which the first Adam's destructive error was both refused and made good by the last Adam, thus opening the way for the fulfillment of God's purpose for man (see Heb 2:6-15)."[8] But what is this act of obedience and how does it affect human beings causally? These questions are not answered directly by the verses in question. Paul simply says that on the basis of Jesus' obedience sinners are constituted or declared just.[9] But we can get some clues to the historical dynamics from the preceding passage (Rom 5:1-11). There Paul speaks of Jesus Christ's dying for sinners (vv. 6, 8), so that we are justified and reconciled by his going to his death, and will be saved by his resurrected and exalted life in the future (vv. 9–10). By faith in God's action for us in Jesus Christ we are justified, and by hope and the movement of God as Spirit, we know we will not be disappointed (vv. 1–5). Jesus Christ's act of obedience is his faithfulness to his mission which ended in his death. Its further entailment is Jesus' resurrection and exaltation and our faith and hope in the power of God's love poured out as the Spirit (v. 5).

Who, then, is Jesus Christ in this christology? He is the second and final Adam. The comparison with Adam makes it clear that Jesus is a human being. This is not a pre-existence christology, but a two-stage christology in which the one compared with Adam is Jesus of Nazareth who went to his death in obedience, was raised and exalted, and is now the one who determines humanity into the end-time.[10] Jesus Christ, the human being, was the vehicle of God's action of love for humankind (Rom 5:8), and now Jesus Christ is risen and exalted with God.

---

8. Dunn, *Romans 1-8*, 297.

9. Joseph A. Fitzmyer, *Romans: A New Translation with Introduction and Commentary* (New York: Doubleday, 1993), 421–22. Brendan Byrne, in *Romans* (Collegeville, Minn.: Liturgical Press, 1996), 179–80, stresses the superiority of Christ in the comparison-contrast with Adam. It is not a balanced contrast, because Christ is the overwhelming love and grace of God invading history to reverse the tide of sin.

10. "In other words, it is not Christ's birth and ministry which is in view, but his death as the eschatological counterpart to Adam's sin: as Adam's transgression introduced death, so Christ's death introduced life. It is the risen and heavenly Christ who characterizes the age to come, just as it is the fallen Adam who characterizes the present age." Dunn, *Romans 1-8*, 292.

Some exegetes see Philippians 2:6-11 as another major witness to a Last Adam christology.[11] Most are agreed that this passage reflects an early Christian hymn which Paul has inserted into his letter. It is thus read not as an autonomous unit, but precisely in terms of Paul's thought reflected throughout his corpus. When it is read in this context the passage runs parallel with Paul's Last Adam christology which was just analyzed. Such an interpretation is accompanied by significant implications. It shifts what is often taken as an early witness to a pre-existence, or three-stage christology, to a two-stage christology. "Paul's christology, therefore, should be described as one of agency whereby the lordship of God finds its domain of power in the Christ's activity first on the cross and then, as a result and in conjunction with the Christ's resurrection, in the lives of believers who await the end of the ages."[12] How the text is interpreted also has a bearing on one's notion of the pace of the development in christology. If, by contrast, this hymn is read as an autonomous text representing a wisdom christology, one has an early pre-Pauline witness to what may be a three-stage christology reflecting some notion of a pre-existence theme.[13] I will return to this text when I consider wisdom christology.

I now want to turn to the hermeneutical issue of how the theologian might interpret a Last Adam christology in a way that is both faithful to its logic and yet correlates roughly with present-day language and understanding. A first point to note is that the fundamental structure of this christology is based on a negative experience of contrast that calls out for salvation. The parallelism between Adam and Jesus Christ contains the framework, but what dominates are the differences of the actions and their effects: sin versus righteousness; disobedience versus obedience; death versus life; the present negative situation and the hoped-for future of salvation. The christology unfolds within the tension of negativity and salvation. It contains a theology of sin and death. But this is the parenthetical contrasting background for the point, the superabundant life-giving effect of the event of Jesus Christ.[14] Moreover, one can find traces in the language of Paul's own personal, enthusiastic experience of God's grace coming to him through Jesus Christ. Here lies the deeper structure of the experience from which this christology arises, and it is a perennial framework for religious discourse. The religious question arises out of the negativities of

---

11. Thus interpreting Phil 2:6-11 in the light of Rom 5:12-21 are, for example, Dunn, *Christology in the Making*, 113–25 and Richard, *Jesus: One and Many*, 328–29. Karl-Josef Kuschel, *Born Before All Time? The Dispute over Christ's Origin* (New York: Crossroad, 1992), 243–66, is in this line of thought. By contrast, Brendan Byrne interprets Rom 5:12-21 in the light of Phil 2:6-11, and finds reflected in the Romans text Paul's vision of a pre-existent Son. Brendan Byrne, "Christ's Pre-Existence in Pauline Soteriology," *Theological Studies*, 58 (1997), 328–29.

12. Richard, *Jesus: One and Many*, 328.

13. For example, Witherington, *Jesus the Sage*, 257–66.

14. Fitzmyer, *Romans*, 407.

human existence in this world, and it hopes for a new reality effected by transcendent power. Without the religious question, one cannot even approach the religious meaning of Jesus of Nazareth.

Secondly, how is this christology related to Jesus of Nazareth? We have seen that obedience is an important, if not central, element of this christology, and the obedience was that of Jesus of Nazareth going to his death. Nevertheless, what Paul envisions transcends Jesus of Nazareth and his death; it includes Jesus risen and exalted and out in front of human beings. But it is not necessary to understand Jesus' obedience as a single act in a particular moment of his life. Jesus' obedience can be construed as an attitude that characterizes the whole person and his career: purposefulness, fidelity, loyalty to God's cause or reign. Resurrection and exaltation, then, are not simply the reward for an act of obedience, but the end and consummation of Jesus' life and mission. Thus the totality of Jesus, the identity which was forged by his action, were assumed into the glory of God's life. Not only Jesus as a person, but all that he did entered into eternal life.

Thirdly, soteriology does not lie behind this christology but constitutes it. It may be read as a soteriology of fidelity, loyalty, faith in the sense of commitment, all of which are connoted by the concept of obedience. Jesus did what Adam should have done but failed, and he did it in the new situation of sin and death which surrounds the present epoch. Jesus lived his life committed to the end. It is not the death of Jesus in itself that is pleasing to God. God cannot be construed as being pleased with death. Rather, resurrection, life, and salvation correlate with the positive, loyal dedication of Jesus' freedom to God's cause to the end.

What, then, is a possible mode of life that this christology holds out as an invitation to faith? Does this christology thematize a possible human experience and life that makes sense today? An answer to this question, I believe, must reflect the simple and primal structure of this christology: the contrast between evil and good, death and life, sin and freedom freed from the confines of self-absorption. When it is approached on this level, the experiential meaning latent in this christology is both perennial and very close to the actual experience of Paul. The fundamental revelatory pattern Paul finds in Jesus is that his life of absolute fidelity to God's will ends in resurrection, life, and glory close to God. This is the original pattern of creation; sin and death are intruders; these negativities of human existence and history are not meant to be; and they will be defeated and transcended. This is a christology that provides grounds for hope by transforming the character of how one envisages the whole of creation and history. The second and final Adam thus stands at the head of a race of people who in this world can live lives transformed by hope in the absolute future.

JESUS CHRIST AS SON OF GOD IN MARK

The meaning of Jesus' title, "Son of God," escapes exact definition. It is subject to many connotations and clearly differs in its meaning in different authors, for example, Mark and John. It is an example of a title that contains different christologies which cannot be rationalized in a single meaning. I shall direct attention to Son of God in Mark's gospel, but in a narrow analysis that only reveals one aspect of Mark's christology. It may be noted that Son of God not only interprets Jesus Christ, but the Jesus Christ of the whole of Mark's gospel also interprets the meaning of Son of God. I will consider the five most important texts in which Son of God appears in Mark (Mark 1:1; 1:11; 9:7; 14:61; 15:39).

The gospel of Mark begins with what could be taken as a title and summary of its content: "The beginning of the gospel of Jesus Christ, the Son of God" (Mark 1:1).[15] The gospel thus has a thesis: Jesus is messiah and Jesus is Son of God. This joining of Son of God with messiah occurs again in Mark 14:61.

Mark 1:11 concludes the tersely narrated scene of Jesus' baptism by John at the beginning of his public ministry. After his baptism Jesus sees the Spirit descend upon him and hears the voice from heaven: "Thou art my beloved Son; with thee I am well pleased." This declaration is modeled upon Psalm 2:7 where, to the newly enthroned king of Israel, God says: "You are my Son, today I have begotten you." But the king is representative of the nation, and a more fundamental Jewish usage of Son of God describes the nation Israel as God's chosen people. Jesus is thus characterized as the one in whom Israel's sonship is being realized. Jesus is a beloved son; he has a unique status. God delights in him because of his obedience to the divine will. The scene depicts Jesus as the one uniquely representing the obedience to God's will to which all Israel is being called by John.[16]

Twice in the course of Jesus' exorcisms Mark has the evil spirits recognize Jesus' true identity. In crying out they say: "You are the Son of God" (Mark 3:11), and they address Jesus as "Son of the Most High God" (Mark 5:7). But the story of Jesus' transfiguration (Mark 9:2-8) is a more significant text as elements of the story accrue to the connotation of Son of God. On the mountain before Peter, James, and John, Jesus' garments became glistening and intensely white, thus reflecting God's glory. Two of Israel's most important religious figures appear in testimony to him. And, finally, God's presence makes itself felt in a cloud from which God speaks: "This is my beloved Son; listen to him" (Mark 9:7). Jesus' authority, already established at his baptism in Mark 1:11, is enhanced by further manifestations of God's presence to him and by the religious lineage he continues.[17]

During the course of the passion narrative, Mark has Jesus being led before the high priest: "and all the chief priests and the elders and the scribes were assembled" (Mark 14:53). During this interrogation the high

15. Morna D. Hooker, *The Gospel According to Saint Mark* (London: A & C Black, 1991), 33–34. Although the phrase "the Son of God" is missing from a few manuscripts, and may have been added or accidentally dropped, the collocation of Jesus as messiah and Son of God reflects accurately Mark's thought. Ibid., 34.

16. Hooker, *Saint Mark*, 44–48.

17. Hooker, *Saint Mark*, 216–18.

priest stood up and asked Jesus directly: "Are you the Christ, the Son of the Blessed?" (Mark 14:61) Here the linkage between being messiah and Son of God is explicit. Son of God or the Blessed is used "in order to fill out the meaning of the term 'Christ'. For Mark, however, the phrase 'the Son of God' was itself a title—indeed, the title which best expressed Jesus' identity—and he uses it here as though it were equivalent to 'Christ'. In this way he is able to link his belief that Jesus was the Jewish messiah with the confession that he was the Son of God. . . ."[18] But what does this say about the status of the Son of God, since messiahship was a human office? In the context of the question of the high priest, Son of God "connotes divine appointment rather than divine nature."[19]

Finally, at the end of his life, indeed, the moment after Jesus dies on the cross, Mark has the centurion, who stood facing Jesus, exclaim: "Truly this man was the Son of God" (Mark 15:39). It is generally agreed that the sense of "Son of God" should be read through the intentionality of Mark and not the centurion. One thing is certain, Mark closes Jesus' life with the same designation found in the "title" and in the inauguration of Jesus' ministry at his baptism. The title thus embraces the whole of Mark's presentation of Jesus' life. In sum, Jesus was Son of God, and for Mark this means one specially chosen and loved by God, designated to be messiah, filled with God's presence and power as Spirit, which the evil spirits readily recognize, and thus endowed with final authority in the tradition, superseding Moses and introduced by Elijah as was expected. Despite his suffering and death, Jesus was the Son of God. Jesus shared in God's power which was present to him and worked through him. But messiahship defines Jesus' status as Son of God in functional rather than metaphysical categories. It should not be construed in the sense it gained by the time of the patristic christological debates. In the end, one cannot say exactly everything that Son of God entails in Mark, but at least it means "a unique relation to God."[20]

How may a Son of God christology such as Mark's be appropriated today? Although this christology reflects a faith already in place, one can recognize in it a structure that parallels the way people might begin to appreciate Jesus in our own time. The faith behind the christology is committed to the proposition that God acted in Jesus, that Jesus' life and the impact it had were events in which God was present, active, and encoun-

---

18. Hooker, *Saint Mark*, 360.

19. Robert H. Gundry, *Mark: A Commentary on His Apology for the Cross* (Grand Rapids: Eerdmans, 1993), 909.

20. Gundry, *Mark*, 975. One should also be attentive to the accrued sense of Son of God that comes from the whole gospel of Mark mentioned earlier. Mark communicates clearly that God was present to and at work in Jesus' "exorcisms, miraculous healings, nature miracles, magnetic attraction of crowds, predictive ability, overpowering authority in teaching, irresistible skill in debate, exercise of divine prerogative of forgiving sins, dying to the accompaniment of supernatural events, and being raised from the dead. . . ." Ibid., 34.

tered. The language of Son of God indicates that Jesus is designated as God's agent; messiah further specifies this agency. People experienced or encountered God in Jesus. This experience overflows the person of Jesus, and the title Son of God draws its meaning from the experience that Jesus is empowered by God's *shekinah* or presence or dynamic power. The works of Jesus show the Son of God to be an agent in the sense of a medium of God; the title reflects the experience of God at work in Jesus.

Since not only Mark but all of the synoptics are centered on Jesus, this christology has Jesus of Nazareth as its focal point. Mark knows that Jesus is risen and exalted, but his christology begins with the human being Jesus. This Son of God christology, as distinct from others, is a two-stage christology; there is no mention of pre-existence in the understanding of Jesus as Son of God.[21]

The soteriology lying behind Mark's Son of God christology is more clearly tied to the idea that Jesus was the Son of Man. Two key texts are enough to indicate the line of thought here. The first occurs as Jesus instructs the twelve about serving others. He holds himself as an example by saying: "For the Son of man also came not to be served but to serve, and to give his life as a ransom for many" (Mark 10:45). This prediction of Jesus' death contains a very generalized account of how Jesus' death was effective. "In some mysterious way, which is not spelt out, the sufferings of one man are used by God to bring benefit to others."[22] And, second, to the pointed question of the high priest concerning Jesus as "Christ, the Son of the Blessed" which was reviewed earlier, the next verse contains Jesus' response: "I am; and you will see the Son of man sitting at the right hand of Power, and coming with the clouds of heaven" (Mark 14:62). Here Mark identifies Jesus with the Son of man from Daniel 7:13: in contrast to his present situation of humiliation and suffering, Jesus will be vindicated. The crucifixion notwithstanding, Jesus shares in the power and glory of God. This vision is generalized in Mark 8:38 and 13:26 when the Son of man comes in glory and final justice.[23]

Can such a christology be appropriated and stimulate a realistic Christian life today? The themes of discipleship and support of the Christian community are major interests in Mark's gospel. Beneath these

---

21. According to Dunn, "there was no real evidence in the earliest Jesus-tradition of what could fairly be called a consciousness of divinity, a consciousness of a sonship rooted in pre-existent relationship to God." Only in John's gospel does a "personal pre-existence fully emerge, of Jesus as the divine Son of God before the world began sent into the world by the Father. . . ." Dunn, *Christology in the Making*, 60, 61.

22. Hooker, *Saint Mark*, 249. Hooker is not quick to read this verse in terms of Isaiah 53. It may be related to other traditions but, in any case, it is not fully clear how the ransom works.

23. Hooker, *Saint Mark*, 361–62; Gundry, *Mark*, 886–87. Richard, in *Jesus: One and Many*, 126–28, synopsizes Mark's christology around three concepts, cautioning that it is not quite this neat: Jesus is messiah in virtue of his ministry, Son of God in virtue of his resurrection, and Son of man in virtue of his future coming in glory.

religious symbols from another age lie a concern that the community not be discouraged, but that it know that Jesus is risen, and that he has gone before, ahead of his disciples (Mark 16:7). In the end the Christian community of disciples, even in these dark days while Jesus is absent,[24] has grounds for hope in final vindication and justice. Once again, this particular Son of God christology leads back to basic options in human existence. This christology counsels hope in the meaning, coherence, and justice of reality on the basis of its faith in Jesus as a representation and agent of God. This christology responds to situations in which God seems absent and negativity seems to have the upper hand; it looks toward the future to give meaning to the present.

JESUS CHRIST AS EMPOWERED BY THE SPIRIT IN LUKE

I turn now to Spirit christology in Luke. I want to emphasize the limits which both terms impose on this sketch. Spirit christology is only one aspect of Luke's presentation of Jesus Christ, but it is a foundational aspect. Joseph Fitzmyer counts fourteen distinct titles of Jesus used by Luke, and, when they are all predicated of the same person, their meanings begin to qualify each other.[25] Luke's gospel is only one representative of Spirit christology in the New Testament, but it is a major one. Paul and John contain developed, nuanced, and complex languages of the Spirit with regard to Jesus during his lifetime and as resurrected. Luke's Spirit christology is also complex, because it cuts across the titles of Jesus and Luke's view of Jesus' salvific work. But despite this extension and wealth of meaning, one can get an idea of Luke's Spirit christology adequate for my purpose from a series of texts representing the period of Jesus in the gospel and the period of the church in Acts. By Spirit or Holy Spirit Luke assumes the meaning from Jewish tradition: "God's active, creative, or prophetic presence to God's world or God's people."[26]

The first text, from the infancy narratives, is a crucial element of the annunciation story. After the angel announces to Mary that she will bear a son, and Mary wonders how, the angel says to her: "The Holy Spirit will come upon you, and the power of the Most High will overshadow you; therefore the child to be born will be called holy, the Son of God" (Luke 1:35). In Luke's view, then, God as Spirit was active in the very coming into existence of Jesus. The verbs "coming upon" and "overshadowing" are vague, figurative terms; there is no question of physical begetting here.

---

24. Schillebeeckx, *Jesus*, 417–23, analyzes the idea in Mark's christology that Jesus' being exalted means that he is absent from history and from the Christian community until his return in the end-time.

25. These are Messiah or Christ, Lord, Savior, Son of God, Son of Man, God's Servant, Prophet, King, Son of David, Leader, Holy One, Righteous One, Judge, Teacher. See Joseph A. Fitzmyer, *The Gospel According to Luke: Introduction, Translation, and Notes* (Garden City, N.Y.: Doubleday, 1981, 1985), 197–219.

26. Fitzmyer, *Luke*, 228; also 350, 484.

But at the same time, God and not Joseph is presented as the agent of Jesus' conception. With this move Luke is, as it were, moving back Jesus' sonship from his resurrection (Rom 1:3-4) and his baptism to his very conception. Moreover, the idea of Son of God is given a new meaning associated with God's direct action.[27]

We move now to the Lucan account of Jesus' baptism, which Luke borrows from Mark, but renders distinctively his own. After Jesus was baptized and was praying, heaven opened "and the Holy Spirit descended upon him in bodily form, as a dove, and a voice came from heaven, 'Thou art my beloved Son; with thee I am well pleased'" (Luke 3:22). With the phrase, "in bodily form," Luke calls attention to the descent of the Spirit implying its importance. That importance lies in its being God's anointing of Jesus for his mission. In Acts, Luke has Peter relate "how God anointed Jesus of Nazareth with the Holy Spirit and with power; how he went about doing good and healing all that were oppressed by the devil, for God was with him" (Acts 10:38). The verse is almost a self-contained christology that comments on Jesus' baptism. The Holy Spirit is God's own power; Jesus' ministry of healing and exorcism is made possible by God's being with and working within him. Thus the promise in Isaiah 42:1, that God would bestow the Spirit on God's servant, is fulfilled: "Behold my servant, whom I uphold, my chosen, in whom my soul delights; I have put my Spirit upon him, he will bring forth justice to the nations." In this way the anointing at Jesus' baptism equips Jesus with God's power for his ministry. What is going on here is more than the appointment of a king.[28]

According to Luke, after his baptism Jesus was "full of the Holy Spirit" (Luke 4:1), and after his temptation in the wilderness, he began his ministry "in the power of the Spirit" (Luke 4:14). This active presence of God gives authority to his teaching, and bestows the power to do wondrous good works, as seen in the next two texts.

The first full account of an incident in Jesus' ministry deals with his returning to Nazareth, reading in the synagogue, and commenting on the text from Isaiah: "The Spirit of the Lord is upon me, because he has anointed me to preach good news to the poor. He has sent me to proclaim release to the captives and recovering of sight to the blind, to set at liberty those who are oppressed, to proclaim the acceptable year of the Lord" (Luke 4:18-19). With a dramatic turn, Luke has Jesus sit and draw to himself the absolute attention of those present. He speaks: "Today this scripture has been fulfilled in your hearing" (Luke 4:21). This amounts to a powerful and comprehensive declaration by Luke. In stunningly direct terms Luke's statement says "the fulfillment of Scripture is to be found in

---

27. I. Howard Marshall, *The Gospel of Luke: A Commentary on the Greek Text* (Exeter: Paternoster Press, 1978), 70–71; Fitzmyer, *Luke*, 337–40.

28. Marshall, *The Gospel of Luke*, 150, 154; Fitzmyer, *Luke*, 481–82.

the person of Jesus himself, who has been anointed with the Spirit and appears as the eschatological prophet—a figure who is to be identified with the Messiah and the Servant of Yahweh."[29]

We move to a saying that comes from the account of the "Beelzebul Controversy" (Luke 11:14-23). Here God as Spirit enables Jesus to act with power. After performing an exorcism, someone says that Jesus "'casts out demons by Beelzebul, the prince of demons'" (Luke 11:15). Jesus responds with a taut logic: his power cannot be of Satan, for then Satan would be destroying himself. The alternative is the positive power of God. Signs do not need further signs. "But if it is by the finger of God that I cast out demons, then the kingdom of God has come upon you" (Luke 11:20). The "finger of God" is God's power, the equivalent of the Spirit of God (Exod 8:19). This generally recognized authentic saying declares that the kingdom of God is arriving now, in Jesus' very works. Where Satan's power is overcome, there is the kingdom of God.[30]

I conclude with a series of texts from Acts which, when presented together as a narrative, communicate the connection between the risen and exalted Jesus and God as Spirit. First, before he ascends, the risen Jesus promises the bestowal of the Spirit: "'But you shall receive power when the Holy Spirit has come upon you; and you shall be my witnesses in Jerusalem and in all Judea and Samaria and to the end of the earth'" (Acts 1:8). This promise is fulfilled at Pentecost when "they were all filled with the Holy Spirit and began to speak in other tongues, as the Spirit gave them utterance" (Acts 2:4).[31] In the speech which follows, Peter comments on what has happened by citing the prophet Joel: "And in the last days it shall be, God declares, that I will pour out my Spirit upon all flesh . . ." (Acts 2:17ff.; Joel 2:28-32). The sending of the Spirit is the eschatological event beginning the new time preparatory to the day of the Lord. The position of Jesus Christ in this economy is also stated by Peter: "Being therefore exalted at the right hand of God, and having received from the Father the promise of the Holy Spirit, he has poured out this which you see and hear" (Acts 2:33). Jesus Christ risen and exalted has been made Lord and messiah, and is now the one who pours out the Spirit.[32]

An appreciation of this christology for today's understanding might begin by noticing how it remains close to the career of the historical person Jesus. This Spirit christology is a narrative christology; the focus remains on Jesus of Nazareth and his ministry of the kingdom of God. It begins with his conception by the overshadowing, creative presence of God as Spirit, so that Jesus is conceived and born God's Son. This chris-

---

29. Marshall, *The Gospel of Luke*, 178.

30. Marshall, *The Gospel of Luke*, 471, 475–76.

31. Luke Timothy Johnson, *The Acts of the Apostles* (Collegeville, Minn.: Liturgical Press, 1992), 42.

32. Johnson, *Acts*, 55.

tology follows his ministry from its inauguration in the Spirit through to its end in exaltation. And the narrative continues in the history of the church where the exalted Jesus Christ is now the Lord of the age of the Spirit. This is a two-stage christology: it begins with Jesus coming into existence on earth, and it ends with Jesus' exalted reign.[33] In Lucan theology the question of Jesus' pre-existence or incarnation is never raised.[34]

A crucial element in any appreciation of this christology lies in an understanding of the symbol "Spirit." The symbol has its roots in a metaphor that characterizes God as immanent in the world; it points to the visible power and effects of God's invisible presence. As Dunn puts it, "on this understanding, Spirit of God is in no sense distinct from God, but is simply the power of God, God himself acting powerfully in nature and upon human beings."[35] The figurative, symbolic character of such terms as Spirit, Wisdom, Glory of God, Finger of God, Word of God is crucial for grasping the structure of christology generally.

In this case, the structure is found in the focus on Jesus and the recognition of God's presence and action in him symbolized as Spirit. Jesus was a person in whom was recognized the presence, power, and action of God in such a measure that Jesus was conceived as God's agent; God acted in history in and through him. At this point commentators become explicit in pointing out that, although it involves more than mere adoption, this is still a "low" christology.[36] This is so when measured against the background of other specific conceptions of Jesus' divinity. For example, Fitzmyer notes that Jesus' divine conception "does not yet carry the later connotations of physical or metaphysical sonship or identity of substance associated with the later Nicene or Constantinopolitan creeds."[37] It is also less explicit than the pre-existence, descent, and incarnational christology found in John. But one may also insist on transcendent characteristics

---

33. "In this two-stage Spirit christology we have a clear parallel with the early (pre-Johannine) Son of God christology and with the Adam christology. In each case the pre-resurrection stage *cannot* be expressed in terms of incarnation because only with his resurrecting does Jesus become Son of God (in power), last Adam, life-giving Spirit." Dunn, *Christology in the Making*, 161.

34. Fitzmyer, *Luke*, 197. These two stages Fitzmyer characterizes as four: 1) the first phase begins with Jesus' conception and lasts until his appearance in the desert for baptism; 2) the second is from his baptism to the ascension; 3) the third is from the ascension to the parousia; 4) the fourth is the parousia. Ibid.

35. Dunn, *Christology in the Making*, 133. In the intertestamental period, one finds personifications of Spirit when Spirit becomes associated or identified with Wisdom. But in Dunn's view, all these instances are not other than figurative language to express God's immanence and transcendence at the same time. Ibid., 134–35.

36. "The unusual or virginal conception of Jesus in Luke indicates not a higher christology (as in Matthew) but meets the requirements of Hellenistic biography where heroes are routinely attributed divine origins or unusual births announced by prophetic omens." Richard, *Jesus: One and Many*, 178.

37. Fitzmyer, *Luke*, 207.

exhibited by the human being Jesus.[38] In the end, the structure of this christology leaves the ontological status of Jesus open, and largely a function of the imagination and the concepts one brings to the task of understanding the presence and activity of God as Spirit in Jesus' life.

The theory of salvation that is incorporated in this Spirit christology is best represented by the very term "salvation." "'Salvation' denotes the deliverance of human beings from evil, physical, moral, political, or cataclysmic. It connotes a victory, a rescue of them from a state of negation and a restoration to wholeness or integrity."[39] This broad concept of salvation allows one to incorporate into it analogously the many ways in which Jesus is the agent of salvation both during his historical life and from his position as the exalted one. Jesus' offer of forgiveness of sin is salvation, and Jesus' exorcism, healing, and welcoming of excluded people is salvation. In other words, Jesus' works for the integrity and humanization of people at all levels of their human existence in this world are part of God's salvation mediated by Jesus. Jesus is also savior from his position of exaltation as the one who pours out God's saving Spirit. "Indeed, Jesus' whole life is considered redemptive by Luke, for it is this agent of God who has made possible universal salvation in the community of believers through the power of the Spirit."[40] Today, Jesus provides a way of pointing to the saving character of God's power of salvation present in human life and history. Salvation lies in the many effects of God's being present to human existence, and Jesus' life and resurrection reveal them.[41] Finally, the Christian life that is opened up by this christology is best characterized as discipleship. The center of attention is Jesus of Nazareth, his active life, animated by God as Spirit, directed toward the goal of the kingdom of God. This narrative christology is easily converted into the spirituality of an imitation of Christ. Discipleship engages human freedom; the kingdom of God provides a goal; the experience of grace empowers and

---

38. Fitzmyer lists five such characteristics: 1) virginal conception by the power of the Spirit; 2) Spirit-empowered ministry; 3) special relation to the Father; 4) resurrection from death; 5) exaltation. *Luke*, 196.

39. Fitzmyer, *Luke*, 222. Fitzmyer sums up the idea of salvation in Luke's christology, as distinct from but including his Spirit christology, in four effects of the Christ event: 1) salvation from sin, alienation from God, and eternal damnation; 2) forgiveness of sin; 3) the peace of the messianic kingdom; 4) eternal life in resurrection. Ibid., 221–26.

40. Richard, *Jesus: One and Many*, 185.

41. Relative to Lucan christology more generally, it is sometimes said that Jesus' death has little salvific significance. But Fitzmyer points to texts that clearly speak of forgiveness of sin on the basis of Jesus' suffering, even though the resurrection assumes greater importance. Fitzmyer, *Luke*, 219–21. And Jerome Neyrey detects a structure similar to that of Paul's Last Adam christology forming an implicit framework of the passion narratives. This would make the narrative of Jesus' obedience unto death leading to resurrection a significant element in the Lucan story of Jesus. Jerome Neyrey, *The Passion According to Luke: A Redaction Study of Luke's Soteriology* (New York: Paulist Press, 1985), 184–92.

generates courage; resurrection offers hope for the course of human existence. Finally, because this is a two-stage christology, there is a parallelism between Jesus' life and the life of other human beings, so that Jesus is imitable.

JESUS CHRIST AS THE WISDOM OF GOD

Wisdom christology is often considered a bridge to a fully three-stage, incarnational understanding of a pre-existent Jesus Christ. I have chosen three texts to illustrate this christology, although I shall do little more than refer to these texts. I am less interested in exegetical detail, which is quite varied, and more interested in how wisdom christology may have developed. The texts are Philippians 2:6-11, Colossians 1:15-20, and Matthew 11:25-30.[42] The premise here is that there was an active wisdom tradition in place, and it provided a language to shape the experience and interpretation of Jesus of Nazareth by his followers.[43]

The first example is the hymn to a descending, self-humbling, a raised and exalted Jesus Christ in Philippians 2. I cite the first two verses of this well-known passage referring to Jesus Christ:

(6) who, though he was in the form of God, did not count equality with God a thing to be grasped, (7) but emptied himself, taking the likeness of men.

The key to the meaning of this passage is usually taken to rest in the interpretation of "in the form of God." We have already seen that some exegetes relate this phrase to the creation of human existence in the "image of God" in Genesis, and thus read this passage within the context of Paul's last Adam christology.[44] The possibility of the idea of the pre-existence of Christ was generated by Jewish symbolisms or speculations of divine agents working in the world.[45] Some read a pre-existence christology on the basis of an analysis of the words of the text.[46] Those who read a wisdom christology in this hymn do so on the basis of the personification of wisdom that was depicted as a divine companion of God (Prov 8:22-31).

---

42. Other texts are 1 Cor 8:6; 1 Tim 3:16; Heb 1:3-4; 1 Pet 1:19-21, 2:21-25, 3:18-22.

43. See Diane Jacobson, "What Is Wisdom? Who Is She?" *Word and World*, 7 (1987), 241–44, for a definition of the wisdom tradition. Two accounts which largely agree on the development of wisdom christology are those of Dunn, *Christology in the Making*, 163ff, and Elizabeth A. Johnson, "Jesus, The Wisdom of God: A Biblical Basis for Non-Androcentric Christology," *Ephemerides Theologicae Lovanienses*, 61 (1985), 261–94.

44. Peter T. O'Brien, in *The Epistle to the Philippians: A Commentary on the Greek Text* (Grand Rapids: Eerdmans, 1991), 263–68, reviews the arguments supporting Last Adam and pre-existence interpretations.

45. Byrne, "Christ's Pre-Existence in Pauline Soteriology," 312–13.

46. For example, I. Howard Marshall, *The Epistle to the Philippians* (London: Epworth Press, 1991), 50.

They also note the fundamental pattern of affliction and salvation, suffering and exaltation, which corresponds to the structure of the hymn, and which the "righteous one" undergoes in the wisdom tradition.[47] In direct contrast to a low christology, many see this hymn as strictly incarnational. It speaks about the "real humiliation of the incarnation and the cross of the one who is himself God."[48] "The choice being described in Philippians 2 is the choice to take on human flesh, a choice only a pre-existent one could make."[49] Although this reading in terms of a descent christology is gaining wider acceptance, it must still be considered disputed.

The second and clearer example of a wisdom christology is the hymn in Colossians 1:15-20, of which the first three verses are striking:

(15) He is the image of the invisible God, the first-born of all creation; (16) for in him all things were created, in heaven and on earth, visible and invisible, whether thrones or dominations or principalities or authorities—all things were created through him and for him. (17) He is before all things, and in him all things hold together.

The background of this hymn is the wisdom tradition, and in it Jesus Christ is identified with Wisdom.[50] Some of the phrases pick up the very language of personified wisdom, and, on the assumption of the vibrant character of this tradition in first-century Palestine, would have been recognized immediately. "The first-born of all creation" echoes "The Lord created me at the beginning of his work" (Prov 8:22), and personified wisdom saying of herself: "From eternity, in the beginning, he created me" (Sir 24:9). The phrase "in him all things were created" parallels these wisdom texts: "The Lord by wisdom founded the earth" (Prov 3:19), and wisdom is "an associate in God's works" (Wis: 8:4), and the "fashioner of what exists" (Wis 8:6). Those who prayed the psalms knew that "In wisdom thou [God] made all [creatures]" (Ps 104:24). The basic teaching of wisdom literature is that all things are held together in and by God's wisdom. "If 'in the beginning God created heaven and earth', Christ, as the Wisdom of God, is the beginning 'in' whom all things were created."[51]

---

47. "Then the righteous man will stand with great confidence in the presence of those who have afflicted him, and those who make light of his labors" (Wis 5:1). See Wis 3:1-4, 5:15-16. There are references to other traditions as well in the hymn, and no interpretation of this passage is undisputed.

48. O'Brien, *Philippians*, 252.

49. Witherington, *Jesus the Sage*, 263, offers a thoroughgoing wisdom interpretation of the hymn. Also arguing to the pre-existent being of Christ on the basis of pre-temporal choices is Byrne, "Christ's Pre-Existence in Pauline Soteriology," 314–20.

50. James D. G. Dunn, *The Epistles to the Colossians and to Philemon: A Commentary on the Greek Text* (Grand Rapids: Eerdmans, 1996), 88–89; Kuschel, *Born Before All Time?*, 332–33.

51. F. F. Bruce, *Paul: Apostle of the Free Spirit* (Exeter: Paternoster Press, 1977, 1980), 419. This identification of Jesus Christ with God's wisdom personified allows exegetes

Also, the idea of "the fullness of God" (v. 19) dwelling in Jesus fits neatly with both wisdom and Spirit christologies.[52] The significance of these hymns is that they seem to reflect an early pre-Pauline "high" christology or, at least, high poetic christological language.[53]

Wisdom christology also found its way into the gospel of Matthew. Matthew 11:25-30 is a collection of three sayings that relate to the theme of revelation and imply a thematic background of wisdom language. The first has Jesus thanking his Father for hiding "these things" from the wise and revealing them to babies (vv. 25-26). It echoes thanksgiving to God in Sirach 51:1-2. The second is a saying of Jesus that only the Father knows the Son and only the Son the Father, "and any one to whom the Son chooses to reveal him" (v. 27). Here Jesus is presented as "the Son of God whose characteristics of intimacy with the Father are modeled in part on the way Wisdom and the Father are described in earlier sapiential literature."[54] The third puts in Jesus' mouth the language of Wisdom herself inviting those who are burdened to share the light yoke of Wisdom in Sirach 51:23, 26-27. The christological message here is clear: "More than a wisdom teacher (though he is that), Jesus is 'the Son' of 'the Father.' Whoever knows him knows the Father, which is the highest form of wisdom."[55]

What is happening in the development of this wisdom christology is evident: "What Judaism said of Sophia, Christian hymn-makers and epistle writers now came to say of Jesus."[56] And what do these assertions mean? On the one hand, some exegetes plainly regard these texts as representing a pre-existent Jesus Christ. But, on the other hand, some exegetes find that these texts and their parallels fall far short of that. James Dunn, for example, recognizes that in his wisdom christology Paul wanted to show that Jesus is the new and exhaustive embodiment of divine wisdom. He admits that Matthew transcends his source Q, where Jesus is a messenger of wisdom, and identifies Jesus with wisdom. It is clear that Jesus is being equated with the personification of God's wisdom in the hymns like that of Colossians. Moreover, this metaphorical language of personi-

---

to read Col 1:16 as depicting "the agency of the preincarnate Christ in the work of creation." Murray J. Harris, *Colossians and Philemon, Exegetical Guide to the Greek New Testament* (Grand Rapids: Eerdmans, 1991), 50.

52. Dunn, *Colossians*, 99–100.

53. Witherington, *Jesus the Sage*, 249.

54. Witherington, *Jesus the Sage*, 350. See Johnson, "Jesus, the Wisdom of God," 282.

55. Daniel J. Harrington, *The Gospel of Matthew* (Collegeville, Minn.: Liturgical Press, 1991), 170. An even stronger assertion is the following: "11:25-30 is a capsule summary of the message of the entire gospel. In this passage, Jesus reveals that he is the revealer. That is, he reveals that, as the meek and humble Son of the Father, he fulfils the calling of Israel, embodying in his own person Torah and Wisdom and thus making known the perfect will of God." W. D. Davies and Dale C. Allison, *A Critical and Exegetical Commentary on the Gospel According to Saint Matthew* (Edinburgh: T & T Clark, 1991), 296.

56. Johnson, "Jesus, the Wisdom of God," 261.

fication finally led to a christology in which Jesus is different in kind from other mediations of God, and enjoys a metaphysically divine status of personal pre-existence. But Dunn fails to find in the Jewish tradition prior to Jesus any consideration of wisdom as a hypostasis or divine being; this would not fit with Jewish monotheism. Wisdom language remains figurative personification.[57] It is thus at least ambiguous that pre-existence represents the intention of these wisdom christologies, because one cannot really show that this is more than the figurative language of metaphor and personification.[58] Is there a way out of this impasse?

What perhaps cannot be resolved historically, in terms of the intentionality of authors, can be sorted out hermeneutically, in terms of making sense of wisdom christology in our own culture.[59] I begin by addressing the question of the connection of these wisdom christologies with Jesus of Nazareth. The three texts used to illustrate wisdom christology have Jesus as their imagined referent. In other words, they are about and refer to Jesus of Nazareth. This is obvious in the case of Matthew's gospel. But it is no less clear in the two hymns which speak of Jesus' obedience in his suffering and death and resurrection. In Philippians, the text points to the one who was born: "And being found in human form he humbled himself and became obedient unto death, even death on a cross" (Phil 2:8). This is Jesus. Colossians too refers to Jesus as "the first-born from the dead" (Col 1:18). The fullness of God was pleased to dwell in Jesus: the reference is to the one who died on the cross (Col 1:19-20). A first move for interpreting these texts, then, is to bind their meaning to Jesus as to their primary referent. Ideas of "pre-existence" are to be read as extrapolations that spring from an experience of Jesus, and they have their basis in him.

A second question concerns the concept of salvation that is contained in wisdom christology. One notices immediately a high correlation between these wisdom christologies and the theme of revelation. The premise for this analysis is that God was encountered in Jesus. In wisdom christology the character of that encounter is frequently symbolized in terms of God being revealed. The Son knows the Father and reveals him (Matt 11:27). The hymn in Philippians is largely doxological: "Jesus Christ is Lord, to the glory of God the Father" (Phil 2:11). But in the context of

---

57. Dunn, *Christology in the Making*, 170.

58. Dunn, *Christology in the Making*, 205–12.

59. For example, Kuschel works with the genre of these texts. The consensus is that the Philippians hymn is poetry; it therefore should be interpreted as an imaginative expression of the experience of the early disciples, and not as a discursive, analytic statement. The hymn as a whole does not set out to formulate a pre-existence christology, but to encapsulate the experience of Jesus as risen Lord. *Born Before All Time?*, 258–63. Relative to Colossians, he writes: "the language of this text is poetical and not conceptual" (339). It is to be understood as referring to the dynamic action of Jesus Christ in his role as a revelatory mediator of God to humankind, as one who was animated by God as Spirit and who incarnated God as Wisdom. Ibid., 333–34.

the larger text of Philippians, the reason for citing the hymn is to propose a model for the attitudes that should govern the life of the Christian community. In Jesus Christ is revealed the basic pattern of human life relative to God.[60] In Colossians, Jesus "is the image of the invisible God" (Col 1:15). In brief, as the wisdom of God, Jesus reveals both the true nature of human existence and also the nature of God.[61]

The structure of this christology appears in the light of the first two points. Jesus is the new historical medium in whom God is encountered and revealed. The personification borrowed from the language of wisdom should be understood in terms of the structure and logic of the christology. I assume here the view that wisdom or *Sophia* personified is a personification of an attribute of God, and that a personified attribute of God, by metonymy, is reductively a personification of God. In other words, wisdom personified can be traced back to God as the subject of this wisdom, and God's wisdom is not other than God, so that the action of God's wisdom is God acting wisely.[62] I am also assuming with many exegetes that the wisdom tradition constituted a living or current language. Therefore the affirmation that Jesus was "in the form of God" (Phil 2:6) or "the first-born of all creation" (Col 1:15), in whom "all things were created" (Col 1:16), or allowing Jesus to be wisdom by speaking the words of wisdom, are instances of symbolic language in a double sense. In the first instance, because all religious language about transcendent reality is symbolic. In the second, because this is consciously developed language of personification: God or God's wise intelligence is treated figuratively as a person, and Jesus is identified with that intelligence of God because it is manifested in him. Descriptively these assertions are saying that in Jesus is embodied and therefore revealed the very wisdom of very God. One encounters God in Jesus by encountering the consummation of God's wise economy for the world which has been revealed in him.

It is mistaken to read this wisdom language as though it were straightforward descriptive language that told the story of a divine being that descended to become Jesus.[63] To understand this language as descriptive language about a being who is "on the side of the creator in the creator-

---

60. O'Brien, *Philippians*, 262.

61. O'Brien, *Philippians*, 216. Commenting on Phil 2:7, O'Brien says that Jesus manifested the form of God in the form of being a human being; as a human being Jesus reveals what it means to be God.

62. Personified divine attributes were basically vivid ways of speaking of God's own powers and activities. It was standard Jewish linguistic practice to personify a quality of God and to describe it as an agent of God. To conceive Spirit, Wisdom, Word as literal language about entities "is a misunderstanding of this particular type of ancient Jewish religious language." Larry W. Hurtado, *One God, One Lord: Early Christian Devotion and Ancient Jewish Monotheism* (Philadelphia: Fortress Press, 1988), 46. See 41–50.

63. I will deal with the narrative in John 1:1-18 in the next section.

creature distinction"[64] is to misinterpret the kind of language that is being used and its epistemological provenance. These texts are not providing unknowable information about transcendent realities from some secret source of knowledge. The epistemology of these christologies begins from below, with Jesus, and their content is based on the encounter of God in and through Jesus. Their revelatory character in epistemological terms is ascending. To the question about God and what God is like, these texts testify that Jesus mediates an answer. God is encountered in Jesus; God is revealed in Jesus; God is like Jesus; the wisdom of God is made manifest in Jesus; Jesus is the wisdom of God.[65] Jesus himself responds to the questions, what is God's wisdom and where is it found?

Finally, revelation also provides the manner in which this christology can be seen to open up possibilities for Christian life. Christian life should correspond to God's wisdom, the rhythm of life revealed as God's will in nature, to be sure, but now narratively and dramatically for historical life in Jesus of Nazareth. This is what Paul intended when he drew upon the extraordinary and, in some quarters, probably well-known poetic hymn and told the Philippians: "Have this mind among yourselves, which you have in Christ Jesus" (Phil 2:5).

JESUS CHRIST AS THE LOGOS OF GOD

No biblical text has had more influence on the development of christology than the Prologue to John's gospel. Here Jesus Christ is presented as the Logos of God incarnate. I cite only a few of the most relevant verses of John 1:1-18 in order to recall the whole and focus the analysis.

> (1) In the beginning was the Word, and the Word was with God, and the Word was God. (2) He was in the beginning with God; (3) all things were made through him, and without him was not anything made that was made. . . . (14) And the Word became flesh and dwelt among us, full of grace and truth; we have beheld his glory, glory as of the only Son from the Father.

Because of its distinctiveness and importance, not to mention its soaring beauty and transcendence, this text is the subject of continuous, extensive study and debate. Most agree that one can distinguish a hymn, perhaps composed within the Johannine circle,[66] from the final redaction of the gospel. But there is disagreement on some very fundamental issues. Some see the structure of the Prologue consisting in a long chiasm that

---

64. Witherington, *Jesus the Sage*, 269.

65. Jesus is the historical symbol through which Christian religious faith experience is mediated. Without some such theory, one cannot transcend naive revelational positivism.

66. Raymond E. Brown, *The Gospel According to John* (Garden City, N.Y.: Doubleday, 1966), 19–20.

"descends" and then "ascends."[67] Others see it as consisting in a three-part summary of the history of salvation.[68] Still others isolate the original hymn as consisting in four strophes.[69] The precise subject matter is also debated: some see the hymn directed toward Logos or Sophia, who then becomes incarnate (v. 14); others read it from beginning to end as referring to the Word incarnate in Jesus; still others want to hold both at the same time.[70] The background or context for reading the hymn is also disputed. All agree that there are strong parallels with the wisdom tradition. A comparison with the hymns in Philippians and Colossians already considered will show analogous patterns of development from being with God, descent into the world, and ascent to God's sphere. But are the parallels with the wisdom tradition enough to sustain a hymn about *Logos*? Some striking parallels with the thought of Philo, for example, suggest a broader background that includes Hellenistic influences for reading this christology.[71] This raises questions of how such a Greek influence was brought to bear. Despite these and other differences of expert interpretation, however, a brief commentary on the verses cited can show the distinctiveness of the christology contained in this hymn.

On one reading, the opening verses are about the Logos:[72] in the beginning, at the dawn of creation, the Logos simply was. This Logos appears to be distinct from God because it was with God or in God's presence. This Logos shared the character of God, for it was "God," but not the Father nor Yahweh, and yet without there being two Gods. This Logos, in the beginning, was the agent of God's creating. How did the Logos cause creation? There are several parallels from Jewish scripture. Creation is by the word of God: "And God said" (Gen 1:3). "By the word of the Lord the heavens were made" (Ps 33:6). God is addressed as the one "who hast made all things by thy word" (Wis 9:1). But the word also causes by being the model or exemplar of reality, for in many respects the Logos here per-

---

67. Neal M. Flanagan, *The Gospel According to John and the Johannine Epistles* (Collegeville, Minn.: Liturgical Press, 1983), 6–8.

68. Thomas L. Brodie, *The Gospel According to John: A Literary and Theological Commentary* (New York: Oxford University Press, 1993), 136–47.

69. For example, George R. Beasley-Murray, *John* (Dallas: Word Books, 1987), 4-5. Also Brown, *John*, 1–3.

70. As, for example, John Ashton, in "The Transformation of Wisdom," *Studying John: Approaches to the Fourth Gospel* (Oxford: Clarendon Press, 1994), 5–35.

71. For example, Brown minimizes the influence of Hellenistic literature in general and Philo in particular on the Prologue. Brown, *John*, lvii–lviii, 519–20. But a good case for considering Philo and "the tradition of Hellenistic Jewish biblical interpretation and speculation" as part of the background for reading the Prologue is made by Thomas H. Tobin, "The Prologue of John and Hellenistic Jewish Speculation," *Catholic Biblical Quarterly*, 52 (1990), 252–69.

72. The central figure of the Prologue is the Logos, and Logos does not appear as a christological title in the gospel. Brown, *John*, 19. The counter view: "As the Gospel is wholly concerned with Jesus, so the prologue is wholly taken up with him." Beasley-Murray, *John*, 5.

forms the same functions as Sophia. One also finds close parallels with Philo's commentary on creation in Genesis: the Word of God is the agent of God by whom the universe came into being.[73] Dunn is convinced that Logos in Philo is not a distinct or real being acting as an intermediary of God, but a metaphor for God's reaching out to the world.[74] Despite that, the early verses of the Prologue give an impression of just such a person-ification become individualized or hypostatized.

We jump forward to verse 14 which reaches back to verse 1 by inclu-sion: (v. 1) the Word *was*, (v. 14) the Word *became*; (v. 1) the Word was *with God*, (v. 14) the Word dwells *among us*; (v. 1) the Word was *God*, (v. 14) the Word became *flesh*.[75] The poetic device brings out quite forcefully that the point is incarnation. All three contrasts reinforce the central and dramatic essence of this christology, that the Sophia-Logos of God has become vis-ible. For the term "flesh" is straightforward and direct; it emphasizes the materiality of human existence, and that God's revealing Logos is really available: "we have beheld his glory" (v. 14). The Logos does not enter into or take on flesh, but "became" flesh: another touch of startling realism that underlines incarnation. The creative Word which came to the prophets has now become personal in Jesus. Jesus is therefore divine Sophia-Logos, pre-existent, but now come among human beings.[76] Jesus Christ is therefore the mediator, for this is the character of the Logos in creation. But by incar-nation Jesus Christ becomes the mediator of a new creation.[77]

Despite its parallelism with other wisdom christologies, Dunn believes that the christology of the Prologue is new and distinctive. The writer is the first "to conceive clearly the personal pre-existence of the Logos-Son and to present it as a fundamental part of his message."[78] In other words, this is the first three-stage, incarnational christology in which Jesus Christ is identified as one who pre-existed as a personal Logos-Sophia, and who as one continuous subject became a human being. The development was made possible, first of all, by the wisdom christologies which projected Jesus back into the sphere of God's intelligence and wisdom as one who was foreknown and planned. In John, personified wisdom language is combined with Son of God language, with the result that Sophia-Logos began to be thought of in realistic, individual personal terms.[79] These

---

73. Tobin, "The Prologue of John," 257–58.

74. Dunn, *The Making of Christology*, 220–30.

75. Brown, *John*, 31.

76. Brown, *John*, 524.

77. Beasley-Murray, *John*, 16.

78. Dunn, *Making of Christology*, 249.

79. Dunn, *Making of Christology*, 245. A three-stage Logos christology is intrinsically ambiguous because, by incarnation, the Logos became Jesus Christ. Therefore, the one who is Jesus Christ pre-existed. Yet it is clear that the human nature and bodily exis-tence of Jesus did not pre-exist. For this reason the phrase "the pre-existence of Jesus Christ" appears to be intrinsically monophysitic. A positive constructive Logos chris-tology today must deal with this issue.

developments were aided by cultural conditions that included speculation about heavenly beings. Whether or not Dunn's time-table or his interpretation of wisdom hymns is correct, it does seem that the Johannine
hymn both resembles the other wisdom christologies and transcends them
in the direction of an explicit statement of the incarnation of an hypostatized being. "The prologue of the Fourth Gospel is the fullest and clearest
statement of incarnational christology in the New Testament."[80]

Moving now to a reflective analysis of this christology, how may one
understand its structure, relationship to Jesus, and underlying soteriology? The Logos christology of John's Prologue is closely related to wisdom christologies, and its logic is an imaginative extrapolation from
wisdom language. Wisdom christologies find their basis in the encounter
of God in Jesus, and they still have Jesus as their point of departure and
reference point. Wisdom language, referring to God as reflected in God's
wise and all-encompassing plan of reality, points to the presence of God,
and even the power of God, within Jesus. Jesus embodies God's wisdom.
The Logos christology of the Prologue, although in many respects continuous with wisdom language, breaks out of this logic.[81] Personified wisdom is now hypostatized as Logos and assigned its own distinctive
existence. The Sophia-Word that was a symbol for God, and God present
to Jesus illumining his life, now becomes a subject, distinct from God, and
yet of and "with" God. Unlike Wisdom in Colossians 1:15-20, which
closely resembles the literary personification exhibited in Proverbs 8:22-
31, the Word in John's Prologue assumes the character of an independent
subject and actor on earth. This pre-existent subject is the same continuous subject who is Jesus of Nazareth. Tracing the movement of the mind
back from Jesus, one envisages that the individual subject who was Jesus
was really one who pre-existed. One depicts the individual Jesus as identical with what had been represented as a personification in wisdom language but is now an individual being. Jesus is given a pre-existence as a
cosmic figure, an intermediary between God and creation, God and
human existence. It is difficult to avoid the terms "mediator" and "intermediary," for the very function of the pre-existent Sophia-Logos is precisely to be the agent or instrument by which God acts. The language of
the Logos in the Prologue moves into a new and different logical sphere
which in some ways reverses the logic of the christologies up to this point.

---

80. Robert Kysar, *John, the Maverick Gospel* (Atlanta: John Knox Press, 1976), 29. By
contrast, Kuschel, after his analysis of the Prologue, concludes that "John does not have
an isolated pre-existence christology . . . but a sending and revelation christology, in
which the statement about pre-existence . . . has the function of emphasizing the origin of the revealer Jesus from God and the unity of Jesus with God." *Born Before All
Time?*, 384.

81. It should be noted that there are various examples of wisdom christology in the
New Testament, and they are not identical. What is said here of the Logos christology
of the Prologue may also apply to some wisdom christologies according to the interpretations of some exegetes.

The narrative language begins with Logos, who is a heavenly being, in the presence of God. This heavenly being has cosmic functions. In the course of time, however, this heavenly mediator becomes a human being, Jesus. This is the language of myth,[82] or of "reflective mythology,"[83] or of a vital religious imagination that, in an act of imaginative projection into "in the beginning," creates a story that expresses the religious significance of Jesus. These affirmations about "the cosmic, extra-worldly existence and behavior of the Logos are poetic and imaginative in the most profound sense. They are means of expressing the significance and status of Christ in the personal lives of the Christian community."[84]

The language of this christology is at the same time still closely tied to Jesus of Nazareth, and an experience of salvation in and through him expressed in terms of revelation. The very logic of this christology reaffirms but heightens what was seen in wisdom christologies. The realistic personification of the Logos is meant to emphasize the realism of God's presence in Jesus.[85] And the realism of incarnation in "flesh" is meant to express dramatically the concrete visibility and availability of God's revelation in Jesus.

How are we to understand this christology today? The problem with poetic and imaginative christology lies not in the christology itself, but in a literalist misreading and misunderstanding of it. Everyone knows what a literal-minded grammatical and syntactical reading or analysis can do to a lyric poem. Analogously, it is recognized today that the exalted poetry of Logos should be read as what it is, namely, a poem and a hymn of worship. On a practical level, Jesus research is reinforcing this altogether obvious insight. Epistemologically this christology was generated from below on the basis of an encounter with God in Jesus. And the more the imagination is tied to Jesus, the less possible is it to break the ties with this concrete human being and allow one's analytical thought to begin with a pre-existent Logos. One of the effects of Jesus research, then, is to bind the imagination to Jesus in such a way that a christology beginning from above has to be interpreted on the basis of an account of its genesis and an analysis of its epistemology. At the same time, an analysis of the poetic

---

82. A myth is "the expression in story-form of a deeply held *religious* conviction. . . ." Ashton, "The Transformation of Wisdom," 33.

83. The phrase "reflective mythology" is used by Elisabeth Schüssler Fiorenza in *In Memory of Her: A Feminist Theological Reconstruction of Christian Origins* (New York: Crossroad, 1983), 133, and *Jesus: Miriam's Child, Sophia's Prophet: Critical Issues in Feminist Christology* (New York: Continuum, 1994), 161. The phrase means that the languages of Wisdom, Logos, Spirit, and so on, operate functionally on a linguistic-symbolic level of opening up meaning to reflection.

84. Kysar, *John*, 30.

85. The irony here is that in some respects the very opposite is achieved. The presence of an intermediary or supernatural agent of Yahweh or the Father precisely weakens the sense of God's own presence in Jesus, and the early centuries of christological development will suffer from strong currents of subordinationism.

and revelatory character of Logos christology will show how this faith narrative can open up meaning for life in today's world.

When this poetic christology is interpreted according to its genre, it makes the human spirit soar with it. It brings to christology the power of sacrality; it recalls the awesome claim of Christian faith that it is God who is encountered in Jesus, in the flesh, so that God is truly revealed in him. In a way analogous to Luke's Spirit christology, it is God as Logos, God as Wisdom, who is present to and in Jesus. The symbol of Logos-become-flesh lends a depth and seriousness to creation, especially to the human existence and freedom that share in God's absoluteness. This truly opens up a life full of meaning and direction, that is, salvation.

THE SIGNIFICANCE OF THE PLURALISM
OF NEW TESTAMENT CHRISTOLOGIES

In this final section I want to reflect on the significance of the pluralism of christologies contained in the New Testament. In the face of this pluralism, the questions of the unity of christological assertion and norms for evaluating christologies become important. I will respond to these issues by reviewing some principles that will also have a bearing on the nature of christology and constructive soteriological and christological thinking.

Jesus as a Response to the Religious Question
I begin by analyzing the process of interpretation itself, and asking what is going on in it. What attracted people to Jesus during his lifetime? Why did people bother with Jesus at all after he died? What are the very premises that underlie and account for the dynamics of the religious interpretation of Jesus? Insofar as the interpreter is concerned, the significance of Jesus has its basis in the fact that he raises the religious question. Jesus was relevant to his period and thereafter insofar as there is a religious question to which he responds. The religious question concerns the identity and significance of human existence: what is the meaning of human existence? What is the significance, purpose, and destiny of human life, both my personal life and human life as such? The religious question arises out of human existence itself, and it implies the question of some ultimate transcendent principle or God as the possible object of ultimate concern: whether God is, what God is like, and the relation of God to human existence. If people do not entertain these kinds of questions, with or without the formal concept of God, Jesus will be of little interest to them. In short, Jesus was and is significant because in his lifetime he raised, and confronted people with, the religious question of the nature of God and the meaning of human existence. This recalls the logic of all theology.[86]

---

86. "The question of God only has meaning for us human beings in so far as, being a human question, it speaks to our humanity; that is, if we then come to realize that the whole issue of man is in the end the issue of God himself." Schillebeeckx, *Jesus*, 404.

Christology as Interpretation of Jesus
in the Light of the Easter Experience

A historical approach to christology in itself makes it clear that formal christological interpretation began in the context of the conviction that Jesus was risen. But I wish to call attention to the import of the circular character of interpretation for christology. Interpretation is a circular, dialogical process. On the one hand, the New Testament communities had certain traditions, concepts, understandings, words, symbols which they applied to Jesus of Nazareth, now experienced as alive and with God. Jesus was the new Adam, the new creation, the Son of God, the prophet animated by God as Spirit, the sage or teacher of wisdom, the embodiment of God's wisdom, the Word of God the Father. By projecting the light of these notions on Jesus, early disciples began to construe his identity on a deeper level. On the other hand, the concepts that interpret Jesus are also interpreted by him. In every case, the categories do not fit his historical life perfectly; they do not completely sum him up. He changes the meaning of the categories; his life and person, his individuality and distinctiveness, alter the traditional titles of the religious figure. For example, the idea of messiah would have to take into account that he was crucified and thus died as a criminal, for these are the historical data.[87]

This structure of interpretation reinforces the necessity that Jesus not be left behind in christology. Jesus is interpreted in the context of the Easter experience, but Jesus of Nazareth cannot be replaced by a risen Christ. Interpretations of Jesus Christ now risen cannot prescind from, but must be modified by, the concrete datum they interpret, namely, Jesus. One has to ask how a given interpretation of Jesus Christ leads back or can lead back, as it were, to Jesus himself. Thus Jesus research provides a way of checking whether a christology has some realistic, historical connection with Jesus. Christology, then, consists in this circle of interpretation, this dialogue or back and forth movement between Jesus and the titles or categories that are used to interpret him. New titles or concepts or characterizations are conferred on Jesus to illumine his work and person; and the earthly Jesus now risen, as the referent of these titles or understandings, modifies the concepts to conform to the historical reality of what he was on earth.[88] Thus in the development of christologies one can see displayed the principle that Jesus in his earthly life is a norm and criterion for what should be said about him. Christology is interpretation of Jesus the risen one.

---

87. "The notion of a suffering Messiah is not found in the OT or in any texts of pre-Christian Judaism." Fitzmyer, *Luke*, 1565.

88. Always understood in these statements of Jesus being a norm for christological interpretation are two qualifications: first, regarding positive content, one must implicitly add the phrase "insofar as something can be known historically." Second, and more importantly, christological interpretation must be regulated by the imaginatively retrojected possibilities of Jesus as a human being.

Development within a Liturgical Context

It is becoming clearer that the development of christology did not happen by way of inference from Jesus' teaching and sayings. One cannot trace a clean development by isolating Jesus' sayings in Q, and from there tracing stages of development. Nor is there a gradual development from low christologies to a later high christology. The development of christology is uneven, different in different communities and contexts. The development of christology is not a logical development of the message of Jesus or the message about Jesus risen. The context for situating the development of christology is better envisioned as the worshiping community, and the logic as one that moves from religious experience of Jesus now risen to the use of various strands of tradition to give new expressions of that experience. Communities used the language that was available. The development of christology consisted in "putting into words," and using the language of tradition, to express "convictions which were already fundamental to the worshiping life of the Christian community."[89] In other words, "the cultic veneration of Jesus in early Christian circles is the most important context for the use of the christological titles and concepts."[90] Cult and ritual would include at least in part the eucharistic meal which has its roots in the common meals that Jesus celebrated with his disciples. It can be argued historically that the eucharistic memorial was operative very early after Jesus' death. If the eucharistic celebrations were part of the context in or for which early pre-Pauline hymns were first formulated, one has a plausible scenario for the composition in poetic language of the wisdom hymns which eventually became "high" christologies.

Larry Hurtado provides one explanation of the development, against the background of preserving Jewish monotheism, in terms of divine agents. Divine agents are heavenly figures that occupy a position second to God and act on God's behalf in the world. This is a generalized, analogous category since there are many different kinds of agents and agency: angels, exalted patriarchs, and so on. In the light of the experience of Jesus' exaltation, the Christian community relates to him as to a heavenly being. But he is not portrayed as God with a cult of his own. "Jesus is praised and acclaimed as their Lord 'to the glory of God the Father' (Phil 2:9-11). Devotion to Jesus did not involve confusing him with God or making Jesus a second God."[91] He is rather linked to the tradition of being an agent of God. He acts by divine authority and power, and is also assigned certain divine attributes. Jesus, exalted in such a way that he was God's chief agent of salvation, thus becomes the object of devotion and worship that is ultimately directed toward God. "This concept, that God has a chief agent in heaven above all other divine servants, served the early

---

89. R. T. France, "Development in New Testament Christology," *Themelios*, 18 (1992), 7.
90. Hurtado, *One God, One Lord*, 13.
91. Hurtado, *One God, One Lord*, 121.

Christians in their attempt to accommodate the exalted Jesus alongside God."[92]

The Soteriological Structure of Christology

Interest in Jesus was motivated by the religious question, and christology began to develop out of an Easter experience that was continually nourished by worship. But the religious question is none other than the question of salvation. Although salvation is conceived specifically in a variety of ways, generally it consists in a positive response to the negativities that threaten the existence, meaning, purpose, and destiny of human life. This involves God or the equivalent of God. The reason why people were and are interested in Jesus is that in some experiential manner he mediates salvation from God. Thus the fundamental structure of Christian faith and christology is soteriological, and, from an anthropological perspective, the whole of christology rests on soteriology.

This soteriological structure of christology is displayed in the New Testament christologies reviewed here. All of them are concerned with interpreting the person or identity of Jesus now risen, of answering the question of who Jesus is. But they always answer the question by saying what he does, namely, bring salvation. "The New Testament hardly ever speaks of the person of Christ without at the same time speaking of his work." When the New Testament asks "Who is Jesus Christ," it means primarily and first of all "What is his function?"[93] And that function is to respond to the religious question, to proffer salvation. Thus in all the christologies in the New Testament, there is an underlying concern for salvation and for how Jesus has mediated or brought or brings that salvation. This view can and should be generalized beyond the New Testament to christology as such. All christology is based on and functions in relation to the question of human salvation.

The Necessity of Pluralism in Christology

One of the purposes of this chapter is to illustrate the fact that there is a pluralism of christologies in the New Testament. The christologies that have been surveyed are not the same; they are different. At certain points one may be in opposition to another; they cannot be reduced to each other. If, for example, the christologies of Mark and Matthew were taken simply as positive affirmations, pronounced from the same perspective, in nonsymbolic language, one could not hold both integrally at the same time. At certain points these christologies contradict each other. But, of course, this is contrary to fact: one can hold all of the New Testament christologies together. This is so precisely because they are symbolic affirmations, about transcendent aspects of Jesus Christ, conceived from different perspectives, and not adequately "containing" their object.

---

92. Hurtado, *One God, One Lord*, 50.

93. Oscar Cullmann, *The Christology of the New Testament* (London: SCM Press, 1959), 3–4.

It is important to see the reasons for the historical necessity of this pluralism, over and above the transcendent character of their subject matter. These reasons stem from historicity. As the Jesus movement spread to new peoples, and new communities were formed, one can imagine how christological development took on a certain life of its own in each community. Each community had its own culture into which it appropriated Jesus. Each had a distinctive set of problems that generated questions peculiar to it. Each possessed a particular religious tradition which supplied a language to interpret Jesus. Different communities appreciated different aspects of the person or message of Jesus. In short, Jesus was interpreted from within the context of the specific tradition and language of the various communities to whom he was introduced, thereby producing of necessity different understandings of him.[94]

Significance of the Christological Pluralism of the New Testament

The pluralism of New Testament christologies raises some deep questions about the relative adequacy of any given christology. The various christologies are not all of equal value. How are we to envisage the logic by which such judgments can be made? I use the term "orthodox" here in a simple and non-technical, formal sense to mean correct belief. And I limit the discussion here to the logic of orthodoxy. Later, in Chapter 15, I shall take up the criteria of orthodoxy in a pluralistic situation in somewhat greater detail. At this point, however, I simply want to underline what is going on in christology in the light of the New Testament christologies just surveyed.

The pluralism found in the New Testament, it seems to me, leads to a negative and a positive conclusion. It should be clear that, negatively, the criterion for the adequacy of one christology cannot be another christology. The nature of pluralism consists in differences held together in unity, or unity amid differences. In this view of the pluralism reflected in the New Testament, one cannot raise up one objective christology and make it the norm for the others. This is so because the pluralism of New Testament christologies lies in this very diversity, and there is no objective reason in the christologies themselves to prefer one over the other. On what basis, for example, would one maintain that John's christology is normative in such a way that Luke's, which disagrees with that of John at several points, is unorthodox? Nor does Luke disqualify John. The process of judging the orthodoxy of a christology, therefore, cannot be reduced to an external comparison of differences in such a way that the objectively developed portrait, language, and belief structure of one christology can be the measure of another christology. This is the inescapable significance of the pluralism of New Testament christologies.

---

94. See Schillebeeckx, *Jesus*, 401–515, for a description of the development of christology that provides reasons for the pluralism of the development, and at the same time relates various strands of the development back to the historical Jesus.

Therefore, positively, one must look to the internal structure of christology itself to find the logic of orthodoxy. Is there a rationale intrinsic
to christological interpretation itself which serves as the basis for the
unity of all orthodox christologies and can serve as the internal measure
of their adequacy? Turning to the New Testament, what is the principle
that holds all of the christologies found there together? In what do they
all agree? This question finds a response in the soteriological structure
of christology just described. All of them express an existential relationship to the person of Jesus, or to God through Jesus, as the bringer of
salvation from God. Every christology implies a personal or existential
lived relationship to the person of Jesus such that Jesus means salvation.
Or, to put it in still another way, each christology explains why or how
Jesus is a savior for human beings, that is, what he did or does for our
salvation. But since this is something that ultimately deals with absolute
transcendent mystery, with God, it necessarily yields to a variety of
interpretations.

This logic may be generalized into an axiom or formula for understanding christology itself. What christology must explain or express
directly is Christian faith in God's salvation mediated through Jesus. An
adequate explanation of who Jesus Christ is, on the basis of his mediating
God's salvation, represents the foundational logic of christology. Christology must express or explain the work and person of Jesus in such a way
that the Christian's faith itself is being explained. Or better, what is being
expressed and explained in christology is the Christian's being saved by
God as mediated through the person of Jesus. This soteriological structure
represents the intrinsic logic of christology. Christology is an expression
or explanation of the Christian community's faith, its existential faith relationship to God mediated by Jesus.

Another axiom flows from this: every christology that does explain this
existential and salvific relationship of the Christian to Jesus is orthodox. An
explanation within faith of who Jesus Christ is, on the basis of his mediation of God's salvation, constitutes an orthodox christology; an unorthodox christology is one that fails this soteriological test.[95] Salvation from God
through Jesus represents the experience that is to be expressed and
explained. The logic of orthodoxy is internal to Christian faith itself: Jesus
of Nazareth, who can be known through history, but is now experienced
as alive, is the bearer of God's salvation for humankind. Every christology
that explains this adequately is orthodox. This is obviously not an objective criterion against which existing christologies can be empirically measured. The New Testament is also pluralistic in its understanding of
salvation. Its meaning will have to be closely compared with the corporate
experience of the Christian community. But this experience of salvation

---

95. For example, as will be shown, Arius's christology was declared unorthodox
because it was judged to have failed to account for Jesus' bearing salvation that was
truly from or of God.

defines the logical framework within which the discussion of the adequacy of christologies must take place.

Judgment about the adequacy of such an "explanation" or christological expression will require more objective criteria beyond this fundamental logic. These criteria are multiple and no one norm is sufficient. To be adequate, christology must correspond to what we can know of Jesus and to the interpretations of him in the New Testament; it must attend to the classic doctrines which have been normative for the churches for so long; it must be in communion with other Christian churches and not isolated or idiosyncratic; it must be coherent and intelligible for the world of those to whom it would communicate and whose faith it would represent; it must posses an ethical credibility and the power to generate a Christian life. All of these more objective criteria will come into play in the construction of the christology which follows.

These four chapters represent an interpretation of such biblical data as are considered essential for a genetic understanding of the place of Jesus Christ in the Christian imagination. This material provides the constant and ever-present source for constructive christology. Implicitly, as we move forward to consider classical and current soteriology and christology, the data of the scriptures are always at work precisely as the historical source and origin of a tradition of life and thought out of which reflection is operating. We pass now to the next stage of our reflection which begins with a methodological recapitulation of the structure of christology implicit in the New Testament development.

PART III

CLASSICAL TRADITION

CHAPTER 7

The Structure of Christology

Having considered the data of the New Testament on Jesus of Nazareth, his resurrection, and the development of various christologies, I shall in this third part consider the development of classical soteriology and christology. But before taking up this material I propose a reprise that will outline the structure of christology. This broad formal category refers to several things at once. The structure of christology includes the experience that lies behind christological assertion, as well as a conception of religious epistemology. On the most general level, the structure of christology should reflect the nature of christology itself. It includes, therefore, the logic that accounts for the meaning of christological language. The structure of christology also points to the theoretical framework within which the method and arguments for a particular christological position are mounted. The structure of christology is thus the systematic framework that accounts for a particular christology.

An analysis of the structure of christology at this point in the overall argument is designed to accomplish several things. On the one hand, looking backward, this chapter recapitulates some of the foundational questions treated in the first part of this book. But at this point one has the advantage of the analysis of the original genesis of christology as a historical response to Jesus of Nazareth as the prime case in point. This chapter will explain analytically the genesis of New Testament christologies and the theological method involved in the interpretation of that development. All the elements for understanding the structure of christology are contained in the original genesis of New Testament christologies. On the other hand, now looking forward from the New Testament to the continuing development of christology in the patristic period and beyond, this analysis will provide the heuristic framework for understanding what was going on in the patristic period and what is demanded today. With this chapter, then, I shall give a more formal characterization of the specific systematic structure of the christology proposed in this book.

I have organized this analysis into four sections. The first deals loosely with religious experience today in the context of historicity and religious pluralism. It offers a general theory of religion in terms of religious epistemology: all religions are functions of historical media. The second merely announces the principle that Jesus is the medium of specifically Christian faith. The third part subsumes the experiential and mediated basis of religion into a theory of religious knowledge that construes it as symbolic: all religious knowledge is symbolic knowledge. When Christianity and christology are understood within the framework of this theory, one can formulate the thesis that the elementary structure of Christian faith has Jesus as its central mediating symbol in its encounter with God. The fourth part of the chapter draws out some of the consequences of this symbolic structure of christology that shed light on the development of the New Testament christologies and that illuminate the task of constructive christology.

THE EXPERIENTIAL AND HISTORICAL CHARACTER OF EVERY ENCOUNTER WITH GOD

This account of the structure of christology begins by returning to some of the presuppositions and questions involved in constructive theology and christology. What are the implications of the historicity and religious pluralism that characterize our religious situation? In this section I will answer this question in terms of religious experience and a new appreciation of it as the clearing house through which all contact with God is negotiated. If historical religious experience is the anthropological foundation of all religion, an examination of the structure of that experience will provide a first entry into the question of the structure of christology.

HISTORICITY AND A THEORY OF RELIGIONS

The religious situation of western cultures is becoming more and more marked by a sense of historicity and a conscious acceptance of religious pluralism. The awareness that our world is a product of evolution may be too large to have an immediate relevance in predicting the future, but it is accompanied by a sense of openness to change, newness, and differences in human understanding and behavior that was impossible before. In fact, the historical consciousness communicated in western culture is radical. The spontaneous bias of intellectual culture is that pluralism is the "natural" state of religious affairs in our world, and that it will always be so insofar as religion is a function of particular cultures and societies. Any claim about a permanent or universal truth must be proposed apologetically within the context of a supposition of some measure of historical relativism. The very claim for the existence of universal truth has become associated with a narrow, sectarian outlook. This relatedness to particular historical cultures has become so ingrained in western historical consciousness that relativism is an epistemological premise, and all claims to transcend it must be accompanied by extensive argument. This implies that Christianity is not only a product and function of western culture, which it obviously is, but is only or merely that. One must argue for the very intelligibility of a universally relevant revelation of God mediated through the particular person, Jesus Christ.

If this statement in some measure reflects our postmodern situation, and if that situation must enter into the method and logic of any christology that would address it, then christology must be accompanied by at least some general theses concerning a theory of religions. In fact any christology claiming to be in any way comprehensive, coherent, and relatively adequate necessarily implies elements of a theory of the other religions, at least in relation to itself. These christological implications should be made explicit and formally argued. Beyond that, however, one can perceive a new exigency that a general theory of religions constitutes the initial framework for constructive christological interpretation. This seems to be the requirement of a christology that argues consistently from below in dialogue with the situation.[1]

The standard reaction against such a procedure rests on the conviction that it necessarily prejudges the status of Christian incarnation and revelation, and risks leveling them to the plane of other religions. Such a relativization of revelation undercuts revelation itself by implying a pluralism without a higher criterion. But these reactions against beginning christology from below in full recognition of our situation are themselves always based on some particular christology and theology of revelation. They are often enough marked by some measure of alarmism. It is not necessary that a recognition of historicity and pluralism lead to religious relativism. And it remains to be seen whether the recognition of truth in other religions undercuts the universal relevance and truth mediated by Jesus Christ. But it is fairly certain that a christology that does not from the beginning situate its reflection in the context of the religious experience of other peoples and cultures cannot claim to be adequate to today's situation.

EXPERIENCE IN THE WORLD

A point of departure for understanding the structure of theology in the context of historicity and pluralism may be found in an epistemology that appeals to experience. Of course the idea of experience is not without ambiguity, and it is not possible here to probe it in the depth required. But I shall briefly describe what I mean by experience and how it underlies the structure of christology.

---

1. One of the most comprehensive theories of religion has been developed over the years by John Hick in a process of writing, criticism, and dialogue culminating in his Gifford Lectures, published as *An Interpretation of Religion* (New Haven: Yale University Press, 1989). His work will be referred to in Chapter 14. The theory of religion developed here will be limited to an anthropological account of religious epistemology.

By experience I understand human existence being present to itself in the presence of the world. When experience is directed toward a specific object, that object is drawn into the circle of a subject's presence to itself within the context of the material, physical, and sensible world. According to Karl Rahner, the human subject may be characterized as spirit or freedom in the world. This entails human subjectivity possessing an intrinsic relationship to matter and physicality that cannot be escaped. Using Aristotelian language, matter in an ontological sense defines the individuality of the human subject. When this ontology is translated back into the epistemology from which it actually derives, one has a theory of knowledge in which the human spirit in its knowing and willing is tied to the finite world of sense data. "Freedom is always mediated by the concrete reality of time and space, of man's materiality and his history."[2] Experience, therefore, is not primarily a screen or veil that separates the human subject from knowledge of the world. Rather, experience is precisely the openness of the human subject to the objective world, the very process of interchange by which the world is presented to and known by the knowing subject.[3] Rahner is perhaps best known for his analysis of human transcendence in its engagement with the world. In the experience of finitude, one experiences one's own transcendence.[4] But I wish to dwell for the moment on the bond of human experience to the world.

This foundational empiricism can be described in terms borrowed from Thomas Aquinas. In Aquinas the attachment of the mind to the world can be explained through the imagination. All human knowledge enters the mind through the mediation of sense data and the imagination. According to Aquinas, in terms of objective content the human mind is born like a clean slate upon which nothing is written.[5] It stands in relation to the whole of reality as a pure potency ready to be filled with content. This content comes to it through the five senses which mediate external reality to the human spirit. The sensible images from the material world are received in the mind through what Aquinas calls internal senses, two of which are imagination and memory. These provide the immediate resources for intellectual or conceptual knowledge. It is finally the active, spiritual intellect itself that discerns within these concrete and particular images immaterial and universally relevant ideas. This process is termed "abstraction," a drawing out of universal truth or meaning from a material, sensible datum.[6] In christology, this elementary pattern of knowing is

---

2. Karl Rahner, *Foundations of Christian Faith: An Introduction to the Idea of Christianity* (New York: Seabury, 1978), 36.

3. John E. Smith, *Religion and Empiricism* (Milwaukee: Marquette University Press, 1967), 44–45.

4. Rahner, *Foundations*, 32.

5. Thomas Aquinas, *Summa Theologica: Complete English Edition in Five Volumes* (Westminster, Md.: Christian Classics, 1961), I, q. 79, a. 2.

6. Aquinas, ST, I, q. 79, a. 4.

exemplified, as we have seen, in the foundational role of Jesus in the generation of christologies.

The rootedness of experience in sensible data yields the proposition that "the intellect knows nothing but what it receives from the senses."[7] And this can be expanded to include the imagination: all human knowledge is drawn from the material world through the senses and the concrete images that are formed and stored up by the imagination. Thus it follows that there are no concepts or words or, more generally, languages that do not also bear with them an imaginative residue. Abstraction of a universally relevant idea from a particular imaginative datum does not mean leaving all contact with physical, sensible reality behind. Rather, it means discovering and grasping universally intelligible meaning within the concrete and specific. I am suggesting that even our most abstract ideas and propositions always carry along, or imply, or create some concrete imaginative construal. All christology should lead back to Jesus.

Imagination in Aquinas has a passive and an active dimension. It is passive in the sense that it receives and stores images of the external world. It is active in the sense that it divides and combines received images and constructs new ones.[8] On this basis one can speak of a two-fold function of the imagination: it is both conservative and creative. The passive storing of images to which all knowledge is bound keeps our speculative reasoning in touch with reality; it prevents imagination from becoming fancy or fantasy. The active dimension of imagination is the principle of creative discovery and invention in poetry, in art, and in the breakthroughs of science. Given the rootedness of language in sensible contact with the world, one can see the grounds for the normativity of Jesus for christology in the foundations of knowing itself, as well as the basis for the possibility of conceiving a resurrection.

The bonds of human knowing to the external, physical world do not imply a passive mind that contributes nothing to the knowing process. There are strong, internal, neo-Platonic dynamisms in Aquinas's theory of knowledge. Experience is not reducible to sense data. Reason enters into and plays a role in critically appraising sense data. Sense data are always appreciated, interpreted, and drawn into a higher synthesis of understanding. The point of this initial step of a turn to experience is not to develop a theory regarding the complex area of reflection, but simply to establish the principle that human experience is bound to the world even though it transcends the world.[9]

---

7. Aquinas, ST, I, q. 78, a. 4, obj. 4.

8. Recall Aquinas's own example alluded to in Chapter 2: from the received image of gold and the image of a mountain the imagination can construct the picture of a golden mountain. ST, I, q. 78, a. 4.

9. On the self-transcendence of the human subject, see Rahner, *Foundations*, 31–39. Addressing experience in the empiricist tradition, Smith notes that an empirical

The Roots of the Religious Question

The anthropological roots of specifically religious experience can be found in experience itself. Experience is a subject's presence to itself in the world. But this self-presence is dynamic and active. It is presence to itself not only in the world but also in duration, so that the self is also activity in time. The consciousness of self as an active subject in the world and in history is the soil which nurtures the religious question and out of which it grows. For all human beings must "question the *from whence* of our life and the *to where* of our striving."[10] The question of God arises as the problem of the ground and the goal of our striving. Blondel formulated the roots of religion in two theses in his extensive phenomenology of human experience as action. First, human existence cannot escape the question of its own destiny. Second, the phenomenology of immanent human action as a possible answer to the question of human destiny shows that finitude always fails to satisfy action's infinite quest for wholeness. And this inevitably raises the question of ultimacy, of God, whether human completion might lie in a principle, goal, or subject that infinitely transcends human existence itself.[11]

The roots of religious experience lie within the human subject and its experience. Not only is it a question of where we are from, but also why? and what for? The "religious" as a category should not be understood in the first place on the level of content, as though religious experience began with a religious object. The religious question arises as a dimension or characteristic of the givenness of human existence and the sheer experience of being in the world. This dimension or level of experience can be defined further as a dialectical tension between negativity and positivity. The human person raises the question about what is implicitly experienced as absent, missing, and lacking to its integral existence. If it were not lacking, there would be no question. On the one hand, human existence is driven by a positive desire and striving for being; on the other hand, human existence is finite and limited; it lacks full existence and in itself is nothing more than a being unto a death that will ultimately negate existence itself. This dialectic between positivity and negativity, between infinite longing and finitude, which is the metaphysical driving force of human action, is the source too of the religious question. If human existence were characterized by an utter fullness that lacked nothing, there

---

approach "means the return of every conceptual scheme to the experiential level from which it arose, while the mark of rationalism is that a conceptual scheme, once launched, gains autonomy within itself so that the criterion of its validity is made to reside in the conceptual scheme itself, its consistency and coherence." *Religion and Empiricism*, 8–9. The point is to strike a balance between these two.

10. Smith, *Religion and Empiricism*, 58ff.

11. This characterizes one aspect of Maurice Blondel's position in *Action (1893): Essay on a Critique of Life and a Science of Practice* (South Bend, Ind.: University of Notre Dame Press, 1984). See 3–15, 425–46.

would be no religious question. The religious question, then, arises out of negativity, which can only be recognized as negativity within the context of a positive dynamism toward unqualified being. In sum, the religious question is intrinsically the question of salvation.

THE MEDIATED CHARACTER OF THE RESPONSE

Thus far I have outlined a turn to experience, with a broad definition of experience that needs further description, the bond of all human experience to the sensible world, and the internal necessity of the religious question that cannot be answered by the sum total of finite objects. In the light of this initial structure we can describe still further the formal notion of God that arises out of this experience and the structure of how God is encountered.

When it is God who is encountered in religious experience, God is recognized as both transcendent and immanent. To be God, God must be infinite; at the same time God is experienced in relation to the self and as present. If God were not transcendent and infinite, but a part of this world, God would not be the final answer to the religious question. And if God's infinite transcendence were not accommodated to the structure of human knowing, God could not be encountered. If God is really encountered in the world by human beings, then God must be such that God can be so encountered.[12]

But this reflection is only preliminary to the more important question of characterizing the experience of God in this world. I presuppose that every encounter with God should be understood as implying an experiential dimension. This seems self-evident if not tautologous, since, if encounter with God did not occur within human experience, it would not occur at all. But this appeal to an existential notion of religion runs counter to a positivist and notional view of revelation. By this I mean a conception of revelation that objectifies it in positive linguistic or propositional forms in such a way that it can be internalized notionally, or conceptually, or linguistically without a living experience of its object or meaning. In still another view of revelation, religious experience is conceived as a result or consequence of God's internal action of revelation, but not a dimension of revelation itself. By contrast,[13] I accept the theological tradition that insists that revelation and human experience are not oppositional terms. Experience, although it is tied to the world, should not be understood as

---

12. This immanence of God is correlative to the doctrine of creation. Creation means there is nothing between creation and the creator. God is totally present to creation. Edward Schillebeeckx, *God Among Us: The Gospel Proclaimed* (New York: Crossroad, 1983), 93.

13. But without denying some measure of relevance to these views: revelatory experience can be objectified in its expressive forms; God is at work in human subjectivity as a cause of religious experience. It is the reductionist character of these views that is resisted here.

something that blocks awareness of God. Rather, experience opens out toward God, and revelation itself is a form of human experience that welcomes in receptivity the self-communication of God. We have seen that experience cannot be reduced to images of sensible data, that it implies the dynamic action of the self, in insight, reflective self-awareness, and the formulation of the question of its own existence. The experience which forms the basis of the religious question is an experience of transcendence that arises out of the very engagement with the sensible world in its concreteness, materiality, and finitude. Experience reaches out toward transcendence not apart from engagement with the concrete sensible world, but in the very recognition of its finitude and ultimate negativity.[14] And beyond this anthropological basis, the thesis that revelation is a form of human experience estimates that God works within human subjects in a way that corresponds to the structure of human experience itself. The long tradition of witness to just such an internal experience is carried in the language of God as Spirit.

All experience of God, because it is tied to the world, is experience that is mediated by the world. In accordance with the structure of human experience, all positive knowledge of God is mediated to experience through the sensible world. This proposal is best understood in contrast to two other positions in relation to which it appears as an alternative middle position incorporating elements from both sides.[15] On the one hand, rationalism argues that one can know God through objective reasoning processes beginning with the data of this world. God is the object of rational inference. On the other hand, mysticism points to God as so overwhelmingly present that God becomes the object of a direct and immediate intuition or experience of those to whom God's self-communication is given. In the first case, knowledge of God is considered to be a function of objective rational thought; in the second case, knowledge of God is a function of ecstatic experience in which the subject is drawn into the immediate presence of God.

The description of all positive experience and knowledge of God in terms of experience mediated through some historical event in this world borrows themes from rationalism and mysticism at the same time that it provides an alternative to both. Because all experience is tied to the world, this position denies an immediate knowledge of God in this world. This does not deny that God is directly present to the human subject, as the doctrine of creation out of nothing suggests. Nor does it rule out prethematic awareness of transcendence, or a generalized experience of the

14. Smith, *Religion and Empiricism*, 60–61.

15. This placing of positive experience of God between rationalism and mysticism is proposed by John E. Smith, *Experience and God* (New York: Oxford University Press, 1968), 68–98, at 81–83. The point here is not to provide an adequate description of these alternatives.

"Holy" as described phenomenologically by Rudolf Otto. But all reflective awareness of God, all explicit, thematic, and positive knowledge of God that is marked by a specific content, must draw such content through historical mediation because of the primal structure of human experience itself. Thus human beings may experience a religious question, and even have a sense of the holy or transcendent, but such formal notions will receive whatever content or character they possess only through some historical medium. This does not mean that there is no such thing as mystical experience. It means, rather, that one should not speak of an immediate experience of God, that the phenomenal experience of the immediate presence of God is always an experience of mediated immediacy.

Likewise, objective reasoning toward God will only reach God when it thematizes an experiential question and search for God. The conclusion of a reasoning process that convincingly generates a knowledge of God does so on the basis of an inner experiential principle that interprets the conclusion as God. In other words, what is formulated in objective categories will only generate the conclusion, "God," on the basis of an experience of the meaning of God. This does not deny that the human mind can ascend toward God through reasoning and inference, nor the role of reason in critical appropriation of the content of religious experience. It rather explains more adequately what is going on in this process which is at the same time experiential and hermeneutical.

Let me sum up this first step in an analytic description of the structure of christology. A critical, apologetic, and genetic christology from below must incorporate into its point of departure the present situation. This includes a historically conscious sense of religious pluralism. Christology, therefore, must be set within the context of an understanding of religious experience and religion as such; one cannot *begin* christology on the premise that Christianity is *sui generis* and discontinuous from other religions. The turn to experience generally, and to concrete active engagement with the sensible world as the basis of all knowing, generates the conclusion that human experience itself gives rise to the religious question. But at the same time, the physical structure of human existence and the ontology of its knowing as being bound to the world mean that all religious responses to the question, insofar as they include a particular or specific content, will themselves be mediated through some historical medium.

JESUS AS THE MEDIUM OF CHRISTIAN FAITH

Jesus is the medium of Christian faith. This statement, pronounced within the context of the broad theory of religious revelation just described, characterizes the essential structure of Christianity. Jesus is what accounts for its distinctiveness, for Jesus is the central medium and focus for Christian encounter with and faith in God. Jesus is the central source for the content of Christian faith. The fundamental teachings of Jewish faith which are subsumed into Christian faith are refiltered hermeneutically through the lens of Jesus called the Christ. Jesus is not the only or exclusive medium of Christian faith, but he is the central medium in the sense that all other media are peripheral to him. Jesus is the primary hermeneutical principle for interpreting the other symbols that make up the complex movement that is Christianity.

Chapters 3 through 6 reflect this structure. The person of Jesus of Nazareth stands at the source and in the center of Christian faith in God. He occupies this position because he mediates God. Jesus, of course, did not propose an apologetic response to the question of God's existence. Rather, he portrayed in his words and actions God's reign in an already religious culture. The status of Jesus being a medium of God for his disciples was confirmed in the Easter experience. Jesus' exaltation was experienced as God's validation of Jesus' mediation of God. In the light of Jesus being so glorified, formal christologies began to develop. Christology is the interpretation of Jesus Christ as the medium of God's self-communication to human existence.

In his discussion of religious revelation, John Smith characterizes the religious medium in terms that make it clear that religious mediation is symbolic. A religious medium is a symbol. On the one hand, the medium participates in transcendence, in God, so that God is present to and within the medium. Yet, on the other hand, the medium is not the transcendent itself, because it is a finite piece of the world, and thus must point beyond itself to God.[16] On the premises that all religions are structured around public media, and that Jesus is the symbolic medium of God to Christian faith, I now want to return to a further analysis of the character of the religious symbol. This analytic description will at the same time illumine and be illuminated by the New Testament data that has already been surveyed.

THE STRUCTURE OF THE RELIGIOUS SYMBOL

Some decades ago Catholic theologians rediscovered the concept of symbol and applied it to Jesus Christ, and derivatively to the church and the sacraments. Through the ideas of symbol and symbolic causality they revitalized a dogmatic theology from above. In taking up the idea of symbol as a central theological principle I am proceeding in the tradition of Rahner, Schillebeeckx, and others. But at the same time, the insertion of the category of symbol into the framework of an historically conscious christology from below transforms the process of thought and the under-

---

16. Smith, *Experience and God*, 86–87. Smith's view of a medium resembles Paul Tillich's conception of the religious symbol.

standing achieved in the earlier synthesis. This will be apparent in what follows as I review the kinds of symbol that are relevant to christology, the range of their use, and the characteristics of symbolic mediation.[17]

CONCRETE AND CONCEPTUAL SYMBOLS

Symbols do not lack analysis in a variety of disciplines, and use of the concept in theology requires its own definition. I will begin with a simple notion and, in the course of the discussion, build upon it with further analytic description. A symbol may be understood as something that mediates something other than itself. A symbol makes present something else. Often, and this is the case in religious symbols, a symbol discloses something distinctive, something that could not be known without the symbol. It "reveals certain aspects of reality—the deepest aspects—which defy any other means of knowledge."[18]

One can begin to understand the distinctiveness of a symbol by differentiating it from a sign. A sign is referential; it designates something else. But a sign is not mediational, rendering that other present and revealing it; it lacks an intrinsic connection with its referent. A red street light says stop, and that is all it does, even though a sociologist may marvel at how green and red lights around a city organize frenetic human behavior in a relatively safe fashion. There is no deep objective or subjective connection between "red" and "stop." A sign is based on no more than human convention. By contrast, a Christian cannot use the word "cross" simply to refer to Jesus' death without connoting a long tradition of profound feeling, reflection, and meaning. When a symbol looses its power to reveal and evoke a presence, it becomes a sign, and this is the meaning of the phrase "merely a symbol." It needs to be repeated that the phrase "merely a symbol" has no connection at all with the theory of symbol being employed here. For "merely a symbol" has come to mean that something "refers to something else" and "does not mean what it says literally," and, therefore, "is not really true." If something is "merely" a symbol, therefore, it is no symbol at all, for a symbol as it is understood here truly reveals and makes present what it symbolizes.

One should distinguish between concrete symbols and conceptual symbols. These different kinds of symbol mean that the term "symbol" is itself analogous. For the most part I shall be referring here to religious symbols. A concrete religious symbol is an entity which reveals and makes present something else. Ordinarily there is an inner connection between the

---

17. I described the nature and use of symbol in theology in R. Haight, *Dynamics of Theology* (New York: Paulist Press, 1990), 127–66. What is said here inevitably will involve some repetition of that material.

18. Mircea Eliade, *Images and Symbols: Studies in Religious Symbolism* (New York: Sheed & Ward, 1961), 12.

symbol and the symbolized that allows the symbol to reveal and make present. For example, in a world conceived as created by God, a creature can be construed as revealing and bearing the creator's real presence. Bonaventure's *Itinerarium Mentis ad Deum* is an extended hymn to the symbolic real presence of God to all creation. In Israel, Torah is not just an objective set of rules to live by, but the symbol of a covenant which effects God's faithful presence to a people and invites or commands reciprocity. A concrete symbol can be anything, a person, a thing, an event. But as a physical thing or event, it is a being, or has being, and this makes it the possible subject of ontology.[19] Therefore it should be clear that a concrete symbol is a being that mediates a real presence within itself of something other than itself. In the case of the concrete symbol Jesus, we are speaking of the real presence of God to him, and through him to the world, that is mediated by him. We know that Jesus is a concrete symbol of God because people encountered God in him and still do.

A conceptual symbol is a concept, word, metaphor, parable, poem, gospel, or story that reveals something else and makes it present to the imagination and mind. Conceptual symbols, if they are to be revelatory of God, must be more than conventional signs. They must have some inner connection with what is revealed and thus presented to the mind. For example, a conceptual symbol may refer back to a concrete symbol and through it communicate a transcendent truth. This is illustrated by Jesus' working of wonders: "'But if it is by the finger of God that I cast out demons, then the kingdom of God has come upon you'" (Luke 11:20). The exorcism was a concrete symbol; the report of it is a conceptual symbol bearing the event forward through writing; the internal linkage is the causality of the divine power at work in Jesus. Or a conceptual symbol may bear an iconic resemblance by analogy to that which is symbolized or being revealed. For example, when Jesus is called the Wisdom of God, the first basis of such a symbolic predication is the recognition of God's wisdom being represented by Jesus' teaching, embodied by Jesus in his actions, and being played out by the whole course of Jesus' ministry, death, and resurrection. In other words, one recognizes an inner connection between Jesus and the wisdom and plan of God. This recognition does not derive from a knowledge of both and an objective comparison. Rather, the wisdom of God is disclosed in and through the encounter with Jesus.

THE RANGE OF CONCEPTUAL SYMBOLS

The category of symbol is used here as a basis for describing all religious knowledge of transcendent reality. Revelation occurs in human

---

19. See, for example, the ontology of symbol of Karl Rahner in "The Theology of Symbol," *Theological Investigations*, 4 (Baltimore: Helicon Press, 1966), 221–52; Haight, *Dynamics of Theology*, 132–39. I shall say more about the ontology of the concrete symbol in addressing the narrow christological problem in Chapter 15.

experience through symbolic mediation. The response of faith, whose object is transcendent reality, expresses itself symbolically, or in symbols. This makes the category very broad, and it will have a variety of different applications. The three applications of religious symbolism which follow are frequent in christology.

First, all language about God is symbolic. When Jesus called God Father, he was using symbolic language. This symbolic character should not be construed as implying that God is not the father of all, and father in a special way of Jesus. It does not undercut the belief that God is creator and thus the ground and source of fatherhood in a pre-eminent way. Rather, it means that what we know of the fatherhood of God, when it is thus formally expressed, we know through the experience of human fatherhood. And since God is as much mother as God is father, in principle the same could be said of the motherhood of God. The order of our thematic knowledge of God moves through symbols drawn from this world which illumine and structure experience of the absolute mystery we call God. The event and the story of the exodus are symbols that disclose God; the formulation of the law, the story of its gift, the idea of covenant are all symbols that illumine the reality of God and God's dealing with humankind. The story and idea of creation open up to our imagination the vast abyss of the power of being itself that is God. Today's scientific theories of creation, when understood as implying the action of a creator, can be forceful revelatory language about God.

Second, knowledge of God in Jesus or opened up by Jesus constitutes a sphere of specifically Christian symbolic knowledge of God. Jesus' parables are clear examples of such symbolic knowledge. And the story of Jesus' ministry or of himself as a person is often referred to as a parable and hence symbol of God.

Third, language about Jesus as the Christ is also symbolic. This specifically includes New Testament christologies which, in trying to express the special role of Jesus as bringer of God's salvation and thus his status relative to God, must express this transcendent relationship in symbolic language. The christologies reviewed in Chapter 6 are written in symbolic language because we have no immediate access to transcendent reality. The divine dimension that is encountered in Jesus can only be articulated in symbolic language drawn from this-worldly experience, even though this divine dimension is other, different, transcendent.

This range for the use of symbolic language in christology, along with its reference to concrete symbols, means that the term "symbol" has somewhat different meanings in different contexts. The term "symbol" is analogous because there are different kinds of symbols. But the religiously symbolic is always that which reveals something other than itself that is transcendent, and which bears its presence in history and to consciousness.

CHARACTERISTICS OF THE RELIGIOUS SYMBOL

It is especially the characteristics of religious symbols and symbolic knowledge that allow the category of symbol to provide a basis for a systematic christology. The following six qualities or attributes of symbolic mediation are crucial for understanding how the notion of symbol functions in christology.

A first important dimension of symbolic communication consists in the fact that it demands participation. Symbolic communication is not objective in the sense that it can be accomplished without subjective or existential engagement in that which is being communicated. Jesus will not function as a mediation of God for a person with no religious question. The kingdom of God had meaning in a culture with a religious tradition where the symbol bore references to the past and responded to actual religious expectations. It would die in a culture in which it had no tradition, did not take root, and did not respond to actual religious experience and language. Part of the problem of Christianity in modern cultures is that science and technology have replaced the Christian symbolization of reality. Generally "religious traditions across the world have found themselves being edged out of the modern imagination for want of a place in modern experience where their symbols can take hold."[20] Unless people experientially can be drawn into the range of a symbol in such a way that they participate in its meaning because it actually responds to their religious questions, there will be no symbolic communication.

Second, a more specifically cognitive aspect of this participation is that symbols mediate meaning by activating the mind. The most significant difference between sign and symbol is the need for the mind to work to discover a symbol's meaning. The referential meaning of a sign lies on the surface and is conventional and immediate: a one-to-one correlation between the sign-word and a defined meaning has become internalized as a spontaneous association and identification. By contrast, the meaning of a symbol does not lie on the surface, and the mind has to search it out. In the example "The business is running wild!" is this good or is it bad? With such ambiguity the symbol may perform like a metaphor or a simile: the kingdom of God is like the strange justice of the owner of the vineyard who pays the same wage for unequal periods of work; God as Spirit is at work in Jesus; Jesus is the Wisdom of God; Jesus is the Son of God. The mind has to find the sense in the non-sense, the truth in the untruth, the point of identity in the difference. The dynamic character of symbolic cognition arises out of this dialectical tension of "is" and "is not." The disclosure must be discovered through interpretation.

Third, religious symbols participate in and point to *transcendence*. It is most important to recognize that, while symbolic knowledge is cognitive,

---

20. James W. Heisig, "Symbolism," *The Encyclopedia of Religion*, ed. by Mircea Eliade, 14 (New York: Macmillan, 1987), 207.

it does not encompass or adequately control transcendent reality, but is deeply embedded in unknowing, in ignorance and agnosticism. Jesus' parables about God and God's reign respect this transcendence. The pluralism of christological formulations shows the searching character of language about Jesus' identity in function of his mediation of God. Symbolic knowledge cannot be taken as directly representative because, when it is read at face value as readily available information about God, it positively distorts what it purports to reveal. I shall return to this theme in terms of a surplus of meaning.

Fourth, religious symbols reveal the essence of human existence. Symbolic knowledge allows one to penetrate into the primordial, ideal, paradisal character of humanity, which is below and above any particular historical actualization. The kingdom of God, God's Word becoming flesh, Jesus risen, God's beloved empowered by God as Spirit: these disclose archetypal and utopic desires than can never be fully realized historically. These concepts correlate with fundamental aspirations that distinguish human beings from the brutes. Religious symbols mediate a self-knowledge, an insight into the most fundamental meaning of humanity relative to the cosmos, the rest of reality, and one's self.[21]

Fifth, symbols are multivalent in their structure. There is no single meaning of the parables of Jesus. The human mind uses symbols to grasp ultimate reality because ultimate reality shows itself in contradictory ways that will not yield to conceptualization. What exactly does it mean to say that Jesus is Son of God? How many different meanings does this proposition have in the whole of the New Testament? But what appears in conceptual thinking as a tension of opposites can often easily be expressed through symbols. The symbol thus expresses the multiple aspects of reality which are not able to be reduced to a series of propositions. It is not clear exactly what is meant when one says that Jesus was "in the form of God" (Phil 2:6), and the more questions one poses, the more the symbol both reveals and conceals. The symbol succeeds as a vehicle of knowing precisely because, in its multivalence, it can transcend a discursive, conceptual expression of the qualities of transcendence.[22] When one affirms that Jesus was empowered by God as Spirit, or embodied God as Wisdom, or was the incarnation of God's Word, many possibilities of meaning relative to a transcendent reality are being offered. To construe this language as directly representative or non-symbolic discourse is to reduce it, to subtract from and compromise its meaning, and to restrict its cognitive scope.

Sixth, and finally, religious symbols have a dialectical character. It is difficult to exaggerate the importance of this quality of the symbol when it is employed in christology. The dialectical character of symbol allows one to assert contrary things about the symbol, because it is not the symbolized, and yet it makes the symbolized present. Eliade explains this as the

---

21. Eliade, *Images and Symbols*, 13–14.
22. Eliade, *Images and Symbols*, 15, 177.

dialectic of things that are sacred. Something becomes a hierophany, a revealer of the sacred, or a receptacle of the holy, and at the same time it continues to participate in its proper worldly environment. A *sacred* stone remains a *stone*.[23] This dialectic between the holy and the worldly, the tensive unity and difference between the sacred and the profane within the symbol itself, is the key to formal christology. Any attempt to break this tension, to resolve it in favor of either the sacrality or divinity of the symbol on the one hand, or the worldliness or humanity of the symbol on the other, will destroy it as a religious symbol. The theologian encounters God in Jesus; for the historian Jesus is a human being. The mediating truth of these opposites lies in a symbolic interpretation of Jesus as the Christ.

In sum, these six qualities help to define further the character of the religious symbol and especially its relevance to christology.

THE SYMBOLIC STRUCTURE OF CHRISTOLOGY

I now want to move to an analysis of the earliest development of christology with the help of a language that is provided by the theology of symbol. Behind this analysis lies the philosophy of religion that explains revelation in terms of symbolic mediation through particular things, persons, and events in history. The analysis is also dependent on a theology of symbol that borrows from a variety of thinkers such as Rahner, Tillich, Eliade, and Ricoeur. With a dialectical conception of religious symbolic mediation as a heuristic device, I hope to portray in a systematic and constructive fashion a framework for understanding the genesis of christology. The result of this analysis will also provide a general account of the fundamental structure of christology and, as such, a map of what goes on as christology continues to develop through history.

The Ground of Christology: Jesus of Nazareth

Christology begins with Jesus of Nazareth. Jesus is the source and the ground of christology, because christology not only begins with his appearance in history, but also refers back to him as to its subject matter. More has to be said here, as those who fear some kind of reduction of christology to a study of Jesus attest. But the premise cannot be forgotten: christology is in some measure about the human being Jesus of Nazareth.

This focusing on Jesus gives rise to a tension between the particularity of Jesus and his universal relevance. This is true of all religious symbols. The tension between the autonomous identity of a symbol and its bearing

---

23. Eliade, *Images and Symbols*, 84–85. The phenomenology of Jean-Luc Marion of the icon in *God without Being: Hors Texte* (Chicago: University of Chicago Press, 1991), 17–18, describes how the icon or symbol, while remaining finite, is translucent in revealing the transcendent invisible.

of a meaning that transcends itself by pointing beyond itself is intrinsic to a symbol. It is therefore important to note that on an historical level Jesus' being a human being makes him universally available. Because and insofar as Jesus is a human being, he is in that degree able to be understood by all other human beings. In symbolic mediation, the universal is found in the particularity of the medium. In the case of Jesus, he was a particular person in his time, place, context, and religious tradition. His individuality further distinguished him from others in his context, for example, John the Baptist. The first step in a constructive christology, then, is to look not only at Jesus' humanity, but also to his distinctive individuality. Symbols release universally relevant meaning through their concreteness as individuals.

But Jesus the individual human being is a religious symbol. A symbolic interpretation of Jesus releases the universal relevance of Jesus from his particularity even as he remains an individual human being. To interpret Jesus symbolically means, initially, that he is not regarded simply in himself alone, but is approached with a religious question. In its depth the religious question always deals with salvation. And salvation ultimately implies at least the question of God. Jesus' ministry, of course, consisted in explicitly mediating God; he is thus approached not simply in himself but pointedly as a medium or mediator of God. Thus one does not ask the religious question neutrally or in a detached fashion, for it involves the self, and does so in an ultimate way. Religious symbols need this subjective participation to succeed as symbols. The manner in which a symbolic interpretation of Jesus releases his universal relevance, then, is both subjective and objective. On his part, Jesus of Nazareth, the human being, pointed to something other than himself, namely, God and God's rule in history. And on the part of the interpreter, one approaches him with the religious question, looking for salvation that comes from beyond, from God.

On a descriptive and historical level, therefore, one can portray what Jesus did in terms of symbolic mediation. Jesus was one who mediated God, and people encountered God in Jesus. The reciprocity here may be underscored: people encountered God in Jesus, because Jesus mediated God. On the one hand, Jesus' mediation of God occurred on several levels of his activity. Jesus was a teacher. Jesus was an exorcist. Jesus healed. Jesus reconciled. Jesus welcomed the outcast and marginated. Jesus acted like the God he preached. Jesus was a symbol of God in his actions of mediating God. On the other hand, disciples encountered God in Jesus. On the one hand, the religious quest for salvation is universal or transcendental. On the other hand, there can be no specific religious answer to a religious question that is universally relevant that is not at the same time historically mediated.

People came to this religious figure with religious questions. His was of course in a religious culture. But neither this fact, nor some theory of a special religious crisis in Israel, is needed to explain the deep existential religious interest to which Jesus appealed, since religious questions are part of human existence. In his early work, Jon Sobrino stressed the fact that Jesus preached not God but the kingdom of God, and that what he held out to people was not a static possession of God, but a way to the Father.[24] This formula captures well the dynamic character of Jesus' mediation, and how objectivity and subjectivity are interactively bound together. Jesus was not communicating an objective set of doctrines but a presence of God, symbolized in a certain way, and a manner of responding to this presence.

Within the framework of the dialectical structure of a symbol, that to which Jesus points is just as important as Jesus himself. Obviously enough, there is a tendency in christology to become christocentric, if not monothematic in a certain Christ-centeredness. This undercuts the dialectical structure of the religious symbol that Jesus was, and it also contradicts the historical evidence concerning his religious mediation. The focus of Jesus' preaching and ministry was God and God's rule. The God Jesus mediated was personal, in some respects like a father, which was the preferred language of the time and place, and in other respects like a mother, all the more striking in a patriarchal setting.[25] This God was friendly, loving, concerned for each human being, especially those who suffered in any way, judging, saving. Jesus can never be separated from the God whom he mediates. Jesus apart from his symbolizing God generates no special religious interest. Only Jesus the symbol of God is the subject matter of christology.

The thesis here is that christology is essentially dialectical because Jesus, as a historical mediator of God, is a concrete symbol. One of the chief merits of a symbolic understanding of christology is that, because symbol is intrinsically constituted by a dialectical structure, it in turn explains the dialectical nature and dynamics of christology. This dialectical character of christology can be illustrated with a series of questions and answers. They show the importance, centrality, and practical relevance of the tensive quality of symbol to christology.

The first question concerns whether Jesus is the object of christology. A dialectical response to the question is both Yes and No. Jesus is the religious symbol central to Christianity. Jesus mediates God and God's salvation to human beings who grasp them in faith. On the one hand, then, Jesus is the object of christology as its source and ground. Christology is about Jesus of Nazareth. Yet Jesus is of interest because he mediates God and God's salvation. As the human mediator Jesus points not at himself but at God and God's rule. The point of the Yes and the No, however, is not to present alternatives, nor to propose a focus of attention that oscillates between the two poles, although this may be inevitable. Rather, the idea is to suggest an intrinsic and irreducible structure in a religious sym-

24. Jon Sobrino, *Christology at the Crossroads* (Maryknoll, N.Y.: Orbis Books, 1978), 338–40.

25. Elizabeth A. Johnson, *She Who Is: The Mystery of God in Feminist Theological Discourse* (New York: Crossroad, 1992), 79–82, 100–03.

bol that at the same time explains Jesus, the encounter of God in him, and christology as the discipline that studies these phenomena. One must hold together the conviction that, as the symbol who mediates God, Jesus both is and is not the object of christology. This dialectical character was first experienced in the most primitive form of the religious experience with regard to Jesus: the disciples encountered God in Jesus. In other words, the basis of this characterization is religious experience itself, in this case experience directed toward God in Jesus, corresponding to the dialectical structure of a symbol. The characterization of a symbol as a tension between two poles is also a description of how the symbol of Jesus Christ functions in religious consciousness. Christians experience a finite person in history; and they experience God in and through him.[26]

There are other questions which elicit dialectical responses and thereby illustrate further the dialectical structure of symbol and the discipline of christology. We will return to each of these issues in more detail later on. I raise them here in order to illustrate and emphasize the dialectical character of the structure of christology.

Is Jesus the object of Christian faith? Or, to put this in another way, is Christian faith directed to Jesus so that it stops, as it were, and rests in him? Or is it faith in God mediated through Jesus? This question, in its first form, also must be answered with both a Yes and a No. Jesus both is and is not the object of Christian faith. Any attempt to say simply either that Jesus is or is not the object of Christian faith will inevitably be inadequate, because it will relax the tension in Jesus as the symbol of God by denying one of the poles. The Council of Chalcedon is precisely an attempt to preserve this tension between the finite and infinite in Jesus against the tendency of monophysitism. The doctrine of two natures corresponds to the dialectical structure of Jesus as symbol of God.[27] If one says Jesus is the object of faith, one tends to forget he was a human being like us. If one says Jesus is not the object of faith, one tends to think that, because one can know about God independently of Jesus, Jesus may be removed from the center of Christian faith. Rather than answer this question in conceptual terms, however, it is better to understand Jesus as the symbol of Christian faith dynamically: Christian faith is faith in God mediated through Jesus. The question of the object of faith, when it reaches a simple, static answer, instead of a view that is intrinsically dialectical and dynamic, tends to falsify the existential, active, and participatory process of faith.

---

26. See Mircea Eliade, "The Structure of Myths," *Myth and Reality* (New York: Harper & Row, 1963), 1–20, for a description of how the dialectical character of symbols is derived from a phenomenology of how they actually function.

27. The Council of Nicaea may be read as a reaction against reducing Jesus to the status of mere creature. But this creedal statement does not have the dialectical balance that was achieved at Chalcedon with the two-natures symbolism.

Is Jesus the object of Christian worship? As was seen in the development of New Testament christologies, Jesus was interpreted as sharing various degrees of divine election and closeness to God. Some time in the course of the first and second centuries, Christians began to worship Jesus. It was largely on the basis of this worship that the essential divinity of Jesus was defined at the Council of Nicaea in the fourth century. Today Jesus is worshiped and called God. How are we to view this structure of Christian worship?[28]

Once again, one cannot view this worship outside of the dialectical tensions that constitute religious symbols. The structure of this worship is identical to the structure of Christian faith; it is dialectical and tensive. For example, Jesus is not worshiped insofar as Jesus is a human being. Rather, Jesus is worshiped insofar as Jesus embodies God and makes God present, that is, insofar as Jesus is the symbol and sacrament of God. This dialectical tension is expressed in the classical formulas of Christian prayer in which one prays to God through the Son, through the mediator, through the one who is our aperture to God, and who in turn makes God present to us. Exactly how God is present within Jesus will be the subject matter of later discussions.

Is Christianity to become theocentric in view of interreligious dialogue? I have already outlined how Christians find themselves today in a new situation of a dialogical relationship with other religions. And the attitude that is becoming increasingly pervasive among Christians is that these religions enjoy a validity rooted in God's providence. This situation recommends an overall religious worldview that is theocentric, that is, literally, one in which God is the center of all reality, and not Jesus Christ. More will be said about this later. But in the interest of defining further the structure of Christian faith and christology, it appears that a *Christian* theocentric worldview would mean that Jesus is still the center of a Christian perception of and faith in God. Christianity is not a free-floating theism that learns of God from all sources indiscriminately. Rather, the logic of what has been described here is that Jesus is at the center of the Christian view of God, even though God is the center of all reality. The symbolic and dialectical structure of christology thus demands both a positive and a negative answer to the initial question.

Finally one has the formal and narrow christological question of the humanity and divinity of Jesus. Here the dialectical character of a symbol becomes directly relevant to one of the most important questions in the history of christology. What does it mean to say that Jesus is consubstan-

---

28. The discussion of worship of Jesus will be taken up again in Chapter 15. The point of raising it here is simply to illustrate the applicability of the dialectical quality of symbol, specifically a "concrete symbol," to christology. Also, I entertain this question here in terms of an understanding of worship as something that is appropriate to God alone. I prescind from the historical question of the religious intentionality that characterized Christian devotion or worship of Jesus Christ in the early centuries.

tial with God, and thus precisely not a human being, and consubstantial with us, and in that measure other than God, a creature? It should be clear at this point that one will have to deal with ontological questions regarding religious symbols. We have just seen that both human and divine dimensions are found together in the dynamics of symbolic mediation. We will have to ask whether the tradition has resources to express these two dimensions of Jesus Christ in a way that preserves the integrity of both. This along with the other systematic problems will be discussed in later chapters. But one can begin to appreciate how the dialectical structure of understanding that arises out of viewing Jesus of Nazareth as the historical symbol of God will be helpful in sorting out the ontological issues that are implied in christology.

THE CONDITION OF THE POSSIBILITY OF CHRISTOLOGY: RESURRECTION

Let us return to an account of the genesis of christology. Of course there were interpretations of Jesus during his public ministry by everyone who came in contact with him and tried to understand his goals. But critical historical research and speculation tends to discourage the view that the more formal christologies of the New Testament were interpretations proffered by Jesus about himself. It is generally agreed that Jesus was not the object of his own preaching, even though questions of his status and authority would certainly have arisen. But it is difficult to establish the historical status of what are called implicit christologies, that is, christological claims that are inferred to have been present in Jesus' teachings and actions, if not in Jesus' own consciousness. Nor are such implicit christologies necessary for the continuous and coherent development of christology. Christianity is not the religion of Jesus, for Jesus was a Jew. Christian faith transcends the content of Jesus' own religion. It is true that Jesus became the object and medium of Christian faith. But this does not mean that christology is limited positively in its assertions about Jesus Christ to historical statements about Jesus during his lifetime, nor to the interpretations of Jesus about himself.[29]

Formal christological interpretation of Jesus is not Jesus' interpretation of himself, but Christian interpretation of him on the basis of his impact on his disciples. This begins in an explicit way after Jesus' death and in the light of the Easter experience. Christological interpretation has its basis in the experience of salvation from God mediated through Jesus. Although begun and nurtured during Jesus' lifetime, the experience of salvation formally flourishes in a new way in, or through, or in the light of the experience of Jesus exalted and ratified by God. I do not need to stress more than

---

29. I am not suggesting here that the discipline of history has no bearing on christological interpretation. On the contrary, history has a considerable bearing and impact on christology, as a negative norm and as a positive guide to interpretation. See Chapter 1. I will say more about implicit christology further on.

I have already that Jesus risen and savior is no other than Jesus of Nazareth. The memory of Jesus is central to the Easter experience and to christology, and his interpretation of himself defines his individuality. But at the same time it is important to register the epistemological and logical place of the Easter experience in the genesis of formal christology and the structure of christology generally.

The various accounts of Jesus appearing, and possibly the accounts of the empty tomb, are symbolic. They are conceptual symbols as distinct from concrete symbols. This means that they are ways of expressing and communicating something about Jesus of Nazareth, specifically, that he is alive and exalted with God. In this case their symbolic character implies that the stories told about Jesus or the disciples' encounter with Jesus or the absence of his body are not to be taken as descriptive historical accounts, but as statements expressing the community's experience and conviction of the ontological reality that Jesus is alive, risen, exalted, and with God. This is so for at least two reasons: because all talk of transcendent reality is symbolic insofar as the reality referred to is other than the directly representative meaning of language culled from ordinary experience; and because this is probably how these stories were originally designed and intended.

The experience of Jesus as risen, or of something analogous to it, is the condition of the possibility for christology.[30] The resurrection of Jesus implies in a decisive way the connection of God to Jesus and of Jesus to God. From one perspective, this is a special relationship that extends beyond what is entailed in the relationship of creator and creature. From another perspective, what occurs in the career of Jesus reveals the destiny of humankind as such. Part of what is being said symbolically of God relative to Jesus in this affirmation is that Jesus was not abandoned by God, that Jesus was in such a way God's, or of God, that God did not leave him in the power of death. From the point of view of the disciples and human beings generally, resurrection symbolically entails salvation. Salvation is part of what is experienced in the affirmation of Jesus' resurrection. For the reality of the resurrection confirms that Jesus' message was true, and that God is as Jesus reveals God to be. In raising Jesus, God becomes identified with Jesus' ministry and message. These are not inferences from a sensibly perceived resurrection, but are entailed in the experience itself of Jesus risen and exalted. These convictions are part of what is being symbolized in the affirmation that Jesus is really risen.

The symbolic character of the concept of resurrection has a bearing on the present-day affirmation that Jesus is risen. "Resurrection" is a symbolic term. According to symbolic realism, this means that Jesus is really

---

30. The resurrection is not affirmed in the same way by all Christian theologians. Existential theologians, for example, not wanting to transcend the existential witness itself with statements about externally objective states of affairs, tend to speak of the resurrection in terms of Jesus being alive in the faith of the community.

raised by God. But this is an object of faith-hope and not of direct representative knowledge. Further, the symbolic character of this predication releases the logic of Jesus' resurrection from a particular historical event witnessed by individuals, and allows it to be a symbol that corresponds to an experience that is universally available to one who encounters Jesus through scripture and the Christian community. The object of that experience is God as mediated by Jesus, and Jesus in his relation to God. Descriptively it is an encounter of God in Jesus' ministry that recognizes that God is as Jesus portrayed God to be, and that this God did not leave Jesus in the grasp of death, but exalted him into God's own life. Understanding this experience in terms of the dynamics of symbolization and symbolic communication explains how it is potentially available to everyone. The experience of Jesus' resurrection is one of faith-hope; it is also an experience of salvation, and the condition of the possibility of christology. As such it is open to all who encounter Jesus and his message. Christological faith rests on the basis of an experience of the resurrection of Jesus analogous to that of the original disciples.

THE ONGOING INTERPRETIVE STRUCTURE OF CHRISTOLOGY: NEW TESTAMENT CHRISTOLOGIES

The symbolic structure of christology corresponds to the fact that christology is essentially interpretation of Jesus. Its character as an ongoing process is demonstrated by the pluralism of New Testament christologies. The dynamic process that generated different christologies in different communities during the first century did not stop. On the basis of the development of New Testament christologies, viewed now from the perspective of symbolic interpretation of Jesus, a number of conclusions can be drawn about the structure of christology itself.

New Testament christologies are interpretations of Jesus; they are symbolic statements. They bear a reference to Jesus of Nazareth, now experienced to be alive and exalted with God. Their logic moves from the memory of Jesus, conditioned by the experience of him as the mediator of God's salvation, toward the one who is now with God and called messiah or Christ. This description of how christologies developed also applies to their internal structure or logic. One must understand christologies within the framework of this "ascending logic": they move from Jesus, being grounded in a concrete imaginative memory of him, to a Jesus exalted with God.[31] Even John's Prologue, which is the single most explicit affirmation that seems to begin from God's side with a pre-existent Logos, must be understood as being grounded in an "ascending" experience. It is a poetic rendering of an insight whose logic ascends from Jesus. It says

---

31. See P. J. A. M. Schoonenberg, "Trinity—The Consummated Covenant: Theses on the Doctrine of the Trinitarian God," *Studies in Religion / Sciences Religieuses*, 5 (1975–1976), 111.

that the human being Jesus was the one in whom God was present and active for salvation. The symbol used to express God present and active in Jesus is God's "Word," a symbol so richly laden with tradition that it cannot be interpreted neatly without remainder. But one thing is certain, the Prologue of John does not represent direct descriptive knowledge of a divine entity or being called Word, who descended and became a human being. To read a metaphor as literal speech is misinterpretation; to read a symbolic statement in terms of direct descriptive representation is to reduce, distort, and finally trivialize the dynamic, searching character of its meaning.

The foundation of the New Testament symbolic interpretations of Jesus as the Christ lies in encountering God in Jesus. The disciples encountered God in Jesus during his lifetime in a proleptic way that is difficult to determine; they experienced God at work in Jesus for their salvation in a more explicit way after his death in the coming to awareness of his exaltation. The basis and foundation of all New Testament christologies, therefore, as well as christology generally, is the experience of salvation. Salvation comes from God; it is transcendent; and thus all salvation theories will have the same symbolic character as christology. But because salvation lies at the basis of christology, to understand a christology fully one must look to the view of salvation that lies beneath, although often enough it is right on the surface. In any case, some conception of salvation always shapes the logic for the symbolic title or conception of Jesus' origin and identity.

The New Testament is a normative document for Christian faith. It contains a plurality of different and in some cases non-symmetrical christologies. How can it be normative? How can one hold all the christologies of the New Testament at the same time? This problem disappears in the recognition of the symbolic structure of christology. New Testament christologies are only in opposition with each other when they are misinterpreted as discursive, conceptual, and directly descriptive language. As symbolic expressions of the meaning, import, and identity of Jesus, they do not pretend conceptually to exclude other conceptual interpretations of Jesus, but to open the imagination to transcendent aspects of his reality. Because their primary intentionality is expansive and not restrictive, they can coexist precisely in the measure in which they are symbolic and not directly descriptive.

Because New Testament christologies are symbolic, they release in their turn a plurality of interpretations. We have seen this in dealing with New Testament christologies; they cannot easily be pinned down to one interpretation. Most exegetes, although they offer an interpretation, admit that interpretation cannot be definitively rendered. Christological interpretation and commentary on New Testament christologies is an ongoing historical affair, a historical fact that relativizes every systematic christology. The pluralism of New Testament christologies, I shall argue in Chapter 15, is a prescriptive norm governing the ongoing task of christology: Jesus

Christ must be interpreted in religious categories that are relevant to each culture and context.

One can understand ongoing christological interpretation as unfolding in a dialectical tension between faithfulness to Jesus of Nazareth and the relevance of Jesus' mediation of God to ever new contexts. One should note the dynamic, productive, and generative character of this tension. On the one hand, christology should be closely attached to the concrete portrait of the historical Jesus. This imaginative construal acts as a norm and a guide to theological interpretation of him. Yet, on the other hand, christology can and must transcend the Jesus of history in its proposing of interpretations of him that are relevant to new audiences and situations, new cultures and epochs. As was said earlier, the intrinsic meaning of Jesus transcends his own consciousness of himself.

From this tension I draw two conclusions which illumine the dynamics of christological interpretation. The first is that it is not always necessary to project back into Jesus' consciousness the later interpretations of him by his Christian followers. It is impossible to imagine that historically Jesus thought of himself in the terms of Nicaea as consubstantial with the Father. Just as the meaning of a classic text transcends the intention of its author, and is still an intrinsic meaning of the written text, so too, the meaning of this classic person transcends his historical self-consciousness. It is not necessary that Jesus thought of himself as universal savior for that interpretation of him to correspond to the intrinsic character of who he really was and is. It is not necessary for Jesus to have predicted his resurrection for him to be risen. It is not necessary for Jesus to have thought of himself as Son of Man or Lord or redeemer for all of these categories to be legitimate interpretations of who he is. This counters a certain tendency in christology in the face of historical criticism to force implicit christological interpretations on the historical Jesus which in the end are not plausible.

The second conclusion comes from a reflection on where new interpretations of the surplus of Jesus' meaning come from. They originate in the relationship between Jesus and the interpreting community. That is to say, they are precisely not found in the synchronic relationships of Jesus to his own situation, but arise out of the new diachronic relationship of Jesus to a new situation and generation.[32] Therefore these interpretations are symbolic of the experience of Jesus that arises out of his impact on the community at a given time. In this way the legitimate interpretation of the surplus of Jesus' meaning for succeeding generations underscores the historically conditioned character of these later interpretations. These interpretations themselves, therefore, should be judged and interpreted in a contextual and historical way.

But there are commonalities in all New Testament christologies, and these help in locating norms for christology. The most obvious and rele-

---

32. Francis Schüssler Fiorenza, *Foundational Theology: Jesus and the Church* (New York: Crossroad, 1985), 163–64.

vant commonality is that Jesus is the bearer of salvation from God. The pluralism of New Testament christologies thus unfolds within an identifiable, unified framework of common suppositions. And in this framework one can read the fundamental elements pertaining to the structure of christology. There is Jesus. There is the fact that God's salvation is encountered in him. There is the experience of Jesus' being of God, not abandoned by God, but presently being with God. There is an experience that Jesus was and is savior, that he responds to the most basic religious question, and that salvation comes through him. There is, in sum, an encounter of God in Jesus.

In a religion that is concerned with truth, a critical search for it, and an apologetic defense of it, unity in the community's faith that also recognizes a pluralism of christologies will give rise to tensions. Even though it appears that pluralism is a given, that it cannot be overcome, and that it should be considered a value, there is still a drive toward a unity of intelligibility that is integral to the inquiring mind, and a social demand for unity within the community on fundamental matters. How can these two fundamental themes accommodate each other? One can see the lines of reconciliation in the intention of the theologian. The systematic theologian strives for a unity of intelligibility at any given time, in relation to the historical context of his or her Christian community. The goal is to achieve a relatively adequate construal of Jesus Christ that includes values contained in the others. On the supposition of the symbolic character of all theological language, there is no reason to think that a given systematic and constructive christology will clear the field of other interpretations. Christologies must strive to be most relatively adequate from their historical situation. But the most important character of any systematic christology is its ability to draw into itself the values represented in other christologies, and therefore its necessary openness to conversation with other christologies.

The norms for christology are complex; there is no single touchstone except in extreme cases. One must think in terms of a group or a series of criteria. These criteria are internal to the disciplines of theology and christology themselves; they are norms of the very process of interpretation. One cannot imagine external and objective christological interpretations as such functioning as norms, because such a norm itself would be subject to interpretive construal. In broad terms, then, the symbolic structure of christology itself can be regarded as containing the norm of christology. This symbolic structure implies the following general axiom: christology is faithfully Christian in the measure in which it adequately explains how Jesus is the concrete symbol mediating God's salvation to humankind.

With this guideline I now take up the development of classical salvation theory and the christology that was built upon it.

CHAPTER 8

Development of Classical Soteriology

After a representation of the New Testament witness to the genesis of christology and a systematic analysis of its structure in terms of religious symbol, I move now to a consideration of the history of the further development of christology in what may be called the classical period. However limited and barely sufficient this analysis will be, it is absolutely necessary for an adequate christology. Christology cannot be based on the New Testament alone, or on a correlation between scripture and common human experience that bypasses or jumps over the intervening history. For the scriptures are integrally mixed up with the church. In anthropological terms, the scriptures are both the product and the norm of the Christian community. As living documents they continue to produce new meaning through the ages. Christological reflection looks back to the bible as the source of its self-understanding, and draws that witness forward in new interpretive languages. This is a continuing and continuous corporate action of the church. Contemporary christological language of any period, then, is a continuation of its immediate and longer-term past. Theology, to the extent that it means to express and communicate with a contemporary church community, has to appeal to that community's past language, especially this classical language which has had and continues to have a powerful hold on the churches, and then draw it forward into new situations in ways that are recognizable. This historical, social, and ontological role of tradition to constitute a community and define its self-identity is most important today as the world church adjusts to a new pluralism that it has never known before.

The brief discussions of the history of soteriology and christology contained here are not meant as a substitute for substantial study of this tradition which may be found in other sources. The goals here must be understood as a function of systematic and constructive theology. The genesis of christology did not stop with the last writing of the New Testament. In fact some of the most distinctive doctrines of Christianity, to which the large majority of Christians are still loyal, were formulated for the first time in the patristic period. The aim of these discussions is, therefore, to analyze a number of key interpretations of Jesus Christ that emerged in the course of this formative history, and to reflect on the historical experience they represent. The supposition is that a common dimension to the Christian experience of Jesus Christ stretches across the centuries, but it is inseparable from its plural forms of faith,[1] and can never exist apart from some particular historical theological language. The study of history both binds Christians in solidarity with the past Christian community and frees the Christian imagination to produce the distinctive interpretations that are necessary today.

In this chapter I will discuss the development of what may be called classical soteriology, that is, the soteriology of the patristic period and distinctive contributions of the medieval and reformation periods. The pluralism of ways in which Jesus Christ is presented as savior is quite extravagant, so that "modern scholarship has abounded in classifications and typologies of 'atonement theories.' Simply to organize the material seems to be a major achievement."[2] Although I shall refer to some typical alternatives in soteriological thought, my interest does not lie in constructing models. The first three sections of the chapter present the views of some of the more influential theologians on how Jesus Christ saves. I will comment on certain aspects of their thought, their presuppositions and method, trying to be sensitive to the connection between the description of the work of Christ and Jesus of Nazareth. In the concluding section I shall try to describe summarily the experience that underlies these soteriologies insofar as it can be retrieved by analysis. The result of this analysis will be important for the overall project in several ways. This discussion of the development of soteriology will contribute to an understanding of the development of the classical christological doctrines. It will also provide important data for a later systematic and constructive interpretation of salvation for today.

Soteriology is intrinsically narrative.[3] At bottom a narrative involves an event that moves things from one state of affairs to another. In this

---

1. Avery Dulles, "The Changing Forms of Faith," *The Survival of Dogma* (Garden City, N.Y.: Doubleday, 1971), 17–31.

2. Michael Root, "The Narrative Structure of Soteriology," *Modern Theology*, 2 (1986), 146. Perhaps the most famous study of types is Gustav Aulén's *Christus Victor: An Historical Study of the Three Types of the Idea of Atonement* (London: SPCK, 1950). A more adequate typology drawn from early sources is Michael Slusser's "Primitive Christian Soteriological Themes," *Theological Studies*, 44 (1983), 555–69. Slusser is attentive to the relation between soteriology and the historical Jesus. H. E. W. Turner's *The Patristic Doctrine of Redemption: A Study of the Development of Doctrine during the First Five Centuries* (London: A. R. Mobray, 1952) also describes various models of salvation in the early church.

3. This characterization of soteriology as narrative is drawn from Root, "The Narrative Structure of Soteriology." Since I have used the term "structure" in relation to christology as a whole and in particular in reference to the symbolic nature of contact between human existence and God, I will speak of the "narrative character" of soteriology which I intend to be synonymous with Root's "narrative structure."

case, human existence is affected and changed through the event of Jesus Christ. Soteriology is an interpretation of the story of Jesus Christ by retelling, or redescribing, or expanding, or augmenting it, with the result that the particular salvific point of the story is highlighted. The unity or coherence of the story of salvation, its salvific point, is the movement from the problem in which human existence finds itself to its resolution by the event of Jesus Christ. Thus Paul described the career of Jesus as salvific because he provided the new Adamic archetype into which human beings were assumed. An early wisdom hymn retells the story of Jesus as a descent, manifestation, playing out, and ascent of God's wisdom. Luke augments the story of Jesus in terms of the role of God as Spirit active in his life for the effecting of God's rule in history. The retelling of the story is soteriology; it explains by highlighting how human existence is changed in a saving or liberating way. It is successful in the measure in which it corresponds to the event of Jesus, and the people to which it is addressed are drawn into it, and recognize its relevance in their own existence.

This characterization of soteriology provides a guide for the study of the texts in the history of soteriology. It opens up such analytic questions regarding the story such as these: just what is human existence being saved from? What exactly did Jesus do for our salvation, or what did God do in or through Jesus? What is the "being saved," or the saved state of human existence? And how are people involved or drawn up into this story so that they are a part of it, and it is their story?

EASTERN SOTERIOLOGY

The title of this section, "Eastern Soteriology," does not really define its subject matter; it simply identifies Irenaeus and Athanasius as Greek theologians. From them one will be able to note some distinctive themes in contrast to the western theology of Augustine, Anselm, and others. But the first concern here is to pinpoint the particular focus of each of these theologians and not to develop a model of eastern soteriology.

IRENAEUS

I begin with Irenaeus of Lyons because as a second-century theologian he was very influential in the development of Christian thought. He also had a distinctive soteriology that shares a manifest continuity with New Testament soteriology.

Jesus Christ's Salvific Work

Instead of summing up Irenaeus's view of the salvific work of Christ with a series of statements, I represent it in its narrative form. This representation is a synthetic statement because Irenaeus never lays it out in this direct way.[4]

The two hands of God, the Word and the Spirit, existed before creation, and God created through them. First Adam and then Eve were created and lived as children in a garden world where all their needs were met. Before their sin, God's Word intended to become incarnate. They and the human race were destined for a life of development and growth in obedience to culminate in resurrection and glory with God (AH 4.38.1-3, pp. 521-22). But their sin broke this pattern, and the history after them was marked with sin, suffering, corruption, and death; history began moving not toward God and the good but away from its intended goal. Although God's Word and Spirit are operative against this history of sin, true salvation is effected by the incarnation of the Word in Jesus Christ. The pre-existent Word becomes the second and new Adam, the new source and archetype of the new saved phylum of human beings in history. He saves basically by living out an integral human existence; he does what Adam should have done.

But there are many dimensions to the "how" of this salvation: first, by the incarnation the Son or Logos assumes to himself a complete and truly human reality, body and all, thus uniting this humanity to himself. Second, by living the whole course of life from beginning to old age, he sanctifies or saves every aspect of human existence.[5] Third, this sanctification is effected by complete obedience to the will of God, which, on the one hand, reverses the disobedience of Adam, and, on the other hand, defeats the advances and temptations of Satan toward disobedience. This obedience is a key element in the story, for it reverses the whole tide of sin and disobedience of history.[6] The death of Jesus may be salvific for other reasons as well, but a main reason is that it is the supreme test of obedience; Jesus saves "by his blood" means the degree of his commitment to the Father's will. For this life of obedience Jesus is raised from death into glory, and this resurrection is the resurrection of all who cling to him by faith and follow him.[7] These effects of Christ's saving works are appropriated con-

---

4. The sources for this summary are St. Irenaeus, *Proof of the Apostolic Preaching, Ancient Christian Writers*, 16, trans. and annot. by Joseph P. Smith (Westminster, Md.: The Newman Press, 1952) and Irenaeus, *Against Heresies, The Ante-Nicene Fathers*, ed. by A. Roberts and J. Donaldson (Grand Rapids: Eerdmans, 1953). These works will be cited as PAP (by paragraph and page references) and AH (by book, chapter, paragraph, and page references), respectively.

5. "But in every respect, too, He (Christ) is man, the formation of God; and thus he took up man into Himself, the invisible becoming visible, the incomprehensible being made comprehensible, the impassible becoming capable of suffering, and the Word being made man, thus summing up all things in Himself . . ." (AH 3.16.6, p. 443).

6. PAP #31, p. 68; #34, p. 69; AH 3.18.2, 6–7, pp. 446–48.

7. "Inasmuch as Christ did rise in our flesh, it follows that we shall be also raised in the same; since the resurrection promised to us should not be referred to spirits naturally immortal, but to bodies in themselves mortal" (AH 5.7, p. 532). See also PAP #39, pp. 72–73.

cretely through the sending of the Spirit which unites divinity to our humanity, and by baptism and the eucharist which are, as it were, physical participations in this world of the incorruption and resurrection won by Jesus Christ.

Finally, the key term in Irenaeus which sums up all of this is "recapitulation," which means, among other things, to sum everything up. The term is closely connected with Jesus Christ being the second Adam, and it encompasses the whole narrative. Whereas Adam failed, Jesus Christ redid everything rightly, lived out a right living relationship to God, became the new source and head of humanity, and set human history back on the right track.[8]

Commentary

Irenaeus retells the story of Jesus as a cosmic drama of salvation. He does so by combining elements of Johannine Logos, descent, and incarnation christology, Pauline final Adam christology, and the kenotic wisdom christology of Philippians. In Irenaeus one has a massive worldview that integrates creation, human history, sin, and a comprehensive salvation.

There are a number of elements in Irenaeus's soteriology that both distance him from the present-day world and yet are appealing to current sensibilities. Irenaeus, for example, operates in a mythological framework which he takes as literal or historical. One has to explicitly interpret Irenaeus symbolically in order to appreciate his story. Still more generally, Irenaeus uses scripture in a way different than a modern theologian would. It portrays for him information, and this objective information about historical and transcendent data is all mixed up into a common framework. This is a major difference between Irenaeus and current theology, one which will be true of all these classical authors. As long as this narrative is depicted narrowly as directly or descriptively representative of objective history, it will not be credible to a modern or postmodern sensibility.

The context of Irenaeus's *Against Heresies* is influenced by an elaborate gnostic world of teaching that had infiltrated the churches. Without trying to characterize gnosticism, many of the points that Irenaeus makes have to be understood as reactions against this worldview. The absence of these same gnostic forces today sets up a certain ambivalence. On the one hand, most people will not appreciate portions of Irenaeus's polemic. On the other hand, many of the anti-gnostic themes in Irenaeus are what make him especially appealing today. His stress on the goodness of this world, his emphasis on the bodilyness of Jesus Christ, and on historical process and practical truth are elements congenial to present western culture.

---

8. The term appears in many different contexts and takes on a richer significance in each. For incarnation as a way of recapitulating human existence, see AH 3.16.6, p. 443; 3.21.10, p. 454; for recapitulation as a rationale for Christ's suffering, see AH 3.18.6, p. 447.

Several other points make Irenaeus attractive. From the perspective of the symbolic structure of christology, one can enter into the mythological form of Irenaeus's writing and identify with forms of experience that are analogous to experience today. For example, Irenaeus had a developmental historical view of the world. Adam and Eve were children, and the whole human race was growing and developing under divine tutelage. God was constantly intervening to teach, correct, and discipline humanity in the course of its growing toward maturity. This amounts to a view of God as a close and constant caring presence. There are obvious analogies here with an historicist outlook and an evolutionary framework.

For Irenaeus, God is constantly and universally involved in the historical development of God's creation. God has and always had a plan for history, and this plan was not changed by sin. There is no period of history or group of people for whom God is unconcerned or inactive. The incarnation is a climactic intervention within a much larger providential and pedagogical caring by God for the whole human race. This universalism is congenial to our age.

Along with his incarnationalism, which is quite literally depicted, Irenaeus at the same time strongly underlines the authentic humanity of Jesus. His anti-gnosticism and anti-docetism, as well as the whole logic of recapitulating the full range of human experience, make him stress the fully human character of Jesus. Thus Jesus is the archetypal human being, the pioneer of our salvation, the one we can look at and strive to imitate. His saving activity, centered in his freedom and obedience, is imitable.

The narrative conception of how Jesus Christ saves, in Irenaeus, lies open to a correlation with the life of Jesus; it allows one to fix the imagination on the concrete historical figure, Jesus. Jesus Christ saved as revealer and recapitulator in the way Jesus taught, lived, gave example, and was obedient unto death in his ministry. And, as in the case of all other human lives, this involved conflict, temptation, suffering, and in Jesus' case violent death. In other words, one can identify in Irenaeus the actions of Jesus that were salvific, and one can identify with the Jesus in Irenaeus's salvation theory. His suffering and death, his conflict with evil and the demons, these were historical conflicts that were played out in Jesus' historical decisions.

What are we being saved from in Irenaeus? We are not being saved from history, or from matter, or from this world. Creation is good; matter is not evil; the world is not a cage or an entrapment of the human spirit. Rather, we were originally designed to live out the course of an earthly existence and to develop and grow toward union with God. The world is our home during the time of our lives. What we are saved from, then, are the patterns of the sin of the world, and the corruption and death that flow from this. In this respect Irenaeus is classic: divine salvation is from sin, suffering, mortality, physical and moral corruption, and final death.

How does Jesus save? Jesus is the pre-existent Word incarnate. He saves by becoming incarnate and revealing, but especially by his obedience which reverses the pattern of sin after Adam, by being the pioneer of our resurrection in his own, and by sending the Spirit as the agent of the rebirth of another line of humanity.

What is the saved state? In this world it is life in the Spirit. This inspirited life leads to resurrection and eternal life.

ATHANASIUS

In this consideration of Athanasius I will focus on what is usually considered a more or less early work, his *On the Incarnation*.[9] Clearly Athanasius is in the same line of thought as Irenaeus; the story line of the descent of the Word in incarnation is the same. But he also has his distinctive vision.

Jesus Christ's Salvific Work

Is there a dominant or central line of thought in Athanasius' conception of the work of Jesus Christ? Is J. N. D. Kelly right in saying that incarnation is the key to a kind of physical notion of salvation?[10] Or is Jaroslav Pelikan correct in saying the central metaphor is illumination?[11] One of the reasons for the difficulty in pinpointing a center of gravity in this work is that the whole reasoning process is presented in the form of a narrative. I will present an analytic account of some of the major aspects of what Athanasius says Jesus Christ did for our salvation.

I begin with some of Athanasius's premises. One such premise for Athanasius's theory of salvation is the reason and logic behind it. The occasion is the fall and the reason is God's love: "the reason of his coming down was because of us, and that our transgression called forth the loving-kindness of the Word . . ." (DeInc 4, pp. 58–59). Salvation, then, is a renewal or restoration or recreation of what God had originally intended human existence to be (DeInc 7, pp. 61–62).

Another premise is that "the renewal of creation has been the work of the selfsame Word that made it at the beginning. For it will appear not inconsonant for the Father to have wrought its salvation in him by whose means he made it" (DeInc 1, p. 56).[12]

---

9. Athanasius, *On the Incarnation of the Word*, in *Christology of the Later Fathers*, ed. by E. R. Hardy with C. C. Richardson (Philadelphia: Westminster Press, 1954), 55–110. References to this version of the work are cited as DeInc by paragraph and page references.

10. J. N. D. Kelly, *Early Christian Doctrines*, Fifth Revised Edition (London: Adam & Charles Black, 1977), 377–80.

11. Jaroslav Pelikan, "Salvation as Illumination [in Athanasius]," *The Light of the World: A Basic Image in Early Christian Thought* (New York: Harper & Bros., 1962), 73–92.

12. "For being the Word of the Father, and above all, he alone of natural fitness was both able to re-create everything, and worthy to suffer on behalf of all and to be ambassador for all with the Father" (DeInc 7, p. 62). In Athanasius, reversing the argument, the Word must be fully divine to effect salvation, because it is a kind of re-creation.

To understand salvation, one has to understand what it is we are saved from. In Athanasius there are several aspects of our condition from which we need to be saved, all of which are the effects of the fall. Human beings lost the pristine image of God in or with which they were created. This was both the character of being rational and actual knowledge of God that reflected God's own Word and constituted a condition of blessedness (DeInc 3, 11, pp. 58, 65). Athanasius describes the dissolution of the whole human race that set in with the loss of this image of God (DeInc 5, 11-12, pp. 59–60, 65–67). It leads to death and final corruption.

Athanasius poses the situation as a kind of dilemma for God, a tension between God's goodness and God's justice. On the one hand, God had to be true to the promise of death if human beings disobeyed the original commandment. Yet, on the other hand, it was against God's love to allow human existence to be destroyed after God created it, bestowed reason on it, and made it partaker of God's Word. "It was, then, out of the question to leave human beings to the current of corruption; because this would be unseemly, and unworthy of God's goodness" (DeInc 6, p. 61; also 6–7, pp. 60–62).

In general terms, then, the logic of salvation is clear; with sin humanity lost its knowledge of God and was pursuing a course of corruption and death and eternal loss of being itself. The Word of God would restore human existence to its former state (DeInc 4, p. 59).

When it comes to the ways in which Athanasius conceives this salvation being effected, his thinking is expansive; it overflows the boundaries of the specific images he uses. Jesus Christ saves, first, by *incarnation*. This is the title and main theme of the work. The divine Word assumes flesh or a body, and in so doing utterly transforms it. The divine principle of life heals and restores human flesh by the very assumption of it as his own. Sometimes it appears that all of human nature is re-created;[13] sometimes it seems that those are re-created who adhere to Christ in faith by the Spirit.[14] By assuming human flesh the divine Word instills the divine

---

13. "Athanasius's language often suggests that he conceived of human nature, after the manner of Platonic realism, as a concrete idea or universal in which all individual men participate. From this point of view, when the Word assumed it and suffused it with His divinity, the divinizing force would be communicated to all mankind, and the incarnation would in effect be the redemption." Kelly, *Early Christian Doctrines*, 378. This is seen in such language as this: "And thus he, the incorruptible Son of God, being conjoined with all by a like nature, naturally clothed all with incorruption, by the promise of resurrection" (DeInc 9, p. 63).

14. "His more considered teaching, however, is that divinization through the Word does not come naturally to all men, but only to those who are in a special relation to Him. To be more precise, we are divinized by intimate union with the Holy Spirit Who unites us to the Son of God, and through Him to the Father." Kelly, *Early Christian Doctrines*, 379. For example, in an apologetic account of the reality of the saving power of Jesus Christ, Athanasius points to the concrete effects he has had on believers in history. DeInc 27–32, pp. 81–86.

image and reverses the fateful path of corruption. Incarnation is the most fundamental ground for Athanasius's axiom, "He was humanized that we might be deified" (DeInc 54, p. 107).[15]

Second, Christ saves by *revelation and example*. Athanasius also refers to the restoration of the image of God in human beings by way of Jesus' teaching and example. The invisible Word took flesh to be seen, so that human beings could learn from his works. In other words, there is also a historical reference to Jesus in Athanasius, or at least the Word working through a human body (DeInc 13–19, pp. 67–73).

Third, the divine Word *undergoes a sacrificial death* for our salvation (DeInc 20–32, pp. 73–86). In the reasoning of Athanasius, this had to happen, because God was bound by the promise of death attached to disobedience in the beginning. And so the divine incarnate Word surrenders his body to death in our place. This death is a sacrifice. The idea is one of substitution or representation; as the head of all humanity he represents all; he undergoes death for all of us, and thus pays the debt or the ransom.[16] This is paid in some diffused way to God, to Satan, and to death itself all at once. Athanasius also uses the language of satisfaction here.[17]

In sum, the meta-story that explains salvation in Athanasius is also a descent of the Logos-Son, his taking on human flesh, and his triumphal resurrection. Within this scheme the variety of the works of Jesus are salvific in different ways. The salvation that he accomplished is the overcoming of the effects of sin, including death, the divinization of human existence, and finally resurrection.

Commentary

There is no small distance between this text and our western intellectual culture. Let me begin by pointing to the difficulties people would have appreciating Athanasius's version of the story of salvation. One element is its mythological form; it is presented as a descriptive account of transcendent realities. The framework of the whole presentation is narrative in form; it is a story, and the actors are God the Father, the Word, Adam and Eve, Satan. Indeed all human beings are participants in the plot. The story, however, is not told with modern critical self-consciousness, but as one would narrate objective history. In a word, it has to be demythologized, that is, remythologized in present-day language.

---

15. Athanasius explains this with a metaphor of how a king who, by residing in a city, raises up the honor and prestige of the whole city, and thus protects it from its enemies by making it a place of special attention and care. DeInc 9, p. 63.

16. "Whence, by offering unto death the body he himself had taken, as an offering and sacrifice free from any stain, straightway he put away death from all his peers by offering an equivalent" (DeInc 9, p. 63). See George Dion Dragas, "St. Athanasius on Christ's Sacrifice," *Sacrifice and Redemption: Durham Essays in Theology*, ed. by S. W. Sykes (Cambridge: Cambridge University Press, 1991), 73–100, esp. 92–95.

17. "For, being over all, the Word of God naturally by offering his own temple and corporeal instrument for the life of all satisfied the debt by his death" (DeInc 9, p. 63).

Secondly, one will note the metaphysical and speculative theological language. These characteristics should be understood within the narrative framework. The story is told in terms that are deeply laden with metaphysical premises that are integral to the story. The intentions of God are explained on the basis of Genesis. Scripture has given us information that functions as objectified representative knowledge of God. It presupposes a developed theology of the Word of God, and somewhat pejorative conceptions of matter, change, the pattern of corruption in nature and time, and so on. In other words, underlying the language of this narrative is an integral conception of reality resting on premises about humanity, scripture, and the transcendent order that are quite alien to a twenty-first-century western perspective on reality.

There is also a historical imagination at work in this work. It is plain in many sections that Athanasius is not just making this up, or merely thinking in abstract, speculative, or theoretical terms. He also has a concrete imagination; he is looking at and referring to concrete historical events. For example, his description of the spread of sin in the world is graphic. When he speaks of Christ as the light of the world, he is at certain places referring to Jesus the teacher and his actual teaching of people and the historical spread of Christianity. And the whole scenario of the saving death of Jesus depicts the actual passion and death of Jesus.

But this historical imagination is not the critical imagination of today; it is not, for example, the historical imagination displayed by exegetes or those involved in Jesus research. Rather, it is deeply shaped by a dogmatic conception of the nature of Jesus Christ. Jesus is not for Athanasius a human being like us. The actor in history is God, or the divine Word who was defined as consubstantial with the Father at Nicaea. In many passages one has the distinct impression that his body or flesh is an instrument through which a divine being, in effect God, is the subject or actor in history. By inference, then, Jesus is not a human being identical with all others, but a bodily form or vehicle in which the divine being, the Word, is the actor.[18]

The contrast for today's audience, then, can be underlined simply by indicating the attention given to Jesus as a human being and the quest for the historical Jesus. Scripture scholars who pursue the historical Jesus assume naturalist premises; they reason and decide issues on the basis of Jesus being a human being. In christology the premise is not that Jesus Christ is a divine being, nor is the task to explain how he was a human

---

18. This represents the possible impression of the present-day reader. Grillmeier puts the point in more historical terms when, in reference to Athanasius, he writes: "There can be no doubt that the Logos is not merely the personal subject of Christ's bodily life, but also the real, physical source of all the actions of his life." The Logos is the "physical subject of all Christ's life." Aloys Grillmeier, *Christ in the Christian Tradition*, 1, *From the Apostolic Age to Chalcedon (451)* (Atlanta: John Knox Press, 1975), 312, 314.

being. Rather, the premise is that he was a human being, and the task is to understand how God's salvation was worked through him.

But at the same time, Athanasius represents some fundamental religious experiences, questions, and affirmations that a reinterpretation of the salvific work of Jesus Christ will surely include. I shall return to these aspects of this work in the last section of this chapter.

WESTERN SOTERIOLOGY

Although the goal here is also not to define "western soteriology," it may be noted that the line of thinking stretching between Augustine and Anselm is quite distinctive in contrast to eastern soteriology. Many of the same themes recur, but they are taken up into a new or different framework. In the eastern soteriologies one finds a certain weight on incarnation, the divine entering the physical world and human flesh in order to divinize them; western soteriology leans more on a transaction performed in Jesus.

AUGUSTINE

Augustine is not the source of western soteriology, but his impact on the western theology generally is enormous. Three texts contain condensed forms of Augustine's rereading of the story of the saving action of Jesus Christ.[19] I begin by responding to some questions regarding the narrative as a whole, and then proceed by describing the different versions of Augustine's understanding of salvation.

Salvation from Sin

The premise or supposition of salvation is the need for it. Salvation is from sin and its effects. With the sin of Adam all future human beings were also radically condemned.[20] The effects of sin are an internal bondage of the will; human beings are incapable of self-transcending knowledge

---

19. *Saint Augustine: The Trinity, The Fathers of the Church* (Washington, D.C.: Catholic University of America Press, 1963), Book 4, Chapters 7–19, paragraphs 11–26; and Book 13, Chapters 8–18, paragraphs 11–23 (cited hereafter as Trin by book, chapter, paragraph and page references to this version of the text); Augustine, *The Enchiridion*, in *Basic Writings of Saint Augustine*, I, ed. by Whitney J. Oates (New York: Random House, 1948), 655–730. Cited hereafter as Ench by paragraph and page references to this version of the text. It should be noted that these texts do not fully represent Augustine's view of how Jesus Christ saves. Augustine's corpus of writing offers a large horizon within which Jesus Christ as savior may be situated. These texts, however, portray key symbols that exerted considerable influence on the western soteriological tradition.

20. "Nevertheless, that one sin, admitted into a place where such perfect happiness reigned, was of so heinous a character, that in one man the whole human race was originally, and as one may say, radically, condemned; and it cannot be pardoned and

or love of God.[21] Human existence was under the external domination of Satan. And all human beings were heading for death and eternal damnation (Ench 25-6, pp. 672–4). No major theologian until Luther puts more stress on sin than Augustine.

The Motive of the Incarnation

The motive or reason for the incarnation is the love of God. One sees in Augustine considerable reference to God's wrath and anger. It is not that God was angry with humanity prior to the sending of the Son; rather, God loved humankind prior to the sending of the Son, and this is the reason for the incarnation (Trin 13.11.15, pp. 390–91). But this love of God is not quite as total and universal as in Origen and Gregory of Nyssa. Augustine is far from proposing a doctrine of universal salvation. But for those who are saved, God's love is total, gratuitous, and effective.

The Nature of Salvation

Augustine characterizes salvation in many different ways. Salvation is union with God and thus life victorious over death. It is being cleansed from sin and forgiven; it is reconciliation (Trin 4.10.13, p. 147). It is emancipation from Satan and restoration to the condition before the fall. It is the approach of God's love, and the gift of God as Spirit who enables a response of love.[22]

How Jesus Christ Saves

This salvation from God requires a mediator. And the mediator is Jesus Christ who is the Word become incarnate. In these texts Augustine responds to the question of why God became human by developing two distinct stories of salvation.

First, Jesus' work is a sacrifice. Augustine provides a way of analyzing this conception of the saving work of Christ by enumerating the essential elements of a sacrifice. "Four things are to be considered in every sacrifice: by whom it is offered, to whom it is offered, what is offered, and for whom it is offered" (Trin 4.14.19, p. 155). 1) The sacrifice is offered to God. The logic of this story lies in making satisfaction. Christ's death is a "propitiation" to God for sin; the innocent victim reconciles us with God's jus-

---

blotted out except through the one Mediator between God and men, the man Christ Jesus, who only has had power to be so born as not to need a second birth" (Ench 48, p. 686).

21. "Since we were, therefore, incapable of grasping eternal things, and the stains of sin, contracted by our love of earthly things and implanted in us, as it were, from the root of our mortality, pressed heavily upon us; it was necessary for us to be cleansed" (Trin 4.18.24, p. 160).

22. "But our being reconciled to God through a Mediator, and receiving the Holy Spirit, so that we who were enemies are made sons . . . : this is the grace of God through Jesus Christ our Lord" (Ench 33, p. 678).

tice (Trin 4.13.17, p. 151).[23] 2) The sacrifice is offered on our behalf, for us and in our place. This is, therefore, a substitution theory. Jesus Christ takes on our sin and its consequence, death. "Christ, who was himself free from sin was made sin for us, that we might be reconciled to God" (Ench 41, p. 683). 3) The one who offers the sacrifice is Christ himself. Thus Jesus Christ is a priest who offers the definitive sacrifice for sin. And 4) the sacrifice itself is also Jesus Christ: his death is a sacrifice. But this should not be conceived exclusively as a physical death satisfying God's justice. An external gift without an internal motive is empty; the real sacrifice is the internal obedience of Jesus Christ to the will of God motivated by a desire to unite humankind to God.[24]

In sum, this narrative explanation of the saving work of Jesus Christ consists in a transaction between God and God done on our behalf. The medium of this transaction is the humanity of Jesus, which Augustine can also emphasize. But in the end, with the doctrine of the trinity firmly in place, it is the divine Word who is the subject of Jesus' actions.

Second, Jesus' work is also redemption through a ransom. The view of Jesus' saving activity as a work of redemption is laid out by Augustine in Book 13 of the *De Trinitate* in graphic language. I present it here according to the elements that make up the story. First, because of sin, on the basis of God's justice, human beings are, as it were, given over to the power of Satan.[25] Although Augustine's language here seems strong, Satan's rights

---

23. "Now, as men were lying under this wrath by reason of their original sin, and as this original sin was the more heavy and deadly in proportion to the number and magnitude of the actual sins which were added to it, there was need for a Mediator, that is, for a reconciler, who, by the offering of one sacrifice, of which all the sacrifices of the law and the prophets were types, should take away this wrath" (Ench 33, pp. 677–78).

24. In Augustine sacrifice has two dimensions: On the one hand, every act designed to unite to God is a sacrifice. On the other hand: "'The visible sacrifice is the sacrament, the sacred sign, of the invisible sacrifice' (Augustine, *The City of God*, 10.5)." Gerald Bonner, "The Doctrine of Sacrifice: Augustine and the Latin Patristic Tradition," *Sacrifice and Redemption*, 106. "And then what greater example of obedience could be offered to us, who had perished by disobedience, than that of the Son of God, who became obedient to God the Father even to the death of the cross?" (Trin 13.17.22, p. 402) "Sacrifice, furthermore, is treated by Augustine as an *inward* act of total devotion of mind, heart, and strength . . . , and it is not confined to the death of Christ but pertains to his entire human activity. . . ." Eugene TeSelle, *Augustine the Theologian* (London: Burns & Oates, 1970), 172.

25. "By the justice of God the whole human race was delivered into the power of the devil, the sin of the first man passing originally into all of both sexes, who were born through conjugal union, and the debt of our first parents binding all their posterity" (Trin 13.12.16, p. 391). Augustine uses the following language: ". . . man was delivered into the power of the devil. . . ." "For when He abandoned the sinner, the author of sin immediately entered into him." "The committing of sin, by the just anger of God, subjected man to the devil. . . ." The theme here is not unlike that contained in the Greek theories: Satan was in control by right; we, as it were, sold ourselves out, into slavery; and Satan's control is "just."

over human beings are within the framework of God's absolute power and justice. Augustine's language about God's wrath and anger due to sin is also sharp, but he himself modifies it. The point is not God's alienation from human beings as persons, but human alienation from God; and God's anger is not really anger, but a function of God's justice (Trin 13.16.21, p. 400). Second, God conquers Satan by justice and not power.[26] Third, this comes about in a narrative scenario. Satan brought about the violent death of Jesus. But Jesus was innocent. Therefore Satan's action was wrong and unjust, and by this injustice Satan lost his rights over all who cling to Jesus Christ in faith.[27] Thus, fourth, Christ's death was a ransom which was paid to Satan. Jesus is a redeemer, one who buys back something that is in captivity. Augustine speaks about the blood of Jesus being paid to Satan, thus embellishing the story with sharp contrasts and paradoxes.[28] Fifth, however, not only is Satan deceived and bought off, he is also conquered by Jesus' resurrection. In resurrection Jesus triumphs over death and Satan.[29]

In sum, this ransom or redemption theory is also a transaction, this time between God and Satan on our behalf. Both this theory and the last have a certain exaggerated or extreme character. But both respond to the question of why God became incarnate by showing the seriousness of sin and the extent of God's love.[30]

There are other aspects of Christ's saving work in Augustine's texts. Christ mediates salvation by being our example.[31] As the incarnation of God's Word and eternal truth, Christ saves by revealing God and being

---

26. "But the devil was to be overcome, not by the power of God, but by His justice" (Trin 13.13.17, p. 393).

27. "What is the justice, therefore, by which the devil was conquered? What, unless the justice of Jesus Christ? And how was he conquered? Because, although he found in Him nothing worthy of death, yet he slew Him. And it is certainly just that the debtors, whom he held, should be set free, since they believed in Him whom he slew without any debt. It is in this way, then, that we are said to be justified by his blood" (Trin 13.14.18, p. 395). See also Trin 13.15.19, pp. 396–97 and Ench 49, p. 687.

28. "In this redemption the blood of Christ was as it were the price given for us (but the devil upon receiving it was not enriched but bound), in order that we might be loosed from his chains, and that he might not involve in the nets of sin and so draw with himself to the ruin of the second and eternal death, anyone of those whom Christ, free from all debt, had redeemed by pouring out His own blood without being obliged to do so. . ." (Trin 13.15.19, pp. 397–98).

29. "It is not difficult, therefore, to see how the devil was conquered when He, who was slain by him, rose again" (Trin 13.15.19, pp. 396–97).

30. "The devil was holding fast to our sins, and by means of them was deservedly fixing us in death. He, who had no sins was undeservedly led by him to death, released them. So great a price did that blood have that he who slew Christ for a time by the death that was not due should no longer detain anyone who has put on Christ in the eternal death that was due" (Trin 13.16.21, p. 400).

31. "He also offered Himself to be tempted by him, the devil, so that by also overcoming his temptations, He might be our mediator not only by His help but also by His example" (Trin 4.13.17, p. 151). Also Ench 53, p. 689.

the focal point of our faith in God (Trin 4.18.24, p. 161). Occasionally one sees hints of the idea of deification in Augustine; God became human so we could become divine.[32] But the distinctive weight of Augustine's retelling of the story of salvation rests on the meta-scenarios of the sacrifice performed and ransom paid to overcome sin.

ANSELM

I now turn to Anselm's classic interpretation of how Jesus Christ saves. This entails a jump of almost 700 years, and a passage from a late classical Latin culture, influenced by neo-Platonism, to a feudal culture of the middle ages. A historical description of the context of this soteriology would have to underline the many differences between Augustine and this medieval monk, between their cultural times and their intellectual presuppositions. But Anselm is operating in the Augustinian tradition, and he presents the story of Jesus Christ making satisfaction in such a clearly reasoned way that it became the basis of western soteriology.[33]

Jesus Christ's Salvific Work of Satisfaction

Anselm's redescription of the story of salvation is quite simple in its essence. It responds to the question of why God had to become incarnate for our salvation. Why could God not have saved by willing it, for example, in an act of forgiveness? The problem is set up by original sin which was an infinite offense against God. This sin broke the right order of the relation of human existence to God, and put humanity in an infinite debt toward God. The offense of sin could be dealt with in three ways, by forgiveness, by punishment, or by satisfaction. But the first, gratuitous amnesty, is impossible because it would not restore human beings to their original dignity. Therefore, sin requires either eternal punishment or satisfaction. Satisfaction here means not just returning what was due, but, over and above that, a "more" or a "plus" that repairs the injury done. The problem, then, is this: how is this satisfaction possible? Only God can save; only God can offer an infinite satisfaction for an infinite offense. But only human beings owe it, and therefore they must pay the satisfaction. There is utterly no way in which mere human beings can provide the "more" entailed in satisfaction, because every act of obedience they perform is already owed.

---

32. The Son of God, divine by nature, became human, so that "sons of man by nature [might] become the sons of God by grace, and dwell in God in whom alone and from whom alone the blessed can be made sharers of His immortality. . ." (Trin 13.9.12, p. 387).

33. Anselm of Canterbury, *Why God Became Man?*, in *A Scholastic Miscellany: Anselm to Ockham*, ed. and trans. by Eugene R. Fairweather (New York: Macmillan, 1970), 100–83. Hereafter referred to as CDH; references in the text are to the book, chapter, and page of this translation.

The necessary solution is a God-man. By a certain "necessity" God must carry through on the original intention for human beings at creation. And this salvation in turn requires an incarnation and the God-man Jesus Christ, as that was understood by Chalcedon. How does Jesus save? The act of surrendering his life freely for the sake of justice, of choosing death, is an act that is not owed to God because Jesus was sinless. Thus this offering provides an infinite "more" than what was owed or due to God, and it renders satisfaction to God for sin. In sum, Jesus acted as a human being and a representative of all human beings. And his unrequired free choice of death is also an infinite satisfaction because it was simultaneously an act of God.

Commentary

Anselm's *Cur Deus Homo?* is a jewel; it is simple and translucent, but cut in such a way that it can be viewed from many angles. As one considers it more closely it gives off different colors in different relationships and seems to become more and more complex.

The relation of faith and reason in Anselm has occasioned a great deal of discussion. On the one hand, Boso, the student who asks the questions in the text, is posing the questions from a non-believer's point of view, so that the work is apologetic. But at the same time the reasoned responses come from a faith already possessed (CDH 1.3, p. 104). The work is a model of the idea that theology is faith seeking understanding.

Sin is every act that does not render to God what is due to God. The will of every creature should be subject to the creator, and any failure is a sin. It is like stealing God's property (CDH 1.11, pp. 118–19). The weight of the least sin, because a sin against the infinite God, by the logic of infinity becomes infinite (CDH 1.21, pp. 138–39). What original sin took away from God is God's plan for humankind (CDH 1.23, p. 141). This must be restored to God.

There are few, if any, words that appear more in this text than the word "just" and its cognates. God's justice, or justice itself, which has its very basis in God, forbids forgiveness of sin without either punishment or satisfaction. God cannot act the same toward sinners and those who do not sin. God is sovereign and free, but God is not arbitrary; God necessarily operates within a framework of what is fitting and just (CDH 1.12, pp. 120–21). This quality of justice in God cannot be reduced to legal justice. One should regard this notion within the framework of a monastic and contemplative theology. God's justice is a dimension of the beauty, order, and harmony of the universe (CDH 1.15, p. 124).[34] Anselm was an

---

34. This is the deeper reason why God cannot grant a gratuitous amnesty and simply forgive sins. God's mercy cannot bypass but must work within a justice that reflects the order of the universe of which God is the basis. "Such forgiveness would do nothing to correct the disturbance of the order and beauty of the universe caused by sin." R. W. Southern, *Saint Anselm: A Portrait in a Landscape* (Cambridge: Cambridge University Press, 1990), 212.

ascetic, and monastic life was governed by rules. But a larger framework is at work here.

Another major notion that guides this retelling of the story of Jesus saving is the honor of God. This should not be understood in a merely personal sense of being esteemed, implying a desire or need for it. "It is impossible for God to lose his honor" (CDH 1.14, p. 123). Nothing can be added or subtracted from God's honor (CDH 1.15, p. 123). Rather than a subjective need, God's honor is connected with the order of the universe and justice within that ordering. It is objective; it characterizes the running of things ontologically the way they should be. "Regarded in this way, God's honour is simply another word for the ordering of the universe in its due relationship to God."[35] Since nothing is greater than God, and God is the very foundation of justice, God "maintains nothing more justly than God's own honor, in the ordering of things" (CDH 1.13, p. 122). This is most important because God's honor is the main reason why God cannot simply forgive sin, and either punishment or satisfaction is an absolute requirement (CDH 1.13, p. 122). The reasoning here is based on the coherence and integrity of reality itself for which God is the ground. The feudal context should not be overly stressed.

Satisfaction is obviously a central term, since it characterizes the logic of the story. Satisfaction presupposes injury done. It consists not in rendering to God what is owed to God in due course, but in making up for an injury done and repairing damage. In terms of theft, this means going beyond restitution of what is stolen. It entails that one "give back more than one takes away" (CDH 1.11, pp. 118–19). This satisfaction must be ordered or measured according to the offense. This puts finite human beings in an impossible situation, for their sin is infinite because it is against an infinite God (CDH 1.19-24, pp. 134–44).

Another major background concept, closely related with faith and reason and the whole order of things, is "necessity." Anselm knows the way things are with God because of revelation, scripture, and faith. But he is looking for the internal reasons why they are the way they are. Theological understanding requires knowing internal logic and necessity. But he also knows that predicating necessity of God and God's sovereign freedom requires care. The idea of necessity is continually implied in the discussion of whether God can abandon creation after sin, of whether an incarnation was necessary, of whether Christ necessarily submitted to his death. In each of these cases necessity is not a strictly logical or metaphysical concept, but either a logical entailment of a certain concept of God, or an argument based on what is called fittingness: given such a God, one cannot conceive otherwise. God must do what is God-like. Anselm is dealing with something as paradoxical as a "free necessity." For example, God cannot lie and be God. But God is not constrained not to lie by an outside force

---

35. Southern, *Saint Anselm*, 227. See also Jasper Hopkins, *A Companion to the Study of St. Anselm* (Minneapolis: University of Minnesota Press, 1972), 192.

(CDH 2.4-5, pp. 148–50). The necessity of God saving lies in God's own goodness: "in creating human beings out of God's own goodness, God freely bound God's self, as it were, to complete the good work once begun" (CDH 2.5, p. 150).

Salvation is a restoration of union with God. As in Augustine's story of sacrifice, human beings are reconciled with God by the free choice of Jesus Christ to undergo a death that he did not owe, because he was sinless. And this "more," this gift of self over and above what was owed to God, is of infinite value because it was the act of a God-man. It thus rendered a satisfaction that infinitely transcends all the sins of all humankind (CDH 2.10-14, pp. 156–64).

When Boso heard Anselm describe the human predicament of sin, infinitely in debt without the possibility of repaying it, he was near to despair; he wondered whether anyone could be saved (CDH 1.21-23, pp. 139–40). When he heard the account of the efficacy of Christ's saving action he wondered whether anyone who turned to Christ could not be saved (CDH 2.19, p. 181). This reflects a tension in Anselm's thought. On the one hand, he did not think many people would be saved. For the most part, one would, practically speaking, have to be a monk to be saved. This is the ascetic side of Anselm.[36] But on the other hand, Anselm argues forcefully that God must (necessity) bring to completion what God intended with creation. This is consistent with the order and harmony of the universe and its ground and creator. "It is certainly incongruous for God to let any rational nature perish altogether" (CDH 2.4, p. 148). Anselm, it seems, restricts his thinking here to human nature, and does not apply it to individuals: God had to save some representative human beings. But it is hard to see the logic of that restriction. Why not everyone? His story really tends toward universal salvation.[37]

ABELARD

One way of characterizing the salvation theory of Abelard is to see him as an heir to the work of Anselm. One of the major contributions of Anselm was that he explicitly denied Satan any rights over humankind. This in effect removed Satan from the drama of salvation, and posed the problem in terms of God and human beings in relation to each other.[38] With Satan no longer in the equation, Abelard drew Anselm's premises to their opposite conclusion: "since human beings could make no payment to God, and God need make no payment to the Devil, the purpose of the

36. "Few will be saved, he reiterated; and most of these will be monks, he implied, for they alone have achieved a complete surrender to God's will." Southern, *Saint Anselm*, 215.

37. Southern, *Saint Anselm*, 215.

38. Southern, *Saint Anselm*, 211.

Incarnation could not be that of making any payment at all. It could only be an act of love."[39] "Love" is the key word that sums up Abelard's telling of the story of salvation, even as his recapitulation summed up Irenaeus's.

Jesus Saves by Revealing and Being an Example

Abelard's salvation theory is laid out succinctly in a passage in his commentary on Romans.[40] It consists in Jesus being a revelation and effective demonstration of God's love for humankind. Jesus teaches us and gives us an example of how to love God and our neighbor in response to God. Jesus Christ thus binds human beings to God in love by being God's love toward us and enkindling our love of God and neighbor in return. The kernel and point of the story, retold in contrast to Anselm, is thus straightforward and simple:

> Now it seems to us that we have been justified by the blood of Christ and reconciled to God in this way: through this unique act of grace manifested to us—in that his Son has taken upon himself our nature and persevered therein in teaching us by word and example even unto death—he has more fully bound us to himself by love; with the result that our hearts should be enkindled by such a gift of divine grace, and true charity should not now shrink from enduring anything for him.[41]

More Than a Moral or Subjective Theory of Salvation

Gustav Aulén calls this a subjective and a moral theory of salvation. By this he means that the change that is effected in salvation is not a changed attitude on the part of God, but a change that takes place in human beings, that is, a conversion.[42] Abelard's view is extended further as a moral theory in nineteenth-century liberal thought, according to which salvation becomes human movement toward God.[43]

These characterizations do not seem to be accurate. First of all, Abelard embraces a high christology; the Logos is incarnate in Jesus. Thus God's approach to human existence is ontological. It is love incarnate, a love of God for human existence and the world that is realized or effected in action. Moreover, the love that is aroused in the human person to respond to God is also ontologically caused by God. It is the effect of the gift of God as Spirit. Abelard is an Augustinian: where there is love of God, it is the effect of the work of God as Spirit or grace. And Abelard explicitly refers to this working of the Spirit by citing Paul: "'Because the charity of God

---

39. Southern, *Saint Anselm*, 210.

40. Peter Abailard, "Exposition of the Epistle to the Romans (An Excerpt from the Second Book)," *A Scholastic Miscellany*, 276–87.

41. Abailard, "Exposition of the Epistle to the Romans," 283.

42. Aulén, *Christus Victor*, 18, 112–13.

43. Aulén, *Christus Victor*, 139–59.

is poured forth in our hearts, by the Holy Ghost, who is given to us.'"[44] In the end, Aulén slights the interpretation of Abelard because he has another interpretation as his standard, one closer to that of the reformers.

THE REFORMERS

The reformers are, of course, very much within the western tradition of theology; they are singled out here because of the distinctive readings they bring to the story of salvation. In the tradition of Augustine and Anselm, their interpretations lay a certain emphasis on the themes of substitution and vicarious punishment.

LUTHER

Luther's religious worldview consistently reflects his religious insight into the antithesis between law and gospel, and into justification by pure grace through faith. Luther was in many respects more anti-Pelagian than Augustine himself. But it is not possible to situate his interpretation of salvation into the whole of his thought. I shall appeal to a few representative texts.[45]

We Are Saved from Sin and the Wrath of God

We are saved from the wrath of God which is due to sin. Luther presents a number of negativities from which human existence is saved: sin, death, Satan, God's curse, and even the law. But most fundamentally salvation is reconciliation with God. And what is reconciled is God's wrath against sin, for sin is the contradiction of God's holiness, righteousness, and justice. In a way, the work of Christ is God reconciling God's self in order to accept human beings in love. The larger framework for understanding God is as a God of love and mercy. But this can be grasped only in faith. While in sin, the conscience of the sinner can only see God's justified anger at sin.[46]

The Logic of Christ's Work: Substitution and Satisfaction

The most fundamental logic of Christ's work is summed up in the two words, substitution and satisfaction. Substitution means that the Logos or

---

44. Abailard, "Exposition of the Epistle to the Romans," 284, citing Rom 5:5.

45. Martin Luther, *Luther's Works*, 26, *Lectures on Galatians 1535*, ed. by J. Pelikan and W. A. Hansen (St. Louis: Concordia, 1963), 276–96, 359–74, representing Luther's commentary on Gal 3:13ff. and Gal 4:1ff.; Martin Luther, "The Freedom of a Christian," *Luther's Works*, 31, *Career of the Reformer*, ed. by Harold J. Grimm (Philadelphia: Muhlenberg Press, 1957), 343–77. Cited hereafter as LW 26 and LW 31 with pages.

46. "To the extent that Christ rules by His grace in the hearts of the faithful, there is no sin or death or curse. But where Christ is not known, there these things remain" (LW 26, 282). See Paul Althaus, "Man Under the Wrath of God," *The Theology of Martin Luther* (Philadelphia: Fortress Press, 1966), 169–78.

Word of God, Christ, becomes incarnate and takes the place of human beings. In his love of paradox and sharp language of dialectically related or opposing themes, Luther states plainly that Christ becomes a sinner, one who is cursed (LW 26, 277–80). He even goes so far as to say that Christ, despite being divine, experienced himself as sinner, cursed, abandoned, and so on. Luther maximizes the pain and suffering of Christ, especially internally.

How is this salvific? Christ, in substituting for all human beings, and in being our representative, is obedient to death in our place. "For Anselm, there were only two possibilities, either punishment or satisfaction. For Luther, satisfaction takes place through punishment, not of the sinner but of Christ."[47] After Jesus Christ, God no longer regards the sinfulness of human beings, but only looks upon the righteousness of the representative. "But when sin and death have been abolished by this one man, God does not want to see anything else in the whole world . . . except sheer cleansing and righteousness. And if any remnants of sin were to remain, still for the sake of Christ, the shining Sun, God would not notice them" (LW 26, 280).[48]

The Cosmic Battle

Within the framework of Christ as our substitute making satisfaction, Luther develops the idea of a cosmic battle between the forces of evil and good. This is an early doctrine of Luther, and is found in his "Freedom of a Christian" (LW 31, 352, 357-58). The duel represents symbolically the dynamics of the work of Christ, and interprets what was going on, especially in Jesus' suffering and death. Luther portrays this as a duel between the incarnate Logos and a whole series of personified forces: sin, death, God's curse, God's wrath, the law. But Christ the innocent, obedient, holy, and divine one overcomes and defeats all of these forces. Although he accomplished this in his humanity, it was the work of divinity. "For to conquer the sin of the world, death, the curse, and the wrath of God in Himself—this is the work, not of any creature but of the divine power. Therefore it was necessary that He who was to conquer these in Himself should be true God by nature" (LW 26, 282).

Although the description of the duel seems like mythological language, it may be read as personification. The place where this duel took place is within the person of Jesus Christ; in this sense, he is the referent. In other words, there is room here for an historical imagination. These forces of evil

---

47. Althaus, *The Theology of Martin Luther*, 203.

48. "If the sins of the entire world are on that one man, Jesus Christ, then they are not on the world. But if they are not on Him, then they are still on the world. Again, if Christ Himself is made guilty of all the sins that we have all committed, then we are absolved from all sins, not through ourselves or through our own works or merits but through Him. But if He is innocent and does not carry our sins, then we carry them and shall die and be damned in them" (LW 26, 280).

were being engaged within the person of Jesus, in some sense within his consciousness.

Appropriation of Salvation: The Wonderful Exchange

This objective salvation must be appropriated by Christians to be effective; it is not automatic. How are people included in Luther's retelling of the story? The believer clings to Christ in faith. And by this existential union there is effected a "wonderful exchange" in which what is Christ's becomes mine, that is, innocence and righteousness, just as what was mine becomes Christ's, that is, sinfulness, fear, condemnation by the law, being the object of God's wrath and curse.[49] This exchange is based upon a kind of interpersonal Christ mysticism in which the believer and Christ become one.[50]

Exemplarism in Luther: The Duel within the Christian

The idea of exemplarism is not prominent in Luther; he will attribute nothing salvific to human freedom. But there is exemplarism in the sense that the conflict and duel that went on in Christ's suffering and death also goes on in the life of the Christian. In the Christian the struggle or duel is between the forces of sin, death, and condemnation by law that lead to despair and faith in Christ. The difference is that whereas Christ conquered by his divine nature, human beings conquer by simply attaching themselves to Christ by faith. "So long as sin, death, and the curse remain in us, sin damns us, death kills us, and the curse curses us; but when these things are transferred to Christ, what is ours becomes His and what is His becomes ours. Let us learn, therefore, in every temptation to transfer sin, death, the curse, and all the evils that oppress us from ourselves to Christ, and, on the other hand, to transfer righteousness, life, and blessing from Him to us" (LW 26, 292).

---

49. See Jared Wicks, *Luther and His Spiritual Legacy* (Wilmington: Michael Glazier, 1983), 137–41.

50. "But because He took upon Himself our sins, not by compulsion but of His own free will, it was right for Him to bear the punishment and the wrath of God—not for His own Person, which was righteous and invincible and therefore could not become guilty, but for our person.

"By this fortunate exchange with us He took upon Himself our sinful person and granted us His innocent and victorious Person. Clothed and dressed in this, we are freed from the curse of the Law, because Christ Himself voluntarily became a curse for us. . . .

"We must look at this image and take hold of it with a firm faith. He who does this has the innocence and the victory of Christ, no matter how great a sinner he is. But this cannot be grasped by loving will; it can be grasped only by reason illuminated by faith. Therefore we are justified by faith alone, because faith alone grasps this victory of Christ" (LW 26, 284).

CALVIN

Just as Thomas Aquinas was an Augustinian because everyone was, so too Calvin was converted to Lutheran ideas, and central themes from Luther's theology reappear in Calvin. But at the same time they were very different men in different socio-cultural settings, and a number of these differences give Calvin's theology a different cast from that of Luther. For Luther's theology, the antithesis between law and gospel is a fundamental axiom; law, although in itself good and from God, is a negative category because it exposes and condemns our sin and, by appealing to our will, is a temptation to further sin and a curse. In Calvin, however, law is positive and, after justification, becomes a guide for the Christian life and a salutary agent for ordering the community. Differences such as these give a distinctive meaning to Calvin's view of how Jesus saves. Calvin narrates the story of salvation in his *Institutes*.[51]

God's Wrath, Substitution, Obedience, Satisfaction
The logic of salvation is laid out clearly by Calvin in terms of Christ being a sacrifice; he substitutes for us, and, by his obedience unto death, he satisfies God's anger and wrath against sin. This is in the particular line of Augustine that I have traced, the one taken over and developed by Anselm. As for God's anger: "No one can descend into himself and seriously consider what he is without feeling God's wrath and hostility toward him. Accordingly, he must anxiously seek ways and means to appease God—and this demands a satisfaction" (*Institutes*, 2.16.1, p. 504). "This is our acquittal: the guilt that held us liable for punishment has been transferred to the head of the Son of God. We must, above all, remember this substitution, lest we tremble and remain anxious throughout life—as if God's righteous vengeance, which the Son of God has taken upon himself, still hung over us" (*Institutes*, 2.16.5, pp. 509–10). The curse of God upon us because of sin was lifted from us and placed on Christ. And then: "Christ was offered to the Father in death as an expiatory sacrifice that when he discharged all satisfaction through his sacrifice, we might cease to be afraid of God's wrath" (*Institutes*, 2.16.6, p. 510). Finally, Calvin is clear that Christ's satisfaction was the work of his whole life: "Christ has redeemed us through his obedience, which he practiced throughout his life" (*Institutes*, 2.16.5, p. 507).[52]

---

51. This account of Calvin's view of salvation relies chiefly on his treatment in *Calvin: Institutes of the Christian Religion*, ed. by John T. McNeill (Philadelphia: Westminster Press, 1960), Book II, Chapter 15–17, 494–534. References are to this edition as *Institutes*, by book, chapter, paragraph, and page.

52. Calvin sums up his interpretation of salvation this way: "By his obedience, however, Christ truly acquired and merited grace for us with his Father. Many passages of Scripture surely and firmly attest this. I take it to be a commonplace that if Christ made satisfaction for our sins, if he paid the penalty owed by us, if he appeased God by his

Resurrection, Intercession, Sending of the Spirit

Calvin looks for a salvational aspect in all the phases of Christ's life. He looks upon Christ as prophet, king, and priest. As prophet his teaching is salvific, as king he rules through the Spirit, and his principle work as priest is the sacrifice just considered. Calvin also draws out the salvific aspects of Christ's burial, descent into hell, resurrection, ascension, and sending of the Spirit. In short, Calvin finds an aspect of salvation in every aspect of the narrative of Christ's life.[53]

Appropriation: Sanctification, Law, Christian Life in the World

One finds a major difference between Luther and Calvin in the way they envision the bearing of salvation on the Christian life. How is salvation appropriated by each Christian? In Luther this happens by faith; by the union with Christ effected by faith, Christ's justice becomes that of the believer. This is true of Calvin as well. But Calvin, after distinguishing sanctification and justification, gave sanctification a prominent place in his theology. Calvin emphasized that the Christian, once justified, should lead a holy life in the world, guided by the law, and within the context of the calling that was assigned each by providence. Thus in Luther salvation in this world lies in a relationship of union with God right now, constituted by grace and grasped in faith; in Calvin, however, salvation was played out in Christian life in society.[54]

---

obedience—in short, if as a righteous man he suffered for unrighteous men—then he acquired salvation for us by his righteousness, which is tantamount to deserving it. But, as Paul says, 'We were reconciled, and received reconciliation through his death.' But reconciliation has no place except where an offense precedes it. The meaning therefore is: God, to whom we are hateful because of sin, was appeased by the death of his Son to become favorable toward us. And we must diligently note the antithesis that follows shortly thereafter. 'As by one man's disobedience many were made sinners, so by one man's obedience many are made righteous.' This is the meaning: as by the sin of Adam we were estranged from God and destined to perish, so by Christ's obedience we are received into favor as righteousness" (*Institutes*, 2.17.3, pp. 530–31).

53. Calvin ends Book II, Chapter 17 with a paragraph that sums up its development. Salvation is found only in Christ. And one can find an aspect of the salvation that he mediates in all aspects of his life, as represented by each clause or phrase in the creed. "If we seek salvation, we are taught by the very name of Jesus that it is 'of him.' If we seek any other gifts of the Spirit, they will be found in his anointing. If we seek strength, it lies in his dominion; if purity, in his conception; if gentleness, it appears in his birth. For by his birth he was made like us in all respects that he might learn to feel our pain. If we seek redemption, it lies in his passion; if acquittal, in his condemnation; if remission of the curse, in his cross; if satisfaction, in his sacrifice; if purification, in his blood; if reconciliation, in his descent into hell; if mortification of the flesh, in his tomb; if newness of life, in his resurrection; if immortality, in the same; if inheritance of the Heavenly Kingdom, in his entrance into heaven; if protection, if security, if abundant supply of all blessings, in his Kingdom; if untroubled expectation of judgment, in the power given him to judge" (*Institutes*, 2.16.19, pp. 527–28).

54. The distinctiveness of Luther and Calvin in relation to each other is drawn out

In sum, in the stories of both Luther and Calvin salvation is from sin. And the dynamics of how Jesus saves is focused in Jesus being a substitute for the rest of humankind, and absorbing in himself the punishment due to our sin. But these two reformers emphasized different aspects of what it means to be saved, with Luther emphasizing faith's clinging to Christ's salvation, and Calvin drawing out the implications of sanctification for life in the world.

EXPERIENCE OF SALVATION IN THE TRADITION

I move now to a second level of reflection, one that inquires into the experience that generated these symbolic stories. What is the experience of salvation that is codified in these symbolic rereadings of the story of Jesus Christ? What aspects of the experience of salvation from God mediated by Jesus are preserved in this symbolic language? These salvation theories are dependent upon a variety of New Testament images, which in turn rest upon a memory and experience of Jesus as the bringer of God's salvation. These dependencies must be kept in mind, for they are the historical predecessors of the texts in question: ultimately these salvation theories and the New Testament accounts of salvation are interpretations of Jesus. Many of them appear today as bizarre, extravagant, and at times grotesque. Did God really require the life of Jesus in a Roman crucifixion to set things right with human beings? Indeed some are convinced that the only way to deal with these classical interpretations of salvation is to abandon them altogether. By contrast, the thesis at work here is that the point of these stories may be retrieved by interpreting them, and by retelling the story of Jesus in terms that make sense today. The first step in such a process, after analyzing the traditional stories themselves, is to estimate the experience that they represent. By this I do not mean an attempt to reach the psychological experience of the author, but rather to interpret the experience opened up by the stories themselves.

The interpretation that follows is formulated in terms of broad, generalized statements. These descriptions try to universalize this experience. The point is to characterize the particular experience that is embedded in these readings of salvation in such a way that it can be appreciated more generally. For the most part, the texts that I have analyzed here are classics.[55] In their particularity they have a transcendental quality that appeals to common human experience.[56] The interpretation here, therefore, aims

---

neatly by Ernst Troeltsch, *The Social Teachings of the Christian Churches* (New York: Harper Torchbooks, 1960), 467–511, 576–630.

55. See Chapter 3, pp. 56–57, above.

56. By common human experience I refer not to actual experiences but to possible experiences that are analogously open to all. The basis for this potentiality resides not in a survey of the sum total of actual human experiences, but in a transcendental analy-

both at representing the past historical symbols and at the same time bridging the historical distance between them and us by an appeal to a human experience reflected in them that potentially can be appreciated by all. The experience embedded in the texts is thus idealized, beyond the objectification of the language of these texts; it is released or placed at another remove from the particular psyches or intentions of the authors.[57] This interpretation will serve as a bridge to a later chapter which will address Jesus as savior today. There we will want to look back in solidarity with the experiential tradition of the community to learn how to face the future. At this point, however, the aim is not to build a meta-story of salvation from common experiences of the past. It is simply to highlight aspects of the specifically Christian experience which is carried by these diverse classical interpretations of Jesus' work of salvation.

Jesus the Teacher Is Experienced as Revealing God

All of the stories either state or imply the experience of Jesus as a revelation of God. In his teaching, in his way of acting, in the whole story of the unfolding of his destiny, Jesus communicates the things that are of God. In his parables Jesus presents God's wisdom. In his ethical teaching he represents God's values. No matter what particular logic thematizes the story of salvation in a given theologian, Jesus is always recognized as the revelation of God.[58] The "knowledge" thus mediated was salvific in a pagan world of polytheism and multiple and diverse religions; it is salvific today for the same reasons in an analogous situation.

God Is Encountered in Jesus

Beyond the experience of revelation, one can discern an experience of encountering God in Jesus in these classical salvation narratives. There are various ways in which scripture and later writers express the idea that Jesus makes God present or that God is present in Jesus to be so encountered: God is present to Jesus as Wisdom and as Spirit. In the hymn intro-

---

sis of the structure of human existence that uncovers its openness to a transcendent salvation.

57. An example of the interpretive logic employed here is Paul Ricoeur, "'Original Sin': A Study in Meaning," *The Conflict of Interpretations: Essays in Hermeneutics*, ed. by Don Ihde (Evanston, Ill.: Northwestern University, 1974), 269–86.

58. A good example of this is seen in Origen who uses an image that correlates nicely with the theory of symbolic mediation proposed in the last chapter. As a replica might reveal an immense reality, thus as a globe might reveal the planet earth, so too has the Son, replica of the Father, become our size to reveal the incomprehensible God. Origen, *Origen on First Principles*, ed. by G. W. Butterworth (Gloucester, Mass.: Peter Smith, 1973), 1.2.8, pp. 21–22. I shall represent Origen's salvation theory in the next chapter, for it has direct bearing on his christology. In Athanasius and others this revelation restores knowledge of God, and thus the image of God that was lost by sin. This was accomplished through Jesus' teaching, and this illumination is salvation. DeInc 13–19, pp. 67–73. See also Pelikan, *The Light of the World*, 73–92.

ducing John's gospel, Jesus is presented metaphorically as the Word of God. In early patristic writers Jesus is a second God, an Angel of God, the anointed of God. This "making God present" reflects Jesus acting in power in his healing and exorcisms; Jesus is depicted in the gospels as being empowered by God as Spirit. In the Greek Fathers God's being present to Jesus physically transforms flesh, or humanity; it divinizes it. Human existence in its turn becomes God's or attached to God in a new way. In Jesus God assumes every aspect of human existence so that it is healed, cleansed, cured, saved.[59] The experience is one of meeting with God's power in this man. Incarnation is a typical conceptual symbol for this; it means that God has come close and identified with humanity by assuming a human being, and thus the human race as such, as God's own.[60] All who are united with Jesus by faith and baptism and receive the Spirit of God participate in God's presence.[61] One can generalize by pointing to the experience lying behind all of these formulas: Jesus makes God present, and God is encountered in or through him. This is the existential and experiential basis for the theory that Jesus is the concrete symbol of God.

God Is Experienced as a Loving Creator

Salvation is always presented as a narrative, and in a story one thing happens after another. Thus the ordinary way of thinking of salvation is as something that occurred after creation, usually because sin required a new initiative of God. But the classical interpretations of salvation also state clearly that the God who works through Jesus is the one creating and saving God. Two things are happening here. On the one hand, Jesus mediates an experience of a God who is benevolent, loving, accepting, forgiving, as well as judging all dehumanizing conduct. The experience is that God is "for us." On the other hand, Jesus in mediating this God is clearly associated with God. Frequently the authors state that only the creator can save, that the creating and the saving are done by the same God.[62] This experience is important because in it lies the principle that generates the close association of Jesus with God and finally the idea that Jesus is divine.

---

59. See, for example, Gregory of Nyssa, "An Address on Religious Instruction," *Christology of the Later Fathers*, ed. by E. R. Hardy (Philadelphia: Westminster Press, 1954), # 27, 304.

60. Recall Athanasius's illustration of divinization with the metaphor of a king who resides in a city and raises its prestige, thus protecting it from its enemies by making it a place of special attention and care. DeInc 9, p. 63.

61. In the case of Luther, salvation happens now by a mystical union with Christ: "We must look at this image and take hold of it with a firm faith. He who does this has the innocence and the victory of Christ, no matter how great a sinner he is. . . . Therefore we are justified by faith alone, because faith alone grasps this victory of Christ" (LW 26, 284).

62. For Athanasius, "the renewal of creation has been the work of the selfsame Word that made it at the beginning. For it will appear not inconsonant for the Father to have wrought its salvation in him by whose means he made it" (DeInc 1, p. 56).

What Jesus reveals, then, is a God who is both creator and savior; as savior God is also creator, and the creator God is also savior. As God's mediation, Jesus begins to be interpreted symbolically as being associated with both creation and salvation. But it is crucial to see that the experience of God as creator and savior are not separable, even if one can distinguish the two ideas. God is experienced simply as God who is simultaneously loving and saving creator. Salvation is restoration of union with God, but God is experienced as a God who "must" bring to completion what God intended with creation. "It is certainly incongruous for God to let any rational nature perish altogether."[63] It will be important in our day to see salvation as inseparable from creation, and thus the scope of salvation as universal and extending to all people.

The Devil Represents an Experience of A Priori Evil to Which Human Existence Is in Bondage

Behind the mythological ransom and redemption stories involving Satan lies an extensive belief in a world of demons.[64] But the point of these stories is not to provide objective information about the world.[65] When these beliefs are interpreted symbolically and existentially, they can be seen to represent the experience of being victims or in bondage to historical and natural forces of which people have little knowledge and over which they have no control. Many of these forces are experienced as sinful and operative within the self prior to freedom.[66] But these experiences are not merely individual, any more than there is such a thing as an isolated, autonomous person. The bonds which hold human freedom in captivity are largely historical and social: the constraints of poverty, social marginalization, war, slavery, disease, sickness, and early death. Thus the demons are everywhere and control everything. Yet Jesus is experienced as a mediator of freedom; he is a savior from the bondage of a fated and externally controlled existence. The commonality of this experience of a

---

63. Anselm, CDH 2.4, p. 148. This echoes similar sentiments all along the tradition, both Greek and Latin.

64. Origen cites abundant testimony to a whole world of external spirits and demons. "The opposing powers and the devil himself are engaged in a struggle with the human race, provoking and inciting men to sin." *On First Principles*, 3.2.1, p. 211.

65. "The real purpose of myth is not to present an objective picture of the world as it is, but to express man's understanding of himself in the world in which he lives. Myth should be interpreted not cosmologically, but anthropologically, or better still, existentially." Rudolf Bultmann, "New Testament and Mythology," in *Kerygma and Myth: A Theological Debate*, ed. by H. W. Bartsch (New York: Harper Torchbooks, 1961), 10.

66. We have seen that Luther and Calvin place great emphasis on the experience of sin within the person. The heightened consciousness of sin generates in inverse proportion a heightened experience of liberation from sin: in the wonderful exchange between Christ and the sinner in Luther, and the release in the Spirit for a constructive life in society in Calvin. But the experience of sin and salvation from it is universally attested to in classical soteriology.

release of freedom is all the more striking because of the different ways in which it is expressed, for example, by Origen,[67] Augustine, with his doctrine of cooperative grace,[68] Luther, and Calvin.

Divine Fidelity Is Experienced in Jesus' Human Fidelity

The language of Jesus suffering for us, of being a sacrifice to God, of absorbing punishment for sin in our place, of being required to die to render satisfaction to God, hardly communicates meaningfully to our age. These concepts do not intersect at all with present consciousness. More seriously, the images associated with this talk offend and even repulse postmodern sensibility and thereby form a barrier to a salutary appreciation of Jesus Christ. Feminist theology has analyzed the implications of the idea of a God who needed satisfaction, or needs to punish, or would send his Son to suffer, in the context of patriarchy. It has also uncovered the damaging gender bias contained in the ideals of self-sacrifice and submission to the Father. From a historical perspective, the passivity that is often, although not necessarily, associated with this account of Jesus' saving work does not correspond with the aggressive prophetic teaching that caused his execution. And from a present-day perspective, the tendency to focus Jesus' saving work in his actual dying blunts the relevance of Jesus' salvific ministry for people's full and active lives of freedom.

One has to ask why the death of Jesus became so central in the Christian imagination. I suggested earlier that perhaps Jesus' death as a criminal was such a shock to the first disciples that apologetic discussion became focused here, and the ideas which were generated took on a life of their own. However that question is answered, in the sacrificial theories of salvation it is not physical slaughter that is important. Jesus' physical death per se is not salvific, but represents the degree of God's love and Jesus' obedience which are salvific. Augustine, for example, proposes a high christology. Thus Jesus is God's gift of God's self to human beings, and this death on a cross is a most radical dramatization of the extent of God's condescension and love.[69] On another level, external sacrifice for Augustine is the symbol of the inner reality of giving oneself to God.[70] Jesus' obedience unto death was considered his ultimate fidelity to God.[71] In other words, Jesus' voluntary passion and death are symbolic of the

67. Freedom is an important concept in Origen's system, and it controls his view of how Jesus saves. Jesus is savior by revealing God and being an exemplar of human existence in its return to God.

68. Augustine, "On Grace and Free Will," *Basic Writings*, 1, Chap. 33, 761.

69. John Burnaby, *Amor Dei: A Study of the Religion of St. Augustine* (London: Hodder and Stoughton, 1938), 172; also Irenaeus, AH 3.18.2, p. 446.

70. Bonner, "The Doctrine of Sacrifice," 106.

71. In Irenaeus, for example, Jesus' death was the external sign of a fidelity that reversed Adam's disobedience: "So by the obedience, whereby He obeyed unto death, hanging on the tree, He undid the old disobedience wrought in the tree." PAP #34, p. 69. Irenaeus frequently uses the language of Jesus redeeming us by his blood.

strength of his attachment to God. What is expressed in these exorbitant views of ransom and sacrifice is that this Jesus, who came from God bearing God's presence and power, symbolizes the radical extent of God's self-gift to human beings and, from the human side, the equally radical kind of commitment this communication should draw forth as a response.

Jesus Is Experienced as the Archetypal Human Being, the Final Adam

And so Jesus himself appears as the saved person, the first of many. He saves by showing the way. One of the most important of the Pauline images for salvation for the whole tradition is that of the final Adam. It is a diffuse and open-ended symbol, and it is taken up in many different ways. We have seen that it appears as recapitulation in Irenaeus. It expresses the experience of Jesus as the new creation, the new archetypal human being who responds to the desire for some guidance, and who embodies what it means to be human.[72] In Irenaeus it is God acting for our salvation in a way that respects human freedom; Jesus is the pioneer of our salvation whom we are to follow. This exemplarism is usually slighted in favor of the more intricate symbols of salvation, but it is basic and virtually present in every classical appropriation and revision of the story.[73] This foundational experience of how Jesus saves underlies the equally fundamental dynamics of Christian spirituality as *imitatio Christi*.

Jesus' Resurrection Is the Promise That Meets the Hope of Human Existence

Intrinsic to the human condition is the desire to exist and to exist permanently. I underscored in Chapter 5 that the resurrection of Jesus is experienced as salvific in the meeting between the basic human trust in life and God's promise of eternal life. The experience of salvation that is implicit in an affirmation of God raising Jesus is absolutely fundamental; it marks the point of departure of formal soteriology and christology. God's resurrection of Jesus is God's response to human hope. Resurrection represents salvation from death, triumph over all the forces that lead so inevitably toward extinction and nothingness.[74] This basic condition, disposition,

---

Its rationale is that the saving dimension lies in Jesus' fidelity, the free commitment of his obedience even to the extent of a bloody death.

72. In Origen this exemplarism has a universal cosmic structure. As God is that according to which Christ exists as God's image, so too Christ is that according to which human beings should exist. Jesus is the paradigmatic human being. See James A. Lyons, *The Cosmic Christ in Origen and Teilhard de Chardin* (Oxford: Oxford University Press, 1982), 127.

73. For example, in Augustine: "He also offered Himself to be tempted by him, the devil, so that by also overcoming his temptations, He might be our mediator not only by His help but also by His example" (Trin 4.13.17, p. 151).

74. Resurrection plays a prominent role in the salvation theory of Gregory of Nyssa whom I did not consider here. His is a complex theory of the reunification of body and

and attitude of hope, nourished by Jesus' final resurrection, lies beneath the whole variety of scenarios of victory.[75]

To sum up, collecting these themes is an effort at generalizing the experiences of the Christian community that are reflected in the classical symbolic interpretations that describe God's salvation mediated through Jesus Christ. They have been restated in a way that takes into account that Jesus of Nazareth is the focal point of these theories, and that explanation today of how Jesus saves must also refer back to the Jesus of history. These experiences have been expressed in terms of common human experience; they can be appreciated by all human beings and thus have potentially universal significance.

This first interpretation of experience as it comes from the past must still be retold in a story of the salvation mediated by Jesus for our own time. What form will the narrative take within the context of the present-day world? This is the task of constructive christology. But before moving to that stage I want to examine the development of classical christology.

---

soul by the incarnate Word to form an indissoluble immortality. "An Address on Religious Instruction," ##8, 16, *Christology of the Later Fathers*, 282–86, 292–94.

75. The victory is over flesh, sin, mortality, death, Satan, the law, and so on. The point is that Christ's victory is also ours. "Inasmuch as Christ did rise in our flesh, it follows that we shall be also raised in the same . . ." (Irenaeus, AH 5.7, p. 532).

CHAPTER 9

Development of Classical Christology

Unlike soteriology, the development of classical christology reached a certain plateau with the doctrine of the Council of Chalcedon in 451. Although the doctrine of Chalcedon was not accepted by churches representing the extremes in the contemporary christological debate, this doctrine became a central teaching of most of the Christian churches and has remained a touchstone of orthodoxy. Chalcedon is a classic symbol of Christian faith.

The history of how the church arrived at this christological doctrine four hundred years after the death of Jesus is well known; the story has been analyzed many times.[1] At the beginning of the second century, Ignatius of Antioch wrote confidently: "There is only one physician—of flesh yet spiritual, born yet unbegotten, God incarnate, genuine life in the midst of death, sprung from Mary as well as God, first subject to suffering then beyond it—Jesus Christ our Lord."[2] During the course of the century Justin Martyr and the other apologists began building bridges between Christian self-understanding and Greco-Roman culture, and Irenaeus defended a bible-based christology against gnostic novelties. The third century witnessed reactions against modalism and patripassionism, and the development of a conception of God's inner life that was differentiated and of which Jesus Christ was a part. It also developed what is sometimes called a "non-heretical" subordinationism.[3] The fourth

---

1. Aloys Grillmeier, *Christ in Christian Tradition*, 1, *From the Apostolic Age to Chalcedon (451)* (Atlanta: John Knox Press, 1975); Adolf von Harnack, *History of Dogma* (New York: Dover Publications, 1961); J. N. D. Kelly, *Early Christian Doctrines* (London: A & C Black, 1977); Jaroslav Pelikan, *The Christian Tradition: A History of the Development of Doctrine*, 1, *The Emergence of the Catholic Tradition (100–600)* (Chicago: University of Chicago Press, 1971); Reinhold Seeberg, *Text-Book of the History of Doctrines*, 1, *History of Doctrines in the Ancient Church* (Philadelphia: Lutheran Publication Society, 1905); Frances M. Young, *The Making of the Creeds* (Philadelphia: Trinity Press International, 1991), and *From Nicaea to Chalcedon: A Guide to Literature and Its Background* (Philadelphia: Fortress Press, 1983).

2. Ignatius of Antioch, "Letter to the Ephesians," 7.2, in Cyril C. Richardson et al., eds., *Early Christian Fathers* (New York: Macmillan, 1970), 90.

3. Grillmeier, *Christ in Christian Tradition*, 167.

century was marked by the controversy between the Arians and the Nicenes, and Athanasius was the interpreter and defender of the doctrine of the first ecumenical council which established the divinity of Jesus against a radical subordinationism. And, finally, during the first half of the fifth century, a controversy concerning the constitution of the person of Jesus Christ came to a head. It pitted an incarnational, Word-flesh christology that depicted Jesus Christ as a divine subject clothed in human nature, against an "assumed human being" christology that depicted Jesus Christ as a human being in whom the divine Word dwelt. Relying heavily on a letter of Pope Leo, the Council of Chalcedon used a language of person and natures, a language marked by tensions and paradoxes, in order to preserve the values contained on each side of this debate. As a practical formula, the teaching of Chalcedon succeeded remarkably well.

My aim in this chapter is not to try to represent this four-hundred-year history in an objectively adequate way. Rather, I will presuppose knowledge of the main lines of this development and comment upon it within the framework of four themes which are relevant to the task of systematic christology. The themes are, first, inculturation and the tensions that are involved in it; second, the dynamic character of christological development and the role of soteriology in it; third, the problem of the relation of Jesus, insofar as he is recognized as divine, to God; and, fourth, the narrow christological problem of the constitution of Jesus Christ as human and divine. In the light of this commentary on the historical development of the theology, the next chapter will present a more pointed analysis and interpretation of the doctrines of Nicaea and Chalcedon. These doctrines make little sense apart from the theological conflicts that generated them.

NEW TESTAMENT SOURCES AND CULTURAL INTELLIGIBILITY

Christology continued to develop after the first century as Christianity spread and entered into contact with new communities. At the same time, the writings of the first century were gradually gathered into a canon which served as a touchstone for authentic Christian belief. The relation between these two developments is interactive, forming a tension between the New Testament sources of christology and the intelligibility of christology for new cultural situations. I want to comment on how this tension manifested itself in the second century, for it had a lasting effect on the whole future development of christology.

Aloys Grillmeier notes how during the second century Christian belief moved from being a set of religious beliefs, more or less integrated with other knowledge of the world, to a generalized Christian religious view of reality. By this he means a more inclusive vision that responds to fundamental questions such as those of God, human existence, life, death, destiny, matter, and spirit. This development occurred alongside of gnosticism, a loose movement of thought that emphasized a religious doctrine of dualism and a system of salvation based on gnosis.[4] The solidification of the vision was carried forward by a questioning, reflective, and constructive mode of thinking that aimed at ever more comprehensive understanding. Inevitably this was accomplished by entering into dialogue or interaction with the culture in which Christians found themselves, the culture which new Christians brought with them into the church. Christian beliefs were placed in conjunction with the broad system of language, culture, and knowledge that was in place at the time. This movement can be seen in the Apologists generally and in Justin Martyr in particular, especially with reference to the area of christology.

This process of interaction with Greek and Roman cultures occurred in tandem with the formation of the canon. This means that the dialogue with culture was not a free interchange, but one that was already bound by Jewish tradition in its scriptures, and by a New Testament tradition that had become objectified in writing. Whether or not it was the intention of its authors, scripture assumed the function of preserving the foundational experience of the church, what was taken to be the classic expression of its faith, so that it provided a decisive norm against corrosive innovation. Unlike an oral tradition that retains more freedom to move forward and change, writing objectifies and preserves a privileged moment in the historical life of the community, so that development into the future doubles back on the classic record which functions precisely as a canon or rule of faith.[5] The canon of scripture was by no means closed in the early second century, but its contents were almost all written, and they were appealed to as an authority.

Christian reflection moves forward in an attempt to integrate beliefs within a wider framework of knowledge. At the same time, Christian reflection is bound to its origins in Jesus and the first formulations of the community's faith in him. These two poles exist in tension with each other. Christology has to be formulated in the language of the culture to which it is addressed, if it is to be understood. But at the same time, that which is reformulated is based on particular historical sources or media and has the scriptures as its norm. There will always be a tension between these

---

4. According to Grillmeier, gnosticism represented a common religious experience of the time. Grillmeier, *Christ in Christian Tradition*, 80–81.

5. See Paul Ricoeur, "Speaking and Writing," *Interpretation Theory: Discourse and the Surplus of Meaning* (Fort Worth: Texas Christian University Press, 1976), 27–30, for a brief analysis of what occurs socially in the transition from an oral tradition to a written tradition. James Barr explains the formation of the canon as a social act of formulating and preserving a classical account of the church's foundational religious experience in *The Bible in the Modern World* (London: SCM Press, 1973), 114–18.

two poles in christology. The norm that is scripture enters into a tensive relationship with a new linguistic tradition and culture, a broad intellectual matrix, a different form of community experience. This will demand a new form of intelligibility, new language, new thought forms, and new forms of life. The result is a tensive structure in the quest for intelligibility, as Jesus Christ is interpreted in a new language and culture, and the New Testament sources act as a controlling norm.

Two features in the process of christological thought in the post-New Testament period had a decisive impact on the future of its development. The first is the objectification of the tradition which is effected by writing. By objectification I mean the turning of the record or witness of a participatory form of religious encounter into an objective source for what appears to be representative religious knowledge and data. On the one hand, the scriptures are able to serve as an objective norm or reference precisely because they rendered the tradition universally available by their written form. On the other hand, the scriptures almost inevitably perform their function by being appealed to as an objective source of directly representative knowledge. Scripture functioned as more than a theological norm; it was read at liturgy and nurtured the spiritual life. But insofar as it served as a source and norm for theological reflection, its content tended to be regarded as containing revealed information and data that was continuous with worldly knowledge.

The second decisive feature of the period concerns the understanding of Jesus of Nazareth, who is the final norm in christology because he is its source and object. After the New Testament period, the understanding of Jesus Christ became governed by the framework and language of the Prologue of John's gospel. The Jesus who was the subject matter of christology ceased to be the Jesus of the synoptics. Or, to put it in another way, the Jesus of the synoptics became understood in Johannine terms. The three-stage christology of the Prologue became the standard framework or form of thought within which Jesus of Nazareth was construed. The process of a genetic growth in interpretation and understanding of the human being Jesus of Nazareth was reversed, and a descent-ascent christology from above became the dominant schema. The pluralism of New Testament christology was gradually but effectively blunted, and a particular model of incarnational christology, involving a pre-existent Logos, developed into the controlling paradigm for all christological thinking. John's christology quickly became not one christology among others but the controlling framework within which mainline christology unfolded. Because of the identity of the subjects, Jesus and Logos, one could even speak of a pre-existent Jesus. This was not a difficult transition in a culture for which the world of transcendence was densely populated with various levels and kinds of invisible beings, and for which Logos was a philosophically meaningful category.

The christology of Justin Martyr exemplifies these trends.[6] He frequently appeals to scripture as a source of objective, other-worldly or transcendent data about Jesus Christ.[7] Johannine christology lies at the basis of his speculative account of the Christian vision of reality. Justin operates within the framework of a three-stage, descent-ascent christology. The pre-existent Logos, or Son, or "our Savior Jesus Christ became Incarnate and took upon Himself flesh and blood for our salvation . . ."(1 Apol 66, p. 105). Although this incarnation is a definitive self-presence of the Logos, the same Logos is the agent or subject of other interactions with the world. It was Christ, for example, who addressed Moses "under the form of fire" (1 Apol 62, p. 101; Trypho 59, pp. 241–42). Christ, then, is one title among many for the Logos who in principle is God's agent interacting with the world, and who finally became incarnate in the flesh of Jesus.[8]

The Christ or Logos was generated from within the Godhead itself: "God has begotten of Himself a certain rational Power as a Beginning before all other creatures" (Trypho 61, p. 144). This hypostatized rational power of God is the principle of the intelligibility of the created universe. Each instance of human reason is formed according to it, and actively participates in it when it acts reasonably. Analogous to a Platonic form, then, Christ as Logos and as Reason is immanent in the whole universe, and present to human beings who, in their turn, are engaged with Christ in their knowledge of truth. Christ "was and is the Logos who is in every person . . ." (2 Apol 10, p. 130). In another place Justin says:

> We have been taught that Christ was First-begotten of God [the Father] and we have indicated above that He is the Word of whom all humankind partakes. Those who lived by reason are Christians, even though they have been considered atheists. . . . So, also, they who lived before Christ and did not live by reason were useless people, enemies

---

6. Justin Martyr, "The First Apology," "The Second Apology," "Dialogue with Trypho," *Saint Justin Martyr*, ed. by Thomas B. Falls (New York: Christian Heritage, 1948). All references to Justin are to this edition of his works.

7. Justin, 1 Apol 45, pp. 82–83, is an example. Here Justin uses Ps 109:1-3 as a prophecy that depicts events that happened later or were happening at his time of writing. This is of course part of a general pattern of arguing from prophetic fulfillment.

8. Justin cites many names and many appearances of the Logos. "Now, the Word of God is His Son, as we have already stated, and He is called Angel and Apostle . . . What has been written has been here set down to prove that Jesus Christ is the Son of God and His Apostle, being of old the Word, appearing at one time in the form of fire, at another under the guise of incorporeal beings [i.e., as an angel], but now, at the will of God, after becoming man for mankind, He bore all the torments which the demons prompted the rabid Jews to wreck upon Him" (1 Apol 63, p. 102; also Trypho 61, p. 144). Grillmeier judges Justin's christology subordinationist on the basis of these inferior names. There are other indications as well, one of which is the transcendence of the Father compared with the Son who is the mediator between heaven and earth.

of Christ, and murderers of those who did live by reason. But those who have lived reasonably, and still do, are Christians, and are fearless and untroubled. (1 Apol 46, p. 83; also 2 Apol 13, p. 133)

Thus Justin took the christology of John's Prologue and fused it with a Greek conception of the world. He combined the Platonic idea of a world-soul with the doctrine of the immanent seeds of the Logos as the source of reason in each human being. "According to the Platonists, the world-soul is the principle at work in ordering the world, both at creation and in sustaining the world. It has a rational element which is termed Nous, Logos or even *he logike*."[9] Jesus Christ is this Logos. In this christology he has assumed the function of the cosmological principle of intelligibility as God's ordering intelligence; and in the incarnation this Logos has appeared in history.

Let me sum up this first point as it is illustrated in Justin Martyr. Theology is a continued effort at inculturation. This involves reformulating christological doctrine in a way that addresses the questions of the culture and uses the language of the culture in response. These responses are in tension with their source and norm, scripture. In going back to scripture, christology during this period employed it as a source of objectified revealed knowledge. And it built christology on the basis of a model taken from the Prologue of John's gospel. Thinking unfolded within this framework in such a way that it became established as the controlling paradigm. This framework then operated as a presupposition, or a "given." Thus two premises of this christology clearly distinguish it from christology in our time: one is the hypostatization of the titles of Jesus, such as Wisdom and Logos; and the other is the use of scripture as a source of objective representative knowledge. These developments, when they are contrasted with the historical development of New Testament christology, also illustrate a shift from a christology "from below" to a christology "from above."[10]

DEVELOPMENT AND THE SOTERIOLOGICAL NORM

There is a tendency to read the history of the development of patristic christology as though it unfolded along a teleological trajectory that led

---

9. Grillmeier, *Christ in Christian Tradition*, 93.

10. I have not used the term "Hellenization" because of the negative connotation it bears, that is, a compromise of authentic New Testament teaching. Those who view this development positively argue that the patristic councils actually saved rather than compromised the New Testament message about Jesus. But either way, no one can deny that this case of inculturation involved a significant change in the manner of thinking about Jesus Christ. An analytical comparison between the material of Chapters 3 through 6 and Chapters 8 through 10, respectively, would show significantly different christological languages and modes of thinking, resulting in different understandings of the content of faith.

to Chalcedon; the doctrine of Chalcedon simply needed time to be discovered. Thus the earlier centuries are read as preparatory to the denouement in the mid-fifth century. A present sense of the contingency of history calls this view into question. History contains more particular occasions of sheer chance than the inner logic of ideas can control. As a result, the history of interpretation is open, so that Chalcedon, however true and however important as a marker in the history of doctrine it may be, is neither the goal nor the end of interpretation.

Although the process of Christian interpretation never ceases, it is not without criteria and norms. Attention has been called to two of them operative in the christology of Justin: scripture, especially the New Testament which was then being constructed, and intelligibility, which implies inculturation. The dialectical interaction between inculturation and the normative sources of faith is the motor of theological development. Here we consider a third theological norm, the Christian life, which correlates with an existential-historical conception of salvation.[11] When salvation is not reduced to an objective situation, but is also appreciated as an experienced and appropriated relationship with God, it becomes a factor of the Christian life. And a conception of Christian encounter with God in historical life is foundational to christological construal. I have already illustrated the close relationship between the experience of salvation and christology in the consideration of New Testament christologies.

One can distinguish two distinct paradigms or trajectories of salvation in the Greek and the Latin traditions, respectively. For example, J. Patout Burns develops the contrast by employing four sets of variables in the two traditions of understanding the process of salvation. One of these variables is whether the grace "through which God works the process of salvation might be operative or co-operative."[12] Another way of stating the same factor would be in terms of the degree to which human freedom is engaged in the process of salvation. Burns measures the distance between eastern and western soteriologies according to this criterion along with the others. However, because of the correlation between soteriology and christology generally, I believe that differences in christology itself can be also charted or measured according to the lines of differences in the underlying anthropology and soteriology. Especially important is the degree to which human freedom and activity are given a place in human salvation. In order to test this correlation, I will analyze the relationship between the soteriologies and the christologies of Irenaeus and Origen.

---

11. Recall that in Chapter 6 I showed how the situation of a pluralism of christologies requires a norm for christology that is internal to the genesis of christology itself, namely, the experience of salvation mediated by Jesus.

12. J. Patout Burns, "The Economy of Salvation: Two Patristic Traditions," *Why the Church?*, ed. by W. J. Burghardt and W. G. Thompson (New York: Paulist Press, 1977), 56.

Irenaeus

I examined the way Irenaeus interpreted the story of how Jesus saves in the last chapter. He combines the incarnational Logos christology of John's Prologue with the final Adam soteriology of Paul. The Logos recapitulated a full human existence first by becoming fully human and then by living out a full human life. Jesus Christ both divinizes human existence and acts as a revealer and new model for human existence. It is clear that Irenaeus delicately balances the two types in question. But in order to illustrate the objective side of salvation, I will highlight those aspects of his christology that correspond most closely with his incarnation-divinization soteriology.

Irenaeus's christology falls into the Logos-sarx type of soteriology. He spoke of the Word becoming flesh, and did not insist on the human soul of Jesus. The stress is on the flesh which needs salvation.[13] Given this premise, three aspects of Irenaeus's christology directly correlate with his incarnational soteriology. By this I mean that he draws the christological conclusion on the basis of a soteriological argument that is incarnational. The first point is his insistence on the divinity of Jesus Christ against the Ebionites. That which was incarnated in Jesus Christ is the Son of the Most High God the Father. The basic rationale for this lies in mediatorship, uniting God and human existence: if Jesus Christ is not divine, we would not receive "God so as to have union with Him, but [would] . . . remain in that Adam who had been conquered and expelled from Paradise. . . ."[14]

Second, Irenaeus argues in the same vein for the authentic and full humanity of Jesus against Docetists. "For He would not have been one truly possessing flesh and blood, by which He redeemed us, unless He had summed up in Himself the ancient formation of Adam" (AH 5. 1. 2, p. 527). According to the final Adam christology of Paul, expounded as recapitulation by Irenaeus, salvation is not accomplished unless the Son fully enters into the real cycle of human flesh and blood life.

---

13. Grillmeier, *Christ in Christian Tradition*, 103.

14. Irenaeus, *Against Heresies*, 5.1.3, in *The Ante-Nicene Fathers: I. The Apostolic Fathers, Justin Martyr, Irenaeus*, ed. by Alexander Roberts and James Donaldson (Grand Rapids: Eerdmans, 1953), 527. Further references to *Against Heresies* in the text are to this edition. Irenaeus says again: "For it was for this end that the Word of God was made man, and He who was the Son of God became the Son of man, that man, having been taken into the Word, and receiving the adoption, might become the son of God. For by no other means could we have attained to incorruptibility and immortality, unless we had been united to incorruptibility and immortality. But how could we be joined to incorruptibility and immortality, unless, first, incorruptibility and immortality had become that which we also are, so that the corruptible might be swallowed up by the incorruptibility, and the mortal by immortality, that we might receive the adoption of sons" (AH 3.19.1, p. 448). See also AH 5.1.1, p. 526, where Irenaeus reasons that only a divine Word could reveal things pertaining to the inner life of God.

Third, and perhaps redundantly, Irenaeus also argues to the unity of the divinity and humanity in the person of Jesus Christ on soteriological grounds. The argument is as follows: Jesus Christ binds the divine and the human together. If he were deficient in either regard, the uniting would not have been effected. "For it was incumbent upon the Mediator between God and human beings, by His relationship to both, to bring both to friendship and concord, and present man to God, while He revealed God to man. For, in what way could we be partakers of the adoption of sons, unless we had received from Him through the Son that fellowship which refers to Himself, unless His Word, having been made flesh, had entered into communion with us" (AH 3.18.7, p. 448).

In sum, there is a balance in Irenaeus's christology between the humanity and the divinity of Jesus Christ, despite its being of the Logos-flesh variety. And this balance correlates neatly with his soteriology. On the one hand, he insists on the divine character of Jesus, because only a divine Logos can reveal God and divinize flesh. On the other hand, because it is precisely humanity that needs divinization, and because the final Adam recapitulates human life, he must be one of us.

ORIGEN

Since Origen's theology of salvation was not analyzed in the preceding chapter, I shall begin with a brief interpretation of Origen's account in his *De Principiis*.[15] This work expresses a complex worldview or cosmology in which Christ, as God's personified Wisdom, Word, and Son, plays a role from the very beginning.[16] I presuppose the expansive framework of creation, the falling away of rational souls, the creation of the world as the region from which they must work their way back to God and find salvation. In this schema Jesus Christ, who is identical with the eternally begotten Son, or Wisdom, or Word, is the mediator. He is, first of all, the principle who binds created reality to God, because God creates through God's Word or Wisdom. But after the fall, the Son is mediator in a second way as incarnate savior. All things will return to God through the saving mediation of Wisdom, Word, or Son incarnate in the human soul and flesh of Jesus.[17] The question, then, is how is Jesus savior?

---

15. The purpose of the *De Principiis*, according to Origen, is to integrate and systematize into "a single body of doctrine" by the use of "clear and cogent arguments" applied to data drawn from the "holy scriptures" and what can be deduced from them by reason, logic, and correct interpretation. Origen, *Origen on First Principles*, ed. by G. W. Butterworth (Gloucester, Mass.: Peter Smith, 1973), 1. Pref. 10, p. 6. Hereafter cited in the text by book, chapter, paragraph, and page in this volume. See Joseph Wilson Trigg, *Origen: The Bible and Philosophy in the Third-Century Church* (Atlanta: John Knox Press, 1983), 94.

16. Christ is the only begotten Son of God, God's Wisdom, and God never existed without God's Wisdom. This Son, Word, or Wisdom is eternally begotten. He is truth itself because the image of the Father. Prin 1.2.1-6, pp. 15–20.

17. The basic role of the Son is to mediate between the Father and creation. The Son

Two prior issues largely determine the answer to the question of how Jesus is savior. One is the centrality of freedom in Origen's thinking. The fall is due to human freedom; the return to God will be through human freedom; God is not savior against but only through human freedom (Prin 1.6.1, pp. 52–53). The notion of human freedom thus acts in a decisive way in Origen's thought.[18] The other prior issue concerns what human existence is saved from. For Origen, despite our freedom, we cannot save ourselves. Rather, we must be saved from ignorance, from an attachment to this world,[19] and from a certain bondage to sin and the power of Satan who inclines or encourages human beings to sin. "The opposing powers and the devil himself are engaged in a struggle with the human race, provoking and inciting people to sin" (Prin 3.2.1, p. 211).[20]

In relation to these conditions Jesus Christ is savior first of all by revealing God; Jesus Christ is the image of the Father.[21] Thus Jesus as the incar-

---

mediates by doing God's will, carrying out or effecting God's plan in creation and in salvation, the divinization of rational creatures. James A. Lyons, *The Cosmic Christ in Origen and Teilhard de Chardin* (Oxford: Oxford University Press, 1982), 115. Lyons summarizes this mediation in two functions: first, Christ is the instrument of creation; second, Christ is the exemplar of creation. Ibid., 129.

18. The just, impartial, and egalitarian character of God together with the principle of human freedom and merit have cosmic implications for Origen. The inequalities in the world stem from lapses of human freedom before worldly time, *"in illo tempore"* (Prin 1.8.1-2, pp. 66–69). On the creation of this world and the explanation of each rational being occupying his or her place or situation according to the principles of prior freedom and merit, see Prin 2.9, pp. 129–37. In brief, he writes that "divine providence arranges all creatures individually in positions corresponding to the variations in their movements and the fixed purposes of their minds." God thus "placed everyone in a position proportionate to his [or her] merit . . ." (Prin 2.9.6, p. 134). This position is held as a Christian view against Greek conceptions that this "world is governed either by chance movements or by a fateful necessity . . ." (Prin 3.5.5, p. 242). "God's providence and the free will of rational creatures shape Origen's understanding of the world. God leaves souls free but in the creation of the material world sets conditions for them which will ultimately lead them to return to God willingly." Trigg, *Origen*, 110.

19. The antitheses of materiality and spirituality, of descent or fall and ascent to salvation, and of correlated evil and good are very clear in Origen. The cosmic fall and devolution calls for ascent, escape, and salvation. And these antitheses govern the ideal Christian life. Origen speaks of human souls who rise above their bodily natures by an ascetic life, mortifying their bodily members and rising above their bodily nature and reaching for a truly spiritual life (Prin 1.8.4, pp. 71–72).

20. Origen also cites abundant testimony to a whole world of external spirits and demons (Prin 3.2.1, pp. 211–13). But sin also has its roots in internal inclinations to sensual excess of every kind. External forces are not the only source of human sin and Origen honors the principle of human freedom in sin as well as salvation. And, finally, saving goodness can never be brought to completion without God's help. Thus he writes: "So I think that a man can probably never by himself overcome an opposing power, but only by the use of divine help" (Prin 3.2.5, p. 220). Thus Origen's insistence on freedom does not amount to human autonomy. See Prin 2.3, pp. 211–22, passim.

21. As a replica might reveal an immense reality [for example, as a globe might

nation of the Son is the light of the world, the Word who interprets the mysteries of reality. He is the way, the truth, and the life (Prin 1.2.7, pp. 20–21).

Second, Jesus saves by being exemplar. He is to be imitated; he is the archetypal human being; he is the pioneer of our salvation whom we are to follow. This respects human freedom; we are to follow Jesus in his obedience.[22]

Third, Jesus saves by his obedience all the way through death and resurrection, and in so doing he conquers Satan and other demons.[23] His obedience is a victory over the power of Satan and his resurrection is the goal toward which human freedom is destined and can now knowingly strive. This imitation of Christ's obedience calls for a certain asceticism; salvation may not be from an evil world, but it is a liberation from attachment and bondage to a world of matter, and a movement toward perfect spirituality even in this world.

But, fourth, the Spirit also has a role in salvation; the Holy Spirit is the agent by which one becomes united to the Father and the Son. Jesus the Word reveals, but it is the Spirit which sanctifies (Prin 1.3.5, pp. 33–4). It is true that the Spirit too "reveals God to whom he will" (Prin 1.3.4, p. 33). But the principal function of the Spirit is to bind a person to the Word of God and to sanctify. For "it is impossible to become partaker of the Father or the Son without the Holy Spirit" (Prin 1.3.5, p. 33).[24] In sum, Jesus reveals and the Spirit sanctifies and empowers, not against freedom, but always in and with freedom.

Origen's christology is also complex; it involves a pre-existent Logos, who is eternally begotten (Prin 1.2.4, p. 18), a descent-ascent pattern, and roughly a two-"natures" composition of Christ. But just as freedom has a

---

reveal the planet earth], so too has the Son, replica of the Father, become our size to reveal the incomprehensible God (Prin 1.2.8, pp. 21–2).

22. The divine Son, Word and Wisdom of the Father "emptied himself, and taking the form of a servant became obedient even unto death in order to teach them obedience who could in no other way obtain salvation except through obedience . . ." (Prin 3.5.6, p. 242). This exemplarism has a deep cosmic structure. As God is that according to which Christ exists, and Christ is God's image, so too Christ is that according to which human existence should exist. This makes Jesus the paradigmatic human being. See Lyons, The Cosmic Christ, 127.

23. Jesus the Son also "'subdues all enemies under his feet'; and by the fact that he must reign till he puts his enemies under his feet he teaches the rulers themselves the arts of control" (Prin 3.5.6, p. 242).

24. In Origen "the working of the power of God the Father and God the Son is spread indiscriminately over all created beings, but a share in the Holy Spirit is possessed, we find, by the saints alone" (Prin 1.3.7, pp. 36-37). In other words, the Spirit does not initiate holiness, but bestows it in the wake of the revelation of Jesus or the cosmic Christ and a free turning of a person toward God. God sanctifies by the Spirit "all that is worthy of sanctification" (Prin 1.3.7, p. 37). This is another sign of Origen's respect for human freedom. The Spirit does not cause holiness but indwells and makes holy those who have chosen through their freedom the God who has been revealed.

large role in Origen's anthropology and soteriology, so too does it have a role in his christology, and it is to this that I call attention. For in Origen Jesus Christ does have a human soul; his is not a Logos-sarx christology. The human soul is the point of connection between the Word and the flesh. The result is that Origen has a broader notion of Jesus' humanity: his union with God and his being the Christ involve human freedom.

"The Son of God, therefore, because for the salvation of the human race he wished to appear to men and to dwell among them, assumed not only, as some think, a human body, but also a soul, in its nature indeed like our souls, but in will and virtue like himself, and of such a kind that it could unswervingly carry into effect all the wishes and plans of the Word and wisdom . . ." (Prin 4.4.4, p. 318). Origen proves this with scriptural texts where there is reference to Jesus' soul. The human soul of Christ is incapable of sin because of its union with the Logos. The human soul of Christ is filled with God's presence, having "received into itself the whole wisdom of God and his truth and life . . ." (Prin 4.4.4, p. 319).

It is because he had such a human soul which was so attached to the Word that Christ can be a model, pioneer, and exemplar. "This is why Christ is set forth as an example to all believers, because as he ever chose the good, even before he knew the evil at all . . . so too, should each one of us" follow his example, take him as "a leader for the journey" and proceed along the way of virtue. "This Word, then, and this wisdom, by our imitation of whom we are called wise or rational, becomes 'all things to all men, that he may gain all'" (Prin 4.4.4, p. 319).

Origen's salvation theory, then, provides a place for the exercise of human freedom. Jesus Christ is revealer of God and guide in the human return to God. "For as the word in us is the messenger of what the mind perceives, so the Word of God, since he has known the Father, reveals the Father whom he has known, because no creature can come into contact with him without a guide."[25] This soteriology of revelation and exemplarism requires a Jesus Christ who is truly human and imitable, a Jesus Christ whose humanity includes the rationality and freedom of human beings. Irenaeus, whose anthropology and soteriology do not stress the role of human freedom the way Origen does, was content with the Johannine formula, "the Word became flesh," and thus a Logos-sarx christology. Origen's stress on human freedom called for and correlates with a Logos-anthropos christology. I want to suggest that the differences exemplified in the soteriologies and christologies of Irenaeus and Origen are paradigmatic. I will continue to argue this thesis when I deal with the competing christologies of the fifth century that lead to the formula of Chalcedon. The paradigm will also help in the understanding of the differences between Arius and Athanasius, and thus in the interpretation of the Nicene Creed.

---

25. Origen, *Commentary on the Gospel According to John Books 1–10* (Washington, D.C.: Catholic University of America Press, 1989), 1.277, p. 91.

JESUS AND GOD

What is the relation between Jesus of Nazareth and God? This question focused one of the major problems that Christian theology had to face in the development of its christology. We have seen that this relationship was conceived in a variety of ways in the New Testament. But in all of its christologies at no point in the New Testament is Jesus identified with the transcendent God without ambiguity. The Prologue of John's gospel, which seems to be the most straightforward statement of Jesus being divine, has to be read according to its genre as poetic, figurative language. In a Greco-Roman world of polytheism, the monotheism of Jews and early Christians was self-conscious, and the transcendence of God carefully guarded. Young suggests that Jesus was not a case dissimilar from other messengers of God on the cosmic or ontological map: servants, prophets, angels, kings. Jesus was never a rival of the one God of Abraham.[26] Jesus was not Yahweh; Jesus was not the Father, who was preeminently the one transcendent God. The question of Jesus' relation to God, then, was clearly not settled by Johannine christology but remained a problem until the fourth century.

And yet Jesus was experienced as divine. At some time during the first century, probably early in the formation of a Christian community, Jesus became the center and the object of Christian cult, and an object of worship.[27] We have seen the development of the wisdom hymns. In John's gospel the author has Thomas say to the resurrected Jesus, "My Lord and my God!" (John 20:28). In John's gospel an exalted Son of God christology is combined with a wisdom and Word christology to express belief in a Jesus who is in some sense divine. But this leaves the question of how this divine Jesus is related to the transcendent God of monotheistic faith.

---

26. Young, *Creeds*, 34. Summarizing the thrust of eastern christology, Young underlines the desire for the distinction of the Father and the Son and the transcendence of the Father. "The one Lord Jesus Christ was the incarnation of the pre-existent Logos, the creative instrument used by God to generate his creation and communicate with it. He was a second *hypostasis*, a distinct existence, never to be confused with the one ultimate, ingenerate God." Ibid., 45.

27. In Chapter 6 I referred to the work of Larry W. Hurtado. He investigates how early Jewish Christians venerated Jesus in cult while at the same time preserving their monotheism. He examines the precedents and conceptual models in Jewish tradition that facilitated this accommodation. He concludes that Christian devotion to God included Jesus as the chief agent of God for salvation. Jesus was an object of worship, not independently but always "to the Glory of God the Father" (Phil 2:9-11). "Devotion to Jesus did not involve confusing him with God or making Jesus a second God." Hurtado, *One God, One Lord: Early Christian Devotion and Ancient Jewish Monotheism* (Philadelphia: Fortress Press, 1988), 121. Hurtado views this material as a basis for the development of the doctrine of Nicaea. But the data he presents are also quite consistent with Arianism. The New Testament remains ambiguous. I will return to this material in Chapter 15 when I consider worship of Jesus.

How is this development to be understood? And how did it unfold?

From a historical perspective one can understand the genesis of the problem of Jesus' relation to God by the hypostatization of symbolic language about God, in this case the symbols "wisdom" and "word." Hypostatization generally means making an idea or a concept into a real thing. In its broad sense the term "hypostasis" means the individuality of a something: a hypostasis is an individual instantiation within a class or species. To hypostatize is to interpret a concept as an existing being, to concretize or materialize an idea. It is to reify, in which process reification means to construe the object of a figure of speech as a reality. By contrast, the symbols Wisdom, Word, and Spirit, which are found in the Jewish scriptures and refer to God, are not hypostatizations but personifications. Personification is a figure of speech in which the symbol is consciously or deliberately treated or spoken of as a person. Proverbs 8 contains a clearly intended personification of God's intelligence or wisdom as a pre-existent person and agent of God. As a figure of speech, it does not intend that wisdom is a distinct or discrete entity or being.

A major development occurred when a personification became transformed into a hypostatization, that is, when what was a figure of speech became intended not as a figure of speech but as referring to "a real being."[28] Wisdom is no longer a linguistic symbol referring obliquely to an attribute of God, but a real being; Logos is no longer a figure of speech but a distinct being; Spirit is no longer a constructive exercise of the human poetic imagination that metaphorically depicts the effects of God as the invisible power of the wind, but a literal something. The hypostatization of a pre-existent Logos and Wisdom creates a problem. As long as Logos and Wisdom remain what they were originally, personifications, that is, figures of speech used to say something about God, it makes sense to say that God's wisdom was actualized in Jesus, and that Jesus embodies God's wisdom. But when the Logos is understood to be a reality in itself, distinct from the Father, and yet somehow divine, and as a divine entity to have assumed flesh, a far different assertion is being made. This language becomes analogous to the thinking of the polytheistic culture which was familiar with hierarchies of divine entities populating the invisible world. Was Jesus the incarnation of "a second God"?[29] And yet how else could Christians, who were monotheists, express their distinctive experience in worship that Jesus was of God? When this development is

---

28. Referring to Logos or Wisdom as "a real being" in the Christian context is at best ambiguous and misleading. Just what such a hypostatization might mean constituted a major problem. The development of language indicating distinction and individuation of the Logos within the Godhead required a great deal of time and discussion before any consensus was achieved.

29. Justin Martyr referred to the Logos as a "second God." Kelly, *Early Christian Doctrines*, 148. Origen, too, occasionally used this language. See his "Dialogue with Heraclides," *Alexandrian Christianity*, ed. by J. E. L. Oulton and H. Chadwick (Philadelphia: Westminster Press, 1954), 438.

placed within the context of the objectification of Christian language that occurred with the writing of the New Testament, and of the decisive influence of John's Prologue in christology, one can understand the problem that was to be taken up in the second century.

One can define the problem in terms of the relation of Jesus to God: how should Christians understand and express the divinity of Jesus and at the same time preserve their monotheism? There is little doubt that Christians used the transcendent language of divinity in speaking of Jesus. Grillmeier finds the principle of "the exchange of predicates," which is based on the human and divine character of Jesus within the unity and identity of the one subject, operative in Ignatius of Antioch.[30] In Tertullian the practice was used to express sharp paradoxes: "And the Son of God died; it is by all means to be believed, because it is absurd."[31] But it is another matter to give an account of the rationale for this language. The manner in which early theology explained the divinity of Jesus while retaining belief in one sole God involved three moves: a transferral of the problem to the inner life of God, a conception of differentiation within the Godhead, and the subordination of the Logos-Son to the Father. This reasoning can be illustrated in the theology of the second and third centuries.

First, a solution to the problem caused by the conviction that Jesus is in some way divine was sought within the framework of the one God of monotheism. To know God, according to Justin, is to know the Father, and to know "that the Father of all has a Son, who, as the First-born Word of God, is also God" (1 Apol 63, p. 102). This move of Justin, which was dictated by John's Prologue, reflects the common thinking of the patristic period. From the very beginning, then, monotheism was never compromised, because the question of Jesus' divinity was from the beginning considered within the framework of the inner life of the one transcendent God. Here, too, one finds the roots of trinitarian reflection, which is strictly christological in its origin, and is always oriented back toward the question of the divinity of Jesus of Nazareth.

The second element in addressing the issue of Jesus' divinity, then, was to find differentiation within the life of God. The differentiation was suggested by the hypostatized Word and Wisdom, which were in turn conceived as incarnated in Jesus. The Father generates a Son. Now theologians began to reflect on the nature or character of this generation. Justin, for example, thinking within a context of Greek philosophy that was current, but also reflecting the wisdom tradition, suggests that "God has begotten of Himself a certain rational Power as a Beginning before all other creatures" (Trypho 61, p. 144). This is confirmed by Proverbs 8 when it is read objectively as referring to a hypostatization (Trypho 61, pp. 144–45).

---

30. Grillmeier, *Christ in Christian Tradition*, 86–89. See the citation of Ignatius at the beginning of this chapter.

31. Grillmeier, *Christ in Christian Tradition*, 122, citing Tertullian, *De carne Christi*, 5.4.

Differentiation within God is the supposition of Tertullian's response to the suggestion of an incarnation of the Father: it is the Son who is incarnate. The Son or Logos (*Sermo*) already has a reality, a certain individuality, and a divine status within the life of the Godhead.[32] By the time of Origen reflection on the generation of the Son within the life of God had advanced. "Wisdom, therefore, must be believed to have been begotten beyond the limits of any beginning that we can speak of or understand" (Prin 1.2.1, p. 16).[33] This generation is internal, eternal, spiritual.[34] The internal generation of the Word is not merely posited on the basis of scriptural data but is also justified by Platonic reasoning: "how could rational beings exist, unless the Word or reason had existed before them? Or how could they be wise, unless wisdom existed?" (Prin 1.2.4, p. 17). Both philosophy and the scriptures, then, suggested a living God with internal differentiation and movement.

The third element in this development was the subordination of the Son to the Father. In other words, although Jesus was divine and of the inner life of God, he was of lesser rank than the Father. This reflects and continues the tradition of the New Testament which stops short of equating Jesus with the Father. This subordination is communicated in a variety of indirect ways since, for the most part, the point of christology was to show Jesus' divinity. In Justin, for example, statements such as the following only suggest this subordination: "For we worship and love, after God the Father, the Word who is from the Unbegotten and Ineffable God, since He even became Man for us, so that by sharing in our sufferings He also might heal us" (2 Apol 13, p. 134). A strong tradition that also suggests subordination was the inability to imagine the Father as incarnate in the world: "no one with even the slightest intelligence would dare to assert that the Creator and Father of all things left His supercelestial realms to make Himself visible in a little spot on earth" (Trypho

---

32. Grillmeier, *Christ in Christian Tradition*, 129. Modalism, which denies distinctions within God between Father, Son, and Spirit, holding them to be aspects or modes of the one divine Person, was also a way of asserting forcefully the divinity of Jesus Christ and, at the same time, preserving the unity of God. But one does not sense that modalism ever gained a serious hearing because of two factors: first, the absolute transcendence of God, localized in the Father, forbade the Father-God's descent into the world; second, it seemed to contradict the New Testament witness when it was read as direct representative information, for the Father and the Son were clearly distinct beings, and it was the Son not the Father who was incarnate.

33. Origen says that "he [the Word] does not *come to be* 'with God' as though previously he were not with him, but because he is always with the Father, it is said, 'And the word *was* with God,' for he did not *'come to be* with God'" (Origen, *Commentary on John*, 2.8, p. 97). He continues: "before all time and eternity 'the Word was in the beginning,' and 'the Word was with God'" (ibid. 2.9, p. 97).

34. This is an eternal begetting as brightness is begotten from light. For he does not become Son in an external way through the adoption of the Spirit, but is Son by nature. The begetting proceeds spiritually and internally "as it were an act of his will proceeding from the mind" (Prin 1.2.4-6, pp. 18–19).

60, pp. 242–43).[35] The Father enjoyed the highest transcendence, which was a distinguishing character of God, not the Son. As Irenaeus put it, it was the Word of God who was constantly present to human beings throughout history. "It is not the Father, for He is transcendent and unseen" (PAP 45, p. 77). This emphasis on the transcendence of God which, given the differentiation within God, is now focused in the Father is the reason why modalism, especially with its implication of patripassionism, failed. Tertullian rejects any suggestion that it was the Father who was in Jesus Christ; it simply does not fit the testimony of the New Testament which speaks of the Son or Word becoming flesh, not the Father.[36]

This subordination is well developed in Origen. God the Father is absolutely transcendent, unknowable, utterly incomprehensible. But the Son can be known and the qualities of the Son mediate a certain knowledge of the transcendent properties of the Father.[37] The Son is the "image of the invisible God" (Prin 1.2.6, p. 18). This subordination is clear in Origen's hierarchical arrangement of Father, Son, and Spirit, and his description of their different functions in his *On First Principles*. In his *Commentary on John* he is also explicit: God the Father, with the article, *the* God, is truly God. But "everything besides the very God, which is made God by participation in his divinity, would more properly not be said to be *'the* God,' but 'God.' To be sure, his 'firstborn of every creature,' in as much as he was the first to be with God and has drawn divinity into himself, is more honored than the other gods beside him . . ." (*Commentary on John*, 2.17, p. 99). For Origen, the Father is truly and absolutely God, while the Son is the Word, the archetype of all other realities, the medium and way back to the Father, him in whom the qualities of the transcendent Father are known because he participates in them.[38]

---

35. This comment of Justin is instructive. On the one hand it reveals a profound experience of God's transcendence. On the other hand, the naive, materialistic, and objectivist form of expression so limits the conception of God's infinite capacity that it becomes impossible to take the statement at face value today. When the transcendence of the Father is thought of in these terms, modalism is automatically ruled out.

36. Tertullian, *Tertullian's Treatise against Praxeas*, ed., intro., trans., and com. by Ernest Evans (London: SPCK, 1948), 27, pp. 172–75. Subordinationism in christology is linked by Grillmeier to too much stress on the absolute transcendence of God. "God the Father was thought to have such an absolute transcendence that he could not possibly deal actively with men (R. Holte). The danger of subordinationism was not far off." Grillmeier, *Christ in Christian Tradition*, 110. But not only subordinationism. Differentiation within God and the need of mediation itself are also dependent upon growth of an idea of a kind of absolutist transcendence of God. If this were considered in the light of a concept of God as subject today that is more malleable, and that can tolerate language about God suffering, the premises of the traditional reasoning would be considerably weakened.

37. Grillmeier, *Christ in Christian Tradition*, 142.

38. "Origen insisted that only God is to be worshiped, and worship is offered to him *through the Son*." Young, *Creeds*, 42.

Is Jesus God in the theology that extended from the second into the fourth century? The answer to this question is yes, but an attenuated yes. What makes it difficult to appreciate this answer is the historical framework in which the answer is given and the intricate process by which the answer was generated. This is christology from above in its pure form, in which conclusions about Jesus of Nazareth are being expressed in terms of the authority of a reading of scripture that communicates directly referential and transcendent information, and a speculative reasoning about the inner life of God.[39] Jesus was an incarnation of the distinct but subordinate aspect or "person" from within the differentiated life of God, that is, the Word or Son. The characteristics of the Son are identical with Jesus because in a three-stage christology Jesus is the Son enfleshed. And the Son is the image of the Father.[40] Jesus is thus truly God, but less than the transcendent Father from whom he is eternally begotten. This solution is not Arian, because the Son is not a creature, but in the light of the Arian controversy, it will be revised. I will look more closely at the Arian formula and its formal contradiction at the Council of Nicaea in the next chapter. I pass now to the development of the question of Jesus' person.

THE CONSTITUTION OF JESUS CHRIST

"Christology" in the narrow and formal sense of the term is the understanding of the constitution of Jesus Christ. In its classical form this question involves the understanding of the divinity and the humanity of Jesus Christ, and how they are interrelated in the single individual with his proper identity. This question was entertained during the second and third centuries of the development of classical christology in both an implicit and an explicit way. But the discussion was clearly intensified after the formulation of the Nicene creed, and we pick up the debate at that point. If the Logos or Son is of the same substance as the Father, the question of his being changeable, passible, and generally involved in the material sphere of human existence becomes newly problematic.[41]

A standard strategy for describing fourth- and fifth-century christology is to present two broad traditions or lines of thinking that began to take shape during this period. The first is a Word-flesh and incarnational christology associated with Alexandrian theologians; the second is the

---

39. It should be clear that the conviction of the divinity of Jesus did not come from this theology; this theology is rather an attempt to express and "explain" the faith experience of the Christian community.

40. This distinction of the Son from the Father, along with the subordination of the Son to the Father, which were pervasive themes in eastern christology, explain the tendency of the East to be sympathetic to Arianism during the fourth century. Young, *Creeds*, 43–45.

41. Young, *Creeds*, 65.

Word-human being and indwelling christology associated with Antioch.[42] I shall work within this framework as I consider the christologies of Athanasius, Apollinaris, and Cyril of Alexandria on the one side, and Theodore of Mopsuestia and Nestorius on the other. I will also note the interpretation of Jesus' work of salvation in these authors and how it correlates with the christology. The goal here is not to lay out an integral picture of these two traditions, but to use these developments to illustrate the following theses: christology is intrinsically linked to soteriology, and it involves a tension between the humanity and the divinity of Jesus that cannot be resolved. These theses both reflect the development of this period and help to explain it.

It was pointed out earlier that the doctrine of Chalcedon was not a datum of revelation that would inevitably have been discovered by reflection and formulated in the terms it actually took. But there is another side to that issue. The symbolic character of Jesus Christ, his being a medium of God's presence and salvation, entails an intrinsic dialectical structure, a tension between Jesus being a finite human being and creature, and Jesus being or mediating the presence of God in history. In the measure in which Chalcedon reflects this dialectical structure of christology, some form of a Chalcedon-like doctrine is essential to christology. The intrinsic tension between the humanity and the divinity, therefore, corresponds to the structure of religious symbols generally, and to Jesus being the concrete symbol who mediates God to Christian faith. From this perspective, I turn to the two distinct lines of theology that provided the language, concepts, and distinctions that form the background for the doctrine of the Council of Chalcedon.

The christological trends associated with Alexandria and Antioch share much in common. Both are christologies from above; they are three-stage christologies; they presuppose the doctrine of Nicaea that the Logos or Son is of the same substance as the Father. They unfold by means of reflection on the objective data of revelation proposed in the scriptures. Their goal is to understand the character or constitution of the figure Jesus Christ. How does his defined divinity cohere with his earthly appearance as a human being? What does it mean to say that this one figure, Jesus Christ, is both divine and human? If it was unthinkable that God the Father should be mixed up in the corruptible world of matter, what does it mean to say the Son, who is of the same nature as the Father, "suffered, died, and was buried"?

ALEXANDRIAN LOGOS-SARX CHRISTOLOGY

The core of Alexandrian christology lies in the consistent unity or continuous self-identity of the Logos or heavenly Son through the three stages

---

42. These two paradigms are thus identified with two historical traditions. The second section of this chapter suggests that these two traditions of christology reflect different experiences of salvation.

of "his career," so to speak. There is one single subject in this christology, that of the Logos. This Logos-Son is the eternal Son of God who, in a manner that seems to have been understood quite literally, took on human flesh for the span of a human lifetime, and then rose from death and ascended to his place within the Godhead. For example, John 1:1-3, 14 directly characterizes Athanasius's christology: the Word is God and the Word became flesh. The Philippians hymn (Phil 2:6-11) also characterizes this descent christology. Both are cited together as proof texts.[43] When one reads Athanasius on Jesus of Nazareth, it is quite clear that the real subject is the divine Son; he who acts is God. "There can be no doubt that the Logos is not merely the personal subject of Christ's bodily life, but also the real, physical source of all the actions of his life."[44] This unity and identity of the subject, Jesus Christ, is an explicit concern of Apollinaris, another Alexandrian theologian who underlines it. He cannot conceive of two intellects or rationalities in one person. The conscious subject in Jesus is the Logos itself, continuous with its divine pre-existence. "Therefore, it is inconceivable that the same person should be both God and an entire man. Rather, he exists in the singleness of an incarnate divine nature which is commingled [with flesh], with the result that worshipers bend their attention to the God inseparable from his flesh and not to one who is worshiped and one who is not. . . ."[45] This paradigm explains why Cyril of Alexandria reacted so strongly against what he perceived in Nestorius, namely, an adoptionism that divided the unity of the divine subject who is Jesus Christ. This paradigm cannot accept any hint of worshiping a man "along with" the Word, or dissociating the body of Christ from the Word. Any separation leads in the end to division, to two Sons of God, the Eternal Son of God and Jesus the Son of God.[46]

The unity and continuous self-identity of the divine Logos as the subject who is also Jesus of Nazareth is emphasized still further in this Alexandrian christology by a deliberate minimization or denial of a human soul in Jesus. It is as though a "Word-flesh" paradigm were to be taken in a literal or physical sense, with the Word functioning as the "rational soul" of Jesus' flesh. Discerning the measure of such an understanding in Athanasius is difficult, because the term "flesh" is a broad and inclusive symbol for "humanity" or "human existence." But even if he did allow for a human soul in speaking of Jesus' humanity broadly, Athanasius was systematic in not assigning a specific function for a ratio-

---

43. Athanasius, "Against the Arians: Discourse III," *Nicene and Post-Nicene Fathers of the Christian Church*, IV, *St. Athanasius*, ed. and trans. by Philip Schaff and Henry Wace (Grand Rapids: Eerdmans, 1961), 3.29, p. 409. References to this work in the text by discourse and paragraph are to this translation.

44. Grillmeier, *Christ in Christian Tradition*, 312.

45. Apollinaris, in a text presented by Richard A. Norris, ed. and trans., *The Christological Controversy* (Philadelphia: Fortress Press, 1980), 108.

46. Cyril of Alexandria, "Second Letter to Nestorius," *Selected Letters*, ed. and trans. by Lionel R. Wickham (Oxford: Clarendon Press, 1983), 6, p. 9.

nal soul in Jesus.[47] Apollinaris is much more explicit in denying a human rationality in Jesus Christ. Divine Wisdom functions as the rational part of Jesus. Christ "is not a human being but is like a human being, since he is not coessential with humanity in his highest part."[48] Speaking of the sanctification of the flesh of Jesus, he describes this as taking place by direct presence: "For in these circumstances the body lives by the sanctification of the Godhead and not by the provision of a human soul, and the whole is completely joined in one."[49] Cyril in a certain sense represents a break with this tradition since he admits a rational human soul in Jesus Christ. We affirm, he wrote, "that the Word substantially united to himself flesh, endowed with life and reason, in a manner mysterious and inconceivable, and became man. . . ."[50] This human soul in Cyril's christology served as a link between the Logos and flesh, and helped him to explain Jesus' suffering. But Cyril remains in the tradition by insisting that "'God the Logos did not come into a man, but he truly became man, while remaining God.'"[51] The significance of this tradition is that the principle of the activity of Jesus Christ is entirely God's or the Word's; there is no human initiative here.

This is confirmed by the use of language that suggests that the flesh of Jesus Christ is an instrument of the Logos. "In the word *organon* Athanasius sums up the whole significance of the Logos-sarx relationship."[52] This is still more pronounced in Apollinaris: "God who has taken to himself an instrument of activity is both God insofar as he activates and human with respect to the instrument of activity which he uses. Remaining God, he is not altered. The instrument and its user naturally produce a single action, but if the action is one, the essence (*ousia*) is one also. Therefore, there has come to be one essence of the Logos and his instrumental means of activity."[53] The implied passivity of the instrument is mitigated somewhat in Cyril. But in each case, when one has recourse to a concrete historical imagination and asks who was acting in the seemingly thoroughly human actions of Jesus, such as his ignorance and suffering, the responses are strained. Was Jesus Christ ignorant? No, for the Word was God and knew all things. But the Word feigned ignorance, because ignorance was proper to the flesh. Did Jesus Christ suffer?

---

47. See Grillmeier's nuanced discussion of Athanasius on this point in *Christ in Christian Tradition*, 320–28.

48. Apollinaris, in Norris, *The Christological Controversy*, 109. "In their irrational body, people are coessential with irrational animals, but insofar as they are rational, they are of a different essence. So also God, who is coessential with men in his flesh, is of a different essence insofar as he is Logos and God." Ibid., 111.

49. Apollinaris, in Norris, *The Christological Controversy*, 106.

50. Cyril, in Wickham, *Select Letters*, 3, pp. 5–7.

51. Cyril, quoted by Grillmeier, *Christ in Christian Tradition*, 477.

52. Grillmeier, *Christ in Christian Tradition*, 317. See Athanasius, "Against the Arians," 3.35, p. 318.

53. Apollinaris, in Norris, *The Christological Controversy*, 110.

Literally no, for the Word is impassible; but yes, in a certain sense, one could say "he suffered" by indirection. For the Word assumed flesh, and the flesh suffered, and thus by appropriation this christology can say that Jesus Christ suffered, that is, insofar as his flesh did.[54] Some of Cyril's responses to the question of Christ's suffering, however, are practically impenetrable. He says that "since his own created body suffered these things he himself 'suffered' for our sake, the point being that within the suffering body was the Impassible."[55] The idea seems to suggest suffering by external appropriation or attribution on the part of the essentially impassible Logos. The Logos is impassible, but "he is seen to attribute to himself the passions that occur in his own flesh. . . . In order that he may be believed to be the savior of the universe, Christ refers the passions of his own flesh . . . to himself by means of an appropriation which occurs for the sake of our salvation."[56] The problem in this tradition is that it is a christology of only one subject, and, that subject being impassible, it leaves no other subject who can suffer.

But underlying this christology is not a soteriology whose center lies in Jesus Christ suffering for our salvation. Although that is not excluded, for it came with the larger tradition, the centering conceptual image is divinization and revelation. It is flesh that needs saving, and it is saved by the Word assuming it. Athanasius says that by nature

> the Word Himself is impassible, and yet because of that flesh which He put on, these things are ascribed to Him, since they are proper to the flesh, and the body itself is proper to the Saviour. And while He Himself, being impassible in nature, remains as He is, not harmed by these affections, but rather obliterating and destroying them, human beings, their passions as if changed and abolished in the Impassible, henceforth become themselves also impassible and free from them for ever. . . .[57]

The very assumption of flesh by the Logos constitutes the gradual salvation of flesh. Apollinaris expresses this in terms of a fallen human rationality. "What was needed was unchangeable Intellect which did not fall under the domination of the flesh on account of its weakness of understanding but which adapted the flesh to itself without force."[58]

---

54. Athanasius, "Against the Arians," 3.37–56, pp. 414–24, passim.

55. Cyril, in Wickham, *Selected Letters*, 5, p. 7.

56. Cyril of Alexandria, "Letter to John of Antioch," in Norris, *The Christological Controversy*, 144.

57. Athanasius, "Against the Arians," 3.34, p. 412.

58. Apollinaris, in Norris, *The Christological Controversy*, 109. For Apollinaris, saving revelation and divinization required that Jesus Christ be God as Logos enfleshed as opposed to an inspired human being. His conception of salvation entailed a christology of "mixture," in which Jesus Christ was like a cross-breed or *tertium quid, between* God and human existence. Jesus Christ "is neither wholly man nor wholly God, but a

The process of divinization is expressed beautifully by Athanasius as a gradual growth and assimilation of flesh to Wisdom. This is seen in his response to the question of what it means to say Jesus grew in wisdom, since divine Wisdom cannot advance. The advancing or growth took place in the flesh, as the flesh was in the Word and was the Word's and is called His. "Neither then was the advance the Word's, nor was the flesh Wisdom, but the flesh became the body of Wisdom. Therefore, as we have already said, not Wisdom, as Wisdom, advanced in respect of Itself; but the manhood advanced in Wisdom, transcending by degrees human nature, and being deified, and becoming and appearing to all as the organ of Wisdom for the operation and the shining forth of the Godhead."[59]

In sum, one sees a remarkable correspondence between a conception of salvation and this christology. And despite the variations among these influential Alexandrians, there is a steady consistency in the fundamental insight. This is centered in the one divine Logos taking on flesh as his own. This "flesh" originally signified all that is entailed in being a human. But in the Alexandrian tradition Jesus does not seem to be conceived as an integral human being. He lacks a rational soul, or is not a human subject, or is without a principle of human individuality, freedom, and action. All of these elements would undermine the effective presence and initiative of God for our salvation. Commentators usually affirm that the strength of this christology lies in the unity of the being of the savior that controls the conception. There is but one Logos through three distinct phases: preexistence, earthly existence, new glorified existence. While this view of a single continuous being across three stages of existence was undoubtedly credible in its time, the monophysitic tendency of this christology appears as a weakness today. For from a historical perspective, any and all symbolic mediation of God in our world must be dialectical in structure. Such a dialectical structure is the condition of the possibility of a historical mediation of God. The tendency of Alexandrian christology is to dissolve this necessary tension into a single divine nature. Its theological conceptions seem directly to represent, and thus communicate to the imagination, an understanding that borders on the mythological: Jesus existed in eternity; Jesus came down on earth, Jesus returned to eternity. The weakness of this position appears at the point where it touches history, specifically in the issue of the suffering of Jesus. The real strength of this christology lies in the religious experience and conviction that salvation can only come from God, and that Jesus is the mediator of God for human salvation. Its strength is what it emphasizes to a fault, namely, the divinity of Jesus Christ.

---

mixture of God and man. He is God by the enfleshed spirit and man by the flesh assumed by God." Young, *Nicaea to Chalcedon*, 188.

59. Athanasius, "Against the Arians," 3.53, p. 422.

ANTIOCHENE LOGOS-ANTHROPOS CHRISTOLOGY

The core of Antiochene christology lies in a consistent vision of Jesus Christ as an historical figure or person who bore two distinct natures. Whereas the focus of attention or referent of Alexandrian christology is the divine subject, the Logos who became flesh, Antiochene christology has as its imaginative referent the historical figure, Jesus of Nazareth, and this entails a different view of things. In contrast to "Word-flesh," this christology is called "Word-human being" and an "indwelling" christology, in which Jesus Christ is the "human being assumed" by the Word. It is not, however, adoptionist. Theodore of Mopsuestia explicitly rules this out: "The one who was assumed according to foreknowledge was united with God from the very beginning, since he received the foundation of the union in his very fashioning in his mother's womb."[60] The guiding theme, then, is the duality of divinity and humanity held together in the one figure Jesus Christ.

A number of texts from the work of Theodore depict the duality in Jesus Christ in a pointed way. "Let the character of the natures stand without confusion, and let the person be acknowledged as undivided—the former in virtue of the characteristic property of the nature, since the one assumed is distinct from the One who assumes him, and the latter in virtue of the personal union, since the One who assumes and the nature of the one assumed are included in the denotation of a single name."[61] The point is to preserve the distinction and integrity of each nature, as opposed to confusion or mixture of one into the other or the formation of a third thing. Each of the natures is conceived as remaining indissolubly in itself. "Moreover, it is also quite evident that the notion of 'union' is thoroughly congruous, for by means of it the natures which are brought together make up one person according to the union."[62] This duality in Jesus Christ held together in union was behind Nestorius's calling into question whether God had a mother. A distinction must be maintained: "A creature does not produce him who is uncreatable."[63] On the one hand, Jesus Christ from the beginning is an assumed human being in whom God dwells. On the other hand, this

---

60. Theodore of Mopsuestia, *De Incarnatione* 7, in Norris, *The Christological Controversy*, 119.

61. Theodore, *De Incarnatione* 5, in Norris, *The Christological Controversy*, 113.

62. Theodore, *De Incarnatione*, 8, in Norris, *The Christological Controversy*, 120. "In the same way we say that the essence of God the Word is his own and that the essence of the man is his own, for the natures are distinct, but the person effected by the union is one. In this way, when we try to distinguish the natures, we say that the person of the man is complete and that that of the Godhead is complete. But when we consider the union, then we proclaim that both natures are one person, since the humanity receives from the divinity honor surpassing that which belongs to a creature, and the divinity brings to perfection in the man every thing that is fitting." Ibid. 8, pp. 120–21.

63. Nestorius, "First Sermon against the Theotokos," in Norris, *The Christological Controversy*, 124.

indwelling produced a unity who was the figure Jesus Christ. "We confess both and adore them as one, for the duality of the natures is one on account of the unity."[64] In responding to Cyril, Nestorius says he fears a confusion of natures in his work, and for his part speaks of the "conjunction" of natures.[65] The language of both Theodore and Nestorius shows that they intend more than a mere moral union of two natures constituting the person of Jesus Christ. The thought is moving in the direction of a distinction of levels in which ontological union is preserved on one level and distinction of "natures" on another. But no clear, stable, and commonly recognized terms for expressing this have been found.[66]

A Word-flesh christology depicts the humanity of Jesus Christ as a passive instrument of the Word. What kind of language is used by Word-human being christology to characterize Jesus Christ in history? Jesus Christ is an integral human being within whom the Logos dwells. When contrasted to an extreme form of Logos-flesh christology, Antiochene christology provides a logic for a language that speaks of Jesus Christ's human intelligence and freedom. The idea that the humanity of Jesus Christ is an instrument of the Logos, however, is not completely abandoned; it is relevant especially in actions that display divine power, such as miracles. But at the same time the indwelling Logos permeates, shapes, and informs the entire human nature and thus all its actions.[67] One can appreciate the different way in which this christology envisions Jesus in history by contrasting the account of Theodore of Jesus' growth in wisdom with that of Athanasius just cited:

> On the one hand, he held fast to this way [of being oriented to the good and hating evil] by his own will, while on the other hand this purpose was faithfully guarded in him by the cooperating work of God the Logos. And he progressed with the greatest ease toward a consummate virtue, whether in keeping the Law before his baptism or in following the citizenship in grace after his baptism. He furnishes us a type of this citizenship and is himself a way, so to speak, established for this end. Thus, later, after the resurrection and ascension, when he had shown himself worthy of the union by his own

64. Nestorius, "First Sermon against the Theotokos," in Norris, *The Christological Controversy*, 131.

65. Nestorius, "Second Letter to Cyril," in Norris, *The Christological Controversy*, 136–37.

66. Grillmeier, in *Christ in Christian Tradition*, assesses Nestorius's christology quite positively. His christological formulas "could compete with any christology of their time" (457). His christology "shows quite an orthodox conception of the incarnation" (462). At certain points Nestorius's language fell short of his intentions, but on the whole Grillmeier believes that Nestorius was misunderstood and misjudged (468, 472). Young concurs, after representing Nestorius's christology as fairly close to that of Chalcedon. Young, *Nicaea to Chalcedon*, 229–40. Similarly Kelly, *Doctrines*, 316–17.

67. Grillmeier, *Christ in Christian Tradition*, 432.

will (having received the union even before this in his very fashioning, by the good pleasure of the Lord), he also unmistakably fur-
nished for ever after the proof of the union, since he had nothing to
separate and cut him off from the working of God the Logos but had
God the Logos accomplishing everything in him through the union.[68]

The conception of Jesus Christ communicated in this text combines a
recognition of Jesus' human freedom and decision making with a sustaining and efficacious presence of God as Logos to him.

As in Word-flesh christology there lies beneath this christology a conception of the way Jesus Christ is savior. Salvation received involves
human freedom, and salvation accomplished by Jesus Christ is achieved
in and through the working of Jesus' freedom. This conception is hinted
at in the text of Theodore just cited: Jesus Christ is a type for life in grace
and provides a way for our imitation. In Theodore, the created soul of
Jesus Christ's human nature is a source of human actions that are decisive
for human salvation.[69] Since salvation is a divine work, this is the work of
the Logos, but the instrumentality involved implies a Logos which draws
up into itself real, rational, and free human actions. This allows Jesus
Christ to be a type and an exemplary "way."

Nestorius proposed an interpretation of Jesus' work of salvation in
terms that integrate human freedom into the story. It combines a narrative
of redemption and a final Adam christology within a Nicene framework.
Jesus Christ in his humanity struggles with Satan to repay the debt
incurred by the first human being, Adam. "Our nature, having been put
on by Christ like a garment, intervenes on our behalf, being entirely free
from all sin and contending by appeal to its blameless origin, just as the
Adam who was formed earlier brought punishment upon his race by reason of his sin. This was the opportunity which belonged to the assumed
man, as a human being to dissolve, by means of the flesh, that corruption
which arose by means of the flesh."[70]

In sum, one finds a mutual consistency between a conception of salvation and the main lines of this Word-human being christology. On the
premise that the story of salvation lies close to the way Jesus Christ is
experienced, one can say that this christology is informed by a conviction
that Jesus Christ was a full and model human being. One looks to Jesus
Christ for direction on how to lead a life that leads back to God.
Descending Logos christology is combined with an integral anthropology

---

68. Theodore, *De Incarnatione* 7, in Norris, *The Christological Controversy*, 118.
Commenting explicitly on Jesus' growth in age, wisdom, and grace (Luke 2:52), he uses
the language of cooperative grace which is based on the union of Jesus' integral freedom with the Logos. Ibid., 119.

69. Grillmeier, *Christ in Christian Tradition*, 427–28.

70. Nestorius, "First Sermon against the Theotokos," in Norris, *The Christological
Controversy*, 128.

that includes a mind and freedom in Jesus, and the two, divinity and humanity, are held together in a union that is never quite satisfactorily conceived. This particular strand of the pre-Chalcedonian debate is much closer to modern, historically conscious sensibilities, but it is still pre-critical. Its strength lies in its preservation of the humanity of Jesus Christ together with his divinity. Its weakness lies in its inability to present a coherent characterization of the unity of the figure Jesus Christ. But it may be that this problem is not the fault of this line of thought, but of the constraints which the received tradition had imposed upon it. Logos-anthropos christology faced an intrinsic problem because of the suppositions under which it was working, namely, the hypostatization of the Logos and a pattern of objectivist thinking. The conception of Logos as a hypostasis creates a problem that defies a solution. With the individualization of the Logos, there are "two," Logos as an individual and the individual human being Jesus, out of which one cannot make "one" without compromising one or the other. What one finds in this christology is not dialectical thinking but an impossible conceptual dilemma.

CONCLUSION

The historical development of what turned out to be classical doctrines about Jesus Christ is, needless to say, important for the understanding of the classics themselves. I will in the next chapter focus attention on the doctrines of Nicaea and Chalcedon as the most important and influential products of this period. But there are other lessons to be learned from this early period of development after the first century.

A comparison between patristic christology and New Testament christology indicates that there were real changes in christology from one period to the next. A major change is effected by the writing of the New Testament. The christology that is reflected in the New Testament as a whole is fluid and open; the pluralism reflected there is far-ranging. Also the christology of the New Testament literature is still in dialogue with Jesus or a memory of Jesus which is quite recent. Even in the New Testament literature that does not focus imaginatively on Jesus of Nazareth, such as the letters of Paul, one must reckon that Jesus is not forgotten, and that memory of him is a constitutive dimension of the life of the community. As history moves away from the event of Jesus, memory of him is objectified and recorded in writing. Then, in the wake of the dominating influence of John's gospel in christology and the hypostatization of Logos as a discrete divine being, christological thinking undergoes some major shifts. Reflection, doubling back on New Testament writings, tends to make this literature into a source book for revealed representative information about God. One finds a tendency "to treat the Bible in an 'atomic' way as if each verse or set of verses was capable of giving direct information about Christian doctrine apart from its context. . . ."[71] The framework for christological thinking becomes narrowed down to a Johannine pattern of thought. Logos or the Son becomes the subject matter of christology, subtly displacing Jesus of Nazareth as the referent of christological imagination. The list of New Testament paths for christological thinking that were not followed is long.

Another real and significant change in christological thinking was mediated by the change of language, that is, the shift from a way of thinking that is rooted in a Jewish, religious cultural tradition to one that is more self-consciously philosophical and Greek in its roots. I refer to forms of questioning and a tradition of meaningful linguistic categories that shape a conceptual worldview. The shift of a cultural matrix involved new questions that generated answers that were not found in the New Testament literature in any explicit way. The point, however, is not made against change and in favor of retaining an alien language in a new culture. The point is simply the recognition of the newness of these conceptions and their changeability in turn.

The overview of this history has demonstrated that this development was historically contingent. This contingency is frequently illustrated, if not proved, with the following rhetorical question: what would have been the result if Christianity had spread toward the East? Yet despite the contingency and the pluralism of patristic christologies, one can detect below the surface a series of perennial questions or problems that are structural. There are topics in christology that necessarily arise and will have to be addressed in any cultural context. Some examples of these that are exemplified in the patristic development are worthy of note. The soteriological structure of christology is constant. The question of the relationship between Jesus and God arose early in the Christian tradition and, on the basis of the New Testament witness, is a fundamental question that cannot be avoided. The relationship between what came to be called Jesus' divinity and the historical fact of Jesus' humanity is also a constant factor in the development of christology after the first century, and it was accentuated by the Nicene formula. And, finally, there is the persistent methodological question concerning criteria and norms for christological judgments. Amid the various interpretations of Jesus as the Christ, how are decisive judgments to be made? All of these issues are addressed in different ways, but the questions that are being asked are intrinsic to christology.

Thus this theological development, when it is analyzed, begins to reveal the intrinsic criteria of theological reflection itself. By intrinsic criteria I want to point again to elements in the structure of the exercise itself as distinct from external criteria, such as other theologies or church doctrines. Throughout this development there is a constant citation of the sources of scripture as a norm; christology has to be faithful to the first witness to

---

71. R. P. C. Hanson, *The Search for the Christian Doctrine of God: The Arian Controversy 318–381* (Edinburgh: T. & T. Clark, 1988), 848–49.

Jesus and to the person of Jesus as he appears in that witness. The process of inculturation, of using the categories of Greco-Roman intellectual culture to understand and explain Jesus Christ, indicates that intelligibility is a norm for christology. And, finally, the consistent correspondence of christology with a conception of how Jesus saves indicates that experience and the Christian life are inner criteria for assessing the point of christology. These criteria will come to bear on an analysis and interpretation of the two monuments of patristic christology, the doctrines of Nicaea and Chalcedon.

CHAPTER 10

Interpreting Nicaea and Chalcedon

This chapter will discuss the two most important christological documents of the patristic period, the creed of the Council of Nicaea and the christological doctrine of the Council of Chalcedon. These teachings are taken to be authoritative and normative for Christian faith. But as classical christological doctrines, they have to be reinterpreted in every age. The goal of this chapter is to offer positive, intelligible, and constructive interpretations of Nicaea and Chalcedon that are at the same time faithful to the intent of these doctrines.

Educated people today are at least implicitly aware of the need to be explicit in reinterpreting classical christological language. Indeed, no adequate christology can fail to include a critical evaluation of these doctrines. At least three issues relating to intelligibility separate the ancient language from our Christian life in postmodern western culture. The first is a changed worldview, one that is mediated by a scientific and technological way of thinking, and that contains data never imagined even a century ago. The body of knowledge that was available to the church fathers has changed. Methods of inquiry and understanding are also different. Just as patristic understanding was an inculturation of Christian beliefs into the Greco-Roman world of the time, so too must christological doctrine make sense to twenty-first-century culture with its science, technology, and cosmology.

Second, from a more explicitly theological point of view, and recalling the reflections of the last chapter, the language of these doctrines appears fantastic. The technical language, which like all language carries an imaginative residue, seems to encourage an anthropomorphic view of the incarnation of God in Jesus Christ. The identification of Jesus with the Logos, the distinction of Logos from the Father, and the three-stage christology seem to justify speaking of a pre-existence of Jesus. In a historically conscious period, where Jesus refers to the flesh and blood figure who lived in Palestine in the first century, this language, when it is taken at face value, depicts a mythological fable. Christology must begin to lay the groundwork for a language that remains incarnational, but at the same time protects the human character of Jesus and avoids any caricature of incarnation.

Third, reinterpretation of classical christology must bring these doctrines into conjunction with Christian life and spirituality. This involves questions of human freedom in history, and how Jesus of Nazareth, the human being, stands in front of human freedom today in an offer of salvation. Christology cannot be approached from above in a way that leaves human beings merely passive before divine salvation. Such a view cannot communicate with an authentic Christian historical consciousness that is simultaneously an awareness of human freedom as responsibility for self, others, and the world.

These three broad considerations are offered as a general rationale for the need of a thoroughgoing reinterpretation of classical doctrine. Such a need is simply stated, but the project itself is filled with ambiguity: how can christological doctrine transcend the boundaries of the fourth and fifth centuries, engage the human questioning of the twenty-first century, and at the same time be faithful to the intentionality of the New Testament and these classic doctrines? No reinterpretation can possibly satisfy everyone. In this attempt to reappropriate these doctrines I shall deal first with the Nicene creed and then the christological doctrine of Chalcedon. In each case I shall briefly outline the well-known doctrine, offer a more explicit critique of it from a current standpoint, and propose an interpretation of its meaning that is both intelligible in today's world and consonant with the intentionality of the classical doctrines.

THE MEANING OF NICAEA

THE HISTORICAL DOCTRINE OF NICAEA

The Nicene creed is a reaction against Arian doctrine. It was most probably constructed on the basis of a local Syro-Palestinian baptismal creed into which key words and phrases were interpolated in order to negate the doctrine of Arius and his followers. Thus, ordinarily, one begins a historical explanation of the meaning of Nicaea with an exposition of Arian theology because "the principal aim of those who manufactured the creed was to call a halt . . . to the Arian heresy. . . ."[1]

---

1. J. N. D. Kelly, *Early Christian Creeds* (London: Longmans, Green and Co., 1950), 231; also 211, 229. For a brief history of the development of the Nicene creed, see Lorenzo Perrone, "De Nicée à Chalcédoine," *Les Conciles Oecuméniques*, 1, *L'Histoire*, ed. by Giuseppe Alberigo et al. (Paris: Éditions du Cerf, 1994), 19–48; Jaroslav Pelikan, *The Christian Tradition: A History of the Development of Doctrine*, 1, *The Emergence of the Catholic Tradition (100–600)* (Chicago: University of Chicago Press, 1971), 172–210; Frances M. Young, *The Making of the Creeds* (London: SCM Press; Philadelphia: Trinity Press International, 1991). R. P. C. Hanson, *The Search for the Christian Doctrine of God:*

The contentious elements of Arius's theology, insofar as it is known from short texts that have survived and the reactions against it, can be reduced to a few propositions. A good example is this extract from a letter of Arius to Eusebius of Nicomedia. Arius held:

> that the Son is not unbegotten, nor a part of the unbegotten in any way, nor [formed out] of any substratum, but that he was constituted by [God's] will and counsel, before times and before ages, full (of grace and truth), divine, unique, unchangeable. And before he was begotten or created or ordained or founded, he was not. For he was not unbegotten. We are persecuted because we say, 'The Son has a beginning, but God is without beginning.' For this we are persecuted, and because we say, 'he is [made] out of things that were not.' But this is what we say, since he is neither a part of God nor [formed] out of any substratum.[2]

In another letter that took the form of a common creedal statement endorsed by many of like belief, the Arians referred to the Son as "a perfect creature of God." Arius continued in this way:

> Thus there are three *hypostases*. God being the cause of all things is without beginning and most unique, while the Son, begotten timelessly by the Father and created before ages and established, was not before he was begotten—but, begotten timelessly before all things, he alone was constituted by the Father. He is neither eternal nor co-eternal nor co-unbegotten with the Father, nor does he have his being together with the father. . . . But as Monad and cause of all, God is thus before all.[3]

Although it is not entirely clear who are the historical ancestors of these views, there is some consensus on the logic of the Arian position. A fundamental value was attached to the idea of the oneness and transcendence of God. God is singular, simple, undivided, undifferentiated, the one and only first principle of all else. Since the Son was distinct from the Father, to grant him divine status was to divide God. On a seemingly materialist premise, if the Son was formed out of the substratum of God, there would

---

The Arian Controversy 318–381 (Edinburgh: T. & T. Clark, 1988) is a thorough study of the unfolding of the fourth-century Arian controversy.

2. Arius, "Letter of Arius to Eusebius of Nicomedia," *Christology of the Later Fathers*, ed. by E. R. Hardy (Philadelphia: Westminster, 1954), 330–31.

3. Arius, "The Confession of the Arians, Addressed to Alexander of Alexandria," *Christology of the Later Fathers*, 333–34. For a sympathetic reconstruction of Arianism, showing the coherence of its appeal to scripture, tradition, and reason, see Maurice Wiles, *Archetypal Heresy: Arianism through the Centuries* (Oxford: Clarendon Press, 1996), 9–26.

be two. God is also absolutely transcendent, one in power so that there can be no equal to God. Everything else comes from God's singular power and is created.

All christology, we have seen, implies a view of salvation. Tacit in the Arian view, although able to be discerned in what is said in the writings, is the conviction that Jesus saved by being obedient to God and that we are saved by imitating him.[4] If Grillmeier is right in assigning a Logos-sarx christology to the Arians, the Son or Logos accounts for the rationality and freedom of Jesus Christ. This creates a strong reason for viewing the Logos who is incarnate in Jesus in such a way that he be imitable. Although above all human beings, still, as a free and rational creature, the Son incarnated in Jesus is imitable.

The Arian position is captured by the phrase or slogan: "There was when he was not." Although pre-existent to all created reality, which was made through the Son, still, the Son too was created. Given the doctrine of God as single source of all, and a salvation theory which saw the Logos as subordinate in being, even though the Logos was called "divine" in some sense, the bottom line of Arianism is that the Logos is actually a creature.

Once the Arian doctrine is laid out in its principal assertions, the historical meaning of Nicaea can be read in the discrete underlined phrases that are aimed directly at Arian teaching and were inserted into the framework of a typical creed for the period: "We believe . . . in one Lord Jesus Christ, the Son of God, begotten from the Father, only-begotten, that is, *from the substance of the Father*, God from God, light from light, *true God from true God, begotten not made, of one substance with the Father. . . .*"[5]

The phrase or term "only-begotten" is of no real special import, "because it was accepted by all parties in the Arian quarrel and no special dogmatic significance was read into it."[6] By contrast, the phrase "from the substance of the Father" directly contradicts the Arian view that the Logos was created out of nothing, and not begotten out of the same divine being as the Father, and thus not the same kind of being as the Father. The phrase "true God from true God" directly counters the undifferentiated, monadic God of Arius. On the supposition of the distinction between the Son and the Father, it affirms that the Son is equally true God, or that the Son is God in the same sense as the Father is God. The phrase "begotten

---

4. This thesis is developed by R. C. Gregg and D. E. Groh, *Early Arianism—A View of Salvation* (Philadelphia: Fortress Press, 1981). "The redeemer's free obedience in the performance of virtuous acts is what wins him divine approval. . ." (162). Jesus Christ becomes only-begotten son; he is savior as exemplar, providing a perfect creaturely model for human willing and obedience. Following Jesus Christ entails progress in virtue leading to final salvation. There is a certain continuity with Origen in this respect.

5. The text of the Nicene creed here and in the quotations which follow is from Kelly, *Creeds*, 215–16.

6. Kelly, *Creeds*, 235.

not made" makes the distinction between being begotten by, as it were, a natural and spiritual process within the internal life of God, and being engendered or generated out of nothing, so that existence is contingent. The phrase directly attacks Arius's view that, because the Son is begotten, the Son is constituted by God's will. And, finally, there is the single word which came to summarize the doctrine of Nicaea, "*homoousion* with the Father." The Son is of the same substance as the Father. The term *ousia*, which is usually translated as substance, could have meant several different things at the time, and the creed's assimilation of its meaning to that of *hypostasis* complicated matters. Were the Son and the Father one and the same identical being, as eastern theologians were wont to fear? That ambiguity was left in place, to be fought over at a later date. But a generalized meaning of substance was defined by contrast with the Arian position: the Son is of the same stuff, the same kind or level of divine being, as the Father. With reference to deity, as the Father is God, so too is the Son.

The creed is followed by a series of anathemas that simply negate Arian positions, repeating in a formal way, as it were, the point of the anti-Arian phrases that were added to the original creed. In a conciliar or doctrinal teaching that reacts against a threatening position, such anathemas define the hermeneutical perspective by which one can discern the intention of the teaching as a whole.[7] The anathemas, indeed, are a reprise of the fundamental propositions of Arian theology in a negative form: "But as for those who say, There was when He was not, and, Before being born He was not, and that He came into existence out of nothing, or who assert that the Son of God is of a different hypostasis or substance, or is created, or is subject to alteration or change—these the Catholic Church anathematizes."

One can be more sure of the overall vision sustaining the position of Arius than of the mind of the council's bishops, since there are no surviving acts or official records of the deliberations. But some things seem to be apparent from the position itself. The central, controlling idea and value for Nicaea is the strict divinity of the Son or Logos. This explains the reaction against Arius, why bishops who tolerated and even endorsed the subordinationism of Origen reacted against Arius.[8] By proposing that the Logos was a creature, Arius crossed a line. If one takes Athanasius's vigorous defense of the creed some thirty years later as representative of its vision, this is what one finds.[9] All his arguments flow from this premise

---

7. Hanson reminds us that Nicaea is an anti-Arian document. Athanasius tells us that in his "De Decretis," but "we do not need Athanasius to tell us so." Hanson, *Christian Doctrine of God*, 164.

8. Even if the Son were inferior to the Father, the Son was intrinsically of God and not a creature. But such Origenism is also reinterpreted, and the Son is understood to be equal in divinity with the Father within the Godhead.

9. Athanasius, "De Decretis or Defense of the Nicene Creed," *Nicene and Post-Nicene Fathers of the Christian Church*, 4, *St. Athanasius*, ed. and trans. by Philip Schaff and Henry Wace (Grand Rapids: Wm. B. Eerdmans, 1961), 150–72.

and seek to justify it: the Son is of the same essence, same substance, same stuff, same being as God the Father. The Son is consubstantial with the Father and equal with the Father in divinity. There never was when he was not, because he is of the very being of God.

What is the soteriology of the Nicene creed? Salvation is cited as the explicit reason behind the incarnation: "Who because of us and because of our salvation he came down and became incarnate, becoming man. . . ." But there is no development of the logic of salvation. However, once again, if Athanasius represents what is going on in the creed, one would find behind the theological position, not hidden but clearly up front, a soteriology and an axiom for salvation. This says that God alone saves, so that if the Logos or Son incarnate in Jesus is not strictly divine or of God, then there is no salvation. Athanasius's own interpretation of the story of salvation is developed more extensively in other writings, as we have seen. But the axiom appears clearly enough: being God, the Son revealed God, deified human flesh, and sent the Spirit. And by the Spirit we are deified or saved. God became human that we may become divine.[10]

In sum, the pre-existent Son or Logos, which is incarnate in Jesus, is consubstantial with the Father. God is Father and always Father so that there always was a Son. The Son is of the essence and being of God.

CRITIQUE OF NICENE LANGUAGE FROM TODAY'S PERSPECTIVE

It must be expected that a formula designed sixteen centuries ago in a different cultural and intellectual milieu will be found at certain points to be at odds with postmodern culture. The criticism which follows is not proposed from within the system of understanding that generated the creed. That kind of criticism would also be relevant. For example, if it was unthinkable that the Father God be incarnate in the world of finitude and matter, how is it that the Son, who is of the same nature as the Father, can be so incarnate? There are some unexamined presuppositions about the nature of a transcendent God, mediation, and implicit subordination that could be fruitfully examined from a historical perspective. But when such a critique was concluded, one would still have to place the Nicene formula in conjunction with the questions of those who encounter it today. This is the perspective of this critical reflection. It will become clear that these reflections are not limited to the language of Nicaea, but apply more broadly to the patristic theological culture which produced it, including the Arians who rejected it and Athanasius who defended it. The intent of these critical reflections is not negative; they are rather an attempt to appropriate reflectively what is going on in this crucial creedal statement so that it may faithfully be reinterpreted.

An obvious reflection on Nicene theology is that it relies almost exclusively on a Johannine framework. In itself, this is not a negative develop-

---

10. Athanasius, "De Decretis," 14, p. 159.

ment, because every consistent christology must have some overarching or integrating framework. But when the Johannine framework of a descending and self-incarnating Logos is combined with other features that will be discussed presently, it overrides and excludes themes contained in other New Testament christologies, especially those christologies of the synoptic gospels that clearly depict Jesus as an integral human being.

The doctrine of Nicaea appeals to scripture, but it employs scripture in a way that is not acceptable today. Scripture provides a source of directly representative information, like facts or objective data, about transcendent reality. This is not peculiar to the Nicene fathers; the Arians too had their favorite proof texts. When the Nicenes argued that the Son was "from God" (John 8:42), for example, the Arians would counter that all things created are also "from God" (1 Cor 8:6; 2 Cor 5:18). Indeed, patristic theology in general, despite considerable sophistication in the use of scripture,[11] still used scripture in a way that implied that it communicated what amounted to representative knowledge about transcendent reality. There is no other way to explain the subjects that were discussed and the amount of knowledge the fathers seemed to possess about them. I have already briefly discussed the process of objectification that is entailed when past experience is codified in writing and becomes the object of reflection. Today, a battery of different forms of criticism and hermeneutics is brought to bear on the epistemology of theoretical knowledge generally. Relative to this theology, people have to ask how the Nicene fathers knew that the Father had a Son, that he was or was not eternally generated, and that he was or was not subordinate to the Father. From where did these conceptions and judgments about the transcendent God come? To a large extent, the answer to these questions is the authority of scripture. Scriptural texts are cited in such a way that, in their propositional form, they provide premises for inferential reasoning. But theology as a critical discipline cannot be satisfied with such a use of scripture. On the premise that conclusions are no better than the arguments that sustain them, one has to reckon that many of the conclusions of both Arius and Athanasius, the defender of the Nicene creed, need to be reinterpreted on other methodological grounds.

The doctrine of Nicaea also gives rise to a confusion about its subject matter. Is the object of the doctrine Jesus? or the Logos? or God? This problem has its roots in the displacement of the problem of the status of Jesus, recognized as somehow divine in cult and New Testament language, to a problem of the place of the Logos within the life of God. The result is the ambiguity of Nicene doctrine. Is it doctrine about Jesus? There are more than one answer to this question. 1) No, it is about the Son, begotten before all ages. The language of Nicaea rarely leads one to refer imaginatively to

---

11. See, for example, the extensive hermeneutical reflections of Origen in *On First Principles*, ed. by G. W. Butterworth (Gloucester, Mass.: Peter Smith, 1973), 4.2.1-9, pp. 269–87.

Jesus of Nazareth but to a heavenly, eternal Son. 2) No, it is consistently called trinitarian doctrine because it is about the differentiated life of God. 3) Yes, it expresses belief in "one Lord Jesus Christ." It is about Jesus because the Logos, the being of God differentiated from the Father, is precisely the subject of the earthly figure Jesus. But is this the Jesus of Nazareth that is being described by contemporary Jesus research? At this point there arises a profound clash of images between the Jesus that is portrayed by Nicene doctrine and the Jesus that is portrayed by critical reconstruction of the figure Jesus.

This critical reflection on Nicene doctrine does not entail abandoning the point of Nicene doctrine in the face of historicism. Rather, it requires being clear about what is being said by this doctrine, and about how the doctrine is saying it. The original problem concerned the meaning of Jesus' divinity for monotheists. At bottom, Nicaea is first of all a doctrine about Jesus: this is where the problem came from, and reflection about God is oriented back to this problematic. Trinitarian doctrine is completely dependent upon soteriology and christology and makes no sense apart from these foundations. Arius caused a crisis because, in affirming the creaturehood of the Logos, he seemed implicitly to deny that true God was present and at work salvifically in Jesus. Arius undermined Jesus' divinity. To that suggestion, Nicaea in its turn said No. In its first instance, Nicene doctrine is about Jesus Christ and has to lead back to him. Speculation about the inner life of God has no grounding in Christian tradition apart from the encounter with God in Jesus.

To sum up, therefore, the underlying problem of the doctrine of Nicaea from a postmodern perspective lies in the hypostatization of the Logos and the shift from the New Testament's christology from below to a second-century christology from above. And the solution to this problem consists in reinterpreting the meaning of Nicaea in terms of a christology from below that is faithful to it and consistent with the New Testament.

An Interpretation of Nicaea

The critical reflections on the doctrine of Nicaea as it stands at least indicate that there is a considerable distance between the framework in which it was generated and that of some Christians today. In order that the point of the doctrine of Nicaea be communicated and appropriated, there must be a conscious shift in the suppositions for understanding what is being said in it, and a new language for "explaining" its content. The strategy here calls for accomplishing that reinterpretation in two stages: the first is an interpretation of the meaning of Nicaea, and the second is a theological explanation of that meaning. The first hermeneutical task of understanding the Nicene formula will be engaged presently; the second, which consists in an "explanation" of the divinity of Jesus Christ and the doctrine of the trinity, will be the subject of Chapters 15 and 16.

Presuppositions

We begin by a characterization of the new framework into which the doctrine of Nicaea is to be appropriated. What are the suppositions that are at work in the interpretation which follows? If the premises and arguments on which a certain conclusion is based are no longer valid, it would be difficult to continue to hold the conclusion itself. If the conclusion is itself valid, one must find a new rationale for it, a new plausibility structure in which the belief can make sense. With this in mind, I begin with a generalized account of the suppositions or premises that underlie this interpretation of Nicaea.

First, the interpretation of the meaning of Nicaea should be one that is not exclusively dependent upon a Johannine linguistic framework, much less one that is limited to the parameters of the christology of the Prologue of John's gospel. It is not that Johannine christology among others should be excluded from one's consideration of the meaning of Nicaea. It is rather that the pluralism of New Testament christologies does not allow the exclusionary hegemony that the language of Logos held in the patristic period. The point of Nicaea should be expressed in a language that transcends the boundaries of the incarnation of Logos, while remaining faithful to the creed itself. The symbol Logos is not essential to the creed, and not itself something that was defined. Because Logos language was never called into question, it never entered into the dogmatic intent of the conciliar fathers. All parties accepted that there was a Logos who pre-existed and who became incarnate in Jesus. The language of a hypostatized Logos constituted the milieu of the discussion. But that very framework has become part of the problem; it has lost its plausibility and power in a postmodern intellectual culture. One should thus seek an interpretation that transcends the narrowly defined framework dictated by Johannine language.[12]

Second, an interpretation of such a fundamental doctrine as Nicaea cannot prescind from a critical theory of religious experience, knowledge, language, theology, and doctrine. All interpretations, even those which purport to be based on commonsense appearance, imply conceptions of these fundamental issues. Even though these topics cannot be explicitly reviewed at every stage of theological argumentation, theology cannot proceed by simply quoting scripture as a revealed authority for affirmations that have bearing on human existence in our context. The interpretation offered here is consistent with an understanding of faith, revelation, and religious knowledge that is symbolically structured. This symbolic realism appeals to the religious experience of those to whom it is meant to communicate.

---

12. It is primarily the objectified and hypostatized sense of Logos that causes the problem. In Chapter 15 I will propose a reinterpretation of Logos christology within the framework of symbolic language that largely overcomes these problems.

Third, then, the term "Logos" is most fundamentally a religious symbol used for referring to an aspect of God, or, more comprehensively, referring simply to God, but from a certain specific perspective, point of view, or formality. This is how such symbols as Wisdom, Spirit, and the Word of God originally came to be and functioned. This original sense is also a foundational sense; when the religious symbol was reified and projected as a real, objective entity, this mental process did not destroy the foundation itself. Logos remains a symbol that formalizes in language a human experience of God. The interpretation offered here prescinds from whether or not the reifications of Wisdom, Word, and Spirit correspond to discrete, objective identities outside the human mind. That question will be taken up in later chapters. The point here is that the supposition of this interpretation is that Logos should be understood first of all on the foundational level of the dynamics of religious symbolic knowledge.

Fourth, Nicaea must be reinterpreted today from the perspective of christology from below. I have explained in Chapter 7 a christology from below in historical, genetic terms according to the layers of witness in the New Testament, and in the formal, structural terms of the dynamics of symbolic historical mediation. A shift in perspective from the christology from above, in which Nicene doctrine is presented, to a perspective that begins with and has continual imaginative reference to Jesus of Nazareth is a major one. It entails rearranging the elements of an integral christology into a new framework. This can be a difficult process psychologically, and it often needs considerable self-conscious reflection. The perspective of its interpretation is not part of the teaching of Nicaea; perspective and framework are given with history as the standpoint and horizon of the interpreter. To effect a transition, one consciously has to ask how the point of Nicene teaching would appear within the new framework of a christology from below. The developing christologies of the New Testament are helpful at this juncture because they reflect a pattern of an ascending christology.

Fifth, the return to a christology from below clarifies the relationship between the issues of Jesus' divinity and the nature of God, at least as this relationship should be understood today. Given the structure of Christian faith as an encounter with God mediated historically by the event of Jesus of Nazareth, Nicaea cannot represent a movement of thought from the nature of God to the divine character of Jesus. This movement from above makes little sense, neither in terms of religious epistemology, nor in terms of a historical reconstruction of how New Testament christology developed. Rather, Nicaea represents, first of all, a movement toward understanding Jesus Christ and the nature of God on the basis of God's being encountered in Jesus. This encounter rests on the basis of Jesus' representation of God in his teaching, action, and person. What is learned of God entails both the positive content about God mediated by Jesus, and a reflection on God's nature that flows from the event of encountering God in Jesus. It is of the character of God to be present to God's creation. Nicaea also represents a reflection on the status of Jesus as divine, because God was encountered in him. Symbolically, the point of Nicaea's Logos language about God is such that God could be present to and encountered in Jesus. And from the perspective of christology, the point is that Jesus must be considered divine because God is encountered in and through him for human salvation.

Logic of Interpretation

Something should be said about the logic of interpreting this central conciliar formula. This logic can scarcely be separated from the suppositions just enumerated, but one can distinguish between premises, method of interpreting, and the conclusions drawn. On the premise that theology, doctrines, and creeds not only shape the experience of the community but express and represent it, because they are based on it, the method employed here consists in discerning and reconstructing the experience that is contained in the Nicene symbol. What is the experience of the Christian community that has come to public expression through these formulae, and not independently of them? The referent of the Nicene creed is both a corporate experience, in the sense of representing a way of being in the world of a community, and a construal of reality or the world consonant with the existential engagement. The community's experience of Jesus is an experience of salvation. Therefore one may read the meaning of the doctrine in terms of the salvific experience it represents. Using this logic, the point of the doctrine of Nicaea can be summarized in three propositions: 1) Jesus mediates God's salvation; 2) God is such as Jesus reveals God to be; and 3) Jesus is divine because he is the medium of God's salvation.

1) The interpretation offered here sees Nicaea as a confession of Jesus' divinity on the basis of his bearing salvation, that is, an encounter with God. The christological position of Nicaea implicitly rests on soteriology, concretely on an experience of salvation mediated by Jesus. The thesis that this relation to soteriology is intrinsic to christology has been argued consistently on the basis of theological foundations and positively from New Testament and patristic evidence. The creed itself contains a reference to salvation as the motive of the incarnation: "because of us and because of our salvation he came down and became incarnate." The logic of salvation, a way of understanding how it unfolded, is absent in the creed. But the role of salvation in the understanding of God and Jesus Christ is explicit.

2) On the basis of encountering God in Jesus, in his mediation, in his life and teaching, death and resurrection, Nicaea is making a statement about God. But the differentiations within God, Father, Son, and Spirit, only indirectly get at the point of Nicaea. For this terminology was not disputed, not questioned. What was denied by Arius, however, was that God was such as to be involved, engaged, or otherwise mixed up with the finite world of physicality, change, corruption, and finally death. In response,

Nicaea affirms, on the basis of the Christian experience of God in Jesus Christ and through the symbol of the Logos which truly represents God, that God is such a God. God is immanent and present to God's creation and to human existence.

3) Also on the basis of its salvific encounter with God in Jesus, Nicaea affirms the divinity of Jesus Christ.[13] As was said, the creed does not develop in any way what it means by salvation. But one would not be far from an accurate understanding of the creed if one interpolated the fundamental reasoning of Athanasius into the logic of its christology: since salvation comes from God, the Jesus Christ who brings this salvation must be true God.

Interpreting Nicaea

On the basis of these presuppositions and premises, and according to the logic of salvation, the following propositions or statements can be taken as paraphrases of the content of the doctrine of Nicaea: the meaning of Nicaea is that no less than God was and is present and at work in Jesus. This means that the God encountered in Jesus for our salvation is truly God. And this statement of the divinity of Jesus implies a second statement about God: God is immanent in and personally present to human existence. This is how God is revealed to be in Jesus.[14]

A brief commentary on these terse interpretations of Nicaea will show how they preserve the historical meaning of the conciliar statement and at the same time attempt to accommodate the conditions for interpretation today.

Both interpreting propositions preserve the negative, anti-Arian intentionality that generated the Nicene creed. Arius affirmed that less than God, that is, a creature Logos, was incarnate, present, and at work in Jesus. And he proposed a closed notion of an impassive, transcendent God, attached to the symbol Father, but who was not quite fatherly, because separated and distant from creation. By contrast, Nicaea affirms against Arius that it was true God that was united to and at work in Jesus of Nazareth, whether true God here be called Sophia, Shekinah, Glory, Word, Spirit, or simply God. And, therefore, God is as Jesus reveals, a God who by being revealed is made available as salvation for humankind.

This interpretation begins with the encounter of God in Jesus; it is christology from below. It includes a Johannine perspective. It is not itself

---

13. Hanson points out the newness of this doctrine. That Jesus is *homoousios* with the Father had never been said before. *Christian Doctrine of God*, 166–67. "There is no theologian in the Eastern or the Western Church before the outbreak of the Arian controversy, who does not in some sense regard the Son as subordinate to the Father." Ibid., 64.

14. These interpretive propositions are proposed from a christological perspective. More could be said about this doctrine from the perspective of the doctrine of God regarding the notion of God that is being rejected and what is being affirmed. One might call what is offered here a restricted christological interpretation.

mythological, but attends to the true content of the symbolic language by an interpretation relying on what Christians experience religiously. It does not hypostatize the Logos, for there is no need for this to get at the core faith of the New Testament and the point of patristic christology and Nicaea. It represents accurately the faith of the New Testament community, and is based on it, without staking its claim to authenticity on proof texts. It is clear in its logic; it is neither esoteric nor complicated. It distinguishes between the experience of salvation, the issue of the nature of God, and the question of Jesus' humanity, and it provides a way to see how these issues are interrelated. There is more to be said on these issues, but Nicaea did not attempt to say everything. Its intentionality was strictly and self-consciously limited to the narrowly defined goal of refuting Arian propositions. It left many questions unaddressed, most notably the issue of the constitution of Jesus Christ. Let me move, therefore, to the Council of Chalcedon and the other side of the christological question concerning the true humanity of Jesus.

THE MEANING OF CHALCEDON

The Historical Doctrine of Chalcedon

Whereas the doctrine of Nicaea was a reaction against the teaching of Arius, and is to be interpreted thus, the doctrine of Chalcedon is a compromise, a positive formula of union between two quite different visions of the person of Jesus Christ, and should be so interpreted. These positions, Alexandrian and Antiochene, were reviewed in the last chapter, but a summary statement of their salient points will not be out of place. What are the viewpoints each assumes regarding the constitution of Jesus Christ, the fundamental insight that sustains the doctrine, its correlative estimation of the dynamics of God's salvation mediated by Jesus, and the problem inherent in the position vis-à-vis the alternative view? I begin with Cyrillian christology because, even though many of the relevant texts of Cyril of Alexandria are reactions against Nestorius, Antiochene christology can also be read as a reaction against the monophysitic tendency of Alexandria.

The viewpoint of Cyril is the divine economy. This means that his imaginative reference point and point of departure is the divine reality of the Logos, distinct from the Father, who came into this world by taking on "flesh" or a human existence, and who lived on earth as the human being Jesus. The fundamental insight of this christology is that Jesus of Nazareth, the Jesus of this world, is really the heavenly Logos; they are one and the same, because the fleshly human existence is precisely that of the divine subject, the Logos or eternal Son of God. This numerical identity is what was behind Cyril's reaction against any compromise of Mary's being *theotokos*, as if one could divide or separate the Logos from his own flesh.

Cyril's conception of salvation is embedded in the christology itself, for salvation occurs by the very assumption of human existence by the Logos. If human existence were not completely taken up and vivified by the divine Word so that it was his own, there would have been no salvation at all. This is the strength of this christology. But it also bears an inner weakness, one that is accentuated today: the integral humanity of the historical figure Jesus is rendered passive and all but disappears within the divinizing reality of the divine subject, the eternal Son.

Nestorius, by contrast, even though he too was faithful to Nicaea, focused his attention on the historical figure Jesus Christ; the point of departure of his thinking and the imaginative referent of his christology is the Son as he appeared incarnate in history. Jesus Christ is one "person" or *prosopon* who unites in himself two natures.[15] This viewpoint, in a post-Nicene framework, attempts to take into account the integral divinity and humanity together in Jesus Christ. Jesus Christ is a single person who combined within himself distinctly and without confusion two radically different elements or *ousiai* or modes/kinds of being, divinity and humanity, each possessing all the characteristics of these natures complete and intact.[16] It followed for Nestorius that, insofar as the Logos is God, he did not have Mary as a mother in any literal sense. As far as Nestorius's conception of salvation is concerned, it correlates cleanly with his christology, because it involved integral human action, supported and assisted by divine power, but still human, free, and responsible in its initiative.[17] The weakness of this position appears most clearly in contrast to Cyril: where does Jesus Christ's unity of being lie? What is his metaphysical identity? In the Johannine framework of a descent christology within which he operated, and by contrast with Cyrillian predilection for thinking in terms of "one nature" even though he admitted two natures, Nestorius's emphasis on the integrity of Jesus Christ's humanity and its qualities and powers did not leave a clear picture of the kind of being Jesus himself was.

The doctrine of the Council of Chalcedon is the result of an attempt to forge a common christological doctrine with which both sides could live. It did not come all at once and many other voices intervened. The Council of Ephesus of 431 condemned Nestorius, but Cyril and John of Antioch reached something of a rapprochement the following year.[18] The controversy then remained relatively latent until after the deaths of John and

---

15. J. N. D. Kelly, *Early Christian Doctrines* (London: A & C Black, 1960), 315.

16. Kelly, *Doctrines*, 314.

17. Kelly explains this with the following syllogism: "if the redemption was to be effected, the second Adam must have been a real man. Yet an authentically human experience would have been impossible if the Lord's humanity had been fused with, or dominated by, His divinity. Hence the two, divinity and humanity, must have existed side by side, each retaining its peculiar properties and operation unimpaired." *Doctrines*, 312–13.

18. See Cyril's "Letter to John of Antioch," in Richard A. Norris, ed. and trans., *The Christological Controversy* (Philadelphia: Fortress Press, 1980), 140–45.

Cyril in 442 and 444, respectively. In 448 it flared up again with the case of Eutyches whose monophysitism was condemned in Constantinople. But the case would not go away, despite the intervention of Pope Leo from Rome with his "Letter to Flavian of Constantinople."[19] Leo's negative view was ignored, and Eutyches was rehabilitated in a hastily arranged synod that leaned toward monophysitism. Once again, as in the time of Arius, the empire was threatened with religious splintering. It took the authority of a new emperor, Marcian, to summon another council and to insist that the council fathers draw up a definition of faith to complement the Nicene-Constantinopolitan creed.[20] Although the formula of Chalcedon draws on multiple sources, the fundamental historical meaning of the doctrine lies in its delicate balancing of the one divine subject christology of the Alexandrians and the two-nature christology of the Antiochenes, supported from Rome by Leo. Among its most fundamental affirmations are these three:

First, Chalcedon teaches that the oneness of the subject who is Jesus Christ lies in the eternal, divine Son, the Logos. This divine Son and Jesus Christ are "one and the same," a refrain that runs through the entire decree.[21] This one and the same Son is the "only-begotten, divine Word, the Lord Jesus Christ." This oneness is defined as pertaining to the metaphysical subject which is named person or *prosopon* and, by a synonymous usage, hypostasis or *hypostasis*. This teaching represents the framework of Cyril and the Alexandrians; the position of the Antiochenes is drawn into an Alexandrian framework by the use of the Antiochene word, "person," and its being equated with "hypostasis." The personhood of Jesus Christ, the principle of his metaphysical individuality or his identity as a hypostasis, is numerically identical with the being of the divine Son or Logos. Thus Jesus Christ in technical terms is not a human person but a divine person, and the human nature of Jesus subsists in or is the human nature of a divine subject, person, individual being, or hypostasis.

Second, Chalcedon affirms the duality that characterizes the one subject Jesus Christ. This duality is dramatically conveyed by a series of paradoxically juxtaposed characteristics of the God-man in the style of Leo's letter: "the same perfect in Godhead and the same perfect in manhood, truly God and truly man, . . . consubstantial with the Father in Godhead, and the same consubstantial with us in manhood." The duality is also summed up by the use of the category "nature." The one person Jesus Christ is "made known in two natures without confusion, without change,

---

19. "Pope Leo I's Letter to Flavian of Constantinople," in Norris, *The Christological Controversy*, 145–55.

20. For an account of the history leading to the Council of Chalcedon, see Perrone, "D'Éphèse (431) à Chalcédoine (451): La question christologique et la rupture de l'oecuméné," *Les Conciles Oecuméniques*, 1, *L'Histoire*, 71–104; Pelikan, *Emergence of the Catholic Tradition*, 226–77.

21. The text of Chalcedon is quoted from the version presented by Kelly, *Doctrines*, 339–40.

without division, without separation, the difference of the natures being by no means removed because of the union, but the property of each nature being preserved and coalescing in one *prosopon* and one *hyposta-sis*." This is Antiochene; monophysitism is a rejected language; the integrity of the two natures is preserved; and with it the consubstantial-ity of Jesus Christ with all other human beings is affirmed.[22]

Third, the communication of idioms is taught by the council in more than one way. The exchange of predicates about Jesus Christ is strikingly displayed by the series of contrasting affirmations about him: "the same perfect in Godhead and the same perfect in manhood." Logically, it is because Jesus Christ is "the same" subject sharing both natures that the exchange of qualities works. The doctrine is also implied by the reference to Mary's being the bearer of God: "begotten from the Virgin Mary, the *Theotokos*, as regards His manhood." Both human and divine predicates can be affirmed about Jesus Christ, but, in the spirit of compromise in the direction of the Antiochenes, the motherhood of God is clarified somewhat by the phrase "as regards his manhood."

In the judgment of most students of this council it proposes a genuine compromise. Both parties in the christological debate could find their posi-tion represented in it.[23] Perhaps a good sign of its fairness is that both sides would also believe that the other side was overly represented, and in fact neither extreme Nestorians nor extreme monophysites would accept the decree. But it was received in the large middle ground as an acceptable compromise. On the one hand, the Antiochene view of Jesus Christ as a union of two distinct and integral natures was preserved; on the other hand, the Alexandrian framework controls the whole vision: the one, divine subject took on a human nature so that the very identity of Jesus of Nazareth was the Logos.

CRITIQUE OF CHALCEDON

The christological doctrine of Chalcedon is prefaced by the doctrine of Nicaea which it considered authoritative and to which it proposed its own teaching as faithful commentary or extension. Thus all the criticisms aris-ing out of our situation and directed to Nicaea apply here as well: an

---

22. R. V. Sellers, *The Council of Chalcedon: A Historical and Doctrinal Survey* (London: SPCK, 1961), 207–28, divides the formal definition of faith into two parts correspond-ing to these first two points.

23. There are dissenting voices here. Reinhold Seeberg reads Chalcedon as an asser-tion of western christology which left many of the questions of the East unanswered. *Text-Book of the History of Doctrines*, 1, *History of the Doctrines in the Ancient Church* (Philadelphia: Lutheran Publishing Society, 1905), 272. Harnack's judgments are more severe: according to him, it is not a compromise document; it rather contradicted the spirit of Athanasius and Cyril, and abandoned christology based on soteriology. Adolf von Harnack, *History of Dogma*, 4 (New York: Dover Publications, 1961), 222.

exclusively Johannine perspective, outmoded argument from scripture, hypostatization of biblical symbols, christology descending from above in method and content, ambiguity about the object of christology. To these may be added some serious reservations about the specific language of Chalcedon. It is important to recall that the intent of this critique is to open up the space necessary for a faithful retrieval of this doctrine in a language more suited to our time.

A common criticism of Chalcedon is that its doctrine, like the theological mode of thought that generated it, has abandoned Jesus as he is portrayed in the synoptic gospels. It deals with Jesus in the abstract or general metaphysical categories of nature, person, substance, and being. When this kind of language controls the subject matter, it compromises an imaginative focus on Jesus of Nazareth. At some points the doctrine of person and natures even seems to contradict the vital, existential, and historical quality of Jesus' union with God as this is displayed in the synoptic gospels. In other words, this doctrinal language has not simply been added on to the historical language about Jesus, it has tended to displace it. The language directs attention to how in Jesus there is a union between his human nature and the principle of divinity or Logos that is within him, controls him, is him. The result is that, despite his being consubstantial with us, Jesus is unique and unlike us in his union with God. But the synoptic gospels do not portray Jesus as a divine person, or as relating to a divine principle within him, but as one like us relating to the transcendent God, his heavenly Father.[24]

The statement of Chalcedon has been construed as teaching that Jesus is a divine person with a human nature. That is to say, Jesus is not really a human person, a human being; he is rather a divine being, person, or hypostasis who, besides his divine nature, also possesses an integral human nature. This human nature is abstract in the sense of not qualifying or being the nature of a human person, or hypostasis, or individual. One has to be careful here not to confuse personhood with psychological identity or ego-consciousness or a sense of self. The human nature that is intended by Chalcedon is not abstract in the sense of being a mere notion or a generalized conception of characteristics.[25] The human nature of Jesus of Nazareth refers to his concrete and fully human appearance in history. But his human nature is abstract in the sense that it is not the nature of a human person or a human being, but subsists in another, the Logos or Son who assumed this nature. This means that the human nature of Jesus subsists in the divine hypostasis. The human nature of Jesus does not have a hypostasis of its own. The decree does not say this in a direct or explicit

---

24. This generalization can stand despite the fact that the synoptics include traces of christologies of various "elevations." An example is the wisdom christology that appears in Matthew's gospel and was examined in Chapter 6.

25. Kelly, *Doctrines*, 319.

way, but it seems implied, and interpretation thereafter confirms the tendency in this direction.[26]

The principle of oneness in Jesus Christ, then, is divine; it is the Logos who is God. As subject, the Logos assumes an integral human nature but not an integral human existence or *esse*, lest there be two: "not parted or divided into two *prosopa*." The divine Logos, the distinct divine person, assumes as its own a human nature as its instrument. Thus the subject, the actor in history, that which acts and moves in history, is not finally a human being, Jesus, but God. With this language it is difficult not to think of Jesus as simply God, God made to be a conscious actor in history, a participant in the finite, creaturely system of causality as a creaturely actor, within a humanity that does not have its own human *esse* and individuality. In short, that Jesus was an integral human being is compromised.[27] In this view, Jesus' consubstantiality with us is reduced to sharing a common kind of being. Because other human beings do not have as the basis of their being the Logos or Son, he must be conceived as radically other than us. This criticism is telling most especially because it really describes the consciousness of many Christians. As Rahner has pointed out, even though we have the doctrine of two natures, many Christians are really monophysites in practice, because the human nature has become a mitigated reality and does not define the person or ontological identity of Jesus integrally.[28]

But the main criticism of the form of this doctrine, one that is comprehensive and pervasive in all that follows, originates from the postmodern situation of christology, which entails a change of viewpoint that leaves the Chalcedonian problematic behind. Central to Chalcedonian language, because central to the debate which led up to it, is an incarnational Logos christology, whether Logos-sarx or Logos-anthropos, which required sorting out in metaphysical terms the unity and interrelationships of Jesus' divinity and humanity. This way of conceiving the christological problem has given way to a new problematic. The point of departure is no longer the Logos and its incarnation, but the historical Jesus. Christology has to deal not with the "humanity" or human nature of Jesus, but with the his-

---

26. Piet Schoonenberg traces the scholastic doctrine that Jesus' humanity had an enhypostatic union, or subsistence within the divine being or hypostasis of the Son, to Leontius of Byzantium. "Chalcedon and Divine Immutability," *Theology Digest*, 2 (1981), 104.

27. "Chalcedon leaves no doubt that the one Logos is the subject of both the human and the divine predicates. . . . In the view of Chalcedon, Christ is not just a '*homo deifer*' or a human subject, *habens deitatem*, but the God-Logos, *habens humanitatem*, or rather, *habens et deitatem et humanitatem*. The person of Christ does not first come into being from the concurrence of Godhead and manhood or of the two natures, but is already present in the person of the pre-existent Logos." Aloys Grillmeier, *Christ in Christian Tradition*, 1, *From the Apostolic Age to Chalcedon (451)* (Atlanta: John Knox Press, 1975), 552.

28. Karl Rahner, "The Position of Christology in the Church between Exegesis and Dogmatics," *Theological Investigations*, 11 (New York: Seabury Press, 1974), 198.

torical appearance of the person, Jesus of Nazareth.[29] The mode of thinking is no longer, in the first instance, metaphysical but historical. The problem is not holding together a human and divine nature in a subject that is metaphysically one, but of conceiving the distinctive character of a historical human being. There is no need here to outline the shift in western culture from classical to historically conscious modes of thought that accounts for the emergence of this new framework. More to the point in our time is the amount of research and general diffusion of discussion about the Jesus of history. Gradually the naturalistic and historicist premises of historical research are becoming internalized broadly. A result of this development, then, is a shift in the problematic for christology. Dealing with the material on the historical Jesus, and especially with the imaginative construal of Jesus as an integral human being, elicits a question which is analogous to but finally not the same as that of Chalcedon. The premise and starting point are not an eternal Logos, but Jesus of Nazareth. The problem and question do not lie in trying to explain his humanity after a consensus about his divinity. The supposition and point of departure are defined by the human being, Jesus, and the question concerns what it can mean to say that Jesus is divine. Ultimately the response to this question will be no less metaphysical than that of Chalcedon, but the approach to such a solution has been reversed: the divinity of Jesus must be understood in such a way as to be compatible with his empirical and historical human existence.

Once this new framework and problematic is understood, one can begin to recognize as well other points at which the classical christological categories and language are showing signs of severe stress. For example, Karl Rahner pointed out many years ago that the quality of the affirmations about Jesus' being human and being divine, or having a human and a divine nature, are logically different.[30] We know in concrete ways what it means to be human, or, since human existence remains a mystery, we participate in it and have some concrete data to rely on. Divinity, what "divine nature" refers to, what it means to have a divine nature, all remain ultimately opaque to objective thought. Reflection here depends on participatory engagement in a mediated revelation of transcendence; affirmations express faith and hope. In the classical debate and in the Chalcedonian formula these natures are "moved around" in an objective, conceptual way that is deceptive against the background of the sense of transcendent mystery that obtains today.

Other examples of how the traditional language does not work in the new situation are provided by the communication of idioms. In the

---

29. John Galvin, "From the Humanity of Christ to the Jesus of History: A Paradigm Shift in Catholic Christology," *Theological Studies*, 55 (1994), 252–73, analyzes this change.

30. See Karl Rahner, *Foundations of Christian Faith: An Introduction to the Idea of Christianity* (New York: Seabury, 1978), 290–91.

Chalcedonian framework, the unity in one person of two integral natures allowed divine qualities to be assigned to the one subject, Jesus of Nazareth, who was the Logos incarnate. Thus Jesus was omniscient, omnipotent, impassible, and, finally, God. Anyone schooled in the literature of the critical, historical investigation of Jesus will find this language inappropriate. There was a logic behind Chalcedonian language; it made sense within the framework of the suppositions, premises, and thought forms of classical christology. But it is clear that the whole system is abstracted from the historical Jesus, so that its logic unfolds at a level that is removed from a concrete, historical imagination. When confronted with one of the criteria of christology, the image of Jesus as a real human being, this predication does not work; it simply breaks down. The subject Jesus, the person, was ignorant, weak, vulnerable to suffering, and did not in the least appear to be Yahweh or the Father or God. The shift of the framework for understanding has rendered the traditional language incredible.

The principal criticism of Chalcedon, in sum, does not go directly to its content but to the theoretical context within which it is delivered. It is the framework, the suppositions, the premises, the language, and the method of argument that have changed. Once this is recognized, the principal discrete affirmations of the council are themselves called into question. The shift to a historical imagination and point of departure undercuts the plausibility of the Johannine framework which in turn dictated the metaphysics of the divine subject, persona, and hypostasis. The historical consciousness that fixes the imagination on the historical person of Jesus calls into question a free license to predicate divine qualities of Jesus. On the positive side, the teaching of Chalcedon that rings most true today is the unambiguous statement of Jesus' being consubstantial with human beings. Against the monophysitism that tended toward making Jesus of Nazareth less than fully human because of his one divine nature, Chalcedon, in its own way, and within its particular framework, calls christology back to the Jesus of history.

INTERPRETING CHALCEDON

After enumerating the common criticisms that are leveled against the form and language of the doctrine of Chalcedon, one must begin to reformulate the suppositions and premises that will shape an understanding of it, and that will in turn be relevant to the present and immediate future. What are the premises and logic for reinterpreting the meaning of Chalcedon, and where do they lead?

Presuppositions

A first supposition and premise for interpreting the doctrine of Chalcedon is that Jesus was and is a human being. There are several reasons why the fact that Jesus' being a human being has to be kept in the forefront of one's interpretation of the meaning of Chalcedon. One is the present intellectual, cultural situation which forms the context in which people understand and shapes the content of a general picture of reality. In this context the fact that Jesus was a human being is not a datum for faith; it is something historians and people generally know to be the case. The facticity of Jesus' human existence is what makes this a premise. Moreover, the Jesus material in the New Testament testifies to this. Jesus was a human being.

In fact, too, Jesus was a man, but no generalized significance can be assigned to his sex. This can be shown on the basis of the soteriological axiom of Gregory of Nazianzus: "What has not been assumed cannot be restored. . . ."[31] This axiom operates in the framework of incarnation christology. It says that, if God has not assumed the whole of humanity, the whole of humanity is not touched by God and hence not saved. The principle helped to establish that Jesus must have had a rational human soul since, if not, integral humanity would not have been saved. In an analogous manner, if one says that God is present and active in a male human being precisely in distinction from a woman, one implies that womanhood is not included in what has been assumed. The axiom is a way of saying that God has approached all humanity, wholly and integrally, in and through Jesus, and not a segment of human beings or an aspect of the human condition. From a theological perspective, Jesus could have been a woman, and to make specific theological points from the facticity of his manhood without further warrant would seem to be fundamentally wrong.

Second, God's presence to Jesus must be regarded as a presence within his humanity. By this I mean that the divine in Jesus does not appear over and above Jesus' being a human being, but rather precisely within the way Jesus was human, the way he lived and taught. Jesus' divinity was not added on top of his humanity, nor was his humanity an abstract human nature added on to or assumed by his divinity. The divine is not apparent in Jesus in any recognizable way, because it does not subsist in him apart or separate from the integrally human life that Jesus lived.[32] Once again, he was a human being, and one must begin to understand the presence of God to him and within him beginning with this premise of integral human existence. In terms of the theory of symbol, the finite, created integrity of human existence must be preserved in Jesus.

Third, Jesus' freedom is integral and autonomous. In other words, one cannot see God acting in Jesus as through a blind instrument. In Rahner's words, God's action physically in Jesus "may not be understood in any

---

31. Quoted in Kelly, *Doctrines*, 297.

32. This is a strong theme in the christology of Edward Schillebeeckx. See, for example, *Jesus: An Experiment in Christology* (New York: Seabury Press, 1979), 626–36. His views are supported by a doctrine of creation in which God is immediately present to created reality, and the transference of this model to christology: christology "is *concentrated* creation: belief in creation as God wills it to be." Edward Schillebeeckx, *Interim Report on the Books Jesus & Christ* (New York: Crossroad, 1981), 128.

other way except the way this influence is exercised by God on free creatures elsewhere."[33] This rules out monophysitism or the idea that Jesus'
human nature is a passive instrument for a divine actor.

Logic of Interpretation

Given these suppositions, which are in some respects quite different
from those lying behind the formulation of Chalcedon, by what logic can
one claim to grasp its authentic meaning? The key to interpreting
Chalcedonian doctrine, as in christology generally, lies in its soteriological structure. For embedded in the soteriological logic of a christology lies
the experience which gives rise to or generates the christology in the first
place. In principle, then, salvation theory lies close to the experience upon
which christology is based. An appeal to salvation, therefore, opens up an
area of experience that is common to the doctrine of Chalcedon, the theologies that generated it, and Christian understanding today.

The first common experiential theme is that salvation must have its origin in God, that God alone can effect the ultimate salvation of humankind.
This generally and passionately held conviction is central to the
Alexandrian conception of divinization and the tendency to regard human
nature as passive in its regard. The search for salvation that can come from
God alone allows one to recognize and encounter God in Jesus. And the
experience of God at work in any salvation mediated by Jesus is responsible for the doctrine of Nicaea that is preserved in Chalcedon. The first
fundamental experience underlying the doctrine of Chalcedon, therefore,
is that it is truly God who is encountered in Jesus.

The second common theme is that human salvation must be effected in
such a way that human freedom itself is engaged in a participatory way.
This tradition is found all along the route of the development of classical
soteriology and its corresponding christology. Jesus Christ is exemplar.
God does not effect human salvation against human freedom, but precisely as a salvation of human freedom. "What has not been assumed cannot be restored." Human freedom is engaged in both God's medium of
salvation, Jesus, and the humankind that participates in this salvation. If
salvation offered to human freedom enjoined no human response, it is difficult to see how it would be salvation of human freedom and not an
imposition upon it. For human freedom entails reflection, responsibility,
decision, and action. Freedom is not mere acquiescence, acceptance, or
consent, but the exercise of the powers of critical reasoning, choice, commitment, and doing. This soteriology requires that Jesus be free, and
imitable, and thus, as the Last Adam, human even as Adam was human.
God acts for human salvation in and through Jesus' integral human existence. The second fundamental experience underlying Chalcedon, therefore, is that Jesus is a human being consubstantial with us.

---

33. Karl Rahner, *Foundations*, 287.

Interpreting Chalcedon

Using soteriological logic as a key to disclosing the point of Chalcedonian doctrine, one can summarize the fundamental meaning of the doctrine in three propositions. First, the doctrine of Chalcedon asserts that, within and through the fully human existence of Jesus of Nazareth, no less than God is present and active for human salvation. Second, the Chalcedonian formula of two natures in one person, and the description of one who, although he is truly divine or consubstantial with God, is also truly human and consubstantial with us, recovers Jesus as a human being. Because Jesus is a human being like all others, what he bears of God is authentic revelation and salvation of human existence.[34] Third, these two points together express the dialectical structure of Jesus as a historical symbol of God's salvation of humankind.

These interpretive paraphrases of the point of Chalcedon need some commentary. First of all, they do not reproduce an explanation of how God was present to Jesus in terms of person and nature. The theological account of how God may be conceived as being present to Jesus will be taken up in a later chapter. This interpretation is not an explanation but a descriptive account of the meaning of Chalcedon. That meaning is found in the faith experience that underlies the whole doctrine. The object of this engaged, participatory experience is Jesus as the medium of God's salvation. The doctrine expresses this experience; without it, there would be no doctrine at all. It is the point of the doctrine, which cannot be identified with the language of persons and natures. Rather, the ontology of person and nature, of hypostasis and substance, functions as a tool in order to express in the language of the fifth century the conditions necessary for ensuring this meaning.

Some theologians, looking for explanatory language that remains close to the Chalcedonian language of one person and two natures and at the same time responds to the exigency and logic of a christology from below, may reverse the Chalcedonian reference for the term "person." Instead of saying that Jesus is a divine person with two natures, they might say he was a human person with two natures. Thus they preserve the one person, two natures language, but the individuality and discrete personhood of Jesus is that of a human being, which subsumes under itself both integral divine and human natures. Such a formula comes close to reproducing an Antiochene type of understanding, and at the same time preserves the unity of the person, Jesus, which Chalcedon insisted upon. This way of reinterpreting the Chalcedonian language is also much closer to the

---

34. Frances Young's interpretation of the significance of Chalcedon runs parallel to these first two propositions: "That it is really *God* who is revealed and at work in Jesus is one fundamental of the Christian tradition which Chalcedon sought to preserve, and that Jesus was truly human, and therefore able to relate to us and ultimately save us is the other fundamental issue." Young, *Creeds*, 78.

reality of Jesus, and is consistent with the demands of a christology from below. And since many commentators today judge the Antiochene christology as exemplified in Theodore of Mopsuestia and Nestorius, but not Nestorianism, as orthodox,[35] this provides a possible route for the refinement of the language of person and nature.

Interpretation of the meaning of Chalcedon in a historically conscious postmodern context will highlight the humanity of Jesus. Such a reading of the doctrine corresponds to its historical development, since it arose as part of a reaction against post-Nicene monophysitic trends. Nicaea affirmed that no less than God was incarnate in Jesus. When this was understood in a Johannine framework of a descent christology, and joined with the Logos-sarx christology of Alexandria, it resulted in a monophysitic tendency that undermined the understanding that Jesus was an integral human being. Against this trend, Chalcedon affirmed the consubstantiality of Jesus with human existence using the language of nature. But at the same time, the human nature of Jesus was subsumed into a divine subject, person, or hypostasis. Therefore, despite the intentionality of Chalcedon itself, the picture of Jesus as a human being presented in the synoptic gospels is not fully represented. One may conclude that the doctrine of Chalcedon was intended as the dialectical complement of Nicaea; but in order for it to succeed, its language needs reformulation. The reality of Jesus as a human being needs to be stated with sharper historical force in our day: Jesus was a human person.

The interpretation of Chalcedon offered here preserves its distinctive theology, and it may be called a christology of unity in diversity.[36] As Chalcedon put it, in the one person there are two natures, united but unmixed, inseparable but distinct and not confused. But it is important in our time to prevent the impression that this formula provides a description of the constitution of Christ. The formula of interpretation, namely, that it is through the fully human existence of Jesus of Nazareth that no less than God is present and active for human salvation, is a historically conscious statement that sums up a narrative. This is the story of human salvation that was effected by and through Jesus. It involves a concrete, historical imagination which has its focus on Jesus of Nazareth. And this historically referential formula incorporates into itself the symbolic structure of Jesus the mediator. Jesus, as a human being like us, makes God present to us and not just to him. And Jesus is relevant to us as revealing and imitable savior because he is consubstantial with us. The interpretation of Jesus as symbolic mediator is intrinsically dialectical, echoing exactly in

---

35. See n. 66 in Chapter 9 above. Edward Schillebeeckx also stays close to an Antiochene understanding of Jesus Christ by suggesting a mutual enhypostatic identification between Logos and Jesus. This conceptualization allows Jesus his individual human identity, but without an autonomy over against the Logos. Schillebeeckx, *Jesus*, 667.

36. Kelly, *Doctrines*, 341.

this respect the teaching of Chalcedon. Jesus is the human symbol who makes present that which is other than himself, God. This duality does not consist of two abstract natures lying side by side, or of two concepts or dynamic principles of action in parallel or in tandem. The mind will have to work in order to conceptualize how God is present to and active for our salvation in Jesus, how the human being Jesus makes God present. But this is the work of a later chapter.

CONCLUSION

Nicaea and Chalcedon together are the classic legacy of the christology of the patristic period. They represent the first major inculturation of the Christian message regarding Jesus Christ into Greek and Roman cultures in the early centuries of the Common Era. Although the Chalcedonian settlement required still further debate and clarification, these doctrines have become authoritative and normative touchstones for the christological faith of both the eastern and the western mainline Christian churches.

Because they have become and remain classics of the Christian faith, these doctrines have to be interpreted. As classics they continue to have bearing on the Christian community. But to make sense and illumine faith today, they must be reinterpreted. Because of the serious differences between the frameworks of this classical period and the modern and postmodern periods in the West, these doctrines, whose language is a function of a past culture and pattern of thinking, are practically unintelligible without extensive study. Because of their inaccessibility to the broad range of Christians, not to mention others, there is a certain temptation to bypass or ignore them. But Christianity cannot drop its past history or forget its tradition; one cannot really understand the situation of christology today without taking into account the past that has shaped it. One must seek to understand these doctrines. But to understand is to interpret. These doctrines, like all classics, are certainly not to be merely learned by rote and recited without understanding, because this too is an interpretation, one which in the current context distorts their meaning and Christian faith itself.

The interpretation of these doctrines that has been proposed here is founded on a conception of religious symbols in two ways. First, it conceives of all religious language as symbolic. Therefore the decrees of Nicaea and Chalcedon should be read in symbolic terms that open up their religious meaning through an appeal to the transcendence of religious experience. This symbolic language is, of course, amenable to more than one theological explanation. Second, Jesus, who finally is the subject matter of both of these doctrines, is himself a concrete, historical, religious symbol who mediates salvific contact from God and with God in history. The basis of this conception is the historical datum of an encounter with God in Jesus by the earliest disciples. This encounter was salvific, and

New Testament christology is the record of the development of various interpretations of Jesus on the basis of this fundamental and perennial encounter. The genesis of christology is replicated in the structure of christology in every age. The very structure of Christian faith is soteriological and christological, because Christian faith is an attachment to God that is mediated through the concrete symbol Jesus Christ.

Chalcedon and Nicaea together represent in a formal way the dialectical structure of Christian faith: Jesus Christ, a historical symbol of God, makes God present in history. Jesus of Nazareth was a human being with a human existence and identity consubstantial with us. But Jesus, as the religious symbol that constitutes Christian faith, makes God present in the world. Nicaea represents and defends the divine dimension of Jesus Christ; Chalcedon reasserts his integral human existence. Nicaea occurred prior to Chalcedon because the accidents of history brought forward in a formal and serious way the erroneous interpretation that true God was not made present in Jesus. Chalcedon followed Nicaea because a dominant line of interpretation threatened to represent Jesus as not a human being like us. Chalcedon had to define the fact that Jesus is consubstantial with us. In our own historically conscious day, however, the logic of christology almost self-evidently begins with Jesus and presupposes his integral humanity. This is how christology actually originated. The problematic doctrine concerns the reality of Jesus being divine in his capacity of mediating God's salvation.[37] In the end, therefore, the authoritative and normative symbolic meaning of Chalcedon and Nicaea involve the necessary dialectical tension between Jesus' being a human being and his being divine because he mediates God and God's salvation.

This concludes a too brief consideration of the classical forms of fundamental christological theology and doctrines. Together with the data of scripture, this will provide a background for a constructive account of soteriology and christology in our own day.

---

37. It may also be the case that among certain Christians the idea of Jesus' divinity is so prominent that a real recognition of his being a human being has been lost. In this case, the problematic of Chalcedon is reproduced. Given the dialectical tension of the religious symbol, one can expect leanings on one side or another.

PART IV

CONSTRUCTIVE CHRISTOLOGY

CHAPTER 11

Beyond Schleiermacher and Barth

This chapter begins the fourth part of this work, an essay at a systematic and constructive christology. It represents something of a leap from the period of the classical christological councils into the modern period. This should not be construed as a silent suggestion that nothing of import was generated in the intervening period, especially with medieval and reformation theology. It is simply a case of having to work within the limits of one volume. Protestant and Roman Catholic theologians will recognize their broad traditions in the descriptions of twentieth-century christology contained in this chapter.

All theology and christology are culturally situated. The pluralism of contemporary christologies requires that every christological proposal take stock of the situation, context, and social location out of which it arises. This chapter will present a more detailed interpretation of the current situation of christology in the West which was schematically outlined in Chapter 2. My goal here is to represent and interpret the situation of christology at the beginning of the twenty-first century. This seems like an absolutely necessary step in this project, for it will describe a context for the constructive christology which follows, explain the sources for categories and distinctions employed, and generally ensure a certain continuity with the immediate past.

The chapter is divided into three sections. The first is dedicated to brief interpretations of the christologies of Friedrich Schleiermacher and Karl Barth. No two theologians have influenced the nineteenth and twentieth centuries more than these two theologians, especially in the Protestant world which first and most thoroughly responded to modernity. Dwelling on the christology of these two reflects a conviction that the breadth of modern christology can aptly be illustrated by the contrasts between them and the polar tensions that arise from viewing them together. There are analogies relating the clash between these two christologies to the opposition between the classical Antiochene and Alexandrian traditions.[1]

---

1. Charles T. Waldrop, in *Karl Barth's Christology: Its Basic Alexandrian Character* (New York: Mouton, 1984), shows in what respects Barth's christology is Alexandrian. A par-

301

Schleiermacher and Barth were both theological giants who spawned any number of "followers" in varying degrees and in diverse respects, so that one can locate within the polarity represented by these two theologians, somewhat uneasily to be sure, a wide variety of the modern christologies of the twentieth century.

The second section gives an account of some of the many other christologies that have appeared in the course of the twentieth century. Despite the extensive, embracing reach of Schleiermacher and Barth, the second half of the century also witnessed movements in christology that cannot be contained within the parameters loosely defined by their method and content. World-wide political and social developments after World War II, along with developments in science, technology, and intellectual culture, are responsible for a newly emerging situation which has been labeled postmodern. The second section of the chapter, therefore, will survey in more detail some of the christological movements mentioned in Chapter 2. My intention is to be attentive to the appearance of new themes, issues, and christological problematics, especially in the last three decades.

Whether or not postmodernity can stand on its own as a clearly defined and distinct cultural matrix, christology is still facing some new and rather fundamental issues that must be factored into the method and content of the discipline. In the third concluding section, therefore, I shall give a brief account of the term "postmodern," which I have elected to use throughout this book. Reflection on what this code-word points to will serve as the bridge and rationale for the constructive effort that will follow.

In sum, the first two sections of this chapter will deal with modern christology from the perspective of the contrast between the christologies of Schleiermacher and Barth, and the broader field of christologies across the stretch of the twentieth century. The analysis will show a certain consistency among modern christologies as well as the emergence of new problems requiring new strategies. The schematic definition of the category of postmodernity will help to explain the need for discussing a new christology that responds to the issues that are emerging in the twenty-first century.

PARAMETERS OF MODERN CHRISTOLOGY

How does one go about uncovering the contours of modern christology?[2] An analytic description of modern christology in a short space can be no more than tentative and suggestive; it will also be highly interpre-

---

allel thesis could be written showing the analogies of Schleiermacher's christology to the Antiochene tradition.

2. John Macquarie's *Jesus Christ in Modern Thought* (London: Trinity Press International, 1990) is an important contribution to an analysis and assessment of modern christology.

tive. The interpretation begins with the choice of Schleiermacher and Barth as representatives of two thematics in christology that together and in contrast with each other embrace a good part of the field. A second interpretive feature consists in placing these two theologians in relation to each other. In sketching these christologies, I do not intend to compete with the able secondary literature that interprets these theologians at length by objective, historical, and reconstructive analyses. The intention here is more evocative; it seeks to use the christologies of these theologians to illustrate two very diverse and in many respects contrasting options that run through twentieth-century christology.[3] This is not an essay at creating types, for the contrast is between two particular theologians. But the distinctive character of these two christologies and the impact they have yielded allow one to view them as representatives of integral lines of thought.

I will use four categories or topics as axes for the analysis of each christology and hence as a device for comparison and contrast. The first is a very broad theme entitled foundational issues; this includes the premises and method that control the christology. The second topic is the view of the work of Christ or salvation. The third focuses on the person of Jesus Christ, that is, christology narrowly conceived. And the fourth is the place of the doctrine of the trinity in each christology.

THE CHRISTOLOGY OF FRIEDRICH SCHLEIERMACHER

I must presuppose data essential to an accurate historical representation of Schleiermacher's christology: the influence of Immanuel Kant on his thinking, both positively and negatively by eliciting reaction, the Berlin circle of Romantics, his classic apologetic work, the *Speeches on Religion*,[4] his development over the next twenty years before the publication of his systematics, *The Christian Faith*.[5] I shall describe his christology as it appears in this work.

Foundational Issues[6]

Let me begin with a characterization of the fundamental problem to which Schleiermacher's theology was addressed. Schleiermacher endeav-

---

3. Schleiermacher and Barth do not represent extremes. There are christologies to the left of Schleiermacher, for example, D. Strauss, A. Ritschl, A. von Harnack, E. Troeltsch, and to the right of Barth, such as fundamentalists. See the distinction between fundamentalism and postliberal conservative theology in David Tracy, *On Naming the Present: God, Hermeneutics, and Church* (Maryknoll, N.Y.: Orbis Books, 1994), 11–15.

4. Friedrich Schleiermacher, *On Religion: Speeches to Its Cultured Despisers*, ed. and trans. by Richard Crouter (New York: Cambridge University Press, 1988).

5. Friedrich Schleiermacher, *The Christian Faith* (New York: Harper Torchbooks, 1963). References in the text to Schleiermacher will be to this edition as CF by paragraph number and page.

6. The term "foundations" and its cognates are not being used in a way that sup-

ored to reestablish the credibility of the Christian message in the wake of certain elements in the critique by the Enlightenment. In his *Speeches* Schleiermacher established that religion is an autonomous sphere of human experience, distinct from knowledge of this world and from morality. Religion, and hence theology, find their anthropological basis in a form of experience of transcendence prior and irreducible to knowing or doing. Later, in *The Christian Faith*, Schleiermacher refined the basis of his theology by a transcendental analysis or phenomenology of human consciousness and freedom. He argued that all human beings have a potentiality for an experience of absolute dependence on God (CF, ##2–4, pp. 3–18). The very structure of human self-consciousness entails at the same time a world-consciousness or consciousness of the world around us. And these two together also entail a deeper level of consciousness that Schleiermacher calls alternatively an experience of absolute dependence, or a dependence on God, and "God-consciousness." He holds that God is present in or to this God-consciousness, giving a certain epistemological realism to the whole system.[7]

A second premise of his theology is that this anthropologically common experience of absolute dependence is always mediated historically (CF, #11, pp. 52–60). Although a structure that is common to human existence, the potential experience of absolute dependence is not experienced in the same way by all people, any more than vision, which is a feature common to human beings, means that all people see the same thing. Foundational religious experience is experienced in history differently according to its particular historical mediations. Thus there are a variety of religions or religious communities in human history. Christianity is the community which has its source, starting point, and continuing basis in Jesus Christ. It is a form of community piety or religious experience in which everything is related back historically to the mediation of God-consciousness accomplished by Jesus Christ.

Third, Schleiermacher proposes that "Christian doctrines are accounts of the Christian religious affections set forth in speech" (CF, #15, p. 76). This sentence typifies the revolution in theology that Schleiermacher wrought. Doctrines are not revealed propositions; they do not contain a propositional knowledge of God in the objective form of statements; they do not contain information about God or refer directly to a transcendent object. Their basis is piety, the historically mediated Christian form of the experience of absolute dependence, or God-consciousness, or religious

---

ports "foundationalism," the search for a universal material foundation for human knowing generally or in the field of theology. See John E. Thiel, *Nonfoundationalism* (Minneapolis: Fortress Press, 1991).

7. See the analysis of Schleiermacher's understanding of religious consciousness by Louis Roy, "Consciousness according to Schleiermacher," *The Journal of Religion*, 77 (1997), 217–32.

"affections." Doctrines consist in these experiences transposed into speech. The basis of theology is religious experience, not the experience of an individual, but the corporate experience of the community of faith.

Fourth, Christian revelation and redemptive experience is supernatural and supra-rational because it comes from God; it is mediated through a particular person, Jesus Christ, and cannot be deduced from common human experience.[8] But at the same time revelation is experienced and appreciated by human beings. The expressions of doctrine are to be set forth rationally and in order so that they can be understood. This is the task of theology (CF, #13, pp. 62–68).

Schleiermacher's method, therefore, consists in a critical examination of the doctrines of the church. His data lie in scripture, which is a record of the inspired and historically mediated foundational experiences of Christian faith, and the confessional statements of the churches. Theology's aim is critically to analyze these doctrines as expressions of the faith of the Christian community, to put forward their meaning in the highest possible declarative definiteness, internal coherence, and consistency. Theology is thus a critical discipline, but it has its basis in the experience that is given within the community. Relative to his analysis of redemption, for example, he explains that his "exposition is based entirely on the inner experience of the believer; its only purpose is to describe and elucidate that experience" (CF, #100, p. 428).

Salvation

Turning now to Schleiermacher's formal christology, I begin with his conception of the saving activity of Jesus Christ.[9] Schleiermacher locates salvation within a broad vision of human history which, *mutatis mutandis*, bears some resemblance to that of Irenaeus. The vision involves a developmental worldview. God did not complete the creation of the human race all at once but in two stages. This is symbolized by the first and the final Adam. Jesus Christ, therefore, was envisioned by God from eternity. In response to the classical medieval question, whether or not Christ would have come had there been no sin, Schleiermacher says Yes, Christ

---

8. Space does not allow a fuller account of Schleiermacher's theology of revelation. But it should be noted in passing that there is no complete antithesis between Schleiermacher and Barth on God's initiative in revelation.

9. After proposing a division between the person and work of Jesus Christ, Schleiermacher begins with the person of Christ. I propose to consider first the work of Christ for a number of reasons: first, in fact Schleiermacher introduces his whole christology with a brief consideration of the consciousness of grace and how this redemption is mediated by Jesus Christ (CF, ##86–90, pp. 355–70; #91, pp. 371–73). Second, the person and activity of Jesus Christ mutually imply each other, and must be systematically correlated, so that either can serve as the starting point for treating the doctrine of Christ (CF, #92, pp. 374–76). Third, treating the saving work of Christ first legitimately highlights a contrast between Schleiermacher and Barth.

would have come, because redemption is not simply a response to sin, but the completion and perfection of creation.

Thus from the beginning, humankind enjoys a certain "receptivity" for God-consciousness; human nature is open to and oriented toward receiving a higher consciousness of God. The plan of creation consists in an evolutionary movement toward an ever higher God-consciousness of which Jesus Christ is the fulfillment: Jesus is the goal of creation (CF, #89, pp. 366–68; also #93, p. 377; #101, p. 437).

The formula of Schleiermacher on the redeeming work of Christ is straightforward: "The Redeemer assumes believers into the power of His God-consciousness, and this is His redemptive activity" (CF, #100, p. 425). This first statement is quite general: Christ's redeeming activity is that which precedes all activity on our part; it is "that by means of which He assumes us into this fellowship of His activity and His life" (CF, #100, p. 425). This fellowship with Christ is the essence of the "state of grace." It is effected within the sphere of the corporate life of the community and through its mediation. Christ is the cause of salvation through "the act of His sinlessness and perfection as conditioned by the being of God in Him" (CF, #100, p. 425). The question is how to explain more exactly what Jesus Christ does and how He accomplishes it.

The redeeming action of Jesus Christ is an action of God, but an action of God channeled and mediated historically through Jesus. It is limited to those individuals who enter into the sphere of his historical influence as that is extended in history by the church (CF, #100, pp. 426–27). The key to this formula is how God is at work in Jesus' action. Christ's redeeming action is more than an empirical influence of Jesus the human being on people. For Jesus' human action is itself "the creative divine activity which established itself as the being of God in Him"; all of Jesus' actions flow from this and continue to have a "person-forming divine influence on human nature." The intended goal of this influence is all human nature, all human beings: "the activity of the Redeemer too is world-forming, and its object is human nature, in the totality of which the powerful God-consciousness is to be implanted as a new vital principle." He takes hold of individuals, and they others, and this stimulates a dynamic spreading effect. The total effective influence of Christ is "only the continuation of the creative divine activity out of which the Person of Christ arose." This is a continuation of God's original creative activity, but now with Christ as a historical organ (CF, #100, p. 427).

On an empirical, historical level Schleiermacher describes the influence of Jesus as similar to a founder of civil community, an influence which shapes and reforms the consciousness of those who join it. Jesus' saving activity is neither ahistorical, a kind of magical influence of God independently of Jesus, nor merely empirical, that is, what is communicated simply by teaching and example, and resulting in an intellectual or moral reform. Rather, through the historical influence of Jesus, people are drawn by the power of God into a new God-consciousness that amounts to the forgiveness and removal of sin (CF, #100, pp. 430–31).[10]

This state of God-consciousness is called redemption, which means being released from a consciousness of sin. Consciousness of sin is overcome. It is also called reconciliation, which means a blessedness that comes from union with God. One is drawn into union with God by being united to Jesus Christ so that one shares in Christ's blessedness. The beginning of this reconciliation, this blessedness of union with God, is the forgiveness of sin (CF, #101, pp. 431–33).

In sum: "The historical redeemer stands as the author of Christian faith and as the medium through which the man informed by his faith apprehends his relation to God, to the world and to himself."[11]

The Person of Christ

Schleiermacher's formal christology can be described in a series of propositions. The basis for his reflections rests on the experience of God's salvation in Jesus in the community and follows from the strict correlation of the dignity of Jesus' person with his redeeming activity (CF, #93, p. 377). The logic is thus analogous to the classic Athanasian principle that christology rests on soteriology, that Jesus is divine because he is mediator of God's salvation. I represent this christology in a series of points in order to highlight some of its features.[12]

First, the foundational conception is that Jesus Christ had an ideal or perfect God-consciousness. It had no imperfections (CF, #93, pp. 378–79). This God-consciousness controlled Jesus' life; all aspects of his life were informed by his consciousness of God (CF, #93, p. 383).

Second, this God-consciousness did not come from below, from Jesus' own resources, from nature. It is due to a "creative divine act" (CF, #93, p. 381). More strongly, Schleiermacher speaks of God being present to Jesus. It is a perfect "indwelling of the Supreme Being as His peculiar being and His inmost self" (CF, #94, p. 388). Designating Schleiermacher's position as merely a "consciousness christology" seriously misrepresents him.

---

10. Schleiermacher takes a position against two extremes, a magical, "which destroys all naturalness in the continuous activity of Christ, and an empirical, which reduces it altogether to the level of ordinary daily experience" and thus misses its supernatural beginning and distinctive peculiarity (CF, #101, p. 434). The empirical, in its fundamentalistic and reductionistic interpretation, somehow gets caught up in belief in the improvement of history and so on, or, in despair of this, posits blessedness in another life and world exclusively (ibid.). The magical imagines blessedness imparted independently of vital fellowship with Christ in community. That is, it is somehow infused into each person, without historical mediation, from without, and thus arbitrarily and magically (ibid., p. 435).

11. Richard R. Niebuhr, *Schleiermacher on Christ and Religion* (New York: Charles Scribner's Sons, 1964), 228.

12. See Martin Redeker, *Schleiermacher: Life and Thought* (Philadelphia: Fortress Press, 1973), 131–37, for a brief statement of his christology.

Third, this presence of God to Jesus is the power by which he was sin-less. Sinlessness is thus a symbol of Jesus' divinity, because he was so only by the power of God. Yet this sinlessness does not separate him from other human beings, because to be sinful is not part of human nature, but an aberration of it.

Thus, fourth, Jesus is truly a human being; he is the perfection of humanity in his sinlessness (CF, #94, pp. 385–86).

Fifth, how is God present to Jesus? Sometimes Schleiermacher uses the language of Spirit christology (e.g., CF, #94, pp. 388–89). His whole christology is consistent with a Spirit christology. But he also uses Logos language in the context of the phrase "the Word was made flesh" (CF, #96, p. 397).

Sixth, if Jesus is fully human like us except for his perfect God-consciousness, how is he different from other human beings? He is so anthropologically because of his sinlessness and because his God-consciousness was perfect. "Christ was distinguished from all other men by His essential sinlessness and His absolute perfection" (CF, #98, p. 413). This perfection is of course due to the perfect presence of God within him. For "to ascribe to Christ an absolutely powerful God-consciousness, and to attribute to Him an existence of God in Him, are exactly the same thing" (CF, #94, p. 387). Jesus is different from other human beings because of the perfect presence of God to him.

Seventh, Schleiermacher is hostile to the christological language of two natures found in Chalcedon. This is either misleading or, worse, inconsistent language, and he subjects it to an extended criticism (CF, #96, pp. 391-96).[13]

Schleiermacher's christology is recapitulated in the following thesis: "The Redeemer, then, is like all men in virtue of the identity of human nature, but distinguished from them all by the constant potency of his God-consciousness, which was a veritable existence of God in Him" (CF, #94, p. 385).

The Trinity

Schleiermacher is critical of the doctrine of the immanent trinity as it is usually understood. He makes two points. The first is that what is essential in the doctrine is already framed in an integral christology and eccle-siology. That essence consists in affirming clearly and ontologically that what is present and active in Jesus Christ and the church is truly God (CF, #170, pp. 738–39). He thus retrieves the logic of Nicaea seen in the last chapter. The second point is that this is a derivative doctrine; it comes from an inference from the experience of God in Jesus and in the community as Spirit. The doctrine itself is not a datum that is given in Christian self-

---

13. "He construes the perfectly regnant God-consciousness as the dwelling of God in Christ, and this then is Schleiermacher's equivalent for the notion of the divine nature of the redeemer." Niebuhr, *Schleiermacher on Christ and Religion*, 157.

consciousness which is the basis of theology.[14] Schleiermacher thus approaches a modalist position. But in his view the doctrine of the immanent trinity has a function, namely, to protect the reality of the divinity of Jesus and the Spirit in the church. From there, however, he does not go on to affirm the reality of the differentiation of persons within the Godhead. This sketch represents no more than an outline of the essentials of Schleiermacher's christology. I shall return to comment on its significance after a parallel sketch of Barth's christology.

THE CHRISTOLOGY OF KARL BARTH

Karl Barth's christology can be justly characterized as a reaction against the liberal tradition at whose head stood Schleiermacher. The contrast, therefore, is built into the very fabric of his thinking. The differences in these two theologians is nowhere more apparent than in the reversal of the order of the topics of trinity, christology, and soteriology. I begin with a general characterization of Barth's theological style.[15]

Foundational Issues

It is difficult to characterize Barth's method in theology. He does not have a method in the sense of a formal hermeneutical principle brought to bear on the tradition to mediate the content of revelation. He distrusts formal methods that mediate the content of God's Word or Logos. By contrast, Barth comments on scripture, at least in a wide sense; he expounds, using traditional sources, the content of the scriptural witness to God's revelation. Theology is the inner-church discipline of reflection on the Word of God found in scripture; it is accountable to no other human science or discipline. One has no leverage over the content of scripture other than the scripture itself.

Some of the characteristics that define his style of theological exposition will help bring out the contrast with Schleiermacher. Barth's theology is *theocentric*. Theology is based on God's objective Word to us. This Word reveals God's perspective on things; there is no appeal to human experience as though one had a positive basis for construing God's revealing.

---

14. "All that is essential in this Second Aspect of the Second Part of our exposition is also posited in what is essential in the doctrine of the Trinity; but this doctrine itself, as ecclesiastically framed, is not an immediate utterance concerning the Christian self-consciousness, but only a combination of several such utterances" (CF, #170, p. 738).

15. Jesus Christ lies at the center of all of Barth's theology, so that it is not contained by the boundaries of a specific section in the *Church Dogmatics*. Also, his christology developed. The representation of Barth's christology here in no way communicates its full scope. For a brief account of the expansiveness of Barth's christology, see John Thompson, *Christ in Perspective: Christological Perspectives in the Theology of Karl Barth* (Edinburgh: St. Andrew Press, 1978).

Barth's theology is *ecclesiocentric*; it is not apologetic and makes no effort to mediate or bridge God's Word and human culture. The direction of this theology is from the authority of scripture and God's Word, from above; God's Word addresses us, we do not discover God's Word.

Barth's theology is *christocentric*: Jesus Christ is the absolute center of history, and there is no authentic knowledge of God apart from Jesus Christ.

Barth's theology is *supernaturalistic*; he makes little overt effort to demythologize scriptural or classical theological language, even though it is understood with nuance. God is envisioned as coming down from above and entering the human condition in stark judgment as the first moment of salvation.

Barth's theology is a theology of *proclamation*; it is an outgrowth and reflection on the preached Word of God. Barth's theology is expository; it reads like pure assertion; explanation is at a minimum, for human reason has the tendency of distorting God's Word addressed to human existence. God is conceived as over against human existence which is sinful. The antithesis between God and human existence gives his theology a consistent tone of paradox; Barth loves to offend human reasoning. His theology is thus profoundly prophetic and counter-cultural. Simply on the level of foundational presupposition and overall vision, Barth represents another and different theological world than that of Schleiermacher.

The Trinity

Barth's christology is pure christology from above. The first volume of the *Church Dogmatics* deals with method, the Word of God, scripture and revelation of God.[16] But God is revealed as trinity. The first doctrine to be treated in the Dogmatics, therefore, is the doctrine of the trinity, its unity and then its threeness, that is, each of the three persons are considered. The first treatment of Jesus Christ, therefore, is as the Son, the second person of the trinity, God as Reconciler. The "from above" of this christology implies two things: first, methodologically, christology begins with and expounds upon classical authoritative texts of scripture and doctrine. Second, "from above" implies a decisive theological vision. Barth's theology envisages and presupposes God coming to human beings in revelation, judgment, and self-disclosure. There is utterly no ascent or even point of contact between human nature or experience and God. God comes in total freedom and surprise to human existence.[17]

---

16. Karl Barth, *Church Dogmatics*, I, 1, *The Doctrine of the Word of God* (Edinburgh: T. & T. Clark, 1975). This work will be cited in the text as Church Dogmatics according to part and volume, "paragraph," and page.

17. This generalized statement, most typical of Barth during his middle period prior to WW II, is appropriate even though the sharpness of these antitheses were softened somewhat in his later theology.

Barth speaks of the eternal Son as distinct from the Father, of the activity of the Son as an action of self-communication distinct from God's action of creation. Revelation or reconciliation is the activity of the Son. In contrast to Schleiermacher, Jesus Christ is not a completion of creation, but an unexpected miracle in a fallen world. Having his origin as the second person of the divine trinity, Jesus of Nazareth is the Word of God. "The movement of thought here is not from below upwards but from above downwards" (CD I-2, #13, p. 21).

The Person of Christ

The question of the person of Christ, the formal christological problem of the divinity and humanity of Jesus, is logically prior to salvation in Barth's descending christology. Who is Jesus Christ? He is the human being who is also God. The doctrine of the two natures is a given; it defines the mystery of Jesus Christ. To slight either is to destroy the mystery (CD I-2, #15, pp. 122–32). The second section of the paragraph just cited contains Barth's explanation of the divinity and humanity of Jesus. This is done in an extended exegesis of John 1:14, "the Word was made flesh." It has three parts: the *Word* was made flesh; the Word was made *flesh*; and the Word *was made* flesh.

It was the *Word* who was made flesh. It is the Logos who becomes flesh and not God indiscriminately. The Logos is "the entire fullness of deity" (CD I-2, #15, p. 133). Barth is clear that the divine Word is the subject, the actor, in the person Jesus Christ. "The Word speaks, the Word acts, the Word prevails, the Word reveals, the Word reconciles. True enough, He is the incarnate Word, i.e., the Word not without flesh, but the Word in the flesh and through the flesh—but nevertheless the Word and not the flesh. The Word is what He is even before and apart from His being flesh" (CD I-2, #15, p. 136).

It was *flesh* that the Word became. "Flesh" means human nature, humanity, in its full human condition, including the condition of sin. Barth is quite realistic in describing Jesus Christ as human, "a man," "a human being"; he is also quite subtle. "We must note that primarily and of itself 'flesh' does not imply a man, but human essence and existence, human kind and nature, humanity, *humanitas*, that which makes a man man as opposed to God, angel or animal" (CD I-2, #15, p. 149). What he means is that Jesus is not an individual human being over against the Logos or Word. Rather, the human being that is Jesus, "this man, is itself the work of the Word, not His presupposition" (ibid.). "God Himself in person is the Subject of a real human being and acting. And just because God is the Subject of it, this being and acting are real" (CD I-2, #15, p. 151).

The meaning of *became* or "was made a human being," Barth says, should not be construed as implying passivity in God. Rather, God assumes a human nature so that the Word is the subject and bearer of this human nature. He proposes a classical enhypostatic union, that is, the human nature of Jesus Christ has no personhood or existence of its own, but subsists in the person of the Word, and exists by the power of the Word.

Salvation

The doctrine of the saving work of Jesus Christ, which Barth calls reconciliation, is analyzed at length. Two particular presentations, however, stand out: one in which he describes God's saving activity generally as Emmanuel, or God with us; the other, a presentation of Barth's redemption theory.

Barth calls the phrase "God with us" the short formula for the central message and very core of Christianity (CD IV-1, #57, pp. 3–4). He draws this out in a series of points. God's reconciling action is the central act of God, and in it and by it God draws human existence into God's own sphere of life; God is a God with us and for us. In Barth's vision, salvation is prior to creation in the sense that salvation is the prior purpose for creation. God intends to save; therefore God creates. Barth's universe is thus christocentric. Sin of course separates human existence from God, but grace overcomes sin and exceeds restoration of the antecedent condition. Human existence is fulfilled by being drawn into the life of God. God's participation in our human existence, God with us, means that we are with God and made free for God. Finally, all of this is focused in Jesus Christ; all of this came to pass as an event in the historical phenomenon of Jesus Christ (CD IV-1, #57, pp. 3–21).

Barth also depicts the work of Christ in terms of a redemption theory (CD IV-1, #59, pp. 211–73). Characterized generally, Barth's depiction of salvation is a substitution theory. Although there are some differences, it fits within the general pattern of Anselm as modified by Luther and Calvin. The overall scheme has Jesus Christ as the second Adam. Several elements define this general framework further.

The motive for the incarnation and God's action of salvation is directed toward God's own glory. God manifests God's glory in saving humankind. But this does not suppress human existence as a goal: God acts for us and out of love for humankind. As a second Adam, the Word becomes incarnate to perform an action in our place. Christ will do something that we should do but cannot do. One of those things that the Word or the Son as Jesus Christ does is positive; he is sinless and obedient. Thus he does what Adam and the rest of humankind failed to do. But the Word of God also underwent the punishment due to sin in our stead; he suffered and died. Barth's theory of the work of Christ for our salvation, which he calls reconciliation, is a substitution theory; the second Adam reconciles humanity to God by taking our place and doing what has to be done for us. This involves, positively, a perfect life of sinless obedience and, negatively, undergoing suffering and death which is the price of sin.

Barth spells out his theory of divine reconciliation in great detail around the metaphor of Jesus Christ as the judge who is judged in our place. The logic is schematized in four points by Barth himself (CD IV-1, #59, pp. 230–73).

First, Jesus Christ is God's judge or norm by which we are judged. Jesus Christ in the world is a judgment upon the sinfulness of human beings. But, second, this judge takes our place as sinners and becomes judged in our stead. In this event our guilt and sin are removed from us; they are borne by Jesus Christ. Our sin is forgiven; we are freed. Third, the way in which Jesus Christ is actually judged in our place consists in his assuming the judgment against sin which is death. Thus reconciliation or redemption transpires most pointedly in the passion and death of Jesus Christ. Barth calls this the suffering of God. In a way, the events of Good Friday constitute the turning point of history. In the one day of suffering, the redemptive judgment of God took place; the broken covenant was legally reestablished; and the decisive turning point in the history of creation occurred (CD IV-1, #59, p. 247).[18] Barth sees this happening historically in Jesus. He reads the historical story of Jesus from a dogmatic point of view, that is, he understands his reconciliation theory as unfolding in the empirical historical events of Jesus' life (CD IV-1, #59, pp. 224–28).

Barth represents these events as an objective salvation; it is done entirely by God and for us but entirely without us. "It happened for us, but it happened without us, without our co-operating or contributing" (CD IV-1, #59, p. 249). Why does Jesus Christ have to die for this reconciliation to take place? Sin is not simply a personal affront to God, but also a disruptive breaking of the covenant which sunders the harmony of creation. Also, the price of sin is death. Jesus, to reconcile human existence to God, had to follow out the logic of sin, pay the price, and restore the harmony of creation (CD IV-1, #59, pp. 252–53). Despite the similarity with Anselm at this point, Barth does not want to call this a "satisfaction" theory (CD IV-1, #59, pp. 254–55).

Fourth, however, this suffering and death are not negative; the whole action of God carried out in Jesus is positive; it is God's Yes to humankind. It is God reconciling human existence to God's self.

Such is Barth's christology roughly schematized around the topics of premises, trinity, formal christology, and salvation. I now wish to draw out the expansive symbolic significance of the christologies of Schleiermacher and Barth.

THE PARAMETERS OF MODERN CHRISTOLOGY

In this attempt to describe modern christology, I take the christologies of Schleiermacher and Barth as sources. Both of these figures are modern, post-enlightenment theologians who learned from and reacted against specific aspects of the Enlightenment's definition of modernity. In other words, one may be modern by both adapting to and, in some measure,

---

18. "In this suffering and dying of God Himself in His Son, there took place the reconciliation with God, the conversion to Him, of the world which is out of harmony with Him, contradicting and opposing Him" (CD IV-1, #59 pp. 250–51).

reacting against the culture of modernity. The significance of these theologians lies in the magnitude and paradigmatic influence of their theological achievements. Although what have been described are not types but particular christologies, each gave rise to methodological patterns in theology. Each, then, has a symbolic significance of representing elementary insights, tendencies of thought, and traits that have influenced and in some measure defined twentieth-century theology. Their christologies function in a manner analogous to the Antiochene and Alexandrian "schools" in the fourth- and fifth-century controversies. These christologies, loosely construed, indicate certain parameters, that is, outer limits, within which the modern christology of the twentieth century has unfolded. When they are so considered, one can immediately identify multiple themes or elements for interpretation in christology which find polar and contrasting construals in Schleiermacher and Barth. I shall consider a number of these themes which, together with the options they represent, will serve as categories for a loose characterization on a formal level of the christology of the first half of the twentieth century. It is important to note that these polarities are not logical contradictories; they represent alternatives only at their extremes. They really describe two ends of a spectrum of various possible positions.

Consider, first, the perspective, imaginative standpoint, and consequent point of departure. Schleiermacher's is a christology *from below*, and Barth's a christology *from above*. These characterizations are quite basic, and other differentiations may find their source here. Barth partly understood the difference between himself and Schleiermacher in these terms. "My own theology," he said, "may be looked upon as a complete reversal of his. I try to look from above, he from below. There is a difference of vantage points."[19]

Regarding the nature and method of the discipline of theology, one finds a polarity defined by the tension between the appeal to *experience* and to the *objective tradition*. Schleiermacher reflects the growing conviction, implied in the turn to the subject, that philosophy, and now theology, and in fact all disciplines of human knowledge must be critically attentive to the very presuppositions of knowing itself. By contrast, Barth accepts the absolute priority of God in revelation, and trusts the objective tradition of theological language in the community. In so doing, he reflects the axiom of the sociology of knowledge that we cannot escape the historical tradition of a community; at best we can only join another one. In both of these theologians, in their different ways, one has a declaration of the independence of theology; in neither is theology merely a function of human knowing, doing, or culture. But they were reacting to different reductions, and the point of departure is so different at the extremes that

---

19. Barth, cited by Terrence N. Tice, "Interviews with Karl Barth and Reflections on His Interpretations of Schleiermacher," *Barth and Schleiermacher: Beyond the Impasse?* ed. by J. O. Duke and R. F. Streetman (Philadelphia: Fortress Press, 1988), 49–50.

one can almost say that Schleiermacher and Barth inhabit different worlds of discourse. Their understanding of Christianity is fundamentally different. Other polarities will reinforce this difference.

A dominant sensibility for either side of *the immanence and the transcendence* of God leads theology in a distinctive direction. In Schleiermacher's view God is present to human religious experience; God is thus not distant from culture. This theology is historically conscious. Theology should be inculturated in the forms and languages of the cultures of any given time.[20] Barth is famous for his retrieval of the theme of the transcendence of God, the divine One who, as infinitely and qualitatively other, looms over human existence and culture. But this God has come close and addressed us once and for all in Jesus Christ. And the language that witnesses to this event is not adapted to culture; human culture adapts to it as we are drawn into God's world. The very process of the thinking of Christian theology is "from above"; one accepts the shape and definition of the world in the terms of the revelation given by God's Word.

Another polarity is derivative of the first two and may be formulated in a question: is the structure of theological language such that it refers directly to human experience, or does it give witness to a more directly received revelation?[21] For Schleiermacher, God is present to the experience of absolute dependence, and this is where God is encountered. In Christian faith this is a God-consciousness that is mediated by Jesus Christ. It is important to note that Barth too understands revelation transpiring within human subjects; revelation is not identical with the words of scripture or the propositions of doctrine. But Barth calls attention to a directness with which God reveals God's own self, and the words of scripture, like sacraments, bear witness to this divine self-gift. Human beings *receive* revelation, and they do not have the right or the ability to shape it to their own ends. Schleiermacher begins his theology with a philosophically mediated anthropology; Barth begins with the reading of scripture and the proclamation of the Word.[22]

Behind much of twentieth-century theology lies *a positive or a negative appreciation of human existence* which deeply colors the conception of the whole of reality and the whole range of theological subjects. Are we to be optimistic or pessimistic about the human project? Can one risk an apolo-

---

20. Historical consciousness is a broad, analogous term, and one could argue about the degree of Schleiermacher's historical consciousness in relation to other theologians and to other periods of time.

21. David Tracy has provided a key to the differentiation of liberal and neo-orthodox theology by an analysis of this distinction in terms of subject and object reference. See David Tracy, *Blessed Rage for Order: The New Pluralism in Theology* (New York: Seabury Press, 1975), 25–31.

22. One could say that Barth's theology begins with a negative experience of culture, a negative experience of contrast, itself a gift of grace, that opens the subject to transcendence. This negative experience, however, does not function as a positive principle for interpreting revelation, but as the occasion of God's self-communication.

getic theology, or does the undertaking of mediation distort the Christian message? How are we to assess the very idea of inculturation which is demanded by the greater portion of western Christians who live outside the West? How is one to locate and define the sin that everyone admits is a power in history? Schleiermacher has a doctrine of sin, a rather strong one, since redemption itself is explained in the context of the consciousness of sin. But strength and weakness are relative terms, and in contrast to Schleiermacher Barth shares the radical doctrine of the reformers. A doctrine of sin is a most significant axis for understanding the variations of modern theology and christology during the twentieth century.

One can differentiate modern christologies across the spectrum of *a historical and this-worldly or a metaphysical and eschatological language of salvation*. This polarity is correlative to those already described, but it refers directly to the content of soteriology. Schleiermacher took some large steps toward a demythologization of the classical theories of salvation. He called for an internal, tensive, and mutually conditioning influence between the supernatural and the empirical-historical. He explains how the Jesus of history effected salvation during the course of his ministry. The language of Barth is decidedly mystical or supernatural, but not without reference to Jesus of Nazareth. There is a genuine polarity here, for both theologians include both sides of the tension. But the emphasis on the different sides results in another major difference between these two theologies.

The same is true for a stress or defining interest in *the humanity or the divinity of Jesus Christ*. Such a focus consistently differentiates christologies, even though both may be consistent with the tradition. Both Schleiermacher and Barth have subtle, dialectical understandings of the relation between the humanity and divinity of Jesus Christ. But for Schleiermacher, Barth's christology would appear docetic; for Barth, Schleiermacher comes nowhere near his conception of the transcendent divinity of Jesus Christ. Schleiermacher's christology begins from below, even though the material of his life of Jesus is not integrated into his dogmatics. Barth's is a christology from above. Schleiermacher was critical of classical doctrine, and he creatively designed a new language in order to communicate and preserve its intent. Barth worked within the classical terms of nature and person in christology but not in trinitarian theology.

Finally, another tension in twentieth-century christology revolves around the polar dimensions of *individuality and sociality* in the historical makeup of human existence. This tension is not reflected in the contrast between Schleiermacher and Barth, and an emphasis on either individuality or sociality does not differentiate the movements they spawned.[23] But the themes of this tension buzz about all the theology of the twentieth century. As religion became more privatistic in a more secular and pluralistic society, theology itself employed a language directed to individual persons.

---

23. Liberal theology is often accused of individualism, but this is not necessarily the case. There is nothing in its fundamental premises or method that is *per se* individualistic.

And as the social conditions of especially modern urban societies deteriorated, the demand for a social and public relevance grew. The social gospel movement in the United States was liberal; it was Barth who stood up to National Socialism in Germany. An overview of twentieth-century theology makes it apparent that either term of this particular polarity can dominate in a theology resembling that of either Schleiermacher or Barth. We move then to a further description of the present situation of christology by means of an overview and analysis of some essays of the past century.

TOWARD POSTMODERN CHRISTOLOGY

The point of this chapter is to map the terrain of modern christology in the twentieth century and, more particularly, to represent the situation of christology as we begin the twenty-first century. The results will serve as a definition of the point of view that guides this constructive christology. One reading of this development is as follows: the modern christology of the twentieth century is loosely contained within the parameters reflected in the christologies of Schleiermacher and Barth. At the same time, during the second half of the twentieth century, a number of christological problems, methods, and proposals have arisen which reflect a new situation in western intellectual culture which is characterized as postmodernity. On the one hand, I have no interest in defending this title, for it may lend too much substance to intellectual developments which singly have not yet come to maturity or collectively coalesced in such a way that a clear cultural threshold or boundary has been crossed. On the other hand, I have no doubt that new and generally held foundational premises and convictions have arisen which far transcend the framework defined by the tensions between Schleiermacher and Barth. It is this shift that I want to document in the second section of the chapter and characterize formally in the third.

Various strategies might be used to describe twentieth-century christology in a few pages of analysis. One would be to highlight the development by chronicling in a narrative form the various christologies that have appeared in this century. Another would be to bring out the similarities and differences of these many christologies by constructing types around a few representative figures. The analysis which follows is organized around the four headings used to compare Schleiermacher and Barth. It attends in some measure to the historical development across the century and to the variety of different christologies that have been developed. But the distinctiveness of the christologies of the second half of the twentieth century is contained in the emergence of new problematics which are challenging modern christologies and opening up new creative interpretations of Jesus Christ. Let me begin, then, with a consideration of how christology has been dealing with foundational issues.

FOUNDATIONAL ISSUES

The problems a christology is facing help to explain its method and approach. The problems underlying the christologies of Schleiermacher and Barth are shared by much of the christology of the first part of the twentieth century. These are the problems of modernity. On the one hand, one finds a deep mistrust of authoritarian religion, and more deeply of extrinsicism, the idea that religion itself comes from outside the human condition and is alienating. The grounds of religious conviction must be found within the human as such. This issue is addressed epistemologically: within the framework of faith and reason, the question of how one knows religiously is a central issue. On the other hand, one finds an almost equal distrust of anthropocentrism, a conviction of the truth of the word of God, and of a distortion of the word of God by cultural interpretations. The experience and doctrine of sin call attention to the need for theology to attend to the initiative of God in Christian revelation. These divergent approaches to the basic problems underlying theology and its method, however, shared some common convictions. Both forms of theology transcend fundamentalism: revelation does not consist in objective propositional knowledge, but occurs within subjective or personal encounter. Both forms of theology are reckoning with an emergent historical consciousness. They defend the uniqueness and superiority of Christian truth. They are secure in a vision of reality that is Christian and western.

A great deal of the christology of the twentieth century shares much in common with the issues debated within the modern paradigm. The christologies of Pannenberg and Moltmann fall within the broad tradition represented by Barth; they are evangelical and retain close ties to the reformers.[24] The christologies of Tillich and Rahner share much in common with Schleiermacher; they appeal to experience and mediate their theology with philosophical reflection.[25] The christologies of Bultmann and Ogden fall neatly into neither camp but can claim analogies with both.[26] But at the same time there are new problems, or new critical edges to old problems, that are emerging within these same theologies. And in the course of the last third of the twentieth century these new problems gradually begin to gain the attention of the christologies of the period.

Much of modern theology and christology presupposes the stability of Christian truth in history, even though it may be expressed in new forms.

---

24. Wolfhart Pannenberg, *Jesus—God and Man* (Philadelphia: Westminster Press, 1977); Jürgen Moltmann, *The Way of Jesus Christ* (Minneapolis: Fortress Press, 1993). Citations in this section are restricted to representative works.

25. Paul Tillich, *Systematic Theology*, 2 (Chicago: University of Chicago Press, 1957); Karl Rahner, *Foundations of Christian Faith* (New York: Seabury Press, 1978).

26. Rudolf Bultmann, *Jesus Christ and Mythology* (New York: Charles Scribner's Sons, 1959); Schubert M. Ogden, *Christ Without Myth* (New York: Harper & Row, 1961) and *The Point of Christology* (New York: Harper & Row, 1982).

It seeks to understand the consistent truth of Jesus Christ against the implied relativism of history. In process theology and christology, however, change and novelty are understood metaphysically as constitutive of reality itself. John Cobb's christology is developed against the background of the inherent diversity of things, and the Logos is interpreted as the very principle of creative transformation.[27] A process view of reality opens up a new look at things; change, which is personally threatening and socially disruptive, epitomizes the natural condition of reality.

Liberation theology in its multiple forms bears many analogies to the theology of the social gospel a century ago in North America and to the social theology of Europe. This was a liberal theology, informed by emerging social science. Liberation theologies have a different immediate historical background but are structurally close to the theologies of the social gospel. The reemergence of this socially mediated christology in the last third of the twentieth century has had a dramatic impact on the discipline. Liberation theology has spread through the whole Christian world; it has been generalized to take on analogous forms for a variety of oppressed and marginalized groups; it has incorporated critical social theory; it thus represents a new understanding of religion, faith, revelation, and the church. Moreover, once human existence is understood as socially constituted, the problematic of liberation becomes the problematic of the meaning of history itself and human responsibility for it. Historical consciousness in this view has been reappropriated: it is not merely the threat of relativism, it is also the very context of understanding and the premise for opportunity and hope.

Another new development in christology is the growth and flourishing since the Second World War of churches outside the West and the demand for and gradual emergence of christologies that reflect these various cultures. Inculturation, archetypically demonstrated in the transition from Palestinian-Jewish-Christian discipleship into the Greco-Roman church, is beginning to take hold in a new self-conscious and dedicated way. But the problematic of sameness and difference entailed in the process of inculturation is profound and new, partly because of the new historical and social consciousness that underlies and propels it. Pluralism in christology is now a desired ideal for which christology consciously strives. This turns the problematic of unity and diversity inside out: christology has been a unity tolerating diversity; it is becoming diversity in the quest of unity.

Finally, the recognition and positive valuation of other religious faiths, the study of other religions, and the practice of interfaith dialogue have stimulated the deeply engaging issue of the Christian theology of religions. A more radical historical consciousness shared by most educated people today raises major intellectual problems concerning the intelligibility of Christian claims about Jesus Christ in a religiously pluralistic

---

27. John Cobb, *Christ in a Pluralistic Age* (Philadelphia: Westminster Press, 1975).

world. Troeltsch raised this issue a century ago. But during the past three decades the issues of religious pluralism have been the subject of lively and engaged debate, and it is still an open question.

These problems that lie at the basis of christology help define the distinctiveness of the discipline at the beginning of the third millennium. The question of salvation too has taken on a distinctive form.

SALVATION

The next two chapters will examine constructively and in more detail an understanding of salvation. At this point I wish to establish in some limited degree the state of the question in the twentieth-century discussion. I have noted the parameters represented by Schleiermacher's philosophically and anthropologically conditioned view of Christian salvation on one side, and Barth's sophisticated return to evangelical and classical soteriological language. How this polarity has been both retained and transcended in the second half of the twentieth century can be illustrated by noting the orientations of various theologians.

Pannenberg follows Barth in his insistence that soteriology flows from christology and in retaining evangelical and classical soteriological language. But he is historically conscious enough to want the historical Jesus to be a norm for soteriological language. Constructively he proposes an Anselmian-Lutheran substitution and penal or punishment theory. "Jesus' death on the cross is revealed in the light of his resurrection as the punishment suffered in our place for the blasphemous existence of humanity."[28] Moltmann is another theologian who works within the framework of evangelical language, but as a political theologian he is attentive to the social dimension of salvation that I will highlight further on. Earlier, Moltmann proposed that God suffered for our salvation in the death of Jesus.[29] Although this idea has been severely criticized, he still defends it in his formal christology. Moltmann focuses on the death of Jesus in explaining the how of Jesus' saving, but he is explicitly insistent that Jesus' death be understood as joined to his resurrection as one whole event. This being said, Moltmann summarizes the saving significance of Jesus' death around four ends or goals: Jesus' death causes the justifying faith of the believer in himself; it forms a bond of memory and responsibility between the living and the dead; united with the resurrection it promises victory over death itself; it renders glory to God and restores justice to those who did not know it in their lifetime.[30] Although Moltmann's soteriology is recognizably Lutheran and evangelical, it is also quite imaginative and distinctive.

---

28. Pannenberg, *Jesus—God and Man*, 245. The fact that Pannenberg elaborates a salvation theory around Jesus' death should not obscure the fact that his whole christology is centered around the resurrection which implicitly has decisive saving power.

29. Jürgen Moltmann, *The Crucified God* (New York: Harper & Row, 1974).

30. Moltmann, *The Way of Jesus Christ*, 183.

Also evangelical are such existential theologians as Rudolf Bultmann, Schubert Ogden, and Paul Tillich. But their biblical language is conditioned in varying degrees by the framework of an existentialist philosophy. For example, in Bultmann and Ogden salvation consists in the existential encounter and being in relationship to God through Jesus Christ, God's Word. This encounter itself is a justification by faith, and an authorization and impulse for exercising freedom into the future. In Tillich, whose whole theology is mediated by an elaborate existential ontology, salvation is represented in terms of being, non-being, estrangement from being, and New Being. Jesus Christ is the bearer of New Being from God: "The doctrine of atonement is the description of the effect of the New Being in Jesus as the Christ on those who are grasped by it in their state of estrangement."[31]

Karl Rahner's theology of salvation is a blending of an incarnation theory of divinization and a transactional theory. Although Rahner's view can only fully be understood within the terms of his system, from a certain perspective it can be summarized in three propositions. The question is how Jesus' death is salvific, or how it *causes* salvation. To understand this, one must first realize that Jesus' dying was an act, not merely a passion, but an intentional commitment and action. He accepted his death positively; he gave his life. Secondly, this final action is a summary of his whole life; it recapitulates and culminates his life. It is the act which sums up the whole Yes to God that constituted his life. Thirdly, then, this final Yes to God is the response that climaxes God's definitive Yes to human existence in the incarnation and hypostatic union. The whole of history moves toward the self-communication of God to human existence. That union is absolutized in God's presence to human existence in Jesus Christ, and in an absolute human acceptance in Jesus' death on the cross. This acceptance by Jesus in faithfully enduring his mission to the end is what is sealed and ratified in the resurrection.[32]

Still more intricately the product of a philosophical correlation and mediation is the salvation theory of a process theologian such as John Cobb. In some respects what he proposes is analogous to an exemplary theory of salvation, one which bears a certain resemblance to that of Schleiermacher. But it is expounded in categories inspired by Whitehead's philosophy. The question is how the historical events of Jesus' life can be understood to have salvific efficacy into the future? Cobb responds that these events set up a historical field of force that radiates into the future. But this causality must be appropriated by freedom to become effective. This provides Cobb with a model for interpreting what Paul meant by a salvation that is effected by being "in Christ." The force of Jesus Christ's union with God from the past is carried into the present by the conformation of the present to it in people's

---

31. Tillich, *Systematic Theology*, 2, 170.
32. Rahner, *Foundations*, 282–85.

appropriation of the historical influence of Jesus.[33] Thus Cobb presents an exemplary theory of salvation, but it transcends a subjective, moral theory by being explained in the ontological terms of a process philosophy of the efficacy of historical causality.

Another theme prominent in process theology is the role of human freedom in the dynamics of salvation. God's salvation does not work against human freedom, but within it as a liberating power. The autonomy of human freedom is a thoroughly modern premise which forms a bridge to some of the notions of salvation that transcend modernity.

These views of salvation are more or less contained within the paradigm of modernity as that is embraced in the representative positions of Schleiermacher and Barth. But one can discern dimensions in these and other theologians that are opening up new aspects of the meaning of salvation, mainly by thematizing negativities to which salvation responds in a new way.

The narrative christology of Edward Schillebeeckx in many ways represents an antithesis to a metaphysical and systematic understanding of salvation. His two volumes, *Jesus* and *Christ*, provide, respectively, an account of Jesus and a survey of interpretations of the salvation he wrought.[34] In *Christ* he analyzes exhaustively New Testament imagery for salvation and current social-political interpretations. But if one asks, what finally is salvific about Jesus, one would have to return to the *Jesus* book for the answer. Schillebeeckx seems to cut through all the elaborated theories of salvation by a return to the story of Jesus as the parable of a saving God. The stress in this narrative christology is precisely the logic of Jesus' historical ministry, how it reveals God's presence and God's vision for reality, and how it calls out to be internalized by conversion and externalized through a following of Christ. One finds in this soteriology a reflection of the deep impact of historical consciousness on theology, a *reductio ad simplicitatem*, a resistance to universal theorizing, an appeal to a concrete classic figure in history.

There is a whole range of theologians who are committed to a view of the salvific work of Jesus Christ that has a bearing on the social human existence in this world. The analogies between these different soteriologies, responding to different forms of social injustice and oppression, in different times and places, are striking. For example, Shailer Mathews proposes a portrait of Jesus as one who had an interest in and impact on social forms of existence.[35] Walter Rauschenbusch developed an atonement the-

---

33. Cobb, *Christ in a Pluralistic Age*, 121.

34. Edward Schillebeeckx, *Jesus: An Experiment in Christology* (New York: Seabury Press, 1979); *Christ: The Experience of Jesus as Lord* (New York: Seabury Press, 1980).

35. Shailer Mathews, *The Social Teaching of Jesus: An Essay in Christian Sociology* (New York: Macmillan, 1897) and *Jesus on Social Institutions*, ed. by Kenneth Cauthen (Philadelphia: Fortress Press, 1971); William D. Lindsey, *Shailer Mathews's Lives of Jesus: The Search for a Theological Foundation for the Social Gospel* (Albany: State University of New York Press, 1997).

ory in which it is precisely the social sins of humankind and individual participation in them that were the cause of Jesus' death and are the object of salvation.[36] Jon Sobrino turns to the Pauline language of salvation, while at the same time keeping in view an image of the historical Jesus, to generate a revelatory and exemplary view of the saving work of Jesus Christ.[37] Racism, sexism, and a combination of the two are the foci for black, feminist, and womanist views of the saving work of Christ, respectively. In the case of each of these soteriologies, however, the salvation that Jesus Christ mediates is understood as engaging concrete social history, as judgment against injustice, and as exemplary incentive to overcome it by creating just, emancipatory patterns of social existence.

The demand that salvation be understood in social terms is not new in the Christian tradition. But these soteriologies contain a number of suppositions which make them distinctive. First of all, given the growth of human population and the complexification of societies, the social negativities calling out for salvation find no precedent for their sheer size and weight. These calls for salvation presuppose with modernity that history is in human hands; but they also presuppose a certain human impotence at being able to deal with the overwhelming social suffering we experience today. These soteriologies address the temptation to nihilism of the rich and the temptation to despair of the poor. These views of salvation, like utopia, open up the contingency of social arrangements and imply a critique of society and culture. The premises of a social interpretation of salvation have increasingly been characterized by a radical historical consciousness.

The historical sense of contingency increases under the impact of the ecological crises that the human race is encountering. Jesus Christ is being interpreted by being placed in conjunction with the physical cosmos, in the context of a new and ever-expanding scientific understanding of creation and the universe.[38] This soteriology tries to incorporate a concern for nature and care of our material environment. It has developed out of a deep contrast experience that the human species is destroying itself by destroying its environment in a corporate act of selfish, inattentive, and sinful domination. Moltmann believes that this ethical imperative needs a spiritual and religious vision to support it, and the Christian vision is interpreted in this direction. Christology must transcend its being centered on the person and church in order to find Christ in the cosmos itself. "A *new* cosmic christology must end the historical christology of modern times, not abolishing it but gathering it into something more which will overcome its limitations and preserve its truth."[39]

---

36. Walter Rauschenbusch, *A Theology for the Social Gospel* (Nashville: Abingdon Press, 1945), 240–79. See Darlene Ann Peitz, *Solidarity as Hermeneutic* (New York: Peter Lang, 1992).

37. Jon Sobrino, *Jesus the Liberator* (Maryknoll, N.Y.: Orbis Books, 1993), 219–32.

38. Moltmann, *The Way of Jesus Christ*, 274–341; Denis Edwards, *Jesus the Wisdom of God: An Ecological Theology* (Maryknoll, N.Y.: Orbis Books, 1995).

39. Moltmann, *The Way of Jesus Christ*, 275.

Finally, another area in which soteriology is being subjected to thorough revision is the theology of religions and theological reflection from the perspective of interreligious dialogue. It is true that many theologians simply apply their already fashioned christologies and soteriologies to the phenomenon of religious pluralism. Others, however, are allowing the practice or the imperative of dialogue, along with the seemingly intrinsic necessity of religious pluralism, to shape their view of salvation and through it their christology. In some cases this has generated strikingly new views of salvation. For example, John Hick, as a philosopher of religion who occasionally writes as a Christian theologian, sees salvation as a universal process, one that is fostered and mediated *in principle*, though not necessarily in fact, equally by all the major religions. In order to hold this, since salvation is so differently conceived by different religions, and because those conceptions are really conflicting, he must define salvation expansively and abstractly in order to view it as a single reality. This generic idea of salvation is one of the most controversial aspects of Hick's theory of religious pluralism. As he states it: "I suggest that these different conceptions of salvation are specifications of what, in a generic formula, is the transformation of human existence from self-centeredness to a new orientation centered in the divine Reality."[40] Within this context Hick proposes an exemplary theory of the salvific work of Jesus. But, more importantly, this problematic has opened up a new horizon for thinking about salvation that transcends the particularity of the Jewish-Christian tradition. On a theological level it forces a reconsideration of the relationship between creation and salvation. The particular salvation mediated by Jesus Christ becomes resituated in a broader and pluralistic context.

It is clear that these developments are beginning to transcend modern soteriology, at least insofar as it may be understood to lay within the parameters represented symbolically by Schleiermacher and Barth. The logic which says that the salvation mediated by Jesus Christ is responsive to the concrete or specific historical evils of human existence leads in the direction of an open-ended soteriology which is intrinsically pluralistic. Let me now turn my attention to the various parallel responses to the formal christological question in the same theological terrain.

CHRISTOLOGY

The narrow christological problem deals with an understanding of the person Jesus Christ, specifically with his status relative to God and human beings. The classical symbol balancing the humanity and divinity of Jesus Christ is the two natures, one person doctrine of Chalcedon. In what follows I wish to illustrate the variety of different approaches to under-

---

40. John Hick, *The Metaphor of God Incarnate* (Louisville: Westminster / John Knox, 1993), 136.

standing the person of Jesus Christ that are in many respects contained within the parameters of Schleiermacher and Barth.

Pannenberg describes his conception of how God is in Jesus as a "revelational presence." The position is inspired by Karl Barth. Pannenberg's explanation of it centers on the resurrection of Jesus and unfolds on two levels. First, as it were epistemologically, he holds that God is ultimately revealed in Jesus in the resurrection, and revealed precisely as the One who bestows life. But with a concept of revelation in which revelation is self-presence and self-gift, such a revelation entails the essential unity of the revealer and the revealed. Jesus belongs to the definition of God and thus shares in God's divinity. On a second level, also beginning with the resurrection, Pannenberg meditates on how the resurrection of Jesus entails that Jesus was always or eternally of the essence of the Godhead. He explains how "the resurrected Lord's essential unity with God leads to the idea of preexistence through its own intrinsic logic."[41] Thus Pannenberg presents a high and in this sense classical christology while at the same time subjecting the person and nature language of the classical councils to strong negative criticism.

Moltmann is another evangelical theologian with a high christology who virtually bypasses conciliar doctrine as contributing no light at all on the person of Jesus Christ. He develops his christology on two parallel tracks: as a narrative theologian he develops a thoroughgoing Spirit christology; as a cosmic theologian he exploits wisdom language. Moltmann begins the history of Jesus with God as Spirit. "Jesus' history as the Christ does not begin with Jesus himself. It begins with the *ruach*/the Holy Spirit."[42] The efficacy of God as Spirit is the "first facet" of the mystery of Jesus. Moltmann finds no antithesis between a Spirit christology and incarnation, between an adoption christology and a pre-existence christology. Spirit language is simply the dominant way of talking about Jesus' relation to God. Moltmann presupposes a trinitarian God and writes from within the framework of traditional Christian language. When he takes up the theme of Jesus Christ relative to the cosmos, he exploits another line of biblical symbols. Jesus Christ is identified with pre-existent Wisdom, and as such Christ is the ground of the original creation of all things, and the moving power of the continual evolution of reality, and the redeeming power of a new creation.[43] Moltmann does not systematically synthesize these languages.

In contrast to Moltmann, Tillich defends the classical christological doctrines as defining and protecting the substance of christology: the humanity and the divinity of Jesus Christ. At the same time Tillich is critical of two-natures language as inadequate: it is static and ultimately leads to

41. Pannenberg, *Jesus—God and Man*, 153–54.
42. Moltmann, *The Way of Jesus Christ*, 73.
43. Moltmann, *The Way of Jesus Christ*, 286.

internal contradictions. In order to protect the dynamic union between humanity and divinity in Jesus Christ, Tillich proposes a thoroughgoing Spirit christology. "Though subject to individual and social conditions his human spirit was entirely grasped by the Spiritual Presence; his spirit was 'possessed' by the divine Spirit or, to use another figure, 'God was in him.' This makes him the Christ, the decisive embodiment of the New Being for historical mankind."[44] Geoffrey Lampe, representing an Anglican tradition, also presents a thoroughgoing Spirit christology and Donald Baillie provides a theological rationale for this move.[45]

The transcendental christology of Karl Rahner contains far too many facets to be characterized briefly. It is both a function of his method and of multiple probes from different points of view over a long career. For example, he can propose an analysis of the proposition that "God became man" which investigates each of the three terms in a fashion parallel to Barth. This is pure christology from above, a classical descending christology. And yet Rahner's christology also employs a transcendental analysis that seeks to establish an a priori, coherent, and intelligible basis for understanding Christ with reference to the structure of common human experience. This is a philosophically mediated christology.[46] One can never lose sight of Rahner's humanism; in contrast to much of Barth's language, Rahner's christology is an apotheosis of human existence. God becoming a human being reveals what human existence is: what God utters into the void in love, the self-expression of God in love, that which would express God's love. "When God wants to be what is not God, man comes to be."[47] This is the depth of the mystery of human being. It is forbidden for human beings to think little of themselves, for then they would be thinking little of God. The mystery of God and human existence are entwined together; christology is anthropology, and through Christ anthropology is theology. Rahner accepts the language of one person and two natures and a hypostatic union, but not without criticism. Despite the classical character of Rahner's christology, he also endorses a christology "from below," proposes strong statements of Jesus's humanity, and encourages critical examination that prohibits a facile use of the communication of idioms. This christology is faithful to the tradition but also genuinely open to new developments. I shall develop Rahner's christology further in Chapter 15.

---

44. Tillich, *Systematic Theology*, 3, 144.

45. G. W. H. Lampe, *God as Spirit* (Oxford: Clarendon Press, 1977); Donald Baillie, *God Was in Christ: An Essay on Incarnation and Atonement* (New York: Charles Scribner's Sons, 1948), 106–32.

46. Rahner, *Foundations*, 212–14. Bruce Marshall, in *Christology in Conflict: The Identity of a Saviour in Rahner and Barth* (Oxford: Basil Blackwell, 1987), contrasts this apologetic approach of Rahner with the fideism of Barth regarding Jesus' particular role in mediating a universal salvation.

47. Rahner, *Foundations*, 225.

Narrative christologies may or may not entertain the narrow christo-logical question in explicit and formal terms. We have seen the example of Moltmann's narrative christology where he takes up a New Testament Spirit christology. By contrast Hans Küng uses the language of Jesus being God's representative, but without a deeper analysis of the ontology implied in such a phrase.[48] Schillebeeckx, using the language of God's Word, appended a brief reflection on the status of Jesus to his narrative portrayal of Jesus, but it seems out of place.[49] Although Schillebeeckx explicitly holds the divinity of Jesus Christ, his narrative christology implicitly raises the question of whether it is necessary to treat the chris-tological question as a formal and metaphysical issue, or even whether it is possible. Is it sufficient for an adequate christology to develop a concept of salvation as encounter and discipleship without posing further ques-tions about Jesus' status as some narrative and existential christologies seem to do?

Liberation christologies tend to be narrative christologies, with an emphasis on the human character of Jesus, because they make strong appeal to ethical commitment and discipleship. They may or may not develop the formal christological question in depth or at length. Shailer Mathews proposed a thoroughgoing Spirit christology: the divinity of Jesus Christ is accounted for by God as Spirit resident within him.[50] Jon Sobrino has addressed the divinity of Jesus Christ both in functional terms as the way to the Father and in the more metaphysical symbols of the tra-dition.[51] Juan Luis Segundo accepts the language of Chalcedon but inter-prets it dynamically to represent how Jesus reveals God.[52] Liberation christology, therefore, in no way rules out either formal considerations of the narrow christological problem or the proposal of a high christology.

John Cobb sets forth a process christology in the metaphysical cate-gories of Whitehead. His thesis is simple enough in the enunciation. The Logos as a divine principle of being is incarnate in all creation and thus in every human being. Jesus, however, must be a unique case. "In the fullest incarnation of the Logos, its presence must constitute not only a necessary aspect of existence but the self as such." "In Jesus there is a distinctive incarnation because his very selfhood was constituted by the Logos."[53]

48. Hans Küng, *On Being a Christian* (Garden City, N.Y.: Doubleday, 1976), 444–50.

49. See Schillebeeckx, *Jesus*, 652–69. Schillebeeckx says that the addition of this sec-tion was an afterthought. Edward Schillebeeckx, *Interim Report on the Books Jesus & Christ* (New York: Crossroad, 1981), 97ff.

50. Shailer Mathews, *The Gospel and the Modern Man* (New York: Macmillan, 1910), 109–39.

51. Sobrino, *Christology at the Crossroads* (Maryknoll, N.Y.: Orbis Books, 1978), 338–40; *Jesus in Latin America* (Maryknoll, N.Y.: Orbis Books, 1987), 3–54.

52. Juan Luis Segundo, *The Christ of the Ignatian Exercises* (Maryknoll, N.Y.: Orbis Books, 1987), 11–40. Segundo also has a developed narrative christology represented by *The Historical Jesus of the Synoptics* (Maryknoll, N.Y.: Orbis Books, 1985).

53. Cobb, *Christ in a Pluralistic Age*, 138, 139.

This is supported by an explanation that bypasses categories of substance. The Logos, which represents metaphysically God's aim and the optimum path for the future, is present to Jesus in such a way that God coconstitutes Jesus' selfhood in the dynamics of his existing; the Logos is identical with the center of being that constitutes Jesus' self. Jesus' human freedom is not diminished but enhanced by God's presence. With this metaphysical language and within the framework of process thought, Cobb satisfies the exigencies of orthodoxy, that is, ensuring the integral humanity and divinity of Jesus.

Attention to the exigencies of religious pluralism and the imperative of dialogue has had a variety of effects upon christology. In the case of John Hick the effect has been a diminishment of the traditional claims of christology. He adopts a thoroughgoing Spirit christology to explain the divinity of Jesus. But instead of this representing a strong christological understanding equivalent to incarnation, Hick is so concerned with transcending particular claims to accommodate all religions that incarnation and God's presence as Spirit in Jesus are reduced to a weak metaphorical sense.[54] Yet other christologies combine positive affirmations about the autonomous significance of other religious mediations with loftier christological formulations. John Cobb, Schubert Ogden, and Paul Knitter are examples of such christologies.[55]

In sum, one must conclude that the exigencies of historical consciousness, of process, of liberation, of religious pluralism, of a new cosmic consciousness have not changed the christological problematic of holding a tension between the humanity and the divinity of Jesus Christ. But at the same time these problem areas have introduced new contexts for thinking, new languages for analysis, and new frameworks for understanding. This is seen most clearly at two precise points: the distinct discussions of the Jesus of history and the relation of Jesus to symbolic mediators in other religions. The first discussion tends to fix the imagination on a thoroughly human Jesus; the second discussion opens up the horizon of understanding and relativizes the context of interpretation. These discussions together so reinforce a historical consciousness that christology beginning from above has become highly problematic. As christology addresses the traditional narrow christological problem, it seems to have transcended in this respect the modernity which obtained in the middle of the twentieth century.

---

54. Hick, *The Metaphor of God Incarnate*, 99–111.

55. Among Cobb's many essays on christological pluralism, see for example "The Meaning of Pluralism for Christian Self-Understanding," *Religious Pluralism*, ed. by Leroy S. Rounder (Notre Dame, Ind.: Notre Dame University Press, 1984), 161–79 and "Christian Witness in a Plural World," *The Experience of Religious Diversity*, ed. by John Hick and Hasen Askari (Brookfield, Ver.: Gower, 1985), 144–62; Schubert M. Ogden, *Is There Only One True Religion or Are There Many* (Dallas: Southern Methodist University Press, 1992); Paul Knitter, *One Earth Many Religions: Multifaith Dialogue & Global Responsibility* (Maryknoll, N.Y.: Orbis Books, 1995) and *Jesus and the Other Names: Christian Mission and Global Responsibility* (Maryknoll, N.Y.: Orbis Books, 1996).

TRINITY

The doctrine of the immanent trinity is wholly derivative from christology; it is unintelligible apart from a christological development that simultaneously entailed reflection on God. I will develop this further in Chapter 16. But once the doctrine of the trinity was established, because it deals with the nature of God, it tended to function as a premise for christological thinking. When this occurs, the genetic structure of christology is reversed; in its place is a holistic symbol system in which christology emerges out of the trinitarian character of God. We have seen in the brief sketch of the christologies of Schleiermacher and Barth that the way the doctrine of the trinity is handled mirrors the structure of a theologian's christology. The chief concern in this brief overview is not with the doctrine of the trinity *per se*, but with the way it relates to christology, for this is another clue for understanding modern christology.

Of the twentieth-century christologies that we have been considering there is a group which either simply presupposes the doctrine of the trinity in their christology or which includes it in their thinking. Moltmann, although he develops his theology of the trinity in a distinct work, seems to presuppose this doctrine even while he sketches a narrative christology from below. As in Barth, so in Pannenberg, the trinity takes a place early in his systematic christology. He endorses the classical doctrine of the trinity in the sense of an internal differentiation in the very life of God. But, on the one hand, he argues to the trinity on the basis of Jesus' resurrection and divinity: since the resurrection entails Jesus' divinity, "then the distinction that Jesus maintained between himself and the Father also belongs to the divinity of God."[56] And, on the other hand, he is severely critical of classical Logos language applied to Jesus Christ; Jesus is not Logos but the revealing Word of God. Rahner too develops his christology within the framework of classical trinitarian doctrine, for his strategy is always to retrieve classical doctrines. But things are never so simple in Rahner. His very influential axiom, that the economic trinity is the immanent trinity, can be seen to reverse a naive descent christology and imply a genetic approach to the trinity. Paul Tillich too argues to the importance of the immanent trinity, to an internal differentiation in the single life of God, because a living, dynamic God cannot be conceived without such differentiation. He is critical of Schleiermacher for his modalism, but also of Barth for beginning his theology with this doctrine.[57]

John Cobb is a kind of bridge figure to the next group of theologians. He has a doctrine of the trinity, but he is severely critical of the doctrine in place. The church went wrong when it used the term "person" or "hypostasis" for each of the three in the trinity. This forced a parallel metaphysical conceptuality for each of the three "persons" that does not cor-

---

56. Pannenberg, *Jesus—God and Man*, 159.
57. Tillich, *Systematic Theology*, 3, 283–94.

respond to the bible. The New Testament asserts a precedence to the Father, and in worship this precedence is obscured by the metaphysical doctrine. But Cobb agrees with the substantial underpinning of the doctrine, namely, that the Son and the Spirit are of God. Cobb manipulates the language in such a way that, although his usage is distinctive, it corresponds to the point of the doctrine.

Christology in the second half of the twentieth century has moved away from christology from above, away from placing a doctrine or theology of the trinity at the source of christology. Jesus research and narrative christology, liberation, political, feminist, and inculturated christologies, and christologies in the face of religious pluralism have all tended toward a historical and genetic understanding of Jesus Christ. This does not mean that there has been no liberationist or feminist work on the trinity;[58] nor that one cannot address the theology of religions from a Christian trinitarian perspective.[59] It simply means that, in responding to the problems with which they are concerned, these movements also reflect a gradual internalization of a postmodern consciousness of historicity and pluralism.

CHRISTOLOGY IN AN INCREASINGLY POSTMODERN CONTEXT

The aim of this chapter is to provide a more extensive reflection on the present situation of christology than was presented in Chapter 1. The analysis of the discipline in terms of representative authors and the problems they are addressing has shown that christology is beginning to transcend the boundaries of modern christology. Our western intellectual culture is increasingly being called postmodern. To conclude the chapter I want to characterize this postmodernity as it is reflected in christology, and in terms of the correlative challenges and opportunities it presents to this discipline.

I understand postmodernity from two perspectives, one material and the other formal. From one perspective, the term refers to the actual world in which people of developed western societies live.[60] The point of this

---

58. For example, Leonardo Boff, *Trinity and Society* (Maryknoll, N.Y.: Orbis Books, 1988); Elizabeth A. Johnson, *She Who Is: The Mystery of God in Feminist Theological Discourse* (New York: Crossroad, 1992).

59. Raimon Panikkar, *The Unknown Christ of Hinduism: Towards an Ecumenical Christophany* (Maryknoll, N.Y.: Orbis Books, 1981), 31–61; Gavin D'Costa, "Christ, Trinity, and Religious Plurality," *Christian Uniqueness Reconsidered* (Maryknoll, N.Y.: Orbis Books, 1990), 16–29, and "Toward a Trinitarian Theology of Religions," *A Universal Faith?* ed. by C. Cornille and V. Neckebrouck (Louvain: Peeters Press, 1992), 139–54; Jacques Dupuis, *Toward a Christian Theology of Religious Pluralism* (Maryknoll, N.Y.: Orbis Books, 1997), 280–329.

60. Stanley J. Grenz, *A Primer on Postmodernism* (Grand Rapids: Eerdmans, 1996) and Paul Lakeland, *Postmodernity: Christian Identity in a Fragmented Age* (Minneapolis:

purely material definition is to ensure that, in the characterizations of post-modernity which follow, the imagination remains rooted in present-day experience. Postmodernity often refers to intellectual theory or intellectual culture, a set of premises in guiding various intellectual disciplines and interpretive theories. But postmodernity also refers to the forms of life which influence and are the effects of intellectual thought. Thus I use the term "postmodernity" in this work to refer to aspects of the fragmented cultures that more and more characterize advanced industrialized societies and to the understandings of reality, sometimes quite theoretical and sometimes implicit, that are attendant upon contemporary life.[61]

Lakeland shows that there are a variety of valuations of postmodernity, as 1) radically new, 2) the continuation of modernity and hence not dramatically different from it, and 3) nostalgic and premodern or counter-modern, that is, as a resource for ideas and values in a conservative reaction against modernity.[62] As a culture, however, postmodernity may be characterized without valuation, as neither good nor bad, but as a given. I shall not analyze postmodernity at its extremes of complete relativism and denial of transcendent or universally relevant truth. Christology *per se* does not address these positions. I am more interested in the way postmodernity as a culture exists inside the church insofar as Christians live in secular society and share postmodern sentiments and ideas. What follows, therefore, is less an objective analysis of postmodernity, and more a definition of how this cultural constellation underlies the problems which occupy current christology. The description itself is generated partly through the discipline of christology insofar as it has been responding to contemporary culture. But I also wish briefly to indicate how this situation is not only threatening, but offers new and positive possibilities for christology.[63] In order to provide a short, material, working concept of postmodern consciousness, I characterize it somewhat arbitrarily in four themes.

First, postmodernity involves a radical historical consciousness. Gone is the confidence in progress, goals toward which history is heading, a *telos* that provides a destiny and gives a meaning to movement. The twentieth century, moreover, has added to this sense of the sheer contingency of history a new sense of evil and collective human sin: it has been a century of war and human destructiveness. Under the lightness of much western cultural behavior social psychologists may find a deep pessimism. Adrift in history, after the holocaust, it is difficult to assign a concrete meaning to

---

Fortress Press, 1997) both describe postmodernity at various levels, the most basic being a subculture, an intellectual mood, a constellation of cultural ideas and values that find expression in a variety of forms of life.

61. Lakeland, *Postmodernity*, 1–8.

62. Lakeland, *Postmodernity*, 16–18.

63. Terrence W. Tilley's *Postmodern Theologies: The Challenge of Religious Diversity* (Maryknoll, N.Y.: Orbis Books, 1995) is an example of just such a constructive examination of theology in a postmodern context.

divine providence. History is really open, and human beings as a group have the capacity, and it now seems the tendency, to destroy human history itself. This historical consciousness is convertible with the relativity of the ideas and values one takes for granted. David Tracy refers to this at its extreme in the terms of Nietzsche as "the abyss of indeterminacy."[64] All knowledge is local. The laws and political structures of society are not based on a universally valid knowledge of reality, but on particular cultural appraisal in the light of practical exigencies.[65] In the end, this sheer openness threatens ontic security by depriving one of a basic stability of meaning. In christology a return to the historical Jesus is a sign of historical consciousness, but not of a radical kind. Radical historical consciousness begins when one recognizes how deeply the meaning of Jesus Christ has changed when he is reinterpreted in different epochs and cultures, and why such change is necessary. On the positive side, however, a radical sense of historicity provides the possibility and an opportunity for the creation of new meaning, not out of nothing, but of Jesus Christ. It seems clear that postmodernity demands new interpretations of Jesus of Nazareth.

Second, postmodernity involves a critical social consciousness. This social consciousness is analyzed in a benign way by the sociology of knowledge. The linguistic structure of all thought implies more deeply the social mediation of knowledge. A more radically pessimistic view is proffered by social analysts who find that society is driven by little more than the interests of power, or class, or gender, or greed. This side of postmodernity threatens a loss of the human subject, of the person, who is reduced to a function of impersonal forces. One of the marks of modernity is the turn to the subject, to universal and critical reason, as the foundation of truth. Now the human subject appears to be a function of history, of social arrangements, of unconscious psychological forces, precisely not a transcendental clearing house of truth.[66] The various socially mediated christologies are both a recognition of the fundamental sociality of human existence and a reaction against any reductionism. These christologies recognize that social structures, from linguistic structures to institutions of slavery, are ultimately functions of human interest and freedom, and they can be changed. The dramatic negative experiences of social oppression and annihilation of this century, precisely in their negativity, mediate encounters with transcendent values. By this negative logic, the poor and the oppressed open up the possibility of human freedom, responsibility, resistance, in the name of justice which, by definition, is universally relevant.[67] Liberation christologies are a reassertion

---

64. Tracy, *On Naming the Present*, 16.

65. Thomas Docherty, *Postmodernism: A Reader* (New York: Columbia University Press, 1993), 36.

66. Lakeland, *Postmodernity*, 18–24.

67. Tracy, *On Naming the Present*, 136; Richard J. Bernstein, "Serious Play: The Ethical-Political Horizon of Derrida," *The New Constellation: The Ethical-Political Horizons of Modernity / Postmodernity* (Cambridge, Mass.: The M. I. T. Press, 1992), 191.

of human subjectivity and freedom, but a personal human subject-with-others, a freedom in society, and the sociality of human existence. Socially conscious christologies unfold within a postmodern context and interpret Jesus Christ as standing for a human imperative to exercise corporate responsibility in the creation of just social structures.

Third, postmodernity involves a pluralist consciousness. At no other time have people had such a sense of the difference of others, of the pluralism of societies, cultures, and religions, and of the relativity that this entails. One can no longer claim western culture as the center, the higher point of view, or Christianity as the superior religion, or Christ as the absolute center to which all other historical mediations are relative. The world is pluralistic and polycentric in its horizons of interpretation.[68] This pluralist and relativist consciousness seems to be yet another attack on universal values and shared truth. A reflection of it is found in young people who are unable to define any absolute or universal values; all is reduced to opinion; every opinion must in principle be tolerated. Pluralism spells the loss of any special group identity, any overarching story that provides a privileged place in history to one people. Now peoples and whole nations appear to be reduced to functions of the forces of history. It is impossible in postmodern culture to think that one group of people is a chosen people. Or that one religion can claim to inhabit the center into which all others are to be drawn. These myths or metanarratives are simply gone. Pluralism means the loss of an overarching framework that encompasses the frameworks of others. This loss leaves a vacuum which is deeply threatening, for the group provides a major source of the identity of persons. Christology lies at the heart of the theology of religions and religious pluralism. In addressing this issue christology also finds itself at the heart of postmodernity. No other issue in christology is as vital; no other will have a deeper effect on christological consciousness. But postmodernity provides an opportunity for dramatic new christological meaning. The discovery of pluralism is precisely a discovery of the "other," other peoples who are different and valuable, but who are excluded or suppressed by the grand narratives. Can one interpret Jesus Christ as precisely God's story which is so open to others that it does not coopt their specific identity and does not privilege Christians over against them? Can christology represent a Jesus Christ who is not divisive, but who authorizes the other *as other*, and hence functions as a principle of unity that respects differences? Here postmodernity seems to offer the occasion for a new and deeper penetration into the meaning of Jesus Christ that genuinely transcends the past.

Finally, postmodernity involves a cosmic consciousness. One way of understanding the shift from modernity to postmodernity is through an analysis of science, especially the epistemology of science, its changes and developments, its foundational paradigms and concepts, and the content

---

68. Tracy, *On Naming the Present*, 4, 136–39.

of the worldview it presently lays before us.[69] Astronomy and the physical sciences have transformed the picture of the cosmos and of the place of our galaxy and planet in it. It is no longer possible without the help of mathematical formulas to imagine the size and the age of created reality. If it is not impossible, it is at least difficult and requires a great deal of nuance to imagine that the human species is the center of things. Naive anthropocentrism is dead. The new concern for our own planet has helped in the internalization of this cosmic consciousness. This new expanded consciousness has to become operative in thinking about ultimate realities such as God and the relation between God and human existence. Soteriology will be placed against the background of creation in a new way.[70] One cannot operate with a language that tacitly presumes an Aristotelian universe. This facet of postmodern consciousness, while it relativizes humanity within the universe, at the same time provides a genuinely new perspective upon the unity of the human race and human solidarity. We constitute a common humanity on this planet, indeed, a community, despite all the differences in religion and culture. We need a christology that will confirm the importance of a common humanity, a human community in a common habitat, and a shared process of nature of which all are a part, and at the same time respects human differences in this postmodern world.

The postmodern situation of christology should act as the lure to create new construals of Jesus Christ that meet the temper of our time. The christology which follows will hardly meet the challenge laid down by postmodernity. This can only be realized by a long-term and corporate effort. This constructive and interpretive essay is meant to be a voice in this conversation. It is divided into the following five chapters which roughly correspond to problem areas actively being addressed in christology. These are 1) a consideration of salvation, 2) an analysis of liberation christologies, of social salvation, and spirituality in the light of liberation christology, 3) an estimate of how Jesus Christ may be regarded by Christians in the light of religious pluralism, 4) an interpretation of the divinity of Jesus Christ in the light of Christian spirituality and the exigencies of religious pluralism, and 5) an interpretation of the point of trinitarian doctrine as a function of christology and a concise summary of the economy of Christian salvation.

---

69. James B. Miller, in "The Emerging Postmodern World," in *Postmodern Theology: Christian Faith in a Pluralistic World*, ed. by Frederic B. Burnham (San Francisco: Harper & Row, 1989), 1–19, traces the rise of postmodernity in terms of science.

70. See, for example, Edwards, *Jesus the Wisdom of God*.

CHAPTER 12

Jesus as Savior

The term "salvation" refers to the most fundamental of all Christian experiences. From a historical perspective, the experience of Jesus as savior provided the basis from which the Christian movement sprang. Christianity arose and continues to exist *because* people experience Jesus as a bringer of God's salvation. Christology, in its narrow construal of defining the status of Jesus before God and human beings, depends upon soteriology. Yet despite this centrality and importance the church has never formulated a conciliar definition of salvation nor provided a universally accepted conception. This is not necessarily a bad situation. It encourages a pluralism of the ways in which salvation is conceptualized. A variety of soteriologies attends to the many aspects of this primal Christian experience. Because of the fullness of the experience of salvation, and the amplitude of its existential reality, no single definition of salvation can confine its meaning. The result is that the meaning of salvation remains elusive: every intentional Christian knows what salvation is until asked to explain it.

The problems that surround the concept of salvation are rendered more grave because of its centrality. Many of the traditional expressions of how Jesus saves resemble myths that no longer communicate to educated Christians; some are even offensive. Many of the traditional theological "explanations" of salvation through Christ do no better. Often treatments of salvation are devoted to rehearsing traditional theories or presenting models or types which seem to inject some order in the disarray.[1] But one cannot assume that the traditional language sounds credible today; it may function as an obstacle to faith, and too little attention is given to critical

---

1. See Chapter 8, note 2 for references to some typologies of salvation theories. Other studies in contemporary soteriology include Gabriel Daly, *Creation and Redemption* (Wilmington: Glazier, 1988); F. W. Dillistone, *The Christian Understanding of Atonement* (Philadelphia: Westminster Press, 1968); Sebastian Moore, *The Crucified Jesus Is No Stranger* (New York: Seabury Press, 1981); Norman Pittenger, *Freed to Love: A Process Interpretation of Redemption* (Wilton, Conn.: Morehouse-Barlow, 1987).

reinterpretation of it.[2] Given the pluralism of conceptions, is there a way systematically to establish a center of gravity on the salvation mediated by Jesus that will be clear and definite but open and not exclusive? In the face of the confusion about the nature of salvation, can one formulate today's questions and crises to which Jesus mediates a salvific answer? Given the incredibility of the mythological language when it is read at face value, can one find a symbolic formulation of this doctrine that is intelligible and closer to actual human experience?

This chapter will attempt to give a constructive account of salvation as it is mediated by Jesus Christ. I use the term "salvation" as distinct from "redemption" and "atonement" because salvation carries a more general and neutral meaning. The notion of "redemption" is too closely tied to a ransom theory of salvation; that of "atonement" strongly suggests Anselm's theory of satisfaction or the reformers' emphasis on the suffering and death of Jesus. These themes are not to be ruled out, however, and one should recognize that "salvation" too is a historically conditioned metaphor, not without its own inner trajectories. But the goal of this chapter is to interpret and not presume its meaning. Salvation has both an objective and a subjective dimension and sense. By objective salvation I mean the work of Jesus Christ, that is, that which Jesus Christ did and which had, and has, the effect of human salvation. By subjective salvation I mean the appropriation of this salvific effect by human beings.[3] The next chapter will develop subjective salvation.

The chapter is divided into four sections. A good deal of groundwork has already been laid for a systematic interpretation of salvation in previous chapters, and part of the task here will be to recapitulate that material and relate it to the task at hand. In the first part, therefore, I will simply state some of the hermeneutical principles or premises which are operative in this chapter. The second will synopsize some of the data from the tradition that was laid out earlier. Section three will survey themes from modern soteriology that will find a place in the present interpretation. And, finally, the fourth part will propose an interpretation of the objective saving work of Jesus Christ.

---

2. Some critical and constructive studies on redemption theory are Francis Schüssler Fiorenza, "Critical Social Theory and Christology: Toward an Understanding of Atonement and Redemption as Emancipatory Solidarity," *Proceedings of the Catholic Theological Society of America*, 30 (1975), 63–110; Michael Root, "The Narrative Structure of Soteriology," *Modern Theology*, 2 (1986), 145–58; Elizabeth A. Johnson, "Jesus and Salvation," *Proceedings of the Catholic Theological Society of America*, 49 (1994), 1–18. For a brief account of current soteriology in the evangelical tradition, see Millard J. Erikson, "Evangelical Christology and Soteriology Today," *Interpretation*, 49 (1995), 255–66.

3. See Paul Tillich, *Systematic Theology*, 2 (Chicago: University of Chicago Press, 1957), 170.

FOUNDATIONS FOR A POSTMODERN SOTERIOLOGY

Foundations refers to the premises and presuppositions that form the framework within which this systematic and constructive theory of salvation is presented. Most if not all of these premises have been alluded to or developed along the way in the chapters on method, Jesus, the structure of christology, and classical soteriology. The point here is not to develop these principles further, but to gather them together and briefly to present them as constituting the framework for a soteriology that correlates with postmodern culture.

A first premise for this constructive soteriology was developed in the opening chapters on method and has been repeated with insistence. Jesus of Nazareth is the historical source of Christianity and the focus of the Christian act of faith. A general historical consciousness and the demand today for an apologetic method in theology force the imagination of the theologian to return to the Jesus of history. Only a reactionary and fearful flight from culture will translate this historical consciousness into a sectarian confessionalism that will not enter into dialogue with other witnesses to common human experience.

One can say that the experience of salvation in and through Jesus of Nazareth is the basis of Christianity itself. This way of putting it brings out the elemental or primal character of the term "salvation." Salvation refers to the effect of power for making whole and well that which is negative, corrosive, and damaging to human existence, all the way to death or extinction. Such power on the level of being itself can only be God's power. Thus Tillich speaks of salvation as New Being, or the power that overcomes being that is sick and estranged. Christian faith finds its object in God, the ground of being, mediated by Jesus. But God in Jewish and Christian traditions is Savior. And the faith in God of a Christian is a response to the experience that Jesus mediates God's salvation. The religious question of the origin, purpose, and destiny of human existence is synonymous with the question of salvation. And religious faith consists in being addressed by a salvific answer to the religious question and responding to it.

The symbolic structure of soteriology and christology is already implied in this brief description of a historicist approach to salvation. This symbolic structure of christology was developed at length in Chapter 7. It is important to see that the language of symbol is descriptive of the human event of finding salvation in Jesus Christ. To call Jesus a symbol of God does not entail shifting the structure of christology away from the narrative of salvation. It should rather be seen as capturing in the idea of symbol the dynamic process of coming to a faith that is salvific. The event of encountering salvation is dialectical. On the one hand, one encounters God and God's salvation in *Jesus*, the historical figure. Jesus was an integral human being, a person who lived in history, and who has become the object of historical inquiry, which one does not need faith to pursue. Jesus is available to all. On the other hand, this salvation is an encounter with *God* in Jesus. It is an axiom that only God can save with the ultimate or transcendent salvation with which we are dealing. To experience salvation in Jesus of Nazareth is to encounter God. On the one hand, then, Jesus stands over against God as creature; Jesus is precisely not God but the medium for the encounter with God. On the other hand, that which is encountered in Jesus is God. Thus Jesus makes God present in a saving way, so that it is no less than God with whom we are confronted in Jesus.

One can thus define Christian salvation simply as the encounter with God in Jesus of Nazareth. Christian salvation is no more and no less than the meeting with God in Jesus the Christ. One has, as it were, the kernel of the Christian experience in the following short formula: Jesus makes God present in a saving way. Soteriology may thus be understood as the interpretation of the content of this foundational experience, the interpretation and analysis of the many facets of how Jesus mediates God's saving presence, and thus how he is savior.

This genetic, historical approach from below to Jesus Christ savior implies that the Jesus of history plays a major role in interpreting how Jesus Christ is savior. One way is that, despite all the subtleties and ambiguities of the quest for the historical Jesus, historical consciousness is such that every understanding of how Jesus is savior must be bound to an imaginative construal of Jesus of Nazareth. This does not mean that one has to have accurate and detailed historical knowledge of Jesus of Nazareth in order to encounter God in him or understand how he is savior. Rather, the point is that one must satisfy the demand of historical plausibility in one's construal of the salvific work of Jesus Christ. Salvation is mediated through Jesus, the historical, terrestrial figure apart from whom we know nothing about him as Christ.[4] The salvific character of Jesus' action then must be found precisely in his historical action, his this-worldly comportment. It cannot be understood by projecting actions and behaviors of Jesus outside this world about which in principle we know nothing.

This last point is illustrated in a negative way by some of the considerations of Karl Barth and Jürgen Moltmann. At certain stages of their reflections on Jesus Christ and the salvation he mediates, they turn to the historical narrative about Jesus. In so doing they implicitly recognize that Jesus of Nazareth was a historical person and event in whom God was encountered, and that this encounter was where Christianity began historically. And yet when they describe the actions of this historical person, Jesus, they do so not in critical historical language, but in dogmatic lan-

---

4. Or one could say more strongly, apart from whom there is no Christ, for "Christ" is precisely a title and name used to interpret Jesus of Nazareth. There is no Jewish tradition of a pre-existent messiah.

guage that has drifted away from its historical moorings.[5] The result is a kind of hybrid language of history, doctrine, and myth that robs the confession that Jesus is savior of its credibility for a historically sensitive audience. All human contact with God is historically mediated, that is, through finite things of this world. The dialectical understanding of the historical symbol cannot be collapsed. But this means that Christian salvation must always be understood within the framework of a historical construal of Jesus of Nazareth. To be credible, this must be mediated by a critical understanding of the historical Jesus.

An adequate theology of salvation should include a rereading of Jesus' ministry with attention to how he addressed human suffering. It should attend to classical beliefs of the community. These initial reflections bring together some of the analyses of the earlier parts of this book in relation to salvation.

THE TRADITION

I have already examined a good deal of material concerning salvation. Chapter 4 analyzed Jesus' representation of God; Chapter 5 analyzed the disciples' experience of Jesus exalted and risen; Chapter 6 considered several of the soteriologies contained in the New Testament interpretation of Jesus; and Chapter 8 analyzed and interpreted a number of the classic salvation theories from the tradition of theology. In the section which follows I shall draw some further insights on how salvation might be construed today from modern theologians. But before doing so it will be useful to recapitulate in an abbreviated synopsis the material drawn from the tradition. This is presented here within the framework that stipulates, first, that the idea of salvation arises out of the experience of negativity and means a restoration of wholeness that only God can provide. Second, an understanding of Christian salvation mediated through Jesus Christ must bear a relation to the Jesus of history. Third, the general formula of how Jesus saves is that he makes God present in a saving way. The question which will occupy the rest of this chapter concerns an understanding of exactly how Jesus does this.

JESUS

Historical consideration of Jesus and how Jesus represented God provides data for an answer to this question. Jesus portrayed God and taught about God in sayings and parables, and in his representing God through

---

5. See, for example, Karl Barth's account of Jesus being judge and then judged in *Church Dogmatics*, IV, 1 (Edinburgh: T. & T. Clark, 1975), 224–28, and Jürgen Moltmann's account of Jesus' baptism in *The Way of Jesus Christ* (Minneapolis: Fortress Press, 1993), 87–94.

his mission, action, and general comportment. The God of Jesus is personal; God interacts with human beings. God is transcendent, infinitely beyond what can be named in this world. God is a loving God and this love shows itself in the idea that God is savior; that is, God acts in the interest of the wholeness of human beings. This God too is just and judges in the name of justice precisely because God is loving savior. This picture of God, it turns out, is not substantially different from God in the Jewish tradition which communicated it to Jesus.

A second important aspect of Jesus' representation of God, and something that historians frequently point out, is that Jesus' mission of the kingdom of God and his action conform to his teaching. This means that Jesus did not merely teach about God as one would objectively point to something absent, or distant and neutral. Judging from the earliest witness to Jesus, it appears that the message he preached correlated with his actions. Jesus represented God through his healings and exorcisms and hospitality. This correspondence between the person's teaching and his actions enables one to view Jesus himself as a kind of parable of God. It also provides a historical reference for the ideas of mediation and embodiment of God's salvific power.

These two points sum up the saving work of Jesus in history. But they do so abstractly and schematically. For this reason it is always important to recall the role of history in this understanding. Jesus was a historical figure; the two shorthand reflections point to a historical career, a story in which Jesus encountered people. The abstract characterization always refers back to Jesus' ministry and must, therefore, be supplemented by a historical imagination.

NEW TESTAMENT SOTERIOLOGY

On the premise that soteriology and christology are reciprocally related in such a way that they entail each other, the five New Testament christologies analyzed in Chapter 6 implicitly contain soteriologies. These were Paul's "final Adam," Mark's "Son of God," Luke's "Spirit" christology, the "wisdom" christology that is spread out through the New Testament, and John's "Logos" christology as it appears in the Prologue to this gospel. The interpretation of these soteriologies is based on the premise that there is a close bond between the person and activity of Jesus. This means that people interpreted who Jesus was on the basis of what he did; christology is dependent upon soteriology. This is born out in each of these cases.

In Paul's view, as this is contained in the metaphor of the final Adam, Jesus saves humankind by being obedient. This is the central contrast with Adam. And with his obedience, and an impact on people that attracted disciples, Jesus begins a new current within history, the new, restored humankind that lives according to God's will. This is a large, comprehensive vision of the work of Jesus Christ. Salvation is the salvation of humankind itself, of human history, by launching a new beginning. This was accomplished by a life of fidelity to God's cause, especially through his suffering and death. But it is not suffering in itself that is salvific, but Jesus' commitment, obedience, and fidelity through it.

In the soteriology of Mark's Son of God, Jesus is a chosen and anointed agent of God who acts with God's authority. Jesus being the Son of God includes his being the messiah or the Christ. It also includes, through his death and resurrection, his being the Son of Man who will come again in glory. Thus Jesus saves by revealing to his disciples, and to humankind itself, what is in store for humanity. Jesus saves concretely by being the object of faith, and especially of hope for the future. In this vision final salvation is out in front of human existence; it lies in the future.

In Luke's soteriology a certain emphasis is given to the empowerment of Jesus by God as Spirit. Jesus is not only anointed by the Spirit at his baptism, Jesus' very coming into being was through the influence of God as Spirit. And the Spirit is the consistent power of God that works in and through Jesus for salvation. Because salvation in Luke's view is not just a final state of wholeness, salvation also consists in the concrete works of Jesus' historical career. His physical curing and his exorcisms are part of the power of God as Spirit's salvation at work in Jesus' historical life. One could interpret Luke as implying that God's salvific power in the Spirit is at work wherever there is restorative, recreative, and humanizing effects. Jesus shows by his actions that this occurs not by Satan's but by God's power.

I tried to show by analysis that the wisdom christologies in the New Testament were not really christologies from above, but christologies based on soteriologies, and thus generated epistemologically from below. They find their root in the experience that Jesus taught, revealed, and embodied divine wisdom. These personifications of God's wisdom and metaphorical identification of Jesus with God's Wisdom have their source in a revelational soteriology in which Jesus not only reveals God, but is also the exemplar of human existence.

The Logos christology of the Prologue of John's gospel is also a wisdom christology, but its simple, dramatic, and exalted language sets it apart. The pattern of a hypostatized or individualized Wisdom figure, an intermediary divine agent of Yahweh or "the" God or the Father, who descends and then returns to God's sphere, is cosmic in scope. Yet it too must be seen as having as its genetic referent Jesus of Nazareth; he is behind this hymnic and worshipful poetic language. In the end, epistemologically, even this Logos christology ascends from the experience of God's salvation in Jesus. Jesus saves by revealing and embodying God as Wisdom, that is, making it appear as real in the flesh.

These are different views of salvation, to be sure. But, once again, they all refer to Jesus and his mediating or making present God's salvation by what he did during his public ministry.

CLASSICAL SOTERIOLOGY

In Chapter 8 I proposed first a historical interpretation of various eastern and western salvation theories. Then, within a modern framework of attention to Jesus, and on the premise that these objective theories should be construed as symbolic expressions, I proposed a series of eight propositions that try to capture the experience of salvation that this symbolic language contains and evokes. This is an explicit hermeneutical effort to transform a mythological language that is hardly appreciated today into more direct statements of the ways in which Jesus mediates the experience of salvation. Without going through that whole development, I can synopsize the results of that analysis.

Jesus reveals God, and the God he reveals is the loving creator God who is also savior. All classical authors include this aspect of what Jesus did for our salvation. Some also stress the embodiment of God by Jesus: especially divinization theories emphasize that Jesus makes this God present. The presence of God in and to Jesus means that Jesus represents God. This proposition is crucial for understanding what is going on in much of classical soteriological language. Because Christians encounter God in Jesus, Jesus becomes a representative and bearer of God to the Christian imagination. Jesus' love and concern represents God's love; Jesus' fidelity in his mission through death and into resurrection represents God's commitment to human existence. This logic explains how Christians can see in Jesus' death not only a dramatic act of human fidelity to God, but also God's love for humankind. Symbolically Jesus carries God's fidelity to human existence. And Jesus' resurrection is salvific because it meets human hope with a content that fulfills human existence.

Jesus also reveals human existence. Picking up the theme of the final Adam, Jesus represents a paradigm of human values and goals. This exemplarism is a constant theme in classical soteriology. Jesus appeals to disciples and offers absolute meaning and fulfillment to such a commitment and way of life. But this exemplarism is based on symbolic mediation: "Christ is, first of all, a 'sacrament' (*sacramentum*), only secondly an 'example' (*exemplum*)."[6] All of this must be read within the context of the religious question or the question of salvation. Only those who experience the need and ask the question can grasp God's saving forgiveness and reconciliation manifested in Jesus' ministry, death, and resurrection.

Such a summary of the tradition on salvation is meant to be suggestive. Unfortunately a schematic account automatically flattens out this rich tradition of experience into propositional formulas. No analysis can catch up with the concreteness of these experiences of a saving encounter with God.

---

6. Schubert M. Ogden, *The Point of Christology* (Dallas: Southern Methodist University Press, 1992), 166.

CURRENTS IN MODERN SOTERIOLOGY

Before proposing an understanding of how Jesus saves that may appear credible to a religious sensibility in a postmodern culture, I turn to the modern theology considered in the last chapter. How have the experiences and beliefs about Jesus as savior from the tradition been transformed by modern theologians? What can be learned from modern soteriology? In the last chapter I briefly typified the way in which a variety of different christologies depicted the saving work of Jesus Christ. What follows will not expand the holistic view of any one of these authors. Rather, I will highlight some of the valuable insights found in a number of these authors. This is a way of capitalizing on what can be learned from modern theology without writing a separate volume on modern soteriology. This section will thus serve as a bridge between classical soteriology and the demands of postmodernity.

HISTORICAL IMAGINATION

One of the clear breaks between classical redemption theory and a modern explanation of the salvific work of Jesus Christ lies in a shift from a mythic style of language, describing an objective event of redemption, to the use of more historical language. This shift is found in Schleiermacher's soteriology and represents one of its most significant elements. Many theologians followed his path.

It was mentioned in passing that Schleiermacher wrote a "life" of Jesus; he thus had a historical imagination. He insisted on the historical dimension of Jesus' salvific work. Salvation consists in being conscious of one's union with God. This consciousness cannot come from our own resources, but must come as grace from outside the self.[7] It is ultimately caused by God's self-gift or presence to a person. But specifically Christian salvation is caused by Jesus, and Schleiermacher is careful to delineate this historical causality. Jesus possessed a perfect God-consciousness and sinlessness by virtue of the power of God present to him. Jesus' consciousness of God is communicated to others by virtue of his historical contact with them in such a way that they participate in it. This happened during Jesus' lifetime, and it continues to happen through the historical community which is the church. Salvation continues to be caused in history both by Jesus, in the sense that in terms of content his God-consciousness is being communicated, and by the church, which is the medium of this historical influence. The church as a historical institution is an integral part of Schleiermacher's construal of salvation. Finally, salvation is received by

---

7. Friedrich Schleiermacher, *The Christian Faith* (New York: Harper Torchbooks, 1963), #86, 356.

people being affected by, and drawn into, this historical influence through their own freedom. Jesus influences people "only in accordance with the nature of the free. The activity by which He assumes us into fellowship with Him is, therefore, a creative production in us of the will to assume Him into ourselves. . . ."[8] Christian salvation is a historical influence that appeals to human freedom.

Schleiermacher's language of salvation retains a tension between an empirical-historical dimension and a religious-mystical dimension, or, as he puts it, between the empirical and the magical. On the one hand, Christian salvation is mediated by natural, historical causes, beginning with the concrete influence of the person of Jesus of Nazareth. On the other hand, salvation comes from God, is supernatural in this sense, and comes as grace.[9]

This aspect of Schleiermacher's soteriology provides a number of initial leads for a language of salvation that will be intelligible in postmodern culture. First, it breaks open the mythological symbolism of the classical tradition and retrieves the point of this language in the concrete terms of history: Jesus, disciples, church, conversion, the Christian life, and mission. Salvation is not privatistic but unfolds in and through the community. Second, this salvation language also appeals to human religious experience. Salvation in this world, for this is what Schleiermacher is describing, must be able to be in some measure described phenomenologically. Third, this salvation language preserves the tension between the historical and the mystical, the human mediation and response, as well as the gratuitous, transcendent, and divine character of salvation. Salvation is from God.

SALVATION AS REVELATION

Classical soteriology understood the saving work of Jesus Christ as revelation. This classical thematic was retrieved in the modern period by Karl Barth and other "Word" theologians, and on the Catholic side by theologians such as Karl Rahner.

What becomes clear in these conceptions of Jesus saving by revealing God is that revelation is a deep and intricate symbol. Revelation far surpasses a thin epistemological process of disclosing information, or passing on knowledge, or explaining something. Although revelation includes the idea of "knowledge" of God, it reaches beyond it to the experience of meeting or encountering God. Thus in the conceptions of both Barth and Rahner, revelation is salvation, and salvation is constituted by revelation. This is so because, using Barth's language, Jesus' revealing of God is strictly correlative with Jesus' full divinity. Jesus reveals God because Jesus is the divine Son and Word, because Jesus is God's presence to human

---

8. Schleiermacher, *The Christian Faith*, #100, 426.
9. Schleiermacher, *The Christian Faith*, #100, 430–31.

existence in history. Revelation of this kind already constitutes a reconcil-iation between God and human existence, a restoration of union and fel-lowship with God. Jesus makes present God's self in a second act of love over and above the love of God the creator.[10] Jesus saves because Jesus is God's being for human beings, God's turning in freedom to be with human beings.[11] Barth equates the "what" of revelation, that which is revealed, and God's own self.[12] Jesus is God entering into a personal con-versation, interchange, and communion with human beings. Jesus Christ is God with us and this is salvation.[13] All of these statements find rather close analogies in the theology of Karl Rahner.

These evangelical theologies of the word are not fundamentalistic or literalistic; the concept of revelation is both objective and subjective, and in both cases nuanced. The themes represented here highlight the initia-tive of God in Jesus the revealer, the realism with which Jesus makes God present in history, and how in encountering Jesus one encounters God in him. Although these themes were put forward by Barth in large measure against trends in modern theology, they are not at all necessarily incom-patible with a historical, anthropological, and apologetic strategy, as Rahner's incorporation of them shows.[14] In the concluding section I will show how much of Barth's language, without some of his presuppositions, can be used in a postmodern context.

WHAT JESUS DID FOR OUR SALVATION

What did Jesus do to reveal God and God's salvation? One of the most serious problems for understanding today what Jesus did for human sal-vation is the traditional focus that Christians place on the suffering and death of Jesus. Even more troubling is the positive valuation they place on Jesus' death on a cross. How can the suffering and crucifixion of Jesus be anything but evil? How can the strange and tortuous explanations of how the cross could have been positive and salvific even begin to make any sense to a postmodern imagination?

Jon Sobrino deals with this issue directly by taking up Paul's theology of the cross. He tries to unravel the many problems and misunderstand-ings that any literal construal of the language of sacrifice ordinarily entails. He asks, what could possibly be pleasing to God in the tragic affair of Jesus' painful journey to execution? In his interpretation, Paul's response to this direct question can only be that it was Jesus himself, in his whole

---

10. Barth, CD, I-1, 406–10.
11. Barth, CD, I-2, 1–19.
12. Barth, CD, I-2, 33–35.
13. Barth, CD, IV-1, 3–21.
14. For the degree to which neo-orthodox theology of revelation is also informed by the liberal theology against which it reacted, see Langdon Gilkey, *Naming the Whirlwind: The Renewal of God-Language* (Indianapolis: Bobbs-Merrill, 1969), 82–84.

comportment during this suffering, that was pleasing to God. In other words, Paul does not affirm that it is the pain and suffering that Jesus underwent that produces salvation. According to the New Testament "what was pleasing to God was the whole of Jesus' life—in the words of the Letter to the Hebrews, a life of faithfulness and mercy—and what Jesus' cross highlights . . . is that this is how Jesus' life was."[15] Implicitly Sobrino appeals to Rahner's theology of death, where death is considered an act which sums up and freely disposes the sum total of one's life.[16] In going through his passion to his death Jesus was recapitulating the commitment of a lifetime and sealing it with his death. What was pleasing to God in Jesus' death was not the suffering he underwent, but the person, and precisely the person as that had been constituted by a whole life of choices for the kingdom of God. "Jesus' life as a whole, not one of its elements, is what is pleasing to God."[17] The cross then remains negative when considered in itself. What is positive is Jesus' active fidelity, commitment, and obedience to the end. The cross is the situation and set of events through which the degree of Jesus' commitment is constituted and displayed.

But Sobrino continues to probe: how exactly does this faithfulness of Jesus bear salvation for other human beings? By analysis one can distinguish two distinct responses to this question in the language of the New Testament about Jesus' saving death. The first rests on the conviction that God is at work in Jesus of Nazareth. This presupposition is plainly asserted in the variety of New Testament christologies. Once one enters the arena of meaning that is opened by this conviction, that God is present to and operative in Jesus' life and person, one can begin to understand the logic of Christ's passion and death being revelatory of God's love. "God himself took the initiative to make himself present to save in Jesus, and Jesus' cross is not, therefore, only what is pleasing to God, but that in which God expresses himself as pleasing to human beings. It is not efficient causality, but symbolic causality. Jesus' life and cross are that in which God's love for human beings is expressed and becomes as real as possible."[18] The point, once again, is that, because God as Spirit is at work in Jesus, Jesus' whole life may be considered a parable or gesture of God's communication to human beings. And this reaches its extreme symbolic intensity when Jesus' fidelity to God's cause, through to death itself, becomes an expression of God's love for human beings.

The second aspect of how Jesus' positive confrontation of death in loyalty to the cause or kingdom of God has to do with what it reveals about

---

15. Jon Sobrino, *Jesus the Liberator: A Historical-Theological View* (Maryknoll, N.Y.: Orbis Books, 1993), 228.

16. Karl Rahner, *On the Theology of Death* (New York: Herder and Herder, 1961), 51–52.

17. Sobrino, *Jesus the Liberator*, 229.

18. Sobrino, *Jesus the Liberator*, 230.

human existence. The cross brings to clear focus and intensity the implicit message of Jesus about the nature of human existence, about what is truly important and valuable relative to being human. Insofar as God was active in Jesus, Jesus in turn mediates what God wants human beings to be. Human beings, therefore, have a model to see what the human can be and should be. "This saving efficacy is shown more in the form of an exemplary cause than of an efficient cause."[19] Thus Sobrino proposes a coherent positive meaning to the New Testament's theology of the cross by, first, keeping his imagination tied to the ministry of Jesus in his interpretation, and, second, construing Jesus' activity within the framework of the traditional revelatory and exemplary theories of salvation.

THE RESURRECTION AS SALVIFIC

So much reflection on the saving work of Jesus Christ zeroes in on the suffering and death of Jesus that the salvific power of both his public ministry and his resurrection can go neglected. The salvific meaning of the resurrection of Jesus is certainly recognized in the New Testament and in classical soteriological theory. And no theologian has given the resurrection a more prominent place in christology than Pannenberg; it occupies the center of his constructive christological views. But I look to Jürgen Moltmann for a clean statement of the salvific significance of Jesus' resurrection which will have a relevance for postmodernity.

Moltmann consistently maintains that the cross or suffering and death of Jesus cannot be separated from the resurrection. These two make up aspects of one single event, the one historical and the other transcendent, and the two together constitute one salvific meaning. "Christ's death and his resurrection are the two sides of the one single happening which is often termed 'the Christ event.'"[20] To regard Jesus' suffering and death as salvific is already to place it within the context of the resurrection. The cross of Jesus is the cross of the risen one, the one whom God raised and vindicated.

The salvific power of the resurrection is explained by correlating it with the human experience of hope. I explained in Chapter 5 that an appreciation of the resurrection of Jesus depends upon a transcendental hope; the possibility of such hope structures human existence. Hope in this sense is a radical openness of the human spirit to being into the future. In the resurrection of Jesus this hope is focused or thematized; it is given a concrete reference, and with that object a shape and a content. The death of Jesus as a death into resurrection amounts to a promise by God of salvation in the future that responds to human hope. It is, Moltmann says with Paul, a promise of victory over death itself. Christian hope is founded upon the remembrance of Jesus' suffering and resurrection. This hope is "an

---

19. Sobrino, *Jesus the Liberator*, 230.
20. Moltmann, *The Way of Jesus Christ*, 214.

unequivocally 'joyful hope' for the resurrection and the life of the world to come. It is not a fearful expectation of a Last Judgment whose outcome for the human beings concerned is uncertain."[21]

One can describe the salvific character of resurrection hope by a hypothetical and phenomenological projection concerning the transformation of the disciples before and after they came to the realization that Jesus was risen. Before their Easter experience, as far as the disciples were concerned, Jesus remained dead. What they had hoped for, whatever their confused religious expectations might have been, seemed to be shattered by the sudden and sheerly definitive power of death. The Easter experience reverses this despair and fills an empty void. In the terms of christology, Jesus and his message are vindicated in what Tillich calls the restitution of Jesus as the Christ. For now New Being is permanently associated with Jesus Christ as the one who has conquered death itself.[22] In the terms of salvation, the resurrection of Jesus opens up a new dimension of reality for these disciples. The future now becomes a real dimension of being for the person who transcends living "only in order to die." One can imagine in the disciples a passage from religious or cosmic despair to a fundamental conviction characterized by hope. This hope, however, is not merely a psychic state but the correlate and source of a significantly different vision of reality.[23] In the chapter which follows I will show the direct bearing of this conviction on postmodern views of history.

THE CAUSALITY OF JESUS' SAVING ACTION

When classical accounts of Jesus' saving action narrate events or transactions that occur in another world they appear mythological. Chapter 8 attempted to interpret that classical language by appealing to the experience of salvation embedded in the structure of these mythic narrative symbols. Some twentieth-century soteriologies retain this mythic language. For example, Barth speaks of God and the whole of reality being changed on the day that Jesus Christ died.[24] Pannenberg, who tries to stay close to Jesus in his theology of salvation, still speaks of Jesus absorbing the punishment for sin due to human beings in order to satisfy the demands of justice.[25] This kind of symbolism is plainly unintelligible in a postmodern culture. But neither does an appeal to experience satisfy the question of intelligibility. One still has to be clear about what one understands to be

---

21. Moltmann, *The Way of Jesus Christ*, 224–25.

22. Tillich, ST, 2, 157; also Karl Rahner, *Foundations of Christian Faith: An Introduction to the Idea of Christianity* (New York: Seabury Press, 1978), 280.

23. Paul, in contrasting Christians with others "who have no hope" (1 Thes 4:13), is characterizing two fundamentally different conceptions of reality.

24. Barth, CD, IV-1, 247.

25. Wolfhart Pannenberg, *Jesus—God and Man* (Philadelphia: Westminster Press, 1977), 269.

taking place in talk about Jesus' saving work. This can be discussed under the rubric of causality; it probes further how Jesus saves.

I have already indicated a number of first responses to this question. Schleiermacher sees the direct influence of Jesus on the God-consciousness of his disciples being channeled or mediated through history by the church. John Cobb develops in more detail an analogous theory to explain the meaning of a salvific "being in Christ": Jesus set up a field of influence which is remembered in the community, thereby allowing members of the community to conform themselves to this influence.[26] Sobrino, we saw, understands God present and acting through Jesus symbolically, and Jesus exercising an exemplary causality for our salvation. Narrative christologies envisage those who hear the story of Jesus being drawn into it so that, by participation, the story begins to occur in them. Raymund Schwager understands the saving influence of Jesus Christ in terms of social or cultural anthropology. He uses the anthropological theory of René Girard as a hermeneutical framework for interpreting the way in which the death of Jesus Christ mediates God's salvation.[27] Like a scapegoat, in a collective transfer of energy to a victim, Jesus absorbs the violence of the community, ultimately of humankind, and is thus a cause of harmony and peace.[28] In this variety of conceptions one can distinguish two distinct issues: the relation of Jesus to the salvation of all human beings, and his relation to the salvation of Christians.

Regarding the relation of Jesus Christ to the salvation of all humankind, modern christology is split between those who retain the idea that Jesus caused or causes the salvation of all and those who do not. One of the points of differentiation on this issue lies in the degree to which theologians have internalized a historical matrix for their thinking. Only by means of a theoretical or speculative, metaphysical construction can one attempt to understand how Jesus Christ had a causal influence on the salvation of those who have never come in contact with him historically, or who existed before the appearance of Jesus. Thus, for example, Karl Rahner holds that Jesus is the cause of the salvation of all, because ultimately Jesus is the Word of God, the second person of the trinity. An intricate metaphysics of the trinity backs his understanding. And specifically relative to the human appearance of Jesus, Rahner holds that Jesus is the final cause of the salvation of all: Jesus is the intended

---

26. John Cobb, *Christ in a Pluralistic Age* (Philadelphia: Westminster Press, 1975), 121–22.

27. Most importantly René Girard, *Violence and the Sacred* (Baltimore: Johns Hopkins, 1977).

28. Raymund Schwager, *Must There Be Scapegoats? Violence and Redemption in the Bible* (San Francisco: Harper & Row, 1987). See also John Galvin, "Jesus as Scapegoat? Violence and the Sacred in the Theology of Raymund Schwager," *The Thomist*, 46 (1982), 173–94 and "The Marvelous Exchange: Raymund Schwager's Interpretation of the History of Soteriology," *The Thomist*, 53 (1989), 675–91.

aim or goal that shaped the saving will of God prior to every instance of its actualization.[29] Jesus is also the symbolic or sacramental cause of the salvation of all: the salvation of historical human existence as such requires the actualization of the complete union of God with human existence in an event in history. By contrast, Schubert Ogden, who is in some respects more sensitive to historical consciousness at this point, holds that Jesus normatively represents human salvation wherever it occurs authentically, but such a norm is not the cause of God's saving outside the Christian sphere. Jesus reveals or manifests something that is already going on in history before the advent of Jesus, and therefore is not caused by him.[30]

In commenting on the kind of influence Jesus has on Christians for their salvation I recall the distinction and tension drawn by Schleiermacher between the empirical and the magical. On the one hand, Jesus has an empirical and historical influence on people through the community's memory and its representation of him in story and sacrament. On the other hand, no empirical causality can amount to salvation; only God causes salvation. This action of God as saving Spirit or grace occurs from without, because it is transcendent, but within a person, because it is God's presence as saving power restoring human existence. Thus the causality of Jesus for human salvation is in the genus of symbolic or sacramental causality. By representing God's action for salvation, Jesus makes conscious and explicit to human beings something that would not have been revealed, known, or conscious in the same way without him. Jesus Christ causes the salvation of Christians by transforming God's presence for salvation into an explicitly conscious encounter. Jesus does not cause God's loving presence to human existence which is there from the dawn of creation. But Jesus causes it to be revealed, and thus formally accepted by human freedom, and thus consciously effective.

SALVATION AND CREATION

Another topic that sheds more light on the nature of salvation is its relation to creation. Three different positions here illustrate three different conceptions of salvation.

In his early volumes of the *Church Dogmatics* Karl Barth insisted that creation and salvation were two radically separable and different acts of God. The action of God the Son is "something very different from the

---

29. In God the hypostatic union of God with Jesus is a final cause because it is the final aim of God's creation; in human beings this finality is manifested as an implicit desire of human existence itself. See Rahner, *Foundations*, 315–21.

30. Schubert M. Ogden, *Is There Only One True Religion or Are There Many?* (Dallas: Southern Methodist University Press, 1992), 93–95, and "Problems in the Case for a Pluralistic Theology of Religions," *The Journal of Religion*, 68 (1988), 505.

activity of God the Creator"; salvation is "an inconceivably new work above and beyond creation."[31] This view is analogous to the cosmic vision of Augustine in which salvation repairs an otherwise permanently damaged and fallen nature. For both there is a great divide in reality separating the before and after Jesus Christ: reality itself has been changed.

In Karl Rahner's view the orders of creation and salvation are really distinct but inseparable.[32] With a modern, transcendental ontology, Rahner retrieves the scholastic distinction between the natural and the supernatural orders. These two orders can never be separated. But they represent really different dimensions of God's single relationship to human beings. Over and above God's efficient creative causality, God is personally present in an utterly free gift of his own self to all human beings. Salvation is identified with this personal communication of God to personal human existence, and the supreme instance of this communication is the hypostatic union of God with Jesus.

Edward Schillebeeckx, by contrast, represents a position in which there is no real distinction at all between the creative and the saving activity of God. Although Jesus' life is a historical initiative of God in history, still this saving initiative is the work of God the creator. God the creator is a personal, loving, and saving God who, as creator, offers God's self in loving, covenantal dialogue with human beings. The saving power of God found in Jesus is nothing but a concentrated form of God's creating power and presence.[33]

One can gain a better perspective on the relation of salvation to creation by placing it in a more expansive framework of interpretation. Elizabeth Johnson develops a broad typology of three large matrices of theological reflection and soteriological language. The different ways of thinking about salvation and creation are thus situated in a wider context, and this in turn reveals that a more decisive shift of consciousness is occurring. The premise here is that talk of salvation has a narrative structure, so that these shifts of context correspond to different types of soteriological narrative.

---

31. Barth, CD, I-1, 406 and 410, respectively. In later volumes creation and salvation are related intrinsically in the intentionality of God, for salvation is the goal of creation. "The ordaining of salvation for man and of man for salvation is the original and basic will of God, the ground and purpose of His will as Creator" (CD, IV-1, 9).

32. This unity and difference run all through the theology of Rahner. It is an explicit topic in Karl Rahner, "The Order of Redemption within the Order of Creation," *The Christian Commitment: Essays in Pastoral Theology* (New York: Sheed & Ward, 1963), 38–74. The distinction is also clearly drawn in his early writings on grace, and I shall return to this point.

33. Edward Schillebeeckx, "I Believe in God, Creator of Heaven and Earth," *God Among Us: The Gospel Proclaimed* (New York: Crossroad, 1983), 91–102, and "Kingdom of God: Creation and Salvation," *Interim Report on the Books Jesus & Christ* (New York: Crossroad, 1981), 105–12; Dorothy A. Jacko, "Creation-Faith," in *Salvation in the Context of Contemporary Secularized Historical Consciousness: The Later Theology of Edward Schillebeeckx* (Ph.D. Thesis, Toronto: University of St. Michael's College, 1987), 83–136.

The three are differentiated largely by an increasing degree of internalization of a consciousness of historicity.[34]

The first type of soteriological narrative is mythological. It is found in premodern theology. It lacks historical consciousness, and mixes historical reference with events that are protohistorical or prehistorical or frankly other-worldly.

The second type Johnson calls a "totalizing historical narrative." It is in some measure historically conscious and refers to historical events. But it also seeks to embrace all of history and reality in its scope, and is confident that it can. By telling a meta-story, a story of all reality, this mode of thought shares in the Enlightenment's ideal of classical reason being able to achieve a universal understanding of things. Rahner's all-encompassing interpretation of the story of salvation is a prime example of this type that combines historical and universalist intent.

The third type of thinking is postmodern, where the two salient characteristics are a more radical historical consciousness of particularity and contingency, and a deeper sense of the unintelligible evil that marks history. "Sprung from the disruptive, out-of-control evils of this century, it is aware of the chaotic, contingent, threatened character of existence and the fragility of the human project."[35] The story of Christian salvation in this intellectual context becomes a contingent historical narrative, but one in which God's presence and action are felt. It is a joyful and hopeful story, because it depicts God's concern and presence precisely in the contingent and particular details that make up history. This presence does not lack universal relevance, but neither does the story claim to absorb all of history into itself.[36]

Further reflection on this paradigm will illumine the notion of salvation in its relation to creation. First of all, in the postmodern framework, salvation will not be conceived apart from the concrete events of history. And the basis for this will be a closer identity between the doctrines of salvation and creation. The doctrine of creation itself has its basis in a sense of radical contingency, of a dependence of the self and all things on a source and ground that is transcendent. The root sense of salvation, therefore, the sense of wholeness and restoration of being over against any negativity, whether physical or spiritual, will not be isolated from God's creative power. Wherever there is wholeness, wherever there is healing, whenever things go right, the condition leads back to God's creative, saving power as source and ground. This more expansive and less differentiated sense of God's simultaneously creative and saving power will be

---

34. The three types are developed in Johnson, "Jesus and Salvation," 6–10. Johnson acknowledges, among several sources, especially David Power, *The Eucharistic Mystery: Revitalizing the Tradition* (New York: Crossroad, 1992), 304–16.

35. Johnson, "Jesus and Salvation," 9.

36. This third type relates to the second in a manner that reflects Ogden's critique of Rahner's view of the way Jesus causes the salvation of all.

confirmed by a renewed attention to God's acts of salvation in the Jewish scriptures and the physical saving acts of Jesus' public ministry.

Second, in the postmodern paradigm the relationship between creation and salvation takes on new dimensions of meaning relative to another variable, human freedom. We have seen the maxim of both the later Barth and Rahner that God creates in order to save. In a postmodern framework, one must also say that God saves in order to create, or in order that there be more creativity.[37] This means that God's salvific activity in grace augments human freedom and releases it for creativity. Salvation is not merely salvation from, but also salvation for a renewed exercise of human freedom, not merely passive but also active. By engaging human existence God's salvation is engaging human freedom in its active, creative essence.

Third, the relationship between God's general salvific and creative action and the particular story of God's action in Jesus is rearranged in Christian theology. The particular saving action of God in Jesus Christ remains a particular story; it is a tradition of God's real salvation in and of history. It is also a true story, and therefore it carries a universal relevance for all of humankind. It says something about the nature of God, creator and savior. But it is not the only story of God saving. God's creative and salvific action extends beyond the limits of this story, precisely because it is a story of a God who creates with a universal salvific intent. The universal saving power of God transcends the story of Jesus even as the life of Jesus is revelatory of it. In short, the event of Jesus reveals the salvation of all in revealing God, but it is not the cause of the salvation of all.[38]

Fourth, as we have become aware of the fragility of the planet earth and the damage that we have done to our home in the universe, the biophysical earth and even the cosmos have reentered our ken as an object of salvation. The ancient classical theme of a cosmic salvation has returned on postmodern premises: our world is a finite contingent system which we can nurture or destroy. Given the direction the human race seems to be headed ecologically, there is a strong sense today that the human cooperation needed to save the planet, and at the same time provide a just distribution of resources, will not be achieved without divine help. Thus theologians are calling for a theology of salvation that doubles back on physical creation to make it the object of salvation.[39]

The six themes of this section do not in any way exhaust the many different and rich analyses of the nature of salvation in the Christian theology of the twentieth century. But they represent some of the issues that

---

37. Viewed in the light of an eschatology in which human freedom has a part in constructing final reality, "creation is not initiated for the sake of grace but grace for the sake of creation." Frances Stefano, *The Absolute Value of Human Action in the Theology of Juan Luis Segundo* (Lanham, Md.: University Press of America, 1992), 209. See also Johnson, "Jesus and Salvation," 13–14.

38. See Johnson, "Jesus and Salvation," 10.

39. Moltmann, *The Way of Jesus Christ*, 301–12; Johnson, "Jesus and Salvation," 13.

have been most prominent in the modern theology of that century. They also indicate where Christian theology may be crossing a boundary into a postmodernity.

JESUS AND SALVATION

I propose to interpret in two stages how Jesus is savior. In the first I will formulate some of the religious questions that are pressing today. One cannot, of course, be comprehensive here; there is no way to exhaust the formalities with which the religious question is posed. Salvation takes as many different forms in our time as it has in the past. As Schillebeeckx put it, salvation in the rain forest will be dry; in the desert, it will be wet. But one can try to put in words the large thematic areas which require specific attention. A notion of salvation that reaches toward being integral, comprehensive, and relatively adequate will have to respond at least to the broad exigencies of our day, of postmodernity. In the second part, then, I try to interpret the salvation mediated by Jesus in such a way that it responds to these questions.

THE QUESTION OF SALVATION TODAY

The question of salvation is the religious question. One who is interested in and understands what is going on in religion has in some measure already appreciated the question and the meaning of salvation. Without the question of salvation, there would be no religion at all, because salvation simply gives specific content to the religious question.[40] In what follows I will try to define more precisely but still very generally various parameters that qualify the religious question today. On the one hand, these exigencies are merely aspects of a common human reaching out for transcendence. On this basis they are connected with religious experience generally, and serve as a link with the tradition of the experience of salvation. On the other hand, insofar as these questions represent the particularities of present-day cultures, they call out for responses that are applicable to our situation. These questions, then, are the link which both binds theological interpretation to the past and at the same time generates distinctively relevant applications to the present.

Any or every salvation theory must respond to the negative experiences of *ignorance, sin, guilt, suffering, and death*. Salvation today has to address the foundational experiences of bewilderment at the ultimate meaning of existence, of the evil that characterizes human existence, of

---

40. These propositions are not polemical. This is simply a way of indicating the wide sense the notion of salvation is being assigned here. Broadly defined as the goal of the impulse that reaches toward transcendence, salvation is able to be further qualified in a variety of different ways.

the moral failure in one's own personal existence, and of the finitude that is never secure, but is only diminished through suffering and with time, and culminates in the apparent annihilation that is death. These hard realities set up a constant tension between themselves and the elemental human desire to be, and to trust in the existence which they seem to undermine and finally negate. All salvation theories, and thus any integral theory of salvation for today, must address these issues, for these are that from which salvation is salvation. In stressing distinctive aspects of the question of salvation today, these classical loci of meaning cannot be bypassed. Salvation is "the experience-acceptance of a releasement from the bondage of guilt-sin, the bondage of radical transitoriness and death, the bondage of radical anxiety in all its forms. . . ."[41] But how do these perennial contradictions confront us today? The paragraphs which follow point to six distinctive exigencies which a contempory understanding of salvation must address.

Actual and Real Salvation

Salvation cannot be understood as merely a promise or as an exclusively future reality. Salvation must be something that can also be experienced now. Salvation has to be formulated as a symbol pointing to a reality that is existentially actualized in a person's life. Such a concrete, historical, and existential view of salvation is demanded by a culture that is empirical-minded and aware of pluralism and false promises. Secular societies generate a combination of critical skepticism and naive trust. The skepticism is a function of the thousand promises of salvation which inevitably fail; the tendency toward trust is created by the imperious demand that some meaning-giving salvation must be available somewhere. Any deep and lasting notion of salvation must be drawn from an experience of an objective mediation that is equally solid and enduring.

Integral Salvation

The question of salvation reaches out to include one's freedom and activity in the world. Salvation must be integral; it cannot touch a so-called spiritual dimension of a person's life and not include his or her activity in this world. Salvation today cannot be interpreted as salvation from the world, unless the term "world" is itself construed in a way alien to a common experience of it. Contrary to escapist views, human beings are spiritual freedom in the world in such a way that the world shapes and defines the human spirit. The world is the full measure of the human body, and one's particular world contributes to the identity of each human being. Salvation must incorporate the world insofar as the world, although in one respect over against the self, is also part of the self. We make ourselves by our action, and, in turn, our activity and work, the whole

---

41. David Tracy, "The Christian Understanding of Salvation-Liberation," *Face to Face*, 14 (1988), 39.

integral fabric of the many commitments that make up a human life, have to be touched by salvation.

The Finality of Salvation

The distinctive question of salvation involves a conception of history that gives it, and my freedom in it, ultimate meaning. Since the Enlightenment, human freedom has been seen as more than the ability to choose or even to enter into a lasting commitment; it has taken on the character of creativity. Human existence is intentional action that extends into the future and always effects novelty, new forms of being. Does the innate drive to achieve and to create have any ultimate meaning? And is human history as a whole, that is, the creativity of science, technology, and politics, also meaningful? Salvation in our world must address the connection between human action and the ultimate state of things, the eschaton.

The Comprehensiveness of Salvation

Salvation must be interpreted not only individually but also socially. The idea of an individual salvation apart from the salvation of the species is incoherent. The issue of one's individual destiny necessarily involves the destiny of other people, of society, region, nation, and the whole race. Thus the question of salvation has to be approached with an explicit concern for meaningfulness within the ignorance, sin, guilt, suffering, and mortality of human existence as a collective phenomenon at its various levels. Each person is a social individual who is nurtured by the innumerable social relationships that constitute his or her particular existence. Thus one must be able to see oneself as a part of society, and ask the question of the health, wholeness, and salvation of the various groups of which one is a part and to which and for which one is responsible. There is no salvation apart from being in relation with other human beings.

Salvation in Other Religions

How does a view of Christian salvation accommodate the salvation that is mediated by other religions? Active intercultural and interreligious exchange are an integral part of human life today. This living closer together can only increase, and the number of people who are affected by it can only grow. Interreligious exchange will also increase in intensity as peoples move closer to each other and intermingle more. How does Christianity view others? A test for this lies in the Christian understanding of how the salvation mediated by Jesus Christ bears upon those who are not Christian. This question has had a history as long as the Christian church itself. But as a new historical and pluralistic consciousness becomes internalized, it calls for a new understanding of the place of Christian salvation relative to other religious conceptions of ultimacy.

Salvation and a Scientific Worldview

Does the understanding that Christians have of salvation fit with the picture of reality that is presented to us by contemporary science? In

Whitehead's view, religion has been continually retreating in an undignified way as science marches forward.[42] But what appears negative and embarrassing could be regarded positively as a natural process. Religious conceptions are not more immune from a deepening understanding of our physical universe than are the understandings of the human phenomenon itself. Biblical and classical conceptions of salvation, we have seen, run in close parallel with the conceptions of the world that were in place when they were formulated. One cannot expect less in our own time. We need a conception of salvation that is sensitive to the negative impact human development is having on our life-support system, and that takes account of scientific data concerning the human species within the larger picture of the reality of God's created cosmos.

These are some of the dimensions of the question of salvation that arise out of our present situation. These are the questions that are being addressed by theology today and which have a bearing on the meaning of salvation. We turn now to a description of how they might shape an appropriation of the experience of salvation from the tradition.

JESUS AND SALVATION

How, then, are we to conceive the salvation that is mediated through Jesus Christ? We have collected a good deal of data relative to this question, from an understanding of Jesus' teaching on God, through New Testament and classical soteriology, to a review of topical themes in modern soteriology. How are we to interpret systematically and constructively for a postmodern intellectual culture these data about the way in which Jesus Christ saves? What exactly did Jesus Christ do, and what does he do, that is salvific for human existence today? This is the question, traditionally known as the question of objective salvation, that is posed here. Responding to it will conclude this first probe into the nature of Christian salvation. Of the six thematic areas that need attention only three will be addressed here. The issues regarding the social comprehensiveness of salvation and the impact of religious pluralism on a notion of salvation have generated their own technical subdisciplines with attendant bodies of literature; they will require separate analyses in the chapters which follow. I will be satisfied at this point with making a clear statement of the kind of salvation theory that is being proposed, pointing out those elements that make it able to be experienced as integral and ultimately fulfilling, and describing it in a way which is continuous with the traditions from which it draws.

The formula identifying the salvation theory that is proposed here is the following: Jesus is salvation by being a revealer of God, a symbol for

---

42. Alfred North Whitehead, *Science and the Modern World* (New York: The Free Press, 1967), 188.

an encounter with God, and an exemplar of human existence. An elaboration and clarification of this formula will at the same time indicate how it meets the exigencies of today's postmodern intellectual culture. This exposition can proceed by taking up the terms of the formula. It will be brief since I shall simply be drawing into a summary statement many of the themes that have been developed up to this point.

Jesus

It is Jesus of Nazareth who is the revealer of God to the Christian imagination. This salvation theory focuses attention on the Jesus of history. Jesus as a person is not something static, or an abstract or notional symbol. He is presented in the New Testament in a narrative form, a narrative that, although religiously enhanced, roughly corresponds to his public ministry. Jesus reveals by means of his living a human life, through his teaching and his actions. This means that the teachings, the actions, the valuations, the healings, the confrontational sayings, the acts of hospitality, all of these actions together are what give substance to Jesus. It is that concrete life that focuses the attention and fixes the imagination of the one approaching Jesus of Nazareth. Jesus becomes for the Christian imagination the parable of God.

Revelation

Jesus reveals God. The premise of this understanding is that all knowledge of God is mediated through history. This means that all conceptions of God, all beliefs, all human construals of the shape and meaning of transcendent reality, are mediated through history. All these beliefs, then, can be led back reductively to a source or origin that is this-worldly and historical.

To say that Jesus reveals God means that the Christian understanding of God, insofar as it is specifically Christian, leads back to Jesus as to its source, origin, foundation. This does not mean that the Christian lacks other historical sources or data for reflection on ultimate reality. It does mean, however, that for the Christian Jesus is the central normative witness to the reality of God.

How does Jesus reveal? Although this is not the place to develop a theology of revelation, some things should be underlined.[43] Jesus' revealing influence cannot be explained in merely historical-empirical terms of instruction and personal influence. Revelation is more than teaching about God. Beyond that, the New Testament proposes that Jesus makes God present. The symbol of God as Spirit present and active in Jesus, which from certain perspectives is the dominant christology in the New Testament, portrays God being present to Jesus and active in him in power. But, from the human side, despite Jesus' actions of power, God's

---

43. I have proposed reflections on the nature of revelation consistent with what is proposed here in *Dynamics of Theology* (New York: Paulist Press, 1990).

presence to him does not lie on the surface; it is not an empirical quality of Jesus. Revelation only occurs in response to the religious question and through an epistemology of faith. In this case it requires that one allow one's imagination to be shaped by Jesus' person and actions in such a way that he becomes a source for understanding the what and the who of God.

Revelation of God in the end is a matter of experiential and existential encounter. As such it is dialectical. There is no evidence that anyone during Jesus' lifetime said that Jesus is God. Such a thing is unthinkable in a Jewish context when the term "God" refers to the transcendent One. And yet the whole New Testament testifies that people encountered God's salvation through him and in him, both during his lifetime and afterwards. Revelation is thus a dialectical encounter of God in Jesus in the sense of being mediated in and through his teaching, actions, and person.

Once revelation is recognized anthropologically as consisting in a form of existential encounter arising out of the religious question, one that occurs in existential subjectivity, one can adopt the language of the theologians of the Word such as Barth and Brunner. Revelation is not to be simply identified with words on a page, or even with the overt human actions of Jesus; it occurs within faith experience itself as that which exercises initiative and causes faith. The objective word of God can be encountered only within existential subjectivity.

The event of revelatory encounter can be described in terms of symbolic or sacramental causality. On one level, the influence of the person of Jesus on those around him was historical efficient causality. But on another level, encounter with God relies on God's presence and power in those to whom God is revealed. Symbolic or sacramental causality effects by bringing to consciousness and explicit awareness something that is already present within, but latent and not an object of clear attention or focused recognition. By being a symbol of God, by mediating an encounter with God, Jesus reveals God as already present and active in human existence. Historically he does this both by being and by making God present in a thematic way through his words, actions, and whole person. Jesus reveals by causing in the persons who come to him in faith an analogous reflective awareness of the presence of God to them.

This same historical and sacramental or symbolic causality is carried forward after Jesus' death and resurrection by the disciples who formed a community and which became the church. In other words, the revealing salvation of Jesus Christ continues to be historically mediated: it requires historical agents. The church, by remembering Jesus, continues the causality of his revelatory salvation through history by drawing people into the historical community of the force-field and impact of Jesus.

God

The salvific dimension of the revelation mediated by Jesus must lie in the object revealed. Jesus is savior because the God whom he reveals and makes present for human encounter is a saving God. What is the character of the God whom Jesus reveals? What kind of a God is mediated when one takes the time to consider the teaching and action of Jesus of Nazareth?

Chapter 4 showed that Jesus' teaching about God revolved around the kingdom of God. Ultimately, the God to whom Jesus points is not substantially different than the God he encountered in his Jewish tradition. Jesus communicates a God who is personal and transcendent. Moreover the transcendent one is friend; the creator is loving. What one encounters in Jesus' ministry is that God is love, that the very nature of God is love. And because God is lover of all, God is against all dehumanization or disfigurement of God's creatures. God is sympathetic to human suffering; God is a just judge of sin against God's own human beings. Anselm conceived of God's salvation from within the context, and thus the limits, of God's being the ground of the order and harmony of the universe. Reversing the scheme of Anselm in favor of Abelard, it is more appropriate to the New Testament witness that Jesus reveals a God whose justice unfolds within the larger context of gratuitous and forgiving love.

Jesus reveals a God who is not distant and aloof, but close to human existence, and even immanent and present to it. Such is the force of the symbol God as Spirit. The witness to the career of Jesus is to a God who is present and at work in Jesus' life. The Jesus movement took off and flourished in the new appropriation of God's presence to the community that was mediated by Jesus. The life of Jesus represents a God who assumes human existence as God's own by being present to it in love and power.

Relative to creation, love is the primary affection that God bears God's creation, and although one may make some mental distinction between God's creating activity and God's love for creation, one cannot separate these two as though they were discrete actions of God. Jesus points to a creator who is benevolent, loving savior prior to and in the very act of creating. But creation is not a past event; it is the always present activity of God. This was the very tradition which Jesus received. Creating, providential caring, saving are reductively aspects of the same activity of God. Being in existence, then, is being within the all-embracing power and love of God. The distinction between God's creating and saving does not correspond to separable phases of God's dealing with creation. Salvation flows from the love that is prior to and an integral part of God's creating; it is God's effective loving of what God creates. From the beginning God has always been love. Jesus does not constitute but reveals something that has always been operative. What one finds revealed in Jesus is a God whose salvation is an integral dimension of God's creating.[44]

---

44. This does not entail a rejection of Rahner's language of God offering God's personal saving self-presence to an already semi-autonomous human reality set in existence by God's creative power. This language distinguishes by analysis dimensions of God's relation to human existence; it is also beautiful and powerful language that fully

Exemplar

Jesus saves not only by being a revelation of God but also by revealing human existence. The supposition here is that human existence is mysterious, and its ultimate character and destiny are not universally recognized or agreed upon. Both biblical and classical soteriology contain this fundamental conviction that Jesus is an exemplar of what it means to be human. This means, more concretely, that the same faith that accepts Jesus as the mediator for an encounter with God also allows Jesus to school one's fundamental human values, one's conception of what virtues are most authentically human, one's basic idea of what human life is for and where it is leading, and, even more generally, opening up a pattern or mode of possible existence in the world. The fundamental meaning of human existence needs to be revealed; it is not readily available on the surface of history. Jesus being an exemplar means that this revelation is embodied in the manner in which he lived for God's kingdom.

The conception of human existence that is communicated in Jesus' public ministry is characterized by freedom, a self-transcending freedom that springs from a strong sense of identity and mission. God active as Spirit in Jesus does not compete with human freedom but actualizes, augments, and fulfills human potential. The character of this God is not over against the human existence that God created; God is the sustainer and empowerment of loving human freedom.

This conception of salvation as consisting in revelation and an appropriating faith lies at the basis of the tradition of *imitatio Christi*, the following of Christ, as a formula for Christian spirituality. The mysticism of "putting on Christ" and "being in Christ" may be understood to have an empirical base when persons allow their thinking and whole conduct to be shaped by the model provided by Jesus of Nazareth.

Resurrection

Finally, God saves in Jesus by raising Jesus from death and drawing him into an eternal life within the sphere of God and God's love. The salvation that is entailed here can be understood in a twofold way. Obviously the final destiny itself is a definitive fulfillment of human existence; this is final, eschatological salvation. But also the revelation of this destiny is itself a salvation that has notable transforming effects in this life. When the promise of eternal life meets human hope, the personal world in the two dimensions of time and space that is dead-ended by death is opened

---

endorses human freedom. Nor can Rahner be faulted for separating these phases; they are held tightly together at all times. The ontological distinctions within God that Rahner forges on the models of efficient and formal causality should be understood loosely as further descriptions of aspects or dimensions of God's relation to human existence. These distinctions are found in Karl Rahner, "Some Implications of the Scholastic Concept of Uncreated Grace," *Theological Investigations*, 1 (Baltimore: Helicon Press, 1961), 326–33.

up toward an infinity of possibility and ultimate meaning. Everything about human life is thus transformed by this new dimension of reality, an absolute future. We shall see in the next chapter how this makes a total difference in the estimate of history and the human project.

In conclusion it should be noted how this view of salvation corresponds with the structure of christology that was developed in Chapter 7. Jesus the revealer of God is Jesus the symbol of God, making God present to the world dialectically, and able to be perceived by the religious inquirer. One should also note that although this is a technical understanding of Jesus Christ as savior, it is also fairly descriptive of the process by which christology first arose and of the structure of Christian faith at any given time. As long as postmodernity does not preclude or quench the religious question itself and the openness of hope, it can grasp this view of Christian salvation, and Christian salvation can address and transform this culture.

CHAPTER 13

Liberation and Salvation: Christology and the Christian Life

The last chapter proposed an interpretation of the saving work of Jesus Christ as revelation and example. This includes the strong sense of a concrete symbol which mediates or makes present that to which it points. Jesus makes God present, and people encounter God in Jesus in a saving way. Although this interpretation retrieves the point of traditional mythological language and corresponds to the lived experience of Christians, it barely begins to respond to the demands for intelligibility and relevance in a postmodern culture. These will be developed in more detail below, but a general statement at this point will introduce the movement of this chapter.

In the context of today's world, religion generally and the language of Christian salvation in particular appear individualistic and even privatistic. Some factors in today's secular culture urge this privatism. That whole spheres of secular life in society have been released from the hegemony of any organized religion may be taken as a positive development. And given a pluralism of religions, the freedom of them all seems to depend on their low public profile. Thus the modern period in western culture has witnessed the privatization of religion, its theological language, and the self-understanding of religious people. The religious question has become the intensely personal question of meaning in the face of individual suffering, personal sin and guilt, disorientation, and finally each one's death and ultimate destiny. Once the religious question is conceived in the individual and personal terms of the self-reflective subject, the whole religious superstructure never seems to escape the privatism, even when it is group or corporate individualism. One always ends up with the salvation of individuals.[1] But for the postmodern person this means that religion ceases to make any difference in public social history. Christian salvation really has nothing to offer the public order; as a private affair it appears irrelevant

---

1. It should be clear that this description is being painted in the most general of terms.

to the decisions that structure public social life. Of course Christian groups have their own interests in public affairs, and as institutions they lobby to make their voices heard. But in so doing they are not necessarily speaking the language of salvation that is intrinsic to Christian faith; self-interested institutional concern is far removed from Jesus preaching the reign of God. In fact faith in a purely individual salvation can act as a palliative to social passion; logically it mitigates concern for the social order of this world. Ultimate salvation becomes the ultimate distraction from political engagement. At least this is true: for one passionately concerned about the human project, religion provides no platform through which this passion will be satisfied. An indication of the relative accuracy of this postmodern critique of the language of the churches is the poor reception in the churches of the various forms of liberation theology which echo the critique and try to address the problem.

This chapter will respond to religious privatism and offer an interpretation of Christian salvation that shows it to be a social reality which at the same time addresses the individual person. Such a salvation implies a Christian anthropology: human existence is intrinsically social, and, ideally, the value of the individual person is not compromised but enhanced by social relationships. Human existence entails individual human subjects who are open and in relation to others forming community and society. Christian salvation liberates and fulfills this human reality. The chapter will address these issues by appealing to the liberation theologies that have appeared during the twentieth century. It will represent only schematically these liberation theologies as they developed historically, but will interpret and appropriate them in a way that displays their truth and relevance beyond their immediate applications to their particular situations. An assumption operative in this chapter holds that in many respects these liberation theologies reflect postmodernity in the problems they address and the thematic principles they employ in responding to them.

This chapter thus takes another step in the interpretation of Christian salvation. It moves to a social level of understanding. The chapter also represents a shift to what is frequently called "subjective" salvation as distinct from the "objective" work of Jesus Christ. Subjective salvation refers to the appropriation of salvation, its applicability, its reception into the lives of human beings, its internalization. Subjective salvation is an existential historical reality. This discussion also forms a bridge to the theme of the Christian life or spirituality. When one conceives spirituality in terms of the contours of the life of the Christian, it becomes a corollary or extension of the appropriation of salvation.

The five parts that make up this chapter presuppose a certain familiarity with liberation theologies. I shall begin, nevertheless, with a brief indication of the liberation theologies that serve as resources for this chapter. In a second step I will interpret the dynamics of liberation theologies and propose a way of reading them as responding to the most basic religious questions of our time. The third section outlines how liberation theologies interpret Jesus and the God to whom he points. I will then be in a position, fourthly, to characterize the social character of the salvation that is mediated by Jesus and its bearing on human life, of individuals and of society. And, finally, in the last section, I will interpret the bearing of this salvation on history in the light of an eschatology.

THE VARIETIES OF LIBERATION THEOLOGY

The twentieth century provides an extraordinary witness to a social interpretation of the Christian message. In characterizing the variety of these theological statements as liberationist, I use the term broadly and inclusively. All of these theologies deal with individuals not as isolated persons but as part of definable groups or as members of society. Every concrete individual has a social identity which helps define his or her individuality. All of these "liberation" theologies work out of a social framework and understand the human person in terms of solidarity and dynamic, open interrelationships with others. They thus portray the Christian message of salvation in its bearing on social existence, in its impact on groups, general society, and the political sphere. In most cases these theologies have their origin in movements within society or church which react against specific evils in society that can no longer be ignored or tolerated.

At the end of the nineteenth and the beginning of the twentieth centuries in the United States, the social gospel movement reflected a corporate response of the churches to the social degradation of especially urban life that followed in the wake of industrialization. This primarily pastoral response, using popular rhetoric and reflecting nineteenth-century optimism and enthusiasm for reform, sought to address to the poor and working classes a Christian message of salvation that was relevant to their lives. It also appealed to the middle class and industrial leaders for the changes and reforms that were demanded. Much of the theology that accompanied this movement shared the popular idiom. But some theologians such as Shailer Mathews and Walter Rauschenbusch proposed critically and methodologically sound historical analyses of Christian tradition and analytical presentations of systematic understanding. In christology, they both turned back to a historical portrayal of Jesus' ministry. Using different hermeneutical keys, they both interpreted Christian salvation as having a direct bearing on American society of the time. Rauschenbusch especially had a conception of human existence as socially constituted in solidarity so that a salvation that did not influence the common good was unthinkable.[2]

---

2. Shailer Mathews's interpretations of Jesus are found in *The Social Teaching of Jesus: An Essay in Christian Sociology* (New York: Macmillan, 1897) and *Jesus on Social Institutions* (New York: Macmillan, 1928). For a comprehensive interpretation of these works, see William D. Lindsey, *Shailer Mathews's Lives of Jesus: The Search for a Theological*

Although social interpretations of Christianity were not lacking in the years after the social gospel flourished,[3] several new liberation theologies arose during the 1960s. We begin with political theology. Political theology cannot be understood apart from the cataclysm of World War II in Europe and the promise of Marxism to provide a fairer distribution of wealth. But the holocaust especially called into question the adequacy of individualistic interpretations of Christianity. How could this have happened in Christian Europe? Political theology, of course, is not a theology of politics, nor a reassertion of church power over society. Rather, as a theology, it interprets God and God's salvation in its relevance to human beings in society and their exercise of political responsibility. On the one hand, political theology reacts against an individualistic existential interpretation of human existence and the salvation offered it. On the other hand, it proposes a social, historical anthropology as a lever for lifting up the meaning of Christian salvation in its bearing on the whole Christian community and society generally, but with special attention to the victims of society who suffer and are marginalized. Political theology brings together hermeneutical theory and critical social theory into a creative reinterpretation of the latent emancipatory themes of Christian tradition.[4]

The prehistory of Latin American liberation theology lies in the social concern of Catholic action groups of students and workers, and in the early writings of Juan Luis Segundo in the first part of the 1960s.[5] Two public events served as symbolic stimuli for its flowering at the end of the 1960s. The first was *Gaudium et Spes* which closed the Second Vatican Council and gave the council its distinctive social impact. The second was the Second General Conference of Latin American Bishops in 1968 in which the bishops described the social situation of the poor majority, char-

---

Foundation for the Social Gospel (Albany: State University of New York Press, 1997); Walter Rauschenbusch's interpretation of Jesus may be found most concisely in *The Social Principles of Jesus* (New York: Association Press, 1916) and *A Theology for the Social Gospel* (New York: Macmillan, 1918). For retrieval of Rauschenbusch's interpretation of Jesus in terms of hermeneutical theory, see Darlene Peitz, *Solidarity as Hermeneutic: A Revisionist Reading of the Theology of Walter Rauschenbusch* (New York: Peter Lang, 1992).

3. Reinhold Niebuhr is well known as a critic of the optimistic anthropology he found in the social gospelers, but he extended the tradition of interpreting Christian doctrine in terms of its engagement with society. The social gospel movement continued to be an influential force in the national life of Canada. See Gregory Baum, *Catholics and Canadian Socialism* (New York: Paulist Press, 1981).

4. I am relying on Johann Baptist Metz, *Theology of the World* (New York: Herder and Herder, 1969) and *Faith in History and Society: Toward a Practical Fundamental Theology* (New York: Seabury Press, 1980) as the leading Catholic proponent of political theology, and Jürgen Moltmann, *Theology of Hope* (New York: Harper & Row, 1967) and Dorothee Soelle, *Political Theology* (Philadelphia: Fortress Press, 1974) as the two leading Protestant representatives of political theology. These works represent early definitions of political theology.

5. Alfred T. Hennelly, in *Theologies in Conflict: The Challenge of Juan Luis Segundo* (Maryknoll, N.Y.: Orbis Books, 1979), reviews Segundo's early untranslated work.

acterizing it as institutionalized violence and sin, and promised that the church would address these inhuman conditions. The 1970s witnessed an outpouring of work in liberation theology following Gustavo Gutiérrez's *A Theology of Liberation* which became the movement's classic text.[6] This theology is written on behalf of the poor and to give voice to the poor; methodologically it feeds on the experience of a ministerial praxis with the poor; it deals with the systemic social issues of poverty and oppression; it interprets Christian revelation and salvation as responding to these issues. Whereas political theology fits a European situation in which Christians and Marxists were entering into dialogue, liberation theology reflects a movement from below, an "eruption of the poor," although not without leadership.[7]

The 1960s also gave birth to black theology in the United States. Like the theology of the social gospel and Latin American liberation theology, black theology emerged out of a social movement, in this case the civil rights movement animated by Martin Luther King. Impatient with the lack of progress, one wing of this movement united around the idea of "black power," a phrase that would galvanize people into a more autonomous, self-reliant group with an identity and a destiny distinct from whites. Black theology, as initially formulated by James Cone, reflected this strong sense of identity. He linked together Jesus Christ, freedom, and black power.[8] He reached back into the history of the African American churches to find the common experience, language, and spirituality of a people. Negatively, black theology reacts against the remains of slavery that still deeply affect black society and culture and American society generally. Positively, it retrieves the tradition of Jesus' ministry in order to build a positive conception of the saving power of God mediated through Jesus Christ into the life of this group and into American society.[9]

Feminist theology as it is known today also began in the 1960s, although there have been many feminist theologians without the title

---

6. Gustavo Gutiérrez, *A Theology of Liberation* (Maryknoll, N.Y.: Orbis Books, 1988) is a revised edition of the original of 1971 (Spanish) and 1973 (English).

7. Perhaps the best introduction to liberation theology is Alfred T. Hennelly, ed., *Liberation Theology: A Documentary History* (Maryknoll, N.Y.: Orbis Books, 1990). Some landmarks in christology are Jon Sobrino, *Christology at the Crossroads: A Latin American Approach* (Maryknoll, N.Y.: Orbis Books, 1978), *Jesus in Latin America* (Maryknoll, N.Y.: Orbis Books, 1987), and *Jesus the Liberator: A Historical-Theological View* (Maryknoll, N.Y.: Orbis Books, 1993); Leonardo Boff, *Jesus Christ Liberator: A Critical Christology for Our Time* (Maryknoll, N.Y.: Orbis Books, 1978), and *Passion of Christ, Passion of the World* (Maryknoll, N.Y.: Orbis Books, 1987); Juan Luis Segundo, *The Historical Jesus of the Synoptics* (Maryknoll, N.Y.: Orbis Books, 1985); Hugo Echegaray, *The Practice of Jesus* (Maryknoll, N.Y.: Orbis Books, 1984).

8. James H. Cone, *Black Theology and Black Power* (New York: Seabury Press, 1969).

9. M. Shawn Copeland, "Black Theology," *The New Dictionary of Theology*, ed. by J. Komonchak, M. Collins, and D. Lane (Wilmington: Michael Glazier, 1987), 138–41. J. H. Cone and G. S. Wilmore, eds., *Black Theology: A Documentary History*, 2 Vols. (Maryknoll, N.Y.: Orbis Books, 1993) provides a good introduction to black theology.

across the history of the church, especially in the nineteenth and twentieth centuries. The large body of feminist theology today borrows from a still more massive movement of feminism that takes multiple ideological forms and reaches into every phase of human life and every academic discipline. Early works, such as Mary Daly's *The Church and the Second Sex* of 1968,[10] stand at the head of a movement that gradually generated a corps of women theologians writing in every theological and ecclesial discipline. Feminist theology is sometimes misinterpreted as a theology of women or of feminine themes instead of as a liberation theology that opposes oppressive social structures that implicate both women and men. This theology arises out of an androcentric social and cultural situation in which women are subordinated and treated unequally. The background of this theology, therefore, is society as a whole; its goals are equality among men and women together; its subject matter is theological. Feminist theology reads the sources of theology, scripture and tradition, in order to generate an understanding of Christian salvation that has a social relevance in a patriarchal church and society.[11] Structurally analogous to feminist theology, womanist theology represents the interpretation of Christian symbols by black women who distinguish themselves both from white feminist theologians and male black theologians. Hispanic women too are developing a distinctive theology. Both groups have addressed christology from their distinctive situation and experience.[12]

Some seminal works are James H. Cone, *A Black Liberation Theology* (Philadelphia: Lippincott, 1970); J. Deotis Roberts, *A Black Political Theology* (Philadelphia: Westminster Press, 1974), and *Liberation and Reconciliation* (Philadelphia: Westminster Press, 1971).

10. Mary Daly, *The Church and the Second Sex* (New York: Harper & Row, 1968), followed by *Beyond God the Father: Toward a Philosophy of Women's Liberation* (Boston: Beacon Press, 1973).

11. The following feminist works in christology reflect a variety of perspectives: Anne Carr, *Transforming Grace: Christian Tradition and Women's Experience* (San Francisco: Harper, 1988); Elisabeth Schüssler Fiorenza, *In Memory of Her: A Feminist Theological Reconstruction of Christian Origins* (New York: Crossroad, 1983), and *Jesus: Miriam's Child, Sophia's Prophet: Critical Issues in Feminist Christology* (New York: Continuum, 1994); Rita Nakashima Brock, *Journeys by Heart: A Christology of Erotic Power* (New York: Crossroad, 1988); Rosemary Radford Ruether, *To Change the World: Christology and Cultural Criticism* (New York: Crossroad, 1981), and *Sexism and God-Talk: Toward a Feminist Theology* (Boston: Beacon Press, 1983); Mary Hembrow Snyder, *The Christology of Rosemary Radford Ruether: A Critical Introduction* (Mystic, Conn.: Twenty-Third Publications, 1988); Maryanne Stevens, ed., *Reconstructing the Christ Symbol: Essays in Feminist Christology* (New York: Paulist Press, 1993).

12. Some representative works are Kelly Brown Douglas, *The Black Christ* (Maryknoll, N.Y.: Orbis Books, 1994); Jacquelyn Grant, *White Women's Christ, Black Women's Jesus* (Atlanta: Scholars Press, 1989); Delores S. Williams, *Sisters in the Wilderness: The Challenge of Womanist God-Talk* (Maryknoll, N.Y.: Orbis Books, 1993); Elsa Tamez, ed., *Through Her Eyes: Women's Theology from Latin America* (Maryknoll, N.Y.: Orbis Books, 1989); María Pilar Aquino, *Our Cry for Life: Feminist Theology from Latin America* (Maryknoll, N.Y.: Orbis Books, 1993).

Besides these more or less explicitly liberationist movements of theological and christological interpretation, a broader, world-wide project of inculturation quietly and gradually continues to move forward. Since its inception, western Christianity has remained resolutely western; by definition it has been dominated by the cultural and linguistic traditions of western philosophy and intellectual scholarship. Churches established by western missionaries inevitably transplanted a version of the Christian message modeled on that of Europe and, more recently, of North America. But for some time now, as Christian churches in non-western cultures develop their own identity, they simultaneously demand a theology, and particularly a christology, that reflects the experience, language, traditions, and customs of their own culture. Just as liberation theologies represent forms of inculturation, there are liberationist dimensions to the project of inculturation. This effort implicitly rejects an implied imperialism of western modes of thought as well as the definitiveness of western conclusions and the formulas that represent them. "Why should one be apprehensive, then, about Asian theologians who find both the Hebrew concept of God and the Greco-Roman elaborations of Chalcedon pedagogically misleading and culturally meaningless in the context of Asia's multifarious perceptions of the Absolute?"[13] The implications of this movement are deep and far-reaching. The term of this development will be decisive in establishing a pluralistic framework for christological thought. Already we are witnessing the beginnings of distinctively new interpretations of Jesus Christ and his salvation coming out of Asia and Africa.[14] The relevance of this movement lies in the way culture and society supply the hermeneutical principles upon which new interpretations of Jesus Christ and his salvation turn.

What is going on in all these developments, including the process of inculturation? A fuller answer to this question will be proposed in the next section, but some factors lie right on the surface of these movements, and they are important. Historical consciousness and pluralist consciousness have become world-wide phenomena; they are increasingly marks of a world-consciousness. The method and the content of these theologies will differ around the world in specific theme, depth, and breath; and self-conscious recognition of these differences are the condition of the possibility of intentional hermeneutical appropriation and genuine inculturation. These projects also assume a sense of identity, freedom, and responsibility in shaping the language and content of christology to the

---

13. Aloysius Pieris, "Christology in Asia: A Reply to Felipe Gomes," *Voices from the Third World*, 11 (December, 1988), 162.

14. A sampling of essays at inculturated understandings of Jesus Christ are found in Robert J. Schreiter, ed., *Faces of Jesus in Africa* (Maryknoll, N.Y.: Orbis Books, 1991) and R. S. Sugirtharajah, ed., *Asian Faces of Jesus* (Maryknoll, N.Y.: Orbis Books, 1993). The problematic of inculturation overlaps with issues that arise out of the context of interreligious dialogue which will be treated in the next chapter.

historical thought-forms or structures of thinking that define a situation and a culture. A self-conscious effort at inculturation reflects not only a willingness to undertake the change that is necessary, but also a grasp of the possibility of such a change and the necessity of reinterpretation. This seems to indicate that some of the themes that characterize postmodernity are being felt globally. This will become more apparent in the light of a deeper analysis of what is happening in liberation theologies.

THE DYNAMICS OF LIBERATION THEOLOGIES

What is going on in liberation theologies? I believe that one best understands these theologies as hermeneutical theologies. Of course all understanding is hermeneutical. But with this designation I propose that an identifiable structure of interpretation, one proposed by hermeneutical theorists, clarifies what is going on in each of these liberation theologies. In Chapter 1 this structure was described as a dynamic process according to a three-fold pattern. It begins with a negative experience of contrast. This negative experience elicits a question or set of questions concerning the subject matter to be interpreted. And the object which is being interpreted discloses a response to the question and is thus appropriated into the situation of the questioner.

If the characterization of this structure is at all accurate, it demonstrates the analogy that obtains among these theologies; it shows that on a certain structural or formal level they bear a family resemblance, while concretely and materially they have their own specific identity which renders them distinct and different from each other. This interpretation of these theologies also treats them as processes of continual understanding and appropriation, and thus as dynamic mechanisms of inculturating the Christian message to new situations. This reading of liberation theologies, therefore, preserves this dynamic structure in each case, but, by generalizing the questions that these theologies raise, shows their universal significance.

THE NEGATIVE EXPERIENCE OF CONTRAST

The nature of a negative experience of contrast and its function in theology were explained in the opening chapter of this book. It will be recalled that such an experience is the common one of perceiving a certain event or situation as simply wrong, as something that absolutely should not be. This virtually immediate or direct perception necessarily carries with it, at least implicitly, some vague idea of the way things should be. It also bears a reaction: an implicit desire that the situation not be and a will to change it. The measure in which one is caught up in such a negative situation controls the quality of one's reaction against it. What has to be explained now is how such a negative experience lies at the basis of every liberation theology.

The theology of the social gospel reacted against the negative situation of the poverty, human degradation, unrealized human potential, and generalized human suffering that accompanied the uncontrolled industrial expansion beginning in the last third of the nineteenth century. A negative contrast experience of precisely this situation was dramatically lived out by Walter Rauschenbusch during the first years of his ministry in New York City when he was converted to the social gospel movement. The scriptural symbol of the kingdom of God took on a new social meaning for him that restructured his whole life and thought.[15] God does not will this human suffering, and no authentic preaching of the gospel can fail to make this clear.

Political theology does not have the focused target of the other liberation theologies and the degree of its experiential passion varies with its authors. But it is clear that all its proponents feel the inadequacy and the distorting effects of an individualistic interpretation of Christian revelation and salvation. The very credibility of Christianity depends on its bearing upon history and society. Consequently, this theology carries a practical intent; it unfolds on the premise that the functional or ethical credibility of any theology will depend upon the engagement and praxis it releases.[16]

The negative contrast experience underlying Latin American liberation theology encompasses poverty, or, more concretely, people who are poor.[17] This theology does not romanticize poverty; it is sheer evil of Jobian proportions; worse, it is sin, which need not and should not be. Everything that the scriptures report about the God of life runs counter to this oppressive and deadly poverty. Here the natural impulse to resist this evil dovetails with the will of God revealed throughout the Jewish and Christian scriptures.

An analysis of black liberation theology yields an analogous and parallel structure. For a history of oppressive structures beginning with Latin American colonialism, substitute the system of dislocation, slavery, and the lasting imprint these had on a people and their culture. And for the

---

15. See the account of Rauschenbusch's gradual "conversion" to a belief in the "kingdom of God" that was mediated through his early experience of the poverty of his people as a pastor in New York's West Side in Paul M. Minus, *Walter Rauschenbusch: America Reformer* (New York: Macmillan, 1988), 49–70.

16. Soelle outlines the problem, conceived in terms of Bultmann's existential theology, to which political theology responds in *Political Theology*, 1–9; the same problematic is sketched in terms of apologetic credibility and praxis in the public arena in several essays by Metz in *Faith in History and Society*, 3–83.

17. Gustavo Gutiérrez, "Option for the Poor," *Systematic Theology: Perspectives from Liberation Theology*, ed. by Jon Sobrino and Ignacio Ellacuría (Maryknoll, N.Y.: Orbis Books, 1996), 22–37. Jon Sobrino develops the stark contrast between this death-dealing poverty and the God of life in "Espiritualidad de Jesús y de la Liberación," *Christus*, 44 (December 1979–January 1980), 59–61.

disdain and neglect of the poor, substitute the focused hatred of racism. It takes a particular kind of blindness to rationalize this radical social injustice into a legal system of slavery or apartheid. But many other social practices find some kind of analogous justification. The prophetic dimension of Christianity addresses this social situation directly.

Feminist liberation theology reacts against the sexism built into androcentric cultures, societies, and partriarchal institutions. Often the structures of inequality are blatant and obvious. But when this sexism is written deeply into a traditional culture, it often goes unnoticed, for it has roots in a long-standing memory, often codified into law, and subsists in an intertwined network of instances. In some cases the biases lie so deeply ingrained that they are experienced as precisely what should be, even according to the will of God. Often only the experience of the victims can witness to the negativity, to the demeaning effects of the system.

Finally, the negativity involved in the alien character of the cultural forms in which western Christianity has been spread and preserved in other cultures is less moral in its makeup. In a natural process of adaptation over a long period of time Christianity takes on the cultural forms of its hosts. But in a historically conscious age, where pluralism highlights identity, there is a new pressure, not for adaptation, but for inculturation. This is heightened by the cultural imperialism of the West. It is wrong not to allow Christian faith to come to expression in the indigenous cultural and linguistic forms of a people, even though this necessarily involves change and difference.

In each case, then, one can discern a negative experience of contrast that lies at the core of these liberation theologies. In each case these social experiences are the existential and epistemological basis that generates the movement upon which the theology depends. The logic of these theologies thus entails a dialectical tension between this negative experience and the demand for a positive intelligibility which will, in turn, provide a direction for a reaction against the evil in question.

THE QUESTIONS ADDRESSED BY LIBERATION THEOLOGIES

The negativity of the situations to which liberation theologies respond includes but transcends the harm done to the victims. In each case everyone in a particular society and culture participates in the situation and is implicated in its evil effects. The premise of this observation lies in the social constitution of human existence and an anthropology of solidarity about which more will be said below. But it seems clear enough that the unity of many different people in community and society implies that these negative situations contain multiple layers of meaning and will be appropriated differently by the various groups of people who are involved. These negative situations also spawn a range of questions that touch the life of every individual who lives in a given social situation.

Liberation theology engages the religious questions imbedded in these negative contrasts. These religious questions transcend without leaving behind the practical questions of how to resist and remedy the situation. This becomes especially evident when the situations seem untractable, which is usually the case when religious questions rise to the surface. A problem is something that can be solved. The negative situations addressed by liberation theologies are not simply objective social ethical problems, but involve the existence of the inquirers in such a way that they are drawn into the mystery of evil itself. The ultimately mysterious and unintelligible evil of these situations touches the inquirer and thus becomes a religious question.

One can discern at least three distinct but overlapping religious questions involved in the contrast experiences with which liberation theologies are engaged. In one respect these are not new questions but perennial questions in a new, postmodern form. There is a distinctive shape to the religious crisis that is generated by the postmodern problem of evil and sin.

The Ground of the Human Subject

The first question concerns the ground for maintaining the value of the human subject or person. This question arises out of the conjunction of the social constitution of the individual and the social evils addressed by liberation theologies. We are aware, as never before, of the degree to which the human person assumes an individual identity through the social mediation of the community. Sociologists, social psychologists, anthropologists, linguists, historians, and philosophers, along with geneticists and biochemists, have shown that the human person is a function of genetic inheritance and the particular social relationships that shape each one over the long period of his or her development. But the negative situations addressed by liberation theologies show that these same social relationships can submerge the individual, negate the person, destroy identity, rob whole groups and classes of people of their autonomy, freedom, and creativity.[18] The oppressive structures that keep the poor from participating in society, the structures of patriarchy that subordinate people because of their gender, the dehumanizing apparatuses of racism, these social patterns of behavior attack human beings as subjects: open, free, and equal with all others.

This raises the question for a postmodern culture that reads reality and the human phenomenon in terms of systems and various relationships of power: what is the source of human personhood? Is the person any more than his or her social identity? Are groups of people able to be defined, stereotyped, and relegated to an inferior place in society? These questions,

---

18. See Paulo Freire's description of "massification," naive consciousness, and the passage to critical consciousness in *Education for Critical Consciousness* (New York: Seabury Press, 1973), 32–45.

which have implicit answers in social and political arrangements, reach back to the ultimate origin of human existence and its authenticating ground. The questions that liberation theologies ask can be put dramatically in their negative form. Why should there not be a differentiated society in which some people participate with power and others remain marginalized and passive? Why should society pretend that all are equal when they obviously are not? Why should not society be arranged hierarchically so that some dominate others? Every society has a variety of roles; why not assign some to white people, others to brown people, and still others to black people? Why should it not be the case that some people are ordainable and others are not ordainable? These are religious questions, not only about the existence of a God who is the ground of being, but also about the kind of God, the interest of this God in human existence, and the quality and character of a divine will for human history.[19]

The Meaningfulness of Human History

The new question of the meaningfulness of history arises out of a conjunction of relative perspectives concerning the size of the universe, the length of human history, the amount of evil that plagues it. Postmodernity possesses a radical historical consciousness. Scientific data concerning the age of the universe and of the human race have recently become an added ingredient of this sensibility. The human race has been in existence for a long period of time before the age of recorded history. But the age and breadth of the universe which forms the framework for the formation of our planet, the gradual development of life, and the evolution of the human species are so large that they necessarily relativize human history itself as a unified phenomenon. The data concerning history and the universe work on the imagination. They inevitably expand the transcendence of God; paradoxically the infinity of God seems greater and God "farther away." The world seems cut off, on its own, more and more subject to blind forces and chance, less and less an orderly process of organic growth toward a goal.

These data provide a context in which the evil addressed by liberation theologies threatens the meaningfulness of human history itself. More precisely, it is the amount of innocent human suffering that raises the question so sharply. Everyone can handle a little pain and a small amount of suffering. But how can this relatively tiny human history be reckoned as significant and meaningful when it is in turn filled with so much suffering for so many people? How can people claim today that human life is sacred, or that no person should be used only as a means, when in fact human life is so intentionally abused and treated so cheaply on such a

---

19. In the view of Segundo, the religious question today does not lie in the antithesis between faith and atheism but between faith and idolatry; it is not the question of whether God exists that is important, but what kind of God we believe in. Juan Luis Segundo, *Our Idea of God* (Maryknoll, N.Y.: Orbis Books, 1974), 12–14.

massive scale? It is true that, as these questions press in, people have to protect themselves by building isolated, storm-free zones of meaning. The world of work, of family and friends, and of limited political engagement provide the boundaries of a limited coherence. But like the walls of the rich who seek to shut out the squalor of the surrounding poverty, these accommodations cannot work for any thinking person. Human beings live in the same world. Only frankly incoherent thinking can imagine that life can be meaningful for some when it is so meaningless for others, when it delivers to so many little more than innocent suffering. The question, then, carries a new biting seriousness in a culture that is historically conscious and empirical-minded: is history itself serious? Is it really worthwhile, not because of another world, but in itself? Does human existence, human life, really count?

The Purpose of Human Freedom

The purpose of human life is thrown into doubt in postmodernity by the variety of positive and negative values to which people commit their freedom. This religious question correlates closely with the first two problems, but the theme of human freedom provides a distinct and important focal point for understanding salvation.

The radical historical and pluralist consciousness of postmodernity has a direct bearing on anthropology. It underscores the prominent place of freedom in human self-understanding: human existence, despite its physical and social determinants, shares a measure of freedom that none of the other species do. Ideally, that freedom consists in choice, steadfast commitment, and an actualization that creates new being. This whole process is impelled by desires, guided by interests, and drawn forward by values. Historical and pluralist consciousness adds a wide-open and ultimately confusing range of interests and values to a postmodern conception and exercise of freedom. And the deeply entrenched negative realities addressed by liberation theologies contribute to this mix a profound sense of the ambiguity and potential destructiveness of what otherwise might be taken for values. All of the situations addressed by liberation theologies are areas in which one might assume that systems were constructed by a freedom guided by positive interests and attracted by positive values. But instead of being creative these systems have become destructive of life. A more sinister interpretation would conclude that human beings can be equally attracted by evil as by the good, not to mention the variety of interpretations attached to the Christian doctrine of a fall. At what point does the dynamic energy of freedom to achieve something pass over and become a quest for economic self-interest, or for political privilege, or for male domination, or for white supremacy? Can one distinguish a desire to create new productive forms of being from the desire for power that will in the end sacrifice human life for that goal? The negativities addressed by liberation theology rest on human freedom; they cannot be reduced to products of nature. By exposing and challenging them, liberation theology raises the question of an anthropology of freedom that can be focused still further in two subquestions.

The first question concerns fundamental values. Are there any universally relevant basic values that can act as general criteria for the exercise of human freedom? Is there anything like a scale of values, or of meta-values, that can help sort out and evaluate the many interests that guide human choices, actions, and especially social and cultural systems? Given the pluralism that actual history reflects, and the actual conflicts over fundamental values, are such values necessarily the object of revelation and acceptance of them a matter of conversion?

The second question has to do with vocation and the questions of life-decisions. By life-decisions I mean not only once and for all decisions that determine a specific career, but also the internalization of certain values that will consistently guide a life, act as criteria for future decisions, or be responsible for a radical change of an original commitment in new circumstances. As one looks at the ambiguity of the historical effects of decisions resting on the highest of values, how is one to make any life-decision? What object in this world counts as worthy of a life's commitment? For example, is the empirical institution of the actual church the place to best realize the values reflected in the ministry of Jesus Christ? Indeed, is any way of life worthy of a final commitment of one's freedom? Liberation theologies, by challenging the interests and disvalues of various destructive institutions and ideologies, may be interpreted as trying to cut through the relativism implied in today's pluralism. Liberation christology seeks to retrieve in the Christian message some fundamental positive values for human freedom which will challenge the ambiguous and seemingly free interplay of positivity and negativity in human creativity.

What is going on in liberation theology and christology? As a theology the issue extends beyond the tactics for addressing the concrete problems of the destructive power of the negative situations which they challenge. Because liberation theology begins and ends with praxis this involvement is never left behind. But one must look more deeply to discover a universal relevance of this christology, stemming from a situation in which all human beings are implicated, and which reflects most accurately the current cultural situation of postmodernity. These questions will provide the hermeneutical perspective in the analysis of liberation christology of the rest of this chapter.

THE LIBERATIONIST INTERPRETATION OF JESUS

The third element of the three-fold structure of the dynamics of liberation christology consists in the disclosure and appropriation of the object of interpretation: God as mediated by Jesus Christ. How do liberationists interpret Jesus of Nazareth? A patient survey of a variety of liberation theologians would provide the most adequate response to this question. But in view of the large scope of this chapter, I shall have to be content with a more schematic representation, with references to various liberationists as representative of a more general tendency. I shall examine briefly the basic rationale for the appeal to Jesus in liberation christology, the broad lines of how Jesus is understood, and the conception of God that is mediated by Jesus. This survey amplifies the interpretation of Jesus presented in Chapters 3 and 4.

A FOCUS ON JESUS

Virtually all liberation theologians turn to Jesus of Nazareth as the basis for their christology.[20] They do this for many of the reasons provided at the outset of this book. But the liberationist agenda compounds the necessity for this move. The oppressive situations against which liberation christology reacts require less a *logos* of the cosmos and more a *mythos* of history. The Jesus Christ who centers the Christian religious imagination responds to the lack of intelligibility in history. His ministry forms the basis of a narrative theology that conveys a meaning by appealing to action. Only a historical figure can mediate meaning and salvation to precisely those historical situations that make no sense for either the victims or the community as a whole.[21] These themes are consistent in the liberationist interpretation of Jesus: he responds to historical crises; he mediates a salvation that is itself historical even while it is transcendent; and he appeals to a faith of followers who will continue his historical project.

THE JESUS WHO MEDIATES GOD

Liberation theology does not take up the project of a neutral and objective portrayal of Jesus within the confines of his own society, that is, a strictly historical reconstruction of Jesus' ministry. The liberation theologian does not limit his or her imagination to a description of the relationship of Jesus to the various groups of first-century Palestine and the crises of the time. In every case liberation christology includes but transcends this task as it seeks to bring the relevance of Jesus forward to come to bear

---

20. Some feminist christologies do not make this turn to Jesus foundational to their understanding because they locate the problematic addressed by feminism in the tension between the genders. If a fundamental feminist christological question is how a male figure can be a savior for women and the problem in the question is located in a tension between the sexes, there is less likelihood for an extensive appeal to the historical career of Jesus. By contrast, feminist christology which is explicitly liberationist locates the problem not in gender *per se*, but in the ideological construal of gender, i.e., in androcentrism, patriarchy, and more generally dominating power. This allows feminist liberation christology to retrieve prophetic themes from the historical Jesus. See Elisabeth Schüssler Fiorenza, *Jesus*, 36.

21. See Ignacio Ellacuría, *Freedom Made Flesh: The Mission of Christ and His Church* (Maryknoll, N.Y.: Orbis Books, 1976), 27.

on the oppressive situations at hand. The liberationist intention reaches back into history, not to remain there, but to circle back to the present and bring Jesus into relation with the present-day world. Reconstruction of what and who Jesus was is a complex enterprise, and it is filled with interpretive judgments at every stage of the process. Liberationists make clear the hermeneutical character of their project and the specific perspective they bring to the task.[22]

Given the conflictive situation of oppression and injustice that liberation theologians address, it is not surprising that the prophetic dimension of Jesus' ministry defines his character for many liberation theologians. Jesus appears in the prophetic-liberating tradition of biblical faith that is constant in both the Jewish scriptures and in the Christian testament. As a prophet, Jesus criticizes religion wherever it justifies oppression or exclusion; he defends the poor and warns the rich. "The prostitutes and the tax collectors will go into the Kingdom of God ahead of the Scribes and the Pharisees."[23] Jon Sobrino suggests that Jesus' prophetic activity may be characterized as a consistent stance against any behavior that diminishes life. God is a God of life, who at every juncture wills creation to flourish. This corresponds to God's rule or kingdom. Wherever people or systems curtail or devalue or suppress life, this is anti-kingdom, and Jesus aggressively takes a stand against it. Jesus' prophetic activity is his continuous "direct denunciation of the anti-Kingdom."[24]

The liberationist interpretation of Jesus highlights the political dimension of Jesus' ministry. The political character of Jesus' ministry provides the central hermeneutical key in Juan Luis Segundo's extensive analysis of Jesus' career. He works from the premise that a public figure of Jesus' stature, especially given the fact that he was publicly executed, could not have failed to have had a political impact on his society.[25] Among Jesus' prime constituents were those whom he sought as disciples. Jesus intended to form a cadre or corps of followers who would enlist in a religious historical project that would simultaneously be critical of all historical mechanisms that oppressed and constructive of structures that enhanced human life. The immediate beneficiaries of this historical project would be the poor. As a prophet Jesus clashed with both the religious

---

22. Although this hermeneutical character of the project is clear in all liberation christologists, not all are equally explicit in characterizing their method as such. Most clear is Elisabeth Schüssler Fiorenza, *In Memory of Her*, 3–40; Jon Sobrino in *Jesus as Liberator* is also explicit about his methodology relative to Jesus.

23. Ruether, *Sexism and God-Talk*, 30. See also 120.

24. Sobrino, *Jesus the Liberator*, 161. See also Julie M. Hopkins, *Towards a Feminist Christology: Jesus of Nazareth, European Women, and the Christological Crisis* (Grand Rapids: Eerdmans, 1995), 22–33.

25. Segundo, *The Historical Jesus of the Synoptics*, 71–85. Segundo does not hold that a political hermeneusis exhausts the significance of Jesus, but this aspect is central and others, such as his religious impact, must be read in connection with the political. According to the genres developed in Chapter 3, Jesus was a prophetic figure.

and the civil authorities of his time. "Jesus was not crucified because of his theological teachings but because of their potentially subversive character and the political threat to the imperial colonial system."[26] This political dimension to Jesus' mission should not be controversial; he operated in a public and conflictive way in a society where religious and political issues were intertwined. But just as this dimension is almost self-evident, so too is it crucial for a liberationist appropriation of Jesus. The religiosity of Jesus, the very faith that structured his life, contained no separation, but demanded a dynamic interaction between being in relation with God and being engaged in the public issues of society.

This becomes clear in the meaning and function of the kingdom of God that liberation christology takes to be the centerpiece of Jesus' preaching and ministerial behavior. The reign of God means that God rules in history, and God's kingdom is what comes to pass when God rules: "a history, a society, a people transformed according to the will of God."[27] This kingdom of God, then, is not other-worldly; it is what people hope for in history. It refers to a social condition that transforms people and society. It appears in contrast to the anti-kingdom; it negates the negation of oppression and injustice. Although the kingdom of God comes as a gift from God, it is mediated by human activity and should be understood in conjunction with human freedom. And although the benefits of God's rule are open to all, Jesus addresses his preaching of the kingdom to the poor because of their weakness, to the sick and possessed because of their suffering, to public sinners because they are excluded and marginalized. It is the reign of God the compassionate one.[28]

The actions of Jesus are viewed by liberation theologians as the actions of one who is completely devoted to the kingdom of God. Many of Jesus' works are seen to realize, embody, or actualize the kingdom of God. When Jesus heals, the power being exercised there is of God as Spirit, and this making whole and restoring an integral life represents in an instance God's power, God's rule, God's kingdom. When Jesus offers forgiveness or welcome or hospitality to those who are socially unacceptable, this represents God's posture. When Jesus enters into conflict with religious authorities about the true meaning of the law, this too represents God's rule. As liberationists read Jesus' public ministry, Jesus is acting out the values and attitudes of God as he understood them. Once again, then, one sees in this interpretation how actions, events, actual gestures are also symbolic; the concrete and even physical benefits for those whose lives

---

26. Schüssler Fiorenza, *Jesus*, 93.

27. Sobrino, *Jesus the Liberator*, 71. See the whole of Chapter 6, "Jesus and the Kingdom of God," 67–104.

28. It is interesting to note the close, almost one-to-one correspondence of the dimensions of Jesus' idea of the kingdom of God in the analysis of Elisabeth Schüssler Fiorenza when compared with the dimensions highlighted by Jon Sobrino. Compare *In Memory of Her*, 118–30, and *Jesus the Liberator*, 67–104. I assume that these analyses are independent of each other.

are affected by Jesus' actions are simultaneously laden with religious value. In the Jewish conception of the time, God's own power and action as Spirit were being mediated in history. One can see in this process of interpretation how Jesus reveals a *mythos* of history. Jesus' ministry is regarded as a narrative whole. His ministerial career, including each of the concrete gestures that constituted it, functions as a parable of God. As such this concrete, narrative symbol releases to the religious imagination an encounter with God. In this experience of God mediated by Jesus, his followers gain a glimpse of God's creative and providential will, and how human beings should respond to it.

Liberation theologians, along with many others, are convinced that Jesus is the founder and leader of a movement.[29] In other words, he explicitly seeks followers to expand his preaching and actions in his own milieu. A number of themes gravitate around this nuclear datum. First, Jesus leads the way where others can follow. For Sobrino, this means that Jesus is a person of faith and trust, where these virtues are fashioned by commitment and action. To have followers, Jesus must be imitable.[30] Second, as we saw, Segundo emphasizes the historical project, the political historical activity, that forms the goal of this movement. Third, the band of followers is characterized by Schüssler Fiorenza as a discipleship of equals. This forms a historical basis for criticism of all institutions exercising dominative power, including patriarchy.[31] Fourth, one can expand the idea of a community of equals to reach a more generalized notion of a community whose social relationships are transformed. The fundamental idea of salvation as transformation of society can be envisaged here in concrete historical terms. The Jesus movement is meant to be a community characterized by relationships of love and justice.[32] And, fifth, all of this added up to a relatively new, or at least a renewed, conception of religion. Over against any area where faith has devolved into religious formalism, against any objectification of religious means, and certainly against any forgetfulness of the poor and the oppressed, the Jesus movement inspires a new idealism for religious faith. The kingdom of God is near.

This represents a highly generalized and schematic portrait of Jesus, for the narrative dimension of liberationist interpretation cannot be captured here. In this synopsis, however, one can still clearly identify two dimensions of the liberationist hermeneutic: the one is the Jesus of history, the

---

29. Dean Brackley, *Divine Revolution: Salvation and Liberation in Catholic Thought* (Maryknoll, N.Y.: Orbis Books, 1996), 136, 178 n.30.

30. The faith of Jesus is an important theme in Sobrino's christology. See *Christology at the Crossroads*, 79–145, where he dedicates an entire chapter to the topic. This is not an effort to gain a knowledge of Jesus' psychological consciousness. Rather, because living by faith is a universal human condition, faith is emblematic of Jesus' humanity and forms a bond of identification between him and his followers. Also, *Jesus the Liberator*, 154–57.

31. Schüssler Fiorenza, *In Memory of Her*, 135–36.

32. Brackley, *Divine Revolution*, 102–03.

other is the bearing he is perceived to have on the present-day situation. As to the theme of relevance, it is not difficult to see how this Jesus addresses the situations of oppressive poverty, sexism, patriarchalism, dominative power, racism and the remains of a culture that actively supported or tolerated slavery. In Jesus one can read a religious and moral response to those issues. But at the same time this reading of Jesus is not eisegesis. The bases for this interpretation and appropriation of Jesus lie in the New Testament witness to Jesus of Nazareth. Jesus of Nazareth opens up this reading of his significance, a significance that is not alien to his historical reality as it appears in the historical data.

THE GOD OF JESUS

Jesus preached the reign of God. A good deal of analysis in liberation christology deals with the nature of the kingdom of God. But liberationists also recognize the importance of the conception of God that controls the metaphor. Generally speaking, liberation theologians do not approach christology with a supposition that the character of God is a given, something already known, whatever the source of this knowledge might be. Rather, Jesus himself is taken as the mediation of how God should be construed in the Christian imagination. Liberation theologians express this quite explicitly in a variety of ways. Jesus and his ministry are the answer to the question of the nature of God.[33] There is an epistemological break between what we can know of God by inference from created reality and the encounter with God that is mediated in the life of Jesus through death and resurrection.[34] Jesus is normative for Christian faith insofar as he is revealer of God. Paul's conception of God, for example, must be subordinated to that of Jesus, because Jesus alone places in focus the Christian imagination's conception of God, God's will, and God's authority.[35]

One could survey the range of qualities that characterize the God of Jesus across the writings of liberation theologians. But Jon Sobrino's analysis of how God appears in Jesus' ministry forms a convenient summary.[36] The goodness and graciousness of God are expressed in many ways in the preaching and ministry of Jesus. The main metaphor used by Jesus of God

---

33. Juan Luis Segundo interprets the doctrine of Chalcedon functionally and epistemologically as meaning that we only know the nature of God through the concrete humanity and life of Jesus. The doctrine does not mean "Jesus is God," but "God is Jesus." See *The Christ of the Ignatian Exercises* (Maryknoll, N.Y.: Orbis Books, 1987), 29–40.

34. Sobrino, *Christology at the Crossroads*, 219–24, 370–71. Two of three chapters on the historical Jesus are dedicated by Sobrino to Jesus and God in *Jesus the Liberator*. This represents a development in his christology in which he explicitly formulates his idea of God through a portrayal of the kerygmatic historical Jesus following the pattern suggested by Segundo. See the previous note.

35. Schüssler Fiorenza, *In Memory of Her*, 101.

36. Sobrino, *Jesus the Liberator*, Chapters 5 and 6, 135–79.

is Father which, for Sobrino, points to God's goodness, love, and concern for people as for God's children. God is one who is faithful and can be trusted. God is transcendent; as such God is powerful, but neither authoritarian nor oppressive. God is also close to the world, concerned about it, and active in it. God is loving with a love that actually touches and engages human existence.

But, finally, the specifying aspect that defines the notion of God most characteristic to liberation christology must lie in Jesus' own central metaphor for representing God. This is the kingdom of God, and it draws from a distinct Jewish tradition. God is the one who assures justice for those who are defenseless, and kings take over this responsibility from God as God's agents. With the metaphor of the kingdom, therefore, Jesus is preaching a God who is the liberator of the oppressed, the deliverer of victims from their oppression and oppressors, and the vindicator of the weak. This is Yahweh the righteous one, who is the ground of justice, the redeemer of the oppressed, the One who defends the helpless. "Righteousness and justice are the foundation of thy throne; steadfast love and faithfulness go before thee" (Ps 89:14). Therefore in Jesus' central message one finds the God who is king, the One who is both righteous and merciful, and who acts to save the poor and any group which is oppressed. The kingdom of God is "God's coming vindication of the poor and afflicted in Israel after the manner of the ideal king of the ancient Near East, not because the poor were righteous, but because God is righteous and merciful."[37]

In these appropriations of Jesus, and through him of God, one finds the beginnings of an answer to the questions addressed by liberation christology. God guarantees the value of the human person, promises that history has a meaning, but seeks human collaboration in establishing that meaning.

SALVATION AND THE CHRISTIAN LIFE

Given this interpretation of the historical data about Jesus and his view of God, I now move to the manner in which liberation theology construes salvation. The last chapter depicted the objective work of Jesus within the framework of a revelatory and exemplary conception of salvation, but not without the theme of Jesus mediating God's active presence in history. The following section will complement this interpretation in a number of different ways. First of all, the discussion shifts to the question of subjective salvation, the act of appropriating what is mediated by Jesus Christ. The emphasis falls much more on the human response to God's presence and

---

37. Brackley, *Divine Revolution*, 126. Brackley bases his analysis on the beatitudes which are understood to be a programmatic statement of Jesus by Jacques Dupont, *Les Béatitudes*, 3 vols. (Paris: J. Gabalda, 1969–73).

action in Jesus in such a way that it is received as salvation. Second, the interpretation offered here is particularly attentive to the social character of salvation as that is highlighted by liberation theology. What is social salvation, and how is individual and personal salvation related to it? Third, the three deeper soteriological questions raised by postmodernity will also be operative in this interpretation. These questions concern the grounds of the value of the person, the meaningfulness of history, and the objects and goals worthy for the commitment of human freedom.

THE SOCIAL CHARACTER OF SALVATION

The last chapter described the deep negativities that religiously call out for salvation: salvation from ignorance, sin and guilt, suffering, and finally death. The real and integral character of salvation means that it must comprehend the whole of life. Salvation is an all-encompassing concept that reaches out toward integrated human wholeness. Although it is religious, it cannot be confined to a narrow spiritual sphere that leaves the fullness of life behind.

Regarding the comprehensive character of salvation, liberation theology has shown that an individualistic notion of salvation is impossible. In the Christian framework of a saving God who is compassionate and righteous, universally loving and just, a purely private and personal salvation set off from the salvation of others is self-contradictory. From an anthropological perspective, the premise for the incoherence of a private salvation lies in the social constitution of human existence. Human existence is a social phenomenon, so that even the individual, in his or her quasi-autonomy, is at the same time a function of social relationships, not to mention intrinsic, organic relationships with the world of nature. This anthropology of human solidarity describes an ontological condition; these relationships constitute persons whether or not they are always explicitly aware of their formational character. On the one hand, then, God is the creator and lover of all human beings together as a group and individually as members of the species called human. But, on the other hand, all human beings are caught up in the negative situations of ignorance, sin, suffering, and death; these are characteristics of the race, and individual members of the species are all implicated in specific, historically defined ways. This social solidarity in a single human race prohibits anyone from even conceiving or hoping for a salvation that would leave others behind.[38] It is not conceivable that the Christian God would love one and not the other, or some and not the others, or that some people are left religiously ignorant while others are completely enlightened, or that some are sinners before God and others not.

---

38. For Schillebeeckx, social solidarity would prohibit final happiness if it included knowledge that others were suffering eternally. Edward Schillebeeckx, "God as a Bogeyman for Some Christians," *For the Sake of the Gospel* (New York: Crossroad, 1990), 112.

The deep insight into the solidarity of humankind as creatures of one God is absolutely central to the Christian vision. Its fundamental importance lies in the fact that in modern western cultures a privatized notion of salvation has gained an ascendency. The privatization of religion implies that this is precisely what people hope for: my salvation, whether or not others are saved. All of us want to believe that, fundamentally, before God and the world, "I'm all right." And this may lead to a distorted idea of self-righteousness that allows some to imagine that they can find a presently satisfying and ultimately completed salvation while others do not. Some aspects of postmodernity are beginning to erode this modern and arrogant corruption of Christian belief, especially in the wake of the increased interaction of peoples around the world and the humbling experience in so much war, poverty, human dislocation, and political oppression of which the Christian West has had no small part. We need a realistic, comprehensible, and engaging concept of social finitude, ignorance, and sin to keep up with consciousness of our actual situation.

Such an explicit concept of social sin has been characteristic of liberation theologies beginning with the theology of the social gospel. Although lacking a deep anthropology of sin in the tradition of Augustine, the social gospel theologians were aware of how a pervasive kingdom of social evil can take on a life of its own and shape the lives of all.[39] Social sin may be defined as any social situation or institution that is destructive of human life. As such it is against the will of the creator of life. But since sin is a moral category implying human guilt, other elements need to be appreciated for social sin to make sense. One is that objective social situations and institutions rest on the stuff of human freedom; they have no natural necessity but can be changed. Another is that, since a social institution does not ordinarily depend on the will of a single individual, but is embedded in learned patterns of social behavior, social sin is not a function of the same kind of responsibility as personal sin but is analogous to it.

We have seen the kinds of social sin that inspired liberation theologies: the corruption, greed, and ruthlessness of unregulated capitalism, systems of political economy that exclude masses of people from participation and keep the poor in dependence, racism and sexism that denigrate people on the basis of physical characteristics. These are specific forms of social sin which become materialized in various specific institutions and patterns of behavior. Thus the idea of social sin can act as a formal, heuristic category that sheds light on all social behavior and illumines the ways in which social patterns of doing things can dehumanize and negate life. All know that no perfect society exists; all social life remains tinged with social sin;

---

39. Rauschenbusch used the phrase "kingdom of evil" for what Sobrino now calls the "anti-Kingdom." See Rauschenbusch, *A Theology for the Social Gospel*, 45–94, for his treatment of objectified social sin. See also Edward A. Ross, *Sin and Society: An Analysis of Latter-Day Iniquity* (Boston: Houghton, Mifflin, 1907), for an early, straightforward sociological analysis of the effects of social sin on members of society.

but some forms of society and some actual societies are more humane than others; and some forms of social sin are radically evil in their destruction of life. One has only to analyze the deep cultural patterns of understanding, valuing, and behaving that underlie the various areas of social strife in our world today, many of which involve religious differentiation, to see the destructive power of social finitude, social ignorance, social sin.

In contrast to social sin, liberation theologies conceive of salvation in antithetical social terms; social salvation negates the negation of the anti-kingdom, social sin. Gustavo Gutiérrez has proposed a formula for salvation that is simple and comprehensive: salvation is communion of people with God and among themselves.[40] This social characterization of salvation embraces the human person as unique individual. This conception includes the idea of human fulfillment. It points to a condition that can be realized within history in a partial manner at the same time that it lies open to perfect eschatological completion. Only such a comprehensive social conception of salvation can be adequate today because the social make-up of human beings is now inescapably apparent. And just as social sin is not an external condition that remains outside individuals, but becomes internalized, so too "human beings *constitute* themselves as human only in society, and they are fulfilled as humans only in society."[41] Human beings can live up to their potential and find fulfillment only within relationships which, because they are built on a combination of the values of love and justice, nurture and facilitate human development. To think of an individual human being apart from his or her social situation, as an introspective existential anthropology tends to do, entails a massive abstraction precisely from his or her individuality. By contrast, to think of individuals in terms of their communities, as living within a network of relationships and interactions that make up a whole life, is to grasp more comprehensively and adequately the very individuality of the person.[42] In short, because human existence is social, an integral and comprehensive salvation can only be social.[43]

David Tracy proposes another straightforward characterization of Christian salvation from the point of view of the individual person, but which balances personal responsibility neatly with the social constitution of human existence. Salvation has three dimensions. First, salvation is a release of the human person from bondage and for freedom. The multiple bondages were discussed in the last chapter. In a postmodern context,

---

40. Gutiérrez, *A Theology of Liberation*, 159.

41. Brackley, *Divine Revolution*, 102.

42. Metz, *Theology of the World*, 110–11.

43. This thesis is developed at greater length by Brackley, *Divine Revolution*, 102–22. It ought to be noted that this accent on the social character of salvation is a retrieval in the face of modern, western individualism. By contrast, the overwhelming witness of the bible is to salvation in social terms, but not to the exclusion of the individual person appealing to God, as, for example, in the psalms.

however, the release of the human spirit for freedom assumes a major importance. Second, this release is experienced as a gift and a task from God. The gift of release expands the human spirit in the direction of self-transcendence, enabling it to accept the responsibility of freedom to address the various life-negating situations that deprive us of meaning. The gift thus enables freedom to accept the task of creating meaning. Third, in the Christian dispensation this salvation is disclosed by Jesus Christ. By revealing God and the power of God's salvation Jesus constitutes this salvation in the life of the Christian.[44]

Given a general conception of salvation that is social in such a way that individuals with their uniqueness, freedom, and initiative are in no way compromised, one needs a further distinction relative to salvation in order to grasp exactly how a social situation envelops and engages discrete human persons.[45] Salvation may be characterized as both a condition and as a dynamic process. For example, one speaks of the salvation of a single person as consisting in his or her union with God and with other human beings. But the way in which a person comes to salvation is through a process of conversion. On the social level an analogous distinction helps to clarify the liberationist language of salvation. On one hand, we have just characterized salvation socially as a condition of the community or society in which the social relationships that bind people together are just and humane. They so respect the human subjects involved in them that they approach the general will of God for human life. On the other hand, this ideal society is not descriptive of the real world; the characterization of social sin is much more realistic; and this raises the question of social salvation as a process. It is clear that social sin does not give way easily, if at all, to social salvation. Clear as well is the fact that one cannot expect God to intervene overtly and directly into human history to remedy the situations of social sin. Liberation theologians use the language of liberation to describe the historical mechanisms by which the process of salvation becomes a reality in history. But where is this liberation? Is there any way of understanding this characterization of the process of liberation that can make it appear as more substantive than merely romantic religious language?

---

44. David Tracy, "The Christian Understanding of Salvation-Liberation," *Face to Face*, 14 (1988), 37–39. Tracy goes on to defend the metaphor of "liberation" as the most adequate and relevant for understanding salvation in our time: "if Christian salvation is appropriately described in our period as both freedom from all bondage and freedom for authentic existence, then there is every good reason to suggest that the liberation, political, and feminist theologians are correct to insist that 'total liberation' is a most appropriate metaphor and concept for Christian salvation in our day. Jesus Christ, Liberator, is an appropriate model for a contemporary christology." Ibid., 40.

45. Individualism in theological literature generally is a pejorative term. But in more general usage, especially when contrasted with an implied collectivism, individualism often carries the values of a personal initiative of individuals and a creative courage that opens up new horizons for themselves and others. In other words, individualism can have positive social connotations in other linguistic contexts.

Participation in the Process of Salvation

One way of developing a realistic theological language about liberation and social salvation consists in going back to the Jesus movement and interpreting his preaching and what came of it. Jesus preaches the kingdom of God. In secular terms this kingdom of God is frequently described as a utopic ideal that stands out in front of history and society as a source of hope and of those values meant to govern our actions. But Jesus also appeals to and enlists followers; he stands at the head of a historical Jesus movement. This means that Jesus wants his ministry to be expanded and to continue. The correlate of this side of Jesus' ministry is that the values of the kingdom of God can in some partial degree be realized in concrete communities in specific historical situations. The antithesis between God's reign and the anti-kingdom in this world is always a matter of degree. In varying degrees societies and communities will embody to a more or less extent in their actual social relationships the values of justice and respect for all people.

Just as salvation characterizes a social situation or community in varying degrees across a wide spectrum, from seeming non-existence to a more recognizably just society, so too one must understand participation in this very salvation not as something merely objective, but as consisting in a variety of responses. One can distinguish between a passive and an active participation in the dynamics of social sin and social salvation. In the measure in which people are entirely passive to the social mechanisms that shape their lives, the religious language of salvation must seem unintelligible. As long as people remain passive, so that their consciousness and freedom are submerged, the condition of society cannot be appreciated as a religious matter. Participation in God's salvation as such, therefore, requires a recognition of the religious dimensions of reality, a sense of the social construction of reality, an engagement with the issues of love of God and love of neighbor, and an active response to the utopic values of the kingdom of God.

With these distinctions we are now in a position to give a more accurate and realistic characterization in liberationist terms of the salvation mediated and revealed by Jesus Christ. Jesus in his preaching and action in history revealed the potential of a power of salvation that comes from God and is operative in this world. Over against the kingdom of evil and the forces of death, Jesus reveals a way of life. The power of God for life and salvation is realized concretely in his own life; Jesus makes God present in a saving way especially in his acts in the power of God as Spirit. But the salvation Jesus preaches and exemplifies is a power that must be actualized by human freedom; it remains a merely potential salvation until it is taken up by followers and acted out in history.

Real salvation in history is potential salvation taken up and concretized in action. God is surely at work in creative, saving action apart from the conscious response of human beings. But the recognition of this as precisely God's saving action requires a specifically religious insight. The logic of this awareness consists in a negative experience of contrast, a religious question, an awareness that God is the source of all power that overcomes the destructive forces of sin, and, most importantly, the active participation of becoming a follower, resisting sin, and working to build up social relationships that are just and humanizing. This last element is decisive: salvation is finally mediated through a form of human action. Where there is no resistance to social sin, social salvation does not exist. Where there is no liberating practice in the face of social oppression, then it is nonsense to speak about salvation in this world. The language of salvation is precisely a language that appeals to freedom to make salvation happen; it is not a description of a state of affairs.

This construct may be tested by the questions that are posed by the negativities of history to which liberation theologies are a response. In the framework of androcentrism, patriarchalism, or any other social system of dominative power, in the light of racism or any other virulent form of socially structured human aggression, how does the meaning of social salvation make sense? It makes no sense to point to a prejudice-free society; there is no society without oppression. It does make sense, however, to speak of salvation as a participation in the movement to resist all forms of dehumanizing institutions and behavior patterns. In this case Jesus reveals a potential salvation. This is not a salvation already accomplished but one that is possible and may in some measure be implemented. Jesus opens up a possibility for human life committed to resisting specific dehumanizing structures in society and promoting their opposite. Religious salvation does not lie in the degree of the success of this action, but in the action itself. On the one hand, one can find salvation in the dedication of freedom to human liberation, even when the cause fails in this world. In some respects Jesus fits this pattern. On the other hand, one can wallow in meaninglessness despite every material advantage and complete external emancipation. The meaningfulness of human existence in history lies precisely in the intentional exercise of personal and corporate freedom.

Is history meaningful? Jesus reveals a potential salvation that is dependent upon its being taken up in action by the follower. The possible meaning of history consists precisely in assuming in one's own life the values of the kingdom of God and acting them out in one's own history. Analogously, the history of groups and societies and nations will be as meaningful as the measure in which they incorporate the values of the kingdom into their corporate or institutionalized social lives. History as a whole is partly meaningful and partly meaningless. One participates in its salvific meaning according to the social values that govern one's life and in the measure of one's commitment and action.

In the confusing pluralism of possible values which claim ultimacy, that is, which possess the ability to unify the person and society in a common goal and destiny, what is worthy of human freedom? Jesus' preaching of God's rule holds out a potential salvation to human freedom. The kingdom of God as preached in Jesus' parables, beatitudes, and sayings, and as demonstrated by a variety of his actions, offers a set of values that appeals to the widest possible range of human commitment and also bestows on human freedom a new worth in service to the neighbor and society. But these values must be internalized and acted out in order to constitute a real salvation in history.

It is at this point in the discussion of salvation that the bearing of christology on the Christian life becomes apparent and meaningful. Christology is not only the center of Christian self-understanding and understanding of all reality, it is the ground of Christian spirituality which in its most elementary form is a conception of the Christian life. A traditional phrase for a christological understanding of Christian spirituality and life is "the imitation of Christ." In the light of a revelatory and exemplary soteriology, the imitation of Christ means that Jesus Christ is to be interpreted in a way that opens up possibilities for the commitment and exercise of human freedom in diverse and changing situations. This requires creative, imaginative, and always changing applications of the values of Jesus' ministry to new circumstances.

Few areas in practical theology today are as diffuse and subject to different methods of understanding as the domain of spirituality. One of the roles of systematic theology in this regard is to provide critical norms and theological grounding for Christian spirituality. This can be done in a variety of ways; different doctrines shed light on the Christian life, and each doctrine is subject to a variety of theological methods.[46] But the doctrine of salvation, at the point where Jesus Christ becomes relevant for human salvation, seems to lie at the center of things.[47] In the view of salvation and spirituality represented by liberation christology, these two elements are essential. First, the appropriation of salvation and thus the ground of Christian spirituality consist in action, a form of Christian life that takes its shape on the basis of the revelation God's values in Jesus Christ. Second, this action ought to take place in and be a response to society. The Christian life has to find its place in a social salvation. Such is the necessary conclusion of both a social anthropology and the social implications of the teaching and ministry of Jesus, that is, his mediation of God.

ESCHATOLOGY

This chapter on liberation christologies has made a number of determinations concerning the nature of salvation. It has moved from the objec-

---

46. In *An Alternative Vision: An Interpretation of Liberation Theology* (New York: Paulist Press, 1985), 233–56, I discuss various paths taken by liberation theologians to develop their views of spirituality. See especially 234–39.

47. Together with the doctrine of God as Spirit, which in relation to salvation has been developed in the western church since Augustine as the doctrine of grace.

tive saving work of Jesus Christ to salvation as the appropriation by Christians of what has been mediated symbolically by Jesus Christ. It has considered the necessity of viewing salvation comprehensively: it must be understood to include simultaneously a personal and a social dimension. To encounter God in Jesus and to be united with God conveys salvation in deep, personal terms of acceptance, forgiveness, and being drawn into God's personal love. But an encounter with God in Jesus also means that God is personally immanent and present to the world. The whole world does not lack, but subsists in, the personal presence of God. A construal of either dimension without the other amounts to a distortion of Christian salvation. I have also introduced the distinction between salvation as an objective social condition and as a historical process, a distinction which is analogous to the difference between God's kingdom and God's reign or ruling. In the case of social salvation, the process of God's saving action is not accomplished without human agents. Therefore, one should understand God's saving work in history not as over against human agents but as transpiring through human freedom. This opens the way to seeing the relevance of salvation to Christian life and spirituality, and to understanding how what Jesus Christ reveals and mediates in human history can respond to some of the deepest questions raised by our current human situation.

But one must also say something about eschatology, about the ultimate meaning and value of freedom, of history, and of the human person. Up to this point I have been speaking of salvation as a creative and active power of God healing and empowering freedom within human history. What can be said of the ultimate end and goal of God's saving presence, the eschaton?

The logic of eschatology and the epistemology of eschatological opinion, that is, how one forms judgments about the end-time, require modesty in what is affirmed. Eschatological statements about the reality that will obtain in God's absolute future do not qualify as matters of a specific knowledge. Such convictions are usually considered functions of hope based on the beliefs that arise out of a faith encounter with God in Jesus Christ. In effect, one projects present faith experience into the absolute future, and one extrapolates what seem to be the necessary conditions and implications of the convictions born in a present-day encounter with God's saving presence in Jesus Christ. The bottom line, then, is that human beings do not know anything about the conditions of a final unity with God in God's own sphere of reality. But one has to say something, and it should be consistent with the theology that is thematized in the present situation.[48]

Perhaps the most important eschatological conviction for our time would deal with the continuity between the exercise of human freedom

---

48. Karl Rahner, "The Hermeneutics of Eschatological Assertions," *Theological Investigations* 4 (Baltimore: Helicon Press, 1966), 323–46.

in this world and the final state of things. Several reasons encourage positing such a continuous eschatology in contrast to a total discontinuity
between this world and what is accomplished in it, on one side, and a final
reality which is created totally new by God, on the other.[49] If there is no
continuity between the works of human freedom and the final kingdom
of God, if the whole of the end-time is fashioned anew out of God's own
self, then the creativity of human freedom in this world amounts to nothing. It literally possesses no final significance at all. But this in its turn
appears to contradict the very creation by God of human freedom as we
know it today. It also undercuts God's saving initiative in Jesus Christ,
which in turn reveals God's continuous sustaining and saving power that,
when accepted, frees freedom from itself and opens it up to create new
things in the power of love. The Christian experience of God implies no
negation of the ontological self, and certainly no devaluation of the human
project. One must interpret God's love as moving in the opposite direction. The encounter with God in Jesus Christ entails a recognition that God
has created something other than God's self, and that God so values
human existence that God enters into loving dialogue with it. All creation
and all human beings in it amount to something real. Especially human
beings, although dependent upon God for existence itself, stand within
that dependence as other than God and able to respond in dialogue with
God. Ironically, and dialectically, Christian revelation affirms the reality
and dignity of human beings and their freedom on the basis of their
absolute dependence in existence and their being loved by the transcendent God of power and might. God does not devalue human freedom and
its creativity; God establishes and grounds their importance.

The resurrection of Jesus can be interpreted in such a way that it discloses this logic. The story of Jesus is not a myth about a being who comes
down and goes back up again. One should not think imaginatively of
Jesus of Nazareth as existing in another place before his birth in Palestine.
Jesus is a human being and, as such, a creature. The resurrection of Jesus
is the drawing of this person into God's life. Such a resurrection is a model
of a continuous eschatology. It is not Jesus' soul or spirit alone that is resurrected; the resurrection of the body symbolizes that Jesus' whole life and
person dies into life in God's reality. But the person of Jesus is constituted
by his relations and actions in this world. As with every other human
being Jesus is a product of his culture and society. And Jesus is what Jesus
did. Jesus made himself by the decisions he made, the creative responses
to the people and situations around him, the commitments that structured
his life and to which he was faithful to the end. The standard interpretation of the resurrection as God's validation of Jesus' life implies the preservation of that whole life in the full complexity of his social constitution as

---

49. By a continuous eschatology I mean a partial, not a complete, continuity
between the creativity and production of human freedom and the final reality of the
end-time. Complete continuity makes little sense in the face of death.

a part of final reality. Regarding Jesus as the final Adam effectively means that Jesus' destiny reveals the plan of God for human existence.

A continuous eschatology bestows a new dimension of ultimacy and seriousness on human existence and the exercise of human freedom. Human beings contribute to the material of the final kingdom of God. That which human beings accomplish in love will make up the substance of the kingdom of God. Although we have no idea how this will be, what has been productive and supportive of human existence will be the stuff of the eschaton. What is given to human freedom to do, and is not done, will not be made up by God.[50] This is not meant in a way that preempts God's freedom, but as an entailment of God's gift of human freedom, and of God's effective presence for human salvation that releases freedom in creativity. Thus a continuous eschatology contributes to the three questions underlying liberation christology an answer that ensures an enduring and even absolute significance. The human person is absolutely valuable; human history and the commitments of human freedom in it are absolutely serious. This view of salvation requires a construal of grace which, while preserving God's initiative in salvation, also emphasizes the positive role of human freedom in God's economy of salvation in history.[51]

A continuous eschatology is of a piece with a new alignment of the doctrines of creation and salvation. All of creation, the full range of human behaviors, ordinary and everyday relationships are all the stuff of salvation. Religious salvation is not escape from history but mediated by engagement in history. A tribe escaping from the conditions of slavery and construing it as divine salvation is not mythological language in a pejorative sense. It is rather the language of creation and salvation that understands God's loving and saving power to be the creating ground of all reality. When the separation between creation and salvation is broken down, one will be able to see the whole of life as sustained by God's creating and by God as Spirit's loving presence and saving power because they are the same thing.[52]

---

50. Juan Luis Segundo, *The Humanist Christology of Paul* (Maryknoll, N.Y.: Orbis Books, 1986), 123–25, 157. Also see Frances Stefano, *The Absolute Value of Human Action in the Theology of Juan Luis Segundo* (Lanham, Md.: University Press of America, 1992), where she draws out at length the significance of Segundo's continuous eschatology. Segundo is not the only theologian to hold a continuous eschatology, but few put as fine a point on it.

51. See Roger Haight, "Sin and Grace," *Systematic Theology*, 2, ed. by John Galvin and Francis Schüssler Fiorenza (Minneapolis: Fortress Press, 1991), 75–141, esp. 131–39.

52. Among other things, the doctrine of creation out of nothing means that God is immediately present to all finite reality and thus to human beings. This means that Jesus Christ should not be understood apart from or over above creation, but precisely within the framework of creation. In the final analysis christology is *"concentrated* creation: belief in creation as God wills it to be." Edward Schillebeeckx, *Interim Report on the Books Jesus and Christ* (New York: Crossroad, 1981), 128. See also Schillebeeckx, "I Believe in God, Creator of Heaven and Earth," *God among Us: The Gospel Proclaimed* (New York: Crossroad, 1983), 91–102.

Another eschatological question debated today revolves around whether one can conceive of final salvation as effectively universal, that is, whether all human beings will actually be saved. As in most pointed eschatological matters one cannot conceive a theological argument in any direction which will satisfy all. The western church seemed to have problems with Origen's doctrine of *apokatastasis*, but did not react to the same doctrine in Gregory of Nyssa. Some theologians speculate that human works not accomplished in love will cease to exist, and that people who are so bound in hatred that all love is driven from their hearts will be annihilated.[53] Karl Rahner, along with others, admits the possibility of hell, but does not believe that anyone is in it. In effect, he believes, because he hopes, in universal salvation.[54] The logic behind the faith-hope of universal salvation rests on taking with absolute seriousness the saving love that Jesus reveals God to be. The justice and righteousness of God, upon which especially the victims of this world make a claim, need not be negated by this love. It is simply that we do not know the mechanisms of its fulfillment.[55]

To conclude, liberation theology transcends the themes of social liberation that have guided this reading of it. In some parts of the world the theme of inculturation sublates emancipation into the explicit demand that Christianity take root in the distinctive forms of the local culture. And the exigencies for human liberation and release from social suffering have been enlisted as constituting the common and centering context for communication among religions in interfaith dialogue. The impulse of liberation has also brought this theology to bear upon the threat of ecological disaster and seeks to awaken human consciousness to its responsibility for stewardship of the planet. All of these later developments of liberation theology entail new appropriations of the modern concern for emancipation in a postmodern context.

I have represented liberation theology in terms of social salvation. But as such, liberation christology should not be read merely in the terms of a local theology. Its significance should not be restricted to the particular constituency of those who are victims of the particular evil it addresses. Liberation christologies include but transcend the specific forms of domination and oppression that each one resists. A more adequate reading of

---

53. Schillebeeckx, *For the Sake of the Gospel*, 112. For Juan Luis Segundo, only what is done in love will endure, but it is impossible to sort out the mixture of love and egoism in this world. See *The Humanist Christology of Paul*, 124–25.

54. Karl Rahner, *Foundations of Christian Faith: An Introduction to the Idea of Christianity* (New York: Seabury Press, 1978), 444. Hans Urs von Balthasar is of the same general opinion. See John R. Sachs, "Current Eschatology: Universal Salvation and the Problem of Hell," *Theological Studies*, 52 (1991), 227–54.

55. This is, of course, why the construct of purgatory has had such a long life and still enjoys a certain credibility. It should be added, however, that the responsibility attributed to freedom here, when it is coupled with a recognition of the evil that freedom can effect, always lends a note of holy fear to the idea of God's final justice.

this family of theologies understands them as constituting a theology of history. This leads to an inclusive interpretation that focuses on their dynamic method and the process of inculturation that they represent. As a hermeneutical theology of history, liberation christology engages the negativities of our common life in this world by retrieving the tradition and showing its applicability to a variety of actual situations. As a theology of history, liberation christology reflects the historicity of human existence, the massive unintelligible social evils of our time, and the deep threat to the human person posed by objectification and social control. It represents Jesus of Nazareth as the Christ because in his revelation and making present of God he symbolizes both the Logos of nature and the world, and the *mythos* of history. He is God's story or parable of human existence in the world. Liberation theology thus responds to these negativities with a coherent and comprehensive understanding of Christian salvation. And in so doing it lays theological foundations for Christian spirituality.

But there is another question latent in postmodernity that is still outstanding, that of religious pluralism. Are the positive dimensions of religious pluralism, or its threatening aspects, compatible with the traditional Christian claims about Jesus Christ?

CHAPTER 14

Jesus and the World Religions

An adequate christology today must include an account of the relation of Jesus to other religious mediations of God. Often this topic is addressed at the end of a christology as an addendum or corollary. But this begs a serious question of theological method. Religious pluralism is a characteristic of the situation of Christian life; it thus becomes an intrinsic dimension of the interpretation of Jesus as the Christ. Many theologians now acknowledge that the narrow christological problem must be addressed within the framework of an estimation of the place of Jesus Christ among other religions. Although a great deal has been written on this subject in recent years, the conversation is not over, and the question is still open.

The sheer vitality of the growth of this area within christology makes it difficult to clear a path in what appears as a jungle of different perspectives, methods, and positions. In the first part of this chapter, then, I will present the perspective of this analysis and the question that will be addressed. And in the second I will lay out a convenient overview of the christological discussion and the assumptions and premises I bring to it. The third and fourth parts form the substance of this chapter. In them I show why Christians may regard Jesus as a normative revelation of God, while at the same time being convinced that God is also revealed normatively elsewhere. In the phrase of Paul Knitter, Jesus is the "true" but "not the only" bearer of God's salvation.[1] The chapter concludes with a reflection on the new situation for addressing the formal christological question.

RELIGIOUS PLURALISM AND THE CHRISTOLOGICAL QUESTION

In many respects the recognition of religious pluralism and the new pressure it places on christology falls into place as a piece of the constellation of cultural factors called postmodernity. Christianity has always had

---

1. Paul Knitter, *Jesus and the Other Names: Christian Mission and Global Responsibility* (Maryknoll, N.Y.: Orbis Books, 1996), 72–83.

to reckon with the existence of other religions. But the internalization of the ideas and values that are pressing in from many directions has given rise to a situation or context that is genuinely new, and it calls for a revised understanding of old truths.

It will be helpful simply to recall some currents of postmodernity that form the framework of understanding here. Historical consciousness recognizes that all human ideas and values, and the thought processes by which they are arrived at, have roots in the particularities of historical time and place. Each religion is individual and has its significance within the context of its own situation. Religious pluralism, which suggests relativism, is itself a consequence of historicity. Cosmic consciousness, by adding the component of the sheer age and size of reality, compounds this sense of relativity. A new understanding of the social determinants of personhood and freedom tends to sap people's social expectations. And as people grow accustomed to the evils of social injustice and oppression, and get used to social suffering, energy for corporate resistance slips away. Precisely because religious pluralism adds one more factor to our changing perception and understanding of reality, it carries some negative weight.

But there is also a positive side to postmodernity and its reception of religious pluralism. Theologians and others who allow religious pluralism to germinate in their thinking have passed beyond tolerance of other religions to a positive appreciation of the religious treasures they contain. Other world religions participate intimately in the particular cultures in which they exist. They are sustained by distinctive revelations of reality. Christians are generally more open to other religions than in the past because more people recognize pluralism as part of the historical condition of human existence. A postmodern mentality easily adjusts to religious pluralism. Thus one can say that the new religious pluralism of today, where religions deliberately coexist and actively interact with each other across the world, is experienced as something positive; it is not simply negative.

Two broadly defined theological reactions can be discerned running parallel to the negative and the positive sides of religious pluralism. Both represent an acceptance and internalization of certain elements of postmodernity; but relative to christology they move in opposite directions.

One group of theologians stresses the particular, individual, and specific identity of each religion, and hence the differences and overall diversity that separates one religion from another.[2] Influenced by philosophy, linguistics, and the social sciences, this position has a hard time finding

---

2. For example, Joseph A. DiNoia, *The Diversity of Religions: A Christian Perspective* (Washington, D.C.: The Catholic University of America Press, 1992); Paul Griffiths, *An Apology for Apologetics: A Study in the Logic of Inter-religious Dialogue* (Maryknoll, N.Y.: Orbis Books, 1991); S. Mark Heim, *Salvations: In Search of Authentic Religious Pluralism* (Maryknoll, N.Y.: Orbis Books, 1995).

any common substance represented by the word "religion."[3] What are commonly called religions can be radically different from each other in worldview, content, and ethics. This habit of thinking begins with the specific self-identity of Christianity. While it is not hostile to dialogue among religions, if the parties so wish, the goal of such dialogue is not to come to common understandings. The goal is better understood as explication and defense of the self-understanding of each, terminating in some degree of mutual understanding. But the specific identities of the religions lie in factors that are more likely incommensurable with each other. Different religions do not mediate a "same" salvation. Historicity means that the various religious traditions will each go its own way, preserving its own self-understanding. This particular element of postmodern consciousness tends toward isolationism rather than an interaction that would force accommodations. Ironically, certain postmodern themes are used to defend premodern christological positions against modern encroachments.[4]

Another group of theologians sees the themes of historicity and relativity as breaking down barriers between peoples that used to be thought impenetrable.[5] Pluralist theologians, as the name indicates, do not advocate the reduction of all religions to one, but they look for commonalities among them in either a general anthropology, or a formal structure of religion, or common ethical responsibilities. Behind this impulse lies the technological, social, and planetary development toward a unification of people in terms of travel, communication, and general interaction. This generates an intuition that looks for potential commonalities that reflect the ontological unity of the race. Especially in the face of corporate human suffering around the world, and potential disaster for the whole race, not excluding self-annihilation, the tendency here is to look for degrees of common self-understanding among the religions and especially bases for

3. John Cobb is firm in denying that the religions of the world have any common genus. They all share nothing in common as religions. John Cobb, "Beyond Pluralism," *Christian Uniqueness Reconsidered: The Myth of a Pluralistic Theology of Religions*, ed. by Gavin D'Costa (Maryknoll, N.Y.: Orbis Books, 1990), 81–84. While he makes a good point, Cobb may exaggerate. For Cobb himself is equally firm in asserting that there can be interreligious dialogue in which members of different religions communicate. But they can only communicate by sharing something in common. If the human species is one, for which there is a good deal of evidence, there will be broad, formal, common ground for interreligious communication.

4. See Paul Knitter, *One Earth Many Religions: Multifaith Dialogue and Global Responsibility* (Maryknoll, N.Y.: Orbis Books, 1995), 38–53, for a good description of how postmodern appreciations of particularity and diversity come to bear on the problems of interreligious dialogue.

5. For example, John Hick, *An Interpretation of Religion* (New Haven: Yale University Press, 1989); Paul Knitter, *No Other Name? A Critical Survey of Christian Attitudes toward World Religions* (Maryknoll, N.Y.: Orbis Books, 1985), and Knitter in L. Swidler and P. Mojzes, eds., *The Uniqueness of Jesus: A Dialogue with Paul F. Knitter* (Maryknoll, N.Y.: Orbis Books, 1997); Wilfred Cantwell Smith, *Towards a World Theology* (Philadelphia: Westminster Press, 1981).

a common praxis that resists human suffering.[6] Ironically, this postmodern idealism, one which all would support if they thought it were possible, places demands on Christians for accommodation and change, particularly at the point of christology, and thus becomes a threat.

The fact and the various valuations of religious pluralism, therefore, present a problem for Christian self-understanding, and it comes to a focal point in christology. Is Christianity truly a religion destined for all people? The issue presses in on past christological formulas and, more existentially, on the integrity of the belief of members of the community. How and to what extent can one hold postmodernity and christological belief and commitment together? The bias of this chapter leans on the side of pluralism. It adopts a global consciousness in trying to resist a sectarian temptation; it is driven by the series of contrast experiences of the intolerable suffering of peoples in our world; it looks forward to when the peoples of different cultures and religions will have to exercise a common responsibility for common human problems or suffer disastrous consequences. Human beings must communicate *with* each other on more than economic and political grounds.

This leads to the formulation of the question of this chapter. In the next chapter I will address the formal christological question of the humanity and divinity of Jesus. This chapter is dedicated to describing further the situation within which the christological question has to be posed. While it depends on traditional sources, christology can only be formulated within a situation and on the basis of the experience of the Christian community. Preliminary to the next chapter, then, this chapter will address the following questions: what is a possible attitude of Christians toward other religions and toward Jesus in the context of these world religions? How are we to characterize the disposition of Christians toward Jesus within the context of respect for and dialogue with other religions? More precisely, what *can be* an appropriate stance in our postmodern situation? The *status quaestionis* is thus focused on characterizing an attitude consistent with Christian faith tradition and at the same time sensitive to and coherent with the world in which we live. The christology constructed in the next chapter will have to reflect this experience or existential attitude.[7]

---

6. The theme of dialogue is central to Knitter's project of religious pluralism. See especially Paul Knitter, *One Earth Many Religions*, where the issue of christology is neatly distinguished from the more fundamental issue of the radical need for interreligious dialogue and mutual cooperation in facing the dilemmas of the planet.

7. This comprehensive question entails a host of subquestions which will help to delimit further its range and introduce some of the language used to answer it: is Jesus a unique figure in human history? The term "unique" here does not simply refer to Jesus' individuality but to the character of his level of being. Is Jesus an "absolute" mediator of God by virtue of his relation to God so that by comparison all others are historically relative? Is Jesus, as a mediator of God and hence in himself as a person, final? decisive? definitive? unsurpassable? highest or supreme? normative? one among

ASSUMPTIONS AND PREMISES

Theologians have tried to harness the many different views of the relation of Jesus to other religions by building typologies. Many such typologies have been proposed, some descriptive of positions, others of methods, still others structured by specific variables and axes for comparison.[8] These typologies can be counterproductive in the way they schematize and oversimplify theological views. That being granted, the typology which follows, which is not developed but simply laid out, is meant only to provide a framework for situating the proposals of this chapter.[9] The typology is built around the relation of Jesus to people's salvation, and more will be said about this below.

Four positions marking the relation of Jesus Christ to human salvation range from the right or a conservative position to a more open stance: exclusivism, constitutive inclusivism, a normative non-constitutive position, and pluralism. Viewing Jesus Christ with respect to salvation, exclusivism holds there is no salvation outside of an explicit historical contact with and faith in Jesus Christ. Constitutive inclusivism is inclusive because it holds that salvation is available to all human beings; it is constitutive because it postulates that Jesus Christ is the cause of this salvation. This is explained by a mixture of historical and metaphysical reasoning. By retaining Jesus Christ as the constitutive mediator of the salvation of all human beings, it conceives those not historically connected with Jesus as "latent" or "anonymous" Christians. Moving further to the left, a normative non-constitutive position is less confident in metaphysical reasoning, more influenced by a historical understanding of reality. It says that Jesus provides a norm or representative measure of religious truth and God's salvation for all of humanity, but Jesus does not cause God's action for the salvation that goes on outside the Christian sphere. Moving still further to the left, pluralism formally embraces the multiplicity of religions and the "salvation" mediated through them by holding that other mediations of God's salvation are or can be "on a par" with Jesus Christ. One can notice two distinct ways of holding a pluralist position. One operates primarily with a historical imagination, as in the normative position just

---

many? One must also ask what these designations mean in each case. When theologians prefer one or another of these determinations, what nuances are being excluded and affirmed? One can also expand the question to show more forcefully its implications: is there only one true religion or are there many? This last question is the title of the book of Schubert M. Ogden, *Is There Only One True Religion or Are There Many?* (Dallas: Southern Methodist University Press, 1992). Cited hereafter as *One True Religion?*

8. Scott Cowdell, in *Is Jesus Unique?* (New York: Paulist Press, 1996), 9–20, surveys many typologies and proposes one of his own.

9. This typology is drawn from J. Peter Schineller, "Christ and Church: A Spectrum of Views," *Theological Studies*, 37 (1976), 545–46. I have modified Schineller's "pluralism" into two subtypes.

mentioned. Its framework is a comparison between religions, and of Jesus with other religious mediations. The other employs a metaphysical imagination and a reasoning process that presumes the doctrinal tradition. For example, the divine Logos, who is incarnated in Jesus, is not identical to or limited by Jesus, but may be incarnated in other religious mediations in history.[10] This distinction of subtypes within the pluralist position illustrates that the pluralist position is not *per se* inimical to a high christology.

Given the limitations of typologies, that they oversimplify and thus unintentionally distort, that they conceal differences among theologians who are lumped together, that they normally do not represent clear boundaries so that certain positions may represent more than one type, I shall try to explain further some of the assumptions and premises guiding this chapter. As a first notation, the method determining these reflections is theological; it transpires within the circle of Christian faith and is bound to a tradition of symbols and language. Such a method differs from that of both the philosopher and the historian of religion. The center of gravity here is not comparative religion or interreligious dialogue, but christology. Thus the question entertained here is intimately connected with salvation. The question of salvation is implied in how one regards the relation of Jesus to other religious mediations because the experience of salvation defines the Christian's relation to Jesus. For this reason any comparison between Jesus and other religious mediations from the side of the Christian theologian cannot avoid the language of salvation; being a salvation bringer makes Jesus the Christ.

This discussion presupposes that religious experience and faith are in some measure cognitive. The particular character of this form of knowing was discussed in the opening chapter. The discussion of the place of Jesus among religious mediators generally assumes that there is such a thing as

---

10. This is the position of Raimon Panikkar, *The Unknown Christ of Hinduism: Towards an Ecumenical Christophany* (Maryknoll, N.Y.: Orbis Books, 1981), 45–61. This kind of move seems to be operative in John B. Cobb, *Christ in a Pluralistic Age* (Philadelphia: Westminster Press, 1975), 62–81, and Rita Nakashima Brock, *Journeys by Heart: A Christology of Erotic Power* (New York: Crossroad, 1988), 52, who substitute for Logos, respectively, "Transforming Power" and "Erotic Power" or "Christa / Community." In some respects, those who develop a Christian theology of religions on the basis of God as Spirit at work in the world "apart from" Jesus also justify a religious pluralism. See the trinitarian theology of religions of Gavin D'Costa, "Christ, Trinity, and Religious Plurality," *Christian Uniqueness Reconsidered*, 16–29, and "Toward a Trinitarian Theology of Religions," *A Universal Faith?*, ed. by C. Cornille and V. Neckebrouck (Louvain: Peeters Press, 1992), 139–54, and Jacques Dupuis, *Toward a Christian Theology of Religious Pluralism* (Maryknoll, N.Y.: Orbis Books, 1997). Note that the fact that God is construed as trinity in a distinctively Christian manner has no more bearing on the theology of religions than any other conception of God or theocentrism generally. It facilitates a view of God actively immanent in the world "independently of" Jesus with the use of traditional language. But if a trinitarian theology of religions calls for the incarnation of the Logos or Son in Jesus in a qualitatively unique or exclusive way, it does not qualify as a pluralist position.

religious knowledge which transcends self-knowledge. This assumption is important in any comparison of religious claims, for it allows the logical principle of non-contradiction to become operative. If religious language only refers to subjective experience, then all religions may be equally true to such experience. When religions and religious beliefs are considered from a cognitive perspective as having a referent, the principle of non-contradiction becomes keenly significant. Along the same line I presuppose the unity of being and the unity of the human race. By contrast I do not accept the idea that because religious experiences and corporate religious worlds of construal are subjectively different, these differences correspond to different objective worlds or autonomous spheres of objective reality.[11]

Despite the assumption that there is a fundamental unity in being and commonality among human beings, historical consciousness implies historicity, that is, the historical character of all existence. Historicity entails a distinctive and individual or particular character to all human consciousness. And thus the historical worlds of different traditions are different insofar as these worlds and the objects in them are perceived differently and constructed differently in corporate consciousness. With respect to conceptions of ultimate reality, these are always generated historically through particular, individual, specific historical media. The attachment of all knowing to the sensible historical world accounts for the pluralism of religious experiences.[12]

Historicity means that no experience of ultimate or transcendent reality can be separated from that which mediates or grounds it historically. This implies that every experience of ultimate reality can be subject to reflective critique and reinterpretation because of its being tied to a historical mediation and its limitation. When generalized, every opinion or proposition takes on new meanings as it is mediated within a new situa-

---

11. John Cobb sometimes gives the impression that the pluralism of religious experiences and traditions corresponds to a pluralism of being itself. See, for example, John Cobb, "Toward a Christocentric Catholic Theology," *Toward a Universal Theology of Religion*, ed. by Leonard Swidler (Maryknoll, N.Y.: Orbis Books, 1987), 97–99. Mark Heim's conception of a pluralism of eschatological salvations corresponding to religious pluralism moves in this direction. Heim, *Salvations*, 129–44, and Mark Heim, "Salvations: A More Pluralistic Hypothesis," *Modern Theology*, 10 (1994), 341–59.

12. John Hick begins his account of the pluralism of religious experience and traditions with the epistemological principle of Thomas Aquinas that "The thing known is in the knower according to the mode of the knower" [Thomas Aquinas, ST, II-II, q. 1, a. 2.]. He adapts this principle to the social-historical conditions of the knower, thus accounting for different apprehensions of the Real. See, for example, Hick, "God Has Many Names," in *God Has Many Names* (Philadelphia: Westminster Press, 1980), 49–52, and *An Interpretation of Religion*, 240–46. An accurate appreciation of John Hick, I believe, requires a distinction between his philosophy of religions, on one side, and his christology and Christian theology of religions, on the other side. I touched on Hick's christology in Chapter 11. His theology of religions is represented in Hick, *A Christian Theology of Religions* (Louisville: Westminster/John Knox Press, 1995).

tion and horizon. There is no universal meaning that is not also tied to the situation of the one who entertains it. Two things follow from this. First, all communication implies some analogy, where the understanding of the communicator and that of the one who receives and appropriates are partly the same and partly different. All understanding is interpretation, and appropriation always implies some adaptation of the known to the knower. Second, therefore, all experiences and conceptions of ultimate reality are subject to comparison and valuative judgments in and through study, dialogue, and dialectic. One cannot assume that all religious experience is simply given in such a way that it is not prone to error or exempt from critical scrutiny.

Given the unity of being and the temporal, finite unfolding of it in history, we are left with a fundamental tension underlying this discussion of ultimate religious truth. On the one hand, whatever one's concept or explanation of truth, it cannot be such that it subverts the principle of non-contradiction. Thus if one assumes the unity of the human race and of reality, one cannot affirm that any proposition about ultimate reality is true and its negation in the same respect is also true. And, as Gavin D'Costa puts it, it is not impossible a priori that, when compared, different religious conceptions of ultimate reality are contradictory.[13] And thus, with respect to where the contradiction lies, one view is more adequate than the other. Beyond the demands of logic, this point is important existentially because of the role religion plays in human life.

But, on the other hand, in the light of historical consciousness, because reality exists in time and is a process of becoming, and because of the complexity of any historical and cultural mediation of the experience of ultimate reality, a great many seemingly apparent contradictions concerning ultimate truth may in fact not be so. Religious experience engages absolute mystery, and its concepts and language are recognized as limited and inadequate in their very usage. Because of their historicity, religious ideas are difficult to compare: it can be hard to discover where the commensurability of perspective lies, and it can never be perfect. We are learning more and more how deeply historicity and situation affect a distinctiveness of perception, conception, and evaluation. From this point of view, differences of interpretation and understanding are not to be read *prima facie* as potential contradictions and negative problems to be solved; they can be positive occasions for new learning and transformation.[14]

---

13. Gavin D'Costa, "The Pluralist Paradigm in the Christian Theology of Religions," *Scottish Journal of Theology*, 39 (1986), 221.

14. This is the side that is emphasized by John Cobb. He holds together in a paradoxical but creative tension the autonomy and incommensurability of different religions and the ability of people within these religions to communicate with each other in dialogue. In addition to the work just cited, see John B. Cobb, Jr., *Beyond Dialogue: Toward a Mutual Transformation of Christianity and Buddhism* (Philadelphia: Fortress Press, 1982); "The Meaning of Pluralism for Christian Self-Understanding," *Religious*

In sum, the imagination behind this interpretation of the place of Jesus among the religions is historically conscious in a postmodern way, but it has not completely gotten beyond the classical and modern premise of the unity of being and the existence of dimensions that are common to humanity. On the one hand, the transcendental imagination reflects the power of human freedom to transcend the self and to understand the other *as other*. In dialogue human self-transcendence can even envisage the self from the perspective of other. This means that we are open subjects who can perceive and create *common* meanings *analogously*. On the other hand, however, what such meanings might be in any concrete and material sense can only be established historically in a positive way. But common human meanings can be pointed to or localized in a formal way around certain issues that are constant and constitutive of all life. Birth, community, self, and death, for example, will be construed differently in different cultures and religions; but they present themselves to all to be interpreted, and thus constitute a formal bond of communication and unity, but in tension with the distinctive content given them.

THE NORMATIVITY OF JESUS

This lengthy preliminary discussion is necessitated by the far-ranging, diffuse, and complex character of the question and the literature surrounding it. It is hoped that delimiting a point of view and describing the operative premises will help to clarify the argument. I now pass to the substance of this chapter which consists in explaining why Christians today can relate to Jesus as normative of the religious truth about God, the world, and human existence, and at the same time be confident that there are also other religious mediations that are true and thus normative. But before building this bridge between the normative but non-constitutive conception of Jesus Christ and a pluralist conception of him, it will help to explain why the exclusivist and constitutive-inclusivist positions no longer seem credible.

BEYOND EXCLUSIVISM AND INCLUSIVISM

An exclusivist attitude toward Jesus Christ is so named because it holds that there is no salvation outside of an explicit historical contact with and

---

Pluralism, ed. by Leroy S. Rounder (Notre Dame, Ind.: Notre Dame University Press, 1984), 161–79; "Christian Witness in a Plural World," *The Experience of Religious Diversity*, ed. by John Hick and Hasen Askari (Brookfield, Ver.: Gower, 1985), 144–62; "Beyond 'Pluralism,'" *Christian Uniqueness Reconsidered*, 81–95. For his part, Paul Knitter reinforces the idea of the positive value of pluralism with his notion of relational truth. Because of the limited character of historical understanding and the transcendent character of the religious object, one must see truth as being discovered in the convergence of different experiences and expressions. See *No Other Name?*, 217–20.

faith in the person of Jesus Christ as mediated by the church. This position has less and less adherence among theologians today. It is usually identified with conservative evangelical Christians who read a number of New Testament texts in a literal way.[15] But such texts are not purveyors of direct information about God, and even the experiential religious meaning they mediate must be interpreted in a more nuanced way, if it is to be faithful to the whole witness of the New Testament.

Two arguments against exclusivism seem decisive.[16] First, this position is against the primitive apostolic witness because it proposes a problem relative to God that is insoluble and, in the light of Jesus' message, inappropriate. How is it that the God depicted by Jesus saves only a minority of human beings? Is God either unwilling or unable to save all? This view runs counter to the core of Jesus' preaching of a God bent on human salvation. Secondly, in terms of our experience today, the experience of being saved through Jesus provides no grounds for saying that God cannot save in some other way, or that only Christians are saved. There are thus simply no grounds for exclusivism.

But while exclusivism is clearly a minority position today, the same is not true of the inclusive and constitutive view that Jesus causes the salvation of all. In one form or other this has been the dominant theology of the mainline churches for some time. What developments have undermined this position?

First, regarding the first criterion of theology, the witness of the New Testament, the same texts that are brought forward to support exclusivism also support inclusivism. However, in order to make the point that Jesus is the cause of the salvation of everyone, these texts have to be interpreted in the same literalistic manner. But historically these texts of the past, which in some way suggest "only through Jesus," did not address the present-day situation. Their meaning in the past has its foundation in the actual encounter of God's salvation in Jesus. Their meaning in their historical context is derived from and contained in the actual religious encounter with Jesus. To interpret their meaning so that it includes a reference to the comprehensive discussion of today and supplies a definitive answer to it constitutes a lapse into a propositional view of revelation and fundamentalism. Early Christianity too made its way in a religious situation that was pluralistic, and defined itself over against other religious traditions. But early Christians were not shaped by a postmodern culture. As in early Christianity, Christians today must make judgments of truth and error about matters in their own tradition and in the world outside themselves. But it must do so in a critical, historically conscious way, and in dialogue with other vital religious traditions.

---

15. For example: Matt 11:27, 1 Cor 8:6, John 1:14, John 1:18, 1 Tim 2:5, Heb 9:12, Acts 12:4. Knitter, *Jesus and the Other Names*, 67.

16. The arguments are those of Ogden in *One True Religion?*, 27–52.

A closer examination indicates that the New Testament witness runs in a direction quite contrary to inclusivism. The primary norm for understanding Jesus' role in human salvation is his own preaching. But there is little evidence that Jesus preached himself as the constitutive mediator of God's salvation for all human beings. By contrast, abundant evidence and the common opinion of exegetes indicate that Jesus did not preach himself, but the rule of God. The message of Jesus himself is theocentric: God saves; God is loving, providential creator and the exclusive cause of salvation wherever it occurs. Jesus, I have argued, is a cause of Christian salvation because he is the symbol and mediator of God's salvation in the Christian community. He thus participates in God's saving activity within the church as the instrument or medium or sacrament of God's saving self-manifestation. But by definition no historical causality links Jesus to people outside the Christian community.

Second, one must also consider on a theological level the credibility of the constitutive position. The lack of evidence for the case and positive evidence against it from the New Testament witness lead to the recognition that the causal nexus between Jesus and the salvation of all others is a product of speculation. Only a speculative, metaphysical reasoning process can explain how Jesus' historical actions can be the cause of the salvation of the human beings who lived and died before his existence. At this point one can appreciate a second major argument against a constitutive christology from common experience today. Speculative reasons do not enjoy the credibility they did in a classical philosophical milieu. Historical consciousness has forced a critical thinking that calls into question theology from above, based entirely on inferences that have a dubious logical foundation in confessional faith statements. Statements of faith do not provide premises for deductive reasoning. In the final analysis the constitutive position has been undermined by a straightforward internalization of historical consciousness. People have come to appreciate more deeply that God alone effects salvation and Jesus' universal mediation is not necessary.[17]

THE NORMATIVITY OF JESUS

It was said at the head of the chapter that this is an essay in theology that transpires within the circle of Christian faith. But the essential structure of Christian faith in God is such that it is mediated by Jesus of

---

17. Ogden sums up well the metaphysical conviction that God alone saves: "But, then, no event in time and history, including the event of Jesus Christ, can be the cause of salvation in the sense of the necessary condition of its possibility. On the contrary, any event, including the Christ event, can be at most a consequence of the salvation, the sole necessary condition of the possibility of which is God's own essential being as all-embracing love." Ogden, *One True Religion?*, 92.

Nazareth. Jesus is the center of Christian faith insofar as it is he who was and is the medium and focus of a Christian's faith in God. This accounts for the title of Jesus as the Christ and the name of the religion as Christian. Jesus is thus normative for Christian faith not because an objective judgment understands his role to be important and essential to a Christian's commitment. His normativity can be said to be prior to the content he mediates because it resides in the very structure of Christian faith. Faith is a habitual way of being and an existential commitment, not something one can step out of to examine neutrally in the form of beliefs. And Christian faith is faith in God that is mediated by Jesus. The normativity of Jesus is therefore its logical entailment because Jesus is constitutive of Christian faith itself. This explains why the New Testament, which is the earliest record of Jesus stemming from the first witnesses of faith to him, is normative for Christian theology.

All of this is true for the Christian; but does this normativity extend to or apply to others? And if so, in what sense? The intrinsic logic of every deeply held truth in ultimate and important matters includes a dynamism toward universal relevance. One can conceive of a "truth for me" or "for us" as distinct from others with reference to everyday customs and cultural patterns of appreciation. But there can be no "truth for me" when an issue concerns those issues that touch on the human as such. These truths unfold on a level that reaches out to embrace all human beings; they reveal a region that is universally comprehensive. This experience of universal relevance is one of the features that marks the human, the ability reflectively to grasp what transcends the self and one's group and obtains for the whole range of the species. Despite the fact that every such fundamental conviction will be interpreted analogously because of its historical mediation, it remains universally relevant. This logic, which is given in the phenomenology of the very notion of truth, bestows on Christian faith its universal applicability. Because of the nature of Christian revelation as encounter with a personal God, it is impossible that such an experience not be conceived as having a universal relevance. The God of Christians cannot be conceived by Christians as a local, tribal God only for themselves.

The very idea of a norm has gained negative connotations in developed and open societies and in increasingly historically conscious and postmodern intellectual culture. But normativity is intimately connected to the notion of truth; one cannot really escape the issue of norms in questions of truth. I have already pointed out that truth entails universal relevance and universal relevance constitutes normativity. The meaning of normativity coincides with the relevance and applicability of a given truth to all human beings. Truth and norms entail each other; one cannot critically claim that one's own ultimate concern is true without invoking some standard or norm for its truth. Every critical proposal of truth, every proposal that goes beyond gratuitous affirmation, necessarily involves some appeal to accepted principles and norms and asserts itself as a norm.[18]

To sum up here, it appears that, from inside Christian faith and according to the principles of Christian theology, and insofar as Jesus Christ is the central medium for Christianity's conception of ultimate reality, it is impossible by definition for Christ to be less than normative for a Christian appropriation of ultimate reality. I now want to move from this statement of principle to how this normativity works.

The principle of non-contradiction states that one cannot affirm as true a particular proposition and its simple negation, that is, that which contradicts it in the same sense and respect. According to this principle, the Christian cannot accept that what is contradictory to or less than that mediated through Jesus is true in the same respect or measure. This objection is consistently brought up against pluralists insofar as they affirm that all religions are true or valid, or should they suggest that all religions are equal, although few make this latter claim. Once one admits that religious experience and hence religions make cognitive claims, that we are dealing with one world of being and a common human species, and that religions can thus be compared and found at certain points to contradict each other, it seems that the principle of non-contradiction must rule out the validity of some religions or at least certain religious tenets.[19]

While this usage of the principle of non-contradiction is certainly valid and hence has a great deal of bearing on the function of the normativity of Jesus for Christian faith, it is by no means the end of the story. For contradiction does not function in the matters of religious experience and knowledge, where the object is strictly transcendent, in the same way as it does within the framework of knowledge of this world. In matters of religious faith, the transcendent object is not present and available for comparison with competitive propositions about it; it is transcendent. Therefore the principle does not prevent a seemingly contradictory conviction or belief from another religion from being not really contradictory of the Christian vision and even in some measure true. This can be

---

18. Ogden, *One True Religion?*, 71–77. The need for norms can be seen clearly in dilemmas of praxis, especially in decisions that are matters of life and death or are otherwise ultimate. Langdon Gilkey analyzes the need for "relative absolutes" within our historical condition in order to act responsibly in such cases. A "relative absolute" in history is the equivalent of a norm. See Gilkey, "Plurality and Its Theological Implications," in *The Myth of Christian Uniqueness*, ed. by John Hick and Paul Knitter (Maryknoll, NY: Orbis Books, 1987), 37–50.

19. The objection to early proposals of John Hick's pluralism elicited responses such as the following: if conceptions of ultimate reality of the different religions are cognitive, then they cannot be equally valid; and if they are equally valid, they cannot be cognitive. See, for example, Peter Byrne, "John Hick's Philosophy of World Religions," *Scottish Journal of Theology*, 35 (1982), 289–301; Paul Griffiths and Lewis Delmas, "On Grading Religions, Seeking Truth, and Being Nice to People—A Reply to Professor Hick," *Religious Studies*, 19 (1983), 75–80; Harold A. Netland, "Professor Hick on Religious Pluralism," *Religious Studies*, 22 (1986), 249–61.

explained on several accounts. For the most part I have refrained from offering a theory or phenomenology of religious experience or faith. But insofar as the object of religious experience is transcendent, as is the case in Christian faith, it remains mystery even, paradoxically, in the awareness of it. Such absolute mystery, grasped in such a limited and historical way, does not easily yield overt contradictions. For this reason there is a tradition of expectation that God can contain what, from our limited vantage point, appear to be contradictions in some mode of *coincidentia oppositorum*. Moreover, from the perspective of historical consciousness, we have already discussed the difficulty but not impossibility of discovering strict commensurability of meaning out of radically different contexts.

These considerations negate neither the principle of non-contradiction nor its applicability, but they do modify it. They allow and, in the interest of truth, impel an effort at accommodation, that is, the attempt to discover the dimension of truth that is not contradictory but complementary to what is revealed through the norm. For example, something apparently contradictory to a given conviction can be in some measure true, or in some respect true, or at some distinct level valid.[20] In sum, to employ the principle of non-contradiction in a non-dialectical manner of an either/or in religious matters fails to grasp the distinctive cognitive character of religious truth and the transcendent character of its object.

Three other principles further condition the function of the normativity of Jesus Christ for a Christian appreciation of reality. First, in holding the normativity of the experience mediated through Jesus and hence the person of Jesus Christ, one should specify as far as possible the center of gravity of the content of this experience. It is not the case that everything about Jesus or all of the interpretations to which Jesus has given rise, whether they be valid or not, are normative. Jesus' diet is not normative for Christians or anyone else. It is of course nearly impossible to formulate an essence of Christianity; the effort of the nineteenth century failed. What Jesus mediates is an existential encounter that is diffuse and far-ranging in the experience of individual persons, and that cannot be contained by definable limits within the whole body of Christians. But at the same time one can make distinctions between what is closer and further from the center of faith. When one enters into this calculus, it will become apparent that the normativity of Jesus will be found in the region of simplicity and depth rather than in a host of many truths. There can be con-

---

20. In some respects the classic case of mediating the principle of non-contradiction occurs in the counterclaims of Christians and some Buddhists that ultimate reality is personal or not personal. Many pluralists attempt to mediate these convictions in order to save the truth of both. See, for example, the attempt of Hans Küng in Küng et al., *Christianity and the World Religions: Paths of Dialogue with Islam, Hinduism, and Buddhism*, (Garden City, N.Y.: Doubleday, 1986), 386–98. More significant, because less conceptual and more existential, is the essay of John Cobb, "Beyond Pluralism," the whole of which is dedicated to mediating between the core truths of Buddhism and Christianity.

siderable overlapping with other religions in this simple core truth. This principle is crucial for any realistic grasp of the way in which the normativity of Jesus can actually function. Mutual understanding does not begin with measuring and contrasting propositions about reality; it begins with trying to communicate the simple, deeply held convictions about the ultimate shape of the whole: God, who is personal, who creates, who is friendly, who loves creatures and enters into an interactive relationship with them.

Second, it should be apparent that the faithful of other religions will hold as normative the fundamental experience that is mediated to them through that which is considered central and basic in their religious form of life. More will be said about the significance of the multiplicity of diverse norms in the discussion of dialogue. But being met with the norms of other religions has a bearing on the functioning of Jesus as a norm and the principle of non-contradiction. It forces a distinction between a positive and a negative function of a norm. A positive norm positively rules out what does not agree with it; it asserts exclusively and thereby implicitly denies alternatives. For example, Jesus would function as a positive norm for the Christian imagination by implying that God is exclusively what Jesus reveals God to be and nothing more. By contrast, a negative norm rules out that which contradicts it; when it affirms, it rules out only those alternatives which contradict it. For example, Jesus functions negatively for the Christian imagination by implying that God is not diametrically other or different or less than the core truth existentially encountered in what is mediated by Jesus.

This distinction between a positive and a negative functioning of a norm is important in this discussion. Too often theologians presume that the idea of normativity is self-evident and that the norming function is simple. Neither is correct. Jesus is a negative norm for Christians. And, positively, Jesus is more than a norm: Jesus functions heuristically by opening up the Christian imagination and guiding it into further truth as the community moves through history. For example, Jesus encourages Christians to find God operative in the world beyond the Christian sphere.

Thirdly, given the historicity of our situation, the notion of normativity finds its complement in a notion of relational truth.[21] It was said that deep truths about reality contain an intrinsic dynamism toward universal

---

21. The idea of relational truth means that truth grows both in its meaning and in its actual relevance and normativity by being accepted by others. But this means entering into the horizon of other forms of religion and culture and being modified by the new situation. A given truth is thus both deepened and expanded; it grows as truth. Fundamental truths about humanity and ultimate reality can never be considered as data, or facts, or unchanging pieces of objective information. Truth as the union and identity of objectivity and subjectivity lives, changes, and grows. See Knitter, *No Other Name?*, 217–21.

human relevance. This means that the substance of such truths, insofar as they are true, potentially can be experienced or recognized by all human beings.[22] Indeed the validity or truth of Christian beliefs is displayed by an analysis that shows its reasonability and credibility within common human experience. In other words, there needs to be critical analysis to disclose the relevance and applicability of truth to common human experience and reason.[23] This is the case for the truth of any religion or philosophy. Thus the need for certain common criteria for truth, at least on a formal level, to which an appeal can be made for common understanding and judgment of truth. I shall return to this in the discussion of interreligious dialogue. But the point here is the way "relational truth" comes to bear upon normativity. It would be one thing simply to declare that a truth is universally relevant in the face of rejection of such a claim by others. It would be quite another so to mediate a claim of truth that it actually becomes broadly understood. The normativity of Jesus must be mediated. When this occurs, Jesus is received into an already established framework of understanding and an accepted set of truths. Thus the normativity of Jesus Christ only becomes actually operative by entering into new relationships within other systems of truth. Another way of explaining this is opened up by the discussion of inculturation and the hermeneutical process it entails. Inculturation implies a notion of historical and relational truth; the given normative truth of Jesus operatively becomes normative by being analogically interpreted through its reception into a new situation and horizon.

In sum, from a Christian theological standpoint Jesus is normative for the Christian imagination. But this normativity functions within the context of historicity. Historical consciousness, however, does not negate or undermine the principle of non-contradiction. But any employment of this principle must be sensitive to the historical conditioning and limited character of all human grasp of absolute mystery. Historical relativity forces the Christian to define more exactly the content of what is mediated by Jesus. Jesus as a norm functions primarily in a negative fashion; positively Jesus opens the imagination to God's presence to the world and guides Christian perception to recognize that what is revealed in him can be enriched by other religious truths.

---

22. Edward Schillebeeckx refers to "anthropological constants" which are not univocally understood universal ideas but universal data or coordinates for shared meaning. These data are differently interpreted within various historical contexts and thus analogical in meaning. But they serve as reference points for communication. See *Christ: The Experience of Jesus as Lord* (New York: Seabury Press, 1980), 731–43.

23. This is a standard methodological observation in Christian theology. Relative to this discussion, see Ogden, "Problems in the Case for a Pluralistic Theology of Religions," *The Journal of Religion*, 68 (1988), 497–98.

PLURALISM AND DIALOGUE

Cognitive, moral, and religious pluralism, as distinct from ontological pluralism, in one degree or another is constitutive of the human condition. John Hick has given a reasonable description of religious pluralism in his philosophy of religions which does not prejudice the religions themselves.[24] The point of this section is to move to a positive construal of this pluralism from a theological perspective. I propose the thesis that the normativity of Jesus does not exclude a positive appraisal of religious pluralism, and that Christians may regard other world religions as true, in the sense that they are mediations of God's salvation. This will involve by implication making global judgments about other religions. Some theologians insist that one cannot judge other religions except a posteriori, after studying them, or entering into dialogue with their representatives, or participating in them. On the contrary, Christian theology is obliged to interpret and judge other religions on the basis of its norm, Jesus Christ, in the same way that it is obliged to interpret all reality. This defines what Christian theology is: its task is to interpret all reality in the light of Christian symbols. Theological evaluation of other religions prior to close critical examination, however, remains what it is, assessment on the basis of the norms of Christian theology, and this should not be confused with more nuanced judgments based on close participatory analysis. I am not dealing with such judgments here, but with the attitudes that Christians should bear toward religious pluralism and other religions generally.

After a consideration of the positive character of religious pluralism the discussion will turn to the significance of interreligious dialogue for Christian theology.

THE POSITIVE CHARACTER OF RELIGIOUS PLURALISM

How can one show that the situation of religious pluralism is something positive, not something to be overcome, but rather a good, because

---

24. Hick's theoretical account of the diverse religious manifestations and experiences of the Real is found in several places. See, for example, *God Has Many Names*, 40–59, 88–115; "On Grading Religions," *Religious Studies*, 17 (1981), 451–67; *An Interpretation of Religion*, 233–96. Hick is sometimes criticized for not respecting the individual distinctiveness of each religion, and for reducing religious pluralism to the scheme of a single meta-narrative by his unified theory. For example, Heim, *Salvations*, 23–35. I do not accept this criticism. In principle, Hick accounts for religious pluralism through socio-cultural mediation. Terrence Merrigan, in "Religious Knowledge in the Pluralist Theology of Religions," *Theological Studies*, 58 (1997), 686–707, criticizes the pluralists generally on the basis of a generalized account of their religious epistemology. The generalized account, however, like a typology, applies unevenly to the respective theologians.

other religions are also mediations of God's salvation? The arguments against exclusivism implicitly rely on the Christian conviction that God's will for human salvation is universal. And by arguing against human salvation being universally caused by Jesus Christ, one has gone some distance in establishing the world's religions as agents of God's salvation independently of Christianity and Jesus Christ.

The primary argument for the truth and authentic saving power of other religions comes from the witness of Jesus Christ. And at this point I refer the reader to Chapters 3 and 4 of this book which deal with the person and teaching of Jesus of Nazareth about God. I shall not review here the concrete words, gestures, and actions of Jesus within which the Christian reads the revelation of God. But the content of the revelation of God mediated by Jesus requires that one expect that God acts in the lives of human beings in a plurality of ways outside of Jesus and the Christian sphere. In Jesus God is revealed to be personal and turned toward human beings, God's personal creatures, in unconditional mercy and love. God wills that all God's own be gathered into salvation. Thus, from a Christian perspective and on the basis of the positive indications provided by Jesus, the Christian must reckon that God approaches all human beings in grace. This grace is God as Spirit, and its content is self-gift in mercy and love. These are not empty emotions on God's part; when predicated of God, they can only be understood as being actual, effective initiatives. They involve God's personal presence. From these premises Rahner's argument for the validity of other religions appears sound: because such grace is necessarily mediated, and the religions are the historical and cultural media of transcendence, the religions are the de facto channels of God's saving grace. This global and comprehensive judgment is thus shared by constitutive inclusivists and pluralists.[25]

This same fundamental argument underlies the position of Ogden on the possible salvific value of other religions. The Christian conviction rests on the experience of God as God is mediated by Jesus. Commenting on the pluralist thesis Ogden says that the possibility of this pluralism in the sense proposed by John Hick is "securely grounded in the completely universal reality of God's love, which is savingly present throughout all human existence; and so I have every reason to look for more evidence of the actuality of pluralism than I have so far been able to find."[26] Ogden's judgment, however, differs from Rahner's in this respect: whereas he hopes and expects that God's salvation will be so mediated by other religions as to make them true, such a judgment is really possibile only a

---

25. See Karl Rahner, "Christianity and Non-Christian Religions," *Theological Investigations* 5 (New York: Seabury Press, 1974), 115–34. Rahner's view of the validity of the world's religions is not unconditional. Also there are elements of Rahner's argument that are not endorsed here. For example, we began with the premise that the belief that all God's grace is *gratia Christi* appears to be tenuous and unnecessary speculation when viewed against the background of historicity.

26. Ogden, "Problems in the Case for a Pluralistic Theology of Religions," 505.

posteriori, on the basis of actual experience, of critical reflection and study of the other religions, and of measuring them by the norm of Jesus Christ.

It is important to underline at this point that the conviction that God acts in history through other mediations in no way undermines the Christian commitment to what it experiences God to have done in Jesus. Underneath the demands of truth and logic there seems to be a competitive urge in human beings that spontaneously reckons one's own relationship to God as weakened by the fact that God loves others and deals with them in specific historical ways. But the logic of God's infinite love does not succumb to such division. The Christian experience of what God has done in Jesus Christ does not appear diminished by the recognition of true God at work in other religions. In fact, the Christian case is strengthened and confirmed: the universal love of God that is experienced by Christians is, as it were, manifested in the other religions.

Just what is being said in this judgment that God is at work in other religions? Is this an affirmation that God is present and manifest in the same way that God is revealed in Jesus Christ? Or in an analogous way? And can one say that the other religions are really salvific, that they cause and mediate salvation, with Rahner? Or, with Ogden, should Christians say that they hope, or even expect, that such is the case, but are not really able to affirm it without their own personal research into the matter? In the end, the positions of Rahner and Ogden are not contradictory at this point and one can be sympathetic to both of them. A map of what they are saying will clarify the nature of these judgments.

First, Ogden himself provides a criterion from a Christian standpoint of what constitutes a true religion. Religion is generally defined as "the primary form of culture in terms of which we human beings explicitly ask and answer the existential question of the meaning of ultimate reality for us."[27] Christian religion has its foundation in the experience of salvation mediated through Jesus; salvation is constituted by the unlimited and effective love of God. If God is true and effective love, and this is what human beings confront in their being human, then other religions can be true if they too represent this. When a religion's praxis and form of life is so transformed by God's love that it represents this as that which constitutes authentic human existence, then that religion is substantially true. In brief, from the Christian perspective, other religions "can validly claim to be formally true insofar as they explicitly represent God's love. . . ."[28] And one can add that religions are substantially true when they implicitly mediate God's love, whether or not they formally and explicitly represent it.

---

27. Ogden, *One True Religion?*, 5.

28. Ogden, *One True Religion?*, 100. Two brief summary statements of his position are found in Schubert M. Ogden, "Some Thoughts on a Christian Theology of Interreligious Dialogue," *Criterion*, 33 (1994), 5–10, and "Is There Only One True Religion or Are There Many?" in Schubert M. Ogden, *Doing Theology Today* (Valley Forge: Trinity Press International, 1996), 169–84.

Second, within a similar framework, Rahner stresses the universality and effectiveness of God's love. This is what Christians experience as salvation in their own lives. The encounter with God in Jesus is such that God's nature is understood to be universally effective love. The extension of this universal saving love of God to the religions, therefore, is not an objectively argued inference, but a drawing out of what is entailed in the experience of God encountered in Jesus. By contrast, holding that God is not present and active in and through the mediations of other religions calls into question either the universality or the effectiveness of God's love.

But, thirdly, one must also note the difference between the substantial truth of other religions and the effectiveness of actual religious forms of life to represent and mediate God's saving presence. On the one hand, Christians have the norm of Jesus Christ to make this judgment, a judgment that also judges Christian praxis in this regard. On the other hand, one must expect that, because of the saving presence of God to other religions, they will contain other, and different, but universally relevant norms for measuring the truth of transcendent reality and of salvation.

It follows then that the global judgment of the truth and validity of other religions and critical assessment of the specific life forms of the religions including Christianity are two different kinds of judgment. The judgment of the Christian that other religions are mediations of God is ultimately based on Christian faith experience. Outside of such a faith experience there can be no such judgment at all. It is not, therefore, founded on an analysis of other religions, not even on the fact of their long existence and present vitality, although this last point enters into the calculus. It is rather a purely formal judgment which says nothing concrete or material about any given religion. Particular aspects of the religions will be assessed by Christians dialogically according to the norm of Jesus of Nazareth, even as Christian institutions are also critically examined by Christians and by others in dialogue. The judgment, therefore, does not ratify particular aspects of any specific religion. Rather, this conviction is analogous to a belief that God's providence is not limited to Christians, but is effective in the lives of all human beings through the agency of the institutions and situations that shape human lives. One must expect that the historical religious response to God's effective love, which love is mediated socio-culturally, will in some measure correspond to God's initiative. The content of the judgment that God is at work salvifically in other religions, therefore, derives from Christian experience; its referent and ground is the God mediated through Jesus, and its significance lies in its shaping of Christian attitudes and vision.

One can at this point compare the position represented here with that of Ogden. Ogden distinguishes his view from that of some pluralists. But given the fact that a good deal of study of other religions and actual dialogue have already taken place, his view is itself virtually a pluralist position. He writes that his stance "warrants a certain optimism about all of the specific religions, even as about human existence and praxis otherwise. Indeed, it gives one every reason to look for signs of the actuality of the pluralism whose possibility is securely grounded in the completely universal reality of God's love, which is savingly present throughout all human existence and, therefore, is also at work in all religions."[29] Knitter refers to Ogden's position as a "cautious pluralism."[30] One has to appreciate this caution. Even Rahner, in declaring other religions valid and willed by God, does not mean to endorse the details, the specific concrete life forms, of any religion. The salvific character of actual religious practice can only be verified by constant review, within Christianity as well. But at the same time, when religions are considered holistically, there are compelling reasons that Ogden's hope and expectation be converted into a conviction. For if other religions are not true, then one is thrown back into an unacceptable alternative: either there is no explicit social-historical mediation of God's grace for the vast majority of humankind, so that each person must encounter God's grace in his or her individual human existence and history, or one is left with the dilemma of the exclusivists, of a God who withholds salvation from the vast majority of people during their lifetime.

The ability to recognize other religions as mediators of God's salvation on a par with Christianity requires a number of nuances based on the distinctions that have been made. Up to this point I have spoken of salvation largely in terms of the mediation of Jesus Christ, his work of revelation, and thus as something that is a function of conscious awareness. One encounters God in Jesus. But the foundation of this experience is God and God's loving presence to human beings. This immanent presence and activity of God is symbolized by God as Spirit. The primitive Christian community testified to their experience of God as Spirit present within the community and active in persons. The character of God as Spirit was identified by Jesus. Thus God as Spirit may be conceived as the universal ground of salvation, normatively revealed in Jesus, but also present in other religions and so normatively revealed in them as well.

One also needs some nuanced differentiation in the very notion of the truth of religions. Religions are true and the traditions valid and positively willed by God insofar as they are the actual channels of God's gracious presence. This requires that they open the human spirit out of itself and turn it toward self-transcendence. It does not require that the power of God as Spirit be understood in the same terms as the revelation of Jesus Christ. The primary mediation of God's presence and salvation for Christianity is the person Jesus of Nazareth. But the fundamental mediation of God's salvific presence in other religions need not be a person: it may be an event, a book, a teaching, a praxis. To say that other religions

---

29. Ogden, *One True Religion?*, 103.
30. Knitter, *One Earth Many Religions*, 184, n. 11.

are true only in the measure that they correspond with Christian concepts of God is to make Jesus a positive norm and to slip back into inclusivism. Religions other than Christianity truly and really mediate God's presence, so that God is encountered precisely in other and different ways.

Religions can truly mediate God's presence even though they do not perfectly represent it. Every actual religion is historically limited, ambiguous, and possibly erroneous in any given practice or belief. Yet even as such it can still be an instrument of God's saving grace. Hyperbolic language about the church often conceals from Christians that Christianity itself, in various historical praxes, gives testimony to this possibility. One must insist on the distinction between the substantial witness of a religion to the presence of God as Spirit that causes human self-transcendence and specific religious practices that may obscure this presence and indeed be sinful. It is thus impossible to label a religion simply and comprehensively true, just as it is difficult to imagine an old and vital religious tradition to be simply false or corrupt.[31] Therefore, one must distinguish between the truth which lies in a religion's mediation of an encounter with God's saving love that calls forth self-transcendence and the formal truth of specific beliefs and practices. This latter can only be established by Christians in and through dialogue and study. Historicity makes dialogue the necessary vehicle for all critically established truth.

The prior judgment or bias that God is at work in other religions entails the idea that religious pluralism amounts to a positive phenomenon. The differences among religions entail new and other aspects of God being brought forward for human recognition. Other religions will consider their fundamental religious mediations and conceptions as universally relevant and normative. I have already considered how the principle of non-contradiction is intrinsic to the normativity of Jesus, and how this does not preclude the possibility that seemingly contradictory beliefs from other religions may be either not really contradictory of the Christian tradition or in some respect and measure true and complementary. But this means further that in our historicist situation dialogue becomes an ultimately indispensable vehicle for a critical appropriation of religious truth in the long run. In a positive religiously plural situation normative claims cannot be held critically and in isolation at the same time. This does not mean that Christian conviction is somehow rendered tentative until the dialogue is over, for in fact the dialogue will never end. Nor does it mean that Christian theology cannot be done outside of an actual interreligious dialogue. There is a division of labor in theology as in every other discipline. It is rather a definition of our situation and a testimony to the conviction that human beings have to share their religious experiences and learn from

---

31. Some religious practices may immediately come to mind that seem to call this last statement into question. But one must take into account the historicity of the very criteria or standards by which these judgments are made.

each other what God is doing for humanity. Christian theology must be done within a pluralistic religious context.

To sum up here, the Christian case for religious pluralism, the truth of other religions and other religious mediations of God, can be seen to rest on the deep experience that reaches back into Jewish tradition of the simultaneous immanence and transcendence of God. The step beyond exclusivism and inclusivism is a large one. It cuts the necessity of binding God's salvation to Jesus of Nazareth alone; it moves the Christian imagination from a christomonism to a theocentrism where Jesus mediates a revelatory encounter with a creator God who is immediately and immanently present to all creatures. I believe that people who fail to acknowledge the salvific truth of other religions may implicitly be operating with a conception of God who is distant from creation. Jesus testifies to the immanence of God. When the world's religions allow transcendence to press in upon them and, in turn, open human beings up to self-transcendence, they reflect and mediate the immanent God as Spirit whom Christians know through Jesus. But this God is also transcendent. Knowing this God transpires in an encounter with mystery. Neither Jesus nor Christianity mediates any complete possession of God. Without a sense of God's transcendent mystery, without the healthy agnostic sense of what we do not know of God, one will not expect to learn more of God from what has been communicated to us human beings through other revelations and religions.

INTERRELIGIOUS DIALOGUE

Holding Jesus Christ as normative for the Christian conception of reality does not inhibit dialogue. It will always be the case that all the parties who enter into dialogue will come with convictions about what is ultimately true, and this would be impossible without norms. Therefore openness to dialogue, which may be presupposed as a value, cannot be used as a reason for dismissing the Christian conviction that Jesus Christ represents normative truth for all humanity. Rather, attachment to God mediated by Jesus necessarily impels the Christian to dialogue.[32] In the light of the God revealed in and through Jesus, Christianity is committed to sharing its awareness of God and to being totally open to whatever truth can be discovered or revealed in history.[33] Therefore a total commitment to Jesus Christ, and a correlative appraisal of Jesus as normative of one's vision of reality, is neither logically incompatible with dialogue nor a practical obstacle to it, but a positive impulse toward dialogue.

---

32. This is the thesis of David Lochhead, *The Dialogical Imperative* (Maryknoll, N.Y.: Orbis Books, 1988).

33. Cobb, "The Meaning of Pluralism for Christian Self-Understanding," *Religious Pluralism*, 175–76.

Paul Knitter uses the analogy of a dialogue between a Christian cat and other religious mice when the Christian enters a dialogue with the conviction that Jesus is an absolute or normative mediator of God.[34] What is being said with this analogy is that the logic of dialogue rules out a party who has nothing substantial to learn. If one is not open to learning, one is not really participating in a dialogue that is seeking truth. Such is not the case for the Christian who holds that Jesus is a negative norm and a positive guide into further truth. The goals of dialogue are multiple: mutual understanding, mutual appreciation of the other, mutual learning and transformation on the basis of an appropriation of what is true in other religions.[35] Negatively, the goal is not that one religion be converted to the religion of the other, even though it would be impossible not to hope that individuals of another religion came to share one's convictions about ultimate truth. But an explicit aim at conversions would imply either the eventual collapse of the many religions into one existing religion or the formation of a hybrid religion. These options seem historically impossible and theoretically undesirable. As John Cobb puts it, should a whole religious tradition end, something incalculable would be lost to the human race.[36]

In his discussion of a world theology Wilfred Cantwell Smith envisions a number of different projects. It is worth distinguishing two of them in order further to define the role of Christian theology in a pluralistic situation. On the one hand, Smith envisions world theology as a collaborative effort and thus an ongoing historical task. It cannot be done by an individual or a theologian representative of one religion alone. It is really the endless task of sharing and probing in dialogue, as human beings of faith, the objects of our faiths. But, on the other hand, representative theologians, from their own faith perspectives, also participate in a global theology when they make the whole scope of religious experience and faith the context and the source for their specific theology. In other words, the horizon of the Christian theologian is opened up by dialogue with other religions, and this transforms Christian understanding of self, world, history, and God.[37] This dovetails with a conclusion reached earlier: Christian theol-

---

34. For example, Knitter, "Review Symposium," *Horizons*, 13 (1986), 132–33. Knitter has altered somewhat his use of the term normative. See *Jesus and the Other Names*, 76–80.

35. A range of goals for dialogue are distinguished by Lochhead in *The Dialogical Imperative*, 54–81.

36. Cobb, *Beyond Dialogue*, xi–xii, 47–51, 141–42.

37. Although they differ significantly on many points, Wilfred Cantwell Smith and John Cobb share this view of the task of Christian theology to be open to transforming experiences from other religions. See Smith, *Towards a World Theology*, 124–28, and Cobb, "Toward a Christocentric Catholic Theology," *Toward a Universal Theology of Religion*, 86–100. For Cobb, the goal of dialogue is the expansion of self-understanding and the transformation of each religion by what it learns from other religions. Thus each religion grows in truth through the understanding of others without merging or syncretism. The point of *Beyond Dialogue* is to demonstrate this.

ogy in a situation of historicity cannot proclaim its truth in isolation; it must recognize our pluralistic situation, and this situation must be allowed to enter into Christian theology as an intrinsic historical dimension of the reflection itself.[38]

Three further reflections qualify the significance of religious pluralism and interreligious dialogue for Christian theology and the normative role of Jesus in it. The first is that, because of the solidarity of all human beings in a world grown smaller, more interdependent, and more marked by social human dislocation, poverty, and social oppression, a concern for human suffering and liberation forms a context for interreligious dialogue and for the world context of a specifically Christian theology.[39] Theology must be accountable not only to the experience of transcendence, but also to human existence in this world. Here one finds concrete data; different understandings of this data and different praxes in reaction to it can be compared in more practical and tangible ways than the different conceptions of ultimate reality. These commonalities of the human situation today provide an empirical reference point for the dialogue partners. Human suffering, political and social oppression, and the many forms of dehumanization present a concrete common responsibility, a point of departure, and a constant reference point for theology in an interreligious context. Christian theology, when it allows the global and religiously pluralistic context to enter into its reflection, begins to engage the actual situation of our planet. Suffering binds all human beings together. Social suffering and ecological destruction, which often go hand in hand, seem to have become an intrinsic dimension of the human species. There is no reason to doubt that, where so much common negative experience obtains, there might also be found common ethical and religious experiences of contrast.

Secondly, it would be important to establish more or less universally accepted criteria to formalize the context within which dialogue, and theology generally, can unfold. Of course, each religion has its own norms and criteria on the basis of its scriptures, history, and tradition. But some

---

38. Francis X. Clooney, in *Theology after Vedanta: An Experiment in Comparative Theology* (Albany: State University of New York Press, 1993), provides a concrete method by which the learning and transformation described by Cobb can be accomplished by comparative theology. This consists in close reading of the texts of other religions in order to retrieve, reflectively after comparison, one's own religious tradition. Clooney's contribution is a scholarly textual method for theological learning from the comparative study of religion. Keith Ward, in *Religion and Revelation* (Oxford: Clarendon Press, 1994), justifies and then exemplifies how the content of the religious experience of other religions can be brought into Christian theological reflection.

39. Paul Knitter makes this case forcefully in "Toward a Liberation Theology of Religions," *The Myth of Christian Uniqueness*, 178–200. He elaborates it more fully in *One Earth Many Religions* where he characterizes his approach and position as calling for "a globally responsible, correlational dialogue of religions" (15). On the need of a focus on the *humanum* in interreligious dialogue and theology, see also Gordon D. Kaufman, *The Theological Imagination: Constructing the Concept of God* (Philadelphia: Westminster Press, 1981), 172–206.

common criteria for assessing the significance and truth of various positions would be helpful for mutual understanding. These criteria might include some of the following formal areas and heuristic questions: 1) The ability of beliefs to account for the data of our common life in history today; do the beliefs or theological understandings correlate with the reality we experience? 2) The metaphysical coherence of beliefs; do theological understandings cohere intelligibly with what we know of reality from other sources? 3) The ethical implications of these beliefs and their consequences for the continued existence and flourishing of the *humanum*; what praxis do these beliefs lead to in the face of our situation today?[40]

Thirdly, the conjunction of the dynamics of interreligious dialogue and the problematic of inculturation merits more attention than a single chapter allows. I brought up inculturation briefly in the last chapter in connection with the Christian response to social salvation. But inculturation is intimately connected with the dialogue with the religions which are so imbedded especially in Asian and African cultures. More and more the Christians who participate in these cultures must be allowed by the Christians of the West to have the freedom to enter into this dialogue in the terms that the culture dictates.[41]

In sum, we live in a religiously pluralistic world. Historically, this is a given, and it will not change; theologically, from a Christian standpoint, this pluralism should be interpreted positively. The normative revelation of Jesus posits that God's grace is operative in other religions. Insofar as other religions mediate God's saving grace, they are in that measure true. The normativity of Jesus also mandates interreligious dialogue. Because other religions are real mediations of God's grace, and thus fundamentally not in competition with God's action in Jesus, Christians should approach them with openness and an eagerness to learn more of God's ways in the world. But these judgments made on the basis of Christian experience itself must at the same time be chastened by actual dialogue and critical thought according to public criteria.

---

40. These criteria are generalizations based on suggestions from Hans Küng, "What Is True Religion? Toward an Ecumenical Criteriology," *Toward a Universal Theology of Religion*, ed. by Leonard Swidler (Maryknoll, N.Y.: Orbis Books, 1987), 231–50; David Tracy, *Dialogue with the Other: The Inter-Religious Dialogue* (Louvain: Peeters Press and Grand Rapids: Eerdmans, 1990), 27–47; Ogden, *One True Religion?*, 1–26.

41. Two theologians deeply involved in pursuing an inculturated christology with an eye toward Hinduism and Buddhism, respectively, are Michael Amaladoss and Aloysius Pieris. Representative essays are: M. Amaladoss, "Dialogue and Mission: Conflict or Convergence," *Making All Things New* (Maryknoll, N.Y.: Orbis Books, 1990), 43–56; "The Pluralism of Religions and the Significance of Christ," ibid., 83–99; "Jesus Christ in the Midst of Religions: An Indian Perspective," Lecture given at Catholic University of Leuven, Nov. 20, 1997; A. Pieris, "Christology in Asia," *Voices from the Third World*, 10 (1988), 155–72; "Interreligious Dialogue and Theology of Religions," *Fire and Water* (Maryknoll, N.Y.: Orbis Books, 1996), 154–61; "Does Christ Have a Place in Asia?" ibid., 65–78, and "The Buddha and the Christ: Mediators of Liberation," *The Myth of Christian Uniqueness*, 162–77.

A NEW CONTEXT FOR CHRISTOLOGY

How does this assessment of the possible attitudes of Christians toward Jesus in relation to other world religions come to bear on christology? In this concluding section I will integrate these pluralist attitudes and views with the christology that has been developed up to this point. This will amount to a recapitulation and a description of the context for the formal christology that will be taken up in the next chapter.

The position reflected here can be summarized in two negative propositions. Affirming the validity of other religions does not undermine the normativity of Jesus Christ. And affirming the normativity of Jesus Christ, not simply for Christians but for all human beings, does not undermine the validity and truth contained in other religions. Positively, one can and should affirm together the normativity of Jesus, the true and salvific character of other religions, and thus the positive character of religious pluralism. This foundational position may be described more fully in a series of points.

First, the context of religious pluralism and the imperative for dialogue, which both the situation and Christian faith itself impose, confirm a historical starting point for christology. They also reinforce a focus on the humanity of Jesus of Nazareth. When the subject matter of dialogue is Christian faith, all the participants in the dialogue can share in common an appreciation of the historical Jesus. Since everyone knows or can know and accept that Jesus was a human being, and since all parties in the dialogue can in principle agree upon some one or other historical interpretation of Jesus, the first task of christology in a situation of interfaith dialogue is to present Jesus of Nazareth. What is called for here is an engagement with Jesus research in an effort to represent what one can say of Jesus and his teaching in order to place him squarely within history.

Second, in the view of Jesus represented here, he remains what Jesus has been from the beginning of the Christian tradition, the one who mediates God's salvation to humankind. The task of christology also remains the same in this respect in this new context: christology must explain how Jesus can be considered God's salvation bringer in such a way that he is normative for humankind. Jesus is salvation bringer not for a certain group in history but for all human beings.

Third, Jesus causes salvation among those who encounter him historically when he in turn mediates an encounter with God as loving creator and friend. The salvation that Jesus causes in the Christian community, and which is further mediated by that community, is precisely an explicit awareness of God's love for humankind. And this love includes this specific community and each one in it; God's specific love of individuals is in no way minimized by its infinite expansiveness and scope. This God is revealed as by nature being a present, active, and effective love at work in all humankind, and hence in the religions that explicitly direct human freedom in the direction of self-transcendence and ultimacy. The love of God that is revealed in Jesus cannot be less than this; God the creator loves all creation and enters into active dialogue with all human beings in a historically mediated way. Therefore Jesus reveals something that has been going on from the beginning, before and outside of Jesus' own influence.

Fourth, the key step or point of transition to the pluralist position is the breakdown of a causal connection between Jesus of Nazareth, who is the basis of christology, and the salvation that according to Christian faith goes on outside of the Christian sphere. In the absence of all historical connection, all such connections can only appear as inferential, speculative, and tenuous; in no way do they appear necessary. When one recognizes that God's creative action is always actuality, and that God's personal loving presence cannot be separated from God's creative presence, no reason remains to design a meta-narrative that makes Jesus' historical life a cause of God's constant and ever-present salvific love.[42]

Fifth, because God is salvifically present to other religions, other representations of God can be universally normative, and thus, too, for Christians, even as Jesus Christ is universally normative. All due attention is to be given to the principle of non-contradiction in measuring these norms, as well as to the historicity of all human conceptions and the transcendence of ultimate reality. But the recognition of God's universal saving influence transforms religious pluralism into a positive situation in which more can be learned about ultimate reality and human existence than is available in a single tradition. In a way, the affirmation of the truth of other religions consists in an extension of this simple insight of common sense. It is difficult to believe today that one religion alone can possess the fullness of truth about transcendent reality.

Sixth, as a corollary to christology, the pluralist position provides a grounding for the religious seriousness of interfaith dialogue. The point of interreligious dialogue transcends a pragmatic getting along with others, although this motive should not be slighted. In the Christian pluralist proposal God is not distant from any members of the human family. And as a religion of salvation, the places where God's presence is most clearly recognized are those deep negative contrast experiences that in themselves spontaneously demand reversal and reprieve. The various levels of universal human guilt, oppression, suffering, and death form a

---

42. This is the essence of Maurice Wiles's argument against Rahner's constitutive christology on the basis of Rahner's supernatural existential: the two theological constructs are thematically inconsistent. Maurice Wiles, *Christian Theology and Interreligious Dialogue* (London: SCM Press, 1992), 45–82. And Edward Schillebeeckx, as I reported in the last chapter, being deeply influenced by the doctrine of creation, is convinced that religious pluralism is justified in principle, so that at bottom christology reflects an ideal form of the union between God and human beings willed in creation. Schillebeeckx deals with religious pluralism in *Church: The Human Story of God* (New York: Crossroad, 1990), 164–86. See Chapter 13, n. 50, for references to Schillebeeckx on creation.

human context in which people of different traditions can begin to communicate their conceptions of ultimate reality.

It may seem to some that these theological considerations about God at work in other religions as well as in Jesus are somehow threatening. Do they not undermine the security entailed in the experience that God has worked human salvation in Jesus finally, definitively, unsurpassably, and absolutely? But it is difficult to see how the recognition of God at work in other religious mediations in any way undermines the radically affirming sense of being addressed by God and united to God through Jesus. God's saving presence in Jesus Christ is in no way strengthened by God's absence from the rest of the world. In fact an inability to recognize God's presence in other religions logically renders God's presence in Jesus less likely. If God were absent from all the religions of the world, what would encourage confidence in God's presence in Jesus? By contrast, nothing is subtracted from Christian faith by affirming God's presence in other religions. Jesus remains a norm. Although there may be other real mediations of God's salvation, the Christian cannot expect that they can authentically represent God to be less than God is encountered to be in Jesus.[43] Ultimately, fear that something is lost in conceiving God as being at work in other religions is based on a premise of competition between the religions. If the Christian could depend on God enough to remove this premise and see God at work in all of them, much of the threat would be transformed into open curiosity about other religions. Many people who presuppose historicity and do not know any alternative already experience this. They find traditional doctrines, when they are transliterated instead of interpreted, unintelligible. By contrast, they are open to other religions even while they are committed to God as mediated by Jesus. Religious pluralism need not be threatening to either christology or general Christian faith consciousness. It is rather part of today's context for reflection on the mysterious reality of Jesus Christ.

---

43. Ernst Troeltsch, who in his middle period held a normative but not an absolute christology, was also sensitive to the sensitivities of ordinary Christians. He explicitly strove to mitigate any anxiety produced by historical consciousness. See Ernst Troeltsch, *The Absoluteness of Christianity and the History of Religions* (Richmond: John Knox Press, 1971), 121–29.

CHAPTER 15

The Divinity of Jesus Christ

I now take up the formal and narrow christological question concerning the relation of Jesus to God and to other human beings. How are we to understand constructively what has traditionally been known as Jesus' divinity? This chapter has as its object to "explain" or construe Jesus' divinity in terms that remain faithful to the witness of the New Testament and the classical conciliar doctrines, best portray this doctrine in a credible and intelligible way in present-day postmodern intellectual culture, and empower discipleship. This entails recognizing that pluralism marks contemporary christology both in fact and principle. In keeping with this pluralism I outline two fundamental types of christology that can meet the criteria just mentioned.[1]

I begin, then, with a brief statement concerning pluralism in christology, in the New Testament and today, and the task of christology relative to it. I will then briefly outline a reinterpretation of the Logos christology of Karl Rahner which has had an exceptional impact in the late twentieth century both inside and outside the Catholic Church. This revisionist interpretation will take into account the features of postmodernity. And finally, in contrast to Logos christology, I will present a Spirit christology. I do not intend to give equal time to these two christologies; Rahner's christology is well known and still enjoys a commanding allegiance among many theologians. The case for a Spirit christology, although it has been discussed for some time, still has to be made for the church at large. The point of pre-

---

1. Wesley J. Wildman, in *Fidelity with Plausibility: Modest Christologies in the Twentieth Century* (Albany: State University of New York Press, 1998), presents a detailed map of the present theological terrain relative to the narrow christological question. Christology is currently undergoing a crisis of plausibility, mainly because of the collapse of the credibility of the absolutist claims attributed to Jesus Christ. The solution, attempted in myriad forms, consists in more modest christologies that are intellectually sound, balance this with fidelity to scripture and the classical tradition, and bear religious power. He illustrates two types of modest christology, inspirational and incarnational, that roughly correlate with the types of the christologies outlined in this chapter. This chapter, therefore, represents another attempt at a modest christology.

senting two different christologies is to illustrate each christology as integral, autonomous, and sound, and thereby to clarify the real differences between them. This will in turn exemplify a pluralism of christological understanding that reaches to the formal christological question.

PLURALISM IN CHRISTOLOGY

Pluralism means differences within a wider unity. Pluralism, as I understand it, presupposes a larger unity. Some common denominator, some defining element, or context, or sphere of interaction, constitutes a unity that is differentiated. Pluralism, therefore, means that real, solid, and persistent differences prevail between people, between their views, between who they think they are as human beings, between the ways in which they act, and thus between the peoples themselves. But these differences are not all that characterize the relations between them. The differences are not complete; they subsist within a larger framework of something shared, some sameness or unity: of the species, of historical interaction, of a region, a society, a loyalty to a country, a common religious faith. This means that at some level one can find commonalities among the differing parties that bind them together, even though the term "pluralism" emphasizes differences.[2]

In what follows I want to demonstrate why pluralism is both necessary and possible in christology. As a way of formulating this thesis I will appeal to the criteria of theology discussed in Chapter 2 by asking whether such a pluralism is faithful to the witness of scripture and the early doctrinal tradition, intelligible today, and generative of the Christian life.

THE NECESSITY OF PLURALISM IN CHRISTOLOGY

Each of the three measurements for the adequacy of a theological position urges the necessity of pluralism in christology. I begin with a consideration of scripture. The analysis of New Testament christologies in Chapter 6 was geared to displaying the wide range of different interpretations of Jesus by the first-century Christian communities. The New Testament is pluralistic in its christology. But the New Testament is

---

2. Nicholas Rescher defends a doctrine of cognitive and social pluralism in these terms: "As pluralism sees it, a variety of distinct, mutually incompatible resolutions on any controvertible issue is in principle 'available.'" N. Rescher, *Pluralism: Against the Demand for Consensus* (Oxford: Clarendon Press, 1993), 96. Rescher's emphasis is on differences in understanding. As distinct from consensus, he insists that the common basis for human communication consists in a shared real world outside the self. "Our concept of a *real thing* as a commonly available focus is accordingly a fixed point, a shared and stable centre around which communication revolves, the invariant focus of potentially diverse conceptions." Ibid., 140. This will apply analogously in christology.

normative for all christology and would on that account seem to demand pluralism. But this follows only if scripture is normative in that particular respect. Is it the case that the New Testament is normative precisely in the pluralism of its christologies? It is. The conclusion is sound not because of a necessary logic of the terms as given, but because the reasons for the pluralism in the New Testament are paradigmatic and applicable universally. New Testament christologies differ because they are historical: the texts making up the New Testament were written by different authors, representing different communities, writing for different audiences, facing different problems. These different communities had different cultures, with different traditions, interests, and styles of speaking, understanding, and writing. Also, the subject matter, Jesus, displays any number of different facets for religious interpretation.[3] Each New Testament text is historically situated and contextualized; it is the product of the inculturated interpretation and appropriation of Jesus of Nazareth. The logic of the position, then, is straightforward: christology should be a pluralistic discipline today because Jesus Christ must be interpreted and culturally appropriated by particular communities today even as he was in the formation of the New Testament.[4] To summarize this first point in a sharp phrase, the New Testament does not merely tolerate a situation of pluralism in christology, it prescribes it.

The necessity of pluralism in christology can be argued on the basis of the criterion of intelligibility by a negative and a positive logic. On the one hand, a uniform mode of understanding Jesus Christ by all Christians in the world is historically impossible, so that, on the other hand, it is readily intelligible that the pluralism that characterizes all historical understanding also obtains in christology.

Pluralism is a consequence of the historicity of all human knowledge, including the interpretation of reality resulting from divine revelation. Because the human spirit is tied to matter, and a particular world of space and time, all appreciation of reality is historically mediated and thus shares a measure of particularity. It is this particularity, as determined by historical specificity, that accounts for pluralism. The sociology of knowledge, critical theory, and language philosophy have analyzed the social determinants that bestow particular accents and biases on all human appreciations of reality. Theology, in its methods and resultant interpretations of Jesus Christ, cannot be and demonstrably is not exempt from these social determinants.

But this very situation can also be represented in a positive and constructive rhetoric. Human beings understand reality within the framework

---

3. See, for example, Edward Schillebeeckx's account of the development of christologies in the New Testament period in his *Jesus: An Experiment in Christology* (New York: Seabury Press, 1979), 401–515.

4. The New Testament canon itself illustrates the point. Although the New Testament is a bond of the unity of the early churches, it also symbolizes in its composition the diversity of churches within that unity.

of their language, their situation in their society, and the context of their culture. The principle that Thomas Aquinas laid down relative to personal appropriation of knowledge can be rephrased in social terms: whatever is learned or known is appreciated according to the social historical form of the community who learns it.[5]

A third criterion for the authenticity of a theological position is its ability to empower a moral life in a particular situation. To understand the moral demand for pluralism one must begin one's reflection with a global understanding of the church as one. Christianity is a distinctive religion, not to be confused with religion itself or other religions. I suppose too that the Christian church is a world church, a church that in principle includes people from all places and cultures, including subcultures that cut across ethnic cultures. At the present time the church is on a threshold as people in the West increasingly become a minority of its membership.

From the perspective of the universality or catholicity of the church, two reflections support the moral credibility of pluralism in christology as the doctrine that lies at the defining center of Christianity itself. First, pluralism in the appreciation of Jesus Christ already exists. Moreover, I have argued, it necessarily exists and is positively salutary. It follows that the church, in its public and institutional face, should reflect and promote this necessary dimension of its historical existence. Negatively, efforts by the centers of world churches to impede indigenous appropriations of Jesus Christ at the periphery can only appear, in the light of the ideal of inculturation, as imperialistic and a morally questionable use, or abuse, of authority.

Second, recognition of the historical necessity of pluralism in all human understanding has been gradually undermining an extrinsicist understanding of authority and replacing it with a more intrinsic and dialogical conception. The unity of faith does not depend exclusively upon a this-worldly external and historical authority. Even the most common bond of all Christians, its scripture, does not unite Christians by being interpreted in a monolithic way. Although external bonds are absolutely necessary, Christians are ultimately bound together by their common faith that in every case is appropriated by the human spirit freely as from the grace of God. God as Spirit unites Christians of every age and across the ages with those who first formed the scriptures. Within the context of this growing conviction of religious freedom, institutional churches cannot give the impression that the unity of Christians, and Christianity as such, can be reduced to the adherence to external ritual, discipline, or doctrinal formula. The moral credibility of the church as institution in contexts that are increasingly inculturated depends upon its ability to encourage the

---

5. "Cognita sunt in cognoscente secundum modum cognoscentis." Thomas Aquinas, ST II–II, q. 1, a. 2. See John Hick's appropriation of this in his *An Interpretation of Religion: Human Responses to the Transcendent* (New Haven: Yale University Press, 1989), 240–41.

freedom of a distinctive appropriation of Jesus Christ. In brief, an explicit openness to pluralism on the part of the world church can serve as a model for a morality of belief in the postmodern world that is credible.

THE POSSIBILITY OF PLURALISM IN CHRISTOLOGY

By the possibility of pluralism in christology I mean its ability to meet the demands of truth and fidelity to Christian belief against the negative threats of historicity: relativism, syncretism, and reductionism. The point, then, is to show that within a situation in which pluralism obtains, one can still appeal to the criteria of theology to measure the adequacy of any given christology. This can be shown by a consideration of each of the criteria.

Although the New Testament prescribes pluralism in christology, it also provides norms for christology. Two elements of the New Testament's representation of Jesus function criteriologically: the portrait of Jesus that can be reconstructed from them, and the series of christologies that interpret him.

All christology must be faithful to Jesus. Jesus, as Jesus can be known by historical research, offers a first criterion for an adequate christology. This normativity functions in two ways. Negatively, a christology cannot contradict something that is established about Jesus on the basis of historical research. Docetism is a good example of a christology ruled out by the historical Jesus. More positively, because christology is precisely an interpretation of the historical person Jesus of Nazareth, and because ordinarily interpretation must keep close to the object of interpretation, the historical person of Jesus as he is depicted by the consensus of historians must enter into the imagination in any portrayal of Jesus Christ. A christology must represent the historical fact that Jesus was a human being like all others and, to the extent possible, the historical figure himself.

Christology must also be consistent with the point of New Testament christologies. The other way in which the New Testament provides a criterion for christology centers on the christologies that are found in the New Testament. Because there are many such christologies, this normative function cannot consist in making one of these christologies a norm for all others. Rather, the christologies of all ages must compare themselves with the point of all New Testament christologies, namely, that God was so encountered in Jesus that salvation from God is mediated through him. I will deal with this point further on under the criterion of intelligibility. What needs to be underlined relative to norms for christology is that an adequate christology must consider, interpret, and appropriate the classical christologies of the New Testament in order to be faithful to the foundational statement of Christian faith.

Christology today has to be congruent with classical christology as well. The foundational expression of christological faith did not really end with the New Testament. Certain questions not answered by the New Testament were entertained in the patristic period. The formal doctrines of Nicaea and Chalcedon, for example, have been considered classical expressions of Christian faith by the majority of the Christian churches. Because of this historical status, an adequate christology must enter into dialogue with this classical language, and allow itself to be shaped by these doctrines in the act of interpreting and appropriating them.[6]

This dialogue with and interpretation of the tradition represent the way any given christology in any given community should enter into dialogue with other communities and the church at large at any given time. The pluralism of christology should not be understood as a movement toward an isolation of a particular community, or breaking communion with the wider church. Communion and dialogue could readily be developed as a distinct criterion for christology.

A second norm for the adequacy of christology is its intelligibility. The criterion of intelligibility explains the necessity of pluralism when a given christology is understood in relation to the intellectual context in which it is proffered. But the criterion of intelligibility guards the unity of christology when it is applied to the intrinsic structure of christological belief, that is, the inner logic of faith in Jesus as the Christ.

Working "from below," from a consideration of the epistemology of faith, the historical genesis of christology, and a conception of its structure or logic, one can discover the *intrinsic* norm for christology in the recognition of what a christology must express or explain. On this premise, a christology must "explain" two things: how Jesus is a mediator of God's salvation, and why he is the object of Christian worship. This proposal introduces those elements in the experience of the Christian community which are distinctively christological. These two elements also isolate the basic christological experience, that which provides the basis for the full range of the conceptions of salvation and Jesus' divinity found in the New Testament.

The first element of the intrinsic intelligibility of christology lies in the common conviction, despite the pluralism of soteriologies and christologies in the New Testament, that Jesus is the mediator of a salvation that comes from God. The genesis of New Testament soteriologies and christologies all stem from the primal experience of an encounter with God in Jesus in such a manner that Jesus mediates God's salvation. The recognition of Jesus' divinity is a function of an experience that he is the bearer of a salvation which is from God and would not be salvation were it not. A second element lies in the cult of Jesus, which began quite soon after his death and the experience of his resurrection or exaltation. This worship of Jesus was the principal reason which lead to the clear and explicit affir-

---

6. Ultimately, the reason why Chalcedon achieved the status of a classic doctrine is that its fundamental symbolic meaning represents the internal logic of christological faith itself. Chalcedon, therefore, must be interpreted in such a way that it is consistent with its own norm, that is, the intrinsic intelligibility of New Testament christology: God is encountered in and through Jesus.

mation of the divinity of Jesus in the patristic period. These two elements are common within the pluralism of New Testament christologies. Because they represent the experiential data upon which christology rests, they represent as well the groundwork for the intelligibility of any christology. And because they represent the genetic basis out of which all christology arises, they are precisely that which is being expressed and explained in all christology. This aspect of the norm of intelligibility in christology is experiential and as such intrinsic to the discipline itself.

The criterion of intelligibility includes an understanding of the very logic and coherence of christological faith. Intrinsically, the faith that generates christology is an encounter with God mediated by Jesus in such a way that Jesus is recognized as the bearer of God's salvation. Therefore, any christology which explains within a given context how Jesus mediates salvation from God and is therefore the object of Christian worship is orthodox, and christologies that fail to do so are inadequate. This structure also explains how the doctrine of Chalcedon, which insists on the humanity and divinity of Jesus, can be formally normative without implying an extrinsicist normativity of its specific language.

The third criterion of an adequate christology is its ethical credibility and its ability to empower a moral Christian life. A descriptive explanation of this criterion entails a formulation of the relationship between theory and practice. The scope of this discussion prevents me from dealing with this relationship in any detail, and I will have to be content with a definition of praxis as a form of life or pattern of behavior that is driven by a fundamental faith commitment to a certain vision of reality and shaped by theory. Praxis thus integrates understanding and knowledge on the one hand and action or practice on the other.

Because of the close interdependence of knowing and doing, and because of the structure of human existence itself in which they are bound together, action, in the sense of a free moral behavior that is consistent with christological faith, becomes another criterion for the adequacy of a given christology. This criterion allows one to suspect that a christology that allows or consistently generates behavior that is commonly judged to be unethical is less than adequate.[7] Conversely, one probably cannot say that a christology that generates certain religious and moral behavior is by that criterion alone orthodox. But a christology that is consistent with and encourages certain practical attitudes, convictions, and patterns of religious attachment to Jesus, as well as concern for justice on religious grounds, is at least morally credible.

This criterion has roots in the New Testament; the pragmatic principle is enshrined in the gospels. Axioms such as the love of neighbor being the

---

7. Many questions concerning the character and meaning of the "ethical" are being begged at this point. But this is consistent with the largely formal character of these reflections.

measure of love of God (Luke 10:29-37), and principles such as "You will know them by their fruits" (Mark 7:16), are explicit and formal. Although this criterion is quite general, it is nonetheless practicable and effective in certain situations. For example, the rise of the social gospel movement at the turn of the twentieth century and its reprise as liberation theology in the last third of that century show that in situations of social suffering that mark our world an individualistic christology is simply inadequate. An adequate christology in an interdependent world cannot fail to represent Jesus Christ in a morally credible way that engages people's freedom at the point where they are inserted into the social, political world.

Such is the demand in our time for pluralism in christology, a pluralism that at the same time allows for the critique of christologies that do not measure up to the intrinsic logic of Christian faith. In what follows I will outline two different christologies which are viable today.

LOGOS CHRISTOLOGY

Given the theoretical rationale for the necessity and possibility of a pluralism of christologies, I intend to exemplify that pluralism with two different christologies, a Logos and a Spirit christology. My goal is to represent these christologies as two viable options in a postmodern context. The representation of these christologies follows a similar pattern or order of topics that allows comparison and contrast. These two christologies are significantly different; yet both may be understood as corresponding to the criteria for a relatively adequate christology. It should be noted, however, that these descriptions bear more resemblance to types of christology than to developed christologies. They should be regarded as schematic representations of paradigms of christology that are abstracted from the specific christological proposals of theologians today. I see them as working models open for critique, further discussion, and development by the theological community. Space does not allow anticipating the questions that these abbreviated representations will provoke. But the point of this chapter may still be achieved, namely, to illustrate that the way Jesus' divinity is experienced and conceived is subject to plural representations.

Behind the generalized account of the Logos christology which follows lies the christology of Karl Rahner. Rahner's is among the christologies which have been most successful in retrieving traditional language and doctrine and responding to modern western culture. Because his christology is "modern," however, it does not correlate neatly with a postmodern context in several respects. For this reason I begin this section by pointing to aspects of Rahner's christology that are susceptible to critique in a postmodern situation. This will lay open the way to a positive retrieval of a Logos christology.

CURRENT QUESTIONING OF RAHNER'S
CHRISTOLOGICAL LANGUAGE

It should be clear that this is not the occasion for a critical study of Rahner's christology. I shall presuppose a general familiarity with Rahnerian christological language, and not develop at length these areas where his thought is being subjected to questions. Many of the questions addressed to Rahner's christology apply to Logos christology generally. I do not presume that these critiques lack rejoinders. Indeed, in some respects the second part of this section responds to them. The purpose of positing these five problematic areas is to open up the space for a retrieval of Logos christology in the spirit of Karl Rahner in the face of new exigencies.

1) Rahner's christology is in many but certainly not all respects a christology "from above." Methodologically, Rahner accepts the major doctrines of the church on the basis of their ecclesial authority. For example, he accepts Nicaea and Chalcedon as given. He then seeks to "explain" these doctrines with creative hermeneutical retrievals of traditional language. Other aspects of his vision and method give it a quality of arguing from above. One is the way his christology unfolds within the framework of an understanding of the immanent trinity. The Logos is the second person of the trinity, who is the self-expression of the Father, and who alone could become incarnate. The metaphysical character of the language that forms the framework which Rahner brings to christology stands in contrast with beginning christology with a historical curiosity about Jesus of Nazareth. Rahner represents a modern version of the metaphysical christology of the patristic and medieval periods.[8]

2) Rahner's Logos christology raises some questions about Jesus' consubstantiality with us. This is not Rahner's intention; his explicitly conscious intent is to show the continuity and not the difference between Jesus and us. But despite his intentions and his strong affirmations of Jesus' real humanity, the suspicions arise at several points. Jesus is not like us insofar as God is present to Jesus as Logos and God is present to us as Spirit. In other words, God's presence as Logos to Jesus is a qualitatively different mode of presence than God's union with human beings generally. It seems metaphysically inconceivable that this different presence to Jesus would not make a substantial, ontological difference in him relative to God's presence to us. It would be an odd metaphysics that could

---

8. By christology "from above" and "from below" I refer to the suppositions and point of departure of one's theological method. The metaphysical nature of Rahner's christology is not the issue here, since all christology is metaphysical by implication, but the way this particular metaphysical framework gives his christology its character of unfolding "from above." This is illustrated by Karl Rahner, "The Theology of the Symbol," *Theological Investigations*, 4 (Baltimore: Helicon Press, 1966), 221–52.

imagine God assuming a human nature without ontologically transforming that human nature.[9] Although Rahner does not usually refer to Jesus
as a human person, he always refers to his humanity as an integral human
nature. Indeed, his description of this integral human nature is realistic.
But Rahner's hypostatic union seems to be an "enhypostatic union," that
is, Jesus' integral humanity is borne and sustained by the divine being of
the Logos. Such is not the case with other human beings, so that, once
again, Jesus appears different from other human beings.

3) Another question raised by Rahner's christology concerns his view
that God can be incarnate only once.[10] This is not indigenous to a Logos
christology, because others with a Logos christology disagree.[11] But
Rahner's view is typical. His reasoning is less a function of Jesus as
revealer, and more a function of the view that, in the Jesus event, God's
pact with humanity is closed and sealed in a definitive, irrevocable way.
Irrevocability implies "only once" because a plurality of incarnations
would seem to mean that the one was not enough. But a consciousness of
historicity makes this difficult to hold. Rahner's position rests on the speculative premise that Jesus does not only represent and reveal the saving
love of God but constitutes and causes it for all people, even when there
is no historical contact with Jesus. But there is massive evidence across the
whole bible that God as savior possesses always and from the beginning
an irrevocable love for human beings. Rahner strongly insists on this universal saving love of God. But he holds that this love becomes effective in
history only because it is sacramentally constituted in the one-time event
of hypostatic union in Jesus Christ. But why is not this transcendental love
of God sacramentally actualized in history in many instances? Why is
Jesus not one of many symbolic actualizations of God's loving presence
to humankind? Cannot "more" of God be revealed in other "incarnations"? There is no hard reason why God could not approach humankind
in a variety of ways and in more than one medium, so that such a restriction seems inappropriately predicated of God. In principle a Logos christology is open to this view, but its tendency has been to tie God's saving
action in history exclusively to Jesus as its unique cause.

4) Rahner's christology has been criticized for containing a certain thematic inconsistency. This is not quite a contradiction or paradox, but an
inconsistency between the language of universal grace, as in the supernatural existential, and the language of Jesus of Nazareth, a particular

---

9. Rahner himself makes an analogous point in the context of understanding the
relation between nature and grace. God's love and the destiny God intends for human
existence utterly transform what would have been the metaphysical structure of
human existence without that love and destiny. Karl Rahner, "Concerning the
Relationship of Nature and Grace," *Theological Investigations*, 1 (Baltimore: Helicon
Press, 1961), 302–03.

10. Paul Knitter, *No Other Name?* (Maryknoll, N.Y.: Orbis Books, 1985), 186–88.

11. For example, Raimon Panikkar, *The Unknown Christ of Hinduism* (Maryknoll, N.Y.:
Orbis Books, 1981), 31–61.

event in history, being the constitutive cause of this grace. The logic for Rahner's reasoning on this point is closely bound to the language of supernaturality, a conception which characterizes God's saving initiative as transcending the dynamics of God's creating and the power of human nature. But Rahner holds these two dimensions of God's relationship to the world closely together, so that God's gracious and saving love is concomitant with God's creating. Thus when one reaches behind this conceptuality to the essence of Rahner's position of the consistent unity of nature and grace from the beginning, it seems to clash with the idea that this was constitutively caused by the relatively recent event of Jesus.[12] Thus a constitutive christology seems gratuitous and unnecessary.

5) Finally, the argument that Rahner mounts to show how the event of Jesus Christ might be conceived as causing this universally available salvation has also come under critical scrutiny. Rahner explains that Jesus Christ is constitutive of all human salvation because he is the incarnation of the Logos or Son, and all saving grace proceeds from the Father and the Son. All grace is the grace of Christ. The Jesus of history is also constitutive because of his free, obedient, and faithful acceptance of God's self-communication. The event of the death of Jesus is where this final acceptance is acted out. The union between God and Jesus that was effected in that death is the final cause and thus intrinsic to the salvation of every human being, before and after the actual life of Jesus. This does not imply that for Rahner there are no other savior figures or other saving religions: he explicitly argues that there are. But Jesus Christ and the union of God with human existence that was achieved in him make up the goal of human existence itself. Thus all fragmentary historical realizations of communion between God and human beings, for example, in other religions, are oriented toward this hypostatic union as toward their meaning-giving end.[13]

Schubert Ogden, however, argues that final causality is not causality at all, but representation.[14] At all events, it is at best a weak causality. Jesus

---

12. Maurice Wiles, *Christian Theology and Inter-religious Dialogue* (London: SCM Press, 1992), 45–63.

13. Karl Rahner, "The One Christ and the Universality of Salvation," *Theological Investigations*, 16 (New York: Seabury Press, 1979), 199–224. Also Rahner, *Foundations of Christian Faith* (New York: Seabury Press, 1978), 315–21. Otto Hentz explains the bearing of Jesus Christ on all of history in terms of the metaphor of God courting human existence in a love relationship leading toward marriage. The end of the narrative is what gives the whole story its meaning. Jesus Christ, in the hypostatic union and the human acceptance of God's definitive self-communication, is like marriage, the final, irrevocable sealing of God's love relationship with humanity. "The savior, then, is decisive for the whole of history, the cause of salvation, because in and through him the goal of our hope becomes a real part of our lives and history." Otto Hentz, "Anticipating Jesus Christ: An Account of Our Hope," *A World of Grace*, ed. by Leo J. O'Donovan (New York: Crossroad, 1987), 112–13.

14. Schubert M. Ogden, *Is There Only One True Religion or Are There Many?* (Dallas: Southern Methodist University Press, 1992), 94–95.

Christ seems to play the role of a "centering" causality in Rahner's thought: like the keystone in an arch, Jesus is the central piece in his meta-narrative and vision. But there can be other such visions as well. These criticisms of Rahner's christology are not mortal, but they do ask for some reconfiguring of his language to meet new problems.

LOGOS CHRISTOLOGY IN THE SPIRIT OF KARL RAHNER

The following account of Logos christology is not a representation of Rahner's christology. But in laying out the elements of a viable Logos christology in a postmodern context I will implicitly or explicitly appeal to themes that occur in Rahner's christology. By attending to the criticisms that were just described, and by being attentive to the demands of histor-ical consciousness for a christology from below, I will recast Rahnerian themes in ways that Rahner would not call his own. But this reinterpre-tation is meant as a retrieval of Rahner.

Contemporary Logos Christologies

Rahner is not alone in proposing a Logos christology. Virtually all chris-tology from the second century onward drew its inspiration from the lan-guage of John's Prologue, combined with a particular construal of Son of God, to provide a framework for christological thinking. Today Logos christology still dominates the mainline Christian churches and the text-book theology taught in seminaries. But as we saw earlier, the applicabil-ity of the historical doctrine of the great councils has been criticized since the beginning of modern theology, most severely by those who wish to remain faithful to it. Thus classical Logos christology without modifica-tions is losing ground today. Rahner has made some of those modifica-tions. One finds parallels to Rahner's Logos christology in the Word christology of Karl Barth.[15] Walter Kasper and Brian McDermott are indebted to Rahner in their portrayal of an incarnational Logos christol-ogy.[16] John Cobb radically transforms the traditional Logos christology by replacing the Greek philosophical themes carried by the symbol with the transcendent principle of "dynamic transformation" inspired by process philosophy.[17] And the liberation theologian Jon Sobrino appeals to the symbol Logos or the Son in his explanation of the divinity of Jesus Christ.[18]

---

15. Barth's Logos or Word christology was outlined in Chapter 11.

16. Walter Kasper, *Jesus the Christ* (New York: Paulist Press, 1976); Brian O. McDermott, *Word Become Flesh: Dimensions of Christology* (Collegeville, Minn.: Liturgical Press, Michael Glazier, 1993). The "kenotic" christology of Lucien Richard, *Christ: The Self-Emptying of God* (New York: Paulist Press, 1997), is also essentially a Logos chris-tology.

17. John B. Cobb, Jr., *Christ in a Pluralistic Age* (Philadelphia: Westminster Press, 1975).

18. Jon Sobrino, *Jesus in Latin America* (Maryknoll, N.Y.: Orbis Books, 1987), 21–31, 40, 46–51. Logos language is not Sobrino's commanding idiom; the Son who leads the way to the Father is more common.

Method and Point of Departure

There is no intrinsic reason why Logos christology must begin "from above." On the contrary, the transcendental method of Karl Rahner in some respects embodies a critical hermeneutical method of correlation. It begins from below with an anthropology, including a phenomenological archaeology of the religious question. Christology must address the anthropocentrism of modernity by going beneath a mere reliance on religious authority and by opening the doors of the religious question inside the autonomously human. Jesus Christ as God's Word comes as a response to the religious question, to human beings who are intrinsically oriented to and looking for God's self-communication in history.[19] I will return to this theme when I address the intelligibility of Logos christology.

There is no reason why Logos christology should not be a christology from below in the further sense that it begins its constructive work with a consideration of the historical Jesus and the plurality of interpretations of him that were generated in the various communities represented in the New Testament literature. The intelligibility of Logos christology must include an account of the historical origin of this symbol, an investigation of Jesus of Nazareth whom it interprets, and a correlation between these two. Interpretations of wisdom and Logos christology, such as those in Chapter 6, are relevant here as a bridge between Jesus and present-day Logos christology.

Fidelity to New Testament Sources

A Logos christology finds its major scriptural support in the Prologue of the Gospel of John which was considered in Chapter 6. Genetically, Rahner's Logos christology is a development of Johannine christology, but one that has gone through two major metamorphoses. The first is the elaboration in the Greek patristic tradition and the great christological councils. This was a thoroughgoing inculturation. The second is Rahner's own reappropriation of this tradition through the modern turn to the subject and a certain anthropocentrism. This oversimplifies a long history of the effects and the ongoing interpretation of this passage. But the point is clear: Logos christology today dialectically unites the christology of John's Prologue and dramatic reinterpretations of it. In order to underline the character of the New Testament symbol, a few remarks of a general nature concerning its origin are necessary.

The biblical symbol, Word. The biblical symbol, the Word of God, ultimately refers to God. But it refers to God under a particular formality and not indiscriminately. The Word of God is God speaking and effecting things by God's command. The symbol of the Word of God is thus a metaphor that ultimately refers to God. God is not other than God's Word; God's Word is God acting outside of God's self in creation. God's Word, in the Prologue of John's gospel, is closely associated with the metaphor

---

19. Rahner's philosophy of religion and propaedeutic to christology are found in his *Hearers of the Word* (New York: Herder and Herder, 1969).

of God's Wisdom, so that the resonances of that metaphor accrue to the Word of God. And, finally, by the time these symbols came to be used in John's gospel, they also carried with them connotations of Greek speculation concerning the intelligibility or "reason" that is responsible for the order of the cosmos. Few symbols in biblical literature are packed with deeper and more widely inclusive sources of meaning.

It is important to underscore the metaphorical and symbolic character of this term "Word," and this can be highlighted by comparing it with other symbols of God's presence in the world, such as God as Spirit, or God as Wisdom, or the hands of God. In one respect these are different symbols, for they are different words and different metaphors. One could analyze a number of specific characteristics of each metaphor and by contrast show the different nuances and subtleties communicated by each of these symbols. For example, the Word of God is responsible for creation: God speaks, commands, or utters God's Word, and it comes to be. God as Wisdom underlies all of creation and especially the right ways of human life. God as Spirit is the source of life and an immanent power at work in prophets and charismatic leaders. Each of these metaphors contains imaginative virtualities that reveal aspects of God. But in another respect, all of these symbols are basically the same insofar as they point to the same generalized experience of God outside of God's self and immanent in the world in presence and active power. The differences of the symbols express various manifestations and characteristics of this primitive datum. This common core is not merely arrived at by abstraction and generalization of a dimension of religious experience, for in many instances in the scriptures the symbols appear to be interchangeable.[20]

In some instances these metaphorical symbols in the Hebrew scriptures are personified, and this personification became a very significant factor in the development of christological and trinitarian doctrine. Personification is a figure of speech: the literal meaning of a personification, that is, the meaning intended by the author of the personification, is not that the "hands of God" refer to two actual hands, or that the Word of God is

---

20. G. W. H. Lampe, *God as Spirit* (Oxford: Clarendon Press, 1977), 37, 115–16, 179; Paul W. Newman, *A Spirit Christology* (Lanham, MD: University Press of America, 1987), 79; James D. G. Dunn, *Christology in the Making* (Philadelphia: Westminster Press, 1980), 131, 266. From a biblical standpoint one could say that Logos christology is not radically distinct from Spirit christology, for the symbol Wisdom can be identified with God as Spirit (Wis 1:7, 7:25) and Wisdom provides a scriptural context for the meaning of Logos. See Addison G. Wright and Pheme Perkins, *The New Jerome Biblical Commentary* (Englewood Cliffs, N.J.: Prentice Hall, 1990), 513 and 951, respectively. This historical work corresponds with a theoretical understanding of religious language as symbolic and metaphorical. Although this cannot be developed here, it leads to the view that christologies that explain Jesus by distinguishing and objectifying religious symbols such as Logos, Spirit, Wisdom, and so on, and assigning them different tasks, misinterpret rather fundamentally the character of religious language. Also, from this point of view, an explanation of Jesus' divinity that uses both Spirit and Logos language is redundant.

something really distinct from God. When the metaphorical character of personification is not respected, when it becomes hypostatized, that is, conceived as objective and individual, in the same measure the power of the symbol tends to be undermined. The symbol can then be made to point to something distinct from God, which in its turn acts as an intermediary between God and the world.[21] God's transcendence and immanence in the world become separated and competitive; God, as holy and transcendent, cannot be mixed up in this world but needs a messenger, an angel, a Word. This goes against the primitive intention of the symbol as referring in its first instance simply to God experienced in the world. In order to preserve this primal quality of the biblical symbol Word, against the tendency of objectifying a personification, I use the phrase God as Word.

Jesus as Logos. The analysis and interpretation of wisdom and Logos christologies in the New Testament in Chapter 6 showed the fit between these metaphors and Jesus. Jesus embodied God's Wisdom; Jesus was the Word of God symbolically because he embodied God's Word to Israel and to the Johannine community. These symbols have a perennial and classical character intratextually, that is, within the Christian community. But more and more they have to be explained even to Christians in present-day secular society and culture.

Foundational Metaphor

The foundational metaphor for understanding Jesus Christ that underlies Logos christology is "incarnation," which is drawn from John's Prologue: "And the Word became flesh" (John 1:14). This christology is not in the line of Antioch; it is not a divine indwelling christology. It is rather a *Logos-sarx* and hypostatic union christology. For example, Rahner continually uses the language of the Word of God assuming a humanity.[22] This is a strong theme which is expressed with emphasis by Rahner. As the Logos or Word is the symbolic self-expression of the Father within the Godhead, so too the full human reality of Jesus is the self-expression of the Logos or Word. "The man Jesus must be the self-revelation of God through who he is and not only through his words, and this he really cannot be if precisely this humanity were not the expression of God."[23] Jesus

---

21. The concept of an intermediary should not be confused with the idea of a medium developed in Chapter 7. The notion of a medium is an anthropological and epistemological category. The notion of an intermediary coming from God to the world is a cosmological category.

22. As I indicated, Rahner does not normally refer to Jesus as a human person or a human being. It would not be wrong to think of his conception as an enhypostatic union. His dominant language speaks of the Logos assuming a humanity. His christology is thus in the Alexandrian and Cyrillian line of thought. Note that Logos christology could be an indwelling christology, as the Antiochenes prove.

23. Rahner, *Foundations*, 224.

does not only speak *about* God, nor is he merely a message *about* God. He is the very Logos of God made present. Rahner is insistent upon this even while being resolute about the real humanity of Jesus.[24] All of this makes sense within the context of Rahner's theology of symbol which is developed in metaphysical, ontological terms and is truly dialectical. As a symbol makes present something other than itself, so Jesus makes present God as Logos, that is, the self-expression of the Father.[25]

It is worth reiterating at this point that the viability of Logos christology lies not only in the metaphor underlying this symbolic language, but more importantly in its truly symbolic character. The language of incarnation, of God as Logos assuming flesh, is not literal language in which the referent is an object of this worldly knowledge and definition. We do not *know* God as Logos; God is an object of belief, which is an expression of faith-hope. These symbols, therefore, both arise out of and are a function of a religious experience of an encounter with transcendence, and they both awaken and appeal to such an experience as the source of their meaning. Symbols reach into the depth of the question of human existence about the ground of being; and through the openness of the human spirit they reach out into the sphere of transcendent being. The foundational metaphor of incarnation cannot appear credible when it is reduced to digital, empirical, or literal non-symbolic language.

But the main problem with the foundational metaphor of "incarnation" lies in the imaginative, three-stage framework that often accompanies it, as in Alexandrian christology of enhypostatic union. If, however, Logos christology is revised in the Antiochene pattern of an indwelling, Logos-anthropos christology, the duality and integrity of Jesus' humanity and divinity are protected. Moreover, the ontology of the concrete symbol can help overcome the difficulty that many have found with the language of the Antiochenes, namely, accounting for the principle of the unity of Jesus Christ. In what follows, therefore, I wish to preserve the formal structure of Rahner's theology of symbol as it is applied to Jesus Christ, but recast it in the framework of a christology from below and an Antiochene pattern of understanding the duality of Jesus' humanity and divinity. This results in an incarnational christology in which the created human being or person Jesus of Nazareth is the concrete symbol expressing the presence in history of God as Logos.

Conception of Salvation

The conception of how Jesus saves that is implicit in the Logos christology in John's Prologue was examined in Chapter 6. A retrieval of the meaning of the salvation effected by God through Jesus symbolized in a

---

24. "Jesus is truly man, he has absolutely everything which belongs to a man, including a finite subjectivity. . . ." Rahner, *Foundations*, 196. See also 226–27.

25. Rahner, "The Theology of the Symbol," 235–40.

Logos and incarnation christology revolves around the concept of revelation and God's self-communication. This is consistent with John's gospel generally.[26]

On the level of religious experience, Christians encounter God in the life, ministry, and person of Jesus, and in the conviction that Jesus was raised by God. Jesus reveals God and makes God present. And the Christian is one who encounters God in Jesus, and allows his or her experience and conception of God to be mediated by Jesus and the community that was formed around his revelation. But this function of Jesus entails and must include a conception of the person of Jesus himself. Who is Jesus of Nazareth that he can play this role in history? Jesus as concrete symbol of God responds to this question. The person of Jesus as symbol of God is thus a revealer of God. I noted under the heading of "Foundational Metaphor" the strong, realistic language that Jesus being the symbol of God stimulates in the theology of Rahner: Jesus does not merely speak about God, but is in his person the medium of God's actual self-gift. For one who is drawn into the participatory knowledge of faith-hope that is directed to God as encountered in Jesus this language contains no exaggeration. Jesus saves by revealing and making God present. And in so doing, at the same time, Jesus reveals and actualizes the fundamental character of human existence in its being related to God. Jesus is paradigmatic exemplar of the nature of human existence. He is God's Word about God, the world, and human existence.

Jesus and Other Religions

In the typology employed in the last chapter, Rahner's christology represents the primary example of a position that reckons Jesus Christ as constitutive and inclusive savior of all human beings. This has been subjected to extensive criticism in Chapter 14, and the critique of Ogden reported above has merit. But these criticisms do not necessarily undermine incarnational Logos christology. And an incarnational Logos christology need not undermine the autonomous legitimacy of other religious mediations of God. The symbol of Logos refers to God's immanence to created reality; it was recognized at Nicaea that God as Logos is God and nothing less. And the symbol of incarnation, referring to God's intelligent presence and power within Jesus, encourages the idea of God being near and available to all human beings. If Jesus is the revelation and self-communication of God, and if the character of God is what the Jewish and Christian traditions maintain it is, that is, a loving God of salvation, and if God's love is effective, one must expect that God is present and available to all of God's creatures, and in a personal way to human beings. Incarnational Logos

---

26. The thematic statements on salvation in this section and the next should not be understood in a reductionist way. Salvation may be the richest and broadest category in Christian vocabulary; it cannot be narrowly restricted. What are in play here are particular, expansive christological foci of interpretation.

christology depicts Jesus Christ as revealing the immanent, saving presence of God to all human existence. It therefore leads the Christian to expect God's revelatory presence in other religious mediations and traditions. This does not canonize all religious forms, but it provides an a priori impulse in Christian experience for a positive openness toward and an appreciation of other religions. In simple terms, the Christian expects that the one whom they know as God is also present to and at work in other religions. Other religions are judged valid in principle by Christians on the basis of their religious experience of God as Logos or God's Word in Jesus.

Worship of Jesus

Logos christology accounts for and justifies the worship of Jesus dialectically. In Rahner's incarnational Logos christology the explanation for this worship of Jesus is provided by his theology of symbol: worship is directed to God in Jesus symbolically. God as Logos is really present in Jesus in such a way that Jesus is the symbolic self-expression of the Logos. As was said earlier, Rahner emphasizes the fact that Jesus does not merely speak about God as though pointing away from himself to God. Jesus is the self-presence of God as Logos to human history. Rahner does try to preserve the integral humanity of Jesus. He does not call Jesus a human being or a human person, but on the axiom that the closer one is to God the more the freedom and autonomy of the creature is preserved, Rahner asserts the truly human character of Jesus. Rahner's Logos christology thus allows worship of God present in Jesus symbolically or sacramentally. This same structure and language are operative within an Antiochene pattern of understanding, but with this difference: by beginning with a consideration of the historical Jesus, such a christology does not strain to respect the human character of Jesus.

Essential to the viability of Logos christology at this crucial juncture is to insist on the symbolic character of all human contact with God. This symbolic structure is operative at two distinct levels here. First, the *conceptual* symbol "Logos" does not refer to an objectified entity independent of or distinct from God; the hypostatization and reification of Logos is a fundamental distortion of religious epistemology and predication. For example, incarnation should not be parodied by a literal three-stage descent and ascent narrative involving a divine being. This objectification tends to reduce the meaning of God as Logos to something less than God. Second, the *concrete* symbol Jesus, who makes God's presence actual in history, must be understood dialectically. This means allowing Jesus to remain a human person, a human being like all other human beings. It means at the same time allowing God as Logos to be present and at work in Jesus in a way that makes God publicly revealed and present to humanity. The "is" and "is not" involved in the dialectics of symbol thus explain incarnation in a way that accounts for Christian worship of Jesus.

Fidelity to the Conciliar Tradition

Logos christology is generally faithful to the conciliar tradition insofar as it continues the same tradition of doctrine. How is Rahner's christology faithful to Nicaea and Chalcedon? And how does an incarnational Logos christology revised in an Antiochene mode preserve the divinity and the humanity of Jesus, the ability to say that not less than God is at work in the human being Jesus?

Incarnation and the divinity of Jesus: consubstantial with God. Rahner's Logos christology rests on the conviction that God's self-expression or self-communication, to which the terms "Logos," "Word," and "Son" all refer, was embodied in the person of Jesus Christ. In one sense his is a classical three-stage christology. Rahner also uses the traditional expression, hypostatic union, that is, an enhypostatic union in which the human reality of Jesus is assumed, sustained, and supported by the "person," the hypostasis, the reality, the being of the Logos. His christology thus falls within the framework of a christology of two natures and one divine person. Two of the problems in Rahner's christology noted at the outset, however, appear at this point: the criticism of his approach "from above," and the suspicion that the Alexandrian framework of his thinking does not allow him finally to do justice to Jesus' being a human being like us.

These two problems are overcome in a christology "from below," which adopts an Antiochene christological framework, and insists on Rahner's dialectical notion of symbol within that framework. Christology that begins with research into the historical Jesus is led to presuppose not the "humanity" of Jesus, but the concrete image of him as a historical figure, a human being. Thus Jesus was empowered by God as Logos within him. That which dwells in the human being Jesus, from the first moment of his existence, is God as revealing presence and Word. Thus the human being Jesus is the symbol and expression of God as Logos present to him. The enhypostatic union is the union of no less than God as Word with the human person Jesus.

Humanity of Jesus: consubstantial with human beings. Rahner is also quite aware of the monophysitic tendencies of a descent christology and a Cyrillian enhypostatic union. He is, therefore, critical of "two natures" language as not representing parallel and equally familiar realities. The term "nature," when predicated of both God and a creature, is at best roughly analogous. He thus strongly and realistically asserts the full human character of the human being Jesus Christ. Jesus had a genuine human freedom and was not a puppet of God as Logos; God did not operate in Jesus independently of his freedom any more than in any other human being.[27]

---

27. "In accordance with the fact that the natures are unmixed, basically the active influence of the Logos on the human 'nature' in Jesus in a physical sense may not be understood in any other way except the way this influence is exercised by God on free creatures elsewhere." Rahner, *Foundations*, 287.

Because the human reality of Jesus is the symbol of the Logos in history, the truly human Jesus is the self-expression of the Logos. From God's side, God as Word assumes an integral human reality through which it expresses itself or communicates itself to history. Rahner's theology of symbol facilitates a dialectical understanding of Jesus Christ: Jesus both is and is more than a human reality, both is and is not, because he is other than, the reality of God.

Although Rahner attends to the dialectical character of Chalcedon through his theology of symbol, the criticisms of his christology as unfolding "from above" and threatening Jesus' consubstantiality with us still obtain. His christology is filled with unresolved tensions because, in terms of its imaginative framework, Rahner's christology is a three-stage descent christology in which the hypostasis of the Logos assumes a human nature. But many of these problems disappear when Rahner's christology is shifted from the classical Alexandrian paradigm of hypostatic union to an Antiochene paradigm of divine indwelling. Chapter 9 showed the potentiality of this scheme to protect the humanity of Jesus while presupposing Nicene orthodoxy. When christology begins from below, with the historical Jesus, Jesus' consubstantiality with us does not need argument: it is presupposed at the outset and consistently throughout. The unity of Jesus Christ is the unity of this human person in whom the fullness of divinity, God as Word, dwells. In short, Rahner's Logos christology can be retrieved as a christology from below, and objections regarding Jesus' consubstantiality with us are answered by reinterpreting it within an Antiochene framework.

Intelligibility

The basis for the intelligibility and credibility of Rahner's Logos christology lies in his conception of human existence as open to God's presence. This appears against the background of the problem that his christology addresses, namely, extrinsicism. Extrinsicism is a conception of the Christian economy that proposes no intrinsic connection between the event of Jesus Christ and the inner nature and aspirations of human existence. Jesus Christ is an altogether unpredictable and, from our point of view, arbitrary incursion into human affairs, an external authority that stands over against human existence. This conception sees the Word of God and the human as discontinuous and at odds because of sin, and in competition because of a conception of the relation between nature and grace as one over against the other.

Against this view, Rahner is at pains to show that the whole point of Jesus Christ, his God, and the salvation he mediates is completion of the human. Reality itself and humanity in particular are so oriented and open to God that the incarnation fulfills the human. The problem with humanity is not the inability to recognize God, but the failure to recognize the God-given and guaranteed dignity of the human. "It is forbidden to man to think little of himself because he would then be thinking little of God. . . ."[28] Human nature is precisely that which is able to be united with God. And this union in Jesus, because it is symbolic of the self-communication of God to all human beings by grace, constitutes the very source and the finality of creation itself. The event of Jesus Christ is not only coherent with evolution, the intimate union represented in him but realized in the first appearance of human existence is the goal toward which evolution from the beginning has been moving. The fulfillment of reality is the final union of all history and creation with God in glory.

Is such a vision intelligible in a postmodern context that distrusts all meta-narratives as ultimately totalizing and excluding? I believe it is when it is understood exactly as Rahner intends it, namely, as a function of an inclusive faith-hope for humankind. The equivalent of extrinsicism in some currents of postmodern culture is an intratextuality that tends to reduce the power of the human subject to transcend its social-cultural matrix.[29] Christianity is construed as a sect; it cannot really learn from and communicate with those who are "other." By contrast, Logos christology predicates of Jesus universal relevance. An apologetic, anthropocentric starting point in christology seeks to discover how Jesus has a bearing on all humankind. Jesus Christ cannot really be savior and reconciler at all unless he is significant for all. Logos christology, therefore, appeals to the utopian dimension of human yearning in all human beings. It seeks to provide the very grounds that forbid totalizing systems that exclude certain persons or groups. It understands Jesus as the historical symbol for faith-hope in a theistic vision that seeks to give meaning to all existence. But this vision cannot be internalized without praxis.

Empowerment

This apologetic conception of the intrinsic relation between incarnation, or hypostatic union of God as Logos with Jesus, and the general condition of human existence is what is empowering in Rahner's christology. Human freedom and autonomy are ratified and apotheosized. The human is more free and more autonomous when closer to God and more at God's disposition.[30] Rahner's christology is typically modern. It presents a modern deification theory of salvation where the human is raised to an unimaginable dignity and importance because God has assumed it as God's own. Rahner's christology provides a solid basis for a Christian humanism and anthropocentrism.

---

28. Rahner, *Foundations*, 225.

29. A description of intratextuality as defining a linguistic-cultural approach to theology and hence christology is found in George A. Lindbeck, *The Nature of Doctrine: Religion and Theology in a Postliberal Age* (Philadelphia: Westminster Press, 1984), 113–24.

30. The basic axiom is that "closeness and distance, or being at God's disposal and being autonomous, do not vary for creatures in inverse, but rather in direct proportion." Rahner, *Foundations*, 226.

But Rahner's christology has to be adjusted to a postmodern situation. I have suggested a thoroughgoing method from below and a shift to an "indwelling" christology. I also suggested in Chapter 13 that Jesus reveals not only God's Logos of nature and the cosmos, but also the narrative Mythos of history. Jesus is the symbol of where human existence is headed and a parable of transcendent values which can draw human freedom forward in a meaningful life. Jesus' message of the kingdom of God is historical. Logos christology, therefore, can be adjusted to speak to a postmodern situation and, more than any other, liberation christology has done this.

SPIRIT CHRISTOLOGY

I now turn to a description of a Spirit christology. This Spirit christology is not proposed in opposition to a Logos or Word christology but in contrast to it. The development runs parallel to the one just concluded. What is characterized here is a thoroughgoing Spirit christology, one that "explains" the divinity of Jesus Christ on the basis of God as Spirit and not on the basis of the symbol Logos. This distinguishes it from a number of christologies which employ both symbols, but unevenly, to express Jesus' divinity. I present Spirit christology at some greater length because for many it is still not fully established as a viable christology.

Contemporary Spirit Christologies

A substantial literature is dedicated to the topic of Spirit christology.[31] But I wish to call attention to essays more generally dedicated to systematic christology that have turned to a Spirit christology. In Chapter 11 I indicated the symmetry between the christology of Schleiermacher and a Spirit christology. His understanding of the experience of absolute

---

31. Some essays that may serve as an introduction to Spirit christology are the following: Dunn, *Jesus and the Spirit, Christology in the Making*; F. X. Durrwell, "Pour une christologie selon l'Esprit Saint," *Nouvelle revue théologique*, 114 (1992), 653–77; Olaf Hansen, "Spirit Christology: A Way out of Our Dilemma?" *The Holy Spirit in the Life of the Church*, ed. by P. Opsahl (Minneapolis: Augsburg, 1978), 172–203; Norman Hook, "A Spirit Christology," *Theology*, 75 (1972), 226–32; Harold Hunter, "Spirit Christology: Dilemma and Promise," *Heythrop Journal*, 24 (1983), 127–40, 266–77 (This essay is hostile to Spirit christology on the basis of a reading of scriptural and early Christian sources.); Lampe, "The Holy Spirit and the Person of Christ," *Christ, Faith and History*, ed. by S. W. Sykes and J. P. Clayton (Cambridge: Cambridge Univ., 1972), 111–30, *God as Spirit*; Newman, *A Spirit Christology*; John O'Donnell, "In Him and Over Him: The Holy Spirit in the Life of Jesus," *Gregorianum*, 70 (1989), 25–45; Philip J. Rosato, "Spirit Christology: Ambiguity and Promise," *Theological Studies*, 38 (1977), 423–49; P. J. A. M. Schoonenberg, "Spirit Christology and Logos Christology," *Bijdragen*, 38 (1977), 350–75.

dependence is realist; the experience corresponds to the perfect "indwelling of the Supreme Being in [Jesus'] peculiar being and His inmost self."[32] Thus his christology, which assigns Jesus Christ the highest God-consciousness, is not merely a "consciousness christology." Rather, Jesus' supreme God-consciousness is due to the supreme presence of God to his person, and Schleiermacher sometimes uses the language of Spirit to express this.[33]

Shailer Mathews, who was both a biblical scholar and a systematic theologian, also proposed a thoroughgoing Spirit christology. The divinity of Jesus is due to the "resident Spirit" who dwells within him.[34] Perhaps a more significant example is Paul Tillich who combines a knowledge of classical philosophy and an existential ontology with a Lutheran tradition. Nevertheless Tillich explicitly develops at some length a Spirit christology. "Though subject to individual and social conditions [Jesus'] human spirit was entirely grasped by the Spiritual Presence; his spirit was 'possessed' by the divine Spirit or, to use another figure, 'God was in him.' This makes him the Christ, the decisive embodiment of the New Being for historical mankind."[35] Tillich is against any theology of Jesus that would make the man Jesus the object of Christian faith. It is "not the spirit of the man Jesus of Nazareth that makes him the Christ, but . . . the Spiritual Presence, God in him, that possesses and drives his individual spirit."[36]

Still another contemporary theologian, this time with an evangelical perspective, Jürgen Moltmann, has a thoroughgoing Spirit christology expressed in the language of the synoptics. For him the christological language of the gospels is necessary and sufficient. From the very beginning of his existence Jesus was filled with God as Spirit. "Jesus' history as the Christ does not begin with Jesus himself. It begins with the *ruach*/the Holy Spirit."[37] For Moltmann there is no antithesis between a Spirit christology and incarnation, between an adoption christology and a pre-existence christology. Spirit language is simply the dominant way of talking about Jesus' relation to God. The kenosis of the Spirit in Jesus means that "God's Spirit becomes *the Spirit of Jesus Christ*. It surrenders itself wholly to the person of Jesus in order to communicate itself through Jesus to other men and women. So the reverse side of the history of Jesus Christ is the history of the Spirit."[38] This means, in Moltmann's view, that the Spirit *always* is

---

32. Friedrich Schleiermacher, *The Christian Faith* (New York: Harper Torchbooks, 1963), #94, 388. He adds that "to ascribe to Christ an absolutely powerful God-consciousness, and to attribute to Him an existence of God in Him, are exactly the same thing." Ibid., #94, 387.

33. As in *The Christian Faith*, #94, 388–89.

34. Shailer Mathews, *The Gospel and the Modern Man* (New York: Macmillan, 1910), 109–38.

35. Paul Tillich, *Systematic Theology*, 3 (Chicago: University of Chicago Press, 1963), 144.

36. Tillich, *Systematic Theology*, 3, 146.

37. Jürgen Moltmann, *The Way of Jesus Christ* (New York: HarperCollins, 1990), 73.

38. Moltmann, *The Way of Jesus Christ*, 94.

the Spirit of Jesus; the Spirit is, as it were, bound to Jesus. "Liberal theologians liked to use this fact [that the Spirit is found beyond the person
and work of Jesus] to relativize Jesus, as the one bearer of the Spirit among
many others. But by so doing they overlooked the unique character of
Jesus' imbuement with the Spirit, which led to his divine Sonship and his
special mission."[39] In Moltmann's christology, therefore, Jesus is the
unique incarnation of God as Spirit; there is no bearer of God as Spirit
comparable to Jesus. He complements this Spirit christology with a reflection on the exaltation of Jesus and the cosmic Christ.

This range of theologians, from philosophically oriented systematicians
to those who rest content with evangelical language, testifies to the strain
that began to afflict classical patristic language in the modern period. All
who criticize patristic language do not necessarily turn to the symbol
Spirit. But it provides a way of remaining faithful to the scriptural and
doctrinal language while meeting today's exigencies.

Method and Point of Departure

A Spirit christology may be characterized as proceeding "from below"
in several senses. First, it begins with a historical consideration of Jesus of
Nazareth and the integrity of this Jesus is never compromised by later
interpretations. Second, the method of this christology is genetic; it traces
historically the genesis of various interpretations of Jesus, including the
conciliar, and the process of these developments. In a third sense this christology is "from below" because it appeals to the Christian experience and
language of grace as an analogy for understanding what is going on in
christology. This methodological move is based on the premise that the
understanding of Jesus cannot simply be based on authority, but must
appeal to experience to become credible. I draw this out further in the following section.

Fidelity to New Testament Sources

Chapter 6 considered the Spirit christology of Luke. But this is merely
part of the large role that Spirit language plays in the bible generally and,
in the New Testament, in characterizing Jesus' person and his relation to
God and to us. It will be useful to present an overview of Spirit language
as it pertains to Jesus and to present-day Christian experience.

The biblical symbol, Spirit. The biblical symbol, the Spirit of God, refers
to God. God as Spirit, or the Spirit of God, is simply God, is not other than
God, but is materially and numerically identical with God.[40] God as Spirit
is God. But God as Spirit refers to God from a certain point of view; it indicates God at work, as active, and as power, energy, or force that accom-

---

39. Moltmann, *The Way of Jesus*, 94.

40. Lampe analyzes the pre-Christian concept of Spirit in *God as Spirit*, 41–60.
Newman's account, which is more hermeneutical, is found in *A Spirit Christology*,
69–94. See also Schoonenberg, "Spirit Christology and Logos Christology," 351–55.

plishes something. Thus God as Spirit refers to God, as it were, outside of the immanent selfhood of God. God as Spirit is God present to and at work, outside of God's self, in the world of God's creation. God as Spirit is like the wind; one does not see it, but one feels its presence; the wind is not tangible, but is a force which one sees in its effects. So too, the metaphorical symbol of God as Spirit expresses the experience of God's power and energy in creation; this power is seen in its effects. The verbal or conceptual symbol points to the way God is present in the world. What does God as Spirit do? The effects of the Spirit are many. God's Spirit is not so much a distinct agent of creation but the creative power itself of God. God as Spirit is life-giving; where there is life, it comes from God's being actually present and sustaining that life. God as Spirit is responsible for remarkable events in the world. God as Spirit inspires human beings and is thus responsible for the dramatic saving events that are accomplished by God's agents. In brief, the metaphorical symbol God as Spirit refers simply and directly to God. It points to God as immanent in the world. And in the measure in which God is personal and is present to human beings, one may think of that presence of God as personal presence. God as Spirit points to God as active. God's personal presence is also power, activity, force, and energy within the world and within people.

Jesus and the Spirit. Can one say anything about Jesus and his experience of God as Spirit? Despite all the difficulties of getting back to Jesus, James Dunn thinks that one can make some general assertions about Jesus' experience of God in terms of God as Spirit. Dunn tries to show that the source of Jesus' convictions and self-understanding, his authority, and some of his powerful actions all stemmed from an experience of God as Spirit present and at work in his life.[41]

There are several places where these facets of Jesus' career seem to be reflected in the synoptic gospels. Chapter 3 showed that Jesus was undoubtedly a healer and an exorcist. Some passages indicate that Jesus was aware that whatever power he exercised was to be attributed to God as Spirit at work through him, and that others recognized this in these terms. "His power to cast out demons was the Spirit of God."[42] This power of God as Spirit at work in the world is closely associated with the kingdom of God, and Jesus' sense of mission too is understood in terms of anointing and empowerment by the Spirit. The synoptics also lead one to understand the presence and action of God as Spirit in his life as the ground of Jesus' sonship and to look upon "consciousness of sonship and consciousness of Spirit as two sides of the one coin."[43]

---

41. Dunn, *Jesus and the Spirit*, 41–67. See also Newman, *A Spirit Christology*, 103–37.
42. Dunn, *Jesus and the Spirit*, 52.
43. Dunn, *Jesus and the Spirit*, 66. See also Lampe, *God as Spirit*, 26–31. Newman is convinced that "Jesus' language of the Reigning of God could be transposed legitimately into language of God's active presence as Spirit." *A Spirit Christology*, 116.

In all of this Dunn is attempting to make general statements about Jesus' consciousness. He speaks in terms of Jesus' experience and aware-ness. On the other side, however, it is notoriously difficult to get into Jesus' mind; at best we can establish probabilities on the basis of some reckon-ing of the historicity of the language that is used. Dunn's conclusions, then, may be taken as broad generalizations about the contours of Jesus' self-understanding. These have, moreover, a certain a priori plausibility. The assumption must be that Jesus had some experience of God. And the term for God being experienced in one's life is "God as Spirit." One does not have to judge the intensity of this experience or the kind of empow-erment by the Spirit or how it was actually manifested in order to arrive at some solid historical conclusions. What seems to be established is this: that Jesus experienced the power of God as Spirit in his life; that he was aware of this in these terms; that this empowerment was manifested in his actions; that these empowered actions were construed as the ruling of God; and that people recognized this even during his life-time.

This implicit christology, however, is no more than that. The point here is not to establish a full-blown Spirit christology during the life of Jesus in Jesus' self-understanding or others' understanding of him.[44] I will argue later that one must assume that Jesus' experience of the Spirit was analo-gous to our experience of the Spirit. The point is simply to see foundations and establish points of continuity between Jesus and later christological interpretation of him. Dunn, it seems to me, establishes a basis for later interpretation of Jesus in terms of God as Spirit at work in him.[45]

Jesus and the Spirit in the early Christian communities. The symbol of the Spirit for God acting immanently in the world and in people remains sub-stantially the same in the New Testament writings as in the Hebrew scrip-tures. But in the wake of the events of Jesus' life and death, and within the framework of the experience of Jesus as alive, as with God, and as God's mediator of salvation, the Spirit is experienced in a new way as being poured forth in the abundance of eschatological salvation through Jesus. God as Spirit is thus thoroughly reinterpreted.[46] The saving Spirit of God is, as it were, let loose in a final, climactic, and saving way through the life, death, and resurrection of Jesus, and is vividly experienced in the com-munities of the Jesus movement that became "Christian." The Spirit is experienced; the Spirit is grace; the Spirit is salvation. The effects of the Spirit in the community and the individual lives of its members can be named: they are faith, love, forgiveness, redemption, justification, sanctifi-cation, adoption by God, reconciliation, freedom from sin, illumination, lib-eration, empowerment, and charismatic gifts of service to the community.

---

44. Recall the conviction registered in Chapter 2 that christology, as interpretation of Jesus, is not dependent upon Jesus' explicit self-consciousness or self-understanding.

45. See James Dunn, *Unity and Diversity in the New Testament* (London: SCM Press, 1977), 213–17.

46. Lampe, *God as Spirit*, 62.

How are we to characterize the Spirit christology that is reflected in the New Testament writings? Once again, James Dunn provides a sketch.[47] This Spirit christology must be seen as developing in two stages and thus having two distinct dimensions. The one is Spirit christology that sees Jesus during his lifetime as one in whom God as Spirit was at work. The second stage or dimension of Spirit christology applies to the risen Jesus, Jesus alive, with God, and called the Christ. In this stage one finds at times a kind of identity or conflation of Christ risen and the Spirit. This can be seen from two points of view. On the one hand, one can say that Christ is the Spirit. Sometimes, especially in Paul, the risen Jesus and the Spirit seem to be identified; Christ is spoken of as though he were the Spirit. With the resurrection Jesus, as it were, functionally becomes God's life-giving Spirit.[48] On the other hand, the Spirit is the risen Jesus. This means that Jesus identifies the Spirit, because it was God as Spirit that was at work in Jesus. One does not know the true Spirit of God except through Jesus, that is, through the mediation of Jesus.

In all of this one sees Jesus and the Spirit placed in close conjunction with each other. First, God as Spirit is at work in Jesus' life, and, then, in the case of Jesus risen, the conjunction tends toward identification. God as Spirit was at work in Jesus so that, after his death, when he is experienced as alive and with God, Jesus is still closely mixed up with the very experience of God as Spirit in the early community. Jesus identifies and specifies what is of the Spirit. This correlates with the theory that all experience of God must have a historical medium to take on content.

At this point one must ask whether one has enough data here to begin to think of a full-scale Spirit christology. This question must be placed against the background of the pluralism of New Testament christologies. Whether one investigates the titles of Jesus, or confessions about him, or the views of what he did for our salvation, or the fundamental models within which his identity was construed, or the symbols used to express God present and at work in him, all of these ways of framing the question yield varieties of conceptions, many of which are incompatible with others. One has to begin with the recognition that there "is no single coherent understanding or presentation of Christ which meets us after Easter."[49] On the basis of this pluralism Dunn criticizes Lampe's Spirit christology as reductionistic; it fails to take into account the second stage of the Spirit

---

47. Dunn, *Christology in the Making*, 129-162. For Lampe's analysis of the concept of God as Spirit in relation to Christ, especially in Paul, Luke, and John, see *God as Spirit*, 5-10, 61-94. O'Donnell, in "In Him and Over Him," 27-39, provides a sketch of Spirit christology. Durrwell's essay, "Pour une christologie selon l'Esprit Saint," provides far-ranging New Testament witness to the role of Spirit in christology without proposing a consistent theory.

48. See, for example, David Greenwood, "The Lord Is the Spirit: Some Considerations of 2 Cor 3:17," *Catholic Biblical Quarterly*, 34 (1972), 467–472.

49. Dunn, *Unity and Diversity*, 216.

christology of the New Testament and to see that one comes closest to Jesus by considering all the New Testament christologies.[50]

In response to this criticism it may be recalled that the task of systematic theology is not to recite the New Testament but to interpret it, and to do so in terms that are comprehensible in our own world. Moreover, insofar as it is systematic, this task is bound by the principle of internal coherence; it cannot simply repeat contrary notions. More positively, Spirit christology seeks to present a consistent interpretation of Jesus in a way analogous to the Logos christology that has ruled Christian consciousness since the second century. But unlike the Logos christology, which tended to place other christologies in a shadow, a Spirit christology can be understood as a basis for considering, interpreting, and appropriating other New Testament christologies. Spirit christology should be understood as functioning not in an exclusive but in an inclusive way. God as Spirit working in the life of Jesus can form the basis for the multiple interpretations of him by explaining why he was the Wisdom of God who spoke and even represented God's Word.

Beyond the historicity of the experience of the Spirit of God at work in Jesus, another reason, also internal to the New Testament, recommends Spirit christology. The symbol of the Spirit more forthrightly makes the claim that God, God's very self, acted in and through Jesus. This stands in contrast to the symbols of God's Word and Wisdom which, insofar as they became personified and then hypostatized, tend to connote someone or something distinct from and less than God that was incarnate in Jesus, even though it is called divine or of God. By contrast, the symbol of God as Spirit is not a personification of God, but refers more directly to God, so that it is clear from the beginning that nothing less than God was at work in Jesus.[51]

Experience of God as Spirit today. At this point I should develop at some length how the symbol God as Spirit is meaningful today. This is essential for a number of reasons. Without some experience of God as Spirit today, the symbol would lack coherent meaning and reference. One needs a paradigm for understanding the operation of God in Jesus, one which bears an analogy with our own experience. In other words, one must try to mediate the meaning of traditional doctrines in terms of common

---

50. Dunn, *Christology in the Making*, 266–67.

51. I have tried to overcome this tendency in the representation of Logos christology. Although this cannot be demonstrated here, in some respects the symbol Logos, insofar as it moved from being a divine personification, that is, a recognized figure of speech, to a hypostatization, that is, the identification of a distinct, objective, and individuated mode of being, caused the problem of subordinationism that Nicaea finally attempted to resolve. In other words, the subordinationism that is typical of the christology until the fourth century was dictated by the symbol Logos itself when its metaphorical character was neglected and it became objectified. See Lampe, *God as Spirit*, 12–13, 41, 132, 140–44; Dunn, *Christology in the Making*, 161. I will develop this further in the next chapter.

human experience.[52] Also one needs some appreciation of the paradoxical character of this experience if it is to illumine the dialectical tension in the doctrine of Chalcedon. Although it is impossible to deal with this issue adequately, I can outline how one might go about addressing this crucial issue.

The remarkable convergence between the biblical language of God as Spirit and the theology of grace of Karl Rahner may serve as a premise to this discussion.[53] In Rahner's view, grace is God's personal-being-present to human beings in love, and this self-communication outside of God's self correlates with the doctrine of God as Spirit. Grace is God as Spirit, God's gift of self, which is at the same time a presence to, and implicitly a being active in, the human spirit or freedom that constitutes every person. And this grace, or God as Spirit, can be experienced and in fact is commonly experienced in this world.

This correlation between the symbol God as Spirit and the theology of grace creates a framework in which elements of an experience of God as Spirit can be considered. Among these I shall single out, first, some fundamental human experiences that may be interpreted as human freedom reaching out toward grace; second, ways in which the theology of grace across the tradition points to a variety of experiences of grace; and, third, the effects of grace or the movement of God as Spirit in human lives as this has been attested to in Christian life.

First, without proposing a transcendental anthropology, one can point to any number of deep but common human experiences that anticipate an experience of God's immanent presence to the world. A fundamental trust in life, in the worth of existence, in the resistance to death and whatever attacks life, seems to imply an inner ground of existence as the basis of its value. A desire for truth and goodness, which ultimately transcends all limited possessions of them, seems implicitly to posit absolute goodness and truth as a human goal. This natural ascent of human freedom, as Augustine envisaged it, reflects an even more fundamental desire, the desire to be, that drives human existence spontaneously to reach out and attach itself to various forms of "absolute being" in which it finds salvation. Analyzing human existence from different angles, one can find a variety of elementary preconscious desires that underlie much of our behavior and open the human spirit to transcendent aims. The human spirit resists radical fragmentation and disorder in personal life and in the broader

---

52. For a brief statement of this principle of analogy underlying hermeneutical theory, see Roger Haight, *Dynamics of Theology* (New York: Paulist Press, 1990), 172–73. "Common human experience" does not refer in the first instance to actual experience in any statistical sense, but to experience that is common because it is structurally indigenous to the human and thus virtual and possible at any given time. Thus one understands sight as indigenously human even though some may be born blind.

53. For a discussion of the correlativity of the notions of "Spirit" and "grace" in Paul, see Dunn, *Jesus and the Spirit*, 201–05. An account of Karl Rahner's theology of grace is found in *Foundations of Christian Faith*, 116–33.

social context of public behavior. Personal identity and moral integrity seem to require a more or less stable system of meaning and an encompassing set of values. These internal mechanisms appear most clearly when these things are lacking; one can see them at work in negative experiences of contrast. Positively, they open the human spirit to a possible experience of an encounter with God as Spirit.

Second, an analysis of the experience underlying the classic theologies of grace reveals some broadly relevant ways in which people encounter grace or God as Spirit.[54] Augustine provides a vivid example. Against the background of so much evil in the world, he asked why was there any goodness at all? What is the ground of goodness, and especially the source of love? He became utterly convinced on the basis of the dynamics of his own life that genuine self-transcendence did not come from himself and could not be initiated by himself. Augustine experienced God as Spirit as the prevenient and sustaining power within that opened up his freedom into self-transcending desire and love. Luther provides another analysis of how God is encountered within by using the language of an interpersonal relationship. Here the experience transpires against the background of a diminished self, a consciousness of self without worth because of sin and, by extension, without significance because headed for death. Against this background, God within is experienced as a love that transforms the self by the sheer fact that this self is loved by God. Here God, as an absolute, loving, and accepting embrace, authorizes the human person and grants human existence an absolute identity. Aquinas's teleological account of grace implies an experience of one's freedom directed toward a new transcendent goal and of being empowered to move toward it by a divine energy within that activates one's freedom and action. Experiences of God as Spirit within the self or within the world can be multiplied. Creation itself, all that is, appears to be an unreasoned gift; it and we are there gratuitously. And when it is so construed, logic turns one toward recognizing the giver within the gift. The symbol of creation conceals and reveals in itself a conception of grace or God's Spiritual presence.

Third, a consideration of the effects of grace, of God as Spirit in human life, provides an analogy that will be helpful in understanding christology. It has been claimed that grace or God as Spirit can be experienced. But this experience has to be understood dialectically, because it is always mediated, so that its object cannot be experienced directly or clearly differentiated from worldly objects and natural movements of the human spirit. Also, scripture and the history of Christian hagiography make a variety of claims about the charisms that accrue to life empowered by God as Spirit. This should not be understood as a suppression of human talent but of God working within. Such confessions are always dialectical. Beginning with the classic statement of Paul, who insisted that in his life

---

54. I am drawing upon previous analyses of classic theologies of grace in Roger Haight, *The Experience and Language of Grace* (New York: Paulist Press, 1979).

of faith "it is no longer I who live, but it is Christ who lives in me,"[55] the whole history of the theology of grace bears witness to the paradoxical tension between God as Spirit and human freedom. Notions of cooperative grace make this explicit. The dialectical character of these experiences can be understood in terms of symbol. Human experience encounters God as Spirit not on the other side of ordinary human experience, but within it; the object of the encounter is made present by ordinary experience. In terms of action, there are not two actors in the person animated by God as Spirit. But such genuine human action makes God's power and presence actual in the world by symbolic causality. D. M. Baillie has shown how this has a bearing on the question of the humanity and divinity of Jesus.[56] It allows an appreciation from within Christian experience of the paradoxical and dialectical character of God's action in the world. The paradox is precisely that one is more oneself, more autonomous, more self-possessed, the more one is within the possession of God and buoyed up by God's power.

To summarize here, one finds theological resources for a Spirit christology at every juncture of the Christian tradition: in its prehistory reflected in the Jewish scriptures, in the New Testament portrait of Jesus and its theology of the saving influence of the risen Jesus, and in the tradition of the theology of the Spirit that has been carried by the theology of grace right up to the present.

Foundational Metaphor

It is important to consider the foundational metaphor underlying a christology, for it often governs the imagination and thereby controls understanding. Generally, Logos christology is set within the framework of the metaphor of incarnation. It was suggested that the imaginative depiction of this as a three-stage narrative involving a hypostatized Logos and a hypostatic union christology be replaced by an indwelling Logos christology. By contrast, I suggest that the metaphor that best expresses the insight of how God is present to and at work in Jesus in a Spirit christology is empowerment.

John Hick in his Spirit christology speaks of Jesus as an inspired man. But this metaphor of inspiration is too thin for the christology envisaged here. Geoffrey Lampe and Paul Tillich use the metaphor of possession. Both are aware that the metaphor of possession by God as Spirit must be used with the proviso that it not be so understood that God as Spirit takes over the consciousness and freedom of Jesus. But the very fact that this qualification has to be made indicates that it is not an adequate symbol to

---

55. Gal 2:20. See Reinhold Niebuhr's development of this theme and the paradoxes it contains in *The Nature and Destiny of Man*, 2 (New York: Charles Scribner's Sons, 1964), 107–26.

56. D. M. Baillie, *God Was in Christ* (New York: Charles Scribner's Sons, 1948), 106–32.

act as foundational metaphor. Jürgen Moltmann and others speak of incarnation. This has the benefit of capturing that in which a Logos and Spirit christology agree, but it fails to differentiate the symbols, and there is a difference.[57] I shall say more about incarnation below. Shailer Mathews speaks of God as Spirit as indwelling and resident in Jesus. This is helpful in bringing out that this Spirit christology is much more in the line of Antioch than of Alexandria. It is not a "Spirit-sarx" or "hypostatic union" christology but a divine indwelling christology. With the substitution of the term "Spirit" for "Logos," the orthodox language of Theodore of Mopsuestia can be applied here almost verbatim.[58] But this indwelling of God as Spirit is also dynamically active, and this is not communicated by the word "indwelling."

I believe that the metaphor of empowerment might provide a fundamental imaginative conception that expresses positively the dynamics of this christology. But this is not said in a way that seeks to exclude completely the other suggestions. For example, while different from some understandings of incarnation, this christology can also be referred to as incarnational. Empowerment presumes the indwelling of God as Spirit to the human person Jesus. As in Rahner's theology of the Spirit as grace, God's Spirit is the presence of God's personal self in such a way that it dynamically empowers human freedom. God's presence and empowerment does not *over*power, but precisely activates human freedom so that it is enhanced and not taken over; Jesus' human existence is fulfilled and not replaced. But this is not a three-stage christology; and God as Spirit is not present as the subject of Jesus' being and action. This is a more dynamic, interactive conception than can be expressed by the language of a divine Logos or Spirit assuming a human nature. This should also be construed as more than a thin functional or "adverbial" presence of God to Jesus, and truly an ontological presence, because where God acts, God is.[59] In this empowerment christology Jesus is the reality of God.

---

57. For example, O'Donnell speaks of Luke's Spirit christology as involving incarnation. "In Him and Over Him," 28. And Schoonenberg, along the same line of thought, refers to it as a descent christology. In Luke's infancy narrative "Spirit christology abandons the form of an ascending, and takes on that of a descending christology." "Spirit Christology and Logos Christology," 362. An important point is being made here: in the effort to distinguish these christologies, the antitheses between them should not be drawn too boldly.

58. See Aloys Grillmeier, *Christ in Christian Tradition*, 1, *From the Apostolic Age to Chalcedon (451)* (Atlanta: John Knox Press, 1975), 428–37.

59. Lampe refers to Jesus being divine "adverbially" because of the dynamic character of God as Spirit. See Lampe, "The Holy Spirit and the Person of Christ," 124. I accepted this designation in my essay "The Case for Spirit Christology," *Theological Studies*, 53 (1992), 275. But I now agree with the critique of that idea by Schoonenberg, "Spirit Christology and Logos Christology," 365. One cannot separate God's being and function in such a way. Jesus *is* divine dialectically, because the presence of God as Spirit pervades his being and action.

Conception of Salvation

How does Jesus save in a Spirit christology? Generally speaking, one can take the following principle as an axiom: there is nothing that cannot be said of Jesus in a Spirit christology that one would want to say of him in a Logos christology.[60] Thus Jesus' ministry of the reign of God mediates personal and social salvation. And God is present to Jesus, so that Jesus is the revelation of God, the self-presence and gift of God to human existence, history, and the world, and the exemplar of authentic human existence. But while all of these dimensions of salvation are possible with a Spirit christology, that which is most congruent with it is a pioneer soteriology. Jesus is the second Adam in the language of St. Paul which became so influential in the patristic period. As such he is the new pioneer; he goes ahead of us and shows the way. Jesus in Jon Sobrino's early work is the way to the Father who calls forth followers.[61] And since this christology brings out well the human character of Jesus, Jesus remains imitable. One can identify with him and follow him. Just as he was empowered by God as Spirit, so too in an analogous way are members of the Christian community. Salvation, as it has been characterized in Chapters 12 and 13 in its personal and social forms, is drawn up into a Spirit christology.

Jesus and Other Religions

A Spirit christology correlates closely with demands of the new consciousness of Christians regarding other religions that was outlined in the last chapter. On the one hand, it accounts for the normativity of Jesus for humankind generally. For Jesus empowered by God as Spirit offers a salvation that is true, universally relevant, and thus normative. On the other hand, as the Jewish and Christian scriptures testify, God as Spirit has been present and at work in the world for human salvation from "the beginning," without a causal connection to the historical appearance of Jesus.[62] Jesus, therefore, is constitutive and the cause of the salvation of Christians because he is the mediator of Christian awareness of life in the Spirit. But Jesus is not constitutive of salvation universally. Rather, a Spirit christology, by recognizing that the Spirit is operative outside the Christian sphere, is open to other mediations of God. The Spirit is spread abroad, and it is not necessary to think that God as Spirit can be incarnated only once in history.

---

60. There are things that some Logos christologies, combined with hypostatic union, allow one to say about Jesus that are not deemed useful or correct in a Spirit christology. For example, the rule allowing for the communication of properties generates such non-dialectical statements.

61. Jon Sobrino, *Christology at the Crossroads* (Maryknoll, N.Y.: Orbis Books, 1978), 338–40.

62. Jacques Dupuis preserves this universal operation of God as Logos and Spirit with a trinitarian understanding of God. See *Towards a Christian Theology of Religious Pluralism* (Maryknoll, N.Y.: Orbis Books, 1997), 319–21.

Worship of Jesus

The question of Christian worship of Jesus is crucial to christology. Historically, Christians worshiped Jesus, thus revealing their attitude toward Jesus as toward a divine figure, and this formed the life situation out of which the conciliar doctrines about Jesus emerged.[63] Moreover, christology today must account for how Christians continually relate to Jesus in prayer and worship. The question, then, is this: with the new emphasis on the humanity of Jesus, is a Spirit christology, which protects this dimension, able to account for worship of and prayer to Jesus? The question is similar to the issue of Jesus' divinity, but it is posed here first in existential terms.

The first response to this problem can be put in terms of principle: one cannot, or at least should not, relate to Jesus undialectically. One cannot relate to any religious symbol undialectically because the tension described earlier defines the nature of a religious symbol as such. There is always a temptation or an implied effort to break this dialectical tension in christology, but in every case, in the measure one does so, in like measure is the figure of Jesus as the Christ distorted. When this principle is applied to the question of prayer to and worship of Jesus, it results in the following tensive formula: one does not worship or pray to Jesus insofar as Jesus is a human being and creature; rather, one worships and prays to God in and through Jesus. This language of prayer through Jesus, of going to the Father through the Son, has a long liturgical tradition. This reflects the dominant pattern of the New Testament. Although Lampe finds some instances of prayer to Jesus in the New Testament, the predominant idea is that worship is through Jesus because Jesus is the medium of our worship of God. Spirit christology underlines this.[64]

This statement of principle, however, is itself probably inadequate without reference to what it represents, namely, an existential relationship. And this relationship unfolds as a dynamic human process of being related, a praxis of praying, an action of defining oneself in relationship to God in and through Jesus. But a phenomenology of this existentially-being-related would bear out its dialectical quality. For example, it would be difficult to distinguish a description of Christian worship in the terms of the doctrine

---

63. It would be relevant to this discussion to determine the character of the divinity that was predicated of Jesus in various historical settings during the early period of developing christology. It must be remembered that not only was the superterrestrial world heavily populated with all kinds of different levels of heavenly beings, angels and demons, powers and principalities, but also the status of the transcendence of God was developing, for example, in terms of the absolute transcendence implied in an understanding of creation out of nothing. In other words, one cannot presume that the idea of *absolute* transcendence is included in the term "divine." Frances Young, "Christology and Creation: Towards an Hermeneutic of Patristic Christology," lecture given at the Catholic University of Leuven, Nov. 21, 1997.

64. Lampe, *God as Spirit*, 162–66.

of Chalcedon from a description in terms of a Spirit christology. According to Chalcedon, Jesus has two natures which are distinct, unmixed, and unconfused: this is a dialectical conception. In this framework one would not say that one worshiped the humanity of Jesus or Jesus insofar as he was human, but rather insofar as he was divine, insofar as he bore or embodied Logos.[65] Spirit christology allows an analogous descriptive account. Jesus is the real symbol who bodies forth God as Spirit present and at work within him; Jesus as symbol participates in God as Spirit, mediates God, and makes God present. Thus the Christian act of worship directed to the human being Jesus is one that moves through Jesus to its mediated object which is God. But this God is not simply up there, out there, and now separated from Jesus. This God is revealed and encountered by the Christian precisely in and through Jesus. Christian prayer is theocentric, but addressed to a God who is known by the Christian through a focus upon Jesus. This view of prayer and worship, therefore, will be seen to correspond with what was said about salvation and what will be noted about Christian spirituality as discipleship: human action is empowered by God as Spirit who is mediated by Jesus.

Fidelity to Conciliar Tradition

Can Spirit christology live up to the standard set by the classic christological councils of Nicaea and Chalcedon? For many, this is the *crux interpretationis*. Only when measured against these councils can a judgment be made concerning the adequacy of a christology. I have already offered an interpretation of the language of these councils, the doctrines of which I take as normative, and the logic of that interpretation will reappear here. It is most important to recognize that Chalcedon does not offer a solution to the christological problem. "It only indicates the criteria that must be unconditionally observed in every christological theory."[66]

Incarnation. A critical point of interpretation regards the compatibility of the language of God as Spirit with that of incarnation. Of course this will depend upon what one means by incarnation. I have already indicated that a Spirit christology is different from a Logos christology in that it is not to be conceived as a three-stage narrative in which there is strict continuity of a single subject. With the light that historical consciousness and research have shone on Jesus' being a human being, substantially like us in all things, many aspects of the meaning of incarnation too can be clarified. One is that one cannot really think of a pre-existence of Jesus. It was natural and inevitable that the New Testament's understanding of Jesus as God's salvation-bringer caused the understanding of his relation to God to be conceived as constituted earlier and earlier: exaltation,

---

65. "It is, in fact, impossible to distinguish prayer to Christ from prayer to God conceptualized in terms of God's self-disclosure in Christ." Lampe, *God as Spirit*, 166.

66. Wolfhart Pannenberg, *Jesus—God and Man* (Philadelphia: Westminster Press, 1977), 292.

resurrection, baptism, conception, pre-existence.[67] But one cannot think in terms of the pre-existence of *Jesus*; what is pre-existent to Jesus is God, the God who became incarnate in Jesus. Doctrine underscores the obvious here, that Jesus is really a creature like us, and a creature cannot pre-exist creation. One may speculate on how Jesus might have been present to God's eternal intentions and so on, but a strict pre-existence of Jesus to his earthly existence is contradictory to his consubstantiality with us, unless the understanding is such that we too were pre-existent.

Given the starting point of christology with Jesus, incarnation has to be interpreted in such a way that it does not undermine the humanity of Jesus. This is, of course, what Logos christology did in the past and what a revised Logos christology and a Spirit christology seek to undo. The idea of God as Spirit at work in Jesus suggests minimally inspiration and maximally possession. But these extremes can and should be avoided. Jesus was empowered by God's Spirit; the Spirit of God is God present, and thus a personal presence, a power, a force, an energy, so that Jesus is an embodiment of God as Spirit. This is not an impersonal power that takes over and controls, but precisely God who works within human freedom, not from outside and dominating, nor from inside and taking over, but actualizing freedom to its full capacity. These themes are more dynamic than in the case of a three-stage, hypostatized Logos christology, in which Logos assumes a human nature and, as subject, acts through it as an instrument. This conception was revised in the Logos christology proposed earlier. But the symbol of God as Spirit is such that it more easily conveys an incarnation that does not negate Jesus' humanity or manipulate it; the Spirit enhances Jesus' freedom rather than acts in its stead.[68]

Frequently the presence of God as Spirit to Jesus is contrasted to what is depicted in a Logos christology as inspiration to real incarnation. But this need not be the case; there simply is no intrinsic reason for this antithesis. The effect of God's Spirit is surely also inspiration, but it has just been characterized in sturdier terms. No reason dictates why God as Spirit's personal self-communication, presence, and activity in Jesus should not be understood as an ontological incarnation, as long as incarnation is not taken to mean that Jesus' consubstantiality with us is negated.[69] Nor need this incarnation of God as Spirit be understood in an

---

67. See Dunn, *Unity and Diversity*, 228. See also Lampe, *God as Spirit*, 114–15. The problem with a notion of the pre-existence of Jesus is that it is incompatible with the doctrine of Chalcedon that Jesus is consubstantial with us. See Lampe, "The Holy Spirit and the Person of Christ," 119. The point of the doctrine of pre-existence is that salvation in and through Jesus comes from God; this is the point of Nicaea, and this point is sustained and explained by Spirit christology.

68. This very basic point is insisted upon by all who propose a Spirit christology. It is one of the elements that recommends a Spirit christology most highly. See Newman, *A Spirit Christology*, 176–77; Lampe, "The Holy Spirit and the Person of Christ," 117–18; Hook, "A Spirit Christology," 229.

69. It must be recalled that very often in Christian literature this negation of Jesus'

adoptionist sense, even though one might suspect that there is a legitimate sense in which this could be done since it is a conception with New Testament roots. But in contrast to adoptionism, one may think of the presence of God as Spirit to Jesus from the first moment of his existence.[70] In all of this, incarnation takes on the meaning given it by the dynamics of the synoptic gospels and is not made to conform to a speculative model.

Divinity of Jesus: consubstantial with God. Chapter 10 sketched the manner in which the issue of the divinity of Jesus was decided by the Council of Nicaea in 325. The question, then, is whether a Spirit christology conforms to the doctrine of Nicaea. I also explained how the Council of Nicaea and its christological decree were primarily negative: the enemy was the doctrine of Arius, and the canons of the council's creedal decree, which indicate the precise points at issue, are essentially a negation of Arian doctrine. For Arius, that which was incarnate in Jesus, namely, the Logos of God, was, strictly speaking, less than God. In a variety of ways the Nicene creed affirms that the Logos is not less than God. The whole burden of the controversy, as indicated by Athanasius's defense of the creed, shows that the positive meaning of "being of the same stuff or substance of God" has to be interpreted against this negative background.

It is important, too, for establishing a Spirit christology, to show why Nicaea does not entail a ratification of the symbol Logos. This appears from the fact that both Arius and the Alexandrian party shared this symbol in common. Because they agreed on an incarnation of the Logos, because they shared this subject matter of the debate, which was not Jesus directly but this Logos itself, it was never an issue of the debate at all. The issue was subordinationism, which had been around for a long time, even in the New Testament, and was only now being faced universally in these terms. And behind this issue lay a conception of salvation that was effected in and by Jesus upon which they did not agree. From all this it follows that the precise doctrine of Nicaea is not an affirmation of the Logos itself, but of what is entailed in this incarnation. Thus the doctrine of Nicaea can be paraphrased in this way: not less than God was present to and operative in Jesus.

Now it seems clear from what has been said of God as Spirit that this doctrine can in principle be conveyed equally well through this symbol. I say "in principle" because in fact the symbol Spirit can be construed in such a way that it conveys this doctrine more clearly and forcefully than

---

being a human being is exactly what is meant by the incarnation of the Logos. This is especially evident in descriptive or narrative accounts of Jesus. The real actor in history is not a human being but is a divine actor, is God in a human form, because the abstract human nature is no more than a passive instrument of God acting. The divine hypostasis has absorbed the human being Jesus; the divinity of Jesus is not God at work in and through a human being, and a "real presence" in that activity, but a God acting in history in a manner that is conceived non-dialectically.

70. Lampe, "The Holy Spirit and the Person of Christ," 125–26; Hook, "A Spirit Christology," 228.

does Logos. In fact, because of its having become personified, and then hypostatized, Logos was quite extensively understood as being less than God or the Father. As was indicated earlier, the symbol Logos itself caused the problem which Nicaea had to overcome. But in principle there is nothing affirmed by the doctrine of Nicaea that cannot also be affirmed in terms of God as Spirit. God as Spirit is God and thus not less than God.

The divinity of Jesus can be asserted in the same manner as in the doctrine of Chalcedon with its formula of one person and two natures. But some of the theology of the past, attendant upon that formula, would be modified. For example, given historical consciousness and the christological problematic today, people spontaneously accept Jesus as a human person. Therefore, as long as these natures are not conceived in a static and abstract way, one can say that Jesus was one human person with an integral human nature in whom not less than God, and thus a divine nature, is at work.[71] But in the end one cannot be satisfied in this matter with the proposal that Jesus was really a divine person with a true and integral humanity but not a human existence. This position says in effect that Jesus was not a human being, or person, or subject, or individual, but really a divine being, divine person, divine subject, divine individual who has a real and truly human nature apart from personhood. This formula from the theology that surrounded the doctrine of Chalcedon has also broken down in the wake of Jesus research.[72] This formulation does not do justice to the concrete person that one finds in the analysis of the synoptic gospels. It also succumbs to a dissatisfaction with an essentialism in scholastic philosophy which allows that real essences or essential natures can be distinguished from and exist apart from their proper act of existence or corresponding individuality. If Jesus is consubstantial with human beings, one must be able to pose the following critical question to understanding his personal identity and expect a positive answer: was Jesus in this respect like myself?[73] It follows that the logical exchanges that were allowed by the communication of the properties of each nature to the one

---

71. Historical consciousness prevents one from saying that Jesus' being a human being really refers to an integral but abstracted human nature that has as its principle of existence, not a human existence, but a divine person or hypostasis. The suggestion, then, is that one speak of two natures in one human person. Lampe writes that "Spirit christology must be content to acknowledge that the personal subject of the experience of Jesus Christ is a man. The hypostasis is not the Logos incarnate but a human being." Lampe, "The Holy Spirit and the Person of Christ," 124. For a discussion of this issue, see Schillebeeckx, *Jesus*, 652–69.

72. John P. Galvin, "From the Humanity of Christ to the Jesus of History: A Paradigm Shift in Catholic Christology," *Theological Studies*, 55 (1994), 252–73.

73. One cannot consider an essential human nature as a fixed entity or datum. This is of course the tendency in the conception of an enhypostatic union in which the hypostasis of the Logos assumes an integral human nature without, that is, abstracted from, its own proper human act of existence as its subject. Relative to that human nature, one may ask whether being united to and sustained in being by the divine Logos makes any difference to it. If not, there is no reason for the theory. If it does make

person do not work with the same logical precision in a Spirit christology. These are too abstract, inattentive to the concrete person of history, and, in the end, result in statements that are not adequately dialectical. The communication of properties breaks the tensive and dialectical structure of christology. Thus, one cannot say undialectically that Jesus is God, nor that he is merely a human being, because the doctrine is that Jesus is both truly human and divine.

When one asserts the divinity of Jesus with a dynamic Spirit christology, this means that God, and not less than God, is really present to and at work in Jesus, and that this is so in such a manner that Jesus is a manifestation and embodiment of the reality of God. The transition of interpretation moves along a line from a static and abstract ontology of God conceived in terms of a divine nature and hypostasis to a conception of God as personal, dynamic activity who is personally present as Spirit. Newman hesitates to call Jesus divine for fear of undermining his humanity. "It is to be clearly stated that the presence of the Spirit in Jesus did not make Jesus in himself divine. . . ."[74] This account is followed by an understanding of God's being present to Jesus not ontologically but functionally. While I appreciate and agree with the intent of Newman to preserve Jesus' humanity, I believe that his language is not sufficiently nuanced. The distinction between God's ontological and functional presence to Jesus does not really work. In contrast, the ontology of symbol presented earlier allows a truly dialectical language that preserves the point of Newman's argument and the point of the doctrine of Chalcedon which is truly dialectical.

Humanity of Jesus: consubstantial with human beings. It is generally conceded that a classical Logos christology favors the divinity of Jesus, and a Spirit christology favors the humanity of Jesus. In this respect the difference between them is analogous to the contrast between an Alexandrian hypostatic union christology and an Antiochene divine indwelling christology. Another way of getting at this issue is through the category of "qualitative uniqueness or difference." An Alexandrian incarnational Logos christology preserves explicitly the uniqueness of Jesus in the sense

---

a difference, it is an infinite difference that must certainly influence the human nature as such. (See above, n. 8.) This has always been the problem with an enhypostatic union. It is impossible to conceive of a human nature not being infinitely qualitatively transformed by being assumed by the divine subject. The result is that Jesus is not really consubstantial with us. The theological anthropology of Rahner seems to anticipate this problem, since human nature is precisely that which is created for unity with God. Therefore, closer union with God means a fuller humanity, as in Spirit christology. But this works only in the measure in which the union of Jesus with God is of the same class as that of other human beings. A proper parallel with Spirit christology would require of Logos christology an Antiochene indwelling paradigm rather than a hypostatic or enhypostatic union that is *sui generis.*

74. Newman, *A Spirit Christology,* 179; see also 180–82.

of his qualitative difference from all others. What is to be said here on the basis of a Spirit christology?[75]

In a Spirit christology one can and should retain the uniqueness of Jesus in the very measure that one views him as a true manifestation of what God is like and the pattern of what human existence should be. But a Spirit christology may or may not hold a qualitative difference between the union of God with Jesus and the union of God with other human beings depending upon what one means by a "qualitative difference." To common sense, some of the clearest examples of qualitative differences are those between kinds of being, such as the differences between inorganic and organic beings, or between vegetative, animal, and human life. If these are illustrations of qualitative difference, it becomes questionable that such a difference should be affirmed between Jesus and other human beings. For "qualitative" here takes on the meaning of "substantial," or "essential," and such a "qualitative" difference appears to be directly contradictory to the doctrine of the consubstantiality of Jesus with other human beings. In other words, this meaning of qualitative refers to an essential level or kind of being. Thus on this understanding, qualitative difference from us and consubstantiality with us are contradictory notions. A qualitative difference between the union of Jesus and of other human beings with God would mean that Jesus was not consubstantial with us, not the new Adam, not the firstborn of many, nor the pioneer of our salvation, nor imitable by us. All of these doctrines indicate that Jesus is one of us, and that we are not unlike Jesus in the offer of God's presence to us.[76]

And yet the prevalence of this idea of qualitative difference indicates that there is something here that should be preserved, and it will be with a Spirit christology. Two reflections will make this clear. The first begins with the ambiguity of the notion of a "qualitative" in relation to a "quantitative" difference. In our current age of discovery through empirical and quantitative methods, it is becoming more and more difficult to distinguish between a qualitative and a quantitative difference between things, even in terms of their level of being. It is not impossible that qualitative differences may be understood quantitatively, and that in some cases differences of quantity or degree or intensity may constitute a qualitative difference.[77] If one says that the Spirit of God, which is God, is present to

---

75. It may be noted in passing here that, in the context of the discussion of Jesus in relation to the mediations of transcendence of other religions of the last chapter, it is sometimes said that Jesus is unique in his individuality. But this is not a relevant assertion; all people are individuals and unique in this sense. There must be some "qualitative" uniqueness at stake for the term to have any relevance. The problem is how to conceive of this qualitative uniqueness in such a way that Jesus remains consubstantial with us.

76. Newman, *A Spirit Christology*, 182–83.

77. In this usage, which may be associated with the scholastic notion of quality, the term "qualitatively" stands over against the idea of "substantial," "essential,"

Jesus in a complete way, or in a fully effective way, in a most intense manner, need one say more?[78] In short, one may understand that God as Spirit was present to Jesus in a superlative degree, and this is sufficient to convey all that was intended by a qualitative difference.[79]

Secondly, one may also understand the uniqueness of Jesus in terms of his vocation, mission, and appointment by God to be the firstborn of many. These terms are congruous with the New Testament; they correspond with the anointing with God as Spirit and the mission of the kingdom of God to which Jesus was loyal. These notions, then, are not merely extrinsic; they determine the inner identity of Jesus. And they, together with the degree to which God animated Jesus' life, are both sufficient to define his uniqueness and necessary to explain it.[80] But at the same time they preserve Jesus' true humanity and consubstantiality with us.

Intelligibility

What is the basis of the credibility of this Spirit christology? To what does it appeal to make the case for its intelligibility? Spirit christology appeals to experience. As was said in response to the question of method, Spirit christology presumes that one cannot base theology today on mere authority; one must appeal to experience. It also works on the premise that there is continuity between Jesus and us. There must be analogies in our experience if we are to appropriate the truth of past affirmations. Therefore Spirit christology appeals to the Christian experience of the internal working of God's grace as an analogy of how God was at work in Jesus. It should be noted, however, that the apologetic of Rahner's Logos christology as fulfillment of the human may be appropriated here, even as Logos christology may appropriate the experience of God into its rationale.

---

and "of nature." It indicates a difference of quality but not of substance. At the same time it does not in any way exclude the possibility that quality may be constituted by quantity.

78. The difference between Jesus' humanity and the presence to it of God as Spirit and that of other human beings generally is understood in terms of fullness and partiality. "The difference at stake could be labeled gradual, but the grade, the measure in which Jesus differs from others is unique." Schoonenberg, "Spirit Christology and Logos Christology," 364.

79. Hook, "A Spirit Christology," 229. This presence of the Spirit to Jesus, Hook adds, is the equivalent of incarnation. Lampe too explains the "qualitative" difference of the union of God with Jesus from that with others in terms of degree. He describes Jesus' response to God as total; and the assumption must be that that is possible by God's total initiative toward Jesus. This "perfect" union between God and Jesus does not in any way undermine the limitations of Jesus' being a human being, with the exception of sinlessness, which is symbolic for the totality of Jesus' response to God. Lampe, *God as Spirit*, 23–24, 111–12. It should be noted that this conception entails speculative reconstruction; although it is stated in historical terms, it is not historically given.

80. Newman, *A Spirit Christology*, 185–86, 205.

Empowerment

A Spirit christology empowers Christian life on the basis of the continuity between Jesus and us; he is a human being like us in all things except sin. This axiom from the New Testament is taken literally by Spirit christology. Because of this continuity between Jesus and disciples, one can be inspired by and imitate Jesus. There is no gap between him and us. One can project upon him all the weaknesses of human existence in order to retrieve from him the inspiration of the power of his earthly life. Spirit christology gives a solid grounding for a spirituality of following Christ.

CONCLUSION

Fundamental to the New Testament is its witness to many christologies. But relative to the narrow christological question of the divinity of Jesus, two basic alternatives appear, both of which have the systematic potential to draw the many other conceptions of Jesus into themselves. "Stated succinctly, the Logos christology is paralleled by a Son, or a Spirit, christology, and the incarnation christology or descending christology by an elevation, or adoption, or ascending christology."[81] As long as one is aware that this christological language is symbolic, one can coherently hold either a Logos or a Spirit christology. These are not final explanations of the reality of Jesus Christ; this remains mystery. This language is not directly referential or objective language that describes how God is present in Jesus. It is symbolic language that points to the mystery of God's presence as it is encountered in Jesus. This does not mean that this language is mere projection and enjoys no realism; it does correspond to reality. But that reality cannot be adequately objectified or thematized; it remains mystery.

Logos and Spirit christologies are easily contrasted with each other. Logos christology, especially since the Council of Nicaea, favors the divinity of Jesus; Spirit christology more easily accommodates Jesus' humanity. Each must be presented in such a way that it accounts for a dialectical understanding of Jesus as concrete symbol of God. Since the patristic period Logos christology has controlled the Christian imagination. To be viable today, Logos christology must consciously adopt a paradigm analogous to the Antiochenes as distinct from the Alexandrians. Since Logos christology has prevailed within the churches for so long, the case for Spirit christology is made on the basis of the pluralism of christologies found in the New Testament. One christology cannot rule to the exclusion of others. But at the same time, systematic theology must adopt a center of gravity and strive for consistency and coherence. A consistent christology may be constructed around either one of these root metaphors or symbols from the New Testament. Each one is open enough to include themes

---

81. Schoonenberg, "Spirit Christology and Logos Christology," 350.

from other christologies that are deemed essential to understanding Jesus Christ.

This means that a thoroughgoing Spirit christology is a viable option today. Spirit christology satisfies the requirements of the discipline. It thematizes Christian experience of Jesus and "explains" the meaning of Jesus' being the bringer of God's salvation. It is faithful to the dominant New Testament language with respect to the narrow christological problem. It is also faithful to the great christological councils of Nicaea and Chalcedon, affirming with the first that no less than God was at work in Jesus, and with the second that Jesus is consubstantial with us. It preserves the strictly dialectical relationship between Jesus' being human and divine. This Spirit christology is intelligible and coherent with other human experience today: with historical consciousness generally, with the new historical focus on Jesus being a human being, with the experience of the analogy between Jesus and other media or institutions which mediate God's salvation in other religions, while at the same time preserving incarnation, and Jesus' divinity, mediation of God's salvation, universal relevance and normativity. Spirit christology meets the criterion of empowerment because it provides the grounding for discipleship in establishing the consubstantiality and continuity between Jesus and us, between Jesus and our being empowered by God as Spirit. In a Spirit christology it becomes plain that the salvation mediated by Jesus is closely bound up with the way one lives in the Spirit; this salvation thus has a bearing on our lives in history. There is, therefore, a strict coherence between christology, the life of grace, ecclesiology, and Christian spirituality.

Although this is a constructive statement, it stands out against the backdrop of the Logos christology that is in place. A comparative argument has not been drawn out in detail because the point here is not to contest Logos christology and to undermine pluralism itself. The thesis here is that a Logos christology is also a viable option today, as long as it is proposed in a way that is conscious of the symbolic character of Logos language and attentive to Jesus as a human being in history. But one of the main resistances to Spirit christology remains a Logos christology that is tied up with trinitarian theology. One must, therefore, examine the doctrine of the trinity, not only because it tends to crowd out the pluralism of christologies, but also, positively, because it is the short formula expressing the heart of the Christian meaning of God and God's economy of salvation.

CHAPTER 16

Trinity

This final chapter will examine the mutual relationships that link the theology and doctrines of Jesus Christ and trinity. It is evident that these two doctrines are intimately related; some may claim that they logically entail each other. Be that as it may, it is important that christological understanding not be left standing alone, so to speak, that it be situated in the grand Christian vision. In traditional Christian creeds, that vision unfolds according to a narrative drama of salvation, structured by belief in the Father, the Son, and the Spirit. Placing this christology in that larger framework will provide a fitting summary and conclusion to this work.

THE QUESTION

Something of a revival in trinitarian theology has been going on for some time.[1] But it is important to note clearly that my aim in this chapter is not at all to develop even in outline an integral trinitarian theology. Such would not be possible and is not called for at this juncture. In contrast to the several treatises on the trinity which are available today, I will severely

---

1. Recent influential works in trinitarian theology are Joseph Bracken, *The Triune Symbol* (Washington, D.C.: University Press of America, 1985); Ralph Del Colle, *Christ and the Spirit: Spirit-Christology in Trinitarian Perspective* (New York/Oxford: Oxford University Press, 1994); William J. Hill, *The Three-Personed God: The Trinity as a Mystery of Salvation* (Washington, D.C.: University Press of America, 1982); Elizabeth A. Johnson, *She Who Is: The Mystery of God in Feminist Theological Discourse* (New York: Crossroad, 1992); Walter Kasper, *The God of Jesus Christ* (New York: Crossroad, 1984); Anthony Kelly, *The Trinity of Love: A Theology of the Christian God* (Wilmington: Michael Glazier, 1989); Catherine M. LaCugna, *God For Us: The Trinity and Christian Life* (San Francisco: Harper, 1992); James P. Mackey, *The Christian Experience of God as Trinity* (London: SCM Press, 1983); Jürgen Moltmann, *The Trinity and the Kingdom: The Doctrine of God* (San Francisco: Harper & Row, 1981); John J. O'Donnell, *The Mystery of the Triune God* (New York: Paulist Press, 1989); Ted Peters, *God as Trinity: Relationality and Temporality in Divine Life* (Louisville: Westminster/John Knox Press, 1993); Karl Rahner, *The Trinity* (New York: Seabury Press, 1974).

limit this discussion by defining several questions which spontaneously arise out of the christology that has just been developed. An initial description and definition of these questions will clarify the limits of this chapter and the aim of the discussion. There are three of them.

The first concerns the close relationship that obtains between christology and trinitarian theology. Just how is this relationship to be defined? More concretely, since different theologians and theologies envisage this relationship differently, how is this relationship conceived in the christology that has been developed in this work? It is frequently said that the doctrine of the trinity is the very center of Christian faith and belief. But such claims might also be made for christological doctrine. Perhaps the doctrine of Christ lies at the center of a trinitarian vision and further defines that center. But it is more likely that, since every conception of a center remains dependent upon perspective and method, one will find a variety of conceptions of the relationship between trinitarian theology and christology. The issue of whether trinity should be placed at the beginning or the end of Christian theology, whether trinity is a starting point or a conclusion of christology, offers one of the more important sets of alternatives on this issue. It is evident that one cannot address such a question without taking positions on the foundations of a particular theological enterprise and the method of its undertaking. Such is the intention of this chapter.

The second question to be addressed in this chapter arises from the fact that I have proposed alongside a Logos christology the possibility of a Spirit christology as a viable alternative. There is an obvious correlation between Logos christology and the doctrine of the trinity, because Logos language controlled the christology out of which the doctrine of the trinity developed. Any proposal of a Spirit christology as an alternative to Logos christology immediately raises the question of its bearing on the doctrine of the trinity. For a thoroughgoing Spirit christology seems to eliminate Logos as a symbol designating both the discrete "person" or distinct "mode of being" in the Godhead and as incarnate in Jesus. Bluntly put, can one still have a doctrine of the trinity if one adopts a thoroughgoing Spirit christology? This sharp form of the question illustrates just how closely the doctrines of Jesus Christ and trinity are intertwined. Can one have a doctrine of the trinity without a Logos christology? Can Jesus be Son without being Logos? And, looking at it from the direction of trinity, can trinitarian language, which developed out of christological reflection, bend back and determine the meaning of the language that logically precedes it? More directly stated, can the doctrine of the immanent trinity act as a normative criterion for christology? It is evident that raising this question also leads back to foundational issues of religious knowledge and inference.

Third, the theology and doctrine of the trinity have intrinsic problems of intelligibility and credibility of their own that are being addressed with vigor today. Because this chapter is not devoted to developing an integral theology of the trinity, these problems will be addressed somewhat obliquely. Although they do not determine the focus of the chapter, neither can they be avoided. A brief statement of some of these problems which appear in every treatment of the doctrine will be sufficient to illustrate the need that they enter into one's ken.

One issue arises from the sharp difference in meaning between the term "person" as it was used in patristic and medieval theology, and the meaning it has come to assume in the modern period. Today a "person" is a being, most immediately known through self-consciousness as an autonomous human being, who interacts with the world through self-transcending reflection and freedom. The doctrine of the trinity was formulated with a different ontological notion of person, and it did not mean that three conscious, free, and independent subjects made up the Godhead.[2] Use of the term "person" today to indicate the "members" of the trinity almost inevitably communicates misunderstanding and error, some form of tritheism, whether or not it is intended. Thus a number of theologians are dropping the term "person" and adopting others. Schillebeeckx writes: "I reject 'modalism,' because for me the divine nature is trinitarian; it is personally trinitarian. I do not explicitly say three persons because that is ambiguous (tritheism), but I do say that the nature of God is itself personal with a trinitarian structure."[3] This case provides a kind of paradigm of the problem of interpretation. One must reformulate the doctrine in a new situation in order to preserve its original meaning; new language is needed to preserve the point of the original doctrine.

Another issue concerns the way this doctrine relates to Christian life: what is the relevance of this doctrine to Christian living? This problem especially affects the trinitarian theology of the West which, in the tradition of Augustine, became something of a speculative discipline. Analogical reasoning showed how the one God could be differentiated into three "persons," each fully divine and distinct, and yet making up one God. This speculative effort, working from traces of God in the world and especially in the human person, was directed toward ways of construing the constitution of God's inner reality; as such it tended to lose a direct bearing on human life. As a result some modern theologians wish to drop a doctrine of the immanent trinity. But others wish to reform the analogical base or model for envisioning the trinity, so that the doctrine uses language that runs more closely parallel with structures of human existence and seems to bear an analogy with human life on a foundational level.[4] One thing is certain, since theology has shifted from being a cate-

---

2. P. J. A. M. Schoonenberg, "Trinity—The Consummated Covenant: Theses on the Doctrine of the Trinitarian God," *Studies in Religion / Sciences Religieuses*, 5 (1975–76), 113.

3. Edward Schillebeeckx, *I Am a Happy Theologian: Conversations with Francesco Strazzari* (New York: Crossroad, 1994), 52.

4. Catherine M. LaCugna, "Re-conceiving the Trinity as the Mystery of Salvation," *Scottish Journal of Theology*, 38 (1985), 15.

chetical discipline to a critical apologetical discipline, it has had to meet the questions that rise out of a correlation between traditional language and existential historical life and culture. These questions are demanding. What difference for our understanding of God and of ourselves is borne by a threefold differentiation within God? What does God being triune add to one's understanding of a personal God? Does it allow us to say anything about God that one could not say if God were an undifferentiated and infinitely free subject, that is, besides threeness itself?

And, finally, there are problems concerning the historical genesis of this doctrine. How can we gain knowledge about the inner makeup of God? The premises and the arguments on which the development of this doctrine rested do not have the same credibility today as they did in the patristic period. And if these premises, and their suppositions, and the arguments they allow, cannot be accepted today, then the conclusions which they generated can no longer be accepted in the same form. I refer to theories of religious epistemology, implicit views of the relation between scriptural text and revelation, the conception of revelation, the use of scripture in theological argument, presuppositions about the nature of God. Looking back at these loci with present-day understandings will call for some reinterpretations of the patristic arguments and conclusions.[5]

These three problem areas, the relation between christology and trinitarian theology, the openness of Spirit christology to trinitarian thought, and issues in the credibility of trinitarian theology, together form the focus of this chapter. The treatment of trinity is thus narrowly limited.[6] The chapter is intended to entertain foundational issues in the theology and doctrine of the trinity in such a way that its relation to christology generally, and especially Spirit christology, will be clarified. The chapter will also serve as a conclusion to this christology. Along the way I shall have to recall basic principles of method as they come to bear on the development of the doctrine of the trinity. I shall also have to double back on the biblical and patristic sources of the tradition. The goal here is to recapitulate this christology by situating it within the trinitarian Christian vision and language of God. The next section takes up the relation of trinitarian doctrine to christology in terms of the development of trinitarian doctrine "from below." And the section following it analyzes the point of trinitarian theology in order to show its openness and compatibility with Spirit christology.

---

5. Roger Haight, "The Point of Trinitarian Theology," *Toronto Journal of Theology*, 4 (1988), 193–94.

6. By contrast, see the great variety of contemporary methods and approaches to the doctrine of the trinity surveyed by Hill, *The Three-Personed God*, 81–237, and Peters, *God as Trinity*, 81–145.

TRINITY FROM BELOW

I entitle this discussion "Trinity from Below" in order to announce the thesis contained in it, namely, that trinitarian theology is completely dependent upon christology, that the doctrine was generated in the course of the development of christology, and that, as in the case of christology, the only way critically to understand the doctrine of the trinity is to trace its historical development. Such an analysis makes up the core of this part of the chapter, but I introduce it with some basic premises of theological method as they apply to the theology of the trinity.

RELIGIOUS KNOWING AND TRINITARIAN SYMBOLS

Piet Schoonenberg succinctly proposes principles for trinitarian theology that run parallel to principles from the early chapters of this book. He writes:

All our thinking moves from the world to God, and can never move in the opposite direction. Revelation in no way suspends this law. Revelation is the experienced self-communication of God *in* human history, which thereby becomes the history of salvation. With reference to God's Trinity, this law means that the Trinity can never be the point of departure. There is no way that we can draw conclusions from the Trinity to Christ and to the Spirit given to us; only the opposite direction is possible.[7]

This provides the bare bones of a response to some of the questions that have been raised, and the rest of this section will put some flesh on them.

The movement of all theological thought from below toward God proceeds on the basis of religious experience and symbolic language. The symbolic character of all religious images, concepts, and language about God has an importance in trinitarian theology that is enhanced by the degree to which it is ignored. For the purpose of making the same single point, one could refer to religious language as symbolic, metaphorical, analogical, and based on models; each of these frames of reference allow one to recognize that the object of religious language is transcendent and not immediately available. Such language, therefore, is not objectively representational, or immediately referential, or propositionally descriptive, or ostensive in its reference. Thus religious language always has a metaphorical structure, because the referent God is always conceived implicitly "like" what is conveyed by ordinary language about this-worldly objects. This language is symbolic and analogous because at the same time its transcendent object is similar and different from its finite

---

7. Schoonenberg, "Trinity," 111.

symbolic analogue. Such a symbol, therefore, points away from itself to the transcendent other which it makes present to human encounter.

Catherine LaCugna and Kilian McDonnell, writing on the trinity, explain language about God in terms of models. Theological concepts are models. This model language complements the ideas of symbol, metaphor, and analogue by highlighting the dynamic, creative, and tentative character of religious symbols. Religious categories are not precise; they are suggestive and changeable; they inadequately refer to their object. Thus models are metaphorical, but they tend to be taken as descriptive. "Against all protest, models are almost inevitably understood non-metaphorically, taken to replicate in a precise way rather than to image in an iconic manner. For this reason equally viable models are viewed as being mutually exclusive." This implies that one trinitarian model cannot be the norm of another; to use one model against another in this manner is to reduce them to descriptive instead of symbolic language. "The model of reality is never the reality itself. . . . A model of God *in se* is not God as such. A model of 'the trinity' is not the trinitarian God. Models must reflect our unknowing of God; model is reflective vision, not direct beholding." Every model also distorts; it cannot exactly correspond to what is given to consciousness in an experiential and relational way. Theology must resist overinvesting in a certain model, clinging to it, as history moves on.[8]

The view of religious and theological language outlined in earlier chapters was called symbolic realism. The tensive character of religious language does not negate its attaining its object, its "objectivity" in this sense, and hence its cognitive character. This was explained by a theory of religious experience in which transcendent reality is also immanent to creation and to human existence. The nature or character of this experience was described in terms of creation and participatory encounter with God immanent and self-communicating. Such realism and objectivity do not allow religious experience to be disclosive of descriptive information about a transcendent reality or realm. Revelation does not provide premises for tight deductive reasoning. But it is cognitive and carries a self-authenticating meaning that is "realized" or actualized in human action and life.

Five symbols from the Jewish-Christian scripture which figure most prominently in later trinitarian theology provide good examples of these qualities of conceptual or linguistic religious symbols. These are Yahweh, Spirit, Word, Wisdom, and Logos. Yahweh is the name of the absolutely transcendent one. The scriptures are filled with the theme of God's inapproachability and the need of mediation to establish contact. The other symbols may be understood by contrast: they point to indications and traces of God in the world. The Spirit is God's effective presence in the

---

8. Catherine M. LaCugna and Kilian McDonnell, "Returning from 'the Far Country': Theses for a Contemporary Trinitarian Theology," *Scottish Journal of Theology*, 41 (1988), 204–05. See also LaCugna, "Re-conceiving the Trinity," 11–12.

world; the Spirit is God's power of creation hovering over the deep. God's action in the world unfolds as the breath of the wind, invisible but effective. From another perspective, in another image, God creates by the announcement of God's intention; God's speaking creates. God's action in the world is the immediate obediential effect of God's commanding will: God speaks a word, and it is done. The result is that God, who was always accompanied by wisdom, injects this wisdom into reality itself, so that all creation, both nature and social life, are structured by God's wisdom. But wisdom is a woman, and this means that womanly qualities are injected back into God and outward into the world through Sophia's immanent presence.[9] For Wisdom is Spirit (Wis 1:7, 7:25). And what is this Logos that according to the poem of John was with God from the beginning? This Logos is God's wisdom, and God's Word, and God's Spirit, and perhaps God's reflective reason as well. These symbols, metaphors, or models did not have a stable univocal meaning. To understand and use language is to interpret, and these symbols were continually being drawn into new situations and taking on new meaning. Their historical meaning, therefore, was dynamic and cumulative; they "meant" or symbolized by pointing the mind to the traces of God's presence in ever new ways. Trinitarian language cannot be taken as providing objective information about God; such a mistake in categories at this primary level creates insoluble problems. The world of religious symbolism, the world of language about God, is not one of facts and digital information; it is a world of religious experience; it is based on a narrative of a symbolic encounter with God in history.

HISTORICAL GENESIS OF THE DOCTRINE

We now turn to the development of that language into the formal and classical doctrine. In any reconsideration of the trinitarian concepts, "it is desirable that we should retrace and follow through the cognitive process of the early Church."[10] We have seen some elements of this history from a christological perspective; it is recounted in most books on the trinity. But often the impression is given that this development proceeded according to a strict and inevitable logic to a conclusion that was already there in the beginning, entailed in its premises, and only needed time to be discovered.[11] This locates the internally consistent element in the process of development in a proposition that developed from being implicitly pos-

---

9. Johnson, *She Who Is*, 76–103.

10. This is the recommendation of the Faith and Order Commission of the World Council of Churches as cited by LaCugna and McDonnell, "Returning from 'the Far Country,'" 211.

11. See, for example, John Henry Newman's *An Essay on the Development of Christian Doctrine* (Westminster, Md.: Christian Classics, 1968). John Courtney Murray, *The Problem of God: Yesterday and Today* (New Haven: Yale University Press, 1964), also leaves the impression that the development of the doctrine of the trinity was inevitable.

sessed to clear, explicit consciousness. Consciousness of the historicity of reason itself prevents such thinking today. All reasoning is historically conditioned; all historical understanding is new interpretation; new interpretation creates new meaning which is both continuous and discontinuous with the past. The trinity, which technically speaking is a doctrine and not a name of God, is such an interpretation. The analysis which follows presupposes the developments of doctrine seen in earlier chapters. It merely highlights a number of areas that raise more questions and thus open up a historical imagination to the possibility of new interpretations of trinitarian language.

Beginning with the New Testament, amid the wide-ranging pluralism of christologies, two christologies in particular point to God's presence and action in Jesus' life. Spirit christology dominates the New Testament in terms of its pervasiveness: God as Spirit encompasses Jesus' life, before, during, and after. Jesus is God's Son because he was born from the power of God as Spirit, lived by the authority of God as Spirit, and was exalted in God as Spirit who then flooded the Christian communities. Logos christology has its roots in the vital tradition of wisdom language and in early Christian worship. It flowers in the dramatic liturgical poem that makes up the Prologue in John's gospel. In it are merged the Jewish understandings of wisdom and resonances of Greek philosophical notions of the grounds of intelligibility and reason. Logos christology formed the bridge that allowed a transition of thought that accompanied the spread of the church westward into Greek and Latin intellectual culture.

Using a distinction that developed in the course of patristic theology, and which is still useful and illuminating, one finds no doctrine of an immanent trinity in the New Testament, that is, a doctrine depicting the inner reality of God as differentiated. "Not a single New Testament text speaks of God in 'immanent' terms."[12] The language of the New Testament represents God at work in the world for human salvation in "economic" terms such as "Word," "Wisdom," "Angel of the Lord," "Spirit," "Son of Man," and so on. This language is often described as functional, experiential, relational, and narrative; it recounts the experience of God's saving action for us in history. What is important here is that later doctrines of an immanent trinity not be allowed to be read into New Testament teaching. In this doctrine as in others, it is crucial that one preserve the stages in the doctrinal development in their historical integrity in order to ensure critical analysis.[13]

Another fundamental feature relative to trinity in the New Testament is the several occasions where Father, Son, and Spirit are brought together

---

12. LaCugna and McDonnell, "Returning from 'the Far Country,'" 205.

13. This historical integrity protects the doctrine of an immanent trinity against the disappointment of not finding such a doctrine in the New Testament after postulating that it "must" be there. The doctrine of the trinity is a product of development. By contrast, the way not to make a case here is by collecting texts out of context that seem to make objective points in propositional form.

in a single formula or extended phrase. This is found on several occasions in Paul. Probably the most well-known and dramatic instance of it brings to a climax Matthew's gospel when the disciples are commissioned to baptize the nations "in the name of the Father and of the Son and of the Holy Spirit" (Matt 28:19). This collocation of terms can be said to represent the fundamental structure of Christian faith, because it is the narrative structure of Christian faith's experience of God's salvation in history. The event of salvation for the Christian is precisely God saving, first through creation and providence, and then through the Son, Jesus, and in God as Spirit active anew in the community.

During the second century, the term "trinity" appeared to designate this three-fold description of God's action for human salvation. The history of the development of the doctrine of the trinity only gradually generated a clearly conceived meaning for this term. The early patristic development of trinitarian theology contains four elements that constantly interact in ways that are hard to generalize into a pattern. These are the hypostatization of the Logos, the interaction of the problem of Jesus and the problem of God, the problem of modalism, and the issue of subordinationism. I will describe each of these elements briefly without pretending to sort out their relative weights in the final development of trinitarian doctrine. One gets a fairly good idea of the logic of the development through the interaction of these four factors.

Jewish tradition was quite familiar with the personification of various symbols representing God's action in the world. A most influential example of this is the personification of God's wisdom or *Sophia*.[14] But whereas personification is recognized as figurative speech, hypostatization represents a certain literalization of it. Hypostatization means the making of an idea or a concept or a figure of speech into a real thing or entity. Given the idea of hypostasis as representing the individuality of something, that is, an individual substance within a class or species, to hypostatize an idea is to reinterpret it as real. The Latin-based equivalent, to reify, means to concretize or materialize an idea such as a figure of speech as an existing entity. Somewhere in the course of the development of thinking about Jesus Christ, at a place that is not easy to determine, wisdom personified became wisdom hypostatized or Logos hypostatized. The distinction between personification and reification is complicated by the structure of metaphor itself. Metaphor radicalizes a simile by the identification of something with what it is not: *Sophia* is a person, she is, "in fact," a woman. When does personification pass in the user's imagination and understanding into a real individual? Although it is usually presumed that Logos or Word in John's Prologue is a discrete being, given the genre and

14. Elisabeth Schüssler Fiorenza, "Wisdom Mythology and the Christological Hymns of the New Testament," in Robert L. Wilken, ed., *Aspects of Wisdom in Judaism and Early Christianity* (Notre Dame, Ind.: University of Notre Dame Press, 1975), 17–41; Johnson, *She Who Is*, 86–100.

the tradition, it seems difficult to be sure. But it is certain that in early patristic literature Logos is a real being. Wherever it occurred, this hypostatization was largely responsible for the most serious problems of christology and trinitarian thinking. Once Logos is hypostatized, one has the problem of the second God.

The second element in the development of patristic christology and trinitarian theology was briefly outlined in Chapter 9: the tendency of the christological problem to become a problem of the nature of God. Such a tendency makes sense in the Greek and Roman worlds of polytheism, or more generally in Mediterranean cultures containing a vast array of religions, and where the world included a supra-empirical or supernatural sphere which was filled with spiritual beings and lesser deities. In such a context it would have been easy to reckon the Logos a second God. But the more fundamental Jewish and then Christian tradition of monotheism was intrinsically unable to allow a second God in any sense of real parity. The context of polytheism forms a constant pressure on this development, and I shall return to it in developing the point of trinitarian theology.

The third and fourth elements of the development of christology that have a bearing on the nature of God reflect two contrary solutions to the problem of a second God. These are modalism and subordinationism. Modalism denies real distinctions within the Godhead. It builds on the conviction that there is but one God, the sole creator and ruler of the universe, and that this God is indivisible. God does not share deity with another. Modalism also represents a high christology, for it could see no other than this one God as the source of the divine status of Jesus Christ. Strict monotheism is preserved; the divinity of Jesus is ensured. But modalism in the terms of the day failed to preserve God's transcendence. It seemed impossible to imagine that the one high God be incarnate in Jesus and still be God. Incarnation involved limitation of God, and an immanence to matter and suffering that was unthinkable. Subordinationism, by contrast, builds on this premise of the absolute transcendence of God. That which was incarnate in Jesus was a "second God," that is, truly of God, but of a status subordinate to the Father. Here too strict monotheism is preserved, but at the price of a lower christology when compared to modalism, for it was not truly God that was incarnate in Jesus.

I discussed at some length the Nicene solution in Chapter 10. The Son is of the same stuff as the Father; subordinationism is overcome. And while some suspected that "one in substance" sounded like it meant numerically one substance or hypostasis, and thus a relapse into modalism, such was not the intention of the council. Nicaea is a trinitarian council because, while presupposing the distinction and duality between Father and Son, *in directo* it spoke of the very nature of God in defining their consubstantiality; the two were one in a common substance. A threshold was thus crossed, and in a certain sense the explicit or full doctrine of the trinity was then a matter of time. Arguments that showed the divinity of God as Spirit were analogous to those *a propos* the Son. The work of the Cappadocians helped in standardizing trinitarian language and clarifying conceptual distinctions. The formation of the Creed of Constantinople in 381 and the resultant doctrine of the immanent trinity forming the substructure of a tripartite creed fell into place.

Historical analysis of the development of the theology of the trinity today highlights the difference between the western tradition of reflection on this doctrine, beginning with Augustine, and the genesis of the doctrine through the debates of the Greek theologians to which I have just alluded. Augustine begins with the premise of a doctrine already in place: the one God is triune. The nature of such a triune creator must be reflected in creation, especially in the human being created in God's image. Therefore, a differentiation between the three-fold structure of, for example, the being of the self, the intellect, and the will, which together constitute the core of human being, also provides an analogy for understanding the being of God.[15] These prayerful, imaginative, contemplative, and speculative ruminations of Augustine stand at the head of a new and different tradition of trinitarian theology which takes the doctrine as a given, makes its object the divine life itself, and tries by analogy to find an intelligibility in this internal, three-fold differentiation. This form of trinitarian theology has come under severe criticism in recent years in the name of a return to the genesis of the doctrine and a closer linkage between it and its roots in the experience of God's economy of salvation.

THE LOGIC OF THE DEVELOPMENT OF THE DOCTRINE
OF THE TRINITY

The four elements of the problem of the nature of God in the light of Jesus Christ intersect and mutually influence each other during the whole course of the development up to Nicaea and beyond. It is often pointed out that the premises of these debates include ideas and values that are more typically Greek than Hebrew. But, when generalized, these elements are operative today. The debate, then as now, is also complicated by unstable language and different traditions in the larger church. And although the Nicene solution won the day, and its language prevailed into the modern period, it is not without ambiguity. Looking back from a present-day perspective that shares different presuppositions inevitably raises some basic questions. The premise in raising these questions is a historical consciousness that recognizes that words and categories change their meaning in new situations. The example of the word "person" cited earlier is a perfect illustration.

So too, the language of modalism today would not mean the same thing as it meant in the second and third centuries. Patripassionism was

---

15. For example, Augustine, *De Trinitate*, 9.1-4, in *Saint Augustine: The Trinity*, *The Fathers of the Church*, (Washington, D.C.: Catholic University of America Press, 1963), 269–74.

unimaginable then, but theologians regularly speak of God suffering today. Certain forms of *passio* are not considered indications of weakness and limit. Process theology speaks of God becoming. Justin Martyr thought that there must be a distinction between the Lord who appeared in history and the Lord who remained in heaven.[16] Sometimes the reasoning seems to rest on the premise that the immanence of God is an alternative to God's transcendence. The conditions for the possibility of an orthodox conception of modalism are more likely to be in place in a historically conscious thought-world. A comparison between the logic underlying modalism and the logic underlying Nicaea points in this direction. How can the incarnation of the Father be rejected out of hand, while the incarnation of a Logos of the very same nature is imaginable?[17] Does an implied subordinationism still linger on here? Not really, for what was won at Nicaea has to do with the essence of Christianity, namely, that very God is mixed up with creation in behalf of human salvation. But this is what modalism in its clumsy way was also affirming, something that appears more readily from our perspective.[18]

Another area that needs more constructive analysis revolves around subordinationism. One issue concerns the extensiveness of the subordinationist mentality. Apart from modalism, and in the light of the strong reaction against it, subordinationism in one form or another seems to have been the pervasive position in the early patristic period. And unless the early fathers simply failed to understand the New Testament message, it undoubtedly comes from the New Testament period itself. It is logical to infer that the very hypostatization of the Logos entailed its subordination to the Father. It is quite usual to recognize with Athanasius that a new word was added to Christian belief in the Nicene creed. It is probably the case that this new word represented a genuinely new belief for the great majority of Christians of the time.

But "subordinationism" is an undifferentiated term, and a distinction between a heterodox and a more "orthodox" subordination of the Son to the Father helps to clarify what is going on here. A heterodox subordinationism depicts the Son as external to the Godhead and a creature, how-

---

16. The reasoning both for and against modalism thus appears somewhat elementary from a postmodern perspective. See Jaroslav Pelikan's account of debate in *The Christian Tradition*, 1, *The Emergence of the Catholic Tradition (100–600)* (Chicago: University of Chicago Press, 1971), 176–82. The reference to Justin is on 177.

17. Maurice Wiles makes the point relative to patripassionism in this way: "Once the Word or Son was firmly asserted to be coequal and consubstantial with the Father, the same difficulty had to be met once more. In what sense could God in his full 'godness' be understood to be involved in all the sufferings of the incarnate?" "The Holy Spirit and the Incarnation," *The Holy Spirit*, ed. by Dow Kirkpatrick (Oxford: Oxford Institute on Methodist Theological Studies, 1973), 102.

18. The aim of this review of certain elements in the reasoning that carried the development of doctrine forward is not to reassert the classical heresies, but to recall and display the historicity and conditioned character of the development.

ever exalted and godly he may be. A so-called orthodox subordination-ism, however, even though it may speak of the Son as beneath the Father, locates the Son eternally within the Godhead. One is thus not dealing with a creature, but with a distinct mode of being of God.[19] This distinction helps to show in what measure Nicaea is both discontinuous and contin-uous with the tradition. On the one hand, Nicaea corrected language that subordinated the Son to the Father, most sharply in negating heterodox subordinationism. In so doing, Nicaea follows the consistent intent of the tradition in affirming that it was truly God who was at work in Jesus. This is the christological affirmation. But on the other hand, when one shifts the problematic and considers the significance of this language about God, Nicaea affirms God's immanence: God's transcendence is not such that God is aloof from creation, matter, and human suffering; God is such that God can be present to and at work in the world.

THE RELATION OF TRINITY TO CHRISTOLOGY

From these analytical reflections on the historical genesis of the doc-trine of the trinity we can conclude that trinity is a function of christology. Trinitarian language, the logic of trinitarian theology, and the doctrine itself of the trinity, all three are completely dependent upon experience of Jesus as God's bringer of salvation, the primary religious language that expresses this experience, its proliferation in New Testament literature, and the reflective theological language that is more properly called chris-tology. This conglomeration of christological material makes up the source and the origin of trinitarian thinking. This means that the doctrine of the trinity is not a doctrine that can be isolated, that can, as it were, stand on its own; the doctrine and the theology that generated it are derivative.

The archaeology of trinity reveals its dependent and derivative char-acter at a variety of levels. It depends experientially on christology. There is no hint of trinitarianism in the Jewish scriptures; it is generated in the wake of the experience of Jesus as savior and the formation of the Christian community; without that experience, there of course would have been no doctrine of the trinity. Trinity is thus logically derivative from the place that Jesus Christ plays in the Christian life and imagination. Consideration of the divinity of Jesus Christ generates the question of dif-ferentiation within the Godhead. Thus the affirmation of trinity is a func-tion of the place of Jesus as medium of Christian faith in God. Trinity is also historically dependent upon christology. The doctrine is a product of historical development over centuries; that development is confusing, but

---

19. The descriptions of the Son relative to the Father in some passages of Tertullian and Origen illustrate this kind of subordinationism. See, for example, *Tertullian's Treatise Against Praxeas*, ed. and trans. by Ernest Evans (London: SPCK, 1948), 9, 140, and *Origen on First Principles*, ed. and trans. by G. W. Butterworth (Gloucester, Mass.: Peter Smith, 1973), 1.3.5, 33–34.

it is no mystery; God is a mystery, doctrines are not.[20] A sense of historicity and contingency today prevents the view that the doctrine as we have it was there in the beginning and only needed time to be discovered. Rather, this doctrine was generated or produced by human reflection on the foundational Christian premise of the experience of salvation in Jesus Christ.

I thus come back to the starting point of this section: history confirms, or at least corresponds to, the theological premises of the analysis. Theology begins with experience; it ascends to God; the doctrine of the trinity cannot act as a point of departure for theological reflection; it is not an isolated and autonomous doctrine that can bend back and provide an extrinsic norm for christology; its very content is received from christology. Trinitarian theology and doctrine, then, are to be critically understood and adjusted in terms of coherent christological thought.

With these analytical presuppositions in place, I now pass to a discussion of the point of trinitarian theology and doctrine. This discussion will interpret the core meaning of trinity as being such that it defines the language used by Christians to express their expanded vision of the reality of God mediated through Jesus Christ.

THE POINT OF TRINITARIAN THEOLOGY

This next archaeological probe rests on the premise just established: the thoroughgoing dependence of trinity upon christology. On that basis I will investigate the point of trinitarian theology and doctrine. By the point of a doctrine I mean the deeper truth or truths that it represents; I mean the kernel that lies within, the "one thing necessary" that lies below the surface of the affirmations about God. Thus I shall not be speaking of the doctrine of the trinity directly, but of the deeper Christian experience and conviction that lie behind it. The point of the doctrine of the trinity is the reality which grounds it, and hence what should always be aimed at and protected in the theology of the doctrine itself. One can penetrate to the point of a doctrine by reviewing and critically examining its genesis. What is going on in this development? Why is this move being made rather than another? What is at stake in this theological decision? This procedure calls for a review of the development of christology and the theology of the trinity in a reflective way, always with an eye to the experience of God and God's salvation mediated through Jesus Christ which lies at the basis of

---

20. As LaCugna puts it: "By mystery theologians mean the incomprehensibility of God as God. The term is never used to refer to a provisional state of knowledge. Therefore, while it is true that God is (absolute) mystery, it is *not* true that a doctrine is a mystery. Doctrines are simply doctrines, that is, human formulations which are meant to shed light on religious experience." "Philosophers and Theologians on the Trinity," Modern Theology 2, n. 3, 175.

trinity. This analysis of the point of trinity will thus provide a summary of this christology, not in the sense of a repetition of conclusions already offered, but of their recapitulation in a new and higher framework. This framework is trinitarian, in the sense of the Constantinopolitan creed, in which the language of God creator, of the Christ, Jesus, and of the Spirit structures the Christian vision: I believe in God, Father almighty, creator; I believe in Jesus Christ, the Son, savior; I believe in God as Spirit at work in the world for salvation.

The point of trinitarian theology is made up of three subpoints, which do not correspond with each of the so-called persons of God. I shall treat each of these points of the trinitarian language of God.

THE UNICITY AND UNITY OF GOD

By the unicity and unity of God I mean that there is only one sole God, and that God is not internally divided into a plurality of divinities but is one integral God. This first dimension of the point of the trinity can be perceived by viewing the context of the doctrine's development and the crucial issue that underlie the debate.

The question underlying the doctrine of the trinity arose out of the experience of salvation in or through Jesus and in God's Spirit. This seems evident when one assumes a historical, developmental perspective in examining the composition of the New Testament literature. But the question of the trinity did not arise directly out of this experience of salvation but mediately on the basis of historical factors. Some New Testament christologies do not lead in the direction of an immanent trinitarian theology. Rather, reflection that moved in the direction of the doctrine was contingent upon those wisdom and Logos christologies that viewed Jesus not only as a teacher of wisdom but as an incarnation of God's wisdom. To the extent that that wisdom or Logos was hypostatized and conceived as pre-existent and divine, one had to begin asking the question of the nature of God.

The question underlying the doctrine of the trinity, or the issue that was debated, concerned the nature of God. It would not be inaccurate to characterize the context of the debate in terms of the culture in which the growing Christian communities found themselves.[21] On one side, Christianity was heir to Jewish monotheism of a strict kind, but had to account for its worship of Jesus. On the other side lay Greek and Roman polytheism, the religion of the empire, in the face of which Christians were labeled atheists for not recognizing the gods. These two contradictory positions, which may be considered the external parameters of Christian thought, can also be seen to have affected Christian thought itself. The conviction concerning monotheism found an outlet in a stress on the singleness of God and God's rule. This was expressed, for example, in the

---

21. Pelikan, *The Emergence of the Catholic Tradition*, 27–41.

monarchial modalism that refused to concede real differentiations or plurality within the Godhead. The influence of polytheism in the development of Christian thought was registered in a constant concern against the danger of tritheism.

These two outer limits of the trinitarian controversy, however, never existed on an equal footing. The polytheistic or tritheistic side of the dilemma was never a viable option. It served rather as a kind of negative limit, a fear on the part of theologians, or a suspicion about the positions of opponents. No theologian intended a tritheistic conception of God, whereas all theologians wanted to preserve the monarchy of God or more particularly the Father.[22] Thus even when it became clear that there should be some distinctions in the Godhead, it was usually maintained that the Father was the one source, the one unoriginate God. In a certain sense, the conviction that there must be distinctions within the Godhead was concomitant with or entailed subordinationism, which was itself a way of asserting the oneness and transcendence of God in the person of the Father.[23] Thus one can say that, in principle, all parties always accepted the oneness and unity of God, even when their language may have compromised their intentions.

From this it follows that the first point of the doctrine is that God is single and one. The point of the doctrine is to affirm monotheism. A way of emphasizing this would be to say that the doctrine is intended to affirm the oneness of God despite the fact that Jesus is divine and the Spirit too is divine, although this negative formulation is not particularly felicitous.

The progress in the development of the doctrine of the trinity can be measured by a growth of consensus along loosely defined stages, that is, agreement that the Father, Son or Logos, and the Spirit were distinct, then that they were all involved in human salvation, then that the Logos and finally the Spirit were fully divine. But as this development went forward away from monarchian modalism, the one constant was the unicity and unity of God. Whatever was said of the Logos and the Spirit, the oneness of God could not be compromised. In this sense, the point of the doctrine of the trinity, in the assertions of the divinity of the Logos and the Spirit, was such that the oneness of God had to be maintained. Here the point of the doctrine appears as a negative limit: whatever is said of Logos and Spirit, the oneness of God must be preserved intact.

Even though the history of the doctrine has been obsessed with the problem of mathematical threeness and oneness, and that obsession continues today, in reality the doctrine has nothing to do with this issue. It is

---

22. This discussion entails patriarchal language without relief. One cannot reproduce the discussion of the Fathers in any other idiom. But Elizabeth Johnson affords something of a remedy by retrieving three patristic themes: divine incomprehensibility, the analogical and not literal character of this language, the need for other names for God. *She Who Is*, 104–20.

23. For example, Tertullian, *Tertullian's Treatise Against Praxeas*, 140.

often quite difficult not to get drawn into thinking that the issue at stake in trinity is reconciling a numerical three with one in the assertion that the three is one God or that God is differentiated into three distinct "persons." And it is the case that much of trinitarian theology assumes the logical form of making distinctions that will allow for this reconciliation on different levels of being. But if the last proposal is correct, that the first point of the doctrine is to affirm the unicity and unity of God, the mathematical perspective is severely distorted. "As long as the doctrine of the trinity is reduced to a puzzle of the sort, 'how can three be one?' no real advance in understanding can take place."[24] The unicity and unity of God are a given and a constant; the discussion of three principles in the Godhead can only be seen as a discussion of possible differentiation within the one God's life. And this differentiation does not mean multiplicity, because the "persons" cannot be counted, as counting is an operation applicable only to finite beings, and because traditionally there is always a unity of operation of the one God.

Theologies that seek to describe or explain differentiation within God in terms of threeness are suspect when and insofar as they promote a language that undermines the unicity and unity of God. Trinitarian speculations that tried, and still try, to name the differentiations in God as discrete always have had to insist against this that God is one, simple, and indivisible. The persons cannot be added; they *are* one being. The reason for this is that the fundamental and guaranteed datum in trinitarian theology is the oneness of God. Christians, in worshiping Jesus Christ, are not polytheists.

It follows from this that any speculative language that even unintentionally communicates tritheism, despite cautions that seek to soften or overcome it, is suspect. But much of trinitarian theology today does precisely this, despite the intentions and disclaimers of its authors. Notions of God as a community, ideas of hypostatizing the differentiations within God and calling them persons in such a way that they are in dialogical intercommunication with each other, militate against the first point of the doctrine itself.

THE REALITY OF SALVATION

The second dimension of the point of the theology of the trinity is salvational. The doctrine of the trinity is what it is in order to preserve or protect the experience of salvation that lies at its basis.

An unfolding of this view also begins with the language of the New Testament. Given the witness of the New Testament, one can say that Christian language about God is necessarily trinitarian. New Testament language about God is extensively defined by the symbols of God as creator and Father, and by the person of Jesus construed according to the

---

24. LaCugna, "Philosophers and Theologians on the Trinity," 177.

various titles and conceptions of him and his work, and by the symbol of Spirit of God, or God as Spirit, the Holy Spirit, or simply the Spirit. One cannot quite conceive of fully Christian language about God that does not also employ the symbols of Christ and the Spirit. The economy of early Christian encounter with God unfolds within the language of Jesus Christ and the Spirit.

The self-communication of God through Jesus Christ and God as Spirit correlates with the theory of religious experience outlined in Chapter 1 of this work and alluded to again in Chapter 7. The structure of human existence is such that it requires that a salvific self-communication of God have, as it were, a double mediation in order that it be explicitly conscious and effective. This double mediation refers to an external witness to the religious truth in question and an internal witness or principle of internal presence, experience, and appropriation. Since all human knowledge and self-awareness are bound to the world and history, and are mediated to consciousness through the world and history, so too a clear or explicit awareness of God must be mediated by an external objective medium. But that external medium of itself will not actually mediate an effective internal experience of God, without which there is no real self-communication or revelation, unless there be an internal principle of appropriation. This internal principle corresponds to the consistent witness of people who experience transcendence as an internal presence. It also helps to "explain" why one person may be moved by an external mediation of religious truth while another will not be so impressed. Thus the salvific self-revelation and self-communication of God through Jesus and the Spirit may be considered in correlation with the very condition of the possibility of a divine revelation. This three-fold structure is implicitly at work in all existentially engaging encounters with transcendent reality.

The doctrine of the trinity, therefore, rests on this foundation: the historical genesis and intrinsic structure of Christian faith, revelation, and salvation are functionally trinitarian. This summary statement draws a conclusion that is implied in the last two paragraphs. Not only Christian language but the very structure of Christian faith is trinitarian. Christian knowledge of God, insofar as it is specifically Christian, is mediated in history by the historical event of Jesus; its actuality or existential reality, its coming to fruition within human beings, is symbolized by the language of the Spirit that corresponds to God as Spirit at work in the human subject as God's self-communication. The inner logic of Christian revelation, then, is determined by the concrete symbol Jesus and the conceptual symbol Spirit pointing to God's personal presence to human beings. And thus insofar as this self-communication of God is salvific, salvation has a trinitarian structure.

This salvational structure also underlies the formation of trinitarian doctrine. Recognition of this soteriological logic of the trinity allows one to break open an understanding of the doctrine that construes it as a description of a differentiated inner life of God. I recall and appeal to several points made in the interpretation of Nicaea in Chapter 10 to under-line the character of the trinitarian doctrine that resulted from it.

First, the direct intention of the Council of Nicaea is negative, to reject the subordinationist teaching of Arius. Second, the central positive reason for this rejection is soteriological. Since human salvation can come only from God, if the Logos is less than God, human existence is not saved. Third, the hypostatization of the Logos and, more generally, Logos lan-guage are not affirmed by the creed, because this was given by the con-text, accepted by all parties, not debated, and therefore not deliberately intended as an element to be affirmed. Therefore, fourth, the meaning of the council can be fittingly generalized as stating against Arius that no less than God was present and at work in Jesus for our salvation. This pres-ence of true God in Jesus is the supposition behind Logos language: this is not the "ordinary" presence of God as creator, but the intimate presence of God for human salvation. Fifth, what is said of the Logos can be affirmed analogously of the Spirit, as it was at Constantinople. Therefore, again generalizing, one may understand the doctrine of the trinity as reli-gious language, as not affirming two and then three distinct and coequal elements within the Godhead, but as affirming a dramatic view of a God who saves. God symbolized as Father, Son, and Spirit is one God who is loving creator, and who was present and active for the salvation of humankind in Jesus, and who is consistently present in the Christian com-munity, in individuals within it, and, indeed, in all human beings. This loving and saving presence is an extension of the love manifested in God's creating.

The point of the doctrine of the trinity is therefore soteriological. The doctrine that rests on and derives from the experience of salvation has as its point to assert and protect the economy of that experience of salvation. Thus, besides being a doctrine that reasserts monotheism in a Christian context, the doctrine also asserts that God's salvation is really mediated to human existence through Jesus and in the Spirit. The doctrine is not intended to provide information about the internal life of God, but is about how God relates to human beings. It is a formula that guarantees that the salvation experienced in Jesus is really God's salvation; the Spirit is God as Spirit. Because this is the experience and the logic that generates it, the form of the doctrine, the propositional formula, should be understood as expressing this point.

THE NATURE OF GOD AS SAVIOR

There remains a third and still more basic point to the theology and doctrine of the trinity. This can be shown by resuming reflections already put forward. I have argued that trinity emerges out of the experience of salvation through Jesus and in God's Spirit. The historical development of the doctrine and the logic that drove its definition show that it is derived from the experience of salvation though Jesus and in God's Spirit.

I also defended a revelational and transformational view of salvation. Chapter 12 showed that Jesus saved by being a revelation and bearer of God's saving presence in history. God as Spirit was presented as the internal transformative presence of God to human subjects. The witness of the scriptures and the history of the theology of grace confirm that the phrase "Spirit of God" refers to God's personal self-communication.

The dynamics of these two modes of God's salvation have been understood in terms of religious symbols. Jesus, as a human being, is the concrete symbol that mediates God's being revealed to human beings. In epistemological terms, one encounters and construes God in and through the life of Jesus. In objective terms, flowing from the epistemology of symbol, Jesus makes present to or in history the possibility of this encounter with the transcendent God. In the theology of grace, which has as its referent God as Spirit, the term "Spirit" is also a symbol, in this case a conceptual symbol, that points to the immanence, presence, and dynamic activity of God within human experience. The primary effect of grace, illumined by Jesus as he is presented to us in the scriptures and experienced in Christian lives, is to open up human freedom from the egocentrism of sin to hope, faith, and active love.

Another principle is at work in the fundamental logic of all trinitarian theology: one can make assertions about God on the basis of encounters with God in Jesus and the Spirit. The objective validity of the doctrine of the trinity depends on the premise that God must in some way be such that God corresponds to the way God is experienced in Jesus and as Spirit. These experiences of God at the same time reveal the way God communicates God's personal self to human beings. In more technical terms, the experience of the economic trinity provides the grounds for affirmations about God. Some discussion, then, of how this principle is to be understood is crucial for any doctrine of the trinity. The following discussion presupposes some fundamental issues related to experience of and language about God, and is limited to defining a meaning for this principle that lies between two extremes.

On the one hand, this principle opposes the theological view that one cannot make any objective statements about God. In this view one only encounters God; one experiences the effects of God's acting within one's life, but one cannot transfer this experience into statements about God in a generalized and objective way.[25] In contrast to this, one can endorse the position that in an encounter with God, relative and historically limited

---

25. See, for example, Rudolf Bultmann, *Jesus Christ and Mythology* (New York: Charles Scribner's Sons, 1958), 66–70. Much of what Bultmann says on these pages appears true enough. But why cannot the theologian generalize on the basis of his or her own experience, and the experience of others in the community, and across a tradition that, for example, God is indeed objectively creator of the universe? A positive argument for the possibility of such a generalized statement might begin with a phenomenology of the experience of human existence participating in contingent being. Human existence appears as contingent or created being-conscious-of-itself.

though it be, one really encounters God in such a manner that one can make statements about what one has actually encountered.[26]

But, on the other hand, the principle as it is understood here may be contrasted with Karl Rahner's use of the axiom of the identity between the economic and the immanent trinity. As he states it: "The 'economic' trinity is the 'immanent' trinity and *vice versa*."[27] In Rahner's theology of the trinity this principle in its first moment is ontological, characterizing the being of God. As such the trinity is a dogmatic postulate. This means that Rahner already accepts the theology of the trinity in its more or less classical form, and then goes on to postulate the identity of the missions and processions of God, that is, the self-communication of God to us in Word and Spirit, and the self-communication of God with God's self as eternally Word and Spirit. This is not done arbitrarily, but with a carefully worked out theology of self-communication by formal causality in incarnation and grace. From this ontology of salvational self-communication *ad extra* and internal self-communication, Rahner binds together, again ontologically and cosmically, the economic and immanent trinity. Because of this ontological identity, which stems from the acceptance of the doctrine and a theological version of it at face value, the principle then also works epistemologically, so that everything falls into place. The two-foldness of God's self-communication in Jesus and in grace not only corresponds but is identical with the two-fold processions and self-communications within God's own self.

The problem with Rahner's construct is that, from a critical epistemological point of view, the axiom of the identity of the economic and the immanent trinity represents a jump. Epistemologically it is a pure postulate that rests on no more than dogmatic grounds. Rahner accepts the already fashioned doctrine in its speculative form, albeit with his own highly technical and brilliant construal of God's self-communication. This implies that, from a critical apologetic point of view, his further theologizing on the real distinctions within God through processions is purely speculative, of the same nature as those of Augustine and Aquinas, and this does not fit well with his equal but more credible insistence on the absolute mystery and incomprehensibility of God.

In Rahner's view, the self-differentiation within God of Father, Word, and Spirit, the latter two of which are identical with God's self-communication to human existence, is seen as the opening-up and expansiveness of God's nature and freedom as a savior God. This is central. But Rahner also consistently argues that if there were no real self-differentiation in God, then what one experienced in Jesus and the Spirit would not be a *real self*-communication of God. But the force of this argument

26. See H. Richard Niebuhr, "Value-Theory and Theology," in *The Nature of Religious Experience: Essays in Honor of Douglas Clyde Macintosh* (New York: Harper and Brothers, 1937), 99–100, 110–16.

27. Rahner, *The Trinity*, 22.

or assertion is not clear. There is no logical connection that demands a correlation of an internal differentiation within God and God's actual self-communication to human existence. If God were conceived as single, simple, spiritual, conscious, intelligent, and sovereignly free subject, this characterization of God could of itself account for God's *real self*-communication to Jesus and each human being. In other words, a "modalist" position can be understood in a way that accounts for the point of the doctrine of the trinity, and there is no really convincing argument against it. With this observation, however, I do not defend or endorse modalism. I simply wish to underscore the premise that human experience and language about God cannot be correlated with God's inner life in a non-mediated and descriptively literal way.

The result is that Rahner's immanent trinity runs parallel to but is not really determined by the experience of the economic trinity. It is this economic trinity that represents the very essence and structure of the Christian encounter with God. Ultimately, Rahner does not "explain," insofar as such is the task of theology, what difference it makes whether or not there be real differentiations in God, but simply states that it is the case.[28]

The position represented here is an epistemologically more modest use of the principle than that of Rahner. It allows objective talk or predication about God, the assertion of something that is true because faith really encounters no less than God in Jesus and what is experienced as the Spirit. But this encounter does not *necessarily* yield really distinct differentiations within God that can be named. These are objects of speculation which, whether or not they correspond to real differentiations within God, are not the *point* of the doctrine of the trinity.

Rather, the third point of the doctrine of trinity is that God is savior. God really is as God is encountered to be in Jesus and the Spirit. This fundamental assertion is drawn from the principle that one can affirm of God what God is encountered to be in the mediation of Jesus and in conversion by the power of God as Spirit. It asserts that God is savior, objectively in the sense that God really is in God's self as God is revealed to be in God's self-communication in Jesus and the Spirit.[29] This means that the point of the theology and doctrine of the trinity is that the qualities of God revealed in Jesus and experienced within human beings as God's Spirit are elements of the very reality of God, real dimensions of God's being God.

---

28. See the analysis and criticism of Rahner's trinitarian theology by James P. Mackey, *The Christian Experience of God as Trinity*, 196–200.

29. It is to be understood here that in affirming this identity one must always tacitly add the phrase "but not without remainder." There is no simple identity between our language and concepts about God and God's own reality, in itself so to speak, and in the sense that these predications could in any way adequately encompass God or adequately comprehend God. God remains, dialectically, absolute incomprehensible mystery and in that sense unknown. What is known of God is given as gift.

At this juncture it is not necessary to develop further all of the other predicates concerning God's nature that this implies, but some of the most elementary are involved in the very concept of the salvation experienced as mediated through Jesus and the Spirit. God is love; God is gracious; God enters into relation with God's creation; God has revealed God's nature in the life of Jesus because God is encountered as actively present and empowering that life; God is communicative of God's self to creatures able to respond to such a personal initiative. The point of the doctrine of the trinity is that these predicates correspond to the way God actually is.

In sum, therefore, the point of the doctrine of the trinity is that God is absolutely and uniquely one, that God's saving action in Jesus and the Spirit are real, and that therefore God as such is a saving God. This summarizes the point of the doctrine of the trinity. It is not, however, a summary of the doctrine itself. Much more is demanded of a trinitarian theology than a definition of the point of the doctrine. The genesis, the language and logic of the doctrine, and its impact on Christian life require full-length historical and systematic studies such as those cited at the outset of this chapter. Does this involve speculation on whether there are differentiations within God's life, and perhaps a cogent account of how these differentiations may be understood and related to each other? One can certainly speculate. But one will never be able to define such differentiations in any final or satisfying way. The recognition of the absolute mystery and incomprehensibility of God, coupled with the extravagant pluralism of trinitarian theologies, indicate how tenuous the analogies are and how projective the essays. There simply are no data on the inner life of God upon which comparisons and differentiations can be made.[30] But for the same reasons neither does the theologian have the grounds to deny such differentiations in God. But it seems certain that in the measure that trinitarian theology gets completely absorbed in defining and working out the distinctions within God's inner life, in the same measure it misses the point.

---

30. Gregory of Nyssa expresses this well with his theory of religious knowledge which, when it is read today, sounds roughly equivalent to a modern conception of symbolic mediation. We know God through God's operations upon us. These are always concrete and specific, thus generating a language that must point beyond itself to an infinite and transcendent other, which is in no sense, as it were, given in itself, but incomprehensible. The names of God represent human conceptions of God and speculation unfolds these human conceptions. He writes: "As we perceive the varied operations of the power above us, we fashion our appellations [of God] from the several operations that are known to us. . . ." "We, . . . following the suggestions of Scripture, have learnt that that [the divine] nature is unnameable and unspeakable, and we say that every term either invented by the custom of men, or handed down to us by the Scriptures, is indeed explanatory of our conceptions of the Divine Nature, but does not include the significance of that nature itself." Gregory of Nyssa, "On 'Not Three Gods,'" *Nicene and Post-Nicene Fathers*, V, *Select Writings and Letters of Gregory, Bishop of Nyssa*, trans. William Moore and Henry Austin Wilson (Grand Rapids: Eerdmans, 1892), 333a and 332b, respectively.

CONCLUSION

A theology that is written in and for a postmodern intellectual culture cannot begin with the doctrine of the trinity. Rather, trinitarian theology and doctrine reach back over the expanse of the Jewish and Christian witness to God's action in the world and recapitulate that experience in the symbols that bring into focus the events of salvation. It thus summarizes what is in essence a narrative theology of God dealing with the world. What has been offered here in no way encompasses the Christian vision to which the doctrine of trinity points. I have not developed a theology of God and of God's creation, reinterpreted in the context of new scientific knowledge of the universe, the planet, life in its various forms, and human existence. I have not developed a theology of God as Spirit experienced by individual Christians in their lives, in the church as a living movement that represents God's mission in the world, in the religions as they express the experience of the absolute mystery of God through other varied mediations. Trinity recapitulates the Christian vision, and that vision cannot be represented adequately without a fuller theology that goes beyond christology.

What I have tried to show in this concluding chapter is the way in which trinity arises out of this fuller theology of Christian experience. As a doctrine it is itself a symbol that summarizes Christian faith in a threefold confession of belief in God as creator, historical savior, and the inner power of authentic human life that leads to final salvation. As such, trinity represents the very content of the Christian vision of reality. Trinity defines the intrinsic structure of Christian language of God because it corresponds to the Christian narrative of salvation. Trinity summarizes Christian theology, the elaboration of Christian experience. But as a derivative and recapitulating theology and doctrine, trinity is open to and receptive of the other areas of theology which feed it with content. As such, trinity is not closed to the thoroughgoing Spirit christologies found in the New Testament or to Spirit christologies today. But at the same time, more research and refinement of language are needed for a full integration between Spirit christology and a fully developed trinitarian theology.

But the aim of this book is not to propose a Spirit christology, but to begin a systematic conversation about Jesus Christ that addresses the postmodern culture that characterizes the situation of the churches as they begin the third millennium of their existence after Jesus Christ. There are many aspects of today's world that make it quite different from the situation in which past christologies were generated. Christology faces many broad new challenges. Spirit christology has been proposed here only insofar as it appears to be more relatively adequate to meet some of these problems. Far more important for an integral christology today is the ability to balance faithfulness to the tradition and present interpretation that actually engages today's questions, an imagination resolutely focused on Jesus as a historical figure that is simultaneously drawn up into an experience of Jesus as symbolic mediator of God who is alive in God, a conception of Jesus' work of salvation that transforms personal existence and at the same time opens the free human spirit to social engagement, a sense of Jesus Christ's uniqueness as one that gives an identity to the Christian community and at the same time that reveals a God who is in like measure universally present and active in the world, a theological language that combines a symbolic mystical dimension with historical and political realism.

Trinity is a centering doctrine because it structures the creed and sums up the full Christian vision. But at the center of this center is the historical figure of Jesus who is the bearer and revealer of God in the Christian community. Thus at the literal center of the Christian vision of reality lies Jesus symbol of God.

Index